murach's
C++
Programming

Mary Delamater

Joel Murach

murach's
C++
Programming

Mary Delamater

Joel Murach

MIKE MURACH & ASSOCIATES, INC.

4340 N. Knoll Ave. • Fresno, CA 93722

www.murach.com • murachbooks@murach.com

Editorial team

Authors:	Mary Delamater
	Joel Murach
Editor:	Anne Boehm
Reviewers:	John Baugh, Professor and Chair, Oakland Community College
	Prentiss Knowlton, UCLA Extension
Production:	Samantha Walker

Books on popular programming languages

Murach's C++ Programming

Murach's C#

Murach's Visual Basic

Murach's Java Programming

Murach's Python Programming

Books on web and mobile development

Murach's HTML5 and CSS3 (4th Edition)

Murach's JavaScript and jQuery (3rd Edition)

Murach's PHP and MySQL (3rd Edition)

Murach's ASP.NET Web Programming with C#

Murach's Java Servlets and JSP (3rd Edition)

Murach's Android Programming (2nd Edition)

Books on database programming

Murach's MySQL (2nd Edition)

Murach's SQL Server 2016 for Developers

Murach's Oracle SQL and PL/SQL for Developers (2nd Edition)

For more on Murach books, please visit us at www.murach.com

ISBN-13: 978-1-943872-27-5

Contents

Expanded contents

Introduction

C++ was first released in 1985, and it was a difficult language to learn. That's because it required programmers to master low-level techniques to work with memory.

Over the years, C++ has evolved to provide many higher-level techniques that make it much easier to write effective C++ code. But most C++ books haven't evolved with the language.

So our goal in this book has been to rethink the entire approach and make it easier than ever to learn C++ by taking advantage of the higher-level techniques that are now integral to the language. Then, once you've learned how to code object-oriented C++ programs today, this book teaches you the older techniques that you need to maintain legacy code and to work with embedded systems that don't support the newer techniques.

What this book does

To make your C++ training as effective as possible, this book is divided into four sections:

- Section 1 presents a practical subset of modern C++ that gets you off to a great start. This section works for both beginners and experienced programmers because it lets you set your own pace. If you're a beginner, you'll move slowly and do all the exercises. If you have experience, you'll move more quickly, skimming through material you already know to focus on skills that are new to you or that you've never mastered.

- Section 2 builds on the subset to present additional C++ essentials that programmers use every day. These skills include working with structures, enumerations, Standard Template Library (STL) containers and algorithms, built-in arrays, C strings, and exceptions.

- Section 3 shows you how to develop object-oriented programs in C++. This is a critical skillset in today's world, and it complements the procedural skills you learned in section 1. When you complete this section, you'll be able to develop programs that combine the best procedural practices with the best object-oriented practices.

- Section 4 presents some advanced skills that you may need, especially if you're working with legacy code or embedded systems. These skills include using pointers to work with memory at a low level and using templates to allow a class to support multiple data types. By the end of this section, you'll also have learned how to develop custom containers and algorithms that work like the containers and algorithms of the STL presented in section 2.

Why you'll learn faster and better with this book

Like all our books, this one has features that you won't find in competing books, all designed to help you learn faster and better. Here are a few of those features.

- As you page through this book, you'll see that all of the information is presented in "paired pages," with the essential syntax, guidelines, and examples on the right page and the perspective and extra explanation on the left page. This helps you learn faster by reading less...and this is the ideal reference format when you need to refresh your memory about how to do something.

- To show you how C++ works, this book presents over 50 complete programs that build from the simple to the complex. We believe that studying the code for complete programs is critical to the learning process... and yet you won't find programs like ours in other C++ books.

- Of course, this book also presents hundreds of short examples, so it's easy to find an example that shows how to do what you want to do. Even better, our paired pages make it easier to find the example that you're looking for than it is with traditional books that embed the examples in the text.

- At the end of each chapter, there are exercises that give you hands-on experience in practicing what you've learned. These exercises also encourage you to experiment and to apply what you've learned in new ways...just as you'll have to do on the job. Because our exercises start from partial programs, you get more practice in less time because you can focus on the skills you've just learned.

What software you need

To develop C++ programs, you just need to download and install an IDE and a compiler for C++ that you can use for coding, testing, and debugging your programs. Fortunately, some C++ IDEs include a compiler for the current operating system.

For example, installing Visual Studio on Windows as described in appendix A also installs the Microsoft Visual C++ (MSVC) compiler. Similarly, installing Xcode on macOS as described in appendix B also installs the open-source Clang compiler that can be used to compile programs in C++ and related languages. Then, chapter 1 shows how to use Visual Studio and Xcode to develop C++ programs for the Windows and macOS operating systems.

How our downloadable files can help you learn

If you go to our website at www.murach.com, you can download all the files that you need for getting the most from this book. This includes:

- the programs presented in this book

- the starting points for the exercises

- the solutions to the exercises

These files let you test, review, and copy the code. If you have any problems with the exercises, the solutions are there to help you over the learning blocks, an essential part of the learning process. And in some cases, the solutions will show you a more elegant way to handle a problem, even when you've come up with a solution that works. Here again, appendixes A and B show how to download and install these files on Windows and macOS systems.

Support materials for instructors and trainers

If you're a college instructor or corporate trainer who would like to use this book as a course text, we offer a full set of the support materials you need for a turnkey course. That includes:

- instructional objectives that help your students focus on the skills that they need to develop

- dozens of projects that let your students prove how well they have mastered those skills

- test banks that let you measure how well your students have mastered those skills

- a complete set of PowerPoint slides that you can use to review and reinforce the content of the book

Instructors tell us that this is everything they need for a course without all the busywork that you get from other publishers.

To learn more about our instructor's materials, please go to our website at www.murachforinstructors.com if you're an instructor. Or if you're a trainer, please go to www.murach.com and click on the *Courseware for Trainers* link, or contact Kelly at 1-800-221-5528 or kelly@murach.com.

Please remember, though, that the primary component for a successful C++ course is this book. Because your students will learn faster and more thoroughly when they use our book, they will have better questions and be more prepared when they come to class. Because our guided exercises start from partial programs, your students will get more and better practice in lab. And because our paired pages are so good for reference, your students will be able to review for tests and do their projects more efficiently.

Please let us know how this book works for you

From the start of this project, we've had two goals for this book. First, we wanted to make this the best-ever book for beginning programmers who want to learn how to program with C++. To do that right, we knew we not only had to make the book easy enough for beginners, but also had to teach all of the skills that a professional C++ programmer needs to know.

Second, we wanted to make this the best-ever book for experienced programmers who want to add C++ to their skillsets. To do that right, we've carefully selected the content, organized it from simple to complex in each chapter, and packed the book full of code examples and sample programs. That allows experienced programmers to move quickly through material that's familiar from other languages, so they can see how to do it the C++ way. If they already know some C++, it allows them to zero in on features that are new to them or that they need to use right away. And when they're done, this book will be their best-ever on-the-job reference.

Now, we hope we've succeeded. We thank you for buying this book. We wish you all the best with your C++ programming. And if you have any comments, we would appreciate hearing from you.

Joel Murach
Author
joelmurach@yahoo.com

Mary Delamater
Author
maryd@techknowsolve.com

Section 1

Essential skills for modern C++

The eight chapters in this section get you off to a fast start by presenting a complete subset of the essential concepts and skills that you need for C++ programming. First, chapter 1 introduces you to C++ programming and shows you how to use an IDE (Integrated Development Environment) to get started with development. Then, chapters 2 through 7 present the programming skills that you need to develop substantial programs of your own.

After the first seven chapters, you're going to need to improve your testing and debugging skills, and you may want to deploy a program to see how that works. So, that's what chapter 8 shows you how to do. When you complete this section, you'll be able to design, code, test, debug, and deploy C++ programs that can work with data that's stored in files.

1

An introduction to C++ programming

This chapter starts by presenting some background information about C++. Although this information isn't essential to developing C++ programs, it does show how C++ works and how it compares to other languages. So it's important for you to at least skim this information.

After the background information, this chapter shows how to use an IDE (Integrated Development Environment) to develop a C++ program. If you're using a Windows computer, we recommend using the Visual Studio IDE that's developed by Microsoft. If you're using a Mac, we recommend using the Xcode IDE that's developed by Apple. As you'll see, there are many other IDEs that support C++ development, including the open-source Eclipse and NetBeans IDEs. These IDEs run on all modern operating systems, and you can use them if you prefer.

An overview of programming and C++

In 1979, Bjarne Stroustrup began working on the language that would eventually become C++ (pronounced "see plus plus"). Today, C++ remains one of the most important programming languages in the world, with billions of lines of code in production. That includes many applications that are crucial to modern computing as we know it.

Four general-purpose programming languages

C++ is a general-purpose programming language that was originally based on the C language. Figure 1-1 begins by presenting a chronological listing of four popular general-purpose programming languages including C++. Of these languages, C was developed first and had a commercial release in 1972. After that, C++ was developed as an extension of the C language that added the capability for object-oriented programming and had a commercial release in 1985. Since then, many other programming languages have used a syntax that's similar to C++, including Java (first commercial release in 1996) and C# (first commercial release in 2002).

At this point, you may wonder why you should learn C++ when there are newer languages like Java and C# available. To start, C++ is still one of the fastest and most efficient languages available. So, if you're developing a program that needs to be fast and use memory efficiently to conserve system resources, C++ is still a great choice. This is an advantage that C++ has over many other languages such as Java and C#.

Like many other modern languages, C++ is portable, which means that it works with many different operating systems and devices. Like many other object-oriented languages, C++ is ideal for developing large and complex applications. In fact, over the past 30 years, thousands of large and complex applications have been developed using C++ and billions of lines of code have been deployed. All of this adds up to a significant demand for C++ programmers in the job market, both for developing new projects and maintaining existing ones.

So, what types of applications are typically developed using C++? Due to its speed and efficiency, C++ is commonly used for the types of programming listed in this figure, including systems programming, desktop applications, mobile apps, video games, performance-critical applications, science applications, engineering applications, and embedded systems programming. In other words, C++ is commonly used for a wide range of applications, especially where speed and efficiency are critical.

Four general-purpose programming languages

Language	Year of first commercial release
C	1972
C++	1985
Java	1996
C#	2002

Why it still makes sense to learn C++ today

- **Speed**. After all these years, C++ is still one of the fastest and most efficient languages available.

- **Portability**. C++ is designed to work with many different operating systems and devices.

- **Scale**. C++ is an object-oriented programming (OOP) language. This makes it ideal for developing large and complex applications that may have millions of lines of code.

- **Job security**. After all these years, there is still a robust demand for C++ developers from many of the largest companies in the world. Many new C++ projects are started every year, and billions of lines of existing C++ code will need to be maintained for many years to come.

What C++ is used for

- **Systems programming** such as key parts of operating systems, device drivers, Internet routers, web servers, database servers, and even compilers and infrastructure for other languages such as Java and C#.

- **Desktop applications** such as web browsers, word processors, spreadsheets, and image editors.

- **Mobile apps** such as apps that need to run as efficiently as possible on Android devices.

- **Video games** that require extensive computation and graphics processing.

- **Performance-critical applications** such as financial, telecommunications, and military applications.

- **Science and engineering applications** that perform extensive numerical computation and graphics processing.

- **Embedded systems programming** such as applications for medical equipment, flight control software, and automobile software.

Description

- C++ is a general-purpose programming language that was originally based on the C language.

- Many other programming languages have been influenced by C++ including Java and C#.

Figure 1-1 Four general-purpose programming languages

A brief history of C++

Since 1998, C++ has been standardized by the *International Organization for Standardization (ISO)*. Although these standards have a long formal name, they're typically referred to by a short informal name as shown in figure 1-2. So, the C++ standard released in 1998 is typically referred to as C++98. Similarly, the standard released in 2017 is typically referred to as C++17, and the standard that's due to be released in 2020 is typically referred to as C++20.

This book shows how to use C++17. However, C++ is *backwards compatible*, which means that C++17 works with older versions of C++ too. In addition, most of the skills described in this book have been a part of C++ since its earliest versions. As a result, earlier versions of C++ such as C++ 2011 work with most of the skills described in this book.

This figure also presents a brief history of C++. This history shows that Bjarne Stroustrup began developing a language called "C with Classes" in 1979. In 1983, this language was renamed to C++. In 1985, the first commercial implementation of C++ was released, though the language was not yet standardized by the ISO. In 1998, the ISO released the C++98 standard, followed by subsequent standards in 2003, 2011, 2014, and 2017. As you progress through this book, you'll learn more about what these standards mean for you as a programmer.

C++ ISO standards

Year	C++ Standard	Informal name
1998	ISO/IEC 14882:1998	C++98
2003	ISO/IEC 14882:2003	C++03
2011	ISO/IEC 14882:2011	C++11
2014	ISO/IEC 14882:2014	C++14
2017	ISO/IEC 14882:2017	C++17

C++ history

Year	Event
1979	Bjarne Stroustrup begins work on "C with Classes".
1983	"C with Classes" is renamed to C++.
1985	The first commercial implementation of C++ is released.
1985	The first edition of *The C++ Programming Language* is published. This book became the definitive reference for the language, as there was not yet an official standard.
1990	*The Annotated C++ Reference Manual* is published. This book became the basis for the 1998 standard.
1998	The C++98 standard is finalized.
2003	The C++03 standard is released, fixing some bugs with the previous standard.
2011	The C++11 standard is released, adding many new features.
2014	The C++14 standard is released, fixing some bugs with the previous standard.
2017	The C++17 standard is released, adding many new features.

Description

- Since 1998, C++ has been standardized by the *International Organization for Standardization* (*ISO*).
- C++ 2020 is the next planned standard.

Figure 1-2   A brief history of C++

A quick look at C++ development

At this point, you're ready to see the user interface and source code for a C++ program. After that, you'll be ready to learn how C++ converts this source code so it can be run by a computer.

The user interface for a console application

An *application*, or *app*, is computer software that performs a task or related set of tasks. However, an application can also be referred to as a *program*, even though one application may actually consist of many related programs. In practice, most people use these terms interchangeably.

A *desktop application* is a program that runs directly on your computer. There are two types of desktop applications that you can create with C++. The first type of desktop application is known as a *GUI application* because it uses a *graphical user interface* to interact with the user. (In conversation, GUI is pronounced *G-U-I* or *gooey*.) Examples of GUI applications include web browsers, word processors, and spreadsheets. So, if you've ever used a web browser, you are already familiar with GUI applications.

However, you might not be familiar with the second type of desktop application. This type of application is known as a *console application* because it uses the *console*, also known as a *command prompt* or *terminal*, to interact with the user by allowing the user to enter commands and data. In figure 1-3, for example, the console application prompts the user to enter the radius for a circle. Here, the user enters a value by typing a number and pressing the Enter key. Then, the application calculates the diameter, circumference, and area of the circle and displays the results on the console.

The appearance of the console may differ from one operating system to another, but the functionality should be the same. In this figure, for example, the first console is the Command Prompt window that's available from Windows, and the second console is the Terminal window that's available from macOS. However, both get input from the user in the same way and display the same result to the user.

Console applications are easier to code than GUI applications. As a result, they're often used by programmers when learning a language. That's why this book uses console applications to show how C++ works. Once you understand the basics of C++, you'll be ready to move on to writing GUI applications, if that's what you want to do.

A console application

Running in the console for Windows 10

```
C:\WINDOWS\system32\cmd.exe                           —    □    ×
Circle Calculator

Enter radius:  9
Diameter:      18
Circumference: 56.5
Area:          254.5

Bye!

Press any key to continue . . .
```

Running in the console for macOS

```
                joelmurach — circle_calculator — 80×16
Circle Calculator

Enter radius:  7
Diameter:      14
Circumference: 44
Area:          153.9

Bye!

logout
Saving session...
...saving history...truncating history files...
...completed.
Deleting expired sessions...none found.

[Process completed]
```

Description

- An *application*, or *app*, is computer software that performs a task or related set of tasks.

- An application can also be referred to as a *program*.

- A *console application* uses the console to interact with the user.

- The appearance of the console may differ from one operating system to another, but the functionality should be the same.

- A *GUI application* uses a *graphical user interface* to interact with the user. Examples of GUI applications include web browsers, word processors, and spreadsheets.

- Console applications are easier to code than GUI applications. As a result, they're often used by programmers when learning a language.

Figure 1-3   The user interface for a console application

The source code for a console application

When you develop a C++ application, you start by entering and editing the *source code* for the program. To give you an idea of how the source code for a C++ program works, figure 1-4 presents the code for the Circle Calculator program shown in the previous figure.

If you have experience with other programming languages, you may be able to understand much of this code already. If not, don't worry! You'll learn how all of this code works in the next few chapters. For now, here's a brief explanation of this code.

The first two lines are #include directives that specify that this code uses two header files (iostream and cmath). These headers are available from the C++ standard library. Here, the iostream header provides the code for working with input and output (I/O) from the console. The cmath header, on the other hand, provides the code for accessing libraries written in the C language that provide mathematical functions. These functions include the pow() and round() functions used in this source code. Then, the third line makes it easier to work with the code in these headers, which are both available from the namespace named std, which is short for standard.

Most of the code for this program is stored in a function named main(). Before the function name, this code uses the int keyword to specify that this function returns an integer to the operating system. The code for this function is stored between the function's opening brace (\{) and its closing brace (\}). When a C++ program starts, it automatically executes the main() function and runs the code between its braces. Because of that, this function is known as the entry point for the application.

Within the main() function, the source code uses the cout, cin, and endl objects that are available from the iostream header to write output to the console (cout), read input from the console (cin), and specify the end of a line (endl). To help with that, this code uses the stream insertion operator (<<) to insert data into the output stream and the stream extraction operator (>>) to extract data from the input stream. In addition, this code uses the pow() and round() functions that are available from the cmath header to raise a number to the power of 2 and to round a number to 1 decimal place. Finally, the last statement in the method returns a value of 0 to tell the operating system that the program has ended normally.

In the next chapter, you'll learn how to write the code for this program. Then, you'll be able to write comparable programs of your own.

The source code for a console application

```cpp
#include <iostream>
#include <cmath>

using namespace std;

int main()
{
    // print name of program
    cout << "Circle Calculator" << endl << endl;

    // get radius from user
    double radius;
    cout << "Enter radius:   ";
    cin >> radius;

    // make calculations
    double pi = 3.14159;
    double diameter = 2 * radius;
    double circumference = diameter * pi;
    double area = pi * pow(radius, 2.0);

    // round to 1 decimal place
    circumference = round(circumference * 10) / 10;
    area = round(area * 10) / 10;

    // write output to console
    cout << "Diameter:      " << diameter << endl
        << "Circumference: " << circumference << endl
        << "Area:          " << area << endl << endl
        << "Bye!" << endl << endl;

    // return value that indicates normal program exit
    return 0;
}
```

Description

- When you develop a C++ application, you write the *source code* for the program. Later, a program known as a *compiler* converts the source code into machine code that can be run by a computer.

- The two #include directives specify that this code uses two header files (iostream and cmath). These headers are available from the C++ standard library.

- The main() function contains the code that's run when the program starts.

- This code uses the cout, cin, and endl objects that are available from the iostream header to write output to the console (cout), read input from the console (cin), and specify the end of a line (endl).

- This code uses the pow() and round() functions that are available from the cmath header to raise a number to the power of 2 and to round a number to 1 decimal place.

- The return statement returns a value of 0 to the operating system to indicate that the program has ended normally.

Figure 1-4   The source code for a console application

How source code compiles to an executable file

Once the source code has been written, you must *compile* the source code into machine language as shown in figure 1-5. *Machine language* consists of the 1s and 0s necessary to run the program on the computer's operating system.

Machine language is an example of a *low-level language* that's hard for humans to read and understand. In contrast, C++ is an example of a *high-level language* that's relatively easy for humans to read and understand but not usable by a computer until it's compiled into a low-level language.

If you take a closer look at the compilation process, it shows that you typically use an IDE (Integrated Development Environment) to enter and edit the source code for a C++ program. Files that contain C++ source code often have an extension of .cpp. In this figure, for example, the source code file is named main.cpp because it contains the main() function for the program.

In the first step, the *preprocessor* combines your source code with the source code from any header files that haven't already been compiled. This results in a temporary file of expanded source code.

In the second step, the *compiler* converts this expanded source code into machine language. The machine language at this intermediate step is called *object code*, and it's stored in a file called an *object file*. Object files often have an extension of .o or .obj.

In the third step, the *linker* links the machine language in the object file with the object code from other libraries that have already been compiled. These libraries contain prewritten C++ code that performs various operations and tasks. Together, they are known as the *runtime library*.

In the end, the compilation process yields a machine language file that can be executed on an operating system. On Windows, an executable file typically has an extension of .exe. By contrast, an executable file on macOS typically has an extension of .app.

Although this compilation process is complicated, it's done automatically with the push of a single key if you're using an IDE to develop your programs, as shown later in this chapter. For now, all you need to take away from this figure is that C++ source code is compiled into machine language that's run by the computer's operating system.

At this point, you should realize that you must compile your source code on each operating system that you want to run it on. Then, you end up with one executable file for each operating system. If you write your source code correctly, you should be able to use the same source code to create an execut- able file for each operating system. This is known as *cross compiling*. In other words, with C++, the source code is portable between operating systems, but the executable file isn't. One of the goals of this book is to show you how to write C++ source code that's portable.

How C++ compiles source code into machine language

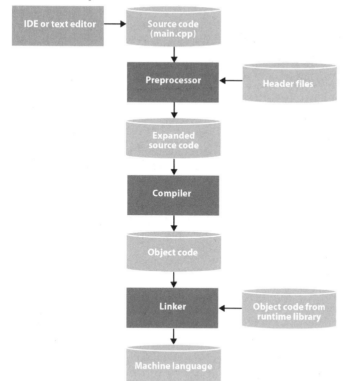

Description

- *Machine language* consists of the 1s and 0s that a computer can run.

- A *low-level language* such as machine language is hard for humans to read and understand but can be run by a computer.

- A *high-level language* such as C++ is relatively easy for humans to read and understand but can't be run by a computer until it is translated into a low-level language.

- A *compiler* is a program that translates a high-level language to a low-level language.

- When you develop a C++ application, you typically use an *Integrated Development Environment* (*IDE*) to enter and edit the *source code* for the application. Files that contain C++ source code often have a .cpp extension.

- The C++ compilation process translates C++ source code into a machine language known as *object code* and then into machine language that can be run directly by an operating system.

- Libraries that contain prewritten and precompiled C++ code that perform various operations and tasks are called the *runtime libraries*.

- For a C++ program to run on different operating systems, you must compile the source code once for each operating system.

Figure 1-5   How C++ compiles code

Four popular IDEs and compilers

Although it's possible to use a simple text editor with command-line tools, an *IDE* (*Integrated Development Environment*) provides features that can make developing C++ programs considerably easier. Figure 1-6 begins by listing four popular IDEs for C++ development. All four of these IDEs are either free or have a free edition. That makes them particularly attractive to students as well as programmers who are learning on their own.

All four of these IDEs provide the features listed in this figure. For example, these IDEs help you complete your code and notify you of potential errors. They automatically compile your code before you run it. And they include a debugger that can help you find and fix errors (bugs) in your code.

Of these IDEs, Visual Studio is the most popular IDE for developing C++ programs for Windows. It's developed by Microsoft and uses the Microsoft Visual C++ (MSVC) compiler by default. This compiler is the most popular compiler for developing C++ programs for Windows. Recently, Microsoft released a version of Visual Studio that runs on macOS, but most Mac users seem to prefer other IDEs, especially the Xcode IDE.

Xcode is the most popular IDE for developing C++ programs for macOS. It's developed by Apple and uses the Clang compiler. This open-source compiler is supported by many major companies including Apple, Microsoft, and Google. It was designed to act as a drop-in replacement for the GNU Compiler Collection (GCC), which is the standard compiler for most Unix-like systems, including Linux.

Eclipse and NetBeans both run on all major operating systems. Both of these excellent IDEs are free and open-source. Neither of them is as popular as Visual Studio and Xcode for developing for Windows and macOS, but both are good options for Linux development.

In addition, other C++ IDEs are available that aren't listed here. These options include commercial products such as the CLion IDE that's developed by JetBrains as well as the open-source Code::Blocks IDE.

When choosing an IDE, keep in mind that you may have to configure it to work with a compiler such as one of the compilers described in this figure. That's especially true if you're using an IDE such as Eclipse or NetBeans that doesn't automatically install and configure a compiler. For example, if you want to use NetBeans for Windows development, you need to install a compiler such as the MinGW compiler separately and configure NetBeans to use it. By contrast, the MSVC compiler is automatically installed and configured when you install Visual Studio, and the Clang compiler is automatically installed and configured when you install Xcode.

When choosing a compiler, keep in mind that different compilers provide different levels of support for the ISO standards. If you choose a compiler that provides good support for the ISO standards, you can use the features specified by those ISO standards. In addition, you can easily port your source code from one compiler to another.

Four popular C++ IDEs

IDE	Description
Visual Studio	A free IDE that runs on Windows and macOS. This IDE is popular for developing C++ applications for Windows.
Xcode	A free IDE that runs on macOS. This IDE is popular for developing C++ applications for macOS.
Eclipse	A free, open-source IDE that runs on most modern operating systems. This IDE is popular for developing C++ applications for Linux.
NetBeans	A free, open-source IDE that runs on most modern operating systems. This IDE is popular for developing C++ applications for Linux.

Features provided by most IDEs

- Code completion
- Error detection
- Automatic compilation
- Debugging

Four popular C++ compilers

Compiler Name	Description
Microsoft Visual C++ (MSVC)	The compiler that comes with the Microsoft Visual Studio IDE. This compiler is popular for Windows.
Clang	An open-source compiler that comes with Xcode. This compiler is popular for macOS. It was designed as a drop-in replacement for the GCC compiler.
GNU Compiler Collection (GCC)	A collection of open-source compilers that includes a compiler for C++. This C++ compiler is standard for most Unix-like systems, including Linux.
Minimalist GNU for Windows (MinGW)	A native Windows version of the GCC compiler.

Description

- To develop C++ applications, you typically use an Integrated Development Environment (IDE). Many other IDEs exist beyond those listed above, including some commercial products such as CLion and more open-source offerings such as Code::Blocks.

- Each IDE must use a compiler to compile the source code for a particular operating system. Many vendors provide C++ compilers, including the Free Software Foundation, Microsoft, Apple, Intel, Oracle, and IBM.

- All of the IDEs and compilers listed here are either free or have free editions.

- Different C++ compilers provide different levels of support for the ISO standards. When choosing a compiler, it's important to choose one that provides good support for the ISO standards.

Figure 1-6   Four popular IDEs and compilers for C++

How to use Visual Studio for Windows development

Now that you have some background information about C++, you're ready to start learning how to use an IDE. In particular, you're ready to learn how to open and run any of the source code provided by this book. You can download this source code as described in the appendixes for this book.

If you're using a Windows computer, you can use Visual Studio as shown in the next four figures to develop programs that run on Windows. Of course, if you're using a Mac, you can skip or skim these figures and move on to the figures that show how to use Xcode to develop programs that run on macOS.

How to open a project and work with source code

Figure 1-7 begins by showing Visual Studio with source code for a C++ project open in its *code editor*. In Visual Studio, a *solution* can contain one or more *projects* where each project is a folder within the solution. In this figure, the solution only contains one project, and both the project and the solution are named circle_calculator.

To open a project in Visual Studio, you can follow the procedure shown in figure 1-7 to open the solution that contains the project. For all of the Visual Studio applications presented in this book, the solutions are in this folder:

```
C:\murach\cpp\vs\book_apps
```

Once you open the solution for a project, you can view the source code for the project in the code editor by double-clicking on its file.

Before you open a source code file in the code editor, you may need to expand the folder for the project and the Source Files folder. To expand a folder, you can click the triangle to its left. In this figure, for example, both the circle_calculator folder and the Source Files folder have been expanded, and the source code file named main.cpp has been opened. This file contains the source code that contains the main() function for the Circle Calculator program described earlier in this chapter.

When you open a source code file in the code editor, it uses different colors for different language elements to make it easier for you to recognize the C++ syntax. In addition, Visual Studio provides standard File and Edit menus as well as keyboard shortcuts that let you save and edit the source code. For example, you can press Ctrl+S to save your source code, and you can use standard menu items and keyboard shortcuts to cut, copy, and paste code.

When you're done working with a solution, you can close it. To do that, you can select the Close item in the File menu. In addition, if you open another solution, Visual Studio automatically closes the current solution.

Before going on, you should realize that the appearance of the IDE as well as the menu structure depend on the Visual Studio development settings. For this book, we used the General settings, which should be the default if you don't have other versions of Visual Studio installed. To check your development

Visual Studio with source code displayed in its code editor

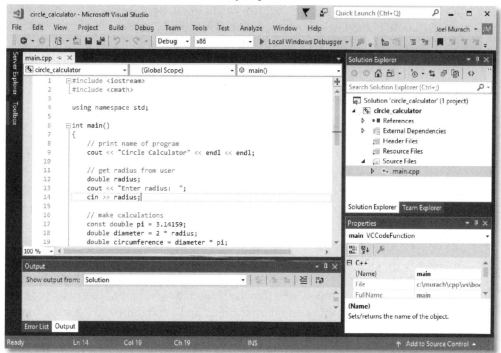

How to open and close a solution

- To open a solution, press Ctrl+Shift+O or select the File→Open→Project/ Solution menu item. Then, use the Open Project dialog that's displayed to locate and select the solution file (.sln) and click the Open button.
- To close a solution, select the File→Close Solution menu item.

How to open, edit, and save a source code file

- To open a source code file in the *code editor*, double-click on it in the Solution Explorer. Before you do that, you may need to expand the folder for the project by clicking on the triangle to its left, and you may need to expand the Source Files folder by clicking on the triangle to its left.
- To edit a source code file, you can use normal editing techniques to enter new code or edit existing code.
- To save a source code file, press Ctrl+S or click the Save button in the toolbar.
- To save all open files, press Ctrl+Shift+S or click the Save All button in the toolbar.

Description

- A Visual Studio *solution* consists of one or more projects where each *project* consists of a folder that contains the folders and files for a program.

Figure 1-7   How to open an existing project and work with its source code

settings, select the Tools→Import and Export Settings menu item to display the Import and Export Settings Wizard. In the first dialog, select the "Reset all settings" option and click the Next button. Then, in the second dialog, select the "No" option and click the Next button. When the third dialog is displayed, the current settings will be highlighted. If those settings aren't General, select General and then click the Finish button. Otherwise, click the Cancel button.

How to compile and run a project

Figure 1-8 shows how to compile and run a project. One easy way to run a project is to press Ctrl+F5. Then, if the project needs to be compiled, Visual Studio automatically compiles (builds) the project and runs its main() function. But first, it may prompt you to make sure you want to build the project. That can happen if you've made changes to the project or if you're running the project for the first time. Since this automatically compiles the project and creates the executable file, this feature is known as *automatic compilation*.

When you use Visual Studio to run a console program on Windows, it starts a Command Prompt window like the one shown in this figure. Then, the program uses this window to display output to the user and get input from the user. In this figure, for example, the program starts by displaying the name of the program on the console. Then, it prompts the user to enter a radius. In this figure, the user entered a radius of 7 by typing 7 and pressing Enter. Next, the program displays the diameter, circumference, and area of the circle. After that, the program displays a message of "Bye!" to indicate that the program has exited.

In this figure, Visual Studio displays the "Press any key to continue…" message after the program exits. This allows the user to view the console output before the console closes. Then, when the user presses any key, the console closes. However, Visual Studio only displays this message when you press Ctrl+F5 or select the Start Without Debugging item from the Debug menu. If you accidentally press F5 or select the Debug→Start Debugging menu item, the console closes when the program exits. For the Circle Calculator program, this would prevent you from seeing the output of the program. You'll learn more about how this works in chapter 8.

When you run a project like the ones for this book that were created by another programmer, you may get a message indicating that there are build errors. In most cases, that's because the version of the Windows SDK that's used by the program is different from the version that was installed when you installed Visual Studio. In that case, you'll see an error in the Error List window indicating that the Windows SDK was not found. (The Error List window is displayed in a tab at the bottom of the IDE as shown in this figure. If this tab isn't displayed, you can use the View→Error List menu item to display it.)

To fix this error, you need to change the Windows SDK version that's used by the application as described in this figure. If you don't know what version to use, you can typically select the most current version, which is likely to be the one that was installed with Visual Studio.

Visual Studio after compiling and running a console application

Description

- To run a project, press Ctrl+F5 or select the Debug→Start Without Debugging menu item. If a dialog is displayed that asks if you want to build the project, click the Yes button to build the project before you run it.

- When you run a project, Visual Studio automatically compiles it. As a result, you don't need to manually compile a project before you run it. This is known as the *automatic compilation* feature.

- The Start Without Debugging menu item automatically displays a "Press any key to continue" message when the program exits. This keeps the console open until you press any key.

- If you accidentally press F5 or select the Debug→Start Debugging menu item, the console closes when the program exits. This might prevent you from seeing the output of the program. You'll learn more about how this works in chapter 8.

How to correct a problem with the Windows SDK version

- If you compile a project and Visual Studio indicates that there are build errors, the problem may be that the Windows SDK version used by the application can't be found. This can happen if a newer version of the SDK is installed with Visual Studio.

- To change the SDK version, select the project in the Solution Explorer and then select the Project→Properties menu item to display the Property Pages dialog. Then, select the General item and set the Windows SDK Version property to the version of the SDK that was installed when you installed Visual Studio.

Figure 1-8   How to compile and run a project

How to use code completion and error detection

Figure 1-9 shows how to use the *code completion* feature. In Visual Studio, the code completion feature is also known as *IntelliSense*. This feature helps you avoid typing mistakes, and it makes it easier to enter code. In this figure, for example, I started to enter the name of a variable. After I entered "rad", Visual Studio displayed a list that included "radius", which is the name of the variable that I wanted to enter. So, I pressed the Down Arrow key to highlight the "radius" option. At this point, I could press the Enter key to automatically enter the rest of the name.

In this case, code completion didn't save me much typing. But, it did make sure that I spelled the name of the variable correctly. This becomes more helpful as you begin working with longer names and more complex code.

In addition, code completion automatically enters opening and closing parentheses and braces whenever they're needed. This makes it easier to code functions like the main() function in this figure.

Code completion can also make it easy for you to enter values for string variables, which consist of a sequence of zero or more characters. If you type a double quotation mark to identify a string value, the code completion feature automatically adds the closing quotation mark and places the cursor between the two quotes. At this point, you can enter the text for the string.

If you experiment with the code completion feature, you'll quickly see when it helps you enter code more quickly and when it makes sense to enter the code yourself. In addition, you'll see that it helps you discover the functions that are available to you. This will make more sense as you learn more about C++ in the next few chapters.

As you enter C++ code, you may introduce syntax errors. A *syntax error* is any code that breaks the syntax rules of C++. If you enter code that contains a syntax error, the code won't compile. For example, if you enter an opening parenthesis without coding a closing parenthesis, your code has a syntax error and won't compile.

As you enter code into the code editor, Visual Studio displays syntax errors whenever it detects them. It does that by marking the error with a wavy red underline. If you position the mouse pointer over the code with the wavy red underline, Visual Studio displays a description of the error. This can provide valuable information that can help you fix the error. This feature is known as *error detection*, and it can help you find and fix errors before you even attempt to compile and run a program.

Visual Studio's code editor with a code completion list

How to use code completion

- When you enter code, Visual Studio often displays a list that attempts to help you complete the code entry. This is generally known as *code completion*, but Visual Studio refers to it as *IntelliSense*.

- If the code completion feature doesn't activate automatically, you can sometimes activate it manually by pressing Ctrl+Spacebar after entering one or more letters.

- To insert an item from a code completion list, you can use the Down and Up arrow keys on your keyboard to select the item and then press the Enter key.

- The code completion feature also helps you enter pairs of quotes, parentheses, braces, and so on. To do that, it enters the closing character immediately after you enter the opening character. For example, after you enter an opening quote, it enters the closing quote and places the cursor between the two quotes.

How to use error detection

- A *syntax error* is any code that won't compile. If Visual Studio detects a syntax error as you enter code, it places a red wavy line under the statement. This is known as the *error detection* feature.

- To get more information about a syntax error, you can position the mouse pointer over the code with the red wavy underline.

Figure 1-9   How to use code completion and error detection

How to create a new project

Figure 1-10 shows a procedure for using Visual Studio to create a new project that works with standard C++ code. To start, you display the New Project dialog and choose the type of project you want to create. In this dialog, you can select the Windows Console Application item as shown in this figure. In addition, you can enter a name and location for the project. In this figure, for example, the project name is "ch01_test" and its location is this folder:

```
C:\murach\cpp\vs\book_apps
```

If you install the source code for this book as described in appendix A, all of the Visual Studio programs presented in this book should be stored in this folder.

After completing the New Project dialog, you can click the OK button. This creates a new project that uses a precompiled header file named stdafx.h. This header file can improve performance of the compiler, especially if you're using many large libraries. However, it isn't standard, and it isn't necessary for the programs in this book, which don't use a lot of large libraries. As a result, we recommend setting the Precompiled Header property to "Not Using Precompiled Headers" as described in this figure. Then, you can use standard headers as shown throughout this book.

Visual Studio's dialog for creating a new project

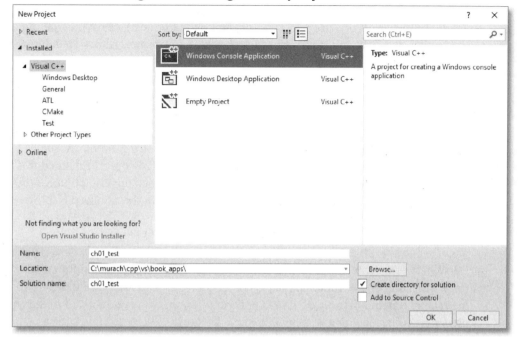

Procedure

1. Click the New Project button in the toolbar or select the File→New→Project menu item to display the New Project dialog.

2. Select the Windows Console Application item, enter a name for the project, select a location for the project, and click the OK button to create the project.

3. Select the project in the Solution Explorer and then select the Project→Properties menu item to display the Property Pages dialog. Expand the C/C++ group, select the Precompiled Headers item, and set the Precompiled Header property to "Not Using Precompiled Headers".

4. Optionally, delete all unnecessary files related to the precompiled header (targetver.h, stdafx.h, and stdafx.cpp).

5. Optionally, rename the .cpp file that contains the main() function to main.cpp.

6. Open the file that contains the main() function and edit the code so it's like the code presented throughout this book.

Figure 1-10   How to create a new project (part 1of 2)

If you set the Precompiled Header property to "Not Using Precompiled Headers", you can use the Solution Explorer to delete all files related to the precompiled header that are no longer needed by the project. These include the targetver.h, stdafx.h, and stdafx.cpp files shown in this figure. Although deleting these files is optional, you can do that if you'd like to omit any unnecessary files. The easiest way to delete a file is to select it in the Solution Explorer and press the Delete key. Then, you can use the resulting dialog to permanently delete the file.

By default, Visual Studio creates a starting source code file that has the same name as the project. For the project shown in this figure, for example, Visual Studio created a source code file named ch01_test.cpp. However, I renamed this file to main.cpp to clearly show that this file contains the main() function for the program. The easiest way to rename a file is to select it in the Solution Explorer and press the F2 key. Then, you can enter a new name for the file. Alternately, you can right-click on the file and select the Rename item from the resulting menu.

When you create a new project, Visual Studio generates some starting code for you. In this figure, for example, Visual Studio generated some of the code for the main() function. However, it also generated some extra code related to the precompiled headers that was unnecessary. As a result, I deleted this code and added some standard C++ code that provides for writing output to the console. At this point, running this program would display a message of "Success!" on the console, which is a good starting point for a new program.

A new project in Visual Studio with some starting source code

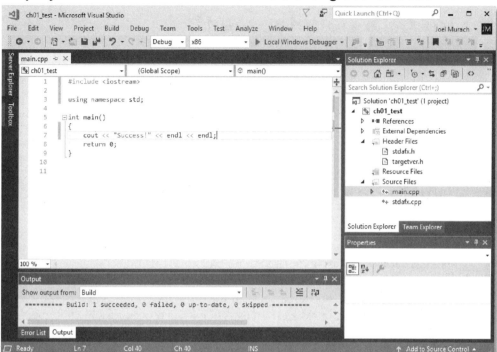

How to rename and delete files

- To rename a file, you can select it in the Solution Explorer, press F2, and enter a new name for the file.

- To delete a file, you can select it in the Solution Explorer, press the Delete key, and use the resulting dialog to confirm the deletion.

Description

- By default, Visual Studio creates a starting source code file that has the same name as the project. However, it's a common practice to use the name main.cpp for this file, as shown by the programs in this book.

- By default, Visual Studio creates a new project that uses a precompiled header file named stdafx.h. This header file can improve performance of the compiler, especially if you're using many large libraries. However, it isn't standard, and it isn't necessary for the programs in this book, which don't use a lot of large libraries.

- If you set the Precompiled Header property to "Not Using Precompiled Headers" as described in part 1 of this figure, you can use standard headers as shown throughout this book. In addition, you can optionally use the Solution Explorer to delete all files related to the precompiled header, including targetver.h, stdafx.h, and stdafx.cpp.

Figure 1-10   How to create a new project (part 2 of 2)

How to use Xcode for macOS development

If you read the first six topics in this chapter and you're using a Mac, you're ready to start learning how to use the Xcode IDE to develop programs that run on macOS. In particular, you're ready to learn how to open and run any of the source code provided by this book. You can download this source code as described in appendix B of this book.

How to open a project and work with source code

Figure 1-11 begins by showing Xcode with source code for a C++ project open in its *code editor*. In Xcode, a *project* is a folder that contains the folders and files for a program. In this figure, for example, the project is named circle_calculator, and it contains a folder named circle_calculator that contains the main.cpp file that stores the code for the program.

To open a project in Xcode, you can follow the procedure shown in this figure. For this book, the Xcode projects for the applications presented are in this folder:

`/murach/cpp/xcode/book_apps`

Once you open the project, you can view the source code for the project in the code editor by clicking on its file.

Before you open a source code file in the code editor, you may need to expand the folder for the project and the folder that contains the file for the source code. To expand a folder, you can click the triangle to its left. In this figure, for example, the circle_calculator folder has been expanded, and the source code file named main.cpp has been opened. This file contains the source code that contains the main() function for the Circle Calculator program described earlier in this chapter.

When you open a source code file in the code editor, it uses different colors for different language elements to make it easier for you to recognize the C++ syntax. In addition, Xcode provides standard File and Edit menus and keyboard shortcuts that let you save and edit the source code. For example, you can press Command+S to save your source code, and you can use standard menu items and keyboard shortcuts to cut, copy, and paste code.

When you're done working with a project, you can close it. To do that, you can select the Close item from the File menu. However, if you open another project, Xcode automatically opens another window for that project. Then, you will have multiple Xcode windows open.

Xcode with source code displayed in its code editor

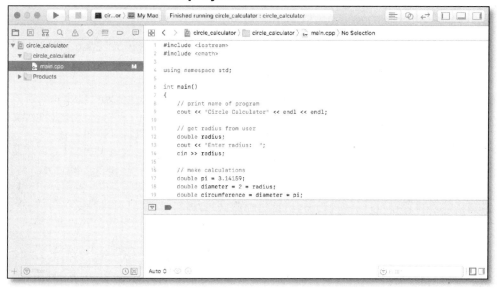

How to open and close a project

- To open a project, press Command+O or select the File→Open menu item. Then, use the dialog that's displayed to locate and select the project file (.xcodeproj) and click the Open button.
- To close a project, select the File→Close Project menu item.

How to open, edit, and save a source code file

- To open a source code file in the *code editor*, click on it in the Navigator. Before you do that, you may need to expand the folder for the project by clicking on the triangle to its left, and you may need to expand the folder that contains the source files by clicking on the triangle to its left.
- To edit a source code file, you can use normal editing techniques to enter new code or edit existing code.
- To save a source code file, press Command+S or select the File→Save menu item.

Description

- An Xcode *project* consists of a folder that contains the folders and files for a program.

Figure 1-11   How to open an existing project and work with its source code

How to compile and run a project

Figure 1-12 shows how to compile and run a project. One easy way to run a project is to press Command+R. Then, if the project needs to be compiled, Xcode automatically compiles (builds) the project and runs its main() function. This feature is known as *automatic compilation*.

When you use Xcode to run a console program, it uses a Console window like the one shown in this figure. Then, the program uses this window to display output to the user and get input from the user. In this figure, for example, the program starts by displaying the name of the program on the console. Then, it prompts the user to enter a radius. In this figure, the user entered a radius of 7 by typing 7 and pressing Enter. Next, the program displays the diameter, circumference, and area of the circle. After that, the program displays a message of "Bye!" to indicate that the program has ended, and Xcode displays some extra information that includes the exit code that the program returned when it ended.

Xcode after compiling and running a console application

Description

- To run a project, press Command+R or select the Project→Run menu item.

- When you run a project, Xcode automatically compiles it. As a result, you don't need to manually compile a project before you run it. This is known as the *automatic compilation* feature.

- When you run a project that writes data to the console, that data is displayed in the Console window in the lower right corner of the Xcode window.

- To display or hide the Console window, you can click the icon on the bottom right corner of the Xcode window.

- When you run a project that requests input from the console, the Console window pauses to accept the input. Then, you can click in the Console window, type the input, and press the Enter key.

- In addition to displaying output and accepting input, the Console window can display other information. For example, the Console window automatically displays a message when the program finishes running, and it can display errors that are encountered when an application is run.

Figure 1-12   How to compile and run a project

How to use code completion and error detection

Figure 1-13 shows how to use the *code completion* feature. This feature helps you avoid typing mistakes, and it makes it easier to enter code. In this figure, for example, I started to enter the name of a variable. After I entered "r", Xcode displayed a list that included "radius", which is the name of the variable that I wanted to enter. So, I pressed the Down Arrow key to highlight the "radius" option. At this point, I could press the Enter key to automatically enter the rest of the name.

In this case, code completion didn't save me much typing. But, it did make sure that I spelled the name of the variable correctly. This becomes more helpful as you begin working with longer names and more complex code.

In addition, code completion sometimes enters opening and closing parentheses and braces whenever they're needed. This makes it easier to code functions like the main() function in this figure.

If you experiment with the code completion feature, you'll quickly see when it helps you enter code more quickly and when it makes sense to enter the code yourself. In addition, you'll see that it helps you discover the functions that are available to you. This will make more sense as you learn more about C++ in the next few chapters.

As you enter C++ code, you may introduce syntax errors. A *syntax error* is any code that breaks the syntax rules of C++. If you enter code that contains a syntax error, the code won't compile. For example, if you enter an opening parenthesis without coding a closing parenthesis, your code has a syntax error and won't compile.

As you enter code into the code editor, Xcode displays syntax errors whenever it detects them. It does that by displaying an error icon and message to the right of the line of code. In this figure, for example, you can see an error icon and message to the right of the line of code that I was entering. If you click on the error icon, Xcode displays more information about the error. This can provide valuable information that can help you fix the error. This feature is known as *error detection*, and it can help you find and fix errors before you even attempt to compile and run a program. In addition, for some errors, the extra information may include a suggested fix and a Fix button that you can click on to automatically implement this fix.

Xcode's editor with a code completion list

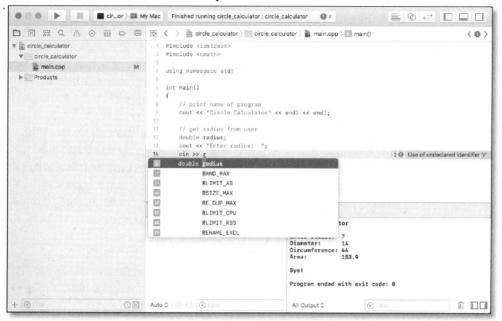

How to use code completion

- When you enter code, Xcode often displays a list that attempts to help you complete the code entry. This is generally known as *code completion*.
- To insert an item from a code completion list, you can use the Down and Up arrow keys on your keyboard to select the item and then press the Enter key.

How to use error detection

- A *syntax error* is any code that won't compile. If Xcode detects a syntax error as you enter code, it displays an error icon and message to the right of the statement. This is known as the *error detection* feature.
- To get more information about a syntax error, you can click the error icon. Sometimes the information that's displayed includes a Fix button that will implement a suggested fix.

Figure 1-13   How to use code completion and error detection

How to create a new project

Figure 1-14 shows a procedure for using Xcode to create a new project for a console application. To start, you display the first dialog for creating a new project and choose the type of project you want to create. In this dialog, you can select the macOS and Command Line Tool options as shown in this figure.

In the second dialog, you must enter a name for the project in the Product Name field. In this figure, for example, the project name is "ch01_test". In addition, you often need to select C++ as the language for the project from the Language drop-down list. If necessary, you can also specify a name for your organization and a unique identifier for it. In this example, I used our website address (murach.com) backwards (com.murach), because that's a common way to uniquely identify an organization. Then, if you ever distribute the program, the organization identifier and the product name will be combined to create a unique bundle identifier as shown in this dialog.

In the third dialog (not shown here), you can specify the location for the project. If you install the source code for this book as described in the appendix, all of the Xcode programs presented in this book should be stored in this folder:

`/Documents/murach/cpp/xcode/book_apps`

After you specify the location, you can click the Create button to create the project. Then, Xcode creates a folder that corresponds with the project name, and it creates some additional files that it uses to configure the project.

Xcode's dialogs for creating a new project

Procedure

1. Select the File→New→Project menu item to display the first dialog for creating a new project.
2. In the first dialog, select the macOS operating system, select the Command Line Tool item, and click the Next button.
3. In the second dialog, enter a product name, select the C++ language, and click the Next button. If necessary, enter an organization name and an identifier for the organization that uniquely identifies it.
4. In the third dialog, navigate to the folder you want to use to store your project, and click the Create button to create the folder for the project.

Figure 1-14   How to create a new project (part 1 of 2)

When you create a new project, Xcode generates some starting code for you. For example, Xcode generated some of the code for the main() function shown in this figure. However, it also generated some extra code that was unnecessary. As a result, I edited this file so it only contains the starting code shown in this figure. At this point, running this program would display a message of "Success!" on the console, which is a good starting point for a new program.

A new project in Xcode with some starting source code

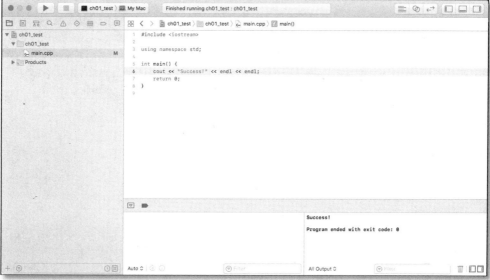

Procedure (continued)

5. In the Xcode window, expand the folder for the project if necessary. Then, click on the main.cpp file to show the main() function that was generated for the project.

6. Edit the generated code so it's like the code presented throughout this book.

Description

*   By default, Xcode generates some starting code for you. You can edit this code so it contains C++ code like the code shown throughout this book.

Figure 1-14   How to create a new project (part 2 of 2)

Perspective

In this chapter, you were introduced to C++ programming. In addition, you learned how to use an IDE such as Visual Studio or Xcode to create and run a C++ program on Windows or macOS. With that as background, you're ready to learn how to write your own C++ programs. But first, I recommend that you familiarize yourself with the IDE of your choice by doing the exercises at the end of this chapter.

Terms

International Organization for
    Standardization (ISO)
application (app)
program
desktop application
GUI application
graphical user interface (GUI)
console application
console
command prompt
terminal
source code
machine language
low-level language
high-level language
preprocessor

compiler
object code
linker
runtime library
cross compiling
Integrated Development
    Environment (IDE)
code editor
Visual Studio solution
project
automatic compilation
code completion
IntelliSense
syntax error
error detection

Summary

- Since 1998, C++ has been standardized by the *International Organization for Standardization (ISO)*.

- An *application*, or *app*, is computer software that performs a task or a related set of tasks. Applications can also be referred to as *programs*, even though one application may actually consist of many related programs.

- A *desktop application* is an application that runs on your computer. A desktop application can use a *graphical user interface* (*GUI*) or the *console* to display output and get user input.

- Applications that use a command line window known as the console to interact with the user are known as *console applications*.

- A *high-level language* such as C++ is relatively easy for humans to read and understand.

- A *low-level language* such as *machine language* is hard for humans to read and understand but efficient for a computer to use.

- A *compiler* is a program that translates a high-level language to a low-level language.

- The C++ compiler translates C++ source code into machine language that consists of the 1s and 0s that can be run directly by an operating system.

- An *Integrated Development Environment* (*IDE*) can make working with C++ easier by providing code completion, error detection, automatic compilation, and a debugger.

- Visual Studio and Xcode are two of the most commonly used IDEs for C++ development.

- A Visual Studio *solution* can contain one or more *projects* where each project is a folder that contains the folders and files for a program.

- An Xcode *project* is a folder that contains the folders and files for a program.

- The main() function of a program is the starting point of the program.

Before you do the exercises in this book

Before you do any of the exercises in this book, you need to have an IDE installed on your system. You also need to download the folders and files for this book from our website and install them on your system. For complete instructions, please refer to appendix A for Windows or appendix B for macOS.

Exercise 1-1   Open and run two projects

This exercise guides you through the process of opening two existing projects, reviewing the code, and building and running the projects. It also has you introduce a syntax error to see what happens.

Open the Circle Calculator project and review its code

1. Use your IDE to open the Circle Calculator project or solution in this folder:
    `book_apps\ch01_circle_calculator`

2. Open the main.cpp file.

3. Review the code to see that it contains two #include directives for the iostream and cmath header files, a using directive for the std namespace, and a main() function that accepts a radius from the console, calculates the diameter, radius, and circumference, and writes the output to the console. Note that the main() function ends by returning a value of 0.

Run the Circle Calculator project

4. Run the project, building it if necessary. (If you're using Visual Studio on Windows and you get an error that indicates that the Windows SDK was not found, use the information in figure 1-8 to fix it and then run the project again.)

5. When prompted, enter a radius. Then, review the output that's written to the console.

Introduce a syntax error

6. Remove the semicolon (;) from the first statement in the main() function to see the errors that are detected.

7. Run the project to see what happens.

8. Add the semicolon back and then run the project again. When you're done, close the project.

Open the Guess Number project and review its code

9. Use your IDE to open the Guess Number project in this folder:
   `book_apps\ch04b_guess_number`

10. Open the main.cpp file and review its code. Note that its code is structured similarly to the code for the Circle Calculator program, but it uses some statements that you haven't learned about yet.

Run the Guess Number project

11. Run the project, building it if necessary. (If you're using Visual Studio on Windows, you may need to change the Windows SDK version for the project.)

12. Enter input when prompted, and review the output that's written to the console. When you're done, close the project.

Exercise 1-2   Create a new project

This exercise guides you through the process of creating a new project that displays a message on the console.

1. Use your IDE to create a project named ch01_success_message in the ex_starts folder.

2. If you're using Visual Studio, modify the project so it doesn't use precompiled headers. Then, delete all the files related to precompiled headers that are no longer necessary.

3. If you're using Visual Studio, rename the ch01_success_message.cpp file to main.cpp.

4. Open the main.cpp file and modify the generated code so it looks like this:

```cpp
#include <iostream>
using namespace std;

int main() {
    cout << "Success!" << endl << endl;
    return 0;
}
```

As you enter this code, use code completion whenever it's helpful.

5. Run the application and view the output. It should display a message that says, "Success!" When you're done, close the project.

2

How to write your first programs

Once you've installed an IDE and the C++ compiler, the quickest and best way to *learn* C++ programming is to *do* C++ programming. That's why this chapter shows you how to write complete C++ programs that get input from a user, make calculations, and display output. When you finish this chapter, you should be able to write comparable programs of your own.

Basic coding skills

This chapter starts by introducing you to some basic coding skills. You'll use these skills for every C++ program you develop.

How to code statements

The *statements* in a program direct the operation of the program. When you code a statement, you can start it anywhere in a coding line, you can continue it from one line to another, and you can code one or more spaces anywhere a single space is valid.

To end most statements, you use a semicolon. In the first example in figure 2-1, for example, all of the lines that end with a semicolon are statements. But when a statement requires a set of braces ({}), it ends with the right brace. Then, the statements within the braces are referred to as a *block* of code. For example, the statement that defines the main() function shown in this figure contains a block of code.

To make a program easier to read, you should use indentation and spacing to align statements and blocks of code. This is illustrated by the program in this figure and by all of the programs and examples in this book.

Note that the first line of code doesn't end with a semicolon. That's because it's a *preprocessor directive*, not a C++ statement. Later in this chapter, you'll learn more about coding this directive.

How to code comments

The *comments* in a program typically document what the statements do. Since the compiler ignores comments, you can include them anywhere in a program without affecting your code. In the first example in figure 2-1, the comments are shaded.

A *single-line comment* is typically used to describe one or more lines of code. This type of comment starts with two slashes (//) that tell the compiler to ignore all characters until the end of the current line. In the first example in this figure, you can see four single-line comments that are used to describe groups of statements. In addition, two single-line comments are coded after the code on a line. This type of single-line comment is sometimes referred to as an *end-of-line comment*.

The second example in this figure shows how to code a *block comment*. This type of comment is typically used to document information that applies to a block of code. This information can include the author's name, program completion date, the purpose of the code, the files used by the code, and so on.

Although many programmers sprinkle their code with comments, that shouldn't be necessary if you write code that's easy to read and understand. Instead, you should use comments only to clarify code that's difficult to understand. In this figure, for example, an experienced C++ programmer wouldn't need any of the single-line comments.

A program that consists of statements and comments

```
#include <iostream>        // a preprocessor directive, not a statement

using namespace std;

int main()
{
    cout << "Welcome to the Calorie Calculator\n\n";

    // get number of servings from user
    double servings;
    cout << "Enter servings per food item: ";
    cin >> servings;

    // get number of calories from user
    double calories;
    cout << "Enter calories per serving: ";
    cin >> calories;

    // calculate total calories
    double total_calories = servings * calories;

    // display total calories
    cout << "Total calories: " << total_calories << endl << endl;

    return 0; // return a value indicating normal exit
}
```

A block comment that could be coded at the start of a program

```
/*
 * Author:  M. Delamater
 * Purpose: This program uses the console to get servings and calories from
 *          the user. It then calculates and displays the total calories.
 */
```

Description

- *Statements* direct the operations of a program, and *comments* typically document what the statements do.

- Most statements end with a semicolon.

- You can start a statement at any point in a line and continue the statement from one line to the next. To make a program easier to read, you should use indentation and extra spaces to align statements and parts of statements.

- Code within a set of braces ({}) can be referred to as a *block* of code.

- To code a *single-line comment*, type // followed by the comment. You can code a single-line comment on a line by itself or after a statement. A comment that's coded after a statement is sometimes called an *end-of-line comment*.

- A *block comment* typically consists of multiple lines. To code a block comment, type /* at the start of the block and */ at the end. You can also code asterisks to identify the lines in the block, but that isn't required.

Figure 2-1   How to code statements and comments

One problem with comments is that they may not accurately represent what the code does. This often happens when a programmer changes the code, but doesn't change the comments that go along with it. Then, it's even harder to understand the code because the comments are misleading. So if you change the code that you've written comments for, be sure to change the comments too.

How to code a main() function

A *function* is a named, reusable block of code that performs a task. The *main() function* is a special kind of function that's automatically executed when your program starts. All C++ programs contain a main() function.

If you use an IDE to create a project, it typically generates a main() function for you. Now, figure 2-2 presents the syntax for declaring a main() function.

The main() function starts with the C++ int keyword. This indicates that the function returns an integer value. You'll learn more about this value in a moment. After specifying the type of data that the function returns, you code the name of the function followed by a pair of parentheses. In this case, the name of the function is main.

For a main() function, you can leave the parentheses empty, as in the first example. Or, you can code two *parameters*, as in the second example. You'll learn more about function parameters later in this book. For now, all you need to know about these parameters is that they are optional, so you don't need to include them. In fact, even though some IDEs generate these parameters by default, the programs presented in this book don't use them. As a result, there's no need to include them for the examples presented in this book.

The next line of code in the main() function is the opening brace for the *body* of the function. This opening brace can be on its own line, as shown in the first and second examples. Many C++ style guides recommend this approach. As a result, this book uses this approach for most of its code. Sometimes, though, to save vertical space, this book may code the opening brace on the first line as shown in the third example. That's an acceptable style too, although coding the opening brace on its own line is more common when working with C++.

The body of the main() function contains the statements that run the program. The last statement in the main() function is a *return statement*. This statement returns an integer value that tells the operating system whether the program exited normally or abnormally. If the main() function doesn't contain a return statement, C++ returns a value of 0 to the operating system by default. Because of this, it's common to omit the return statement to save space.

When you're working with C++11 or later, you can also return the EXIT_SUCCESS and EXIT_FAILURE values. The advantage of this approach is that it makes the return statement easier to read and understand. However, since the main() function automatically returns a value that indicates a normal exit, you typically don't need to code a return statement for your main() function.

A main() function with no parameters

```
int main()
{
    // statements
    return 0;
}
```

A main() function with two parameters

```
int main(int argc, char** argv)
{
    // statements
    return 0;
}
```

A main() function with different brace placement

```
int main() {
    // statements
    return EXIT_SUCCESS;
}
```

Three standard return values for the main() function

Value	Description	C++ version
0	Normal exit	All
EXIT_SUCCESS	Normal exit	C++11 or later
EXIT_FAILURE	Abnormal exit	C++11 or later

Description

- Every C++ program contains one *main() function* that is called by the operating system.

- The statements between the braces in the main() function are run when the program is executed.

- In most cases, you can code the main() function with no parameters. To do that, type an empty set of parentheses after you type the function's name.

- If you need the execution environment to pass arguments to the main() function, you can code the parameters named argc and argv as shown in the second example. However, these parameters aren't necessary for any of the programs presented in this book.

- You can code the opening brace of the main() function on the same line as the parentheses or on the next line. Many C++ style guides recommend coding the opening brace on its own line, and this book follows that convention whenever possible.

- You can end the main() function by coding a *return statement* that returns an integer value that tells the operating system how the program exited. If you omit this return statement, the main() function automatically returns a value of 0, which indicates a normal exit.

Figure 2-2   How to code a main() function

The last line of code for the main() function is the closing brace. Unlike the opening brace, this one should always be on its own line. That's because a common syntax error is forgetting to code a closing brace. Thus, leaving the closing brace on its own line makes it easier to see whether the opening brace has a corresponding closing brace.

How to create identifiers

As you code a C++ program, you need to create and use *identifiers*. These are the names that you define in your code.

Figure 2-3 shows you how to create identifiers. In brief, you must start each identifier with a letter or an underscore. After that first character, you can use any combination of letters, underscores, or digits.

Since C++ is case-sensitive, you need to be careful when you create and use identifiers. If, for example, you define an identifier named subtotal, you can't refer to it later as Subtotal. That's a common coding error.

When you create an identifier, you should try to make the name both meaningful and easy to remember. To make a name meaningful, you should use as many characters as you need, so it's easy for other programmers to read and understand your code. For instance, net_price is more meaningful than nprice, and nprice is more meaningful than np.

Notice here that the name of this identifier is formed by separating two lowercase words with an underscore. This can be referred to as *snake case*, and it's used for most identifiers in this book. However, some developers prefer to name identifiers by capitalizing the first letter of each word. This is called *camel case*.

To make a name easy to remember, you should avoid abbreviations. If, for example, you use nwcst as an identifier, you may later have difficulty remembering whether it was ncust, nwcust, or nwcst. If you code the name as new_customer, however, you won't have any trouble remembering what it was. In addition, that's easy for other programmers to understand. Yes, you type more characters when you create identifiers that are meaningful and easy to remember, but that will be more than justified by the time you'll save when you test, debug, and maintain the program.

On the other hand, programmers often use just one or two lowercase letters for some common identifiers. For example, the letter *i* is often used to identify an integer that's used as a counter variable.

When you create identifiers, you can't use the same name as any of the C++ keywords shown in this figure. These keywords are reserved by the C++ language. To help you identify keywords in your code, most IDEs display these keywords in a different color than the rest of the code. As you progress through this book, you'll learn how to use many of these keywords.

For compatibility with programs written in the C language, you should also avoid creating identifiers that are the same as any of the C keywords. Most of the C keywords are the same as the C++ keywords, so this isn't hard to do. However, there are a few keywords shown in this figure that are specific to C. A C++ compiler might allow you to use one of these C keywords as an identifier, but you shouldn't.

Valid identifiers

```
subtotal        i           TITLE
subTotal        x           TAX_RATE
SubTotal        item1
sub_total       item2
_sub_total      June2011
```

The rules for naming an identifier

- Start each identifier with an upper- or lowercase letter or underscore.

- Use letters, underscores, or digits for subsequent characters.

- Don't use C++ or C keywords.

C++ keywords

alignas	const_cast	module	static_cast
alignof	continue	mutable	struct
and	decltype	namespace	switch
and_eq	default	new	synchronized
asm	delete	noexcept	template
atomic_cancel	do	not	this
atomic_commit	double	not_eq	thread_local
atomic_noexcept	dynamic_cast	nullptr	throw
auto	else	operator	true
bitand	enum	or	try
bitor	explicit	or_eq	typedef
bool	export	private	typeid
break	extern	protected	typename
case	false	public	union
catch	float	register	unsigned
char	for	reinterpret_cast	using
char16_t	friend	requires	virtual
char32_t	goto	return	void
class	if	short	volatile
compl	import	signed	wchar_t
concept	inline	sizeof	while
const	int	static	xor
constexpr	long	static_assert	xor_eq

Additional C keywords

_Alignas	_Bool	_Imaginary	_Thread_local
_Alignof	_Complex	_Noreturn	restrict
_Atomic	_Generic	_Static_assert	

Description

- An *identifier* is any name that you create in a C++ program. These can be the names of variables, functions, classes, and so on.

- A *keyword* is a word that's reserved by the C++ language. As a result, you can't use keywords as identifiers. For backward compatibility, you should also avoid C keywords.

- When you refer to an identifier, be sure to use the correct uppercase and lowercase letters because C++ is a case-sensitive language.

Figure 2-3   How to create identifiers

How to work with numeric variables

The topics that follow show how to work with numeric variables. They introduce you to the use of variables, assignment statements, arithmetic expressions, and two of the built-in data types that are defined by the C++ language.

How to define and initialize variables

Figure 2-4 starts by summarizing two of the built-in *data types* that are available from C++. You can use the int data type to store *integers*, which are numbers that don't contain decimal places (whole numbers), and you can use the *double* data type to store numbers that do contain decimal places.

A *variable* stores a value that can change, or *vary*, as a program executes. Before you can use a variable, you must *define* its data type, which is simply the type of data it will store, and its name. In addition, it's a good practice to *initialize* a variable by *assigning* an initial value to it. To do that, you can use either of the techniques described in this figure.

To show how this works, the first example uses one statement to define an int variable named counter. Then, it uses a second statement to initialize the variable by assigning an initial value of 1 to that variable.

However, it's often easier to define and initialize a variable in a single statement as shown by the second example. Here, the first statement defines an int variable named counter and initializes it by assigning an initial value of 1. The second statement defines a double variable named unit_price and initializes it by assigning an initial value of 14.95.

When you assign literal values to double types, it's a good coding practice to include a decimal point. If, for example, you want to assign the number 29 to the variable, you should code the number as 29.0. This isn't required, but it creates a literal value of the double type, not the int type. In addition, it makes it easy for programmers to see that the variable stores a double type, not an int type.

If you follow the naming recommendations in this figure as you name variables, it makes your programs easier to read and debug. In particular, you should use words formed with lowercase letters and separated by underscores, as in unit_price or max_quantity. This is the standard convention for naming variables when you're using C++.

When you initialize a variable, you can assign a *literal* value like 1 or 14.95 to it as illustrated by the examples in this figure. However, you can also initialize a variable to the value of another variable or to the value of an expression like the arithmetic expressions shown in the next figure.

How to code assignment statements

After you define and initialize a variable, you can assign a new value to it. To do that, you code an *assignment statement* that consists of the variable name, an equals sign, and a new value. The new value can be a literal value, the name of another variable as shown in the last statement in figure 2-4, or the result of an expression as shown in the next figure.

Two built-in data types for working with numbers

Type	Description
`int`	Integers (whole numbers).
`double`	Double-precision, floating-point numbers (decimal numbers).

How to define and initialize a variable in two statements

Syntax

```
type variable_name;
variable_name = value;
```

Example

```
int counter;              // definition statement
counter = 1;              // assignment statement
```

How to define and initialize a variable in one statement

Syntax

```
type variable_name = value;
```

Examples

```
int counter = 1;              // define and initialize an int variable
double unit_price = 14.95;    // define and initialize a double variable
```

An example that uses assignment statements

```
int quantity = 0;             // define and initialize an int variable
int max_quantity = 100;       // define and initialize another int variable

// two assignment statements
quantity = 10;                // quantity is now 10
quantity = max_quantity;      // quantity is now 100
```

Description

- A *variable* stores a value that can change, or *vary*, as a program executes.

- Before you can use a variable, you must *define* the type of data it will store (its data type) and its name. Then, you can *initialize* the variable by assigning an initial value to the variable.

- An *assignment statement* assigns a value to a variable. If the data type has already been defined, an assignment statement does not include the data type.

- A value can be a literal value, another variable, or an expression like the arithmetic expressions shown in the next figure.

- It's considered a good practice to initialize a variable before you use it since that allows you to be sure of the initial value that's assigned to the variable.

Naming recommendations for variables

- Each variable name should be a noun or a noun preceded by one or more adjectives.

- Try to use meaningful names that are easy to remember.

- Use lowercase letters and separate the words with underscores (_).

Figure 2-4   How to define and initialize variables

How to code arithmetic expressions

To code simple *arithmetic expressions*, you can use the *arithmetic operators* summarized in figure 2-5. When you use these operators, you code one *operand* on the left of the operator and one operand on the right of the operator.

As the first group of statements shows, the arithmetic operators work the way you would expect them to with one exception. If you divide one integer into another integer, the result doesn't include any decimal places. This is known as *integer division*. When you perform integer division, you can use the *modulus operator* (%), or *remainder operator*, to return the remainder.

In contrast, if you divide a double into a double, the result includes decimal places. This is known as *decimal division*.

When you code assignment statements, you can code the same variable on both sides of the equals sign. Then, you can include the variable on the right side of the equals sign in an arithmetic expression. For example, you can add 1 to the value of a variable named counter with a statement like this:

```
counter = counter + 1;
```

In this case, if counter has a value of 5 before the statement is executed, it has a value of 6 after the statement is executed. This concept is illustrated by the second group of statements.

If you mix integer and double variables in the same arithmetic expression, C++ automatically converts the int value to a double value and uses the double type for the result. However, if you store the result of the expression in an int variable, the decimal places are dropped as shown by the third group of statements. Here, the double value of 251.0 that's stored in the total variable is divided by the int value 2 that's stored in the counter variable. When the result of the division is stored in the double variable named result10, it's stored as 125.5. However, when the result of the division is stored in the int variable named result11, the decimal value is dropped and it's stored as 125.

It's important to restate that when you divide an integer by an integer, the result is always an integer. This is true even if you store the result of the division in a double variable as shown by the last statement in this figure. Here, the integer value in x (14) is divided by the integer value in y (8). This yields a result of 1, and this result is converted to a double value of 1.0 so it can be stored in the double variable.

Although it's not shown in this figure, you can also code expressions that contain two or more operators. When you do that, you need to be sure that the operations are done in the correct sequence. You'll learn more about that in chapter 3.

Five arithmetic operators

Operator	Name	Description
+	Addition	Adds two operands.
–	Subtraction	Subtracts the right operand from the left operand.
*	Multiplication	Multiplies the right operand and the left operand.
/	Division	Divides the right operand into the left operand. If both operands are integers, the result is an integer.
%	Modulus	Returns the value that is left over after dividing the right operand into the left operand.

Statements that use simple arithmetic expressions

```
// integer arithmetic
int x = 14;
int y = 8;
int result1 = x + y;        // result1 = 22
int result2 = x - y;        // result2 = 6
int result3 = x * y;        // result3 = 112
int result4 = x / y;        // result4 = 1
int result5 = x % y;        // result5 = 6

// decimal arithmetic
double a = 8.5;
double b = 3.4;
double result6 = a + b;     // result6 = 11.9
double result7 = a - b;     // result7 = 5.1
double result8 = a * b;     // result8 = 28.9
double result9 = a / b;     // result9 = 2.5
```

Statements that increment a counter variable

```
int counter = 0;
counter = counter + 1;      // counter = 1
counter = counter + 1;      // counter = 2
```

Statements that mix int and double variables

```
double total = 251.0;
double result10 = total / counter;   // result10 = 125.5
int result11 = total / counter;      // result11 = 125
```

A statement that divides an integer by an integer

```
double result12 = x / y;             // result12 = 1.0 (not 1.75)
```

Description

- An *arithmetic expression* consists of one or more *operands* and *arithmetic operators*.
- When expressions mix int and double variables, the compiler converts, or *casts*, the int types to double types.
- When both operands in a division expression are integers, the result is an integer. This is known as *integer division*.

Figure 2-5   How to code arithmetic expressions

How to use the console for input and output

Most programs get input from the user and display output to the user. The easiest way to do this is with the *console*. Before you learn how to use the console, though, you need to learn how to include header files so you can use the C++ standard library to work with the console.

How to include header files

The C++ *standard library* provides code that's stored in *header files*. To use code from the standard library, you include the header file that contains the code you want to use. This allows you to include only the features of the standard library that you need, which keeps the compile time of your program manageable.

Figure 2-6 lists of some of the commonly used header files. You'll learn how to use all of these headers, and more, as you progress through this book. You can also navigate to the URL shown here to see a comprehensive list of the header files available in the standard library.

To include a header file, you use the #include *preprocessor directive*. This instructs the preprocessor you learned about in chapter 1 to include the header file's code in your program. The compiler then treats the code in the header file as if it were typed at the top of your program file.

The example in this figure shows two #include directives. Each of these directives starts with a hash symbol (**#**) and does *not* end with a semicolon. Typically, you code the #include directives at the top of the file before any other code, as shown in this example.

Here, the first directive includes the iostream header. This header contains code that allows you to send data from one location to another. In particular, it contains code that you can use to send output to the console and read input from the console as shown in the next two figures.

The second directive includes the cmath header. This header contains code that you can use to perform common mathematical operations such as getting a square root or rounding a number. Later in this chapter, you'll learn how to use some of this code.

After coding the #include directives, it's common to code a *using directive* that makes it easy to access the code from any headers that are included, as shown in this figure. This works because all of the code that's available from the header files of the standard library is stored in a *namespace* named std. As a result, the using directive in this figure makes all code from the iostream and cmath headers available to the statements in the main() function. Later in this chapter, you'll learn other techniques for accessing the std namespace. These techniques can improve the performance of your code and help you to avoid the naming conflicts that can occur if an object or function is available from more than one namespace.

Common header files of the C++ standard library

Header file	Description
cstdlib	General purpose utilities such as program control, sort, and search.
iostream	Input/output (IO) stream objects.
iomanip	Input/output (IO) helper functions to manipulate how IO is formatted.
cmath	Common math functions.
string	For working with a string of characters.
vector	For working with a sequence of data elements of the same type.

URL for a complete list of C++ header files

http://en.cppreference.com/w/cpp/header

A typical way to include header files and make them easily accessible

```
#include <iostream>
#include <cmath>

using namespace std;    // make code in both headers easily accessible

int main()
{
    // code that uses the headers goes here
}
```

Description

- The *standard library* for C++ provides a library of code that you can use. This library is organized into *header files*.

- To use the code that's available from the standard library, you code an #include *preprocessor directive* for the header file that contains the code you want to use.

- A *namespace* provides a way to organize code to avoid naming conflicts. All of the code that's available from the header files of the standard library is stored in a namespace named std.

- To make it easy to access the code in the std namespace, it's common to add a using directive for the entire namespace. However, to improve efficiency and avoid naming conflicts, you can use other techniques for accessing the std namespace as shown later in this chapter.

Figure 2-6   How to include header files

How to write output to the console

To write output to the console, you can use the cout (pronounced "see-out") *object* that's available from the iostream header. You'll learn more about objects later in this book. For now, all you need to know is that you can use the cout object that's available from the iostream header. To do that, you don't have to create that object or assign it to a variable. All you need to do is to include the iostream header, and the cout object is available the entire duration of the program.

The cout object represents a *stream*, which is a sequence of characters. More specifically, the cout object represents the *standard output stream* that you can use to write a stream of characters to the console.

To do that, you use the *stream insertion operator* (<<) to add data to the output stream. In figure 2-7, for instance, the first example writes a string of "Hello!" to the console output stream. Later in this chapter, you'll learn more about strings. For now, just know that you can code a string of characters by enclosing them in double quotes.

The second example begins by multiplying 4 by 4 and storing the result in an int variable. Then, it writes a string of "4 times 4 is " to the console. Note that this string contains a space at the end to separate it from the output that follows. Next, it writes the integer that's a result of the multiplication operation to the console. Since the output stream is a series of characters, the output stream automatically converts the integer value to a string of characters.

The console output for this example shows how the integer value looks when it's displayed on the console. In addition, it shows that the string and the integer values are displayed on the same line even though the two insertion operations are coded in separate statements and on separate lines.

In the second example, the second and third lines each use the << operator with the cout object as the left operand (or lvalue) and the string or int to be printed as the right operand (or rvalue). However, these insertion expressions can be *chained* as shown in the third example. This example works the same as the second example, but it only uses two lines of code. That can make this code easier to read and understand.

If you want to start a new line in your output, you can write a *stream manipulator* named endl (pronounced "end-L" or "end line") to cout. The endl manipulator adds a newline character to the stream. In this figure, the fourth example uses two endl manipulators to write three lines to the console.

The fourth example uses three statements to write three lines to the console. However, it's possible to accomplish the same task by chaining the insertion expressions as shown in the fifth example. This example only uses one statement, but it splits that statement across three lines. This works because you can use indentation and spaces to make your code easier to read. Since this example only requires you to code one cout object and one semicolon, some programmers prefer it over the technique that's used in the fourth example.

When you work with console programs, you should know that the appearance of the console may differ slightly depending on the operating system. However, even if the console looks a little different, it should work the same.

Two objects available from the iostream header

Object	Description
`cout`	An object that represents the output stream to the console.
`endl`	An object that represents the end of a line. When you insert this object into an output stream, it inserts a newline character into the output stream.

How to send a message to the console

```
cout << "Hello!";
```

The console

```
Hello!
```

How to send text and a number to the console

```
int result = 4 * 4;
cout << "4 times 4 is ";
cout << result;
```

The console

```
4 times 4 is 16
```

Another way to send the same data to the console

```
int result = 4 * 4;
cout << "4 times 4 is " << result;
```

The console

```
4 times 4 is 16
```

How to send multiple lines to the console

```
cout << "This is line 1." << endl;
cout << "This is line 2." << endl;
cout << "This is line 3.";
```

The console

```
This is line 1.
This is line 2.
This is line 3.
```

Another way to send multiple lines to the console

```
cout << "This is line 1." << endl
     << "This is line 2." << endl
     << "This is line 3.";
```

Description

- The *stream insertion operator* (`<<`) lets you add characters to the output stream.

Figure 2-7   How to use the cout object to write output to the console

How to read input from the console

To read input from the console, you can use the cin object (pronounced "see-in"). The cin object represents the *standard input stream* that you can use to get input from the console. Like the cout object, the cin object is available for the entire duration of the program if you include the iostream header.

You use the *stream extraction operator* (>>) to read data from an input stream. In figure 2-8, for instance, the first example reads an integer from the console. To do that, the first statement defines an int variable named value to store the data that's going to be read from the stream. The second statement prompts the user to enter a number. And the third statement uses the >> operator to extract the integer from the console input stream.

After getting the number from the user, the fourth statement calculates the result of multiplying that number by itself. Then, the fifth statement displays the result of that calculation on the console. To do that, it chains several stream insertion expressions that display the number entered by the user, a string, the number, another string, and the result of the calculation.

The second example shows how to read multiple values from the console. To start, it defines two int variables to store the data read from the stream. Then, it prompts the user to enter two numbers. Next, it extracts the values entered by the user from the input stream and stores them in the int variables. As the console output below the code shows, this works the same whether the user enters one number per line or both numbers on one line.

After getting the two numbers from the user, the second example calculates the result of multiplying those two numbers together. Then, it displays that result. Like the first example, this example creates a chain of insertion expressions.

Like insertion expressions, extraction expressions can also be chained together as shown in the third example. This example consists of a single statement that could be used instead of the two extraction statements in the second example.

Since the insertion and extraction operators are similar in appearance, they can be easy to confuse, especially when you're first getting started. One way to keep them straight is to think of them as indicating the direction that the stream is flowing. For example, you can think of the output stream as flowing out toward the cout object. So, the insertion operator points at cout (cout << val). Conversely, you can think of the input stream as flowing in from the cin object. So, the extraction operator points away from cin (cin >> val).

Another object that's available from the iostream header

Object	Description
cin	An object that represents the input stream from the console.

How to read one value from the console

```
// read input from console
int value;
cout << "Please enter a number: ";
cin >> value;

// make a calculation and display output to the console
int result = value * value;
cout << value << " times " << value << " equals " << result;
```

The console

```
Please enter a number: 5
5 times 5 equals 25
```

How to read multiple values from the console

```
// read input from console
int value1;
int value2;
cout << "Please enter two numbers: ";
cin >> value1;
cin >> value2;

// make a calculation and display output to the console
int result = value1 * value2;
cout << value1 << " times " << value2 << " equals " << result;
```

The console when the user separates the numbers with a space

```
Please enter two numbers: 4 5
4 times 5 equals 20
```

The console when the user presses Enter after the first number

```
Please enter two numbers: 4
5
4 times 5 equals 20
```

How to chain extraction expressions

```
cin >> value1 >> value2;
```

Description

- The *stream extraction operator* (>>) gets characters from the input stream.
- When you use the cin object, it doesn't matter if the user enters one value per line or all the values on one line.
- When working with strings and characters, you may need to use some other techniques for reading input that are described later in this chapter.

Figure 2-8   How to use the cin object to read input from the console

The Gallons to Liters program

Figure 2-9 presents a program that reads input from the console and writes output to the console. This program starts with a block comment indicating the author and purpose of the program. Then, it includes the iostream header, so the program can work with the cout and cin objects, as well as the endl stream manipulator. Next, a using directive for the std namespace makes it easy to access the objects in the iostream header.

The main() function starts by writing the name of the program to the console. This line of code ends with two endl manipulators. The first endl manipulator starts a new line after the program title, and the second endl manipulator produces the blank line between the title and the first prompt.

The next group of statements gets the number of gallons from the user. To do that, it starts by defining a double variable named gallons to store the data. Then, it prompts the user to enter the number of gallons, and it uses an extraction expression to read the value the user entered from the console and store it in the gallons variable.

After getting the number of gallons entered by the user, this code converts the gallons to liters by multiplying the number of gallons by 3.7854, and it stores the result of the calculation in a double variable named liters. Then, the next statement displays the number of liters and a message that indicates that the program is ending. To do that, this statement writes the string "Liters: " to the console, followed by the calculated number of liters, two endl manipulators, and the string "Bye!".

As you review this code, note that it uses spaces to format the input and output so it aligns in two columns. Later in this chapter, you'll learn how to use tab characters to align output in columns. Then, in chapter 5, you'll learn how to use stream manipulators to use an even more sophisticated technique for aligning output in columns.

***

If you're new to programming, we recommend that you take a break now and complete exercise 2-1 that's presented at the end of this chapter. This should give you some hands-on practice working with the skills presented so far in this chapter, and it should help you absorb this information. After that, you'll be ready to continue with the rest of the chapter.

The console

```
Gallons Converter

Enter gallons: 10
Liters:        37.854

Bye!
```

The code

```cpp
/*
 * Author:  M. Delamater
 * Purpose: This program uses the console to get gallons
 *          from the user. Then, it converts gallons to liters
 *          and displays the result of the conversion.
 */

#include <iostream>

using namespace std;

int main()
{
    // print name of program
    cout << "Gallons Converter" << endl << endl;

    // get gallons from user
    double gallons;
    cout << "Enter gallons: ";
    cin >> gallons;

    // convert gallons to liters
    double liters = gallons * 3.7854;

    // write output to console
    cout << "Liters:         " << liters << endl << endl
        << "Bye!" << endl << endl;

    // return value that indicates normal program exit
    return 0;
}
```

Figure 2-9   The Gallons to Liters program

How to work with the standard library

So far, you've learned how to do simple arithmetic operations with built-in data types, you've learned how to include headers, and you've learned how to use the cout and cin objects that are available from the iostream header. As you develop more complex programs, though, you'll need to use dozens of different objects and functions that are available from the C++ *standard library*. In addition, you'll need to learn more about how to work with the std namespace.

How to call a function

The C++ standard library provides a large collection of functions that you can use in your programs. As mentioned earlier in this chapter, a *function* is a reusable block of code that performs a specified task. Each function has a name and other code can call the function to execute it.

Figure 2-10 begins by showing five of the many functions that are available from the cmath header. If you include the cmath header as shown earlier in this chapter, these five functions and many other mathematical functions are available to your code.

Once you include the header and the using directive for the std namespace, you can call the functions in the header by using the syntax shown in this figure. To start, you code the function name followed by a set of parentheses. Within the parentheses, you code the *arguments* that are required by the function, separating the arguments with commas. If the function doesn't require any arguments, you leave the parentheses empty.

If the function returns a value, you define a variable to store the return value. You define this variable just like you would any other variable. Then, you assign the result of calling the function to the variable. When you do this, the data type of the variable that stores the return value should be the same data type that's returned by the function. For example, all of the functions in this figure return a double value. As a result, you should assign the values returned by these functions to a variable of the double type.

The first example shows how to use the sqrt() function to calculate the square root of a number. This function requires a single argument. As a result, you can call it by coding the name of the function, a set of parentheses, and a number within those parentheses. Then, you can assign the value that this function returns to a variable. In this example, the first statement assigns the square root of 16 to a double variable named root1, and the second statement assigns the square root of 6.25 to a double variable named root2.

The second example shows how to use the pow() function to raise a number to the specified exponent. This function requires two arguments. The first argument specifies the base number, and the second argument specifies the power of the exponent.

The third, fourth, and fifth examples show how to use the round(), floor(), and ceil() functions to round double values to a specified number of decimal places. These functions all round to the nearest whole number and return a value of the double type. However, a common coding trick for rounding to a specified number of decimal places is to multiply the number by a multiple of ten, round

Five functions available from the cmath header

Function	Description
`sqrt`(number)	Calculates the square root of the specified number and returns the resulting value as a double.
`pow`(base, exponent)	Raises the base to the power of the exponent and returns the resulting value as a double.
`round`(number)	Rounds the number up or down to the nearest whole number and returns the resulting value as a double.
`floor`(number)	Rounds the number down (towards the floor) to the nearest whole number and returns the resulting value as a double.
`ceil`(number)	Rounds the number up (towards the ceiling) to the nearest whole number and returns the resulting value as a double.

How to call a function

Syntax

```
function_name(arguments);
```

The sqrt() function

```
double root1 = sqrt(16);   // root1 is 4
double root2 = sqrt(6.25); // root2 is 2.5
```

The pow() function

```
double pow1 = pow(2, 4);   // pow1 is 16
double pow2 = pow(2.5, 2); // pow2 is 6.25
```

The round() function

```
double x = 10.315;
double round1 = round(x);          // round1 is 10.0
double round2 = round(x * 10) / 10;   // round2 is 10.3
double round3 = round(x * 100) / 100; // round3 is 10.32
```

The floor() function

```
double floor1 = floor(x);          // floor1 is 10.0
double floor2 = floor(x * 10) / 10;   // floor2 is 10.3
double floor3 = floor(x * 100) / 100; // floor3 is 10.31
```

The ceil() function

```
double ceil1 = ceil(x);          // ceil1  is 11.0
double ceil2 = ceil(x * 10) / 10;   // ceil2 is 10.4
double ceil3 = ceil(x * 100) / 100; // ceil3 is 10.32
```

Description

- When you call a *function*, you code its name followed by a pair of parentheses. If the function requires *arguments*, you code the arguments within the parentheses. These arguments must be of the correct data type, and they must be coded in the correct sequence separated by commas.

- A function can return a value to the code that calls it. If a function returns a value, you can store the return value in a variable.

Figure 2-10   How to call a function

the number, and then divide by the same multiple of ten. For example, to get two decimal places, you can multiply the number by 100, round the number to the nearest whole number, and then divide the number by 100. If you review these three examples, you should get a feel for how this works.

As you progress through this book, you'll learn how to use dozens of functions and objects. You'll also learn how to create your own.

How to work with the std namespace

A *namespace* provides a way to organize objects and functions. This helps to avoid naming conflicts. As mentioned earlier, the standard library stores its code in a namespace named std. So far in this chapter, you have been coding a using directive to automatically make all objects and functions in the std namespace available to your code. This is shown by the first example in figure 2-11. The advantage of this approach is that it's an easy way to make all objects and functions in a namespace available to your code.

However, it's considered a better practice to specify individual members with *using declarations* as shown in the second example. This example uses three declarations to specify the objects and functions that are used in the main() function. To do that, these declarations use the *scope resolution operator* (::) to create a fully qualified name. A *fully qualified name* consists of the namespace, the scope resolution operator, and the member of the namespace. For example, the fully qualified name for the cout object is

```
std::cout
```

and the fully qualified name for the sqrt() function is

```
std::sqrt
```

If you don't code a using directive or declaration for an object or function, you can still use it in your code as shown in the third example. In that case, however, you must use a fully qualified name to access the object or function.

There are several advantages to the approaches shown in the second and third examples. First, they should help your code compile more quickly. Second, they should reduce the chance of encountering a naming conflict. Third, they clearly show the objects and functions that your code needs, which makes it easier to read and maintain your code.

Many programmers prefer to use using declarations, since they make it easy to access the specified objects and functions. This is especially true if your code needs to use a namespace member repeatedly. Then, you don't have to qualify the member each time you use it, which saves you typing and can make your code easier to read and maintain. If you're only going to use a member once or twice, though, you might want to use a fully qualified name.

To save space, most of the examples shown in this book use a using directive for the std namespace. However, you should know that using declarations are generally considered a better practice.

A using directive for the std namespace

```
#include <iostream>
#include <cmath>

using namespace std;    // use all elements of the std namespace

int main() {
    int num = 7;
    double root = sqrt(num);
    root = round(root * 1000) / 1000;    // round to 3 decimal places
    cout << "The square root of " << num << " is " << root << endl;
}
```

Using declarations for three members of the std namespace

```
#include <iostream>
#include <cmath>

using std::cout;        // use the cout object
using std::sqrt;        // use the sqrt function
using std::round;       // use the round function

int main()
{
    int num = 7;
    double root = sqrt(num);
    root = round(root * 1000) / 1000;    // round to 3 decimal places
    cout << "The square root of " << num << " is " << root << endl;
}
```

Fully qualified names

```
#include <iostream>
#include <cmath>

int main()
{
    int num = 7;
    double root = std::sqrt(num);
    root = std::round(root * 1000) / 1000;    // round to 3 decimal places
    std::cout << "The square root of " << num << " is " << root << std::endl;
}
```

The console for all three examples

```
The square root of 7 is 2.646
```

Description

- The members of the standard library are grouped in a *namespace* named std.
- You can identify members of namespaces by using the *scope resolution operator* (::).
- You can code a *using directive* for a namespace to make it easy to access all members of that namespace. However, this can lead to naming conflicts.
- You can code a *using declaration* for a specific member of a namespace to make it easy to access that member of the namespace. This significantly reduces the chance of a naming conflict.

Figure 2-11   How to work with the std namespace

The Circle Calculator program

Figure 2-12 presents an enhanced version of the Circle Calculator program that you saw in chapter 1. This program prompts the user to enter the radius for a circle. Then, it uses two functions from the cmath header to calculate the diameter, circumference, and area of the circle with that radius.

This program starts by including the iostream and cmath headers. Then, the first three using declarations make it easy for the program to work with the cout and cin objects, as well as the endl stream manipulator. After that, the last two using declarations make it easy to work with the pow() and round() functions of the cmath header.

The main() function starts by writing the name of the program to the console. This line of code ends with two endl manipulators. The first endl manipulator starts a new line after the program title, and the second endl manipulator produces the blank line between the title and the first prompt.

The next group of statements gets the radius from the user. To do that, it defines a double variable named radius to store the value, it prompts the user to enter the radius, and it uses an extraction expression to read the value the user entered from the console and store it in the radius variable.

After getting the radius entered by the user, this code uses four statements to calculate the diameter, circumference, and area of the circle. Here, the first statement defines a double variable named pi and assigns it an initial value of 3.14159. The second statement calculates the diameter by multiplying the radius by 2. The third statement calculates the circumference by multiplying the diameter by pi. And the fourth statement calculates the area by using the standard geometric formula of pi times radius squared (πr^2).

As you review this code, note that both the third and fourth statements use pi. As a result, assigning the value of pi to a variable named pi makes your code easier for others to read and follow. In addition, if you wanted to use a more or less precise approximation of pi, you could just modify the value that's assigned by the first statement.

After making the calculations, this code uses the round() function to round the circumference and area to 1 decimal place. Then, it displays the results of the calculations and a message that indicates that the program is ending. Note that after it displays the area, this code uses two endl manipulators to print a blank line between the result of the calculations and the end message.

The console

```
Circle Calculator

Enter radius:  9
Diameter:      18
Circumference: 56.5
Area:          254.5

Bye!
```

The code

```cpp
#include <iostream>
#include <cmath>

using std::cout;
using std::cin;
using std::endl;
using std::pow;
using std::round;

int main()
{
    // print name of program
    cout << "Circle Calculator" << endl << endl;

    // get radius from user
    double radius;
    cout << "Enter radius:  ";
    cin >> radius;

    // make calculations
    double pi = 3.14159;
    double diameter = 2 * radius;
    double circumference = diameter * pi;
    double area = pi * pow(radius, 2.0);

    // round to 1 decimal place
    circumference = round(circumference * 10) / 10;
    area = round(area * 10) / 10;

    // write output to console
    cout << "Diameter:      " << diameter << endl
         << "Circumference: " << circumference << endl
         << "Area:          " << area << endl << endl
         << "Bye! ";

    // return value that indicates normal program exit
    return 0;
}
```

Figure 2-12   The Circle Calculator program

How to generate random numbers

When learning how to program, it's often helpful to be able to generate random numbers. They're useful if you want to develop games that involve dice, cards, or other elements of random chance. They're also useful for simulations such as testing a function with a range of random numbers.

To generate random numbers with C++, you can use the functions of the cstdlib and ctime headers presented in figure 2-13. First, you use the time() function to get a seed value for the srand() function. To do that, you can use the nullptr keyword to pass a null pointer argument to the time() function. This returns the number of seconds that have elapsed since Jan 1, 1970. As a result, the time() function returns a different number each time it's called.

Once you have a seed value, you use the srand() function to specify the seed value for the rand() function. Next, you use the rand() function to get a random integer between 0 and RAND_MAX, which is a large integer that varies from compiler to compiler.

After you get the random integer, you can use the modulus operator to specify the upper limit of the random number. In this figure, for example, the code uses the modulus operator to return the remainder after dividing by 6. That way, the result of the operation is from 0 to 5 inclusive. Then, you can add 1 to the result to get the value of a six-sided die (1 to 6 inclusive).

So, why do you need to provide a seed value for the rand() function? Because the rand() function actually generates *pseudorandom numbers*, which are series of numbers that appear to be random but are actually the same for each seed value. As a result, if you don't change the seed value each time you run the program, the program will use the same series of numbers each time, which isn't typically what you want.

The functions presented in this figure provide a simple way to generate a series of pseudorandom numbers. This is adequate for creating programs like the one shown here. However, random numbers that are generated using this technique are not cryptographically secure. As a result, if you need to generate cryptographically secure numbers, you'll have to use a different technique. For example, if you're using C++ 11 or later, you can use the random header to generate random numbers that are cryptographically secure. By the time you finish this book, you should have the skills you need to learn to use the random header on your own.

Two functions of the cstdlib header for generating random numbers

Function	Description
`rand()`	Returns a pseudorandom integer between 0 and RAND_MAX. This function uses a seed to generate the series of integers, and the seed should be initialized to a distinctive value using the srand() function.
`srand(seed)`	Specifies the seed value for the rand() function.

One function of the ctime header

Function	Description
`time(timer)`	If the timer argument is a null pointer, it returns the current calendar time, generally as the number of seconds since Jan 1, 1970 00:00 UTC.

Code that simulates the roll of a pair of dice

```cpp
#include <iostream>
#include <cstdlib>
#include <ctime>

using namespace std;

int main()
{
    // use time() to get an int value
    int elapsed_seconds = time(nullptr);

    // seed the random number generator
    srand(elapsed_seconds);

    // roll the first die
    int die1 = rand() % 6;      // die1 is >= 0 and < 6
    die1 = die1 + 1;            // die2 is >= 1 and <= 6

    // roll the second die
    int die2 = rand() % 6;      // die2 is >= 0 and < 6
    die2 = die2 + 1;           // die2 is >= 1 and <= 6

    // write output to console
    cout << "Your roll:  " << die1 << " " << die2;
}
```

The console

```
Your roll:  6 3
```

Description

- The rand() and srand() functions provide a simple way to generate a series of *pseudorandom numbers*, which is a series of numbers that appears to be random but is actually the same if you specify the same seed value for the series.

- If you're using C++ 11 or later, you can use the random header to generate random numbers that are cryptographically secure. However, this requires advanced programming techniques that aren't presented until later in this book.

Figure 2-13   How to generate random numbers

How to work with char and string variables

As you've already seen, programs often need to work with character data. In the next few topics, you'll learn about char and string variables, you'll learn how to work with special characters, and you'll learn about some functions for reading char and string data from the console.

How to assign values to char and string variables

A *char* is a built-in data type defined by the C++ core language. A char contains a single character, which can be any letter, number, punctuation mark, or special character in the *ASCII character set*. Technically, the char type is an integer type since it actually contains an integer that maps to one of the ASCII characters.

The first example in figure 2-14 shows how to define and initialize a char variable. This is similar to defining a numeric variable. However, the *character literal* that's assigned to a char variable is enclosed in single quotation marks.

A *string*, conversely, is not a built-in data type. Rather, it's an *object* that consists of a sequence of zero or more characters. This object type is defined by the string *class* that's available from the string header file and that's a member of the std namespace. When you include the iostream header, most compilers also include the string header. However, to make sure your code is portable across all compilers, it's a good practice to include the string header file as shown in the second example.

The third example shows how to define and initialize a string variable. Here, the first statement creates a *string literal* of "Invalid data entry" by coding multiple characters within double quotation marks, and it assigns that string literal to a string object named message1. A string variable can also contain an *empty string*. To assign an empty string to a string variable, you code a set of double quotation marks with nothing between them as shown in the second statement in this example.

If you want to *join*, or *concatenate*, two or more strings into one, you can use the + operator. The fourth example shows how this works. Here, two string variables are initialized with first name and last name values. Then, these two values are concatenated with a string literal that contains a comma and a space. The resulting string is assigned to a third string variable called name. When concatenating strings, you can use string variables or string literals.

You can also join a string with a char. This is illustrated in the last statement in the fourth example. Here, the first_name and last_name variables are concatenated with two character literals and a char variable that contains a middle initial. As before, the resulting string is assigned to the name variable.

You can use the + and += operators to *append* a string or character to the end of a string as shown by the fifth example. Here, the second statement uses the += operator to append the last name to the first name followed by a space. If you use

The built-in data type for characters

Type	Description
char	A built-in data type that stores an integer value that maps to a single character in the ASCII character set. This character set includes letters, numbers, punctuation marks, and special characters like *, &, and #.

A class that's available from the string header

Class	Description
string	A class that defines a type of object that consists of a sequence of zero or more characters.

How to define and initialize a char variable

```
char middle_initial = 'M';
```

How to include the string header file

```
#include <string>
```

How to define and initialize a string variable

```
string message1 = "Invalid data entry";
string message2 = "";                        // empty string
```

How to concatenate strings and chars

```
string first_name = "Bob";                   // first_name is Bob
string last_name = "Smith";                  // last_name is Smith

string name = last_name + ", " + first_name; // name is Smith, Bob
name = first_name + ' ' + middle_initial + ' ' + last_name;
                                             // name is Bob M Smith
```

How to append one string to another with the += operator

```
name = first_name + ' ';                     // name is Bob followed by a space
name += last_name;                           // name is Bob Smith
```

Description

- To specify a character value, you can enclose the character in single quotation marks. This is known as a *character literal*.

- A class defines a type of *object*. When you create an object from a class, you can assign it to a variable of the class type.

- To create a string object, you enclose text in double quotation marks. This is known as a *string literal*.

- To assign an *empty string* to a string variable, you can code a set of quotation marks with nothing between them. This means that the string doesn't contain any characters.

- To *concatenate* a string with another string or a char, use a plus sign.

- The += operator is a shortcut for appending a string or char to a string variable.

- If you only need to store a single character, the char type works more efficiently than the string type.

Figure 2-14   How to assign values to char and string variables

the + operator, you need to include the string variable on both sides of the = operator. Otherwise, the assignment statement replaces the old value with the new value.

When working with char and string variables, a string uses slightly more overhead than a char. As a result, if you're working with a single character, you should use a char variable or literal, not a string variable or literal.

How to work with special characters

Figure 2-15 shows how to work with special characters. To do that, you can use the *escape sequences* shown in this figure.

Each escape sequence starts with a backslash. If you code a backslash followed by the letter n, for example, the compiler includes a newline character as shown in the first string example. If you omit the backslash, the compiler just includes the letter n in the string value. The escape sequence for the tab character works similarly as shown in the second string example.

To code a string literal, you enclose it in double quotes. As a result, if you want to include a double quote within a string literal, you must use an escape sequence as shown in the third string example. Here, the \" escape sequence is used to include two double quotes within the string literal.

Finally, you need to use an escape sequence if you want to include a backslash in a string literal. To do that, you code two backslashes as shown in the fourth string example. If you forget to do that and code a single backslash, the compiler uses the backslash and the next character to create an escape sequence. That can yield unexpected results.

When you work with escape sequences, remember that they define special characters, not special strings. As a result, there are times when you may want to assign a special character to a variable of the char data type as shown in the char examples. To do that, you can create a char literal by enclosing the escape sequence in single quotes. This defines a single character that can be assigned to a char variable. Here, the first statement assigns a newline character to a char variable named newline. The second statement assigns a tab character to a char variable named tab. And the third statement assigns a backslash character to a char variable named sep, which is short for separator.

Common escape sequences for special characters

Sequence	Character
\n	Newline
\t	Tab
\r	Return
\"	Quotation mark
\\	Backslash

String examples

A string that uses a newline character

```
"Code: CPP\nPrice: $49.50"
```

Result

```
Code: CPP
Price: $49.50
```

A string that uses tabs

```
"Joe\tSmith\nKate\tLewis"
```

Result

```
Joe       Smith
Kate      Lewis
```

A string that uses double quotes

```
"Type \"x\" to exit"
```

Result

```
Type "x" to exit
```

A string that uses backslashes

```
"C:\\murach\\cpp\\files"
```

Result

```
C:\murach\cpp\files
```

Char examples

```
char newline = '\n';
char tab = '\t';
char sep = '\\';          // use backslash as a separator
```

Description

- You can use *escape sequences* to identify certain types of special characters.
- Within a string, you can code the escape sequence anywhere you want to use the special character.
- A special character is a single character of the char type. As a result, to code a char literal, you code single quotes around the two characters of the escape sequence.

Figure 2-15   How to work with special characters

How to read strings and chars from the console

When you use the extraction operator (>>) to read data from the cin object, it uses *whitespace* (spaces, tabs, or new lines) to separate the data in the input stream into one or more *tokens*. Then, it reads one token per extraction expression. So, if a user enters "Grace M. Hopper",

```
cin >> name;
```

only stores "Grace" in the name variable.

You could fix this by declaring variables for the first name, middle initial, and last name and then chaining the extraction expressions like this:

```
cin >> first_name >> middle_initial >> last_name;
```

However, what if you want to give your users the flexibility to enter only a first name or a first and last name? One way to do that is to use the getline() function that's presented in figure 2-16 to read the entire line of user input.

Unlike an extraction expression, the getline() function only uses line breaks to separate the data in the stream. As a result, it reads all data up to the end of the current line of input. This function takes two arguments. The first is the cin object, and the second is the string variable where the extracted data is stored.

The first example in this figure shows how this works. Here, the first statement defines the name variable, the second statement prompts the user to enter a full name, and the third statement passes the cin object and the name variable to the getline() function. As a result, this code stores whatever the user enters in the name variable, whether it's "Grace" or "Grace Hopper" or "Grace M. Hopper".

When reading strings and chars from the console, you sometimes need to ignore characters. To do that, you can use a special kind of function known as a *member function*, which is a function that's available from an object. For example, this figure summarizes the get() function and two versions of the ignore() function. All of these methods are members of the cin object. As a result, to call them, you start by coding the object name and the *dot operator* (.). Then, you code the function name and its arguments just as you would for any other function.

The examples below the syntax summary show how this works. Here, the first statement calls the get() member function of the cin object. This gets the next character in the stream. The second statement calls the ignore() member function of the cin object. Since this statement doesn't pass any arguments to the function, it just extracts and discards the next char in the input stream. However, the third statement calls the ignore() function and passes two arguments to it. These arguments indicate that the function should discard the next 100 characters or all characters until the next space character, whichever comes first.

The last example shows how to pause program execution until the user presses the Enter key. This is useful if the console for a program closes before the program is done. Here, the first statement discards all data that the user may have entered earlier, up to 1000 characters. This statement isn't always necessary, but it makes sure that this code will work even if there are some extra characters remaining in the input stream. Then, the second statement prompts the user to press Enter. Finally, the third statement extracts and ignores the newline character that's inserted into the input stream when the user presses Enter.

The getline() function of the iostream header

Function	Description
`getline(cin, var)`	Extracts an entire line of console input, including spaces, and assigns it to the specified variable.

How to use the getline() function to read a full name

```
string name;
cout << "Enter full name: ";
getline(cin, name);
cout << "Your name is " << name;
```

The console

```
Enter full name: Grace M. Hopper
Your name is Grace M. Hopper
```

Member functions of the cin object

Member function	Description
`get()`	Gets the next character in the input stream.
`ignore()`	Extracts and discards the next character in the input stream.
`ignore(n, delim)`	Extracts and discards characters in the input stream until either the number of characters discarded is n, or the character in delim is found.

How to call a member function of an object

Syntax

```
object_name.function_name(arguments);
```

Examples

```
char initial = cin.get(); // extract and return the next char
cin.ignore();             // extract and discard the next char
cin.ignore(100, ' ');     // extract and discard the next 100 chars
                          // or all characters up to the next space
```

Code that pauses until the user presses Enter to continue

```
cin.ignore(1000, '\n');   // discard any extra characters
                          // on the current line
cout << "\nPress [Enter] to close the terminal ...\n";
cin.ignore();
```

The console

```
Press [Enter] to close the terminal ...
```

Description

- Many objects in the standard library have *member functions*. To call a member function, code the name of the object, the dot operator (**.**), and the name of the member function.

- You pass arguments to and get return values from a member function just like you do a regular function.

Figure 2-16   How to read strings and chars from the console

How to fix a common problem
with reading strings

In most cases, the getline() function works the way you want it to. Sometimes, though, you can run into a problem if you use getline() after code that uses an extraction operator to extract data from an input stream. Figure 2-17 begins by showing this problem. Here, the first example starts by using an extraction expression to read an account number. Then, it uses the getline() function to read a full name. However, the console doesn't give the user a chance to enter a full name.

What's causing this problem? Well, when a user types a value and presses the Enter key, C++ adds the value and the newline character to the input stream. But, the extraction expression only extracts the value from the stream, not the newline character. That's fine if you're using the extraction operator because this operator ignores a leading newline character. Unfortunately, the getline() function doesn't ignore this character. As a result, getline() reads the leading newline character into the name variable, and program execution continues to the statement that writes the output to the console.

To fix this problem, you can use the ignore() function of the cin object to extract and discard the newline character that's causing the problem as shown in the second example. Once you extract and discard this newline character, the getline() function works correctly.

Some programmers consider it a best practice to call the ignore() function after every extraction expression. That way, the leading newline character is always discarded. But, it's also common to only call the ignore() function when necessary.

A common problem with reading strings
The code

```
int account_num;
cout << "Enter account number: ";
cin >> account_num;          // extracts data but leaves the newline character

string name;
cout << "Enter full name: ";
getline(cin, name);          // reads the newline character left in the stream

cout << "Name: " << name << " | Account: " << account_num;
```

The console

```
Enter account number: 1234
Enter full name:
Name:  | Account: 1234
```

The data in the cin object after the user enters "1234"

1	2	3	4	\n

How to fix the problem
The code

```
int account_num;
cout << "Enter account number: ";
cin >> account_num;

string name;
cout << "Enter full name: ";
cin.ignore();            // discards the newline character left in the stream
getline(cin, name);      // reads the next line

cout << "Name: " << name << " | Account: " << account_num;
```

The console

```
Enter account number: 1234
Enter full name: Mary Delamater
Name: Mary Delamater | Account: 1234
```

Description

- When the user presses the Enter key at the console, C++ inserts a newline character into the input stream.

- When you use the extraction operator to extract data, it skips over any leading whitespace characters (such as spaces and newline characters) and extracts the data up to the next whitespace character, leaving the whitespace character in the stream.

- When you use the getline() function to read data, it doesn't skip over a leading newline character. Instead, it returns an empty string. To skip over a leading newline character, you can call the ignore() member function of the cin object to ignore the leading newline character.

Figure 2-17   How to fix a common problem with reading strings

The Guest Book program

Figure 2-18 presents another program that reads input from the console and writes output to the console. This program accepts string input from the user and displays formatted output.

Like the Gallon Converter program, the Guest Book program starts by including the iostream header. It also includes the string header. In addition, it specifies a using directive for the std namespace so the code doesn't need to use fully qualified names for the objects in the iostream and string headers.

The main() function starts by writing the title of the program to the console. Note that this statement uses the newline character rather than the endl manipulator to add line breaks. Here, the first newline character (\n) starts a new line and the second adds a blank line after the program title.

After the title, this code prompts the user to enter a first name. Then, it uses an extraction expression to get a first name from the user. Next, it calls the ignore() function of the cin object to discard the leading newline character left in the stream by the previous extraction expression as well as any other characters left in the stream, up to 100 characters.

After the first name, the code prompts the user to enter a middle initial. Then, it uses the get() member function to get the middle initial. Next, it calls the ignore() function to discard any characters left in the stream, including the leading newline character.

After the middle initial, the code prompts the user for a last name. Here, the code uses the getline() function to get the last name, so the user can enter a last name that contains spaces. This code continues by using the getline() function to get the user's city and country.

After getting all of the input from the user, the code formats the data and writes it to the console. To do that, it uses the newline character (\n) to start new lines. In addition, it uses the + operator to create a full name by concatenating the first name, a space character, the middle initial, a period, a space character, and the last name. It also uses the + operator to create the line that contains the city and country.

As you review this code, note that each prompt uses a tab character (\t) to align the user's entry. In addition, this code encloses special characters such as the tab character in double quotes if the special character is part of a string. Otherwise, this code encloses the special character in single quotes so it's treated as a char type. That's true for other single characters as well, such as a space. As you learned earlier in this chapter, that makes your code slightly more efficient.

Also, note that this program only extracts the first name that's entered before any whitespace. As a result, if a user enters "Emmy Lou" as the first name, the program only stores "Emmy" as the first name. Similarly, this program only extracts the first character that's entered for the middle initial. As a result, if a user enters "Wiliford" for the middle initial, the program only stores "W". If that's not what you want, you can use the getline() function instead of the extraction operator to get the first name and middle initial. And if you do that, you don't need to use the ignore() function.

The console

```
Guest Book

First name:      Dave
Middle initial: Williford
Last name:      Von Ronk
City:           New York
Country:        United States

ENTRY
Dave W. Von Ronk
New York, United States
```

The code

```cpp
#include <iostream>
#include <string>

using namespace std;

int main()
{
    cout << "Guest Book\n\n";

    string first_name;
    cout << "First name:\t";
    cin >> first_name;              // get first string only
    cin.ignore(100, '\n');          // discard leftover chars and newline

    char middle_initial;
    cout << "Middle initial:\t";
    middle_initial = cin.get();     // get first char only
    cin.ignore(100, '\n');          // discard leftover chars and newline

    string last_name;
    cout << "Last name:\t";
    getline(cin, last_name);        // get entire line

    string city;
    cout << "City:\t\t";
    getline(cin, city);             // get entire line

    string country;
    cout << "Country:\t";
    getline(cin, country);          // get entire line

    cout << "\nENTRY\n"             // display the entry
        << first_name + ' ' + middle_initial + ". " + last_name + '\n'
        << city + ", " + country + "\n\n";
}
```

Figure 2-18   The Guest Book program

How to test and debug a program

In chapter 1, you were introduced to *syntax errors* that are detected by an IDE when you enter code. Because syntax errors prevent a program from compiling, they are also commonly referred to as *compile-time errors*. For example, if you try to compile the code shown in figure 2-19, the compiler returns an error like the one shown in this figure.

This error information is typically displayed by the IDE, and it can help you determine the location of the error. In this figure, for example, the message indicates that a semicolon was expected before the string keyword on line 10. That's because a semicolon was missing from the end of line 8. Once you've fixed the compile-time errors, you're ready to test and debug the program.

How to test a program

When you test a program, you run it to make sure it works correctly. As you test, you should try every possible combination of valid and invalid data to be certain that the program works correctly under every set of conditions. Remember that the goal of testing is to find errors, or *bugs*, so they're not encountered by users when they run the program.

As you test, you will inevitably encounter two types of bugs. The first type of bug causes a *runtime error* (also known as a *runtime exception*). A runtime error can cause a program to crash or to behave erratically.

The second type of bug produces inaccurate results when a program runs. These bugs occur due to *logic errors* in the source code. For example, these types of bugs can cause a program to enter an infinite loop or to display incorrect data. For instance, the console in this figure shows output for the Circle Calculator program that displays incorrect data. Here, one of the calculations is not correct. This type of bug can be more difficult to find and correct than a runtime error.

How to debug a program

When you *debug* a program, you find the cause of the bugs, fix them, and test again. As your programs become more complex, debugging can be one of the most time-consuming aspects of programming. That's why it's important to write your code in a way that makes it easy to read, understand, and debug.

To find the cause of runtime errors, you can start by finding the source statement that was running when the program crashed. To do that, you can start by studying any error messages that you get.

To find the cause of incorrect output, you can start by figuring out why the program produced the output that it did. For instance, you can start by asking why the Circle Calculator program in this figure didn't perform all of the calculations correctly. Once you figure that out, you're well on your way to fixing the bug.

The beginning of a file that contains an error

```
1   #include <iostream>
2   #include <string>
3
4   using namespace std;
5
6   int main()
7   {
8       cout << "Guest Book\n\n"
9
10      string first_name;
11      cout << "First name:\t";
...
...
```

The error that's returned by the compiler

```
main.cpp: In function 'int main()':
main.cpp:10:5: error: expected ';' before 'string'
    string first_name;
    ^
```

The Circle Calculator program with incorrect output

```
Circle Calculator

Enter radius:   9
Diameter:       18
Circumference: 28.3
Area:           254.5
```

Description

- A *syntax* or *compile-time error* occurs when a statement can't be compiled. Before you can test a program, you must fix the syntax errors.

- To *test* a program, you run it to make sure that it works properly no matter what combinations of valid and invalid data you enter. The goal of testing is to find the errors (or *bugs*) in the program.

- To *debug* a program, you find the causes of the bugs and fix them.

- One type of bug leads to a *runtime error* (also known as a *runtime exception*) that causes the program to end prematurely. This type of bug must be fixed before testing can continue.

- Even if a program runs to completion, the results may be incorrect due to *logic errors*. These bugs must also be fixed.

Debugging tips

- For a runtime error, go to the line in the source code that was running when the program crashed. In most IDEs, you can do that by clicking on the link to the line of source code. That should give you a strong indication of what caused the error.

- For a logical error, first figure out how the source code produced that output. Then, fix the code and test the program again.

Figure 2-19   How to test and debug a program

Perspective

The goal of this chapter has been to get you off to a fast start with C++ programming. Now, if you understand how the programs presented in this chapter work, you've come a long way. You should also be able to write comparable programs of your own.

Keep in mind, though, that this chapter is just an introduction to C++ programming. The next few chapters will build upon what you learned in this chapter to expand your knowledge of C++ programming. This will include learning some new skills as well as learning more about data types, arithmetic expressions, input and output streams, strings, and debugging.

Terms

statement	stream insertion operator
block of code	chained expressions
comment	stream manipulator
single-line comment	standard input stream
end-of-line comment	stream extraction operator
block comment	function
main() function	argument
parameter	using directive
body of a function	using declaration
return statement	scope resolution operator
identifier	fully qualified name
snake case	pseudorandom number
camel case	char
keyword	ASCII character set
data type	character literal
variable	string
define a variable	class
initialize a variable	object
literal value	string literal
assignment statement	empty string
arithmetic expression	concatenate strings
arithmetic operator	append to a string
operand	escape sequence
cast a data type	whitespace
integer division	token
modulus operator	member function
remainder operator	dot operator
decimal division	syntax error
console	compile-time error
preprocessor directive	test a program
standard library	bug
header file	runtime error
namespace	logic error
stream	debug a program
standard output stream	

Summary

- *Statements* direct the operations of a program, and *comments* typically document what the statements do.

- The *main() function* is a special type of function that's called by the operating system when it starts your program.

- *Variables* are used to store data that changes, or varies, as a program runs.

- When you *define* a variable, you must code its data type and its name. Two of the most common data types for numeric variables are the int and double types.

- After you define a variable, you can *initialize* it by assigning an initial value to it.

- You can use *assignment statements* to assign new values to variables.

- You can use *arithmetic operators* to code *arithmetic expressions* that perform operations on one or more *operands*.

- The *standard library* uses *header files* to organize and store its *classes*, *objects*, and *functions*.

- The standard library groups its members in the std *namespace*. You can use a *using directive*, *using declarations*, or *fully qualified* names to work with the members of a namespace.

- You *call* a function by typing the function name and a set of parentheses. A function may require one or more *arguments*, and it may *return* a value.

- You can use objects from the iostream header file to work with the *standard input and output streams* of the *console*. The cout object writes output to the console, and the cin object reads input from the console.

- A *char* is a built-in data type that contains a single character.

- A *string* is an object that contains zero or more characters. A string object is created from the string class that's available from the string header file.

- You can use the **+** operator to *concatenate* one string with another string or a char, and you can use the **+** or **+=** operator to *append* one string to another.

- To include special characters in strings, you can use *escape sequences*.

- *Testing* is the process of finding the errors or *bugs* in a program. *Debugging* is the process of locating and fixing the bugs.

Exercise 2-1   Create a Rectangle Calculator program

In this exercise, you'll code a program that accepts the height and width of a rectangle and then displays the area of the rectangle. When you're done, a test run should look something like this:

```
Rectangle Calculator

Enter height and width: 4.25 5.75
Area:                   24.4375

Bye!
```

Open the project, review the code, and add a comment

1. Use your IDE to open the Rectangle Calculator project or solution in this folder:

    `ex_starts\ch02_ex1_rectangle_calculator`

2. Review the code in the main.cpp file to see that it contains an #include directive for the iostream header file, a using directive for the std namespace, and a main() function with a return statement.

3. Add a block comment at the beginning of the file that includes your name, the current date, and the purpose of the program.

Code the main() function

4. Add a statement at the beginning of the main() function that writes the name of the program to the console. The name should be followed by two newline characters.

5. Define two variables with the double data type to store the height and width the user enters. Then, add a statement that prompts the user for a height and width.

6. Add a statement that uses chained extraction expressions to get the height and width values that the user enters at the console.

7. Define a variable with the double data type to store the area. Then, calculate the area of the rectangle (height times width), and assign it to this variable.

8. Add a statement that displays the area on the console, followed by two newline characters, the "Bye!" message, and two more newline characters.

Run the program

9. Run the program to be sure it works correctly. If any errors are detected, fix them and then run the program again.

Exercise 2-2   Enhance the Gallons Converter program

In this exercise, you'll enhance the Gallons Converter program presented in this chapter. When you're done, a test run should look something like this:

```
Gallons Converter

Enter gallons: 2.335
Liters:        8.84
Quarts:        9.34
Ounces:        298.88

Bye!
```

Open the project, review the code, and run the program

1. Use your IDE to open the Gallons Converter project or solution in this folder:
    `ex_starts\ch02_ex2_gallons_converter`

2. Review the code in the main.cpp file. Then, run the program to see how it works.

Add code to round the number of liters

3. Add an include directive for the cmath header file.

4. Add a statement that rounds the number of liters to two decimal places.

5. Run the program to be sure this works correctly. If any errors occur, debug the program, fix the errors, and then run the program again.

Add code to calculate the quarts and ounces

6. Define a variable with the double data type to store the number of quarts.

7. Calculate the number of quarts, and assign it to this variable. (One gallon is equal to four quarts.) The number of quarts should be rounded to two decimal places.

8. Modify the statement that writes the number of liters to the console so it also writes the number of quarts.

9. Run the program, and fix any errors that occur.

10. Repeat steps 6 through 9 to calculate and display the number of ounces in a gallon. (One gallon is equal to 128 ounces.)

Replace the using directive with using declarations

11. Replace the using directive for the std namespace with the using declarations needed by this program.

12. Run the program one more time to be sure it still works.

Exercise 2-3   Enhance the Guest Book program

In this exercise, you'll enhance the Guest Book program presented in this chapter so it accepts additional information. When you're done, a test run should look something like this:

```
Guest Book


First name:      Dave
Middle initial:  Williford
Last name:       Von Ronk
Address:         123 Wall St.
City:            New York
State:           NY
Postal code:     10001
Country:         United States

ENTRY
Dave W. Von Ronk
123 Wall St.
New York, NY 10001
United States
```

Open the project, review the code, and run the program

1. Use your IDE to open the Guest Book project or solution in this folder:
    ex_starts\ch02_ex3_guest_book

2. Review the code in the main.cpp file. Then, run the program to see how it works.

Add code to accept and display the address, state code, and zip code

3. Define three string variables to store an address, a state code, and a zip code.

4. Add statements that prompt the user for the address, state code, and zip code.

5. Add statements that get the data entered by the user for the address, state code, and zip code and assign the values to the appropriate variables. The entire line of data should be retrieved for the address and zip code, but only the first two characters should be retrieved for the state code.

6. Modify the statement that writes the entry to the console so it displays the data as shown above.

7. Run the program and test it with the data shown above. If the program doesn't pause for you to enter a value for the zip code, that's because the newline character after the state code hasn't been retrieved from the console. In that case, you can fix this problem by adding a statement that extracts and discards any additional characters in the input stream.

8. Run the program again to be sure it works correctly.

3

How to make decisions

In chapter 2, you learned how to write programs that get input from a user, process that input, and display output to the user. In this chapter, you'll learn how to write code so your program can make decisions. For example, it's common to make decisions based on the input from a user. To do that, you'll learn how to code control statements such as the if and switch statements.

How to get started with if statements

As you write programs, you need to determine when certain operations should be performed. To do that, you can code *control statements*. In the topics that follow, you'll learn the basic skills for coding one of the most basic control statements, the if statement. But first, you need to learn how to code expressions that compare numeric, string, or character values.

How to use the relational operators

To compare numeric, string, or character values, you code *Boolean expressions* that use the *relational operators* listed in figure 3-1. A Boolean expression is an expression that evaluates to either true or false.

The first group of examples shows how to use relational operators to compare numbers and return a true or false value. Here, the first expression is true if the value of the variable named counter is equal to the literal value 5. The second expression is true if the value of the test_score variable is not equal to 0. And the sixth example is true if the value of the variable named quantity is less than or equal to the value of the variable named reorder_amt.

When you code expressions like these, you must remember to code two equals signs (==) instead of one for the equality comparison. That's because a single equals sign (=) is used for assignment statements. As a result, if you accidentally code a Boolean expression with a single equals sign, it won't work the way you want.

When you compare numeric values, you usually compare values of the same data type. However, if you compare values of different types, C++ automatically converts the two numeric types to the same numeric type. In particular, if you compare an int type to a double type, C++ converts the int type to the double type before making the comparison.

The relational operators work the same way for string and char values as they do for numeric values. However, you typically don't need to use the less than or greater than operators with chars or strings. Instead, you usually use equality tests with chars and strings, as shown in the second group of examples.

Here, the first expression is true if the value in the char variable named choice equals the character literal 'y'. The second expression is true if the value in the name variable equals the string literal "Jones". And the third expression is true if the string value in the name variable does *not* equal the value in the name2 variable.

When working with strings and chars, tests for equality are *case-sensitive*. As a result, the first expression is true if the choice variable is equal to 'y', but not if it is equal to 'Y'. Similarly, the second expression is true if the name variable is equal to "Jones", but not if it is equal to "jones".

However, when working with chars, you can use the tolower() and toupper() functions presented here to do comparisons that are *case-insensitive*. The code example below the table shows how this works. Although there aren't similar functions for string values, you'll learn how to write your own function for doing this in chapter 7.

Relational operators

Operator	Name	Description
==	Equality	Returns a true value if the two operands are equal.
!=	Inequality	Returns a true value if the two operands are not equal.
>	Greater Than	Returns a true value if the left operand (lvalue) is greater than the right operand (rvalue).
<	Less Than	Returns a true value if lvalue is less than rvalue.
>=	Greater Than Or Equal	Returns a true value if lvalue is greater than or equal to rvalue.
<=	Less Than Or Equal	Returns a true value if lvalue is less than or equal to rvalue.

Examples of Boolean expressions

```
counter == 5          // equal to a numeric literal
test_score != 0       // not equal to a numeric literal
years > 0             // greater than a numeric literal
i < months            // less than a numeric variable
subtotal >= 9.99      // greater than or equal to a numeric literal
quantity <= reorder_amt  // less than or equal to a numeric variable
```

How to test strings and chars for equality

```
choice == 'y'         // char equal to a char literal
name == "Jones"       // string equal to a string literal
name != name2         // string not equal to another string variable
```

Two functions that convert a char to lower or upper case

Function	Description
tolower(char)	Returns the lower case equivalent of the char it receives. If there is no lower case equivalent, returns the char unchanged.
toupper(char)	Returns the upper case equivalent of the char it receives. If there is no upper case equivalent, returns the char unchanged.

How to make a test for equality of two chars case insensitive

```
tolower(choice) == 'y'    // true if choice is 'y' or 'Y'
```

Description

- A *Boolean expression* is an expression that evaluates to either true or false. To create a Boolean expression, you can use the *relational operators* to compare two operands.

- To compare two operands for equality, make sure to use two equals signs. If you only use one equals sign, you are coding an assignment statement, not a Boolean expression.

- If you compare an int value to a double value, the compiler casts the int value to the double type.

- When you test chars and strings for equality, the test is *case sensitive*. For chars, you can make the test *case-insensitive* by adding the tolower() or toupper() function.

Figure 3-1   How to use the relational operators

How to code an if statement

Figure 3-2 shows how to use the *if statement*, which is also known as the *if...else statement*, to control the logic of your programs. This statement is the C++ implementation of a control structure known as the *selection structure* because it lets you select different actions based on the results of a Boolean expression.

The syntax summary shows that you can code this statement with just an if clause, with one or more optional else if clauses, and with one optional else clause. In this syntax summary, the ellipsis (...) means that the preceding element (in this case the else if clause) can be repeated as many times as it is needed. And the brackets [ ] mean that the element is optional.

When an if statement is executed, C++ begins by evaluating the Boolean expression in the if clause. If it's true, the statements within this clause are executed and the rest of the clauses in the if statement are skipped. If it's false, C++ evaluates the first else if clause (if there is one). Then, if its Boolean expression is true, the statements within this else if clause are executed, and the rest of the clauses in the if statement are skipped. Otherwise, C++ evaluates the next else if clause.

This continues with any remaining else if clauses. Finally, if none of the clauses contains a Boolean expression that evaluates to true, C++ executes the statements in the else clause (if there is one). However, if none of the Boolean expressions are true and there is no else clause, C++ doesn't execute any statements.

In this figure, all of the if statements use braces to clearly identify a block of statements for each clause. If you define a variable within a block, that variable is available only to the other statements in the block. This can be referred to as *block scope*. As a result, if you need to access a variable outside of the block, you must define it before the block. In this figure, for instance, all of the examples define the discount_percent variable before the block for the if statement. That way, the code after the if statement can access the discount_percent variable.

In this figure, the first example shows an if statement that only contains an if clause. Here, the statement that declares the discount_percent variable initializes it to a value of .05 (5%). Then, the if clause checks whether the subtotal is greater than or equal to 100. If it is, the code sets the discount_percent variable to a value of .1 (10%). Otherwise, the code leaves the discount_percent variable at its default value of .05 (5%).

The second example shows an if statement that contains an if clause and an else clause. This performs the same task as the first example. However, it uses the else clause to set the default value of the discount_percent variable.

The advantage of the second example is that the statements that set the value for the discount_percent variable are all coded at the same level. As a result, some programmers find it easier to read and understand this example. The disadvantage of this approach is that it uses three more lines of code. Since the first and second examples work equally well, you can choose the approach that you prefer.

The syntax of the if statement

```
if (boolean_expression) { statements }
[else if (boolean_expression) { statements }] ...
[else { statements }]
```

An if statement with only an if clause

```
double discount_percent = .05;
if (subtotal >= 100) {
    discount_percent = .1;
}
```

With an else clause

```
double discount_percent;
if (subtotal >= 100) {
    discount_percent = .1;
} else {
    discount_percent = .05;
}
```

With multiple else if clauses

```
double discount_percent;
if (subtotal >= 300) {
    discount_percent = .3;
} else if (subtotal >= 200) {
    discount_percent = .2;
} else if (subtotal >= 100) {
    discount_percent = .1;
} else {
    discount_percent = .05;
}
```

Description

- An *if statement* always contains an if clause. In addition, it can contain one or more else if clauses and one else clause.

- A pair of braces defines a *block* of code. Any variables declared within a block have *block scope*. As a result, they can only be used within that block.

- C++ evaluates the clauses of an if statement from the top down. Once a clause evaluates to true, C++ skips the rest of the clauses. As a result, it's most efficient to code the most likely conditions first and the least likely conditions last.

Figure 3-2   How to get started with if statements

The third example in figure 3-2 shows an if statement that contains multiple else if clauses. When coding a statement like this, it's important to remember that C++ evaluates if statements from the top down. Once a clause evaluates to true, C++ executes the statements for that clause and skips the rest of the if statement. In the third example, for instance, the if clause checks whether the subtotal is greater than or equal to 300. If it is, the discount_percent variable is set to .3 and the rest of the if statement is skipped. Otherwise, the first else if clause checks whether the subtotal is greater than or equal to 200. If it is, the discount_percent variable is set to .2 and the rest of the if statement is skipped. And so on.

Since these conditions are coded in a logical sequence, they're easy to read and understand. As always, the easier your code is to read and understand, the easier it is to test, debug, and maintain.

How to work with braces

In figure 3-2, all of the clauses within the if statements use braces. These braces are required if the clause contains more than one statement, but they're optional if the clause contains just one statement. When you're getting started with C++, we recommend always coding these braces. However, if a clause only contains one statement, you can omit the braces as shown by the first example in figure 3-3.

The second example shows a common error that programmers often encounter when they're first learning C++. Here, the if clause contains two statements. The first statement sets the discount percent, and the second sets the shipping method. However, since this example doesn't include braces, the if clause only includes the statement that sets the discount percent. As a result, the statement that sets the shipping method to "FedEx" is always executed, even if the subtotal is less than 100.

To fix this error, the third example add braces to the if clause. That way, C++ knows that it should execute both statements when the subtotal is greater than or equal to 100. As a result, this statement does not set the shipping method to "FedEx" when the subtotal is less than 100. This shows that braces are optional when a clause only contains one statement, but braces are required when a clause contains two or more statements.

The fourth example shows an if statement that includes multiple statements for its if clause and its else clause. As a result, braces are required for both clauses.

The fifth example works the same as the fourth example, except that the opening braces for the two clauses are placed on their own line. Some programmers prefer this convention because it makes it easier to see how the opening brace corresponds with the closing brace. However, some programmers prefer the convention used in the fourth example since it uses less vertical space and allows the programmer to see more code on the screen.

Both conventions for brace placement are commonly used, and the choice of which convention to use is largely a matter of personal preference. Of course, if you're working with a team of programmers, you should follow any conventions that have been established by the team. For this book, we typically use the convention presented in the fourth example because it saves vertical space and is still easy to read, especially once you get used to it.

An if statement without braces

```
double discount_percent;
if (subtotal >= 100)
    discount_percent = .1;
else
    discount_percent = .05;
```

An if statement without braces that causes an error

```
double discount_percent = .05;
string shipping_method = "USPS";
if (subtotal >= 100)
    discount_percent = .1;
    shipping_method = "FedEx";   // Error! This statement is always executed
```

An if statement that uses braces to fix the error

```
double discount_percent = .05;
string shipping_method = "USPS";
if (subtotal >= 100) {
    discount_percent = .1;
    shipping_method = "FedEx";   // Braces fix error
}
```

An if statement with clauses that contain multiple statements

```
double discount_percent;
string shipping_method;
if (subtotal >= 100) {
    discount_percent = .1;
    shipping_method = "FedEx";
} else {
    discount_percent = .05;
    shipping_method = "USPS";
}
```

Another coding style for brace placement

```
double discount_percent;
string shipping_method;
if (subtotal >= 100)
{
    discount_percent = .1;
    shipping_method = "FedEx";
}
else
{
    discount_percent = .05;
    shipping_method = "USPS";
}
```

Description

- If a clause in an if statement contains just one statement, you don't have to enclose the statement in braces. You can just end the clause with a semicolon.

Figure 3-3   How to work with braces

The Invoice 1.0 program

Figure 3-4 shows the console and code for the Invoice 1.0 program. Although this program is simple, it gets input from the user, makes a decision based on that input, performs some calculations, and displays the results of the calculations.

The code for the Invoice program starts by displaying the program name at the console, followed by a blank line. Then, it prompts the user for the subtotal and stores the subtotal the user enters in the subtotal variable. Next, it uses an if statement to set the discount percent based on the value of the subtotal. If, for example, the subtotal is greater than or equal to 200, the discount percent is .2 (20%). If that condition isn't true but the subtotal is greater than or equal to 100, the discount percent is .1 (10%). Otherwise, the discount percent is .05 (5%).

As you review this code, note that it defines the discount_percent variable before the if statement. As a result, this variable is available to the rest of the code in the block for the main() method, including all clauses in the if statement.

When the if statement finishes, the code calculates the discount amount and the invoice total and rounds the results to 2 decimal places. Then, it displays the discount percent, discount amount, and invoice total on the console.

Although this program illustrates the use of a simple if statement, it could be improved in many ways. For example, this program displays output that doesn't make sense if the user enters an invalid double value such as "x" for the subtotal. To fix this issue, you can check the failure flag after the extraction expression as described in chapter 5. In addition, this program could format and align the numbers so they're easier for the user to read as shown in chapter 5.

In the meantime, if you're new to programming, you can learn a lot by writing simple programs like this Invoice program. Doing that gives you a chance to become comfortable with coding simple if statements.

The console

```
Invoice Total Calculator 1.0

Enter a subtotal: 129.43
Discount percent: 0.1
Discount amount:  12.94
Invoice total:    116.49

Bye!
```

The code

```cpp
#include <iostream>
#include <cmath>

using namespace std;

int main()
{
    cout << "Invoice Total Calculator 1.0\n\n";

    // get subtotal from user
    double subtotal;
    cout << "Enter a subtotal: ";
    cin >> subtotal;

    // determine discount percent based on subtotal
    double discount_percent;
    if (subtotal >= 200) {
        discount_percent = .2;
    } else if (subtotal >= 100) {
        discount_percent = .1;
    } else {
        discount_percent = .05;
    }

    // calculate and round results
    double discount_amount = subtotal * discount_percent;
    discount_amount = round(discount_amount * 100) / 100;

    double invoice_total = subtotal - discount_amount;
    invoice_total = round(invoice_total * 100) / 100;

    // write the results data to the console
    cout << "Discount percent: " << discount_percent << endl
         << "Discount amount:  " << discount_amount << endl
         << "Invoice total:    " << invoice_total << endl << endl;

    cout << "Bye!\n\n";
}
```

Figure 3-4   The Invoice 1.0 program

More skills for coding if statements

Now that you know how to code simple if statements, you're ready to learn how to code more complex ones, such as if statements that use logical operators and if statements that are nested within other if statements.

How to use the logical operators

To code a *compound conditional expression*, you can use the *logical operators* that are shown in figure 3-5 to combine two or more Boolean expressions. If you use the AND operator, the compound expression only returns true if both expressions are true. If you use the OR operator, the compound expression returns true if either expression is true. If you use the NOT operator, the value returned by the expression is reversed.

Below the table of operators, you can see their *order of precedence*. That is the order in which the operators are evaluated if more than one logical operator is used in a compound expression. This means that NOT operators are evaluated before AND operators, which are evaluated before OR operators. Although this is normally what you want, you can override this order by using parentheses.

The examples in this figure show how these operators work. For instance, the first example uses the AND operator to connect two Boolean expressions. As a result, it evaluates to true if the expression on its left *and* the expression on its right are both true. Similarly, the second example uses the OR operator to connect two Boolean expressions. As a result, it evaluates to true if either the expression on its left *or* the expression on its right is true.

The third example shows how to use the NOT operator to reverse the value of an expression. As a result, this expression evaluates to true if the age variable is *not* greater than or equal to 65. In this case, using the NOT operator is okay, but often the NOT operator results in code that's difficult to read. That's why it's a good practice to rewrite your code so it doesn't use the NOT operator.

The next four examples show that compound conditions aren't limited to two expressions. For instance, the fourth example uses two AND operators to connect three Boolean expressions, and the fifth example uses two OR operators to connect three expressions.

You can also mix AND and OR expressions as in the sixth and seventh examples. In the sixth example, the parentheses *clarify* the sequence of operations since C++ would do the AND operation first anyway. In the seventh example, though, the parentheses *change* the sequence of operations. As a result, C++ evaluates the two expressions connected by the OR operator before evaluating the rest of the expression.

When you use the AND and OR operators, C++ evaluates them from left to right, and the second expression is only evaluated if necessary. That's why these operators are known as *short-circuit operators*. If, for example, the first expression in an AND operation is false, the second expression isn't evaluated because the entire expression is going to be false. Similarly, if the first expression in an OR operation is true, the second expression isn't evaluated because the entire expression is going to be true.

Logical operators

Operator	Name	Description
&&	AND	Returns a true value if both expressions are true. This operator only evaluates the second expression if necessary.
||	OR	Returns a true value if either expression is true. This operator only evaluates the second expression if necessary.
!	NOT	Reverses the value of the expression.

Order of precedence

1. NOT operator
2. AND operator
3. OR operator

Boolean expressions that use logical operators

```
// The AND operator
age >= 65 && city == "Chicago"

// The OR operator
city == "Greenville" || age >= 65

// The NOT operator
!(age >= 65)

// Two AND operators
age >= 65 && city == "Greenville" && state == "SC"

// Two OR operators
age >= 65 || age <= 18 || status == "retired"

// AND and OR operators with parens to clarify sequence of operations
(age >= 65 && status == "retired") || age < 18

// AND and OR operators with parens to change sequence of operations
age >= 65 && (status == "retired" || state == "SC")
```

Description

- You can use the *logical operators* to create a Boolean expression that combines two or more Boolean expressions.
- Since the && and || operators only evaluate the second expression if necessary, they're sometimes referred to as *short-circuit operators*.
- By default, NOT operations are performed first, followed by AND operations, and then OR operations. These operations are performed after arithmetic operations and relational operations.
- You can use parentheses to change the sequence of operations. In addition, you can use parentheses to clarify the sequence of operations.

Figure 3-5   How to use the logical operators

If statements that use the logical operators

Figure 3-6 begins with an example that shows another way to code the if statement that sets the discount percent based on the subtotal. In this case, the if and else if clauses use compound conditions. This shows the lower and upper limits for most of the discount ranges.

One advantage of this approach is that the else if clauses can be coded in any sequence. One disadvantage of this approach is that it requires more code.

When coding a statement like this, it's important to remember that C++ evaluates the clauses of an if statement from the top down. Once a clause evaluates to true, C++ executes the statements for that clause and skips the rest of the clauses. As a result, it's most efficient to code the most likely conditions first and the least likely conditions last. In this example, for instance, the code runs most efficiently when the if clause contains the most likely condition (a subtotal greater than or equal to 100 and less than 200), the first else if clause contains the second most likely condition (a subtotal greater than or equal to 200 and less than 300), and so on.

If efficiency isn't your primary concern, you should code the conditions in the way that's most readable. As always, the easier your code is to read and understand, the easier it is to test, debug, and maintain.

The second example shows how an if statement can be used to check whether data entered by a user is valid. This is known as *data validation*. Here, the if statement checks whether the variable named score contains a value that's between 0 and 100. If it does, a message thanking the user for entering a score is displayed. If it doesn't, a message that indicates that the score is not valid is displayed. You'll see more practical and complete examples of data validation starting in chapter 5.

The third example also checks for a valid user entry. Here, an if statement checks whether the customer_type variable is not equal to an 'r' or a 'w'. If this expression is true, an error message is displayed. However, if this expression is false, it means that the customer_type variable is equal to an 'r' or a 'w'. In that case, the statements in the if clause are skipped.

An if statement that uses logical operators in its Boolean expressions

```
double discount_percent;
if (subtotal >= 100 && subtotal < 200) {
    discount_percent = .1;
} else if (subtotal >= 200 && subtotal < 300) {
    discount_percent = .2;
} else if (subtotal >= 300) {
    discount_percent = .3;
} else {
    discount_percent = .05;
}
```

An if statement that validates the range of a score

```
if (score >= 0 && score <= 100) {
    cout << "Thanks for entering a test score.\n";
} else {
    cout << "Test score must be from 0 - 100.\n";
}
```

An if statement that validates the customer type

```
if (customer_type != 'r' && customer_type != 'w') {
    cout << "Customer type must be 'r' or 'w'.\n";
}
```

Description

- If you can code an if statement more than one way and get the same results, you should usually choose the way that's easiest to read and understand.

- If efficiency is a primary concern, you should code the most likely conditions first and the least likely conditions last.

- If statements are often used to choose one option out of several. They are also used to make sure that user entries are valid. This is called *data validation*.

Figure 3-6   Examples of if statements that use logical operators

How to code nested if statements

In many programs, you may need or want to code one if statement within a clause of another if statement in order to get the logic right. The result is known as *nested if statements*.

When you're coding if statements and the conditions get so complicated that they're hard to follow, it often helps to create a table that summarizes the conditions. This is illustrated by the table in figure 3-7. Here, the customer type can be either 'r' for retail or 'w' for wholesale. Then, the discount percent is determined by the customer type and the invoice subtotal.

Once you create a table like this, you can use it as a guide to coding your if statements. In the first example, for instance, the outer if statement checks for two customer type codes. The if clause tests for the 'r' code, and the else if clause tests for the 'w' code. If neither test evaluates to true, the discount_percent variable stays at its initial value of zero.

Within the outer if clause, a nested if statement sets the discount percent based on the value of the subtotal variable. Similarly, the outer else if clause uses a nested if statement to set the discount percent.

When you nest if statements, it's a good practice to indent the nested statements and their clauses, since this makes it easy to identify where each nested statement begins and ends. That's particularly true if you nest more than one level deep. Although there's no technical limit to how deep you can nest if statements, nesting that's more than one or two levels deep can be confusing and hard to follow. So, you should avoid nesting any deeper than that.

To avoid nested if statements, you can use conditional operators as shown by the second example. This code gets the same results as the first example, but it doesn't use nested if statements. Instead, it uses a series of compound Boolean expressions. In addition, it uses comments to describe what the two main portions of the if statement are doing. This makes it easier for other programmers to read and understand this if statement. On the other hand, most programmers would probably say that the first example is considerably easier to read.

One problem with the second example is that it duplicates the Boolean expression that checks the customer type in each clause. As a result, it makes your code more difficult to maintain. If, for example, the code for retail customers was changed from 'r' to 't', you'd have to make that change in three places in the second example. That's both tedious and error prone. By contrast, you'd only have to change the code in one place in the first example. Because of that and because of the reduced readability of this code, it's better to use nested if statements in a situation like this.

A table that summarizes the discount rules

Customer type	Invoice subtotal	Discount percent
r (for retail)	< 100	.0
	>= 100 and < 250	.1
	>= 250	.2
w (for wholesale)	< 500	.4
	>= 500	.5

Nested if statements for applying customer discounts

```
double discount_percent = .0;
if (tolower(customer_type) == 'r') {
    if (subtotal < 100) {                    // begin nested if
        discount_percent = .0;
    } else if (subtotal >= 100 && subtotal < 250) {
        discount_percent = .1;
    } else {
        discount_percent = .2;
    }                                        // end nested if
} else if (tolower(customer_type) == 'w') {
    if (subtotal < 500) {                    // begin nested if
        discount_percent = .4;
    } else {
        discount_percent = .5;
    }                                        // end nested if
}
```

An if statement that gets the same results

```
double discount_percent = .0;
// the discounts for retail customers
if (tolower(customer_type) == 'r' && subtotal < 100) {
    discount_percent = .0;
} else if (tolower(customer_type) == 'r' &&
        (subtotal >= 100 && subtotal < 250)) {
    discount_percent = .1;
} else if (tolower(customer_type) == 'r' && subtotal >= 250) {
    discount_percent = .2;
// the discounts for wholesale customers
} else if (tolower(customer_type) == 'w' && subtotal < 500) {
    discount_percent = .4;
} else if (tolower(customer_type) == 'w' && subtotal >= 500) {
    discount_percent = .5;
}
```

Description

- It's possible to code one if statement within a clause of another if statement. The result is known as *nested if statements*.

- In some cases, you can use the logical operators to get the same results that you get with nested if statements.

- To improve the readability of if statements, you can use comments to describe what various clauses do.

Figure 3-7   How to code nested if statements

The Invoice 2.0 program

Figure 3-8 presents the Invoice 2.0 program. This program uses nested if statements to calculate the discount percent for an invoice. Except for the brace placement, these nested if statements are the same as the nested if statements presented in the previous figure. However, the main if statement in this figure includes an else clause that sets the discount_percent variable to zero.

Here again, the discount percent is based on the customer type (r or w) and the subtotal. Both of these values are entered by the user.

To make the nested if statements easier to follow, comments are used to explain the function of the clauses of the outer if statement. In the nested if statements, the clauses include braces even though each clause only contains one statement. That way, if you ever need to, you can easily add more statements to these clauses without introducing any errors.

The console

```
The Invoice Total Calculator 2.0

Enter customer type (r/w): r
Enter subtotal:            125.75
Discount percent:          0.1
Discount amount:           12.58
Invoice total:             113.17

Bye!
```

The code

```cpp
#include <iostream>
#include <cmath>

using namespace std;

int main() {
    // display title
    cout << "The Invoice Total Calculator 2.0\n\n";

    // get input
    char customer_type;
    cout << "Enter customer type (r/w): ";
    cin >> customer_type;

    double subtotal;
    cout << "Enter subtotal:            ";
    cin >> subtotal;

    // set discount percent
    double discount_percent;
    if (tolower(customer_type) == 'r') {           // RETAIL
        if (subtotal < 100) {
            discount_percent = .0;
        }
        else if (subtotal >= 100 && subtotal < 250) {
            discount_percent = .1;
        }
        else {
            discount_percent = .2;
        }
    }
    else if (tolower(customer_type) == 'w') {      // WHOLESALE
        if (subtotal < 500) {
            discount_percent = .4;
        }
        else {
            discount_percent = .5;
        }
    }
    else {                                         // OTHER
        discount_percent = .0;
    }
```

Figure 3-8   The Invoice 2.0 program (part 1 of 2)

Once the discount percent is established, the program calculates the discount amount and the invoice total. Then, the invoice total is displayed along with the discount percent and discount amount.

This program assumes that if the user doesn't enter a customer type of 'r' or 'w', another type of customer is being processed and the discount percent is set to zero. However, what if you wanted a customer type other than 'r' or 'w' to be considered invalid? Then, you could use an if statement like the last one you saw in figure 3-6 to validate the customer type. In that case, the program would display an error message and end if the customer type was invalid.

In most cases, you wouldn't want a program to end because of an invalid entry. Instead, you would want the program to prompt the user for another entry after displaying an error message. You'll learn how to do that in the next chapter using a while loop.

The code (continued)

```
        // calculate and round results
        double discount_amount = subtotal * discount_percent;
        discount_amount = round(discount_amount * 100) / 100;

        double invoice_total = subtotal - discount_amount;
        invoice_total = round(invoice_total * 100) / 100;

        // display output
        cout << "Discount percent:       " << discount_percent << endl
             << "Discount amount:        " << discount_amount << endl
             << "Invoice total:          " << invoice_total << endl << endl;

        cout << "Bye!\n\n";
    }
```

Figure 3-8   The Invoice 2.0 program (part 2 of 2)

Other ways to make decisions

The if statement is a powerful control structure that allows a program to make decisions. However, C++ provides other ways to make decisions, including the conditional operator and the switch statement. You can almost always accomplish the same task with an if statement, but there are times when using the conditional operator or a switch statement can improve your code. In addition, when you work on code written by other programmers, you're likely to encounter these ways of making decisions.

How to use the conditional operator

Earlier in this chapter, you learned how to use relational operators such as the less than operator (<). These operators are known as *binary operators* because they have two operands. Now, figure 3-9 shows how to use the *conditional operator*. This operator is known as a *ternary operator* because it has three operands. The first operand is a Boolean expression, the second operand is an expression that's evaluated and returned if the Boolean expression is true, and the third operand is an expression that's evaluated and returned if the Boolean expression is false.

The conditional operator requires two symbols to separate its three operands. This is illustrated by the syntax for a conditional expression, which is an expression that uses the conditional operator. As you can see, the question mark (?) is used to separate the Boolean expression and the true expression, and the colon (:) is used to separate the true and the false expressions.

The first example shows a conditional expression. Here the Boolean expression checks if the variable named subtotal is greater than or equal to 100. If so, it returns .1. Otherwise, it returns .05.

The second example shows how you would use a conditional expression in an assignment statement. Here, the statement begins by declaring a double variable named discount_percent. Then, it assigns the result of the conditional expression in the first example to that variable. As a result, if the subtotal is greater than or equal to 100, the discount_percent variable is .1. Otherwise, it's .05.

The third example works the same as the second example. However, it uses parentheses to clearly identify the Boolean expression. These parentheses are optional, but some programmers prefer using them because they make it easier to read the statement.

The fourth example shows the third example after it has been rewritten to use an if statement instead of the conditional operator. This shows that a statement that uses the conditional operator can always be rewritten to use an if statement. Some programmers prefer this approach, since they consider if statements easier to read. Other programmers like to use the conditional operator.

Nevertheless, many programmers like to use the conditional operator because it takes fewer lines of code. As a result, even if you don't use the conditional operator in your code, you still need to understand how it works so you can understand code that has been written by other programmers.

The syntax for a conditional expression

```
boolean_expression ? if_true : if_false
```

A conditional expression

```
subtotal >= 100 ? .1 : .05       // returns .1 or .05 depending on subtotal
```

How to use a conditional operator to set the value of a variable

```
double discount_percent = subtotal >= 100 ? .1 : .05;
```

A statement that uses parentheses to identify the Boolean expression

```
double discount_percent = (subtotal >= 100) ? .1 : .05;
```

An if statement that performs the same task

```
double discount_percent;
if (subtotal >= 100)
    discount_percent = .1;
else
    discount_percent = .05;
```

Description

- The *conditional operator* consists of three expressions that are separated by the question mark (?) and colon (:) symbols. The first expression is a Boolean expression, the second expression is evaluated and returned if the Boolean expression is true, and the third expression is evaluated and returned if the Boolean expression is false.

- The conditional operator provides a way to code simple if...else statements on a single line.

- An operator that works on two operands is known as a *binary operator*. The relational operators such as the less than (<) and greater than (>) operators are examples of binary operators.

- An operator that works on three operands is known as a *ternary operator*. The conditional operator is an example of a ternary operator.

Figure 3-9   How to use the conditional operator

How to code switch statements

The next few figures show how to work with the *switch statement*. This is the C++ implementation of a control structure known as the *case structure*. This structure lets you code different actions for different cases. The switch statement can sometimes be used in place of an if statement.

Figure 3-10 shows how to code a simple switch statement. To do that, you code the switch keyword followed by a switch expression that evaluates to an integer type such as the int or char type. After the switch expression, you can code one or more *case labels* that represent the possible values of the switch expression. Then, when the switch expression matches the value specified by the case label, the statements after the label are executed.

You can code the case labels in any sequence, but you should be sure to follow each label with a colon. Then, if the label contains one or more statements, you can code a *break statement* after them to jump to the end of the switch statement. The *default label* is an optional label that identifies the statements to be executed if none of the case labels are executed.

The first example shows how to code a switch statement that sets the description for a product based on the value of an int variable named product_id. Here, the first case label assigns a value of "Hammer" to the product_description variable if product_id is equal to 1. Then, the break statement exits the switch statement. Similarly, the second case label sets the product_description variable to "Box of Nails" if product_id is equal to 2, and then it exits the switch statement. If product_id is equal to something other than 1 or 2, the default case label is executed. Like the other two case labels, this one sets the value of the product_description variable and exits the switch statement.

The syntax of the switch statement

```
switch (switch_expression) {
    case label1:
        statements
        break;
    [case label2:
        statements
        break;] ...
    [default:
        statements
        break;]
}
```

A switch statement that uses an int variable named product_id

```
string product_description;
switch (product_id) {
    case 1:
        product_description = "Hammer";
        break;
    case 2:
        product_description = "Box of Nails";
        break;
    default:
        product_description = "No product found for specified ID";
        break;
}
```

Description

- The switch statement can only be used with an expression that evaluates to an integer type such as the int type or the char type.

- The switch statement transfers control to the appropriate *case label*. If control isn't transferred to one of the case labels, the optional *default label* is executed.

- The case labels can be coded in any sequence.

Figure 3-10   How to code switch statements

More examples of switch statements

If you don't code a break statement at the end of a case label, the execution of the program *falls through* to the next case label and executes the statements in that label as shown in figure 3-11. Here, the first example shows how to code a switch statement that sets a day variable to "weekday" or "weekend" depending on the value of the integer in the variable named day_of_week. Here, the case labels for 1, 2, 3, and 4 don't contain any statements, so execution falls through to the case label for 5. As a result, day is set to "weekday" for any of those values. Similarly, whenever day_of_week equals 6 or 7, day is set to "weekend".

Although a break statement is coded at the end of the last case label in this example as well as the other examples shown in this chapter, you should know that it isn't required. If you omit this break statement, program execution automatically falls through to the statement that follows the switch statement. However, it's generally considered a good programming practice to code a break statement at the end of the last case label. That way, if you add a new case label after the last case label, your switch statement still works correctly. Similarly, if you move the last case label so it occurs earlier in the switch statement, it still works correctly.

Switch statements are often used for console applications that allow the user to select a menu item as shown in the second example. Here, the first statement displays a list of three menu items with an integer that identifies each item. Then, the code gets the int value for the menu choice from the user. Next, it uses a switch statement to execute the appropriate code for the menu item. Or, if the user doesn't select a valid menu item, it displays a message that indicates that the item wasn't valid.

In this example, the code for the first two menu items just displays a message that identifies the selected menu item. However, as you progress through this book, you'll learn how to write code that implements these menu choices. For instance, in chapter 9, you'll learn how to display a list of the movies that are stored in a file, and you'll learn how to add a movie to that file.

A switch statement that falls through case labels

```
string day;
switch (day_of_week) {
    case 1:
    case 2:
    case 3:
    case 4:
    case 5:
        day = "weekday";
        break;
    case 6:
    case 7:
        day = "weekend";
        break;
}
```

A switch statement for a menu system

```
// display menu
cout << "1. List all movies" << endl
     << "2. Add a movie" << endl
     << "3. Exit" << endl << endl;

// get menu item from user
cout << "Menu item: ";
int menu_item;
cin >> menu_item;

// execute the correct code for the menu item
switch (menu_item) {
    case 1:
        cout << "MOVIE LIST" << endl;
        // code that lists all movies goes here
        break;
    case 2:
        cout << "ADD A MOVIE" << endl;
        // code that adds a movie goes here
        break;
    case 3:
        cout << "Bye!";
        break;
    default:
        cout << "Invalid menu item! Try again." << endl;
        break;
}
```

Description

- If a case label doesn't contain a break statement, code execution *falls through* to the next label. Otherwise, the break statement ends the switch statement.

Figure 3-11   More examples of switch statements

A switch statement for the Invoice 2.0 program

To give you a better idea of how switch statements work, figure 3-12 presents a switch statement that could be used with the Invoice 2.0 program presented earlier in this chapter. Here, the switch statement determines what customer type the user entered. If the user enters 'r' or 'R' for the customer type, the first nested if statement is executed. If the user enters 'w' or 'W', though, the second nested if statement is executed. Otherwise, the default label sets the discount percent to zero.

This example shows that you can use switch statements to work with a switch expression that evaluates to a char type. In addition, it shows that you can nest an if statement within a switch statement. Although it's less common, you can also nest switch statements within if statements, and you can nest one switch statement within another. As always, when you nest statements, you should try to code them with a logical structure that is relatively easy to understand. If necessary, you can also add comments that clarify the logic of your code.

Most importantly, this example illustrates the difference between a switch statement and an if statement. If you compare the switch statement shown here with the if statement in figure 3-8, for example, you'll see that the advantage of the switch statement is that you only have to code the customer_type variable once in the parentheses after the switch keyword. By contrast, you have to code this variable as part of the Boolean expression for every if and else if clause of an if statement. This makes the switch statement easier to read and maintain, especially for a decision that has many branches.

The advantage of the if statement is that it's more flexible and can make decisions that the switch statement can't make. For example, you couldn't use a switch statement for either of the nested if statements shown in this figure. As a result, you must know how to code an if statement to be able to perform certain tasks. A switch statement, on the other hand, isn't absolutely necessary, but it can make your code easier to read and maintain.

A switch statement for the Invoice application

```
double discount_percent;
switch (customer_type) {
    // RETAIL
    case 'r':
    case 'R':
        if (subtotal < 100)
            discount_percent = .0;
        else if (subtotal >= 100 && subtotal < 250)
            discount_percent = .1;
        else
            discount_percent = .2;
        break;

    // WHOLESALE
    case 'w':
    case 'W':
        if (subtotal < 500)
            discount_percent = .4;
        else
            discount_percent = .5;
        break;

    // OTHER
    default:
        discount_percent = .0;
        break;
}
```

Description

- You can often use a switch statement or an if statement to perform the same task.
- You can nest other control statements within a switch statement.

Figure 3-12   A switch statement for the Invoice 2.0 application

Perspective

Now that you've completed this chapter, you should be able to code if statements and switch statements. These are the C++ statements that allow your program to make decisions. In the next chapter, you'll learn how to code loops. Like if and switch statements, loops are a control structure that you can use to control the logic of your program. Like if statements, loops also rely on Boolean expressions to determine how they're executed.

Terms

control statements	short-circuit operators
Boolean expression	data validation
relational operators	nested if statements
case-sensitive comparison	binary operators
case-insensitive comparison	ternary operator
if statement	conditional expression
if...else statement	switch statement
selection structure	case structure
block of statements	case label
block scope	break statement
compound conditional expression	default label
logical operators	execution fall through
order of precedence	

Summary

- A *Boolean expression* is an expression that evaluates to either true or false. To create a Boolean expression, you can use the *relational operators* to compare two operands.

- You can use *if statements* and *switch statements* to control the logic of an application, and you can nest these statements whenever necessary.

- A pair of braces defines a *block* of code. Any variables declared within a block have *block scope*. As a result, they can only be used within that block.

- You can use the *logical operators* to connect two or more Boolean expressions.

- Since the **&&** and **||** operators only evaluate the second expression if necessary, they're sometimes referred to as *short-circuit operators*.

- The *conditional operator* consists of three expressions that are separated by the question mark (**?**) and colon (**:**) symbols. It provides a way to code simple if...else statements on a single line.

- An operator that works on two operands is known as a *binary operator*. The relational operators such as the less than (**<**) and greater than (**>**) operators are examples of binary operators.

- An operator that works on three operands is known as a *ternary operator*. The conditional operator is an example of a ternary operator.

- The switch statement transfers control to the appropriate *case label*. If control isn't transferred to one of the case labels, the optional *default label* is executed.

- If a case label doesn't contain a break statement, code execution *falls through* to the next label. Otherwise, the break statement ends the switch statement.

Exercise 3-1   Enhance the Invoice program

In this exercise, you'll enhance the if statement for the Invoice program so it provides for an additional customer type and additional discounts. When you're done, a test run should look something like this:

```
The Invoice Total Calculator 2.0

Enter customer type (r/w/c):  c
Enter subtotal:               425.42
Discount percent:             0.25
Discount amount:              106.36
Invoice total:                319.06

Bye!
```

Open the project and modify the if statement

1. Open the Invoice project or solution in this folder:
   ex_starts\ch03_ex1_invoice

2. Change the if statement so customers of type 'r' or 'R' with a subtotal that is greater than or equal to $250 but less than $500 get a 20% discount and those with a subtotal of $500 or more get a 30% discount. Then, test the program to make sure it works.

3. Add another else if clause for customers of type 'c' or 'C' (for college). These customers should always get a 25% discount. Be sure to update the message that prompts the user for a customer type. In addition, update the output messages so the data is aligned. Then, test the program again.

Replace the if statement with a switch statement

4. Code a switch statement right after the if statement. This statement should provide for the user entering 'r', 'R', 'w', 'W', 'c', or 'C'. It should also provide a default label for any other entries.

5. Copy the code from the original if statement that provides for the discount percents that are based on the subtotal and paste it into the case labels where appropriate. Then, add break statements to the case labels as necessary.

6. Make the entire if statement above the switch statement a comment. Then, test to make sure the switch statement works correctly. Is this code easier to read and understand?

Exercise 3-2   Enhance the Rectangle Calculator program

In this exercise, you'll enhance the Rectangle Calculator program so it checks the height and width entries to be sure they're greater than zero. When you're done, a test run should look something like this:

```
Rectangle Calculator

Enter height and width: 22.1 0

Height and width must be greater than zero.
```

Open the project and add two if statements

1. Open the Rectangle Calculator project or solution in this folder:
   `ex_starts\ch03_ex2_rectangle_calculator`

2. Add an if statement after the code that gets the height and width from the user that tests if the height is greater than 0.

3. Nest another if statement within the first if statement that tests if the width is greater than 0.

4. Move the code that calculates the area of the rectangle and displays the result within the second if statement. Now, these statements will only be executed if both the height and width are greater than 0.

5. Add an else clause to both if statements that displays an error message if the entry is invalid. Include a blank line before and two blank lines after the error message.

6. Test the program to be sure it works.

Use a logical operator to combine the if statements

7. Create a copy of the nested if statements, and then make the original statement a comment.

8. Modify the copied code so it uses a single if statement. The if clause should use a logical operator to test that both the height and the width are greater than zero.

9. Modify the else clause for the if statement so it displays an appropriate error message if either entry is invalid.

10. Test the program to be sure it works.

4

How to code loops

In chapter 3, you learned how to code if and switch statements to make decisions. Now, this chapter shows how to code a statement known as a loop that allows you to repeat a block of statements multiple times. But first, this chapter presents some more skills for coding arithmetic expressions because these skills are often used when coding loops.

More skills for coding arithmetic expressions

In chapter 2, you learned how to code simple arithmetic expressions that use the addition, subtraction, multiplication, division, and modulus operators. Now, you'll learn some additional skills for coding arithmetic expressions. Once you learn these skills, you'll be ready to learn how to code loops.

How to use arithmetic unary operators

Figure 4-1 shows four operators that work on one operand. These operators are referred to as *unary operators*. For example, you can code the increment operator (++) after an operand to increase the value of the operand by 1.

When you code an increment (++) or decrement (--) operator, you can *prefix* the operand by coding the operator before the variable. Then, the increment or decrement operation is performed before the rest of the statement is executed. Conversely, you can *postfix* the operand by coding the operator after the variable. Then, the increment or decrement operation isn't performed until after the statement is executed.

Often, an entire statement does nothing more than increment or decrement a variable as shown in the first two examples. Then, both the prefix and postfix forms yield the same result. However, if you use the increment and decrement operators as part of a larger statement, you can use the prefix and postfix forms of these operators to control when the operation is performed. This is shown by the third and fourth examples.

If you don't need to postfix the operand to get the code to run correctly, it's considered a best practice in C++ to prefix the operand. That's because postfixing an operand can lead to the creation of temporary variables in memory, which isn't efficient.

If necessary, you can code the negative sign operator (-) in front of an operand to reverse the value of the operand, as shown in the fifth example. Although you can also code the positive sign operator (+) in front of an operand, it doesn't change the value of the operand. As a result, this unary operator is rarely used.

Since each char type is an ASCII character that maps to an integer, you can perform some integer operations on char types. For instance, the sixth example shows how you can use the increment operator to change the numeric value for a char variable from 67 to 68, which changes the character from *C* to *D*.

The arithmetic unary operators

Operator	Name	Description
++	Increment	Adds 1 to the operand (x = x + 1).
--	Decrement	Subtracts 1 from the operand (x = x - 1).
+	Positive sign	Indicates that the value is positive.
-	Negative sign	Changes a positive value to negative, and vice versa.

A typical statement that uses the increment operator

```
int i = 1;
++i;                    // after execution, i = 2
```

A typical statement that uses the decrement operator

```
int i = 10;
--i;                    // after execution, i = 9
```

How to prefix an increment operator

```
int x = 14;
int result = ++x;   // after execution, x = 15, result = 15
```

How to postfix an increment operator

```
int x = 14;
int result = x++;   // after execution, x = 15, result = 14
```

How to reverse the value of a number

```
int x = 14;
int result = -x;    // result = -14
```

How to perform an arithmetic operation on a character

```
char letter1 = 'C';        // letter1 = 'C' (ASCII code 67)
char letter2 = ++letter1;  // letter2 = 'D' (ASCII code 68)
```

Description

- *Unary operators* operate on just one operand.
- When you use an increment or decrement operator as a *prefix* to a variable, C++ performs the increment or decrement operation before other operations.
- When you use an increment or decrement operator as a *postfix* to a variable, C++ performs the increment or decrement operation after other operations.
- If you code an increment or decrement operation as a single statement, not as part of an expression, it doesn't matter whether the operator is prefixed or postfixed.
- Unless there's a specific reason to postfix an operand, it's considered a best practice to prefix the operand. That's because postfixing an operand can lead to the creation of temporary variables in memory, which causes the operation to run less efficiently than prefixing the operand.

Figure 4-1   How to use the arithmetic unary operators

How to use the compound assignment operators

When coding assignment statements, it's common to code the same variable on both sides of the equals sign, as shown by the first group of examples in figure 4-2. That way, you can use the current value of the variable in an expression and update the variable by assigning the result of the expression to it.

Since it's common to write statements like this, the C++ language provides the five *compound assignment operators* shown in this figure. Although these operators don't provide any new functionality, you can use them to write shorter code that doesn't require you to code the same variable on both sides of the equals sign. This is shown by the second group of examples.

If you need to increment or decrement a variable by a value of 1, for instance, you can use a compound assignment operator. For example,

```
month = month + 1;
```

can be coded with a compound assignment operator as

```
month += 1;
```

which is equivalent to

```
++month;
```

Similarly, if you want to add the value of a variable named next_number to a variable named sum, you can do it like this:

```
sum = sum + next_number;
```

which is equivalent to

```
sum += next_number;
```

The technique that you use is mostly a matter of preference, because all of these techniques are easy to read and maintain. However, the compound assignment operators have two advantages over the regular assignment operator. First, the code is slightly shorter. Second, the variable that's being updated is only coded in one place, not two. As a result, the code is slightly easier to write and maintain.

The compound assignment operators

Operator	Name	Description
+=	Addition	Adds the operand to the starting value of the variable and assigns the result to the variable.
-=	Subtraction	Subtracts the operand from the starting value of the variable and assigns the result to the variable.
*=	Multiplication	Multiplies the operand by the starting value of the variable and assigns the result to the variable.
/=	Division	Divides the starting value of the variable by the operand and assigns the result to the variable. If the operand and the variable are both integers, the result is an integer.
%=	Modulus	Derives the value that is left over after dividing the starting value of the variable by the operand, and then assigns this value to the variable.

Code that uses the same variable on both sides of the assignment operator

```
count = count + 1;              // count is increased by 1
count = count - 1;              // count is decreased by 1
total = total + 100.0;          // total is increased by 100.0
total = total - 100.0;          // total is decreased by 100.0
price = price * .8;             // price is multiplied by .8
rate = rate / 12;               // rate is divided by 12
remainder = remainder % 7;      // remainder is set to the value that's left
                                // after dividing remainder by 7
sum = sum + next_number;        // sum is increased by the value of next_number
```

Code that uses compound assignment operators to get the same results

```
count += 1;                     // count is increased by 1
count -= 1;                     // count is decreased by 1
total += 100.0;                 // total is increased by 100.0
total -= 100.0;                 // total is decreased by 100.0
price *= .8;                    // price is multipled by .8
rate /= 12;                     // rate is divided by 12
remainder %= 7;                 // remainder is set to the value that's left
                                // after dividing remainder by 7
sum += next_number;             // sum is increased by the value of next_number
```

Description

- Besides the assignment operator (=), C++ provides for five *compound assignment operators*. These operators provide a shorthand way to code common assignment operations.

- These operators make your code easier to type, and also easier to read. That's because the variable doesn't appear on both sides of the assignment operator, so it's less confusing.

Figure 4-2   How to use the compound assignment operators

How to work with the order of precedence

Now that you have been introduced to all of the arithmetic operators, you're ready to learn more about the *order of precedence* of the arithmetic operations. To start, figure 4-3 lists the order of precedence. This shows that all of the postfixed and prefixed increment and decrement operations in an expression are done first, followed by all of the positive and negative operations, and so on. If there are two or more operations at the same order of precedence, the operations are done from left to right.

When you code arithmetic expressions, this sequence of operations doesn't always work the way you want it to. As a result, you sometimes need to override the sequence by using parentheses. Then, the expressions in the innermost sets of parentheses are done first, followed by the next sets of parentheses, and so on. Within the parentheses, though, the operations are done from left to right in the order of precedence. In general, you should use parentheses to specify the sequence of operations whenever there's any doubt about it.

The first example shows why you sometimes need to use parentheses to specify the order of precedence. Here, the first expression that calculates price doesn't use parentheses. As a result, C++ uses the default order of precedence and performs the multiplication operation before the subtraction operation, which gives an incorrect result. In contrast, the second expression that calculates price encloses the subtraction operation in parentheses. As a result, C++ performs the subtraction operation before the multiplication operation, which gives a correct result.

The second example shows how you can use parentheses in a more complicated expression. Here, the first expression uses three sets of parentheses to calculate the current value of an investment account after a monthly investment amount is added to it, monthly interest is calculated, and the interest is added to the current value. If you have trouble following this, you can plug the initial values into the expression and evaluate it one set of parentheses at a time:

```
(5000 + 100) * (1 + (.12 / 12))
(5000 + 100) * (1 + .01)
5100 * 1.01
5151
```

If you have trouble creating an expression like this for a difficult calculation, you can often break the expression down into a series of statements as shown in the last four lines of code. Here, the first statement adds the monthly investment amount to the current value. The second statement calculates the monthly interest rate. The third statement calculates the monthly interest amount. And the fourth statement adds the interest to the current value. This takes away the need for parentheses, and it makes the code easier to read and debug. On the other hand, after coding statements like these, an experienced programmer might combine them into a more concise expression that's easier to maintain.

The order of precedence for arithmetic operations

1. Increment and decrement
2. Positive and negative
3. Multiplication, division, and modulus
4. Addition and subtraction

Code that calculates a discounted price

```
double discount_percent = .2;          // 20% discount
double price = 100;                     // $100 price
```

Using the default order of precedence

```
price = price * 1 - discount_percent;    // price = $99.8
```

Using parentheses to specify the order of precedence

```
price = price * (1 - discount_percent);  // price = $80
```

Code that calculates the current value of a monthly investment

```
double current_value = 5000;       // current value of investment account
double monthly_investment = 100;   // amount added each month
double yearly_interest_rate = .12; // yearly interest rate
```

Using parentheses to specify the order of precedence

```
current_value = (current_value + monthly_investment) *
                (1 + (yearly_interest_rate / 12));
```

Using separate statements to control the order of precedence

```
current_value += monthly_investment;                       // add investment
double monthly_interest_rate = yearly_interest_rate / 12;
double monthly_interest = current_value * monthly_interest_rate;
current_value += monthly_interest;                         // add interest
```

Description

-   Unless parentheses are used, the operations in an expression take place from left to right in the *order of precedence*.

-   To specify the sequence of operations, you can use parentheses. Then, the operations in the innermost set of parentheses are done first, followed by the operations in the next set, and so on.

-   Another way to specify the sequence of operations is to break a complex expression down into a series of statements. Then, the statements are executed in the sequence in which they're coded.

Figure 4-3   How to work with the order of precedence

How to code while and do-while loops

In the next few topics, you'll learn how to use while and do-while statements to code while loops and do-while loops. These are two of the statements that C++ uses to implement the *iteration structure*, also called the *repetition structure*.

How to code while loops

Figure 4-4 shows how to code a *while statement*. When C++ executes a while statement, the program repeats the statements in the block of code within the braces *while* the Boolean expression in the statement is true. In other words, the statement ends when the expression becomes false. If the expression is false when the statement starts, C++ never executes the statements in the block. Because a while statement loops through the statements in the block as many times as needed, a while statement is often referred to as a *while loop*.

The first example in this figure shows how to code a while loop that adds the numbers 1 through 4 together and stores the result in a variable named sum. Before the loop starts, the first statement defines a *counter variable* (or just *counter*) named i that's equal to 1. When coding loops, the use of a counter is a common coding practice, and a single letter like i is commonly used as the name of the int variable that is the counter. The second statement defines a variable named sum that's equal to 0. Then, the third statement defines a while loop that continues to execute while i is less than 5. Within the loop, the first statement writes the value of i followed by a space to the console, the second statement uses the compound addition assignment operator (+=) to add the value of i to sum, and the third statement uses the increment operator (++) to add a value of 1 to i.

When C++ executes this code, the value of i is 1 the first time through the loop. As a result, C++ adds 1 to the sum so its value becomes 1. The second time through the loop, C++ adds 2 to the sum so its value becomes 3. And so on. However, when the value of i becomes 5, the Boolean expression at the top of the while statement evaluates to false, and the loop ends.

When you code loops, it's important to remember that the code within a loop has block scope. As a result, any variables that are declared within the loop can't be used outside of the loop. That's why the variables that are needed outside of the loop in the first example have been declared before the loop. This allows you to update the counter variable within the loop and to access the sum variable after the loop has finished executing.

The second example shows that you don't need to use braces for a loop that contains a single statement. Although a loop with a single statement is rare, it's possible to code such a loop. However, it's generally considered a good practice to use braces to clearly identify the statement or statements that are executed by the loop.

The second example also shows that it's necessary to use the postfix increment operator to write "1 2 3 4" to the console. If this code had used the prefixed increment operator, the loop would have written "2 3 4 5" to the console.

The syntax of the while loop

```
while (boolean_expression) {
    statements
}
```

A while loop that calculates the sum of the numbers 1 through 4

```
int i = 1;
int sum = 0;
while (i < 5) {
    cout << i << ' ';
    sum += i;
    ++i;
}
cout << "\nSum: " << sum << endl;
```

The console after the loop runs

```
1 2 3 4
Sum: 10
```

A while loop that doesn't use braces

```
int i = 1;
while (i < 5)
    cout << i++ << ' ';
cout << "\nThe loop has ended." << endl;
```

The console after the loop runs

```
1 2 3 4
The loop has ended.
```

Description

- In a *while loop*, the condition is tested before the loop is executed. Because of that, a while loop can be referred to as a *pre-test loop*.

- A while loop executes the block of statements within the loop as long as its Boolean expression is true. If the expression is false when the loop starts, its code is never executed.

- If a loop requires more than one statement, you must enclose the statements in braces. This identifies the block of statements that are executed by the loop, and any variables or constants that are declared in that block have block scope.

- If a loop requires just one statement, you don't have to enclose the statement in braces. However, it's generally considered a good practice to use braces to identify the statements that are executed by the loop.

Figure 4-4   How to code while loops

More examples of while loops

Figure 4-5 shows more examples of while loops. To start, the first example uses a while loop to continue a program while a user enters 'y'. Before the loop, this code creates a variable named choice and sets it to a char value of 'y'. Then, the loop runs while the choice variable equals 'y'.

The first time through the loop, the choice variable equals 'y'. As a result, the loop always runs at least once. Within the loop, the first statement prompts the user. If the user enters 'y', the condition at the top of the loop evaluates to true. As a result, the loop prompts the user again. Otherwise, the condition at the top of the loop evaluates to false, and the loop ends. This displays "Bye!" on the console and ends the program.

The second example uses a while loop to calculate the future value of a series of monthly payments for a specified monthly interest rate that's calculated each month. Before the loop, this code defines and initializes four starting variables, including a counter variable named i. Then, the loop executes one time for each month. In this case, that's 36 times.

Within the loop, the first statement uses a complex arithmetic expression to calculate the future value for each month. To do that, this expression adds the monthly investment and monthly interest to the future value. Then, the second statement in the loop increments the counter variable.

To get the expression that calculates the future value to work correctly, this code uses parentheses to control the order of precedence. For programmers who have a strong mathematical background, this might be easy enough to understand. For other programmers, this expression may be difficult to understand. For those programmers, it may make sense to break down this arithmetic expression into multiple statements like this:

```
while (i <= months) {
    future_value += monthly_investment;
    future_value *= 1 + monthly_interest_rate;
    ++i;
}
```

This isn't as concise, but it makes the code easier to read and debug.

If the condition for a while statement doesn't ever become false, the loop continues indefinitely. This is called an *infinite loop*. When you first start programming, it's common to code an infinite loop by mistake. Then, the technique you use to stop the loop depends on the IDE and operating system you're using. If you're using Visual Studio on a Windows system, for example, you can click the Close button in the upper right corner of the console or press Ctrl+C. Or, if you're using Xcode on a macOS system, you can click the Stop button in the IDE.

It's also a common practice to code an infinite loop on purpose to continue to execute statements repeatedly for as long as a program is running. To do that, you can code a while loop with the true keyword as the Boolean expression as shown by the third example. Then, if necessary, you can use a break statement to end the loop as shown later in this chapter.

A while loop that continues as long as the user enters 'y'

```
char choice = 'y';
while (choice == 'y') {
    cout << "Ask again? (y/n): ";
    cin >> choice;
}
cout << "Bye!" << endl;
```

The console after the loop runs

```
Ask again? (y/n): y
Ask again? (y/n): n
Bye!
```

A while loop that calculates a future value

```
double future_value = 0.0;
double monthly_investment = 100.0;
double monthly_interest_rate = .08 / 12;
int months = 36;
int i = 1;
while (i <= months) {
    future_value = (future_value + monthly_investment) *
                   (1 + monthly_interest_rate);
    ++i;
}
cout << "Future value: " << future_value << endl;
```

The console after the loop runs

```
Future value: 4080.58
```

Code that causes an infinite loop

```
while (true) {
    // any statements in this loop run forever
    // unless a break statement is excecuted as shown
    // later in this chapter
}
```

Description

- If the condition for a loop never becomes false, the loop never ends. This is known as an *infinite loop*, and beginning programmers often code them accidentally. In most IDEs, you can cancel an infinite loop by clicking on a Stop button to stop the execution of the program. Otherwise, you may be able to cancel the loop by closing the console.

Figure 4-5   More examples of while loops

How to code do-while loops

Figure 4-6 shows how to code a *do-while loop* using a *do-while statement*. The difference between a while loop and a do-while loop is that the Boolean expression is evaluated at the beginning of a while loop and at the end of a do-while loop. As a result, the statements in a while loop are executed zero or more times, but the statements in a do-while loop are always executed at least once. Because the Boolean expression is tested after the statements are executed, a do-while loop can be referred to as a *post-test loop*.

Most of the time, you can use either of these two types of loops to accomplish the same task. For example, the four do-while loops in this figure perform the same tasks as the while loops presented in the previous two figures.

One advantage of the while loop is that it puts the Boolean condition at the top of the loop where it's easy to see. Many programmers think this makes while loops easier to read than do-while loops.

Another advantage of the while loop is that it doesn't require the do keyword or a semicolon after the Boolean expression. As a result, it's slightly more concise and streamlined than a do-while loop.

One advantage of a do-while loop is that it always runs at least once, which is convenient in some situations. In the fourth example, for instance, you want to prompt the user at least once. As a result, a do-while loop might make sense. You can accomplish the same task with a while loop by initializing the choice variable to 'y' before the loop starts. With a do-while loop, however, you don't need to initialize the choice variable before the loop starts. Instead, you can start the loop and initialize the choice variable with the first character the user enters.

The syntax of the do-while loop

```
do {
    statements
} while (boolean_expression);
```

A do-while loop that calculates the sum of the numbers 1 through 4

```
int i = 1;
int sum = 0;
do {
    cout << i << ' ';
    sum += i;
    ++i;
} while (i < 5);
cout << "\nSum: " << sum << endl;
```

A do-while loop that doesn't use braces

```
int i = 1;
do
    cout << i++ << ' ';
while (i < 5);
cout << "\nThe loop has ended." << endl;
```

A do-while loop that calculates a future value

```
double future_value = 0.0;
double monthly_investment = 100.0;
double monthly_interest_rate = .08 / 12;
int months = 36;
int i = 1;
do {
    future_value = (future_value + monthly_investment) *
                    (1 + monthly_interest_rate);
    ++i;
} while (i <= months);
cout << "Future value: " << future_value << endl;
```

A do-while loop that continues as long as the user enters 'y'

```
char choice;
do {
    cout << "Ask again? (y/n): ";
    cin >> choice;
} while (choice == 'y');
cout << "Bye!" << endl;
```

The console after the loop runs

```
Ask again? (y/n): y
Ask again? (y/n): n
Bye!
```

Description

- A *do-while loop* works like a while loop, except that the condition is tested after the loop is executed. Because of that, its code is always executed at least once.

Figure 4-6   How to code do-while loops

The Test Scores program

Figure 4-7 shows the console and code for the Test Scores program. This program asks the user to enter numeric test scores from 0 to 100 and ignores numeric data that's not within the specified range. When users signal that they're done by entering -1, the program displays the number of valid test scores entered, the total of all valid scores, and the average of the valid scores. Here, -1 is a *sentinel* value that's used to determine when to stop the loop.

The main() function begins by writing a message to the console that describes how the program works. Next, the code defines and initializes three variables that the program uses to store the current test score as well as the count and total of all valid scores.

After declaring the three variables, the program starts a while loop that continues until the score variable is equal to -1. Since the score variable is initialized to 0, the block of code for the while loop runs at least once. However, if the user enters -1 as the first score, the loop isn't run a second time and no valid scores are entered.

Within the loop, the first two statements prompt the user to enter a score and extract the score from the console input stream. Then, this code uses an if statement to determine whether the score is valid.

If the score is greater than 100, the code displays a message that indicates that the score must be from 0 to 100. This causes program execution to jump back to the top of the loop, which gives the user a chance to enter a valid score.

If the score is greater than -1, then it's valid. That's because the previous if clause handled values that are greater than 100, so the code in this else if clause only runs if the value is between 0 and 100. As a result, the code adds 1 to the current value of the count variable and adds the score to the current value of the total variable.

If the score is less than -1, this code displays a message that indicates that the score can't be a negative number. This causes program execution to jump to the top of the loop, which gives the user another chance to enter a valid score.

If the score is -1, none of the clauses in the if statement are executed and execution jumps to the top of the loop. When the Boolean expression is evaluated again, it evaluates to false, which causes the loop to end. As a result, program execution continues on to the statements after the loop.

After the while loop, the code calculates the average score. To do that, it defines a double variable to store the average score. Then, it uses an if statement to make sure the count variable is greater than 0. This prevents the code from dividing by zero, which is an illegal mathematical operation. Within the if clause, the code calculates the average score by dividing the score total by the score count. After calculating the average score, the code displays the score count, total, and average.

The Test Scores program illustrates many useful skills presented in this chapter, but it could be improved in many ways. For example, this program enters an infinite loop if the user enters an invalid number such as "x". To fix this issue, you can check the failure flag as shown in the next chapter.

The console

```
Enter test scores from 0 to 100.
To end the program, enter -1.

Enter score: 90
Enter score: 80
Enter score: 150
Score must be from 0 to 100. Try again.
Enter score: 75
Enter score: -1

Score count:    3
Score total:    245
Average score: 81.6667
```

The code

```cpp
#include <iostream>

using namespace std;

int main()
{
    cout << "Enter test scores from 0 to 100.\n"
         << "To end the program, enter -1.\n\n";

    // define variables
    int score = 0;
    int count = 0;
    double total = 0.0;
    while (score != -1) {                    // get all scores from the user
        cout << "Enter score: ";
        cin >> score;

        if (score > 100) {
            cout << "Score must be from 0 to 100. Try again.\n";
        } else if (score > -1) {
            ++count;
            total += score;
        } else if (score < -1) {
            cout << "Score can't be a negative number. Try again.\n";
        }
    }

    // calculate the average score - make sure not to divide by zero
    double avg_score = 0.0;
    if (count > 0) {
        avg_score = total / count;
    }

    // display the score count, total, and average
    cout << endl
         << "Score count:    " << count << endl
         << "Score total:    " << total << endl
         << "Average score: " << avg_score << endl;
}
```

Figure 4-7   The Test Scores program

How to code for loops and nested loops

Now that you know how to code while and do-while loops, you'll learn how to code for loops. This is another way C++ implements the iteration structure. In addition, you'll learn how to nest one loop within another loop.

How to code for loops

Figure 4-8 shows how to use the *for statement* to code *for loops*. This type of loop is useful when you need to increment or decrement a counter that determines how many times the loop is executed.

To code a for loop, you start by coding the for keyword followed by three expressions enclosed in parentheses and separated by semicolons. The first expression initializes the starting value for the counter variable. Typically, this expression also defines the counter variable, but it's also possible to define the counter variable before the loop. The second expression is a Boolean expression that determines when the loop ends. And the third expression determines how the counter is incremented or decremented each time the loop is executed.

The first two examples in this figure perform the same tasks as the first two while loops presented in figure 4-4. A comparison of these loops shows that a for loop improves upon a while loop when a counter variable is required. That's because a for loop requires you to code the three expressions that control the counter variable at the top of the loop. This makes the code more concise and, arguably, easier to read.

In the first example, the initialization expression defines a counter variable named i that's of the int type and initializes that variable to a value of 1. Then, the Boolean expression specifies that the loop should be repeated as long as the counter variable is less than 5. Next, the increment expression increments the counter variable by 1 at the end of each loop. Within the loop, the first statement writes the counter variable followed by a space to the console, and the second statement adds the counter variable to the current value of the sum variable.

Like the first example, the second example also displays the numbers 1 to 4 on the console. However, because this loop only contains a single statement, the braces for the loop are optional and have been omitted. This works the same as it does for if statements and while loops. Since it's generally considered a good practice to include the braces even if the loop only contains a single statement, the third and fourth examples include the braces.

The third example calculates the sum of 8, 6, 4, and 2. Within the parentheses of the for loop, the initialization expression initializes the counter variable to 8, the Boolean expression indicates that the loop repeats as long as the counter variable is greater than 0, and the increment expression uses a compound assignment operator to subtract 2 from the counter variable with each repetition of the loop. Within the loop, the first statement adds the value of the counter variable to the current value of the sum variable. As a result, the final value for the sum variable is 20.

The syntax of the for loop

```
for (initialization_expr; boolean_expr; increment_expr) {
    statements
}
```

A for loop that calculates the sum of the numbers 1 through 4

```
int sum = 0;
for (int i = 1; i < 5; ++i) {
    cout << i << ' ';
    sum += i;
}
cout << "\nSum: " << sum << endl;
```

The console after the loop runs

```
1 2 3 4
Sum: 10
```

A for loop without braces

```
for (int i = 1; i < 5; ++i)
    cout << i << ' ';
cout << "\nThe loop has ended." << endl;
```

The console after the loop runs

```
1 2 3 4
```

A for loop that adds the numbers 8, 6, 4, and 2

```
int sum = 0;
for (int i = 8; i > 0; i -= 2) {
    sum += i;
}
cout << "Sum: " << sum;
```

The console after the loop runs

```
Sum: 20
```

A for loop that calculates a future value

```
int months = 36;
for (int i = 1; i <= months; ++i) {
    future_value = (future_value + monthly_investment) *
                        (1 + monthly_interest_rate);
}
```

Description

- A *for loop* is useful when you need to increment or decrement a counter that determines how many times the loop is executed.

- Within the parentheses of a for loop, you code an initialization expression that gives the starting value for the counter, a Boolean expression that determines when the loop ends, and an increment expression that increments or decrements the counter.

- If necessary, you can declare the counter variable before the for loop. Then, this variable is in scope after the loop finishes executing.

Figure 4-8   How to code for loops

The fourth example in figure 4-8 shows how to code a loop that calculates the future value for a series of monthly investments. Here, the loop executes one time for each month.

The Future Value program

Now that you've learned how to code for loops, figure 4-9 presents a Future Value program that uses a for loop that's nested within a while loop. As the console for this program shows, the user starts by entering the values for the monthly investment, the yearly interest rate, and the number of years. Then, the program calculates and displays the future value.

The code for this program begins by using a while loop to determine when the program ends. In this case, the program ends when the user enters a value other than 'y' or 'Y' when prompted if the program should continue. You can see this code at the end of the loop.

The code within this loop starts by getting the three entries from the user for calculating the future value. Then, it converts these entries to the same time unit, which is months. To do that, the number of years is multiplied by 12, and the yearly interest rate is divided by 12. In addition, the yearly interest rate is divided by 100 so it's a decimal value rather than a percent.

Once the code sets up those variables, the program enters a for loop that calculates the future value. When the loop finishes, the program formats and displays the future value and asks whether the user wants to continue.

Because this program doesn't validate the user's entries, it enters an infinite loop if the user enters an invalid number such as "x" or "$100". However, you'll learn how to fix this issue in the next chapter. Otherwise, this program works the way you would want it to.

When testing loops, it can sometimes be hard to tell whether the loop is producing the correct results. In that case, it's sometimes helpful to add debugging statements within the loop while you're testing it. With this program, for instance, you can add this statement as the last statement in the for loop:

```
cout << "Month " << i << ": " << future_value << endl;
```

Then, the program writes one line to the console each time through the loop. This makes it easy for you to check that the calculation for each month is accurate. It also makes it easy for you to tell whether the loop was executed the correct number of times.

Now that you know how to code both while loops and for loops, you may be wondering when you would use each type of loop. In general, it makes sense to use a while loop when you don't know how many times you need to execute the loop. In this program, for example, it makes sense to use a while loop for the outer loop because you don't know how many times the user wants to perform this calculation.

Conversely, it generally makes sense to use a for loop when you *do* know how many times you need to execute the loop. In this program, for example, it makes sense to use a for loop for the inner loop because you know that the loop should be run one time for each month, and you can calculate the number of months from the number of years entered by the user.

The console

```
The Future Value Calculator

Enter monthly investment:   100
Enter yearly interest rate: 3
Enter number of years:      3
Future value:               3771.46


Continue? (y/n):
```

The code

```cpp
#include <iostream>
#include <cmath>

using namespace std;

int main() {
    cout << "The Future Value Calculator\n\n";

    char choice = 'y';
    while (choice == 'y' || choice == 'Y') {
        double monthly_investment;
        cout << "Enter monthly investment:   ";
        cin >> monthly_investment;

        double yearly_rate;
        cout << "Enter yearly interest rate: ";
        cin >> yearly_rate;

        int years;
        cout << "Enter number of years:      ";
        cin >> years;

        // convert yearly values to monthly values
        double monthly_rate = yearly_rate / 12 / 100;
        int months = years * 12;

        // calculate future value
        double future_value = 0;
        for (int i = 1; i <= months; ++i) {
            future_value = (future_value + monthly_investment) *
                            (1 + monthly_rate);
        }

        // round to 2 decimal places and display
        future_value = round(future_value * 100) / 100;
        cout << "Future value:               " << future_value << "\n\n";

        // see if the user wants to continue
        cout << "Continue? (y/n): ";
        cin >> choice;
        cout << endl;
    }
    cout << "Bye! ";
}
```

Figure 4-9   The Future Value program

How to code nested loops

As you saw in the previous figure, you can nest one loop within another loop. In fact, it's common to use nested loops to work with data that's aligned in rows and columns. For example, figure 4-10 shows how to use nested loops to display a table of future value calculations. In this table, the monthly investment is 200, the interest rate varies from 5.0% to 6.5%, and the number of years varies from 1 to 6.

In this example, the first for loop adds the header row to the table. Before this loop starts, the code displays "Year". Then, the loop displays the interest rates from 5.0% to 6.5%, separating each column with a tab character. After this loop, the code ends the row for the header by starting a new line.

After the first for loop, the nested for loops display the rows and columns of the future value calculations for each year. First, the outer loop iterates through the years (1, 2, 3, 4, 5, and 6). Within this loop, the code displays the year in the first column. Then, the nested loop iterates through the four interest rates (5%, 5.5%, 6%, and 6.5%). Within this loop, the code calculates the future value for each interest rate, rounds each result to a whole number, and displays the result of each calculation, separating each column with a tab character. When the nested loop finishes, the outer loop starts a new line, which ends the row.

As you review this code, you might notice that tabs are used to align the data in the columns. In addition, you might notice that the future value calculations have all been rounded to whole numbers (no decimal places). This approach makes it possible to align the results of these calculations in columns. Unfortunately, it doesn't give you much control over how this data displayed, and it doesn't work correctly on all systems. Fortunately, the next chapter introduces skills that give you more control over displaying data on the console, including being able to control decimal places for numbers as well as the width and alignment of each column.

The console

```
Monthly investment: 200

Year    5%      5.5%    6%      6.5%
1       2466    2473    2479    2486
2       5058    5085    5112    5139
3       7783    7844    7907    7969
4       10647   10760   10874   10989
5       13658   13839   14024   14211
6       16823   17093   17368   17649
```

Nested loops that print a table of future values

```cpp
// set the monthly investment and display it to the user
int monthly_investment = 200;
cout << "Monthly investment: " << monthly_investment << endl << endl;

// display header row
cout << "Year";
for (double rate = 5.0; rate < 7.0; rate += .5) {
    cout << '\t' << rate << '%';
}
cout << endl;

// loop through the years
for (int year = 1; year < 7; ++year) {
    // display year at the start of the row
    cout << year;

    // loop through each interest rate
    for (double rate = 5.0; rate < 7.0; rate += .5) {
        int months = year * 12;
        double monthly_rate = rate / 12 / 100;

        // calculate the future value
        double future_value = 0.0;
        for (int i = 1; i <= months; ++i) {
            future_value = (future_value + monthly_investment) *
                (1 + monthly_rate);
        }

        // round to whole number
        future_value = round(future_value);

        // display the calculation for each rate
        cout << '\t' << future_value;
    }
    // end the row for the year
    cout << endl;
}
```

Figure 4-10   How to code nested loops

How to code break
and continue statements

The break and continue statements give you additional control over loops. The *break statement* breaks out of a loop by causing program execution to jump to the statement that follows the loop. This causes the loop to end. The *continue statement* continues a loop by causing execution to jump to the top of the loop. This causes the loop to reevaluate its Boolean condition.

How to code break statements

The first example in figure 4-11 shows how the break statement works. Here, the condition in the while loop is intentionally set to true. Because of that, the while loop never ends due to the condition becoming false. However, you can use a break statement to end the loop.

Within the loop, the first statement asks the user to enter a command. If the user enters a command that is not "exit", the code writes the command to the console. However, if the user enters "exit", this code executes the break statement. This causes execution to jump out of the current loop and execute the statement that follows the loop. This statement writes "Bye!" to the console.

How to code continue statements

The second example in this figure shows how the continue statement works. This example uses a while loop that starts by getting an integer from a user. Then, it checks if the integer is less than or equal to zero. If it is, this code displays a message that indicates that the number must be greater than zero. Then, it uses a continue statement to jump to the start of the while loop. This reevaluates the condition at the top of the loop. Since this condition still evaluates to true, this executes the first two statements in the loop, which prompt the user for a number again.

A break statement that exits the loop

```
while (true) {
    cout << "Enter a command: ";
    string command;
    cin >> command;
    if (command == "exit") {
        break;
    }
    cout << "You entered: " << command << endl;
}
cout << "Bye!";
```

The console

```
Enter a command: add
You entered: add

Enter a command: exit
Bye!
```

A continue statement that jumps to the beginning of a loop

```
char choice = 'y';
while (choice == 'y') {
    cout << "Enter a number: ";
    int number;
    cin >> number;
    if (number <= 0) {
        cout << "Number must be greater than 0. Try again.\n";
        continue;
    }
    cout << "You entered: " << number << endl << endl;

    cout << "Continue? (y/n): ";
    cin >> choice;
    cout << endl;
}
cout << "Bye!";
```

The console

```
Enter a number: -100
Number must be greater than 0. Try again.
Enter a number: 100
You entered: 100

Continue? (y/n):
```

Description

- To jump to the end of the current loop, you can use the *break statement*.
- To skip the rest of the statements in the current loop and jump to the top of the current loop, you can use the *continue statement*.

Figure 4-11   How to code break and continue statements

The Guess the Number program

Figure 4-12 presents a Guess the Number program that uses the break and continue statements. In addition, this program uses three functions from the cstdlib and ctime headers to get a random number as described in chapter 2.

To start, this program declares a variable named upper_limit that sets the highest number that the player can guess. Then, it displays a message that tells the user the range of numbers to guess from.

After displaying this message, the code gets a random number between 1 and the upper limit. To do that, it uses the srand() method of the cstdlib header to seed the rand() method of the cstdlib header. This code passes the int value that's returned by the time() method of the ctime header to the srand() function. Then, it calls the rand() function to return a random int value from 0 to a very large integer, and it divides that value by the upper_limit variable. This returns a random integer from 0 up to but not including the upper limit. Next, it increments that value by 1. This gets a random integer from 1 up to and including the upper limit.

After getting the random number, the code begins a while loop that allows the user to continue guessing until the correct number is guessed. To do that, the condition on this loop is set to true. As you learned in the previous figure, this means that you must end the loop using a break statement.

Within the loop, the first three statements get the guess from the user. Then, this code checks if the guess is less than 1 or greater than the upper limit. If it is, the code displays an error message and executes a continue statement. This causes the rest of the statements in the current loop to be skipped and for execution to continue at the top of the loop, which gets another guess from the user.

If the guess is within the specified range, this code checks if the guess is higher or lower than the number. If it is, this code displays an appropriate message and increments the counter variable. However, if the guess is equal to the number, this code displays an appropriate message that includes the count of guesses, and it uses a break statement to break out of the loop. This jumps over the statement that increments the counter variable and out of the loop.

This program uses the variable named upper_limit to set the highest number that the user can guess because it makes it easier to modify the program later if you decide to change the highest number. In that case, you just need to change the value of the variable, which is used in three places in this code. If you didn't use this variable, you would need to change the limit in each of these three places.

Although this program uses break and continue statements, you should know that it could be coded without them. You'll get a chance to try this for yourself in one of the exercises at the end of this chapter.

The console

```
Guess the number!
I'm thinking of a number from 1 to 10

Your guess: 11
Invalid guess. Try again.
Your guess: 5
Too low.
Your guess: 7
You guessed it in 2 tries.

Bye!
```

The code

```cpp
#include <iostream>
#include <cstdlib>
#include <ctime>

using namespace std;

int main() {
    int upper_limit = 10;
    cout << "Guess the number!\n";
    cout << "I'm thinking of a number from 1 to " << upper_limit << "\n\n";

    // get a random number between 1 and the upper limit
    srand(time(nullptr));                   // seed the rand() function
    int number = rand() % upper_limit; // number is >= 0 and < upper_limit
    ++number;                               // number is >= 1 and <= upper_limit

    int count = 1;
    while (true) {
        int guess;
        cout << "Your guess: ";
        cin >> guess;

        if (guess < 1 || guess > upper_limit) {
            cout << "Invalid guess. Try again.\n";
            continue;
        }

        if (guess < number) {
            cout << "Too low.\n";
        }
        else if (guess > number) {
            cout << "Too high.\n";
        }
        else {
            cout << "You guessed it in " << count << " tries.\n\n";
            break;
        }
        ++count;
    }
    cout << "Bye!\n\n";
}
```

Figure 4-12   The Guess the Number program

Perspective

Now that you've completed this chapter, you should be able to code while, do-while, and for loops. These are the C++ statements that implement the iteration structure. You can use them to perform repetitive processing. In addition, you should be able to use break and continue statements to control how loops operate.

Terms

unary operators
prefix an operand
postfix an operand
compound assignment operators
order of precedence
iteration structure
repetition structure
while statement
while loop
pre-test loop
counter variable
infinite loop
do-while loop
do-while statement
post-test loop
sentinel value
for statement
for loop
break statement
continue statement

Summary

- An operator that works on a single operand is known as a *unary operator*. The increment and decrement operators, which can *prefix* or *postfix* an operand, are examples of unary operators.

- The *compound assignment operators* provide a shorthand way of assigning a simple arithmetic expression to a variable when the variable is part of the expression.

- You can use *while*, *do-while*, and *for loops* to repeatedly execute one or more statements until a Boolean expression evaluates to false, and you can nest these statements whenever necessary.

- You can use a *break statement* to jump out of the current loop, and you can use a *continue statement* to jump to the start of the current loop.

Exercise 4-1   Enhance the Circle Calculator program

In this exercise, you'll enhance the Circle Calculator program from chapter 2 so the user can make more than one calculation and so each entry is validated. When you're done, a test run should look something like this:

```
Circle Calculator

Enter radius:  11
Diameter:      22
Circumference: 69.1
Area:          380.1

Enter another radius? (y/n): y

Enter radius:  -1
Radius must be a positive number.

Enter radius:  17.4
Diameter:      34.8
Circumference: 109.3
Area:          951.1

Enter another radius? (y/n): n

Bye!
```

1. Open the Circle Calculator project or solution in this folder:
    `ex_starts\ch04_ex1_circle_calculator`

2. Review the code in the main.cpp file and run the program to refresh your memory on how it works.

3. Enhance the program so it lets the user repeat the entry and get the diameter, circumference, and area for more than one radius. To do that, use a while loop.

4. Enhance the program so it checks whether the radius is less than or equal to zero. If so, display an error message and jump to the beginning of the while loop to give the user another chance to enter a valid radius.

Exercise 4-2   Enhance the Future Value program

In this exercise, you'll enhance the Future Value program from this chapter so it displays the future value at the end of each year. When you're done, a test run should look something like this:

```
The Future Value Calculator

Enter monthly investment:    100
Enter yearly interest rate: 12
Enter number of years:       5

Year = 1          Future Value = 1280.93
Year = 2          Future Value = 2724.32
Year = 3          Future Value = 4350.76
Year = 4          Future Value = 6183.48
Year = 5          Future Value = 8248.63

Continue? (y/n):
```

1. Open the Future Value project or solution in this folder:
    `ex_starts\ch04_ex2_future_value`

2. Run the program to see how it works.

3. Modify the for loop so it displays the future value for each year. To do that, you can use the modulus operator to determine if the counter variable is evenly divisible by 12.

4. Make any other changes necessary for the console output to appear as shown above.

Exercise 4-3   Modify the Guess the Number program

In this exercise, you'll modify the Guess the Number program from this chapter so it doesn't use a break or continue statement.

1. Open the Guess the Number project or solution in this folder:
    `ex_starts\ch04_ex3_future_value`

2. Review the code for the main.cpp file to see that the while loop contains a break and a continue statement. Then, run the program to see how it works.

3. Modify the code so it works without the break and continue statements. To do that, you can change the condition in the while loop so it's executed until the user's guess is equal to the random number. To get that to work, you need to move the variable that stores the guess before the loop and initialize it so it's outside the valid range of values. You also need to modify the if statement so it works correctly with the new code.

4. Make any other changes that are needed for the program to work correctly.

5

How to work with I/O streams and files

So far in this book, you've learned how to write programs that work with input and output, or I/O, streams to read input from the console and write output to the console. When you use I/O streams, the main memory of your computer stores the data. But when the program ends, that data is lost.

In this chapter, you'll learn how to save the data in main memory so it isn't lost. To do that, you can use an output stream to write data from memory to a file. Then, you can use an input stream to read data from the file into memory. This is known as file input and output, or file I/O.

Before you learn how to work with file I/O, you need to learn a few more skills for working with input and output streams. These skills apply to all types of I/O streams. In other words, they apply whether you're using a stream to work with the console or a file.

How to work with input streams

In chapter 2, you learned the basic skills for getting input from the console. Now, you'll learn some additional skills for working with input streams. These skills include detecting and handling data input errors such as a user entering a string when the program is expecting a number.

An introduction to streams and buffers

Figure 5-1 introduces you to some terms and concepts that apply to streams, including how buffers work. To start, let's review some terms that apply to streams. A *stream* is a sequence of characters that your program can use to work with input or output. *Input* and *output* is commonly abbreviated as *I/O* or *IO*.

An *input stream* contains data that is being *read* from an object. For example, this figure shows the characters that are read from the console when the user enters an integer after the first prompt. Here, the user entered "22" and pressed the Enter key, which adds a newline character (\n) to the stream. When you use the extraction operator to read data from an input stream, it ignores *whitespace* such as spaces, tabs, or new lines. As you'll see in the next figure, however, this whitespace can affect the data that's extracted from the stream.

An *output stream* contains data that is being *written* to an object. For example, this figure shows the characters that are written to the console after the user finishes entering all of the data for the input stream. Here, the code uses the endl manipulator to insert a newline character (\n) before and after "You entered:", and it uses the space character to separate the four values that the user entered.

A *buffer* is a location in memory that temporarily stores stream data as it is being written or read. When a buffer is *flushed*, all the data temporarily in the buffer is sent to its next destination. So far in this book, that destination has been the console. Later in this chapter, though, you'll learn how to send data to a file or a string buffer.

Most of the time, you don't need to know when buffers are flushed. Instead, you just need to know that a stream will flush the buffer according to its own internal logic. As you'll learn in this chapter, though, you can sometimes flush the buffer manually, and you may sometimes want to discard the data in the buffer so it doesn't get flushed.

When you work with streams, you should know that C++ provides stream objects that let you write to and read from many destinations, including the console, a file on disk, or a buffer in memory. Fortunately, once you learn how to work with one type of stream object, most of the same skills apply to other types of stream objects. That's because all stream objects provided by C++ share a similar *interface*. As a result, you can use the same operators and member functions for all streams.

A program that reads input from and writes output to the console

```
int i;
cout << "Enter an integer: ";
cin >> i;

double d;
cout << "Enter a double: ";
cin >> d;

char c;
cout << "Enter a character: ";
cin >> c;

string s;
cout << "Enter a string: ";
cin >> s;

cout << endl << "You entered:" << endl
     << i << ' ' << d << ' ' << c << ' ' << s;
```

The console

```
Enter an integer: 22
Enter a double: 3.14
Enter a character: d
Enter a string: hey

You entered:
22 3.14 d hey
```

The input stream for the first entry

2	2	\n

The output stream with the user's entries

\n	Y	o	u		e	n	t	e	r	e	d	:	\n	2	2		3	.	1	4		d		h	e	y

Description

- A *stream* is a sequence of characters that can be used to work with *input* or *output* for your program. Input and output is commonly abbreviated as *I/O* or *IO*.

- An *output stream* contains character data that is being *written* to an object, and an *input stream* contains data that is being *read* from an object. When data is read from an input stream, *whitespace* such as spaces, tabs, or new lines is typically ignored.

- A *buffer* is a location in memory that temporarily stores stream data as it is being written or read. When a buffer is *flushed*, all the data temporarily in the buffer is sent to its next destination.

- C++ provides stream objects that let you write to and read from many destinations, including the console, a file on disk, or a buffer in memory.

- All stream objects provided by C++ share a similar *interface*. As a result, you can use the same operators and member functions for all types of C++ streams.

Figure 5-1   An introduction to streams and buffers

How unexpected input can cause problems

Figure 5-2 shows how unexpected input can cause problems for a program like the one shown in the previous figure. To start, the first example shows what happens if a user enters all of the data for the program at the first prompt. This causes the code to display the second, third, and fourth prompts without pausing to let the user enter data. To solve this problem, you can discard any extra data as shown in the next figure.

The second example shows a problem that can occur if a user enters data with the incorrect data types. This can also cause the program to display a prompt without pausing to let the user enter data. Again, one solution to this problem is to discard any extra data after each prompt as shown in the next figure.

Notice that even though the program doesn't work correctly when the user enters all of the data at the first prompt, the correct output is still displayed. When the user enters data with the wrong data types, though, the output isn't correct. So, it's especially important to provide for a case like this.

The program when a user enters all the data on one line

```
Enter an integer: 22 3.14 d hey
Enter a double: Enter a character: Enter a string:
You entered:
22 3.14 d hey
```

The string entered by the user and the extracted values

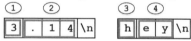

What the program does

1. The program extracts value 1. The whitespace and other values remain in the buffer.

2. The program prompts for value 2, but since there's still data in the buffer, it doesn't pause to allow the user to enter a value. Instead, the program discards the leading whitespace and extracts value 2. Again, the rest of the string after value 2 remains in the buffer.

3. Step 2 repeats for values 3 and 4.

The program when a user enters the wrong data types at two prompts

```
Enter an integer: 3.14
Enter a double: Enter a character: hey
Enter a string:
You entered:
3 0.14 h ey
```

The two strings entered by the user and the extracted values

What the program does

1. For the first entry, the program extracts the first int value (value 1) and stops at the decimal point. The fractional value (value 2) remains in the buffer.

2. The program prompts the user to enter a double, but since there's still data in the buffer, it doesn't pause to allow the user to enter a value. Instead, it extracts value 2, leaving only whitespace (\n) in the buffer.

3. For the second entry, the program discards the leading whitespace and extracts the first character it encounters (value 3). The rest of the string (value 4) remains in the buffer.

4. The program prompts the user to enter a string, but since there's still data in the buffer, it doesn't pause to allow the user to enter a string. Instead, it extracts value 4.

Description

- Extra data on a line or incorrect data types can cause unexpected results in a program.

Figure 5-2   How unexpected input data can cause problems

How to discard data from an input stream

Figure 5-3 shows how to use the numeric_limits class to discard all remaining data in an input stream. This works much like the technique you learned in chapter 2, but it ensures that all of the data in the buffer is discarded instead of just the number of characters you specify. Note that discarding the data in a buffer isn't the same as flushing the buffer. When you flush the buffer, the data in the buffer is sent to another destination. But when you discard the data in the buffer, it isn't sent anywhere.

To use the numeric_limits class, you include the limits header file. Then, you can use the max() function of the numeric_limits class to get the maximum size of the stream. Next, you can pass this value to the ignore() member function of the cin object as its first argument, and you can supply a newline character (\n) as the second argument. That way, C++ discards the rest of the data in the input stream buffer.

When you know that you only want to retrieve the first data value entered by the user, it often makes sense to discard the rest of the data in the buffer immediately after you read the first data element. That way, you can be sure that the extra data won't cause unexpected behavior later in your program. In this example, for instance, the line that discards all remaining data in the buffer is coded after each statement that extracts a data value from the input buffer. In this example, it isn't necessary to code it after the last group of statements, but many programmers consider this a good practice since it makes it easy to add code later without getting unexpected results.

The two consoles presented in this figure show how this code works. At the first console, the code discards all of the extra data that's entered by the user and only extracts the first data value for each prompt. At the second console, the code only extracts an int value of 3 from the "3.14" that's entered at the first prompt, and it only extracts a char value of 'h' from the "hey" that's entered at the third prompt. However, the second and fourth prompts work as expected.

Although these examples extract the data types that the program expects, it still may not produce the intended output. That's because it doesn't check whether the user enters the correct data types. To do that, you can use the techniques shown in the next two figures to detect and handle data input errors.

How to include the header file for the numeric_limits class

```
#include <limits>
```

How to discard all remaining data in the buffer

```
cin.ignore(numeric_limits<streamsize>::max(), '\n');
```

The program updated to clear the buffer after each value is extracted

```
int i;
cout << "Enter an integer: ";
cin >> i;
cin.ignore(numeric_limits<streamsize>::max(), '\n');

double d;
cout << "Enter a double: ";
cin >> d;
cin.ignore(numeric_limits<streamsize>::max(), '\n');

char c;
cout << "Enter a character: ";
cin >> c;
cin.ignore(numeric_limits<streamsize>::max(), '\n');

string s;
cout << "Enter a string: ";
cin >> s;
cin.ignore(numeric_limits<streamsize>::max(), '\n');

// the rest of code is the same as figure 5-1
```

The program when a user enters all the data on one line

```
Enter an integer: 22 3.14 d hey
Enter a double: 3.14 d hey
Enter a character: d hey
Enter a string: hey

You entered:
22 3.14 d hey
```

The program when a user enters the wrong data types at two prompts

```
Enter an integer: 3.14
Enter a double: 3.14
Enter a character: hey
Enter a string: hey

You entered:
3 3.14 h hey
```

Description

- You can use the ignore() member function of a stream object and the max() function of the numeric_limits class to discard all the data that remains in a buffer.

Figure 5-3   How to discard data from an input stream

How to detect data input errors

When you perform an input operation using an input stream, C++ sets the *error bits* of the stream object depending on the result of the operation. Then, you can check the state of the stream using either the cin object or the error member functions of the stream object as shown in figure 5-4.

The first two examples show how to use the cin object to check the state of a stream after an input operation. In the first example, the cin object is used as the Boolean condition for the if statement. Then, if the stream is in a good state (the goodbit is set), C++ converts the cin object to a true value. As a result, the code displays the number that the user entered. However, if the stream isn't in a good state, C++ converts the cin object to a false value. Then, the code displays an error message that indicates that the user did not enter a valid number.

The second example shows a more concise way to extract an input value and check the state of a stream. Here, the extraction expression is coded as the Boolean condition. This performs the same task as the first example, but it uses one less line of code. This is a common coding technique that you'll see used throughout this chapter.

When you use the cin object to check the state of an input stream, you can only check whether or not the stream is in a good state. To check the states represented by the other error bits, you can use error member functions of the input stream. This is illustrated by the third example.

In this example, a different action is performed depending on the state of the stream. If the stream is in a good state, the code displays the number entered by the user. If the stream is in a failed state, the code displays a message that indicates that the number isn't valid and asks the user to try again. And if the stream is in a bad state, the code displays a message that indicates that an unrecoverable error has occurred, and it executes a return statement to exit the current function. If the current function is the main() function, this causes the program to end, which is often what you want if a stream is in a bad state.

One thing to keep in mind when checking the state of a stream is that multiple bits may be set at the same time. For example, if your code reads past the end of a file, the eofbit and failbit may both be set. As a result, when you code an if statement that checks the error bits, you need to be sure to code the conditions in the correct sequence. For example, you typically code the clause that checks the eofbit before the clause that checks the failbit.

Although it's not shown here, you can also use the clear() error member function when working with input streams. This function sets all of the error bits of a stream object to indicate that the stream is in a good state. You'll see how this function can be used in the next figure.

The error bits of a stream object

Bit	Description
`ios::eofbit`	The end of an input stream (eof stands for *end of file*).
`ios::failbit`	An attempted operation has failed but the stream is OK.
`ios::badbit`	An attempted operation has failed and the integrity of the stream itself may be compromised.
`ios::goodbit`	None of the above bits are set and the stream is in good condition.

The error member functions of a stream object

Function	Description
`eof()`	Returns true if eofbit is set. Otherwise, returns false.
`fail()`	Returns true if failbit is set. Otherwise, returns false.
`bad()`	Returns true if badbit is set. Otherwise, returns false.
`good()`	Returns true if goodbit is set. Otherwise, returns false.
`clear()`	Sets all error bits to indicate the stream is in a good state.

Code that uses the cin object to check the state of a stream

```
double num;
cout << "Enter a number: ";
cin >> num;
if (cin) {
    cout << "Your number is " << num << endl;
} else {
    cout << "That's not a valid number!\n";
}
```

A more concise way to extract a value and check the state of a stream

```
double num;
cout << "Enter a number: ";
if (cin >> num) {
    cout << "Your number is " << num << endl;
} else {
    cout << "That's not a valid number!\n";
}
```

Code that uses member functions to check the state of a stream

```
double num;
cout << "Enter a number: ";
cin >> num;
if (cin.good()) {
    cout << "Your number is " << num << endl;
} else if (cin.fail()) {
    cout << "That's not a valid number! Try again.\n";
} else if (cin.bad()) {
    cout << "An unrecoverable error has occurred. Bye!\n";
    return 0;
}
```

Description

- You can use the cin object or the member functions of an input stream to check the *error bits* of the stream. You can also use a member function to reset the error bits of a stream.

Figure 5-4   How to detect data input errors

How to handle data input errors

Figure 5-5 shows how to handle data input errors. To do that, you can use a loop to continue to prompt the user until that user enters valid data. This is known as *data validation*.

The example in this figure contains a loop that continues until the user enters a number from 1 to 100. To start, the code declares a double variable for the number. Then, it begins a while loop that continues until the code within the loop executes a break statement.

Within the loop, the first statement prompts the user to enter a number from 1 to 100. Then, the second statement attempts to extract the number from the input buffer.

After attempting to extract the number, the code checks if the extraction operation failed. If so, it displays a message that indicates that the user didn't enter a valid number and asks the user to try again. Then, it calls the clear() function of the input stream to reset its error bits to a good state. Next, it discards all remaining data in the stream. Finally, it executes a continue statement to jump to the top of the loop and prompt the user to enter a number.

When the user enters a valid number, the second if statement checks whether that number is in a valid range. If it isn't, this statement displays an appropriate error message and asks the user to try again. Since the if statement is the last statement in the loop, this causes execution to jump to the top of the loop and prompt the user to enter a number. However, if the number is within the range, this code executes a break statement to exit the loop, which causes the code to display the valid number on the console.

The console shows how this works. To start, the user enters "eighty six". This string can't be converted to a number, so the console displays an appropriate error message and allows the user to try again. When the user enters -1 and 101, the values are outside of the specified range, so the console displays an appropriate message and allows the user to try again. However, when the user enters 86, the console just displays the number because it's a valid number that's within the specified range.

When you're working with console programs, you don't always need to provide this level of data validation. That's because, in some cases, it's acceptable for the program to only work correctly when the user enters valid data. That's the case for many of the sample programs presented in this book. In other cases, though, you'll need to make sure the user enters valid data by providing robust data validation like that shown here.

Code that loops until the user enters a valid number

```cpp
#include <iostream>
#include <limits>

using namespace std;

int main()
{
    double num;
    while (true) {            // loop continues until break statement
        cout << "Enter a number (1-100): ";
        cin >> num;

        // if extraction operation failed, try again
        if (cin.fail()) {
            cout << "That's not a valid number. Try again.\n";
            cin.clear();
            cin.ignore(numeric_limits<streamsize>::max(), '\n');
            continue;
        }

        // check the range of the number
        if (num < 1) {
            cout << "Number must be greater than 0. Try again.\n";
        }
        else if (num > 100) {
            cout << "Number must be 100 or less. Try again.\n";
        }
        else { // number is in specified range - exit loop
            break;
        }
    }
    cout << "Your number is " << num << endl;
}
```

The console

```
Enter a number (1-100): eighty six
That's not a valid number. Try again.
Enter a number (1-100): -1
Number must be greater than 0. Try again.
Enter a number (1-100): 101
Number must be 100 or less. Try again.
Enter a number (1-100): 86
Your number is 86
```

Description

- You can use a loop to continue to prompt the user until that user enters valid data. This is known as *data validation*.

Figure 5-5   How to handle data input errors

How to work with output streams

In chapter 2, you learned the basic skills for displaying output to the console. Now, you'll learn some additional skills for working with output streams. These skills include how to display data in columns that are left or right justified, and how to control the formatting of floating-point numbers.

An introduction to stream manipulators

Figure 5-6 starts by summarizing the most common *stream manipulators*, which you can use with the stream insertion operator (<<) to format output streams. These manipulators are available from the iostream and iomanip header files, and they include the endl manipulator that you learned about in chapter 2 as well as six more manipulators that you'll learn about in this chapter.

As you review these operators, note that the endl manipulator adds a newline character (\n) to the stream and flushes the buffer. If you manually add a newline character (\n) to a stream, however, the buffer isn't flushed. When you're working with large files, flushing the buffer too often can degrade performance. As a result, if you're worried about performance, you can use the newline character (\n) instead of the endl manipulator whenever it isn't necessary to flush the buffer.

How to specify the width of a column

If you need to display data in columns, you can use the tab character (\t) to separate columns. However, using tab characters doesn't always work correctly, and it doesn't allow you to specify the width of the column. In figure 5-6, for instance, the first example uses tab characters to align two columns of data. Here, the header for each column isn't aligned with the data for the column.

To solve this problem, you can use the setw() manipulator as shown in the second example. Here, the setw() manipulator specifies that each column should be 10 characters wide. In addition, when you use the setw() manipulator, it uses right justification by default, which is often what you want when displaying numbers in columns.

When you use the setw() manipulator, you must code it before each data element. In this example, the output consists of two columns and four rows. As a result, you must code the setw() manipulator eight times.

Common stream manipulators

Manipulator	Header	Description
endl	iostream	Adds a newline character to the stream and flushes the buffer.
setw(n)	iomanip	Sets the width of the column to the specified number of characters.
left	iostream	Positions fill characters to the left of any output.
right	iostream	Positions fill characters to the right of any output.
setprecision(n)	iomanip	Sets the precision of floating-point numbers to the specified number.
fixed	iostream	Formats floating-point numbers in fixed-point notation instead of scientific notation.
showpoint	iostream	Makes decimals always show in floating-point numbers.

How to include the iomanip header file

```
#include <iomanip>
```

How to align columns with tabs

```
cout << "PREVIOUS" << '\t' << "CURRENT" << endl;
cout << 305 << '\t' << 234 << endl;
cout << 5058 << '\t' << 5084 << endl;
cout << 10647 << '\t' << 10759 << endl;
```

The output

```
PREVIOUS        CURRENT
305     234
5058    5084
10647   10759
```

How to specify the width of a column

```
cout << setw(10) << "PREVIOUS" << setw(10) << "CURRENT" << endl;
cout << setw(10) << 305 << setw(10) << 234 << endl;
cout << setw(10) << 5058 << setw(10) << 5084 << endl;
cout << setw(10) << 10647 << setw(10) << 10759 << endl;
```

The output

```
  PREVIOUS   CURRENT
       305       234
      5058      5084
     10647     10759
```

Description

- You can use *stream manipulators* with the stream insertion (<<) operator to format output streams.

- Both the endl manipulator and the '\n' special character add a new line to a stream, but endl also flushes the buffer. This can degrade performance when you're working with files.

- When you use the setw() manipulator, the column uses right justification by default. This is often what you want when displaying numbers in columns.

Figure 5-6   How to specify the width of a column

How to right or left justify columns

As you learned in the previous figure, the setw() manipulator uses right justification by default. However, when using the setw() manipulator, you can use the left and right manipulators to left and right justify the data in a column as shown in figure 5-7.

When aligning data in columns, it's common to use left justification for strings and right justification for numbers. To illustrate, the first example uses the default right justification for two columns of strings that are 14 characters wide. As you can see, this data isn't as easy to read as it could be.

To improve the appearance and readability of this data, the second example specifies left justification for these columns. Since the left and right manipulators are *sticky*, this example only sets the justification to left once. Then, the rest of the code is the same as in the first example.

Often, you need to use left justification for some columns and right justification for others. For this type of data, you need to code the left and right manipulators each time you want to change justification. For instance, the third example switches the justification for every column to create a first column that's left justified and a second column that's right justified. Here, the values in the second column are numbers that contain two decimal places, so aligning them at the right causes the decimal points to be aligned.

Text data displayed with the default right justification

```
cout << setw(14) << "FIRST NAME" << setw(14) << "LAST NAME" << endl;
cout << setw(14) << "Grace" << setw(14) << "Hopper" << endl;
cout << setw(14) << "Bjarne" << setw(14) << "Stroustrup" << endl;
```

The output

```
    FIRST NAME     LAST NAME
         Grace        Hopper
        Bjarne    Stroustrup
```

How to left-justify the text with the left manipulator

```
cout << left;
cout << setw(14) << "FIRST NAME" << setw(14) << "LAST NAME" << endl;
cout << setw(14) << "Grace" << setw(14) << "Hopper" << endl;
cout << setw(14) << "Bjarne" << setw(14) << "Stroustrup" << endl;
```

The output

```
FIRST NAME     LAST NAME
Grace          Hopper
Bjarne         Stroustrup
```

Data that uses left and right justification

```
cout << left << setw(14) << "Total:"
     << right << setw(8) << 199.99 << endl;
cout << left << setw(14) << "Taxes:"
     << right << setw(8) << 14.77 << endl;
cout << left << setw(14) << "Grand total:"
     << right << setw(8) << 185.22 << endl;
```

The output

```
Total:          199.99
Taxes:           14.77
Grand total:    185.22
```

Description

- When using the setw() manipulator, you can use the left and right manipulators to left and right justify the data in a column.

- It's common to use left justification for text and right justification for numbers.

- The left and right manipulators are *sticky*. This means that once you set them, they stay in effect until you change them or the program ends.

Figure 5-7   How to right or left justify a column

How to format floating-point numbers

Figure 5-8 shows how to format floating-point numbers. To start, you should know that, by default, a floating-point number is displayed with no more than six *significant digits*. A significant digit is a digit that carries meaning about the accuracy of a measurement. Significant digits include zeros when they're between other non-zero digits, but they don't include leading zeros or trailing zeros. For example, 109900 has four significant digits (1099). That's because the trailing zeros aren't necessary when the number is displayed in scientific notation (1.099×10^5). Conversely, 0.001099 has the same four significant digits (1099). That's because the leading zeros aren't necessary when the number is displayed in scientific notation (1.099×10^{-3}).

One way to format floating-point numbers is to round them to a specified number of significant digits. To do that, you can use the setprecision() manipulator. The first example shows how this works. To start, it defines and initializes two double values that both have 7 significant digits. Then, it displays these numbers with three significant digits and then five significant digits. If you didn't use the setprecision() function here, both values would be displayed with the default of six significant digits.

In this example, the second number is very large. As a result, C++ uses scientific notation to display it. However, the first number is neither very large nor very small. As a result, C++ uses standard notation to display it.

The second example shows how to use the fixed manipulator to display a specified number of decimal places using *fixed-point notation*. Here, the fixed manipulator indicates that the number should have a fixed number of decimal places. Then, the setprecision() manipulator indicates that the number should have 2 decimal places. As a result, C++ displays all of the numbers in this example with two decimal places. To do that, it rounds the first number, and it adds trailing zeros to the next two numbers.

The third example shows how to use the showpoint manipulator to force the display of trailing zeros. Here, the precision is set to 8. By default, C++ doesn't display trailing zeros that don't add meaning to the number unless you use the fixed manipulator. As a result, this code begins by displaying the double value of 4500.0 without any trailing zeros. However, this code continues by using the showpoint manipulator to display 8 digits, four to the left of the decimal point, and four to the right of it.

When you work with the setprecision(), fixed, and showpoint manipulators, you need to remember that they're sticky. As a result, they stay in effect until you change them or the program ends.

How to set the number of significant digits

```
double d1 = 1.012345;
double d2 = 101234500000;
cout << setprecision(3) << "3 significant digits\n"
     << d1 << endl
     << d2 << endl << endl
     << setprecision(5) << "5 significant digits\n"
     << d1 << endl
     << d2 << endl;
```

The output

```
3 significant digits
1.01
1.01e+11

5 significant digits
1.0123
1.0123e+11
```

How to set the number of decimal places

```
cout << fixed << setprecision(2)
     << 10.125 << endl
     << 19.5 << endl
     << 42.0 << endl;
```

The output

```
10.13
19.50
42.00
```

How to force trailing zeros

```
double d3 = 4500.0;
cout << setprecision(8)
     << d3 << endl
     << showpoint
     << d3 << endl;
```

The output

```
4500
4500.0000
```

Description

- The setprecision() manipulator rounds floating-point numbers to the specified number of *significant digits*, which are the digits that carry meaning about the accuracy of a measurement.

- The fixed manipulator forces the output of floating-point numbers to be in *fixed-point notation*, rather than the default scientific notation.

- The showpoint manipulator forces the display of trailing zeros.

- The setprecision(), fixed, and showpoint manipulators are sticky. As a result, they stay in effect until you change them or the program ends.

Figure 5-8   How to format floating-point numbers

The Invoice 3.0 program

Figure 5-9 shows another version of the Invoice program that you learned how to code in chapter 3. However, this version of the program validates user input. In addition, it displays the calculated output in columns, and it formats the floating-point numbers so they display two decimal places.

The program begins by displaying its title. Then, it gets the customer type from the user. To do that, it uses a while loop that continues until the user enters a valid customer type of 'r' or 'w'. Notice here that after the customer type is extracted, an ignore() function is used to discard any additional data in the input stream to prevent unexpected input from causing problems.

If the user enters a valid customer type, this program executes a break statement to exit from the while loop. Otherwise, it displays an error message and then prompts the user for another customer type.

The second while loop gets a subtotal from the user. Within this loop, the first two statements prompt the user to enter a subtotal and attempt to extract the subtotal from the stream. Then, an if statement uses the good(), fail(), and bad() functions to check the state of the input stream. If the input stream is good, this code cxccutes a break statement to exit the loop.

If the input stream is in a failed state, this code displays a message that indicates that the number isn't valid and that the user should try again. Then, it uses the clear() function to reset the input stream to the good state. Next, it uses the ignore() function to discard the rest of the data in the buffer for the input stream.

The console

```
The Invoice 3.0 program

Enter customer type (r/w): direct
Invalid customer type! Please try again.
Enter customer type (r/w): r
Enter subtotal:          one thousand
Invalid number! Please try again.
Enter subtotal:          973

INVOICE
Subtotal:           973.00
Discount percent:     0.20
Discount amount:    194.60
Invoice total:      778.40

Bye!
```

The code

```cpp
#include <iostream>
#include <iomanip>
#include <limits>
#include <cmath>

using namespace std;

int main() {
    cout << "The Invoice 3.0 program\n\n";

    // get input
    char customer_type;
    while (true) {
        cout << "Enter customer type (r/w): ";
        cin >> customer_type;
        cin.ignore(numeric_limits<streamsize>::max(), '\n');
        if (tolower(customer_type) == 'r' ||
            tolower(customer_type) == 'w') {
            break;
        }
        else {
            cout << "Invalid customer type! Please try again.\n";
        }
    }

    double subtotal;
    while (true) {
        cout << "Enter subtotal:          ";
        cin >> subtotal;

        if (cin.good()) {          // stream good - end loop
            break;
        } else if (cin.fail()) {   // stream OK - try again
            cout << "Invalid number! Please try again.\n";
            cin.clear();
            cin.ignore(numeric_limits<streamsize>::max(), '\n');
```

Figure 5-9   The Invoice 3.0 program (part 1 of 2)

If the input stream is bad, this code displays a message that indicates that an unrecoverable error has occurred and that the program is exiting. Then, it uses a return statement to end the main() function, which ends the program. Since it's extremely rare for an input stream to be bad, you don't need to handle this state for all programs. However, for mission-critical programs, it's a good practice to handle this state by using code like the code shown in this figure.

Notice that this loop doesn't validate the range for the subtotal. However, you could easily add code that makes sure the user enters a reasonable number for the subtotal, such as a number that's greater than 0 and less than 1,000,000.

After getting the subtotal from the user, this code sets the discount percent depending on the customer type and the subtotal. To do that, it uses the same nested if statement described in chapter 3. Then, it uses the discount percent to calculate the discount amount and invoice total.

After calculating and rounding the results, this code displays the output in two columns. Here, the first column is 18 characters wide and left justified, and the second column is 8 characters wide and right justified. In addition, this code displays all numbers with fixed-point notation and 2 decimal places. That makes it easy to read the results of the calculations and check them to make sure they're accurate.

The code (continued)

```
        } else if (cin.bad()) {           // stream bad - exit program
            cout << "Sorry, an unexpected error has occurred. Bye! ";
            return 0;
        }
    }

    // set discount percent
    double discount_percent;
    if (tolower(customer_type) == 'r') {          // RETAIL
        if (subtotal < 100) {
            discount_percent = .0;
        } else if (subtotal >= 100 && subtotal < 250) {
            discount_percent = .1;
        } else {
            discount_percent = .2;
        }
    } else if (tolower(customer_type) == 'w') {    // WHOLESALE
        if (subtotal < 500) {
            discount_percent = .4;
        } else {
            discount_percent = .5;
        }
    } else {
        discount_percent = .0;
    }

    // calculate results
    double discount_amount = subtotal * discount_percent;
    double invoice_total = subtotal - discount_amount;


    // display output
    int col1 = 18;
    int col2 = 8;
    cout << fixed << setprecision(2) << endl    // use 2 decimal places
        << "INVOICE" << endl
        << left << setw(col1) << "Subtotal:"
        << right << setw(col2) << subtotal << endl
        << left << setw(col1) << "Discount percent:"
        << right << setw(col2) << discount_percent << endl
        << left << setw(col1) << "Discount amount:"
        << right << setw(col2) << discount_amount << endl
        << left << setw(col1) << "Invoice total:"
        << right << setw(col2) << invoice_total << endl;

    // display exit message
    cout << endl << left << "Bye! ";
}
```

Figure 5-9   The Invoice 3.0 program (part 2 of 2)

How to work with file streams

At this point, you have most of the skills you need for working with I/O streams. However, you've only learned how to apply these skills to working with the console. Now, you'll learn how to apply these skills to working with a file. This is known as *file I/O*, and it's important because the data that's stored in *main memory (RAM)* is lost when the program ends. However, if you write that data to a file, you can read it from the file next time the program runs.

How to read and write a file

Figure 5-10 shows how to read and write a file. To do that, you can use the three classes of the fstream header file that are summarized at the top of this figure. To start, you can create an object for the file stream. Then, you can use the open() function to open the stream that connects the file.

For the open() function, the filename argument specifies a path for a file. In this book, the examples only specify the filename. As a result, the open() function looks for the file in the working directory. The location of the working directory depends on the IDE that you're using. For example, if you're using Visual Studio, the working directory is the directory where the source code file that contains the main() function for the program is stored. If you're using Xcode, however, the working directory is the directory where the executable file for the program is stored. If you want to work with a file that isn't in the working directory, you can specify the full path to the file as described in appendix B.

When you open a file stream object, some of the operating system's resources are used to work with that object. As a result, when you're done working with the object, you should call its close() function to close it. This frees the resources that the file stream object is using and prevents problems that can occur if you don't close it.

The examples in this figure work with a *text file*, which is a file that stores data as a series of characters. The first example in this figure shows how to write data to a text file using an ofstream object. To start, it creates an ofstream object named output_file. Then, it opens a file named "names.txt" that's in the current working directory. If this file doesn't already exist, this code creates the file. And if this file does exist, any data it contains is deleted by default. In the next figure, though, you'll learn how to open an output file so you can append data to it.

Next, this code inserts three names into the output file stream where each name is followed by a newline character. Finally, this code closes the ofstream object, which frees all resources being used by this object. This also flushes any remaining data in the buffer.

The second example in this figure shows how to read data from a file. To start, it defines an ifstream object named input_file. Then, it attempts to open a file named "names.txt" that's in the current working directory.

If the file opens successfully, the ifstream object returns a true value. In that case, the code uses a while loop to read each line from the file and display each

Three file stream classes

Class	Description
`ifstream`	Creates an input stream object that reads data from a file on disk.
`ofstream`	Creates an output stream object that writes data to a file on disk.
`fstream`	Can create an input stream, an output stream, or both. See next figure.

Two member functions of the file stream classes

Function	Description
`open(filename)`	Opens a file for reading (input file) or writing (output file). If input file doesn't exist, the operation fails. If output file doesn't exist, it's created.
`close()`	Closes the file and flushes the buffer.

How to include the header file for the file stream classes

```
#include <fstream>
```

How to write data to a file

```
ofstream output_file;                    // create output file stream object
output_file.open("names.txt");           // open stream - create file if necessary
output_file << "Grace\n";                // write to stream
output_file << "Ada\n";                  // write to stream
output_file << "Alan\n";                 // write to stream
output_file.close();                     // close stream - flush data to file
```

The contents of the file

```
Grace\nAda\nAlan\n
```

The contents of the file when viewed in a text editor

```
Grace
Ada
Alan
```

How to read data from a file

```
ifstream input_file;                     // create input file stream object
input_file.open("names.txt");            // open stream
if (input_file) {                        // if stream opened successfully...
    string line;
    while (getline(input_file, line))    // read line from stream
        cout << line << '\n';            // write line to console
    input_file.close();                  // close stream
}
```

The console

```
Grace
Ada
Alan
```

How to define a file stream object and open it in one statement

```
ifstream input_file("names.txt");
```

Figure 5-10   How to read and write a file

line on the console, followed by a newline character. After the while loop, this code closes the ifstream object, which flushes the buffer and frees all resources being used by this object.

If the file doesn't open successfully, this code doesn't do anything. That can happen, for example, if the file doesn't exist. In this case, it isn't necessary to close the ifstream object since the code wasn't able to open that object in the first place.

The last example shows how to create an object for a file stream and open a file in one statement. To do that, you code the name of the file in parentheses after the name of the file stream. This coding technique is more concise than the technique presented in the first two examples, and it's commonly used by C++ programmers.

How to append data to a file

Figure 5-11 shows how to append data to a file. To do that, you can pass a second argument to the open() function of an ofstream object that uses a *file access flag* to specify the mode for the stream.

In the first example, for instance, the second statement calls the open() function of the ofstream object and passes "names.txt" as the first argument and ios:app as the second argument. As a result, C++ opens the file in append mode so the existing data isn't deleted. Then, when the third statement writes data to the file, it appends the data to the end of the file. Since the code in the previous figure already added three names to this file, this example appends a fourth name.

How to use the fstream object to work with files

This figure also shows how to use an fstream object for input and output. When you use this type of object, you need to use the file access flags to specify whether the stream will be used for input or output.

The statements in the second example in figure 5-11 illustrate how this works. Here, the first three open() functions open a file for output. The first open() function causes all the data in the file to be deleted, since that's the default. The second open() function is similar, but it includes the default ios::trunc access flag. Notice that to pass more than one flag to the open() function, you separate the flags with the | operator. The third open() function also uses two flags. This time, though, the second flag indicates that data should be appended to the file.

The last two statements in this figure show how to open an fstream object for input. To do that, you use the ios::in flag. As you saw in the previous figure, you can also define and open an fstream object using a single statement.

If you compare the use of the fstream object with the use of the ifstream and ofstream objects, you'll see that the code for opening ifstream and ofstream objects is somewhat simpler. Because of that, you'll use these objects most of

The syntax for the open() member function of a file stream object

```
object.open(file_name, file_access_flag [ | file_access_flag] ...);
```

Common file access flags

Flag	Description
ios::out	Output mode. If the file exists, any existing data in the file is deleted when the file is opened unless ios::app is also specified. If the file doesn't exist, it's created.
ios::app	Append mode. Any existing data in the file is preserved, and new data is written (appended) to the end of the file. If the file doesn't exist, it's created.
ios::trunc	Truncate mode. Any existing data in the file is deleted (truncated) when the file is opened. This is the default mode that's used by ios::out.
ios::in	Input mode. If the file doesn't exist, the open operation fails.

How to use an ofstream object to append data

```
ofstream output_file;
output_file.open("names.txt", ios::app);   // open in append mode
output_file << "Mary\n";                    // write to stream
output_file.close();                        // close stream and flush
```

The contents of the file when viewed in a text editor

```
Grace
Ada
Alan
Mary
```

How to use a fstream object for input and output

Declare the fstream object

```
fstream file;
```

How to open a file stream that deletes existing data from the output file

```
file.open("names.txt", ios::out);
```

Another way to open a file stream that deletes existing data from the output file

```
file.open("names.txt", ios::out | ios::trunc);
```

How to open a file stream that appends data to the output file

```
file.open("names.txt", ios::out | ios::app);
```

How to open a file stream that reads data from the input file

```
file.open("names.txt", ios::in);
```

How to define a fstream object in one statement

```
fstream file("names.txt", ios::in);
```

Description

- The open() member function of the ofstream and fstream classes accept two arguments. The first is the name of the file to open, and the second is a *file access flag* that indicates the type of stream to create.

- To pass more than one flag to the open() function, separate each flag with the | operator.

Figure 5-11   How to append data to a file and use the fstream object

the time. However, an fstream object provides more flexibility since it allows you to change the input/output mode for a stream. So, you might want to use it for a program that needs to open a file in input mode, read and process input data, switch to output mode, and write the processed data to the file.

How to check for errors when working with files

Figure 5-12 shows how to check for errors when working with files. To start, the first example in this figure shows a while loop that doesn't check for errors as it extracts numbers from the file named info.txt. Here, the condition in the while loop extracts the number. This causes the loop to execute until the extraction operation fails. In this case, the loop ends when the extraction operator attempts to extract "three" from the file. As a result, the code displays 100 and 200 on the console, but not 400, which comes after "three" and "hundred".

To fix this problem, the second example uses the error bits described in figure 5-4 to check the state of the file stream after the extraction operation. Here, the while loop continues until the code executes a break statement. If the extraction was successful, this code displays the number on the console.

If the extraction wasn't successful, this code uses the eof() and fail() functions of the ifstream object to check why the operation failed. If the operation reached the end of the file, this code exits the loop. However, if the operation failed for another reason, this code uses the clear() function to reset the stream to a good state, and it discards the rest of the data in the buffer. This discards all non-numeric data such as "three" and "hundred".

When the extraction operation reaches the end of the file, it sets both the eof and fail bits to true. As a result, if you want your code to work correctly, you must check the eof bit before checking the fail bit as shown in this example. If you check the fail bit first, the else if clause for the eof bit will never be executed, and the code will enter an infinite loop.

When you work with files, you often need to check for errors as you process them. That's especially true of files that you get from outside sources that might have inconsistent data. You'll learn more about this as you progress through this chapter.

The data in the file named info.txt

```
100
200
three hundred
400
```

A while loop that displays the data in the text file

```
ifstream input_file;
input_file.open("info.txt");       // open file for reading
if (input_file) {                  // if file opened successfully...
    int num;
    while (input_file >> num) {     // extract int - while no error...
        cout << num << '|';        // display value
    }
    input_file.close();
}
```

The console

```
100|200|
```

How to handle data conversion errors

```
ifstream input_file;
input_file.open("info.txt");        // open file for reading
if (input_file) {                   // if file opened successfully...
    int num;
    while (true) {                  // loop until there's a break statement
        if (input_file >> num) {     // if extraction is good...
            cout << num << '|';     // display number
        }
        else if (input_file.eof()) {     // if end of file...
            break;                       // exit loop
        }
        else if (input_file.fail()) {   // if extraction failed...
            input_file.clear();          // fix stream and try again
            input_file.ignore(numeric_limits<streamsize>::max(), '\n');
        }
    }
    input_file.close();
}
```

The console

```
100|200|400|
```

Description

- You can use the error bits described in figure 5-4 to check the state of the file stream after operations that might fail, such as extracting data.

- You can use the eof() member function to check whether the operation has reached the end of the file.

- You can use the fail() member function to check whether the operation failed.

Figure 5-12 How to check for errors when working with files

How to read and write delimited data

Figure 5-13 shows how to work with a *table* that stores its data in *columns* and *rows*, which are also referred to as *fields* and *records*. When you store a table of data in a file, it's common to separate the columns and rows of the table with characters known as *delimiters*. There are many ways to do this, but one common way is to use a tab character (\t) to separate columns and a newline character (\n) to separate rows. This type of file is known as a *tab-delimited file*.

The first example in this figure defines a string variable named filename that contains a value of "temps.txt". This variable is used by the second and third examples to write and read tab-delimited data.

The second example begins by defining and opening an ofstream object for the file specified by the filename variable. Then, it sets the output stream so it uses fixed-point notation with 1 decimal place.

After setting up the ofstream object, this code writes two columns and three rows of data to the file. Here, the code separates each row with a newline character, and it separates each column with a tab character. Finally, this code closes the ofstream object, which flushes all data to the file and frees all resources being used by the stream.

The third example begins by writing "TEMPERATURES" to the console, followed by column headings of "Low" and "High". Then, this code defines and opens an ifstream object for the file specified by the filename variable.

After opening the file, this code defines two variables to store the low and high temperatures. Then, it checks if the ifstream object was opened successfully. If so, it sets the input stream so it uses fixed-point notation with 1 decimal place.

Next, this code uses a while loop to extract the low and high temperatures from the file into the low and high variables. Within the loop, the code displays the low and high temperatures in two columns on the console. Like the two heading columns, these columns are 8 characters wide and right justified.

After the while loop, this code closes the ifstream object. This flushes the buffer and frees all resources being used by this stream.

As you review this code, note that it will only work if the data in the file always alternates between the low and high temperatures. In some cases, that may be a valid assumption. In other cases, you'll need to write code that checks for errors when reading the data. To do that, you can sometimes use a string stream as described later in this chapter.

Code that defines a filename

```
string filename = "temps.txt";
```

Code that writes tab-delimited data to a file

```
ofstream output_file;
output_file.open(filename);
output_file << fixed << setprecision(1);
output_file << 48.4 << '\t' << 57.2 << '\n';
output_file << 46.0 << '\t' << 50.0 << '\n';
output_file << 78.3 << '\t' << 101.4 << '\n';
output_file.close();
```

The contents of the file when viewed in a text editor

```
48.4    57.2
46.0    50.0
78.3    101.4
```

Code that reads tab-delimited data from a file

```
cout << "TEMPERATURES\n";
cout << setw(8) << "Low" << setw(8) << "High" << endl;

ifstream input_file;
input_file.open(filename);

double low;
double high;
if (input_file) {                     // if file opened successfully...
    cout << fixed << setprecision(1);
    while (input_file >> low >> high) {
        cout << setw(8) << low << setw(8) << high << '\n';
    }
    input_file.close();
}
```

The console

```
TEMPERATURES
     Low    High
    48.4    57.2
    46.0    50.0
    78.3    101.4
```

Description

- When storing a *table* of data in a file, it's common to separate the *columns* and *rows* of the table with characters known as *delimiters*.

- A file that uses tab (\t) and newline (\n) characters to separate columns and rows is known as a *tab-delimited file*.

Figure 5-13   How to read and write delimited data

The Temperature Manager program

Figure 5-14 shows a Temperature Manager program that allows you to view pairs of high and low temperatures that are stored in a file. In addition, it allows you to add temperatures to the file. And when you're done, it allows you to exit the program. To perform these tasks, you can enter a command of 'v', 'a', or 'x' respectively.

The code for this program begins by including all of the necessary header files. This includes the iomanip, fstream, and limits files described in this chapter.

Within the main() function, the first statement defines a string variable named filename and initializes it to a value of "temps.txt". Later in this function, the file streams for input and output both use this filename. As a result, you can be sure that operations for file input and output are both working with the same file.

After displaying the list of commands, this program enters a while loop that continues until the user enters 'x' to exit. Within this loop, the first four statements display the Command prompt and get the char that corresponds with the command entered by the user.

The console

```
The Temperature Manager program

COMMANDS
v - View temperatures
a - Add a temperature
x - Exit

Command: v

TEMPERATURES
      Low     High
-------- ------
    48.4    57.2
    46.0    50.0
    78.3   101.4

Command: a

Enter low temp: 54
Enter high temp: 61
Temps have been saved.

Command: x

Bye!
```

The code

```cpp
#include <iostream>
#include <iomanip>
#include <fstream>
#include <limits>
#include <string>

using namespace std;

int main()
{
    string filename = "temps.txt";

    cout << "The Temperature Manager program\n\n";

    cout << "COMMANDS\n"
         << "v - View temperatures\n"
         << "a - Add a temperature\n"
         << "x - Exit\n";

    char command = 'v';
    while (command != 'x') {
        // get command from user
        cout << endl;
        cout << "Command: ";
        cin >> command;
        cout << endl;
```

Figure 5-14   The Temperature Manager program (part 1 of 2)

After getting the command character, this code checks whether that character is equal to 'v'. If it is, the code continues by reading all the low and high temperatures stored in the file and displaying them on the console. But first, it attempts to open the file and then checks that it was opened successfully. Since this code is similar to code you saw in figure 5-13, you shouldn't have much trouble understanding how it works. After executing this code, program execution reaches the end of the while loop and jumps back to the top of the loop, which causes the program to get another command from the user.

If the command character is equal to 'a', this code gets a low and a high temperature from the user. Then, it defines and opens an ofstream object and uses it to append the low and high temperatures to the end of the file. Since this file is a tab-delimited file, this code separates the two temperatures with a tab and follows them with a new line. Again, after this code is executed, program execution reaches the end of the while loop and jumps back to the top of the loop, which causes the program to get another command from the user.

If the command character is equal to 'x', the code displays a "Bye!" message on the console to indicate that the program is ending. Then, program execution jumps back to the top of the while loop, and the condition for the loop evaluates to false. This causes the loop to end, which ends the main() function and the program.

If the command character isn't one of the characters in the previous if or else if clauses, the else clause displays a message on the console. This message indicates that the command is invalid and that the user should try again. Because this is the last statement in the while loop, code execution jumps to the top of the loop, and the code prompts the user to enter another command.

As you review this code, note that the code that adds the new low and high temperatures to the file needs to use the ios:app file input flag to open the file in append mode. Otherwise, all existing data in the file would be deleted when the file was opened.

Also, note that this code doesn't validate the temperature data that's entered by the user. This helps keep the focus on working with file streams. In general, though, validating this data would be a good practice. In addition, it's a good practice to code functions for data validation and to store those functions in a separate file. You'll learn how to do that in chapter 7.

The code (continued)

```cpp
            if (command == 'v') {
                cout << "TEMPERATURES\n";
                cout << setw(8) << "Low" << setw(8) << "High" << endl;
                cout << "-------- -------" << endl;

                ifstream input_file;
                input_file.open(filename);

                double low;
                double high;
                if (input_file) {        // if file opened successfully...
                    cout << fixed << setprecision(1);
                    while (input_file >> low >> high) {
                        cout << setw(8) << low << setw(8) << high << '\n';
                    }
                    input_file.close();
                }
                else {
                    cout << "Unable to open file.\n";
                }
            }
            else if (command == 'a') {
                double low;
                cout << "Enter low temp: ";
                cin >> low;

                double high;
                cout << "Enter high temp: ";
                cin >> high;

                ofstream output_file;
                output_file.open(filename, ios::app);
                output_file << low << '\t' << high << '\n';
                output_file.close();
                cout << "Temps have been saved.\n";
            }
            else if (command == 'x') {
                cout << "Bye!\n\n";
            }
            else {
                cout << "Invalid command. Try again.\n";
            }
        }
    }
```

Figure 5-14   The Temperature Manager program (part 2 of 2)

How to work with string streams

A *string stream* uses a *string buffer* to hold the characters in a string. When you read input from a text file that may contain unexpected data, it's often helpful to read each line of the file into a string stream. Then, you can use the input and output techniques that you've learned in this chapter to process the data in each line of the file.

How to use a string stream to handle unexpected data

Figure 5-15 starts by summarizing three classes of the sstream header file. These classes work much like the three classes of the fstream header file, except they create a string buffer for input, output, or both. When working with a string stream object, you can use the str() function to get the string that's stored in the buffer or to replace the string that's stored in the buffer with the specified string.

To illustrate how this works, this figure shows a data file that contains unexpected data. To start, the second line has extra data in a third column. In addition, the third line doesn't contain any data. Finally, the fourth line begins with a string of "n/a" where a number would normally be expected.

The code example shows how to use a string stream to handle this type of data. First, the code checks whether the input file was opened successfully. If it was, it defines some variables, including a string variable named line that will be used to store each line of text that's retrieved from the file and a stringstream object named ss that will be used to store the text from the string.

Next, a while loop is used to process the data. Here, the Boolean expression uses the getline() function to read each line from the input file and store it in the line variable. Within the while loop, the first statement uses the str() function of the stringstream object to replace the contents of the string stream buffer with the contents of the line variable. At this point, the line of data from the file is stored in the string stream buffer. Then, the clear() function of the string stream object sets the stream to a good state.

Next, this code attempts to extract the low and high temperatures from the string stream. If this operation is successful, this code displays the low and high temperatures on the console. Otherwise, it jumps to the top of the loop and the next line in the text file is processed. As a result, this code only displays the three lines of the file that it was able to process successfully. In this case, that includes the second line of data, even though it has extra data in the third column. That's because this code was able to extract the low and high temperatures from the first two columns, and the rest of the string stream wasn't processed.

Three string stream classes

Class	Description
`istringstream`	Creates an input stream object that reads characters from a string.
`ostringstream`	Creates an output stream object that writes characters to a string.
`stringstream`	Creates a stream object that can read characters from and write characters to a string.

A member function of the string stream classes

Function	Description
`str()`	Returns a string object that's a copy of the contents of the buffer.
`str(string)`	Replaces the contents of the buffer with the specified string.

How to include the header file for the string stream classes

```
#include <sstream>
```

A data file that contains unexpected data

```
48.4    57.23
46.0    50.0      sensors down

n/a     64
78.3    101.4
```

Code that uses a string stream to handle unexpected data

```cpp
ifstream infile("temps.txt");
if (infile) {                   // if file opened successfully...
    string line;
    stringstream ss;
    double low;
    double high;
    cout << fixed << setprecision(1);
    while (getline(infile, line)) {
        ss.str(line);   // replace string stream buffer with current line
        ss.clear();     // reset string stream error bits
        if (ss >> low >> high) {
            cout << setw(8) << low << setw(8) << high << '\n';
        }
    }
    infile.close();
}
```

The console

```
48.4     57.2
46.0     50.0
78.3    101.4
```

Description

- A *string stream* uses a *string buffer* to hold the characters in a string.

- A string stream is particularly useful when processing each line of a file that may contain unexpected data.

Figure 5-15   How to use a string stream to handle unexpected data

The Temperature Analyzer program

Figure 5-16 shows a Temperature Analyzer program that reads temperature data from a text file, processes the data, and displays the results on the console. To start, this program gets the name of the file from the user. If this file doesn't exist, the program displays an error message and prompts the user to enter the name of another file.

Once the user enters the name of a valid file, the program reads the low and high temperatures from that file. As it does that, it ignores any extra data at the end of the line, and it skips blank lines and lines that contain incorrect data types. As a result, this program is able to handle a file that contains unexpected data, such as the temps.txt file shown in this figure.

For each line that the program can successfully process, this program calculates the average temperature and displays the low, high, and average temperature on the console. In addition, it updates the lowest and highest overall temperature as well as the overall daily temperature average.

When the program finishes, it displays a message that includes the total number of lines (days) as well as the number of lines that were successfully processed. That way, the user can tell how much of the overall data the program was able to process. Finally, the program displays the totals for the lowest, highest, and average temperatures.

By now, you shouldn't have much trouble understanding the code for this program. It works much like the examples in the previous figures. However, it allows the user to specify the name of the file, and it does some additional processing on the data.

In part 2, the code that prompts the user for the name of the file uses a while loop to continue prompting until the user enters the name of a file that can be opened successfully. After this loop, this code displays a message that indicates the file was opened successfully and displays the table header.

Next, this code defines and initializes the variables used by the while loop in part 3. That includes the variables named lowest and highest that store the overall lowest and highest temperatures. Here, the lowest variable is initialized to a high number (1000), and the highest variable is initialized to a low number (-1000). That way, the first two temperatures that are processed should be set as the lowest and highest temperature. After that, this code only sets these variables when a temperature is lower or higher than the current lowest or highest temperature.

Within the while loop, the code increments the number of lines read and the number of lines processed. In addition, when the code successfully processes a line, it calculates the average temperature for the line and displays the low, high, and average temperatures in the console in 3 columns. In addition, it calculates a total of all the daily average temperatures.

After the loop ends, the code calculates the daily average temperature by dividing the total of the average temperatures by the number of lines processed. Then, it displays the overall lowest, highest, and average temperatures in two columns.

The console

```
Temperature Analyzer

Enter input filename: temps
Unable to open input file! Try again.
Enter input filename: temps.txt
Input file (temps.txt) opened successfully.

    Low    High    Avg
--------------------------
   48.4    57.2    52.8
   46.0    50.0    48.0
   45.0    55.3    50.1
   54.0    61.0    57.5
   37.0    52.0    44.5
   37.0    43.3    40.1
   45.0    57.0    51.0
   48.0    55.0    51.5
   54.0    57.0    55.5
   48.1    54.3    51.2

10 of 14 days successfully processed.

Lowest temp:        37.0
Highest temp:       61.0
Avg daily temp:     50.2
```

The temps.txt file

```
48.372 57.23
46      50
45.01   55.273839404
54      61
37      52
37      43.27
45      57
n/a     64
55.34   n/a
50a     59
48.0    55.0
54      57

48.1    54.27
```

Description

- The Temperature Analyzer program opens a text file specified by the user, reads temperature data from that text file, processes that data, and writes output to the console.

- If the file specified by the user doesn't exist, the program displays an error message and prompts the user for another filename.

- When the program reads from the text file, it ignores any extra data on a line, and it skips blank lines and lines that contain incorrect data types.

Figure 5-16   The Temperature Analyzer program (part 1 of 3)

The code

```cpp
#include <iostream>
#include <iomanip>
#include <fstream>
#include <string>
#include <sstream>
#include <limits>

using namespace std;

int main()
{
    cout << "Temperature Analyzer\n\n";

    // open input file
    string filename;
    ifstream infile;
    while (true) {
        cout << "Enter input filename: ";
        cin >> filename;
        cin.ignore(numeric_limits<streamsize>::max(), '\n');

        infile.open(filename);
        if (infile) {               // if file opened successfully
            break;
        }
        else {
            cout << "Unable to open input file! Try again.\n";
        }
    }
    cout << "Input file (" << filename << ") opened successfully.\n\n";

    // start output - set floating-point formatting
    cout << fixed << setprecision(1);

    // output table header
    int col = 7;  // column width for display
    cout << setw(col) << "Low" << setw(col) << "High"
         << setw(col) << "Avg" << endl;
    cout << "-------------------------" << endl;

    // initialize variables used by loop
    double low = 0.0;
    double high = 0.0;
    double avg = 0.0;
    double avg_total = 0.0;
    double lowest = 1000.0;
    double highest = -1000.0;
    int lines_read = 0;
    int lines_processed = 0;
```

Figure 5-16   The Temperature Analyzer program (part 2 of 3)

The code (continued)

```cpp
// loop through each line in the input file
string line;
stringstream ss;
while (getline(infile, line)) {
    ++lines_read;    // increment counter variable

    ss.str(line);    // replace string stream buffer with line
    ss.clear();      // reset string stream error bits

    // extract temps from string stream - if OK, process
    if (ss >> low >> high) {
        ++lines_processed;

        // calculate avg temp
        avg = (low + high) / 2;

        // display low, high, avg temps
        cout << setw(col) << low << setw(col) << high
            << setw(col) << avg << endl;

        // update totals
        avg_total += avg;
        if (low < lowest)
            lowest = low;
        if (high > highest)
            highest = high;
    }
}
infile.close();

cout << endl
    << lines_processed << " of "
    << lines_read << " lines successfully processed.\n\n";

// calculate the daily avg
double avg_daily = avg_total / lines_processed;

// display calculations
int col1 = 17;
int col2 = 7;
cout << left << setw(col1) << "Lowest temp: "
    << right << setw(col2) << lowest << endl
    << left << setw(col1) << "Highest temp: "
    << right << setw(col2) << highest << endl
    << left << setw(col1) << "Avg daily temp: "
    << right << setw(col2) << avg_daily << endl << endl;
}
```

Figure 5-16   The Temperature Analyzer program (part 3 of 3)

Perspective

In this chapter, you learned more skills for working with all types of I/O streams. That includes skills for reading data from and writing data to the console. That includes skills for working with file input and output. And that includes skills for working with string streams, which are often helpful when reading input from a text file.

Although this chapter only presents the skills for working with text files, you should know that you can also use C++ to work with other types of files such as binary files. Beyond that, you should know that most serious applications store their data in databases. However, these C++ skills are beyond the scope of this book.

Terms

stream	file I/O
input	main memory (RAM)
output	text file
I/O	file access flag
input stream	table
whitespace	column
output stream	row
buffer	field
flush the buffer	record
error bits	delimiter
data validation	tab-delimited file
stream manipulators	string stream
significant digits	string buffer
fixed-point notation	

Summary

- A *stream* is a sequence of characters that can be used to get *input* or *output* for your program. Input and output is commonly abbreviated as *I/O* or *IO*.

- An *output stream* contains character data that is being *written* to an object, and an *input stream* contains data that is being *read* from an object.

- When the extraction operator reads data from an input stream, *whitespace* such as spaces, tabs, or new lines is typically ignored.

- A *buffer* is a location in memory that temporarily stores stream data as it is being written or read. When a buffer is *flushed*, all the data temporarily in the buffer is sent to its next destination.

- All stream objects provided by C++ share a similar *interface*. As a result, you can use the same operators and member functions for all types of C++ streams.

- You can use the member functions of an input stream to check the *error bits* of the stream or to reset the error bits of a stream.

- You can use a loop to continue to prompt the user until that user enters valid data. This is known as *data validation*.

- You can use *stream manipulators* with the stream insertion (<<) operator to format output streams.

- The setprecision() manipulator rounds floating-point numbers to the specified number of *significant digits*, which are the digits that carry meaning about the accuracy of a measurement.

- The fixed manipulator forces the output of floating-point numbers to be in *fixed-point notation* rather than the default scientific notation.

- Data that's stored in *main memory* (*RAM*) is lost when the program ends. But if you save that data to a file, you can read it the next time the program runs.

- A *text file* stores data as a series of characters. If you open a text file in a text editor, it's easy for a human to read the characters.

- The open() member function of the ofstream and fstream classes accepts two arguments. The first is the name of the file to open, and the second is one or more *file access flags* that indicate the type of stream to create.

- When storing a *table* of data in a file, it's common to separate the *columns* and *rows* of the table (also called *records* and *fields*) with characters known as *delimiters*.

- A file that uses tab (\t) and newline (\n) characters to separate columns and rows is known as a *tab-delimited file*.

- A *string stream* uses a *string buffer* to hold the characters in a string.

Exercise 5-1   Validate data and create a tab-delimited file

In this exercise, you'll modify a program that calculates miles per gallon so it validates the data entered by the user and stores the data for each calculation in a tab-delimited file. When you're done, the tab-delimited file should look something like this:

```
225.2        17.0
1374.8       64.5
```

Open the program, review the code, and test the program

1. Open the Miles Per Gallon project or solution that's in this folder:
   `ex_starts\ch05_ex1_mpg`

2. Review the code. Note that it validates the miles and gallons entries to be sure they're greater than zero, rounds the MPG to two decimal places, and gets entries for one or more trips.

3. Run the program to see how it works. Test to see what happens when you enter 0 for the miles or gallons. Then, test to see what happens when you enter two values for one of the entries. Finally, test to see what happens when you enter an invalid number.

Validate and handle input errors

4. Modify the program so it discards any extra data entered by the user.

5. Modify the program so it makes sure that the user enters valid numbers. If the input operation fails, the program should display an error message, clear the error bits from the input stream object, and discard any remaining data in the stream.

6. Run the program again. This time, it should ignore any extra data entered by the user. In addition, it should display an error message and prompt for another entry if the user enters an invalid number for miles or gallons.

Write the valid entries to a tab-delimited file

7. Modify the program so it appends valid miles and gallons entries to a tab-delimited file named trips.txt. Both of these values should have one decimal digit. (For this program, you can assume that the user doesn't enter miles or gallons with more than one decimal digit.)

8. Run the program and enter two or more valid sets of entries. Then, use a text editor to view the text file.

9. Close the text file and run the program again. This time, enter valid and invalid entries.

10. Display the text file again to be sure that the program appended valid entries to the original entries and that it didn't write any invalid entries to the file.

Exercise 5-2 Display data from a tab-delimited file

In this exercise, you'll modify the Miles Per Gallon program from exercise 5-1 so it displays the data in the tab-delimited file when the program starts and after each time the user enters data for a trip. When you're done, a test run should look something like this:

```
Miles Per Gallon

    Miles      Gallons         MPG
    225.2         17.0       13.25
   1374.8         64.5       21.31

Total miles:       1600.00
Total gallons:       81.50
Average MPG:         19.63

Enter miles driven:          274
Enter gallons of gas used: 18.5
Miles per gallon:          14.81

    Miles      Gallons         MPG
    225.2         17.0       13.25
   1374.8         64.5       21.31
    274.0         18.5       14.81

Total miles:       1874.00
Total gallons:      100.00
Average MPG:         18.74

Get entries for another trip? (y/n):
```

1. Open the Miles Per Gallon project or solution that's in this folder:
   ex_starts/ch05_ex2_mpg

2. Modify the program so it starts by displaying the data in the trips.txt file as well as the MPG. Be sure to set the column widths and the precision so the values are displayed as shown above.

3. Modify the program so it displays the data in the text file and the MPG after it writes the data to the file. To do that, you can copy the code you just wrote so it's executed after the data is written to the file.

4. Modify the program so it displays the total miles, total gallons, and average MPG both when the program starts and anytime data is written to the file. Be sure to set the column widths, alignment, and precision, and make sure the decimals are always displayed.

Exercise 5-3   Use a string stream

In this exercise, you'll write the code for an Employee Wages program so it uses a string stream to handle unexpected data in the input file. When you're done, a test run should look something like this:

```
Name                Hourly wage      Hours        Total
----------------    -----------   -----------  -----------
Scott                     24.95         32.25       804.64
Angelina                  32.75         41.00      1342.75
Jordan                    18.75         22.50       421.88
Annalise                  16.18         25.00       404.46
Andrew                    22.50         38.00       855.00

5 lines not processed.
```

1. Open the Employee Wages project or solution that's in this folder:
   `ex_starts\ch05_ex3_employee_wages`

2. Review the code to see that all the #include directives you need have been included. In addition, the main() function includes code that defines an input file stream, opens a file named wages.txt, checks if the stream is in good condition, and closes the file.

3. Define the variables that you need to work with the string stream and the data that will be extracted from it. That includes the name, hourly wage, and hours that are stored in each line of the input file.

4. Process each line of data from the file, using a string stream to skip any lines that contain unexpected data. Write the data for any other lines to the console, displaying two decimal digits for each floating point number.

5. Calculate the total wages for each line that's written to the console by multiplying the hourly wage by the hours, and display it in a fourth column as shown above.

6. Keep track of the number of lines that can't be processed because of unexpected data, and display that number on the console after the data for the lines that were processed.

6

How to work with data types, strings, and vectors

In chapter 2, you learned how to use two of the built-in, or fundamental, data types as you defined and initialized variables and coded assignment statements that used simple arithmetic expressions. In addition, you learned some basic skills for working with strings.

Now, you'll learn more skills that will let you work with fundamental data types at a professional level. In addition, you'll learn more about working with strings, and you'll be introduced to vectors, which allow you to store a sequence of values of any data type.

Basic skills for working with data types

The figures that follow review some of the skills presented in chapter 2 for working with data types. In addition, these figures present some new skills that are commonly used by professional programmers.

The fundamental data types

Figure 6-1 shows the *fundamental data types* provided by C++. You can use these data types to store numbers, characters, and true or false values. Since these types are built-in to the C++ language, they're sometimes referred to as the *built-in data types*.

In chapter 2, you learned how to use the int data type to store *integers* (whole numbers). However, C++ provides three other data types for integers. For example, if a value is too big for the int type, you can use the long or long long types. Conversely, if you only need to store small integer values and you want to save system resources, you can use the short type.

In chapter 2, you also learned how to use the double data type for storing numbers with decimal places. However, if you want to save system resources, you can use the float data type. Or, if you want to store numbers that are too large for the double type, you can use the long double type. The values for all three of these data types are stored as *floating-point numbers* that can hold very large and very small values, but with a limited number of *significant digits*. For instance, the double type has 16 significant digits. As a result, it supports numbers like 12,345,678,901,234.56. On the other hand, the float type only has 7 significant digits. As a result, it can still support numbers such as 1,234,567,000,000,000. That's because the digits 1 through 7 are significant in this number but the zeros are not.

To express the value of a floating-point number, you can use *scientific notation*. This notation lets you express very large and very small numbers in a sort of shorthand. To use scientific notation, you type the letter e or E followed by a power of 10. For instance, 3.65e+9 is equal to 3.65 times 10^9 (3,650,000,000). Similarly, 3.65e-9 is equal to 3.65 times 10^{-9} (.00000000365).

In chapter 2, you learned how to use the char type to store one character from the *ASCII character set*. When you use a char type, you should know that C++ only allows the first 128 characters (codes 0 to 127) of this character set. That's because the char type is technically an integer type that stores an integer from 0 to 127 that maps to an ASCII character.

Last, you can use the bool type to store a true or false value. This data type is often used to represent a condition in a control statement such as if or while that can be true or false. Because of that, a bool variable is often referred to as a flag. You'll see examples of how to use bool variables in control statements later in this chapter.

When you work with the bool data type, you should know that the true keyword maps to a non-zero int value, typically 1, but possibly other values such as -1, 2, 3, and so on. On the other hand, the false keyword always maps to an int value of 0.

The fundamental data types and their typical sizes and ranges

Type	Bytes	Range
char	1	Integers from 0 to 127 that map to one of the characters in the ASCII character set.
short	2	Integers from -32,768 to 32,767.
int	4	Integers from -2,147,483,648 to 2,147,483,647.
long	4	Same as int on most systems.
long long	8	Integers from -9,223,372,036,854,775,808 to 9,223,372,036,854,775,807.
float	4	Single-precision, floating-point numbers from -3.4E38 to 3.4E38 with up to **7** significant digits.
double	8	Double-precision, floating-point numbers from -1.7E308 to 1.7E308 with up to 16 significant digits.
long double	8	Same as double on most systems, but sometimes 10 bytes with range of -3.4E4932 to 1.7E4832.
bool	1	A true or false value.

Unsigned integers and their typical sizes and ranges

Type	Bytes	Range
unsigned short	2	From 0 to 65,535.
unsigned int	4	From 0 to 4,294,967,295.
unsigned long	8	Same as unsigned int on most systems.
unsigned long long	4	From 0 to 18,446,744,073,709,551,615.

Description

- The *American Standard Code for Information Interchange* (*ASCII*) assigns an integer from 0 to 127 for the individual *characters* on a keyboard.

- *Integers* are positive or negative whole numbers. *Unsigned* integers only allow for positive whole numbers.

- *Floating-point numbers* provide for very large and very small numbers that require decimal positions, but with a limited number of *significant digits*. A *single-precision number* provides for numbers with up to 7 significant digits. A *double-precision number* provides for numbers with up to 16 significant digits.

- A *Boolean value* can be true or false. The true keyword maps to a non-zero int value, typically 1, and the false keyword maps to an int value of 0.

- The *fundamental data types* are also known as the *built-in data types*.

Technical notes

- The number of bytes a data type uses in memory can vary from system to system.

- To express the value of a floating-point number, you can use *scientific notation*. For example, 2.382E+5 means 2.382 times 10^5, which is a value of 238,200. Conversely, 3.25E-8 means 3.25 times 10^{-8}, which is a value of .0000000325.

Figure 6-1   The fundamental data types

How to define and initialize variables

In chapter 2, you learned how to *define* and *initialize* a *variable*. Figure 6-2 reviews these skills, and it presents some new information.

To start, the first example shows how to define and initialize some of the data types that weren't presented in chapter 2. Here, the third and fourth statements show how to assign values to the float and long types. To do that, you can add a letter after the value to specifically indicate its data type. For a float type, you can add an *f* or *F* after the value. For a long type, you can add an *L*. Although this isn't necessary for the code to compile, it provides clarity and can protect against data loss. You can also use a lowercase *l*, but that letter can easily be mistaken for the number 1. As a result, it's generally considered a better practice to use an uppercase *L*.

The fifth statement shows how you can use scientific notation as you assign a value to a variable. Then, the sixth statement shows that you can assign a character to the char type by enclosing the character in single quotes. The seventh statement shows that, because the characters in the ASCII character set map to integers, you can also assign a character to the char type by supplying the integer for the character.

The eighth statement shows how to define a bool variable named is_valid and how to use the false keyword to initialize it to a value of 0. Then, the ninth statement shows how to define a bool variable named success and how to initialize it to a value of 1, which maps to the true keyword. In general, it's considered a good practice to use the true and false keywords because they make code easier to read and understand.

In most cases, you define and initialize one variable per statement. That's considered a good practice because it usually results in code that's easy to read and modify later. However, it sometimes makes sense to define multiple variables in the same statement as shown in the second example. Here, the first statement defines three double variables with one statement, and the second statement defines two int variables. To do that, these statements separate the variable names with commas.

You can also define and initialize multiple variables in a single statement as shown by the third example. Here, the first statement defines and initializes three double variables with one statement, and the second statement defines and initializes two int variables. To do that, these statements separate each assignment expression with commas.

The fourth example shows how to assign the same value to multiple variables. Here, the first statement defines four int variables. Then, the second statement initializes these variables by assigning a value of 20 to them. To do that, this code uses the assignment operator to chain each of the variables.

The fifth example shows how to use the auto keyword to infer the data type based on its initial value. Here, the first statement initializes an auto variable named hours by assigning an int value of 40. As a result, the compiler infers that it should use the int type for this variable. The second statement works similarly, but it assigns a double value of 40.0. As a result, the compiler infers that it should use the double type for this value.

The assignment operator

Operator	Name	Description
=	Assignment	Assigns a new value to the variable.

Statements that define and initialize variables

```
int counter = 1;                  // initialize an int variable
double price = 14.95;             // initialize a double variable
float interest_rate = 8.125F;     // F indicates a floating-point value
long number_of_bytes = 20000L;    // L indicates a long integer
double distance = 3.65e+9;        // scientific notation
char letter1 = 'A';               // stored as ASCII code 65
char letter2 = 65;                // cout << letter2 displays the letter A
bool is_valid = false;            // false = 0
bool success = 1;                 // 1 = true
```

How to define multiple variables in one statement

```
double pay, subtotal, total;     // define 3 variables
int x, y;                        // define 2 variables
```

How to define and initialize multiple variables in one statement

```
double pay = 0.0, subtotal = 0.0, total = 0.0;
int x = 0, y = 0;
```

How to assign the same value to multiple variables

```
int a, b, c, d;                  // define 4 variables
a = b = c = d = 20;              // assign 20 to all 4 variables
```

How to use the auto keyword to infer the data type based on initial value

```
auto hours = 40;                 // compiler infers that hours is an int
auto hours = 40.0;               // compiler infers that hours is a double
```

Description

- A *variable* stores a value in memory that can change as a program executes. In other words, the value of a variable varies as a program executes.

- Before you can use a variable, you must *define* its data type and its name.

- After you define a variable, you can *initialize* it. To do that, you *assign* a value to the variable with the *assignment operator* (=).

- You can define more than one variable in a single statement, as long as the variables have the same data type. To do that, you use commas to separate the variables. You can also initialize the variables in that same statement.

- When you define and initialize a variable in one statement, you can use the auto keyword. Then, the compiler will *infer* the type based on the value used to initialize it.

- To identify float values, you can type an *f* or *F* after the number.

- To identify long values, you can type an *l* or *L* after the number. The compiler will be able to tell the difference between long ints and long doubles.

- To identify long long int values, you can type *ll* or *LL* after the number.

- For clarity, uppercase *L*s are better because a lowercase *l* resembles the number 1.

Figure 6-2   How to define and initialize variables

When working with the fundamental data types, you usually don't need to use the auto keyword. However, it can sometimes result in code that's shorter and more flexible, especially when working with more complex data types as described later in this book. For example, chapter 10 provides several examples of when it makes sense to use the auto keyword.

How to define and initialize constants

In chapter 2, you learned that a variable stores a value that changes as a program executes. In contrast to a variable, a *constant* stores a value that does not change as a program executes. In other words, the value of a constant remains constant.

Most of the skills for defining and initializing variables also apply to declaring and initializing constants. However, when you define a constant, you begin the statement with the const keyword as shown in figure 6-3. Here, the first statement creates a constant that stores the number of days in November. The second statement creates a constant that uses the float type to store a sales tax percentage. The third statement defines a constant that stores the number of miles per light year. To provide the value for this constant, the code use scientific notation. That's because the number of miles per light year is a very large number that's unwieldy to store in standard notation. And the fourth statement defines three constants that store integer values that correspond to the first three months of the year.

In many programming languages, it's a common coding convention to use all uppercase letters for the name of a constant and to separate the words in the name with an underscore as shown by the fifth statement. This makes it easy for programmers to differentiate between variables and constants. In C++, however, using uppercase letters can cause conflicts with *macros*, which are fragments of code that always have uppercase names. As a result, it's generally considered a good practice to use lowercase letters to name your constants just as you do your variables.

Although using lowercase letters to name both variables and constants means that you won't be able to differentiate between them, that usually isn't a problem. In the unlikely case that a programmer attempts to assign a value to a constant, the code won't compile and the compiler will return a message that indicates that you can't assign a value to a constant. That clearly shows that the name in question is a constant, not a variable.

The second example shows how to use a constant to calculate the area of a circle. Here, the first statement defines a constant to store the value of pi (π) and initializes it to a value of 3.14, which is an approximation of the value of pi. Then, the next three statements get the radius from the user and store it in the variable named radius. Finally, the program calculates and displays the area of the circle. As you review this code, note that the constant named pi remains constant, but the variables named radius and area vary depending on user input.

How to define and initialize a constant

Syntax

```
const data_type constant_name = value;
```

Examples

```
const int days_in_november = 30;
const float sales_tax = .075F;
const double miles_per_light_year = 5.879e+12;
const int jan = 1, feb = 2, mar = 3;
const int COL_WIDTH = 7;                    // all caps is not recommended
```

How to use a constant

```
const double pi = 3.14;

double radius;
cout << "Enter radius: ";
cin >> radius;

double area = pi * radius * radius;
cout << "Area: " << area << endl;
```

The console

```
Enter radius: 6.5
Area: 132.665
```

Description

- A *constant* stores a value in memory that cannot change as a program executes. In other words, the value of a constant remains constant as a program executes.

- To define a constant, you begin the definition statement with the const keyword. A constant must be initialized at the time it is defined.

- In other programming languages, it's common to use all capital letters when naming constants. This distinguishes them from variables. In C++, however, this can cause conflicts with *macros*, which are named fragments of code. As a result, many programmers recommend using lowercase letters when naming constants.

Figure 6-3   How to define and initialize constants

The Light Years Calculator program

Figure 6-4 shows a program named Light Years Calculator that calculates the number of miles, kilometers, and parsecs in the specified number of light years. Then, it displays these calculations in both scientific notation and fixed notation.

To start, this program gets the number of light years from the user. Then, it defines three constants that are used to perform the calculations. First, it defines and initializes the number of miles per light year. Second, it defines and initializes the number of kilometers per light year. Third, it defines and initializes the number of parsecs per light year.

Next, this program calculates the number of miles, kilometers, and parsecs for the specified number of light years. Then, it displays the results in scientific notation. Here, it sets the number of significant digits to 8. As a result, this code displays up to 8 significant digits.

After displaying the results in scientific notation, this code displays the results in fixed-point notation with 8 decimal places, and it uses the setw() manipulator to use 24 characters for this column. This aligns the numbers on their decimal point, which makes it easy to see how the number of miles and kilometers compare to the number of parsecs.

The console

```
Light Years Calculator

Enter light years: 6

SCIENTIFIC NOTATION
Miles:              3.5274e+013
Kilometers:         5.6766e+013
Parsecs:            1.839606

FIXED NOTATION
Miles:                 35274000000000.00000000
Kilometers:            56766000000000.00000000
Parsecs:                           1.83960600

Bye!
```

The code

```cpp
#include <iostream>
#include <iomanip>

using namespace std;

int main() {
    cout << "Light Years Calculator\n\n";

    double light_years;
    cout << "Enter light years: ";
    cin >> light_years;

    // define three constants
    const double miles_per_light_year = 5.879e+12;
    const double km_per_light_year = 9.461e+12;
    const double parsec_per_light_year = 0.306601;

    // calculate miles, kilometers, and parsecs
    double miles = light_years * miles_per_light_year;
    double km = light_years * km_per_light_year;
    double parsecs = light_years * parsec_per_light_year;

    // display the results
    cout << endl << setprecision(8)
         << "SCIENTIFIC NOTATION\n"
         << "Miles:            " << miles << endl
         << "Kilometers:       " << km << endl
         << "Parsecs:          " << parsecs << endl << endl;

    cout << fixed
         << "FIXED NOTATION\n"
         << "Miles:            " << setw(24) << miles << endl
         << "Kilometers:       " << setw(24) << km << endl
         << "Parsecs:          " << setw(24) << parsecs << endl << endl;

    cout << "Bye!\n\n";
}
```

Figure 6-4   The Light Years Calculator program

More skills for working with data types

Now that you've learned the basic skills for working with data types, you're ready to learn some additional concepts and skills. That includes skills that you can use to fix issues with code that works with numeric data.

How to work with type conversion

As you develop C++ programs, you may encounter situations where you need to convert data from one data type to another. This is also referred to as *casting* data from one type to another.

If you assign or perform arithmetic operations with different data types, C++ automatically converts the types following the rules for *type coercion* described in figure 6-5. To start, C++ *promotes* data from a smaller type such as the int type to a larger type such as the long type. With this type of conversion, the new type is always wide enough to hold the original value. For instance, the first statement in this figure converts an integer value of 93 to a double value of 93.0.

If you assign the final value of an expression to a variable that's of a less precise type, C++ *demotes* the data from the more precise type to the less precise type. With this type of conversion, the less precise data type may not be wide enough to hold the original value, which may result in the loss of some data. For instance, the second statement in this figure converts a double value of 93.67 to an int value of 93, which discards the data stored in the decimal digits.

C++ also promotes values in an arithmetic expression if some of the values have more precise data types than other values, as shown by the next three statements. Here, the variable named d is defined with the double type, and the variables named i and j are defined with the int type. As a result, when these variables are used together in an expression, C++ converts both i and j to double values.

When C++ promotes a type, it usually doesn't cause any problems. However, demoting a type can lead to the loss of data. As a result, it's generally considered a good practice to explicitly cast values that you're demoting to make it clear that you intend to perform the demotion. To do that, you can use the static_cast operator shown in this figure.

When you use the static_cast operator, you specify the target data type by coding it within angle brackets (<>) just after the operator name, but before the parentheses. Then, you code the value to convert within the parentheses. In this figure, the first statement that uses this operator explicitly demotes a double value of 93.67 to an int value of 93.

In some cases, you may need to use explicit casting to get your code to work correctly. For example, if you want to use decimal division with two int values, you need to explicitly cast one of the int values to the double type as shown by the second static_cast operator. Here, C++ casts the first integer to the double type before performing the division. That way, C++ uses decimal division and returns a result that has decimal places. Without explicit casting, the expression would use integer division and return an integer value (1) that C++ would then promote to a double (1.0).

The C++ rules for type coercion

- The char, short, and unsigned short types are automatically *promoted* to the int type. If a system allows an unsigned short to hold a value greater than an int can hold, then the unsigned short is promoted to an unsigned int.
- For all other data types, the lower ranking data type is promoted to the next higher data type, as described below.
- The final value of an expression is converted to the data type of the variable to which it is assigned. If the variable has a lower ranking data type, then the result is *demoted* to that data type.

The ranking of the data types

int → unsigned int → long → unsigned long → float → double → long double

Examples of type coercion

```
double grade = 93;                  // promote int to double; grade = 93.0

int grade = 93.67;                  // demote double to int; grade = 93

double d = 95.5;
int i = 86, j = 91;
double average = (d+i+j)/3;         // promote int values to double values
                                    // average = 90.8333
```

How to explicitly convert a value to another type

Syntax

```
static_cast<type>(value)
```

How to explicitly demote a data type

```
int grade = static_cast<int>(93.67);        // grade = 93
```

How to use static_cast to correct integer division

```
int a = 8, b = 7;
double result = static_cast<double>(a) / b;  // result = 1.14286
```

Another way to perform an explicit conversion (not recommended)

```
int grade = (int) 93.67;                     // grade = 93
```

Description

- If you perform assignment or arithmetic operations with different data types, C++ automatically converts or *casts* the types using its rules of *type coercion*.
- You can also explicitly convert types using the static_cast operator.
- C++ also allows you to perform a cast by coding the data type in parentheses just before the value to be converted. However, this syntax forces the compiler to choose from among several types of casts. Since this can lead to unexpected results, it's better to specify the type of cast you want to use.

Figure 6-5   How to work with type conversion

C++ also allows you to perform an explicit cast by coding the data type in parentheses just before the value to be converted as shown by the last example in figure 6-5. However, this syntax forces the compiler to choose from among several types of casts, including a static cast. Since this can lead to unexpected results, it's better to use the static_cast operator to specify that you want to use a static cast.

When you code an explicit cast, an error may occur at runtime if C++ isn't able to perform the cast. As a result, you should use an explicit cast only when you're sure that C++ is able to perform the cast.

Although you typically cast between numeric data types, you can also cast between the integer and char types. That's because every char value corresponds to an integer that identifies it in the ASCII character set. However, there is a possible loss of data when converting integer types such as the int type to the char type. As a result, you should be careful when doing this.

How to work with data type sizes and limits

Data types vary from system to system. For example, the long double type might use 8 bytes on some systems and 10 bytes on other systems. As a result, you may sometimes need to check the number of bytes used by a data type. To do that, you can use the sizeof() operator as shown in figure 6-6. Here, the first two examples show two ways to check the size of a data type or a variable.

In addition, you may sometimes need to get the maximum or minimum value that's allowable for a data type. That way, you can get the data types to work correctly on all systems. To do that, you can use the static min() and max() functions of the numeric_limits class as shown by the first two statements in the second group of examples. When you call these static functions, you begin by specifying the data type within angle brackets (<>) immediately after the name of the class. Then, you code the *scope resolution operator* (::) and the name of the static function.

The numeric_limits class also includes the static constants shown in this figure. These constants provide a way to check whether a value is signed, is an integer type, or is an exact type. The last three statements in the second group of examples show how to use these constants.

When an integer variable is assigned a value that's too big for its type, it will *overflow*, which causes it to wrap around to the type's minimum. Similarly, when an integer variable is assigned a value that's too small for its type, it will *underflow*, which causes it to wrap around to the type's maximum. The third example shows how this works. If that's not what you want (and it usually isn't), you can use the min() and max() functions to make sure the value is within a valid range before you assign it.

When a floating-point variable is assigned a value that's too big or small for its type, the result varies depending on the system. It may cause your program to display errors and stop, display errors and keep running, or keep running with no errors but possibly incorrect data. If you encounter this problem, you can use the min() and max() functions to make sure the value is within an acceptable range before you assign it to a floating-point variable.

The sizeof operator

Syntax

```
sizeof(type)
```

Examples

```
auto size = sizeof(unsigned short);    // argument is a data type
cout << size << " bytes\n";            // displays "2 bytes"

unsigned short us = 100;
size = sizeof(us);                     // argument is a variable
cout << size << " bytes\n";            // displays "2 bytes"
```

The include statement for the numeric_limits header file

```
#include <limits>
```

Some of the static members of the numeric_limits class

Member	Description
`min()`	Returns the minimum finite value that the data type can hold.
`max()`	Returns the maximum finite value that the data type can hold.
`is_signed`	Returns true if the data type is signed.
`is_integer`	Returns true if the data type is an integer.
`is_exact`	Returns true if the data type uses exact representations.

Examples

```
auto result1 = numeric_limits<int>::min();        // -2147483648
auto result2 = numeric_limits<int>::max();        // 2147483647
bool result3 = numeric_limits<double>::is_signed; // 1 (true)
bool result4 = numeric_limits<short>::is_integer; // 1 (true)
bool result5 = numeric_limits<float>::is_exact;   // 0 (false)
```

What happens when you exceed an integer type's minimum or maximum

```
unsigned short s;
s = numeric_limits<unsigned short>::max();    // s is 65535
s += 100;                                     // overflow: s is 99
s = numeric_limits<unsigned short>::min();    // s is 0
s -= 100;                                     // underflow: s is 65436
```

Description

- Data types vary from system to system. You can use the sizeof() operator to determine the size of a type on your system. You can use the members of the numeric_limits class to determine the range of a type on your system.

- When an integer variable is assigned a value that's too big for its type, it will *overflow*, or wrap around to the type's minimum. When an integer variable is assigned a value that's too small for its type, it will *underflow*, or wrap around to the type's maximum.

- When a floating-point variable is assigned a value that's too big for its type, the result varies depending on the system. This may cause your program to display errors and stop, display errors and keep running, or keep running with no errors.

- To access static members of a class, you can code the name of the class, the *scope resolution operator* (::), and the name of the member.

Figure 6-6   How to work with data type sizes and limits

How to fix problems with floating-point data

Because of the way floating-point numbers are stored internally, they can't represent the exact value of the decimal places in some numbers. This is shown by the first example in figure 6-7. This example begins by setting the precision of the cout object to 24 so it can display a more accurate representation of the number. This shows that C++ stores the literal value of .1 as a floating-point number that's extremely close to .1, but not exactly .1. Similarly, it stores the literal value of .9 as a floating-point number that's extremely close to .9, but not exactly .9.

Most of the time, this doesn't cause any problems with your code. However, it can sometimes cause problems with equality comparisons and calculations. In the second example, for instance, the code attempts to use a loop to display the numbers .5, .6, .7, and .8. This loop should end when the counter value is equal to .9. However, since .1 isn't exact, adding it to the counter variable causes the counter variable to become less precise each time through the loop. As a result, the counter variable never equals .9, which causes an infinite loop. Since this example uses the default precision of the cout object, the output looks as if the counter variable is equal to .9. However, if you set the precision to 24, you would see that the counter variable does not equal .9 on the fifth iteration of the loop.

This figure shows two of the many ways to solve this problem. To start, you can avoid using an equality comparison with the floating-point number. In this case, you can use a less than comparison to check whether the floating-point number is less than a specified number.

Another way to solve this problem is to use the round() function of the cmath header to round the floating-point number to a less precise number of decimal places. In this case, you can round the floating-point number to 1 decimal place after incrementing it by .1. Then, the counter variable doesn't become more imprecise each time through the loop, and the equality comparison works correctly.

For intensive calculations, or calculations that require extreme precision, the techniques presented here may not be enough. In that case, you can search the Internet for more information on how to handle floating-point numbers with C++.

Code that shows how some floating-point numbers are not exact

```
cout << setprecision(24);
cout << .0 << endl;
cout << .1 << endl;
cout << .5 << endl;
cout << .9 << endl;
```

The console

```
0
0.100000000000000005551115
0.5
0.900000000000000022200446
```

An infinite loop caused by an issue with floating-point data comparisons

```
double counter = 0.5;
while (counter != .9) {    // counter never equals .9, so loop never stops
    cout << counter << "   ";
    counter += .1;
}
```

The console

```
0.5  0.6  0.7  0.8  0.9  1  1.1  1.2  1.3  1.4 ...
```

Two ways to fix the problem

By not using an equality comparison

```
while (counter < .85) {
    cout << counter << "   ";
    counter += .1;
}
```

By using the round() function of the cmath header to fix the calculation

```
while (counter != .9) {
    cout << counter << "   ";
    counter += .1;
    counter = round(counter * 10) / 10;
}
```

The console for both solutions

```
0.5  0.6  0.7  0.8
```

Description

- Because of the way floating-point numbers are stored internally, they can't represent the exact value of the decimal places in some numbers. This can cause problems with equality comparisons and calculations.

- To fix problems with equality comparisons, you can avoid using equality operators with floating point numbers

- To fix problems with calculations, you can use the round() function of the cmath header to round the floating-point number to a less precise number of decimal places.

Figure 6-7   How to fix problems with floating point data

How to work with vectors

At this point, you have been introduced to the most important skills for working with the fundamental data types that are available directly from C++. However, C++'s *Standard Template Library* (*STL*) provides for more complex data types. Many of these complex data types can contain multiple elements of another data type. As a result, they're known as *containers*. For example, the STL provides a data type known as a *vector* that can contain a sequence of *elements* of the same data type.

How to create a vector and refer to its elements

Figure 6-8 begins by showing how to include the vector header file that contains the vector class. Then, it shows the syntax for defining a vector object. To do that, you code the name of the vector class, followed by angle brackets (`<>`) that contain the data type for the elements of the vector. This is followed by the name of the vector and, optionally, the initial number of elements in the vector enclosed in parentheses.

The examples for defining vectors show how this works. Here, the first example defines a vector object named prices that stores a sequence of double values. The second example works like the first example, but it specifies an initial size of 10 elements. When you specify an initial size, C++ uses a default value for each element. In this case, the elements are double types, so C++ uses a default value of 0.0.

Because the first example doesn't specify the initial size, it creates a vector that has zero elements. Whether or not you specify the initial size of a vector when you create it, though, it's easy to add elements later. However, if you know the initial size of the vector, it's typically more efficient to create the elements when you create the vector.

The third example shows another way to create a vector. Here, a variable whose value is accepted from the user is used to provide the initial size.

To refer to the elements of a vector, you use the *subscript operator* (`[]`) and an *index*. In the example in this figure, for instance, the first statement creates a vector of int values named scores that has 3 elements. Then, the next three statements use the subscript operator to assign values to the three elements of the vector. Here, the first element has an index of 0, the second has an index of 1, and so on. Next, the fifth statement gets the value of the second element (index of 1) and displays it on the console. Finally, the last statement attempts to access the fourth element (index of 3).

Since there isn't a fourth element, this causes *out of bounds access*, also known as *out of range access*. This leads to unexpected results that vary depending on the compiler. Some compilers raise an error that causes the program to crash. Other compilers don't check whether the index is in range. In that case, the code returns or overwrites whatever value happens to be at the out of bounds memory location. This allows code to execute efficiently, but it can lead to bugs that are hard to find and fix.

How to include the header file for the vector class

```
#include <vector>
```

The syntax for defining a vector

```
vector<type> vector_name [(initial_size)];
```

Examples of vector definitions

Code that defines a vector object that holds a sequence of double values

```
vector<double> prices;
```

Code that defines a vector of 10 double values

```
vector<double> prices(10);   // create a vector with 10 elements
```

Code that uses a variable to specify the size of a vector

```
int name_count = 0;
cout << "Enter the number of names: ";
cin >> name_count;
vector<string> names(name_count);
```

The syntax for referring to an element of a vector

```
vector_name[index]
```

How to use the subscript operator to access the elements in a vector

```
vector<int> scores(3);        // create a vector with 3 elements
scores[0] = 99;               // set the value of the first element
scores[1] = 87;               // set the value of the second element
scores[2] = 91;               // set the value of the third element
cout << scores[1];            // display the value of the second element
cout << scores[3];            // BAD! out of bounds access!
```

Description

- The *Standard Template Library (STL)* contains many data types in addition to the fundamental data types. Many of these data types can contain multiple elements and are often called *containers*.

- A *vector* contains a sequence of *elements* of the same data type. You can use the *subscript operator* ([]) with an *index* to access the elements of a vector, where 0 is the index for the first element, 1 is the index for the second element, and so on.

- *Out of bounds access* occurs if your code specifies an index that's outside the range of valid indexes. Since this leads to unexpected results, you should always write code that prevents out of bounds access.

- Vectors, as well as other items provided by the STL, are members of the std namespace. Because of that, a program must include a using directive for that namespace, a using declaration for the specific member of the namespace, or it must fully qualify any references to the member with the name of the namespace.

Figure 6-8   How to create a vector and refer to its elements

How to initialize and loop through a vector

In the last figure, you saw how to define a vector and set the values of its elements individually using the subscript operator. However, you can also define a vector and provide values for its elements using a single statement. To do that, you use an *initialization list* as shown in figure 6-9.

The three examples in this figure show how this works. Here, the initialization list in the first example includes three values, so a vector with three elements is created and assigned those values. Similarly, the second and third examples create vectors with five and four elements. Note that, unlike the first example, these two examples don't include an assignment operator. That's because this operator is optional and is usually omitted.

After you initialize the elements of a vector, you can use a standard for loop to iterate the elements in a vector. In the example in this figure, the counter variable is initialized to 0, the loop is executed as long at the counter variable is less than the size of the vector, and the counter variable is incremented by 1 each time through the loop. Within the loop, the first statement uses the subscript operator and the counter variable to get the element at the specified index. Then, the second statement displays the element on the console.

When coding standard for loops, it's easy to make a mistake that leads to out of bounds access. For example, this can happen if you code the initialization expression or the Boolean expression incorrectly. One way to avoid out of bounds access is to use a *range-based for loop* as shown by the last example. This kind of loop iterates over every element in the vector without using a counter variable or the subscript operator. As a result, it's easier to code and less prone to cause errors.

The syntax for using an initialization list to define and initialize a vector

```
vector<type> vector_name [=] { value1[, value2] ... };
```

Examples that use an initialization list

```
vector<int> scores = { 99, 87, 91 };                        // 3 elements
vector<double> prices { 14.95, 12.95, 11.95, 9.95, 16.95 }; // 5 elements
vector<string> names { "Joel", "Mary", "Anne", "Samantha" }; // 4 elements
```

How to use a for loop to display all the elements in a vector object

```
vector<int> scores { 99, 87, 91, 76 };
for (int i = 0; i < scores.size(); ++i) {
    int score = scores[i];
    cout << score << ' ';
}
```

The console

```
99 87 91 76
```

How to use a range-based for loop to avoid out of bounds access

```
vector<int> scores {99, 87, 91, 76};
for (int score: scores) {
    cout <<  score << ' ';
}
```

The console

```
99 87 91 76
```

Description

- You can define a vector and provide initial values in a single statement by using an *initialization list*. The number of values you include in the list determines the initial size of the vector.

- You can use the size() function of a vector to get the number of elements in the vector.

- When iterating the elements of a vector, you can avoid out of bounds access by using a *range-based for loop*. This kind of loop iterates over every element in the vector without using a counter or the subscript operator.

Figure 6-9   How to initialize and loop through a vector

How to use member functions of a vector

A vector contains many member functions. Figure 6-10 summarizes some of the most common member functions and shows how to work with them.

In the first example, the first statement creates an empty vector of doubles, and the next two statements add elements to that vector by *pushing* them onto the back of the sequence of elements. The fourth statement then calls the size() function, which returns a value of 2 because the vector now holds two elements. Since the exact data type that's returned by this function varies, this statement uses the auto keyword to define the size variable. Then, the C++ compiler can infer the correct data type for this variable.

The next three statements use the front(), back(), and at() functions to get the values of the elements at the front of the sequence, at the back of the sequence, and at an index of 1. For the third statement, you could use a subscript operator to get the same value. However, the at() function is safer to use because it always performs bounds checking. This may not run as efficiently as a subscript operator that doesn't check bounds, but it can prevent bugs that are hard to find and fix.

The next statement removes the element at the back of the sequence by calling the pop_back() function. The three statements after that call the size() function to get the new size of the vector, the empty() function to determine if the vector contains elements, and the back() function to retrieve the new value at the back of the sequence. At this point, there's only one element in the vector. As a result, back() returns the same value that front() did earlier.

The second example shows how to use the insert() and erase() functions to add or delete elements anywhere in the vector. It's important to understand that these functions accept iterators, not indexes. You'll learn more about iterators in chapter 10. For now, just know that an iterator points to an element's location in memory, and you can use the addition operator (+) to advance a vector's iterator to point to other elements.

The code in the second example starts by creating a vector of four strings. Then, it uses the erase() function to delete the third string, which is at the index of 2. To do that, this code uses the begin() function to get the iterator that points to the first element. Then, it uses the addition operator to advance that iterator to point to the third element. Next, this code uses the insert() function to insert an element at the beginning of the vector.

When you use the erase() and insert() functions, the vector object has to move all of the elements that are after the element that's removed or inserted. Because of that, these function are less efficient than the push_back() and pop_back() functions. You'll learn more about this, and about some of the other STL containers, in chapter 10.

Some member functions of the vector container

Function	Description
`size()`	Returns the number of elements in the vector.
`empty()`	Returns true if the vector contains no elements.
`push_back(element)`	Adds the specified element to the back of the vector.
`pop_back()`	Removes the element at the back of the vector.
`back()`	Returns a reference to the last element in the vector.
`front()`	Returns a reference to the first element in the vector.
`at(index)`	Returns a reference to the element at the index. Throws an out_of_range exception if the index is greater than or equal to the number of elements in the vector.
`clear()`	Removes all the elements in the vector.
`begin()`	Returns an iterator that points to the first element in the vector.
`insert(iterator, element)`	Inserts the element at the specified iterator.
`erase(iterator)`	Removes the element at the specified iterator.

Statements that use the member functions of a vector

```
vector<double> prices;              // create empty vector
prices.push_back(9.99);             // add element to vector
prices.push_back(149.99);           // add element to back of vector
auto size = prices.size();          // size is 2

double first = prices.front();      // first is 9.99
double last = prices.back();        // last is 149.99
double second = prices.at(1);       // second is 149.99

prices.pop_back();                  // remove back element
size = prices.size();               // size is 1
bool is_empty = prices.empty();     // is_empty is false
last = prices.back();               // last is 9.99
```

How to insert and erase elements

```
vector<string> names { "Mary", "Joel", "Mike", "Anne" };

int index = 2;                            // index for "Mike"
names.erase(names.begin() + index);       // removes "Mike"
auto size = names.size();                 // size is 3
string name = names.at(index);            // name is "Anne"

names.insert(names.begin(), "Ben");       // insert "Ben" at front
size = names.size();                      // size is 4
name = names.front();                     // name is "Ben"
```

Description

- The size() function returns an unsigned integer, but the exact data type varies. As a result, if you need to store this unsigned integer in a variable, it's a good practice to use the auto keyword to define that variable.

- You'll learn more about the vector class and other STL containers in chapter 10.

Figure 6-10   How to use member functions of a vector

The Test Scores program

Figure 6-11 shows another version of the Test Score program that was first presented in chapter 4. This version of the program stores each valid score entered by the user in a vector. Then, when the user finishes entering test scores, this program loops through the valid test scores and displays the count, total, and average score.

This program begins by including the header files that it needs, including the vector header file. Then, the main() function displays the title and directions for the program and defines a vector named scores.

Next, this code executes a loop that continues until the user enters -1. Within the loop, the first two statements prompt the user for a score and extract the score from the user input. Then, this code checks if the score is valid. If the score isn't a valid number, the code sets the input stream to a good state, discards the user input, and displays an appropriate message. If the score is greater than 100 or less than -1, the code also displays an appropriate message. However, if this code is greater than -1, the value must be a valid number from 0 to 100. As a result, this code uses the push_back() function to append the score to the end of the vector. Since the if statement is the last statement in this while loop, the program executes the appropriate clause and then jumps back to the top of the loop. This prompts the user to enter a score, which is what you want.

The console

```
The Test Scores program

Enter test scores from 0 to 100.
To end the program, enter -1.

Enter score: 97
Enter score: 93
Enter score: eighty two
Invalid number. Try again.
Enter score: 105
Score must be from 0 to 100. Try again.
Enter score: 83
Enter score: -1

Score count:    3
Score total:   273
Average score: 91
```

The code

```cpp
#include <iostream>
#include <vector>
#include <cmath>

using namespace std;

int main()
{
    cout << "The Test Scores program\n\n";

    cout << "Enter test scores from 0 to 100.\n"
         << "To end the program, enter -1.\n\n";

    vector<int> scores;
    int score = 0;
    while (score != -1) {
        cout << "Enter score: ";
        cin >> score;

        if (cin.fail()) {
            cin.clear();                // clear error bits
            cin.ignore(1000, '\n');     // discard input up to end of line
            cout << "Invalid number. Try again.\n";
        }
        else if (score > 100) {
            cout << "Score must be from 0 to 100. Try again.\n";
        }
        else if (score < -1) {
            cout << "Score can't be a negative number. Try again.\n";
        }
        else if (score > -1) {      // valid score - add to vector
            scores.push_back(score);
        }
    }
```

Figure 6-11   The Test Scores program (part 1 of 2)

When the user enters -1 and the while loop ends, the main() function continues by checking if the vector is empty. If so, it displays a message that indicates that the user didn't enter any scores.

However, if the vector isn't empty, the code loops through the scores stored in the vector and calculates the total of all the scores. To do that, it defines an int variable named total and initializes it to 0. Then, it uses a range-based for loop to iterate through each score and update the total variable accordingly.

After calculating the score total, this code uses the size() function to get the count of the scores. Then, it calculates the average score. To do that, this code uses a static cast to convert the score total from the int type to the double type. That way, C++ uses decimal division, which allows the average to contain decimal places. Then, this code rounds the average to 1 decimal place. Finally, this code displays the score count, total, and average.

The code (continued)

```
if (scores.empty()) {                    // vector is empty
    cout << "\nNo scores entered\n.";
}
else {                                   // vector contains scores
    // calculate total of all scores
    int total = 0;
    for (int score : scores) {
        total += score;
    }

    // get the count and calculate the average
    auto score_count = scores.size();
    double average = static_cast<double>(total) / score_count;
    average = round(average * 10) / 10;

    // display the score count, total, and average
    cout << '\n'   // blank line
        << "Score count:   " << score_count << endl
        << "Score total:   " << total << endl
        << "Average score: " << average << endl << endl;
}
}
```

Figure 6-11   The Test Scores program (part 2 of 2)

The Temperature Manager program

Figure 6-12 shows another version of the Temperature Manager program presented in the previous chapter. This version of the program reads the temperature data from a file and stores it in two vectors when the program starts. Then, it allows the user to add or remove data from that vector. In addition, it allows the user to save the data in the vector to the file.

When the Temperature Manager program starts, it displays a list of five characters that correspond to a command. The first three commands let the user view, add, and remove temperatures. The last two commands let the user save changes that have been made and exit the program.

The code begins by importing the necessary header files, including the vector header file. Then, it defines and initializes the filename for the file, and it displays the program title and the list of commands.

Part 2 of the code reads the low and high temperatures from the file and stores them in two vectors of double values named low_temps and high_temps. To do that, this code uses the push_back() function to add the low and high temperatures to the end of the vectors.

After reading the temperatures from the file, this code executes a while loop that continues until the user enters 'x', which causes the program to end. If the user enters 'v', the code uses a standard for loop to iterate through both vectors and display the low and high temperatures on the console. In addition, this loop displays an integer that corresponds to the day for each pair of low and high temperatures.

If the user enters 'a', the code gets a low and high temperature from the user as shown in part 3. Then, it appends each temperature to the end of the appropriate vector, and it displays a message that indicates that the temperatures have been added.

If the user enters 'r', the code prompts the user to enter the number of the day for the temperatures to be removed. Then, it gets the index for that day by subtracting 1 from the day. Next, this code checks if the index is within a valid range. If so, it uses the erase() function to remove the element at the specified index. To do that, it uses the begin() function to get an iterator for the beginning of the vector, and it adds the index to that iterator. After it finishes, it displays a message that indicates that the temperatures have been removed.

If the user enters 's', the code uses a for loop to iterate though each element of the two vectors and write the low and high temperatures to a tab-delimited file. When it's done, it displays a message that indicates that the temperatures have been saved.

If the user enters 'x', the code displays a goodbye message. Then, the condition for the while loop becomes false and the while loop ends. Because there's no code after the while loop, the program also ends.

If the user doesn't enter any of the above commands, the code displays a message that indicates that the user didn't enter a valid command. Then, program execution jumps to the top of the loop, which prompts the user to enter another command.

The console

```
The Temperature Manager program

COMMANDS
v - View temperatures
a - Add a temperature
r - Remove a temperature
s - Save changes
x - Exit

Command: v
TEMPERATURES
Day      Low      High
----  -------  -------
1        48.4     57.2
2        46.0     50.0
3        68.2     73.0

Command: a
Enter low temp: 73.2
Enter high temp: 101.5

Command: r
Enter day to remove: 3
Temps for day 3 have been removed.

Command: s
Your changes have been saved.

Command: x
Bye!
```

The code

```cpp
#include <iostream>
#include <iomanip>
#include <fstream>
#include <string>
#include <vector>

using namespace std;

int main()
{
    string filename = "temps.txt";

    cout << "The Temperature Manager program\n\n";

    cout << "COMMANDS\n"
         << "v - View temperatures\n"
         << "a - Add temperatures\n"
         << "r - Remove temperatures\n"
         << "s - Save changes\n"
         << "x - Exit\n";
```

Figure 6-12   The Temperature Manager program (part 1 of 3)

The code (continued)

```cpp
// read low and high temps from file and store in vectors
double low, high;
vector<double> low_temps, high_temps;
ifstream input_file;
input_file.open(filename);
if (input_file) {        // if file opened successfully...
    while (input_file >> low >> high) {
        low_temps.push_back(low);
        high_temps.push_back(high);
    }
    input_file.close();
}
else {
    cout << "\nUnable to open file. You may need to add temperatures.\n";
}

char command = 'v';
while (command != 'x') {
    // get command from user
    cout << endl;
    cout << "Command: ";
    cin >> command;

    // define variables
    ofstream output_file;
    int day_num, index;

    // execute appropriate command
    switch (command) {
    case 'v':
        cout << "TEMPERATURES\n"
            << left << setw(4) << "Day"
            << right << setw(8) << "Low" << setw(8) << "High" << endl
            << "---- ------- -------" << endl;

        cout << fixed << setprecision(1);
        day_num = 1;
        for (int i = 0; i < low_temps.size(); ++i) {
            low = low_temps[i];
            high = high_temps[i];
            cout << left << setw(4) << day_num
                << right << setw(8) << low << setw(8) << high << '\n';
            ++day_num;
        }
        break;
```

Figure 6-12   The Temperature Manager program (part 2 of 3)

The code (continued)

```
        case 'a':
            cout << "Enter low temp: ";
            cin >> low;

            cout << "Enter high temp: ";
            cin >> high;

            low_temps.push_back(low);
            high_temps.push_back(high);
            break;

        case 'r':
            int day;
            cout << "Enter day to remove: ";
            cin >> day;

            index = day - 1;
            if (index >= 0 && index < high_temps.size()) {
                high_temps.erase(high_temps.begin() + index);
                low_temps.erase(low_temps.begin() + index);
            }

            cout << "Temps for day " << day << " have been removed.\n";
            break;

        case 's':
            output_file.open(filename);
            for (int i = 0; i < low_temps.size(); ++i) {
                low = low_temps[i];
                high = high_temps[i];
                output_file << low << '\t' << high << '\n';
            }
            output_file.close();
            cout << "Your changes have been saved.\n";
            break;

        case 'x':
            cout << "Bye!\n\n";
            break;

        default:
            cout << "Invalid command. Try again.\n";
            break;
        }
    }
}
```

Figure 6-12   The Temperature Manager program (part 3 of 3)

How to work with strings

In chapter 2, you learned some basic skills for working with strings, including how to define and initialize a string variable, how to concatenate string variables, and how to append one string to another string. Now, you'll review some of those skills. In addition, you'll learn some additional skills for working with strings.

How to create and loop through a string

Figure 6-13 begins by reviewing some basic concepts about strings. To start, it shows how to include the string header file, how to define a string, and how to define and initialize a string. Then, the fourth example shows how to initialize a string by including it in parentheses immediately after defining the name.

When you work with a string, you should realize that a *string* is a sequence of char values. With C++98 and later, you can use the string class from the C++ standard library to work with a string. This class is a container type for characters.

So, you can think of a string as a vector of characters. Also, like a vector, you can use the subscript operator to access the individual characters of a string. Like a vector, the indexes for the characters in a string start with 0. In the fifth example, for instance, the code uses an index of 0 to get and display the first character of the string and an index of 1 to get and display the second character of the string. Then, it uses an index of 3 to set the fourth character of the string to 'k'. This changes the string from "Mary" to "Mark".

The sixth example shows how to capitalize the first letter of a name. To do that, this code uses the subscript operator to get the first character of the string, which is at index 0. Then, it uses the toupper() function to convert the letter to an uppercase letter. Next, it uses the subscript operator to set that uppercase character as the first character of the string.

The seventh example shows how to compare strings for equality. To do that, you can use the equality operators, just as you do for char values. However, this comparison is case-sensitive. As a result, "secret" does not equal "Secret".

The eighth example shows how to convert a string to all uppercase letters. To do that, this code uses a standard for loop to loop through each character in the string. This loop defines and initializes a counter variable with a value of 0 that will be used as the index for the characters of the string. Then, it uses the string's size() function to specify that the loop should continue while the counter variable is less than the size of the string, and it increments that variable by 1 each time through the loop. Within the loop, the first statement uses the subscript operator with the counter variable to get the current character. Then, the second statement converts that character to uppercase and uses the counter variable again to replace the current character with the uppercase character.

The last example shows how to use a range-based for loop to create a new string that's the same as the first string, except that it uses all uppercase letters. Before the loop, this code defines a string named name_upper to store the uppercase letters. Then, it uses a range-based for loop to loop through each

How to include the header file for the string class

```
#include <string>
```

How to define a string

```
string name;
```

How to define and initialize a string

```
string name = "Mary";
```

Another way to define and initialize a string

```
string name("Mary");
```

How to use the subscript operator to access individual characters

```
string name = "Mary";
cout << name[0] << endl;      // displays the first character 'M'
cout << name[1] << endl;      // displays the second character 'a'
name[3] = 'k';                // updates last character - name is now "Mark"
name[4] = 'y';                // out of bounds access
```

How to capitalize the first letter of a string

```
string name = "grace";
char letter = name[0];
name[0] = toupper(letter);         // name is "Grace"
```

How to compare strings for equality

```
string password1 = "secret";
string password2 = "Secret";
if (password1 == password2) {      // case-sensitive comparison
    cout << "Your passwords match!\n";
}
```

How to use a for loop to convert a string to all uppercase letters

```
string name = "grace";
for (int i = 0; i < name.size(); ++i) {
    char c = name[i];
    name[i] = toupper(c);
}                                  // name is "GRACE"
```

How to use a range-based for loop to create a new string of uppercase letters

```
string name = "grace";
string name_upper = "";
for (char c : name) {
    name_upper += toupper(c);
}                                  // name_upper is "GRACE"
```

Description

- A *string* is a sequence of char values.

- You can use the string class that's available from the C++ standard library to work with strings. When you do, you can think of a string as a vector of characters.

- You can use the subscript operator ([]) to access the individual characters of a string where 0 is the first character, 1 is the second character, and so on.

Figure 6-13   How to create and loop through a string

character in the string. Within the loop, a single statement converts each character to uppercase and appends it to the string named name_upper.

If you compare the range-based for loop with the standard for loop, you'll see that the range-based loop is easier to code. In addition, it's less prone to leading to out of bounds access. As a result, you should use the range-based for loop whenever it works for your purposes. However, if you need to use an index to access specific characters of a string, it typically makes sense to use a standard for loop.

How to use basic member functions of a string

Like a vector, a string provides many member functions that you can use to work with the string. Since a vector and a string are both containers for a sequence of elements, they both provide many of the same member functions. Figure 6-14 shows how to use many of these member functions, which provide a basic way to work with the characters of a string.

The first example shows that the size() and length() functions of the string class return the same information. As a result, the choice of which one to use is a matter of personal preference. Since the exact data type that's returned by these functions may vary depending on the compiler, this statement uses the auto keyword to define the size and length variables. Then, the C++ compiler can infer the correct data type for this variable.

The second example shows how to use the back() function to check if the last character in the string is a newline character (\n). If it is, this code uses the pop_back() function to remove the newline character from the end of the string.

The third example shows how to use the empty() function to make sure the user has entered a string. To do that, the first three statements get the name of a movie from the user. Then, the fourth statement checks if the move name is empty. If it is, this code displays a message that indicates that the move name is required.

The fourth example shows how to use the clear() function to remove all characters from a string. This example assumes that the variable named line is a string object. If it is, calling the clear() function removes all characters from this string.

Some basic member functions of the string class

Function	Description
`size()`	Returns the number of characters in the string.
`length()`	Returns the number of characters in the string.
`empty()`	Returns true if the string contains no characters.
`push_back(char)`	Adds the specified character to the end of the string.
`pop_back()`	Removes the last character in the string.
`back()`	Returns a reference to the last character in the string.
`front()`	Returns a reference to the first character in the string.
`at(i)`	Returns a reference to the character at index i. Throws an out_of_range exception if i is out of bounds.
`clear()`	Removes all the characters in the string.

How to check the size of a string

```
string name = "grace hopper";
auto size = name.size();        // size is 12
auto length = name.length();    // length is 12
```

How to remove the last character of a string

```
string name = "bjarne stroustrup\n";
auto size = name.size();            // size is 18
if (size > 0 && name.back() == '\n') {
    name.pop_back();                // remove last char
}
size = name.size();                 // size is 17
```

How to make sure a user has entered a string

```
string movie_name;
cout << "Enter movie name: ";
getline(cin, movie_name);

if (movie_name.empty()) {
    cout << "Error! Movie name is required.\n";
}
```

How to remove all characters from a string

```
line.clear();
```

Description

- The string class provides many of the same member functions as the vector class. You can use these functions to work with the characters of the string.

Figure 6-14   How to use basic member functions of a string

How to search a string

Figure 6-15 shows how to search a string for a specified string or character. Here, the first example shows how to use the find() and rfind() functions. To start, this code defines a string named name that contains a value of "grace hopper".

The first find() function searches the name string for a string of "grace" and stores the index that's returned in a variable whose type is automatically inferred by the compiler. Here, using the auto type is helpful because the integer type that's returned by the functions presented in this figure may vary depending on the compiler. Since a string of "grace" begins at an index of 0, the first find() function returns a value of 0. The second find() function searches for a character of 'g'. Since this character is at the index of 0, this function returns a value of 0. This shows that the find() function works with strings or characters.

The next two find() functions show how to search for multiple occurrences of a string or character. Here, the third find() function searches for a character of 'r'. This returns a value of 1, which is the index for the first occurrence of this character. The fourth find() function searches for the same character starting at the index of 2, which is the first character after the 'r' that was found by the previous statement. This returns a value of 11, which is the index for the second occurrence of this character.

Finally, the fifth find() function searches for the character 'g' starting at the index of 1. This returns a value of -1, which indicates that the character wasn't found by this search.

The rfind() function works like the find() function, but in reverse. In other words, the rfind() function begins searching at the back of the string and searches towards the front.

The find_first_of() and find_last_of() functions provide a way to search for the first or last character in the specified string of characters. For instance, the second example shows how to use the find_first_of() function to find the index of the first numeric character. To do that, this code specifies a string that contains all of the numeric characters ("0123456789"). Then, this code checks if this index is equal to -1. If it is, the string does not contain a numeric character.

The find_first_not_of() and find_last_not_of() functions work similarly, but they return the index of the first character that does not match the specified string. For instance, the third example shows how to use the find_first_not_of() function to get the index of the first character in the string that is not a space, tab, or newline character. Here, the indexes of 0 through 5 correspond to a tab character, a newline character, and four space characters. As a result, this example returns an index of 6, which is the index for the 'b' character.

Some member functions for searching strings

Function	Description
`find(str)`	Returns the index of the first occurrence of the specified string or char.
`find(str, i)`	Returns the index of the first occurrence of the specified string or char starting from the specified index.
`rfind(str)`	The same as the find() function except the search starts from the back of the string and searches toward the front.
`rfind(str, i)`	The same as the find() function with an index except the search starts from the index and searches toward the front.
`find_first_of(str)`	Returns the index of the first occurrence of a character that matches any of the characters in the specified string.
`find_last_of(str)`	Returns the index of the last occurrence of a character that matches any of the characters in the specified string.
`find_first_not_of(str)`	Returns the index of the first occurrence of a character that does not match any of the characters in the specified string.
`find_last_not_of(str)`	Returns the index of the last occurrence of a character that does not match any of the characters in the specified string.

How to use the find() and rfind() functions

```
string name = "grace hopper";

// find() function
auto index = name.find("grace"); // index is 0
index = name.find('g');          // index is 0
index = name.find('r');          // index is 1
index = name.find('r', 2);       // index is 11
index = name.find('g', 1);       // index is -1

// rfind() function
index = name.rfind('r');         // index is 11
index = name.rfind('r', 10);     // index is 1
index = name.rfind('h', 5);      // index is -1
index = name.rfind("grace");     // index is 0
```

How to check if a string contains at least one numeric character

```
string password = "superSecret";
auto index = password.find_first_of("0123456789");
if (index == -1) {
    cout << "This password does NOT contain a number. Try again.\n";
}
```

How to get the index of the first character that's not whitespace

```
string name = "\t\n    bjarne stroustrup";
auto index = name.find_first_not_of(" \n\t");  // index is 6
```

Description

- The find() and rfind() functions accept arguments of the string or char type.

- All of these functions return a value of -1 if they can't find what you're searching for.

Figure 6-15   How to search a string

How to work with substrings

A *substring* is a string that's extracted from another string. To extract a substring from a string, you can use the substr() function as shown in figure 6-16.

The first example shows how to get the first and last names of a full name. Here, the first statement defines a variable for storing a full name and initializes it to a name that includes four parts separated by spaces. Then, the second statement defines variables for storing the first and last names and initializes them to empty strings.

After setting up the variables, the next group of statements gets the first name. To do that, it searches the name string for the first space character and gets its index. Then, to make sure that this space character was found, it checks if its index is greater than -1. If so, it gets the first name by using the substr() function to specify a starting index of 0 and a length that's equal to the index of the first space. This works because the index of the space character is 5, which is also the length of the first name.

After getting the first name, the next group of statements gets the last name. To do that, this code uses the rfind() function to search the string for the last space character and gets its index. Then, this code checks if the character was found. If so, it increments this index to get the index for the character after the space character. Next, this code protects against out of bounds access by checking if the index is within a valid range for the string. Remember, a valid index is greater than -1 and less than the length of the string. If the index is within a valid range, this code uses the substr() function to get the string. To do that, it specifies the starting index, but it doesn't specify the length. As a result, the substr() function gets the substring from the starting index to the end of the string.

The second example shows how to strip whitespace from the beginning of the string. To start, it uses the find_first_not_of() function to find the first character that is not a tab, newline, or space character. Then, it checks if the index is greater than zero. If so, it uses the substr() function to return a substring that starts at the first character that's not whitespace and continues until the end of the string.

The third example shows how to get the domain part of an email address from a string that contains an email address. Here, the code starts by getting the index of the first and only at character (@) and the index of the last dot character (.). After getting these indexes, this code checks if they are both greater than -1, which indicates that the characters exist in the string. If these characters are found, this code increments the index for the at character to get the index of the next character. Next, this code checks if the index for the at character is still within a valid range. More specifically, it checks if the at character is less than the size of the string and less than the index of the dot character. If so, this code calculates the number of characters for the length of the domain by subtracting the at index from the dot index. Finally, it uses the substr() function to get the domain by specifying the starting index and the length of the substring.

A member function for getting part of a string

Function	Description
`substr(i)`	Returns a new string starting at the specified index and continuing to the end of the string.
`substr(i, len)`	Returns a new string starting at the specified index and spanning the specified length.

How to get the first and last names of a name

```
string name = "Grace Brewster Murray Hopper";
string first_name = "", last_name = "";

auto index = name.find(' ');              // index is 5
if (index > -1)
    first_name = name.substr(0, index);   // first name is "Grace"

index = name.rfind(' ');                  // index is 21
if (index > -1) {
    ++index;                              // index is 22
    if (index < name.length())
        last_name = name.substr(index);   // last name is "Hopper"
}
```

How to strip whitespace from the beginning of a string

```
string name = "\t\n    bjarne stroustrup";
auto i = name.find_first_not_of(" \n\t"); // get index
if (i > 0)
    name = name.substr(i);                     // strip whitesphace
cout << name << endl;                          // displays "bjarne stroustrup"
```

How to get the domain part of an email address

```
string email = "grace.hopper@yahoo.com";
string domain = "";

auto at_index = email.find('@');
auto dot_index = email.rfind('.');
if (at_index > -1 && dot_index > -1) {
    ++at_index;                                      // get index of next char
    if (at_index < email.length() && at_index < dot_index) {
        int length = dot_index - at_index;
        domain = email.substr(at_index, length); // domain is "yahoo"
    }
}
```

Description

- A *substring* is part of a string. When you use the substr() function to get a substring, it creates a new string and doesn't modify the original string.

Figure 6-16   How to work with substrings

How to modify a string

In chapter 2, you learned how to use the **+=** operator to append one string to the end of another string. Now, figure 6-17 shows some other ways that you can use member functions to modify a string.

The first example shows how you can use the insert() function to insert a string at a specified index in another string. Here, the first statement creates a string named months that contains three-letter abbreviations for two months with each month followed by a space. The second statement inserts a string of "Mar " at index 4, which is just after the first month. This shifts all characters currently in the string from index 4 and on back by four indexes. The third statement inserts a string of "Jan " at the beginning of the string. This shifts all other characters in the string back by four indexes. Although it isn't efficient to shift characters in a string like this, performance is typically adequate for strings that don't contain a large number of characters. The fourth statement inserts a string of "May " at the end of the string. As a result, the final string is "Jan Feb Mar Apr May ".

The second example shows how to use the erase() function to delete part of a string. Here, the second statement deletes four characters starting at the index of 0. As a result, it deletes the first four characters of the string. This shifts all other characters forward by four. Just as when you insert characters into a string, shifting characters isn't efficient, but performance is typically adequate for strings that don't contain a large number of characters.

The third example shows how to replace all instances of a placeholder with a specified string. Here, the code initializes a message string that contains a placeholder of "<st>" in two places. Then, it defines two strings to store a placeholder of "<st>" and a replacement of "Oregon" as well as an index that will indicate the position of the placeholder in the message string. Next, this code begins a while loop that continues until it replaces the placeholders with the replacement string.

Within this loop, the first statement uses the find() function to get the index of the placeholder. The first time through the loop, this search starts at the index of 0, which is the first character in the string. Then, this code checks whether the index of the placeholder has been found. If it has, this code uses the replace() function to replace the placeholder string with the replacement string. Then, it jumps to the top of the loop, which again checks whether the placeholder has been found. This time, it uses the most recent index as its starting point. This continues until all placeholders have been replaced. Then, the find() function returns an index of -1, and the loop ends.

The fourth example shows how to replace all instances of one character with another character. In particular, it shows how to replace the dash character with the space character. To do that, you don't need to use the replace() function, which is designed to work with strings. Instead, you can just use a standard for loop to loop through each character.

In this example, the first statement creates a string that contains a credit card number that separates some numbers with dashes. Then, this code uses a standard for loop to check each character to determine if it's the dash character.

Some member functions for modifying a string

Function	Description
`insert(i, str)`	Inserts the specified string at the specified index.
`erase(i, len)`	Removes the specified number of characters starting at the specified index.
`replace(i, len, str)`	Replaces the characters in the string starting at the specified index and spanning the specified number of characters with the specified string.

How to insert a string into another string

```
string months = "Feb Apr ";
months.insert(4, "Mar ");                 // insert after "Feb "
months.insert(0, "Jan ");                 // insert at beginning
months.insert(months.length(), "May ");   // insert at end
cout << months << endl;                    // displays "Jan Feb Mar Apr May "
```

How to delete part of a string

```
string months = "Jan Feb Mar Apr May ";
months.erase(0, 4);                       // erase "Jan "
cout << months << endl;                    // displays "Feb Mar Apr May "
```

How to replace all instances of a placeholder

```
string message = "Welcome to <st>! <st> is a great state!\n";
string placeholder = "<st>";
string state = "Oregon";
int index = 0;
while (index > -1) {
    index = message.find(placeholder, index);
    if (index > -1)
        message.replace(index, placeholder.length(), state);
}
cout << message; // displays "Welcome to Oregon! Oregon is a great state!"
```

How to replace all instances of one character with another character

```
string cc_number = "4012-881022-88810";
for (int i = 0; i < cc_number.length(); ++i) {
    if (cc_number[i] == '-')
        cc_number[i] = ' ';
}
cout << cc_number << endl; // displays "4012 881022 88810"
```

Description

- You can use member functions to modify a string by inserting another string into it, deleting part of the string, or replacing part of the string with another string.

- To replace a single character with another character, you can use a standard for loop and the subscript operator.

Figure 6-17   How to modify a string

If so, it uses the subscript operator to replace the dash character with the space character. This shows that looping through the characters in a string is sometimes the simplest and most efficient way to process a string.

How to check characters within a string

In chapter 2, you learned how to use the toupper() and tolower() functions to convert a char to uppercase or lowercase. Now, figure 6-18 shows how to use some other functions to get information about a character, such as whether it is an uppercase or lowercase letter, a number, punctuation, or whitespace. It's common to use these functions to check characters within a string.

In the first example, for instance, the islower() function checks whether the first character in a string is a lowercase letter. If it is, this code replaces that letter with an uppercase letter. This isn't necessary for the code to work correctly, but it may improve efficiency since it doesn't execute the statement that converts the lowercase letter to an uppercase letter if the first character of the string isn't a letter or is already uppercase.

The second example, on the other hand, uses the ispunct() function to check whether any character in a string is a punctuation character. Here, the first statement defines a password that contains a punctuation character (the # character), and the second statement defines a bool variable named contains_punctuation that indicates whether the string contains a punctuation character. After the first two statements, this code loops through each character in the string.

Within the loop, an if statement uses the ispunct() function to check whether the current character is a punctuation character. If it is, the first statement sets the contains_punctuation variable to true. Then, since there's no need to continue checking the rest of the characters, this code executes a break statement to exit the loop. This second statement isn't necessary for the code to work correctly, but it improves the efficiency of the code.

When you code the functions shown in this figure as part of a Boolean expression, they work as you would expect. However, you should remember that they indicate true by returning a non-zero int value, which is typically 1. Conversely, they indicate a false value by returning value of 0. As a result, if you display the values returned by these functions on the console, the console displays int values, not the true and false keywords.

Functions for checking the value of a character

Function	Description
islower(char)	Returns true if the character is a lowercase letter.
isupper(char)	Returns true if the character is an uppercase letter.
isalpha(char)	Returns true if the character is a letter of the alphabet.
isdigit(char)	Returns true if the character is a numeric digit (0, 1, 2, 3, 4, 5, 6, 7, 8, or 9).
isalnum(char)	Returns true if the character is an alphanumeric character (a letter or a number).
isspace(char)	Returns true if the character is a whitespace character such as a space, a tab (\t), or a newline (\n) character.
ispunct(char)	Returns true if the character is a punctuation character. This includes every printable character that isn't a letter, number, or whitespace.
isprint(char)	Returns true if the character is a printable character. This includes the space character, but not other whitespace characters.

How to check if a string starts with a lowercase letter

```cpp
string name = "bjarne";
if (islower(name[0])) {              // if lowercase letter
    name[0] = toupper(name[0]);      // convert to uppercase
}
```

How to check if a string contains punctuation

```cpp
string password = "super#Secret007";
bool contains_punctuation = false;
for (char c : password) {                    // loop through each char
    if (ispunct(c)) {                        // if char is number
        contains_punctuation = true;         // set variable to true
        break;                               // exit loop
    }
}
```

Description

- C++ provides functions that you can use to get information about a character, such as whether it is an upper- or lowercase letter, a number, punctuation, or whitespace.

- These functions return an integer that corresponds to a true or false value. For a true value, these functions return a non-zero number, typically 1. For a false value, these functions return 0.

Figure 6-18   How to check characters within a string

The Create Account program

Figure 6-19 shows a Create Account program that prompts the user to enter a full name and a password. To make sure the user enters a full name, this code checks to make sure it contains a space. Then, it assumes that the first name is all characters that lead up to the space character. In addition, this code checks that the user enters a password that has at least 8 characters and includes a number as well as a special punctuation character.

The code for this program starts by including the necessary header files, such as the header file that contains the string class. Then, within the main() function, the code defines variables to store the full name and the first name. It also defines a bool variable named valid_name that's initialized to false. This variable is used by the while loop that follows to determine when the loop ends. Here, the conditional expression for the while loop is coded like this:

```
!valid_name
```

That makes sense if you remember that a bool variable stores a true or false value. In this case, the loop is executed until the variable is not false, or until it is true. This conditional expression could also be coded like this:

```
valid_name != true
```

However, the first technique is more concise and more commonly used by professional programmers.

In this case, the while loop continues until the user enters a full name that includes a space. Within this loop, the first two statements get the full name from the user. Then, a group of statements strips whitespace from the front of this string. To do that, it uses the find_first_not_of() function to get the index of the first character that isn't a tab, newline, or space character. If the string starts with whitespace, this code uses the substr() function to strip the whitespace from the string.

After stripping the whitespace, this code continues by getting the first name from the full name. To do that, it begins by using the find() function to find the index of the first space character in the full name. If this function returns a value of -1, it means that the string doesn't contain a space. In that case, the code displays a message that indicates that the user must enter a full name. Since this if statement is the last statement in the loop, this causes program execution to jump to the top of the loop, which gets another full name from the user.

If the find() function returns a value other than -1, that value is the index of the first space character in the string. Then, this code uses that index with the substr() function to get the first name from the string. Finally, it sets the valid_name flag to true to exit the loop.

As you review this code, note that it works correctly even if the user enters one or more spaces at the beginning of the full name. In that case, the code strips these spaces. That way, the find() function finds the first space that comes after non-whitespace characters. At this point, the user could still enter only a first name by entering a first name followed by a space. However, if you wanted, you could prevent this by adding code that strips whitespace from the end of the string.

The console

```
Create Account

Enter full name: grace
You must enter your full name. Please try again.
Enter full name: grace hopper

Enter password: secret
Password must be at least 8 characters.
Password must include a number.
Password must include a special character.
Please try again.
Enter password: superSecret123
Password must include a special character.
Please try again.
Enter password: super#Secret123

Hi Grace,
Thanks for creating an account!
```

The code

```cpp
#include <iostream>
#include <string>

using namespace std;

int main()
{
    cout << "Create Account\n\n";

    // get full name and parse first name
    string full_name;
    string first_name;
    bool valid_name = false;
    while (!valid_name) {
        cout << "Enter full name: ";
        getline(cin, full_name);

        // strip whitespace from front
        auto i = full_name.find_first_not_of(" \n\t");
        if (i > -1) {
            full_name = full_name.substr(i);
        }

        // get first name
        auto space_index = full_name.find(' ');
        if (space_index == -1) {
            cout << "You must enter your full name. Please try again.\n";
        }
        else {
            first_name = full_name.substr(0, space_index);
            valid_name = true;
        }
    }
    cout << endl;
```

Figure 6-19   The Create Account program (part 1 of 2)

Part 2 of figure 6-19 begins by defining a string variable to store the password and a bool variable named valid_password that's initialized to a value of false. This Boolean flag is used to determine when the while loop that follows ends. In this case, the loop continues until the valid_password flag is true, which means that the user entered a valid password.

Within the loop, the first statement sets the Boolean flag to true. As a result, the loop will exit unless some code later in the loop sets this flag to false.

The next two statements get the password entered by the user. Then, the if statement that follows checks if the password has less than 8 characters. If it does, this code displays a message that indicates that the password must be at least eight characters and sets the valid_password flag to false. Otherwise, the if statement doesn't execute any code. Either way, program execution continues on to the rest of the code in the loop.

The next group of statements check if the password includes a number. If not, this code displays an appropriate message and sets the valid_password flag to false. Otherwise, the if statement doesn't execute any code. Either way, program execution continues with the rest of the code in the loop.

The next group of statements checks to make sure the password includes a special character. To do that, this code loops through each character in the password and uses the ispunct() function to check if it's a punctuation character. If it is, the code sets the special_character flag to true and exits the for loop. Then, it checks whether the special_character flag is false. If it is, the code displays an appropriate message and sets the valid_password flag to false. Otherwise, the if statement doesn't execute any code. Either way, program execution continues to the last if statement in the loop.

The last if statement checks the valid_password flag to determine if the password is valid. If not, it displays a message that asks the user to try again, and program execution continues at the top of the loop. Otherwise, the valid_password flag is true, and program execution exits the loop and continues on to the rest of the code.

After the loop that gets the password, this code makes sure that the first name begins with an uppercase letter but uses lowercase letters for the rest of the name. Here, the first statement gets the first letter (the one at index 0), and the second statement uses the toupper() function to convert the letter to uppercase. Then, a for statement loops through the rest of the indexes starting at 1. Within this loop, the tolower() function converts the letter at each index to lowercase.

Finally, the last statement displays a message that uses the name stored in the first_name variable to thank the user for creating an account. As a result, this message should display the user's first name with an initial cap like "Grace" even if the user entered "grace", "GRACE", or "gRaCe".

As with most programs presented in this book, the Create Account program leaves plenty of room for improvement. As mentioned earlier, you could add code that strips whitespace from the end of the full name. That way, a first name followed by a space would not be a valid full name. Or, you could add code that prevents a user from entering a full name that starts with a number or a punctuation character.

The code (continued)

```cpp
// get the password
string password;
bool valid_password = false;
while (!valid_password) {
    // set valid flag
    valid_password = true;

    // get password
    cout << "Enter password: ";
    getline(cin, password);

    // make sure password has at least 8 characters
    if (password.length() < 8) {
        cout << "Password must be at least 8 characters.\n";
        valid_password = false;
    }

    // make sure password includes a number
    auto index = password.find_first_of("0123456789");
    if (index == -1) {
        cout << "Password must include a number.\n";
        valid_password = false;
    }

    // make sure password includes a special character
    bool special_character = false;
    for (char c : password) {
        if (ispunct(c)) {
            special_character = true;
            break;                          // exit for loop
        }
    }
    if (!special_character) {
        cout << "Password must include a special character.\n";
        valid_password = false;
    }

    // display message if password is not valid
    if (!valid_password) {
        cout << "Please try again.\n";
    }
}
cout << endl;

// make sure first name uses initial cap and then lower case
char letter = first_name[0];
first_name[0] = toupper(letter);
for (int i = 1; i < first_name.length(); ++i) {
    letter = first_name[i];
    first_name[i] = tolower(letter);
}

// display welcome message
cout << "Hi " << first_name << ",\n"
    << "Thanks for creating an account!\n\n";
}
```

Figure 6-19   The Create Account program (part 2 of 2)

The Word Jumble program

Figure 6-20 shows the code for a Word Jumble program that illustrates some of the skills presented in this chapter for working with vectors and strings. This program lets the user guess the word from a jumble of letters. If unable to guess the word, the user can enter "hint" to display the next letter of the word. Or, the user can enter "exit" to exit the program.

The code for this program begins by including the necessary header files, such as the header files that contain the vector and string classes. In addition, it includes the cstdlib and ctime header files that contain the functions needed to get a random number.

Within the main() function, the code defines and initializes a vector that contains the possible words for the jumble. At this point, this list only contains three words. However, it would be easy to modify this code so it included more words. One way to do that would be to read a list of words from a file into the vector.

Once the vector is ready, this code gets a random word from the vector. To do that, it uses the time(), srand(), and rand() functions with the modulus operator (%) to get a random integer that ranges from 0 to one less than the size of the vector. In other words, it randomly picks a valid index for the vector. Then, this code gets the word that corresponds to that index. (If you need to refresh your memory on how to use the time(), srand(), and rand() functions and the modulus operator to get a random number, please see figure 2-13 in chapter 2.)

After getting the word, the code jumbles the word. To do that, it starts by defining a string variable to store the jumbled word and initializes it to the same string that's stored in the unjumbled word. It also defines an auto variable named length to store the length of the word. Then, it executes a loop once for each character in the word. To do that, it uses a counter variable named index1 that will be used to refer to the characters in the unjumbled word, starting with the character at index 0.

Within the loop, the first statement gets a random number between 0 and one less than the length of the word by using the modulus operator with the rand() function and the length variable. The result is assigned to a second int variable named index2 that will be used to get a second character from the word. Then, this code swaps the two characters at the first and second indexes of the jumbled word. To do that, the second statement gets the character at the first index of the word and temporarily stores it in a variable named temp. The third statement gets the character at the second index of the word and assigns it to the first index of the word. And the fourth statement gets the original character from the first index, which is currently in the temp variable, and moves it to the second index. When this loop finishes, the characters in the word should be sufficiently jumbled.

The console

```
Let's Play Word Jumble!

Enter 'hint' for a hint.
Enter 'exit' to exit.

The jumble is...URITGA

Your guess: hint
Hint: G _ _ _ _ _

Your guess: hint
Hint: G U _ _ _ _

Your guess: guitar
Congratulations! You guessed it.
```

The code

```cpp
#include <iostream>
#include <string>
#include <vector>
#include <cstdlib>
#include <ctime>

using namespace std;

int main() {
    cout << "Let's Play Word Jumble!\n"
        << "\n"
        << "Enter 'hint' for a hint.\n"
        << "Enter 'exit' to exit.\n\n";

    // define a vector of possible words
    vector<string> words { "guitar", "violin", "tapestry" };

    // get random word from vector
    srand(time(nullptr));
    int index = rand() % words.size();
    string word = words[index];

    // jumble the word
    string jumbled_word = word;
    auto length = word.size();
    for (int index1 = 0; index1 < length; ++index1) {
        int index2 = rand() % length;
        char temp = jumbled_word[index1];
        jumbled_word[index1] = jumbled_word[index2];
        jumbled_word[index2] = temp;
    }
```

Figure 6-20   The Word Jumble program (part 1 of 2)

Part 2 of figure 6-20 begins by displaying the jumbled word in uppercase characters. To do that, the code uses a range-based for loop to loop through each character and convert it to uppercase. However, the toupper() function returns an int value that corresponds to an ASCII character code. As a result, this code uses a static cast to convert the int value to a char value.

After displaying the jumbled word, this code defines two variables. First, it defines a variable that counts the number of hints that the user has requested. Then, it defines a variable that stores the guess entered by the user. After that, this code begins the main loop of the program.

Within this loop, the first three statements get the guess from the user and discard any extra data in the console input stream. Then, this code checks if the user guessed the word successfully. If so, the code prints a message of congratulations and breaks out of the loop, which ends the program.

If the user enters "hint" instead of guessing the word, the code displays a hint for the user. To do that, the code loops through the indexes for every character in the string. Then, it checks if the index is less than the hint count. If so, it displays the letter in uppercase followed by a space. Otherwise, it displays an underscore character followed by a space. As a result, the first time the user enters "hint", this code displays the first letter of the word. For the word "guitar", this would display:

G _ _ _ _ _

After displaying the hint, this code increments the variable that stores the count of hints. That way, the next time the user enters "hint", the program will display another character in the word.

If the user enters "exit", the code displays a message that indicates that the program is ending. Then, it breaks out of the loop, which ends the program.

Finally, if the user doesn't guess the word or enter "hint" or "exit", the code displays a message that indicates the guess was not correct. Then, program execution jumps to the top of the loop, which prompts the user for another guess.

The code (continued)

```
// display the jumbled word in uppercase
cout << "The jumble is...";
for (char c : jumbled_word) {
    cout << static_cast<char>(toupper(c));
}
cout << "\n\n";

// loop until the user guesses the jumble or enters 'exit'
int hint_count = 1;
string guess = "";
while (true) {
    cout << "Your guess: ";
    cin >> guess;
    cin.ignore(1000, '\n');   // discard input up to end of line

    if (guess == word) {
        cout << "Congratulations! You guessed it.\n\n";
        break;
    }
    else if (guess == "hint") {
        cout << "Hint: ";
        for (int i = 0; i < word.length(); ++i) {
            if (i < hint_count) {
                cout << static_cast<char>(toupper(word[i])) << ' ';
            }
            else {
                cout << '_' << ' ';
            }
        }
        cout << "\n\n";
        ++hint_count;
    }
    else if (guess == "exit") {
        cout << "Bye! Let's play again soon.\n\n";
        break;
    }
    else {
        cout << "Nope. Try again!\n\n";
    }
}
}
```

Figure 6-20   The Word Jumble program (part 2 of 2)

Perspective

Now that you've completed this chapter, you should be able to work with any of the fundamental data types you need in your programs. In addition, you should be able to use vectors and strings whenever you need them.

In this chapter, the Temperature Manager program uses two vectors to store two columns of data for low and high temperatures. For now, this technique is adequate. However, this technique gets unwieldy if you needed to store many columns of data. Fortunately, C++ provides other ways to store and manipulate a table of data, and you'll learn more about how to do that starting in chapter 9.

Terms

fundamental data types	promote data
built-in data types	demote data
integers	scope resolution operator
floating-point numbers	integer overflow
significant digits	integer underflow
single-precision number	Standard Template Library (STL)
double-precision number	containers
characters	subscript operator
Boolean value	index
scientific notation	vector
ASCII character set	element
variable	out of bounds access
define a variable	out of range access
initialize a variable	initialization list
assignment operator	range-based for loop
constant	push an element
casting data	string
type coercion	substring

Summary

- C++ provides *fundamental data types* to store *integers*, *floating-point numbers*, *characters*, and *Boolean values*.

- To express the value of a floating-point number, you can use *scientific notation*.

- *Variables* store data that varies as a program runs. *Constants* store data that remains constant as a program runs. You use the *assignment operator* to assign values to variables and constants.

- If you perform assignment or arithmetic operations with different data types, C++ automatically converts or *casts* the types using its rules of *type coercion*.

- When you use different data types in an expression, C++ automatically *promotes* lower ranking data types to the next higher data type. When you assign a value to a variable that has a lower ranking data type, C++ automatically *demotes* the value to that data type. This can result in the loss of some data.

- When an integer variable is assigned a value that's too big for its type, it will *overflow*, or wrap around to the type's minimum. When an integer variable is assigned a value that's too small for its type, it will *underflow*, or wrap around to the type's maximum.

- The *Standard Template Library* (*STL*) contains many data types in addition to the fundamental data types. The STL types that contain collections of other data types are often called *containers*.

- A *vector* contains a sequence of *elements* of the same data type. You can use the *subscript operator* (`[]`) to access the elements of a vector.

- *Out of bounds access* occurs if your code specifies an index that's outside the range of valid indexes. Since out of bounds access leads to unexpected results, you should always write your code to prevent it.

- A *range-based for loop* automatically iterates over every element in a vector or string without having to specify a counter or use the subscript operator.

- A *string* contains a sequence of char values. You can think of a string as a vector of characters.

Exercise 6-1 Store the values for future value calculations in vectors

In this exercise, you'll modify the Future Value program from chapter 4 so it stores the values for each future value calculation in vectors and then displays a table of those values when the program ends. When you're done, a test run should look something like this:

```
The Future Value Calculator

Enter monthly investment:    100
Enter yearly interest rate:  5
Enter number of years:       10
Future value:                15592.93

Continue? (y/n): y

Enter monthly investment:    150
Enter yearly interest rate:  5
Enter number of years:       10
Future value:                23389.39

Continue? (y/n): n

    Monthly  Yearly
 investment    rate  Years  Future Value
     100.00    5.00     10       15592.93
     150.00    5.00     10       23389.39
```

Open the program

1. Open the project or solution named future_value in this folder:
   `ex_starts\ch06_ex1_future_value`

2. Review the code and then run the program to refresh your memory about how it works.

Store the calculation values in vectors

3. Define four vectors that can be used to store the monthly investment, yearly interest rate, years, and future value for each calculation. To do that, you'll need to include the vector header file.

4. After each future value calculation, add the current values for the monthly investment, yearly interest rate, years, and future value to the end of the corresponding vector.

5. When the user is done calculating future values, use a for loop to display the values in the vectors as shown above. The floating-point values should be displayed in fixed-point notation and rounded to two decimal places. The result that's displayed for each calculation should also be displayed in fixed-point notation rounded to two decimal places.

Exercise 6-2   Enhance the Create Account program

In this exercise, you'll enhance the Create Account program so it accepts an email address from the user and then checks to make sure it's valid. When you're done, a test run should look something like this:

```
Create Account

Enter full name: grace hopper

Enter password: super#Secret123

Enter email: grace@yahoo
The email must include a dot character (.).
The domain name of the email must have two or three characters.
Please try again.
Enter email: grace.hopper@yahoo.x
The domain name of the email must have two or three characters.
Please try again.
Enter email: grace.hopper@yahoo.com

Hi Grace,
Thanks for creating an account!
```

1. Open the project or solution named create_account in this folder:

    ex_starts\ch06_ex2_create_account

2. Add a while loop that gets an email address until a valid address is entered. You can pattern this loop after the loop that gets a valid password.

3. Within the while loop, start by checking that the email includes an at sign (@) and a dot character (.).

4. If the email address includes an at sign and a dot character, check that the rest of the characters in the address are alphanumeric, an at sign, a dot character, an underscore (_), or a dash (-). To do that, you can use a range-based for loop.

5. Check that there is at least one character before the at sign and the last dot character and two or three characters after the dot character. To do that, you can use the indexes for the at sign and the last dot character and the length of the email address.

7

How to code functions

So far, the programs you've seen in this book have consisted of a single function, the main() function. As your programs get longer and more complex, though, you'll need a way to break them down into manageable chunks of reusable code. One way to do that is to code your own functions that can be called by the main() function.

In this chapter, you'll learn a variety of skills for declaring, defining, and calling functions. In addition, you'll learn how to organize your functions into header files and namespaces. When you do that, you'll be able to access these functions from multiple programs just as you can the functions in the C++ standard library.

How to start coding your own functions

A *function* is a named block of code that performs a task. Functions are useful because they provide a way to divide the code for a program into shorter, more manageable chunks of code. This makes your code easier to read, maintain, reuse, test, and debug.

How to define and call a function

Figure 7-1 starts by showing the syntax for *defining* a function. To do that, you code the data type that's returned by the function. Or, if the function doesn't return any data, you can code the void keyword. Then, you code a name for the function, a set of parentheses, an optional list of *parameters* within the parentheses, and a set of braces. Within the braces, you can code one or more statements that are executed when the function is called.

To *call,* or *invoke*, a function, you use the same syntax that you've been using for calling functions from the standard library. That is, you code the function name and a set of parentheses. Then, if the function requires one or more arguments, you code the arguments in the same sequence as the parameters that are defined by the function, and you use commas to separate the arguments.

For instance, since the function in the first example doesn't return any data, you code the void keyword for its return type. And since it doesn't require any arguments, you don't code any parameters within its parentheses. As a result, you call it by coding the name of the function followed by a set of parentheses.

The function in the second example defines one parameter. To do that, it specifies a data type of string and a name of title. As a result, the statement that calls it provides an argument that is a variable of type string. Then, the body of the function displays that string on the console followed by a blank line.

The function in the third example defines two parameters and returns a double value. Then, the body of the function divides the values of the two parameters, rounds the result of the calculation to 1 decimal place, and uses a *return statement* to return the result to the calling statement. In this example, the calling statement assigns the value that's returned to a variable named mpg.

When you code a calling statement, the names that you use for the arguments don't have to be the same as the parameter names in the function definition. In the third example, for instance, the calling statement passes arguments named miles_driven and gallons_used, but the function defines parameters named miles and gallons. However, the arguments in the calling statement must be in the same sequence as the parameters in the function definition.

When you name a function, it's a good practice to start the name with a verb. In addition, the name should do a reasonable job of describing or implying what the purpose of the function is. To do that, you can follow the verb with a noun or an adjective followed by a noun. That makes it easier for you and other programmers to understand what your functions are doing.

Note that this book uses the term *parameter* when referring to a function definition and the term *argument* when referring to calling statements. In practice, programmers often use these terms interchangeably.

The syntax for defining a function

```
return_type function_name([parameter_list]) {
    statements
}
```

A function that doesn't accept arguments or return data

How to define it

```
void display_title() {
    cout << "Miles Per Gallon Calculator" << endl << endl;
}
```

How to call it

```
display_title();                                // displays title
```

A function that accepts an argument but doesn't return data

How to define it

```
void display_title(string title) {
    cout << title << endl << endl;
}
```

How to call it

```
string title = "Miles Per Gallon Calculator";
display_title(title);                           // displays specified title
```

A function that accepts two arguments and returns a double value

How to define it

```
double calculate_mpg(double miles, double gallons) {
    double mpg = miles / gallons;
    mpg = round(mpg * 10) / 10;     // round to 1 decimal place
    return mpg;
}
```

How to call it

```
double miles_driven = 500.0;
double gallons_used = 14.0;
double mpg = calculate_mpg(miles_driven, gallons_used); // mpg = 35.7
```

Description

- A *function* is a block of code that can be *called* by other statements.

- To *define* a function, code the function's return type, name, a set of parentheses, and a set of braces. Within the parentheses, you can code zero or more *parameters*, separating parameters with commas. Within the braces, you can code one more statements for the body of the function.

- To *call*, or *invoke*, a function, code the name of the function and a set of parentheses. Within the parentheses, code any arguments separated by commas. The arguments must be in the same sequence as the parameters in the function.

- If a function uses the void keyword for its return type, it doesn't return any data. If a function specifies a return type, you must code a *return statement* that returns data of the specified type to the calling code.

Figure 7-1   How to define and call a function

The Miles Per Gallon program

Figure 7-2 should give you a better idea of how to code a program that consists of multiple functions. It shows a complete Miles Per Gallon program after it has been divided into a display_title() function that displays the title of the program, a calculate_mpg() function that calculates the miles per gallon, and a main() function. Here, the program starts by defining the first two functions. Then, it executes the main() function, which uses the first two functions.

The display_title() function doesn't return any data or require any arguments. It just contains a single statement that displays the title of the program followed by a blank line.

The calculate_mpg() function returns a double value and requires two double values as arguments. Then, the calling statement passes two arguments to it. In this case, the names of the arguments in the calling statements are the same as the names of the parameters in the function definition. Remember, though, that these names don't have to be the same. However, they have to be in the same sequence as they are in the function definition.

The last statement in the calculate_mpg() function is a return statement that returns the miles per gallon. This value is then stored in the mpg variable in the main() function. After that, the main() function continues by displaying the value stored in the mpg variable.

As you review this code, you might notice that using the display_title() function makes the program longer and more complicated than it would be if you just put its one line of code in the main() function. So, why would you want to create a function like this one? The short answer is that you probably wouldn't. One advantage to this approach is that the name of the function clearly describes what its code does. As a result, there's no need to include comments to describe the code within this function. Still, the code that displays the title is simple enough that there's not much need to describe it with comments anyway, so there's very little advantage to putting the title in its own function.

So, when does it make sense to code functions? For starters, it makes sense to code a function whenever you notice that you are writing the same or similar code in multiple locations in your program. For example, at the end of this chapter, you'll learn how to code a get_double() function to get a double value from the user instead of writing very similar code in multiple places as it is in this program. In programming, this is known as the *Don't Repeat Yourself* (*DRY*) principle. When you do this, your code is easier to debug and maintain.

Beyond that, it makes sense to break your code down into functions whenever it helps you organize your code in a way that makes it easier to understand and maintain. For example, when you have nested loops, it often makes sense to write a function for the inner loop. Because this reduces the depth of the nesting, it often makes the code easier to understand and maintain.

The console

```
Miles Per Gallon Calculator

Enter miles driven:        500
Enter gallons of gas used: 14
Miles per gallon:          35.7
```

The code

```cpp
#include <iostream>
#include <cmath>

using namespace std;

void display_title() {
    cout << "Miles Per Gallon Calculator\n\n";
}

double calculate_mpg(double miles, double gallons) {
    double mpg = miles / gallons;
    mpg = round(mpg * 10) / 10;     // round to 1 decimal place
    return mpg;
}

int main() {
    display_title();

    double miles;
    cout << "Enter miles driven:        ";
    cin >> miles;

    double gallons;
    cout << "Enter gallons of gas used: ";
    cin >> gallons;

    double mpg = calculate_mpg(miles, gallons);

    cout << "Miles per gallon:          " << mpg << endl << endl;

    return 0;
}
```

Description

- The main() function can call other functions that are defined before it.

Figure 7-2   The Miles Per Gallon program

How to declare a function

In the Miles Per Gallon program in the previous figure, the code only works because all functions used by the main() function are defined before the main() function. For example, if you moved the display_title() function after the main() function, the display_title() function wouldn't be available to the main() function because it would not yet be defined. However, if you *declare* a function before the main() function as shown in figure 7-3, you can *define* the function after the main() function.

There are two benefits to this approach. First, it makes it easy for you and other programmers to see the functions that are available to the main() function, along with their return types and parameters. Second, it allows you to code the definitions for these functions after the main() function in any sequence that you want. This allows you to organize your functions in a way that makes sense to you.

To declare a function, you code the function's return type, name, and parameters followed by a semicolon. Although the parameter names are optional, you should include them whenever they improve the readability of the code. In this figure, for instance, the first example shows some possible ways to code the display_title() and calculate_mpg() functions presented earlier in this chapter. Here, the second calculate_mpg() function is easier to read than the first function because the second function clearly shows that the first parameter specifies miles and the second parameter specifies gallons.

Since a well-coded function declaration should describe what a function does, it's also known as a *function prototype*. In this figure, for instance, the second example begins by coding two function prototypes. Then, the main() function uses these function prototypes. Finally, the rest of the program provides the code that defines the prototypes.

The syntax for declaring a function

```
return_type function_name([parameter_list]);
```

Code that declares functions

```
void display_title();

void display_title(string);                            // no param name
void display_title(string title);                      // param name

double calculate_mpg(double, double);                  // no param names
double calculate_mpg(double miles, double gallons);    // param names
```

Code that declares and defines two functions

```
#include <iostream>
#include <cmath>

using namespace std;

// declare two functions
void display_title();
double calculate_mpg(double miles, double gallons);

int main() {
    display_title();                                   // call function 1

    double miles = 500.0;
    double gallons = 14.0;
    double mpg = calculate_mpg(miles, gallons);     // call function 2
    cout << "Miles Per Gallon:              " << mpg;
}

// define function 1
void display_title() {
    cout << "Miles Per Gallon Calculator" << endl << endl;
}

// define function 2
double calculate_mpg(double miles, double gallons) {
    double mpg = miles / gallons;
    mpg = round(mpg * 10) / 10;      // round to 1 decimal place
    return mpg;
}
```

Description

- To *declare* a function, you code the function's return type, name, and parameters followed by a semicolon. In a declaration, the parameter names are optional. However, they're recommended because they improve the readability of the code.

- A function that has been declared is also known as a *function prototype*.

- If you declare a function before the main() function, you can define a corresponding function after the main() function.

Figure 7-3   How to declare a function

When and how to use local and global variables

Scope in a programming language refers to the visibility of variables. That is, it tells you where in your program you can access the variables and functions that you've defined.

In a C++ program, *global variables* are variables that are defined outside of all functions. These variables have *global scope* so they can be accessed by any function without passing them to that function. In contrast, *local variables* are variables that are defined within functions. They have *local scope*, which means that they can only be used within the functions that define them. In general, it's considered a good practice to avoid the use of global variables whenever possible because they often lead to programming problems.

The examples in figure 7-4 show how this works. In the first example, tax is a local variable in each of the two functions. As a result, the calc_tax() function needs to return the tax variable to the main() function that calls it. The main() function can't refer to the tax variable in the calc_tax() function directly. This is the preferred way to work with variables that are used by more than one function.

In the second example, though, tax is defined as a global variable. As a result, the calc_tax() function can access the tax variable directly. In other words, the calc_tax() function can change the same tax variable that's used by the main() function. Because of this, there's no need for the calc_tax() function to return the tax variable to the main() function. This makes the function less modular and can make your code more difficult to understand and maintain. As a result, it's generally considered a best practice to avoid coding functions that modify global variables.

In the third example, a local variable *shadows* a global variable. This happens because the local variable has the same name as a global variable. Then, the statements in the calc_tax() function refer to the local tax variable because it's defined there. But the statements in the main() function refer to the global variable. This can lead to debugging problems. As a result, it's generally considered a best practice to avoid shadowing.

With few exceptions, it's a best practice to use local variables and avoid the use of global variables. This is illustrated by most of the programs in this book.

The last example shows how to use a *global constant* to store the tax rate. Since it isn't possible for any of the functions in a program to change the value of a global constant, using a global constant rarely leads to debugging problems. As a result, it's considered an acceptable coding practice.

Functions that use local variables

```
double calc_tax(double amount, double tax_rate) {
    double tax = amount * tax_rate;      // tax is a local variable
    return tax;                          // return statement is necessary
}

int main() {
    double tax = calc_tax(85.0, .05);   // tax is a local variable
    cout << "Tax: " << tax << endl;      // tax is 4.25
}
```

A function that changes a global variable (not recommended)

```
double tax = 0.0;                        // tax is a global variable

void calc_tax(double amount, double tax_rate) {
    tax = amount * tax_rate;             // change global variable
}

int main() {
    calc_tax(85.0, .05);
    cout << "Tax: " << tax << endl;      // display global - tax is 4.25
}
```

A local variable that shadows a global variable (not recommended)

```
double tax = 0.0;                        // tax is a global variable

double calc_tax(double amount, double tax_rate) {
    double tax = amount * tax_rate;      // tax is a local variable
    cout << "Tax: " << tax << endl;      // display local - tax is 4.25
    return tax;
}

int main() {
    calc_tax(85.0, .05);
    cout << "Tax: " << tax << endl;      // display global - tax is 0.0
}
```

A function that uses a global constant (okay)

```
const double tax_rate = 0.05;            // tax_rate is a global constant

double calc_tax(double amount) {
    double tax = amount * tax_rate;      // OK to use global constant
    return tax;
}
```

Description

- A variable defined inside a function is known as a *local variable*. A variable defined outside of all functions is known as a *global variable*.

- A local variable can only be used within the function that defines it. Global variables can be used by all functions.

- When a local variable has the same name as a global variable, the local variable *shadows* the global variable. In a function that defines the variable, all operations are done on the local variable. Otherwise, all operations are done on the global variable.

Figure 7-4   When and how to use local and global variables

How to plan the functions of a program

As a program gets longer and requires more functions, it gets more difficult to decide what the functions should be and how they should relate to each other. To help you make those decisions, you can use a hierarchy chart to analyze and plan the modules of the program.

How to use a hierarchy chart

Figure 7-5 shows how to plan the functions of a program by using a *hierarchy chart*. Here, the hierarchy chart represents the five functions that are used by the Convert Temperatures program presented in figure 7-6. This shows that the main() function calls the display_menu() and convert_temp() functions. In turn, the convert_temp() function calls the to_celsius() and to_fahrenheit() functions.

If you compare the hierarchy chart in this figure with the code in the next figure, you shouldn't have much trouble understanding how a hierarchy chart relates to the code. But, how do you to learn to create a chart like this for a new program before the code is written? To do that, you can start with the main() function because it's always at the top level. Then, you ask yourself what primary function or functions the main() function needs to call. In this figure, that's the convert_temp() function. Once you identify the primary function or functions, you add them to the hierarchy chart.

After identifying the primary function or functions, you ask yourself what functions, if any, need to be called before or after the primary function or functions of the program. In this figure, that's the display_menu() function that's called before the convert_temp() function. After you add those functions to the chart, the first two levels are done: the top-level with the main() function and the next level. Then, you continue this process for the next levels down, until you've divided all of the functions into their component functions.

When you add a function to a chart, try to use a name that starts with a verb and ends with a noun, perhaps with one adjective between the verb and noun. That name should provide a good indication of what the function does. Later, when you code the functions of the program, you can create the function names by connecting the words on the flowchart with underscores, so "convert temp" on your chart becomes convert_temp in your code.

In practice, programmers often draw hierarchy charts by hand and discard them once the program has been coded and tested. Another alternative is to use a *hierarchy outline* like the one in this figure, instead of a hierarchy chart. An outline like this is a left-to-right view of the structure instead of a top-down view, and it's easy to type into a text editor or word processor.

A hierarchy chart for the Convert Temperatures program

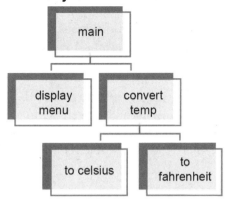

A hierarchy outline for the same program

```
main
     display menu
     convert temp
          to celsius
          to fahrenheit
```

How to build a hierarchy chart

- Start with a box for the main() function.
- At the next level, put boxes for the functions that the main() function needs to call. This usually includes the function that will control the main action of the program, plus any functions that need to be done before or after that function.
- Continue down the levels by dividing the higher-level functions into their component functions until there aren't any more components.

Guidelines for creating hierarchy charts

- The names in a chart should start with a verb and give a good indication of what the function does. Then, the names can easily be converted to function names.
- Each function should do everything that is related to the function name and nothing more.

Figure 7-5   How to use a hierarchy chart

The Convert Temperatures program

Figure 7-6 shows a Convert Temperatures program that corresponds to the hierarchy chart shown in the previous figure. Here, the user enters a 1 or a 2 to indicate what type of conversion should be done followed by the number of degrees to be converted. Then, the program displays the result.

The code begins by declaring the four functions that are used by the main() function. Here, you can see that the display_menu() and convert_temp() functions don't require any arguments or return any data. However, the to_celsius() and to_fahrenheit() functions accept a double value and return a double value.

The console

```
Convert Temperatures

MENU
1. Fahrenheit to Celsius
2. Celsius to Fahrenheit

Enter a menu option: 1
Enter degrees Fahrenheit: 100
Degrees Celsius: 37.8
Convert another temperature? (y/n): y

Enter a menu option: 2
Enter degrees Celsius: 0
Degrees Fahrenheit: 32
Convert another temperature? (y/n): n

Bye!
```

The code

```cpp
#include <iostream>
#include <cmath>

using namespace std;

// declare functions
void display_menu();
void convert_temp();
double to_celsius(double fahrenheit);
double to_fahrenheit(double celsius);

int main() {

    cout << "Convert Temperatures\n\n";

    display_menu();
    char again = 'y';
    while (again == 'y') {
        convert_temp();

        cout << "Convert another temperature? (y/n): ";
        cin >> again;
        cout << endl;
    }
    cout << "Bye!\n";
}

// define functions
void display_menu() {
    cout << "MENU\n"
         << "1. Fahrenheit to Celsius\n"
         << "2. Celsius to Fahrenheit\n\n";
}
```

Figure 7-6   The Convert Temperatures program (part 1 of 2)

When organizing your code, you can put the function definitions in any sequence that makes sense to you. This program organizes the functions by putting them in the sequence in which they're called. To start, the main() function is called first. As a result, this code places it before the definitions for the other functions. Since the main() function calls the display_menu() function followed by the convert_temp() function, that's the sequence in which they're coded. And since the convert_temp() function calls the to_celsius() and to_fahrenheit() functions, they appear after the convert_temp() function.

The code (continued)

```cpp
void convert_temp() {
    int option;
    cout << "Enter a menu option: ";
    cin >> option;

    double f = 0.0;
    double c = 0.0;
    switch (option) {
    case 1:
        cout << "Enter degrees Fahrenheit: ";
        cin >> f;

        c = to_celsius(f);
        c = round(c * 10) / 10;

        cout << "Degrees Celsius: " << c << endl;
        break;
    case 2:
        cout << "Enter degrees Celsius: ";
        cin >> c;

        f = to_fahrenheit(c);
        f = round(f * 10) / 10;

        cout << "Degrees Fahrenheit: " << f << endl;
        break;
    default:
        cout << "You must enter a valid menu number.\n";
        break;
    }
}

double to_celsius(double fahrenheit) {
    double celsius = (fahrenheit - 32.0) * 5.0 / 9.0;
    return celsius;
}

double to_fahrenheit(double celsius) {
    double fahrenheit = celsius * 9.0 / 5.0 + 32.0;
    return fahrenheit;
}
```

Figure 7-6   The Convert Temperatures program (part 2 of 2)

More skills for coding functions

Now that you've learned the basics of coding functions and planning the functions of a program, you're ready to learn more skills for coding functions.

How to use default values for arguments

When you define a function, you can assign default values to one or more of the parameters. To do that, you code the data type and name for the parameter, the assignment operator (=), and the default value for the argument as shown by the first example in figure 7-7. In this function, the second and third parameters assign default values. When you assign default values, though, you need to code the parameters with default values after any parameters that don't provide default values.

When a parameter has a default value, you don't have to code an argument for that parameter when you call the function. Then, the function uses the default value for the parameter. However, if you do code the argument in the calling statement, the argument you pass to the function overrides the default value for the parameter. For instance, the second example shows three ways to call the calculate_future_value() function defined in the first example. Here, the first statement uses both default values, the second statement only uses one default value, and the third statement overrides both default values.

When you code both a function declaration and a function definition, you can't assign a default value in both the declaration and the definition. If you do, you'll get a compile-time error. In this figure, for instance, the third example uses the function declaration to specify the default values, and the corresponding function definition doesn't specify any default values. Since this approach allows other programmers to understand how to use a function by looking at its declaration, many programmers consider this a good practice. However, this is largely a matter of personal preference, and it's perfectly acceptable to code the default values in the function definition.

A function definition that has two default values

```
double calculate_future_value(double monthly_investment,
        double yearly_interest_rate = 3.0, int years = 10) {

    // convert yearly values to monthly values
    double monthly_rate = yearly_interest_rate / 12 / 100;
    int months = years * 12;

    // calculate future value
    double future_value = 0;
    for (int i = 0; i < months; ++i) {
        future_value = (future_value + monthly_investment) *
                       (1 + monthly_rate);
    }

    return future_value;
}
```

How to call the function with default values

```
double fv1 = calculate_future_value(100.0);            // fv1 = 14009.1
double fv2 = calculate_future_value(100.0, 4.0);       // fv2 = 14774.1
double fv3 = calculate_future_value(100.0, 4.0, 11);   // fv3 = 16602.3
```

A function declaration that has two default values

```
// function declaration
double calculate_future_value(double monthly_investment,
        double yearly_interest_rate = 3.0, int years = 10);

// corresponding function definition
double calculate_future_value(double monthly_investment,
        double yearly_interest_rate, int years) {
    // function code goes here
}
```

Description

- You can specify a default value for any argument in a function declaration or definition by assigning a value to the argument. However, the arguments with default values must be coded last in the function declaration or definition.

- When you call a function, any arguments that have default values are optional, but you can override the default value for an argument by supplying that argument.

- You can't assign a default value in both a declaration and a definition. If you do, you'll get a compile-time error.

Figure 7-7   How to use default values for arguments

How to overload a function

When you create two or more functions with the same name but with different parameter lists, the functions are *overloaded*. Then, when you call that function in your code, C++ calls the version of the function that has parameters that match the arguments in the calling code.

When you code a function, the function name plus the number of parameters and the data type for each parameter form the *signature* of the function. You can code more than one function with the same name as long as each function has a unique signature. For example, all three to_celsius() functions in figure 7-8 have different signatures.

For a function signature to be unique, the function must have a different number of parameters than the other functions with the same name, or at least one of the parameters must have a different data type. However, the names of the parameters aren't part of the signature. So using different parameter names isn't enough to make the signatures unique. Also, the return type isn't part of the signature. As a result, you can't create two functions with the same name and parameters but different return types.

One purpose of overloading is to allow a function to work with different data types. For example, the first function in this figure works with a double value, and the second works with an int value. Here, the second function rounds the result of the conversion to 0 decimal places, automatically converts that result from a double value to an int value, and returns that int value.

Another purpose of overloading is to allow a function to provide additional parameters that enhance its functionality. For example, like the first function, the third function converts a double value from Fahrenheit to Celsius. However, the third function includes a second parameter that allows the calling code to specify the number of decimal places for rounding.

Within the third function, the first statement calls the first to_celsius() function to convert the parameter value from Fahrenheit to Celsius. Although this function could have used the same code as the first to_celsius() function to perform this conversion, calling the first function prevents code duplication, which makes your code easier to maintain.

When you refer to an overloaded function, the number of arguments you specify and their data types determine which version of the function is executed. In this figure, the three statements that call the to_celsius() function show how this works. Since the first statement provides a single double value as an argument, it calls the first version of the to_celsius() function. Since the second statement provides a double value and an int value of 2, it calls the third version and rounds the result to 2 decimal places. And since the third statement specifies a single int value, it calls the second version and returns an int value.

An overloaded to_celsius() function

For double values

```
double to_celsius(double fahrenheit) {
    double celsius = (fahrenheit - 32.0) * 5.0 / 9.0;
    return celsius;
}
```

For int values

```
int to_celsius(int fahrenheit) {
    double celsius = (fahrenheit - 32) * 5.0 / 9.0;
    celsius = round(celsius);
    return celsius;
}
```

For double values with rounding

```
double to_celsius(double fahrenheit, int decimal_places) {
    double celsius = to_celsius(fahrenheit);
    if (decimal_places > 0) {
        int multiplier = 1;
        for (int i = 0; i < decimal_places; ++i)
            multiplier *= 10;    // add a zero each time through the loop
        celsius = round(celsius * multiplier) / multiplier;
    }
    return celsius;
}
```

Code that calls these functions

```
double d = 120.0;
cout << d << " Fahrenheit = " << to_celsius(d) << " Celsius\n";
cout << d << " Fahrenheit = " << to_celsius(d, 2) << " Celsius\n";

int i = 120;
cout << i << " Fahrenheit = " << to_celsius(i) << " Celsius\n";
```

The console

```
120 Fahrenheit = 48.8889 Celsius
120 Fahrenheit = 48.89 Celsius
120 Fahrenheit = 49 Celsius
```

Description

- When you create two or more functions with the same name but different parameter lists, the functions are *overloaded*.

- When you code a function, the function name plus the number of parameters and the data type for each parameter form the *signature* of the function. Each overloaded function must have a unique signature.

- When overloading functions, the parameter names aren't part of the signature, and the return type isn't part of the signature. As a result, for a function signature to be unique, the function must have a different number of parameters, or at least one of the parameters must have a different data type.

Figure 7-8   How to overload a function

How to use reference variables as parameters

So far in this book, you have learned to use a variable to store a copy of a value in memory. This type of variable is known as a *value variable*. Now, figure 7-9 shows how to work with a variable that *refers* to a value that already exists in memory. This type of variable is known as a *reference variable*, and it allows multiple variables to work with the same value.

The first example compares how assignment statements work with value variables and reference variables. With value variables, the assignment statement makes a copy of the double value. As a result, the third statement changes the double value that's stored in the variable named p1, but not the double value that's stored in the variable named p2.

With reference variables, the assignment statement does *not* store a copy of the value. Instead, it causes both variables to refer to the same value. As a result, when the third statement uses the variable named p1 to change the double value, this change is also reflected in the variable named p2. That's because both variables refer to the same value. As a result, if you have multiple variables that refer to the same value, you need to be careful about changing its data.

When coding functions, it's common to use reference variables as parameters. This can improve the efficiency of your code, especially if the function uses a parameter to work with a large amount of data. However, this can also make your code more difficult to understand and maintain. As a result, it often makes sense to avoid this technique.

The second example compares how the parameters of a function work with value variables and reference variables. This example uses a function named increase_price() that increases the price by 10%. With a value variable, the price parameter stores a copy of the double value. Then, the first statement increases the price parameter by 10%. However, this doesn't change the price in the calling code. As a result, the second statement returns the price to the calling code so it can access the new price.

With a reference variable, the price parameter refers to the same double value as the calling code. As a result, this function doesn't need to return the double value to the calling code. Instead, changing the value of the price parameter also changes the value of the price variable in the calling code.

The third example shows the code that calls the functions in the second example. If the increase_price() function uses a value parameter, the code that calls it must assign the return value to the variable named price if it wants to change that variable. However, if the increase_price() function uses a reference parameter, the function increases the price that's stored in the calling code. As a result, there's no need for an assignment statement.

Most of the time, you can write your code without thinking too much about the differences between value variables and reference variables. Occasionally, though, you do need to be aware of these differences. For example, you may want to use reference variables to improve efficiency as shown in the next figure.

How reference variables work

Code that uses value variables

```
double p1 = 54.50;
double p2 = p1;             // p1 and p2 store copies of 54.50
p1 = 57.50;                 // only changes p1
```

Code that uses a reference variable

```
double p1 = 54.50;
double& p2 = p1;           // p2 references the value stored by p1
p1 = 57.50;                // changes p1 and p2
```

Another way to declare a reference variable

```
double &p2 = p1;           // p2 references the value stored by p1
```

How reference parameters work

Code that uses a value parameter

```
double increase_price(double price) {
    price = price * 1.1;     // does not change price in calling code
    return price;            // returns changed price to calling code
}
```

Code that uses a reference parameter

```
void increase_price(double& price) {
    // the price parameter refers to the price in calling code
    price = price * 1.1;     // changes price in calling code
}
```

How function calls work

For value parameters

```
double price = 54.50;
price = increase_price(price);  // assignment necessary
```

For reference parameters

```
double price = 54.50;
increase_price(price);          // assignment not necessary
```

Description

- A *value variable* always stores its own copy of the value. As a result, changing the value for one value variable doesn't change the value of any other value variables.

- A *reference variable* stores a reference to the value. This allows multiple reference variables to *refer* to the same value. As a result, changing the value for one reference variable also changes the value for any other variables that refer to that value.

- To define a variable as a reference variable, code the & symbol immediately after its data type or immediately before its name.

Figure 7-9   How to use reference variables as parameters

How to use reference parameters to improve efficiency

If a parameter may contain a large amount of data, you can improve the efficiency of the function by declaring the parameter as a reference variable. That way, the function can refer to the same data as the calling code and doesn't need to make a copy of that data.

For instance, figure 7-10 begins by showing a function named tolower() that converts a string to lowercase. To do that, this code declares a reference parameter for the string. Then, it uses a reference variable with a range-based for loop to change each character in the string to lowercase. Since this modifies the string in the calling code, the function doesn't return a value, and the calling code doesn't need to use an assignment statement.

While this tolower() function runs efficiently, some programmers would consider it bad design to allow the function to modify the string value that's referred to by the calling code. Another option would be to use a value parameter like this:

```
string tolower(string str) {
    string str_lower = "";
    for (char c : str) {
        str_lower += tolower(c);
    }
    return str_lower;
}
```

Then, the calling code would need to use an assignment statement like this:

```
name = tolower(name);
```

This doesn't run as efficiently, but it should work efficiently enough for most programs, especially if the strings being converted aren't too large. In addition, this makes the tolower() function more modular and flexible since it doesn't modify data in the calling function.

If your function doesn't change the value of a parameter, you can improve its efficiency without any downside by using a reference parameter. In that case, you should also use the const keyword to declare the parameter as a constant. That way, other programmers can easily see that the function doesn't modify the reference parameter. As an added bonus, you can be sure that you won't accidentally write code that modifies this parameter.

To illustrate, the second example shows a function named iequals() that performs a case-insensitive comparison of two strings. Here, the parameters for both strings have been declared as constant reference parameters so the code can't modify these strings. Within the function, the code begins by checking whether the two strings contain the same number of characters. If not, the two strings can't be equal, so the code returns a false value, which exits the function.

Otherwise, the code continues by looping through each character in the two strings. Then, it checks whether the lowercase version of each character is equal. If not, the loop returns a false value, which exits the function. However, if all of these comparisons are equal, the loop ends, and the statement after the loop returns a true value to indicate that the two strings are equal.

A function that converts a string to lowercase

A function that changes the value of a reference parameter

```cpp
void tolower(string& str) {
    for (char& c : str) {
        c = tolower(c);
    }
}
```

Code that calls the function

```cpp
string name = "Bjarne";
tolower(name);
cout << name << endl;
```

The console

```
bjarne
```

A function that performs a case-insensitive comparison of two strings

A function that uses constant reference parameters

```cpp
bool iequals(const string& str1, const string& str2) {
    if (str1.size() != str2.size()) {
        return false;
    }

    for (int i = 0; i < str1.size(); ++i) {
        if (tolower(str1[i]) != tolower(str2[i])) {
            return false;
        }
    }
    return true;
}
```

Code that calls the function

```cpp
string name1 = "Bjarne";
string name2 = "bjarne";
if (iequals(name1, name2))
    cout << name1 << " equals " << name2 << " (case-insensitive)\n";
else
    cout << name1 << " does NOT equal " << name2 << endl;
```

The console

```
Bjarne equals bjarne (case-insensitive)
```

Description

- If a parameter may contain a large amount of data, you can improve the efficiency of the function by declaring the parameter as a reference parameter. That way, the function doesn't need to make a copy of the data that's passed to the parameter.

- If you don't want to allow the function to change the reference parameter, you can declare it as a constant.

- You can use the return statement to exit a function at any point in the function.

Figure 7-10   Examples that use reference parameters

The Temperature Manager program

Part 1 of figure 7-11 shows a Temperature Manager program that uses functions to organize its code. To start, this program defines a const to store the filename of the text file that stores the temperature data for this program.

After defining the filename, this code declares the functions used by this program. First, it declares a general-purpose function named get_char(). This function provides a way to get a character from the console. Its only argument is the prompt that's displayed to the user before getting the character from the user.

Next, this code declares two functions for working with file I/O. First, the load_temps() function reads the temperatures from the file for the program and loads the low and high temperatures into the vectors for storing the low and high temperatures. Since this function needs to modify these vectors, it declares them as reference parameters. Second, the save_temps() function writes the temperatures from the low and high vectors to the file for the program. Since this function doesn't need to modify these vectors, it declares them as constant reference parameters.

Finally, this code declares four functions for console I/O. First, it declares the display_menu() function that displays the menu of commands. Second, it declares the view_temps() function that displays the temperatures on the console. Third, it declares the add_temps() function that allows the user to add the low and high temperatures for a day. Fourth, it declares the remove_temps() function that allows the user to remove the temperatures for a day.

Of these functions, the last three accept the vectors of low and high temperatures as their arguments. All three of these functions declare the arguments as reference parameters. However, since the view_temps() function doesn't need to modify these vectors, it declares them as constant reference parameters.

The console

```
The Temperature Manager program

COMMANDS
v - View temperatures
a - Add temperatures
r - Remove temperatures
x - Exit

Command: v
TEMPERATURES
Day     Low     High
----    ------- -------
1       57.2    78.3
2       54.3    75.9
3       55.8    77.0

Command: a
Enter low temp: 53.1
Enter high temp: 74.7
Your temperatures have been added.

Command: r
Enter day to remove: 3
Temps for day 3 have been removed.

Command: x
Bye!
```

The code

```cpp
#include <iostream>
#include <iomanip>
#include <fstream>
#include <string>
#include <limits>
#include <vector>

using namespace std;

const string filename = "temps.txt";

// General purpose function
char get_char(string prompt);

// Functions for file I/O
void load_temps(vector<double>& low, vector<double>& high);
void save_temps(const vector<double>& low, const vector<double>& high);

// Functions for console I/O
void display_menu();
void view_temps(const vector<double>& low, const vector<double>& high);
void add_temps(vector<double>& low, vector<double>& high);
void remove_temps(vector<double>& low, vector<double>& high);
```

Figure 7-11   The Temperature Manager program (part 1 of 4)

After declaring the functions, the main() function shown in part 2 of figure 7-11 provides the code that's executed when the user starts the program. First, this code displays the title of the program. Then, it uses the display_menu() function to display the menu of commands that are available to the user. Next, it defines the vectors for the low and high temperatures and loads the temperatures from the text file for this program into the vectors by calling the load_temps() function and passing the vectors.

After loading the data from the file, this program begins a while loop that continues until the user enters 'x' to exit the program. This loop begins by getting a command from the user. Then, it uses a switch statement to execute the appropriate command. If the user enters 'v', 'a', or 'r', the code executes the view_temps(), add_temps(), or remove_temps() functions by passing the vectors that store the low and high temperatures to the appropriate function. If the user enters 'x', the code displays a message that says "Bye!" and exits the loop. Otherwise, this code displays a message that indicates that the command was invalid and uses the display_menu() function to display the list of commands again.

After the main() function, this code defines the get_char() function that gets a character from the user. To start, this function defines a char variable named choice. Then, it displays the prompt argument on the console. Next, it gets the character entered by the user and stores it in the char variable. Finally, it discards any other data that the user may have entered and returns the character to the calling code.

The code (continued)

```
int main()
{
    cout << "The Temperature Manager program\n\n";

    display_menu();

    // get temps from file
    vector<double> low_temps, high_temps;
    load_temps(low_temps, high_temps);

    char command = 'v';
    while (command != 'x') {
        // get command from user
        command = get_char("Command: ");

        // execute appropriate command
        switch (tolower(command)) {
        case 'v':
            view_temps(low_temps, high_temps);
            break;
        case 'a':
            add_temps(low_temps, high_temps);
            break;
        case 'r':
            remove_temps(low_temps, high_temps);
            break;
        case 'x':
            cout << "Bye!\n\n";
            break;
        default:
            cout << "Invalid command. Try again.\n\n";
            display_menu();
            break;
        }
    }
}

char get_char(string prompt) {
    char choice;
    cout << prompt;
    cin >> choice;

    cin.ignore(10000, '\n');
    return choice;
}
```

Figure 7-11   The Temperature Manager program (part 2 of 4)

The load_temps() function in part 3 of figure 7-11 loads two vectors of double values, one for the low temperatures stored by the program, and one for the high temperatures. Since these vectors could potentially be very large and use a large amount of memory, this function defines them as reference parameters. That way, the code doesn't make a copy of these vectors, which improves efficiency.

To start, the load_temps() function defines double values for low and high temperatures. Then, it attempts to open the input file. If this is successful, the code reads the data for the low and high temperatures from the file and stores them in the appropriate vector. When the loop is done, this code closes the file. Since this function defines the vector parameters as reference variables, this code doesn't need to return these vectors to the calling code. Instead, it can just add the data to these vectors, and it will also be available to the calling code.

The save_temps() function also defines two vectors as its parameters, one for low temperatures and one for high temperatures. Like the load_temps() function, these vectors are defined as reference parameters. Also, since this code doesn't need to change these vectors, this code defines them as constants.

Within the save_temps() function, the first two lines open the output file. Then, this code executes a loop that provides an index for each element of each vector. Within this loop, the code writes each low and high temperature to a line in the file, separating the low and high temperatures for each day with a tab character.

After defining the functions for working with file I/O, this code defines some functions for working with console I/O. To start, it defines the display_menu() function that displays the menu of the four commands for using this program.

The next three functions correspond to the commands that are available to the user. The view_temps() function provides the code that's executed when the user enters 'v' to select the view temperatures command. This function accepts two vectors, one for low temperatures and one for high temperatures. Like the save_temps() function, this function defines these vectors as constant reference parameters to improve efficiency.

The code (continued)

```
void load_temps(vector<double>& low_temps,
                vector<double>& high_temps) {
    double low, high;
    ifstream input_file(filename);
    if (input_file) {
        while (input_file >> low >> high) {
            low_temps.push_back(low);
            high_temps.push_back(high);
        }
        input_file.close();
    }
}

void save_temps(const vector<double>& low_temps,
                const vector<double>& high_temps) {
    ofstream output_file(filename);
    for (int i = 0; i < low_temps.size(); ++i) {
        output_file << low_temps[i] << '\t' << high_temps[i] << '\n';
    }
    output_file.close();
}

void display_menu() {
    cout << "COMMANDS\n"
         << "v - View temperatures\n"
         << "a - Add temperatures\n"
         << "r - Remove temperatures\n"
         << "x - Exit\n\n";
}

void view_temps(const vector<double>& low_temps,
                const vector<double>& high_temps) {
    cout << "TEMPERATURES\n"
         << left << setw(4) << "Day"
         << right << setw(8) << "Low" << setw(8) << "High" << endl
         << "---- ------- -------" << endl;

    cout << fixed << setprecision(1);
    int day_num = 1;
    double low, high;
    for (int i = 0; i < low_temps.size(); ++i) {
        low = low_temps[i];
        high = high_temps[i];
        cout << left << setw(4) << day_num
             << right << setw(8) << low << setw(8) << high << '\n';
        ++day_num;
    }
    cout << endl;
}
```

Figure 7-11   The Temperature Manager program (part 3 of 4)

The add_temps() function in part 4 of figure 7-11 provides the code that's executed when the user enters 'a' to select the add temperatures command. This function accepts two vectors, one for low temperatures and one for high temperatures. To improve efficiency, this function defines these vectors as reference parameters. However, since this function needs to modify these vectors by adding an element to each of them, it doesn't declare these parameters as constants.

Within the add_temps() function, the code begins by getting the low and high temperatures from the user. Then, it uses the push_back() function to add these temperatures to the end of the vectors for the low and high temperatures. Next, it saves this data to the file by calling the save_temps() function and passing both vectors to that function. Finally, it displays a message that indicates that the temperatures have been added.

The remove_temps() function provides the code that's executed when the user enters 'r' to select the remove temperatures command. This function works much like the add_temps() function. However, it includes some range checking to prevent out of bounds access with either of the vectors. To start, this code converts the day that's entered by the user to an index that corresponds to an element in the vector. To do that, it subtracts 1 from the day. Then, it checks if the index is greater than or equal to 0 and less than the size of the vector of high temperatures. If it is, the index is within a valid range for both vectors. As a result, the code continues by using the erase() function to remove the temperature for the specified day from both vectors. Then, it saves this data to the file by calling the save_temps() function. However, if the index isn't valid, this code displays a message that indicates that the day was not valid.

As you review this code, note that it separates the code for the file I/O from the code for the console I/O. In other words, it separates the code that works with the data in the file from the code that works with the user interface. That's generally considered a good design practice because it allows you to change the user interface without having to change the data access code. For example, if you later need to change the user interface from a console program to a graphical user interface (GUI), you could still use the same file I/O code.

In addition, this design leads to code that's more reusable. For example, both the add_temps() and remove_temps() functions call the save_temps() function to save any changes to the data immediately after the data has been changed. That way, the user won't lose that data even if the program crashes after executing these functions.

Similarly, the main() function calls the display_menu() function in two places. First, it displays the commands when the program starts. In addition, it displays the commands if the user enters an invalid command. That way, if a user enters an invalid command, the program shows the user the list of valid commands to choose from.

The code (continued)

```
void add_temps(vector<double>& low_temps,
               vector<double>& high_temps) {
    double low, high;

    cout << "Enter low temp: ";
    cin >> low;

    cout << "Enter high temp: ";
    cin >> high;

    low_temps.push_back(low);    // modifies reference param
    high_temps.push_back(high);  // modifies reference param
    save_temps(low_temps, high_temps);
    cout << "Your temperatures have been added.\n\n";
}

void remove_temps(vector<double>& low_temps,
                  vector<double>& high_temps) {
    int day;
    cout << "Enter day to remove: ";
    cin >> day;

    int index = day - 1;
    if (index >= 0 && index < high_temps.size()) {
        // modify reference params
        high_temps.erase(high_temps.begin() + index);
        low_temps.erase(low_temps.begin() + index);
        save_temps(low_temps, high_temps);
        cout << "Temps for day " << day << " have been removed.\n\n";
    }
    else {
        cout << "Unable to remove day " << day << ". Invalid day.\n\n";
    }
}
```

Figure 7-11   The Temperature Manager program (part 4 of 4)

How to work with header files and namespaces

As you get better at coding functions, you will eventually code some functions that you will want to use in multiple programs. To do that, you can store the functions that you want to reuse in separate files called *header files*. This also has the benefit of allowing you to divide a single source code file that's long and unwieldy into smaller source code files that are easier to manage.

How to create, implement, and use header files

Figure 7-12 begins by showing how to create a header file. To start, you can use your IDE to create a file with an extension of .h such as the temperature.h file shown in this figure. Then, you can add code like the code in the first example. Here, the header file stores the declarations for the to_celsius() and to_fahrenheit() functions. Since these declarations provide the interface for using the header file, a header file is also known as an *interface file*.

To prevent the compiler from including the same header file twice, headers typically use the #ifndef, #define, and #endif preprocessor directives to define an *include guard*. For this to work correctly, the header file must define a unique name for the header file such as MURACH_TEMPERATURE_H. Here the #ifndef (if not defined) directive checks if the specified constant has *not* been defined. In that case, the #def (define) directive defines this constant and the two function declarations are included. However, if this constant has already been defined, execution skips to the #endif directive and the two functions declarations are not included.

When you create a header file, you should not define any constants, variables, or functions. That's because the header file only supplies the interface, not the implementation. In addition, you should not code using directives or declarations. That's because you don't want members of other header files to be included when you include a header file.

Once you've defined the header file, you need to provide a file that contains the source code that implements the header file. This file is known as the *implementation file*. To do that, you can start by using your IDE to create a file with an extension of .cpp such as temperature.cpp file. Then, you add the code that implements the interface. In this figure, the implementation file just provides the definitions for the two functions declared by the header file. By convention, the implementation file has the same name as the header file. In other words, the filenames are the same, but the extensions are different.

When you're ready to use a header file that you've created, you use an #include directive to specify the header file that contains the functions. To do that, the #include directive must enclose the name of the header file in double quotes. In this figure, for example, the main.cpp file includes the temperature.h header file. As a result, the code in the main.cpp file can use the functions declared in the temperature.h file and defined in the temperature.cpp file.

The header file named temperature.h

```
#ifndef MURACH_TEMPERATURE_H    // include guard - if not defined
#define MURACH_TEMPERATURE_H    // define

// declare functions
double to_celsius(double fahrenheit);
double to_fahrenheit(double celsius);

#endif                          // end include guard
```

The implementation file named temperature.cpp

```
// define functions
double to_celsius(double fahrenheit) {
    double celsius = (fahrenheit - 32.0) * 5.0 / 9.0;
    return celsius;
}

double to_fahrenheit(double celsius) {
    double fahrenheit = celsius * 9.0 / 5.0 + 32.0;
    return fahrenheit;
}
```

The main.cpp file that uses these functions

```
#include <iostream>
#include "temperature.h"

using namespace std;

int main() {
    double c = to_celsius(32);
    cout << "Celsius: " << c << endl;

    double f = to_fahrenheit(0);
    cout << "Fahrenheit: " << f << endl;
}
```

A header file should not include

- Any definitions of constants, variables, or functions
- Using directives or declarations

Description

- You can organize functions by storing them in separate files. To do that, you can store the function declarations in a *header file*, also known as an *interface file*, and you can store the function definitions in an *implementation file*.
- To prevent the compiler from including the same header twice, headers typically use the #ifndef, #define, and #endif preprocessor directives to define an *include guard*.
- To use a header that you've defined, you must use an #include directive that encloses the name of the header file in double quotes, not in angle brackets. This indicates that the header file is in the working directory, not the include directory that contains the header files from the C++ standard library.

Figure 7-12   How to create, implement, and use header files

How to define namespaces

When you write code that's going to be used by multiple programs, it's important to avoid naming conflicts. For example, you need to make sure that a function that you define doesn't have the same name as a function that another programmer has defined. Fortunately, you can use *namespaces* to organize your code to avoid naming conflicts. Then, the functions defined within the namespace have *namespace scope*.

Figure 7-13 shows how to define a namespace for the two functions of the temperature header described in the previous figure. The first example shows how to store the declarations for the two functions in this header in the temperature namespace. Here, the namespace keyword specifies a name of temperature for the namespace. Then, the braces surround the two functions.

The second example shows the definitions for the functions that are declared in the header file. Just as they are in the header file, the functions in this file are coded within the temperature namespace.

Once you've put functions in a namespace, you can use any of the techniques described in chapter 2 to identify the members of the namespace. For instance, the third example uses a using directive to make all functions in the temperature namespace available to the code. As a result, this code can call the to_celsius() function without identifying the namespace.

On the other hand, the fourth example doesn't include a using directive for the namespace. Instead, it uses the fully qualified name of the to_celsius() function to access that function. To do that, this code begins with the namespace, followed by a scope resolution operator (::) and the function name.

A header file that declares two functions in a namespace

```
#ifndef MURACH_TEMPERATURE_H
#define MURACH_TEMPERATURE_H

namespace temperature {
    double to_celsius(double fahrenheit);
    double to_fahrenheit(double celsius);
}

#endif // MURACH_TEMPERATURE_H
```

A source code file that defines two functions in a namespace

```
namespace temperature {
    double to_celsius(double fahrenheit) {
        double celsius = (fahrenheit - 32.0) * 5.0 / 9.0;
        return celsius;
    }

    double to_fahrenheit(double celsius) {
        double fahrenheit = celsius * 9.0 / 5.0 + 32.0;
        return fahrenheit;
    }
}
```

Code that makes it easy to access all functions in a namespace

```
#include <iostream>
#include "temperature.h"

using namespace std;
using namespace temperature;

int main() {
    double c = to_celsius(32);
    cout << "Celsius: " << c << endl;
}
```

Code that identifies a specific function within a namespace

```
#include <iostream>
#include "temperature.h"

using namespace std;

int main() {
    double c = temperature::to_celsius(32);
    cout << "Celsius: " << c << endl;
}
```

Description

- A *namespace* provides a way of organizing code to avoid naming conflicts.

- To define your own namespace, code the namespace keyword, a name for the space, and a set of braces. Within the braces, code the functions for the namespace.

- Once you've put functions in a namespace, you can use any of the techniques described in chapter 2 to identify the members of the namespace.

Figure 7-13   How to define namespaces

A header for getting input from the console

Part 1 of figure 7-14 begins by showing a header file named console.h and its implementation, which is stored in a file named console.cpp. Here, the header file begins with an include guard that uses a constant of MURACH_CONSOLE_H. Since this constant begins with MURACH, it's unlikely that this name will be used by anyone else. As a result, this include guard should work correctly. Of course, if you code your own include guard, you should use a unique identifier of your own.

After the include guard, this file includes the string and limits headers. Then, it defines a namespace named console that contains the declarations for three general-purpose functions. All three of these functions display a prompt on the console and get input from the user. Here, the get_double() function gets a double value, the get_int() function gets an int value, and the get_char() function gets a character. The get_double() and get_int() functions both have three parameters and include default values for the second and third parameters. The get_char() function has two parameters and includes a default value for the second parameter. As a result, these functions only require the calling code to supply an argument for the first parameter.

The console.cpp file provides the implementations for these three functions. To start, it defines the console namespace. Then, it declares three helper functions.

After declaring the helper functions, this code provides the definitions for the three functions declared in the header file. These functions get a double, int, or char value that the user enters on the console. For the double and int values, these functions make sure the entry is a valid double or int value that's within a specified range. As a result, you can use these functions instead of having to write validation code for each entry.

The get_double() function begins by declaring a double value named num and initializing it to a value of 0.0. Then, it begins a loop that continues until the user enters a valid double value. Within this loop, the first statement uses the prompt parameter to prompt the user to enter a double value. Then, it attempts to extract a double value from the console input stream. If this is not successful, the code calls the handle_invalid_number() function shown in part 2 to display an error message, clear the failure flag, and discard any remaining characters. Then, program execution continues at the top of the loop. This causes the loop to prompt the user to enter another double value.

However, if the code successfully extracts a double value from the stream, it uses the discard_remaining_chars() function shown in part 2 to discard any remaining characters in the stream. Then, it uses the check_range() function shown in part 2 to check if the double value is within the range specified by the min and max parameters. If it isn't, this code displays an appropriate error message and execution jumps to the top of the loop, which prompts the user to enter another double value. If it is, this code returns the double value to the calling code, which exits the loop and the function.

The console.h file

```
#ifndef MURACH_CONSOLE_H
#define MURACH_CONSOLE_H

#include <string>
#include <limits>

namespace console {
    // declare general-purpose functions
    double get_double(std::string prompt,
        double min = std::numeric_limits<double>::min(),
        double max = std::numeric_limits<double>::max());
    int get_int(std::string prompt,
        int min = std::numeric_limits<int>::min(),
        int max = std::numeric_limits<int>::max());
    char get_char(std::string prompt,
        bool add_blank_line = true);

}

#endif // MURACH_CONSOLE_H
```

The console.cpp file

```
#include <iostream>
#include <string>
#include <limits>

namespace console {
    // declare helper functions
    void discard_remaining_chars();
    void handle_invalid_number();
    bool check_range(double num, double min, double max);

    // define general-purpose functions
    double get_double(std::string prompt, double min, double max) {
        double num = 0.0;
        bool is_valid = false;
        while (!is_valid) {
            std::cout << prompt;
            if (!(std::cin >> num)) {
                handle_invalid_number();
            }
            else {
                discard_remaining_chars();
                is_valid = check_range(num, min, max);
            }
        }
        return num;
    }
```

Figure 7-14   A header for getting input from the console (part 1 of 2)

The get_int() function shown in part 2 of figure 7-14 works like the get_double() function. However, it works with int values instead of double values. Like the get_double() function, the get_int() function uses the helper functions defined at the end of this file.

The get_char() function begins by displaying the prompt and getting the first character that's entered by the user. However, this function includes a second parameter that specifies whether it displays a blank line after the user enters the character. This parameter has a default value of true, so this function displays a blank line after the user input, unless the calling code specifies a second argument of false. Then, it calls the discard_remaining_chars() function to discard all remaining characters on the current line, and it returns the first character that the user entered.

The discard_remaining_chars() function contains a single statement. However, this statement is a complicated statement that uses the ignore() function of the cin object to discard all remaining characters on the current line. As a result, it's easier and more consistent to call the discard_remaining_chars() function than it is to code the complicated statement that's contained within this function.

The handle_invalid_number() function contains three statements. The first displays a standard message for an invalid number, the second clears the failure flag from the cin object, and the third calls the discard_remaining_chars() function to discard any remaining characters on the current line.

The check_range() function returns a Boolean value that indicates whether the specified number is within the specified range. To accomplish this, the body of this function checks whether the specified number is between the specified minimum and maximum values. If not, this code displays an appropriate error message and returns a false value. Otherwise, the number is within the specified range. In that case, this code returns a true value. Since the parameters for this function are double types, you might think that it wouldn't work for int values. However, this function works equally well for int values because C++ automatically converts int values to double values.

As you review this code, note that these files don't use using directives or declarations. Instead, they use the scope resolution operator (::) to access the members of the standard and console namespace that they need. As mentioned earlier in this chapter, that's a best practice when coding header files.

There are several advantages to using functions like the get_double(), get_int(), and get_char() to get valid user input. First, they make it possible to reuse your code within a program. If, for example, your program needs to get 10 valid double values, you can call the get_double() function 10 times instead of repeating its code in 10 different places in your program. Second, since you aren't repeating code in multiple locations, you are following the Don't Repeat Yourself (DRY) principle, which makes your code easier to debug and maintain.

When you put these functions in a header file, it's possible to reuse them in other programs too. One way to do that is to copy the header file and its implementation file into the directory for another program. Then, you can include the header file as described earlier in this chapter.

The console.cpp file (continued)

```cpp
int get_int(std::string prompt, int min, int max) {
    int num = 0;
    bool is_valid = false;
    while (!is_valid) {
        std::cout << prompt;
        if (!(std::cin >> num)) {
            handle_invalid_number();
        }
        else {
            discard_remaining_chars();
            is_valid = check_range(num, min, max);
        }
    }
    return num;
}

char get_char(std::string prompt, bool add_blank_line = true) {
    char choice = 'n';
    std::cout << prompt;
    std::cin >> choice;
    if (add_blank_line)
        std::cout << std::endl;

    discard_remaining_chars();
    return choice;
}

// define helper functions
void discard_remaining_chars() {
    std::cin.ignore(std::numeric_limits<std::streamsize>::max(),
        '\n');
}

void handle_invalid_number() {
    std::cout << "Error! Invalid number. Try again.\n";
    std::cin.clear();                    // clear the failure flag
    discard_remaining_chars();
}

bool check_range(double num, double min, double max) {
    if (num < min) {
        std::cout << "Error! Number must be greater than "
            << min << ". Try again.\n";
        return false;
    }
    else if (num > max) {
        std::cout << "Error! Number must be less than "
            << max << ". Try again.\n";
        return false;
    }
    else {
        return true;
    }
}
}
```

Figure 7-14   A header for getting input from the console (part 2 of 2)

The Future Value program

Figure 7-15 shows a Future Value program that uses functions. Part 1 begins by showing the console when the user enters invalid data for this version of the Future Value program. For example, the first error message is displayed if the user doesn't enter a valid double value for the monthly investment. The second error message is displayed if the user enters a value that's out of range for the interest rate. And the third error message is displayed if the user doesn't enter a valid integer value for the years.

The INPUT section in this figure uses descriptive error messages to identify data entry problems to the user, and it doesn't require that the user re-enter values that have already been successfully entered. In addition, it only uses the first value the user enters on a line and discards the rest, which is usually what you want. For example, if the user enters "100 dollars", the program uses 100 as the input.

After the user completes the INPUT section, the Future Value program calculates the future value and displays it along with the user's entries in the OUTPUT section. This clearly shows the valid values entered by the user, which is useful if the user has entered one or more invalid entries in the INPUT section.

The code for the Future Value program begins by including the header that's defined in the console.h file described in the previous figure. This header contains the get_double(), get_int(), and get_char() functions. Then, the code for the Future Value program declares the calculate_future_value() function that's defined in part 2 of this figure.

The main() function begins by printing the title of the program. Then, it begins a loop that continues if the user enters 'y' or 'Y'. This loop starts by using the get_double() and get_int() functions to get the monthly investment, yearly interest rate, and number of years from the user. To access these functions, this code uses fully qualified names that include the namespace (console), the scope resolution operator (::), and the name of the function.

The calls to the get_double() and get_int() functions include minimum and maximum values that specify a valid range for each entry. In this case, the monthly investment must be a double that's greater than 0 and less than 10,000, the yearly interest rate must be a double that's greater than 0 and less than 30, and the number of years must be an int that's greater than 0 and less than 100. Since the code validates this data, you can be sure that the program can calculate the future value for any values within these ranges.

The console

```
The Future Value Calculator

INPUT
Monthly Investment:    $100
Error! Invalid number. Try again.
Monthly Investment:    100 dollars
Yearly Interest Rate: 36
Error! Number must be less than 30. Try again.
Yearly Interest Rate: 12.0
Years:                 one
Error! Invalid number. Try again.
Years:                 1

OUTPUT
Monthly Investment:    100.00
Yearly Interest Rate: 12.0
Years:                 1
Future Value:          1280.93

Continue? (y/n):
```

The code

```cpp
#include <iostream>
#include <iomanip>
#include <string>
#include <limits>
#include "console.h"

using namespace std;

// declare program-specific function
double calculate_future_value(double monthly_investment,
    double yearly_interest_rate, int years);

int main() {
    cout << "The Future Value Calculator\n\n";

    char choice = 'y';
    while (tolower(choice) == 'y') {
        // get input
        cout << "INPUT\n";
        double monthly_investment =
            console::get_double("Monthly Investment:   ", 0, 10000);
        double yearly_rate =
            console::get_double("Yearly Interest Rate: ", 0, 30);
        int years =
            console::get_int("Years:                ", 0, 100);
        cout << endl;
```

Figure 7-15   The Future Value program (part 1 of 2)

In part 2 of figure 7-15, the main() function continues by using the calculate_future_value() function to calculate the future value. Then, it displays the valid input values and the future value calculated from the input values. Next, it uses the get_char() function to get a character from the user. If the user enters 'y' or 'Y', the condition at the top of the loop evaluates to true, and the loop executes again. Otherwise, the loop ends and the program displays a message that says "Bye!" to the console.

Part 2 also shows the definition for the calculate_future_value() function. This function accepts the three arguments needed to calculate the future value, and it returns the result of the calculation. To do that, it converts the yearly interest rate and number of years to monthly interest rate and number of months. Then, it uses a loop to add the investment for each month and to calculate the interest for each month.

As you review this code, note that it uses fully qualified names to access the functions that are available from the console namespace. This makes it easy to see when the code in the Future Value program calls the functions from the console header. In part 1, the code calls the get_double() function twice and the get_int() function once. In part 2, the code calls the get_char() function once. Of course, if you used this header in a more complex program, you might call each of these functions many times.

The code (continued)

```
            // calculate future value
            double future_value = calculate_future_value(monthly_investment,
                yearly_rate, years);

            // display the output to user
            cout << "OUTPUT\n"
                 << fixed << setprecision(2)
                 << "Monthly Investment:    " << monthly_investment << "\n"
                 << fixed << setprecision(1)
                 << "Yearly Interest Rate: " << yearly_rate << "\n"
                 << "Years:                 " << years << "\n"
                 << fixed << setprecision(2)
                 << "Future Value:          " << future_value << "\n\n";

            // see if the user wants to continue
            choice = console::get_char("Continue? (y/n): ");
        };
        cout << "Bye!\n\n";
}

// define program-specific function
double calculate_future_value(double monthly_investment,
    double yearly_interest_rate, int years) {

    // convert yearly values to monthly values
    double monthly_rate = yearly_interest_rate / 12 / 100;
    int months = years * 12;

    // calculate future value
    double future_value = 0;
    for (int i = 0; i < months; ++i) {
        future_value = (future_value + monthly_investment) *
            (1 + monthly_rate);
    }
    return future_value;
}
```

Figure 7-15   The Future Value program (part 2 of 2)

Perspective

Now that you've finished this chapter, you should have all the skills that you need for defining and calling the functions that your programs require. These are critical skills that become increasingly valuable as your programs get longer and more complex. By applying these skills, you make your programs easier to understand, test, debug, and maintain.

In section 3 of this book, you'll learn how to use object-oriented programming, which provides another way to organize the code in your programs. Fortunately, many of the skills for working with functions also apply to object-oriented programming. That's another reason this chapter is so important.

Terms

function	global constant
define a function	hierarchy chart
parameter	hierarchy outline
call a function	overloaded function
invoke a function	signature of a function
return statement	value variable
Don't Repeat Yourself (DRY)	reference variable
declare a function	header file
function prototype	interface file
global variable	include guard
global scope	implementation file
local variable	namespace
local scope	namespace scope
shadow a global variable	

Summary

- A *function* is a block of code that can be *called* by other statements.
- To *define* a function, code the function's return type, name, a set of parentheses, and a set of braces.
- Within the parentheses of a function, you can code zero or more *parameters* where each parameter consists of a data type and a name and multiple parameters are separated by commas.
- Within the braces of a function, you can code one or more statements for the body of the function. If the function returns a value, the body of the function must use a *return statement* to return a value of the appropriate data type to the calling code.
- To *call*, or *invoke*, a function, code the name of the function and a set of parentheses. Within the parentheses, code any arguments and separate multiple arguments with commas.

- To *declare* a function, you code the function's return type, name, and parameters followed by a semicolon.

- A function declaration is also known as a *function prototype*.

- A variable defined inside a function is known as a *local variable* and is only available within that function.

- A variable defined outside of all functions is known as a *global variable* and is available to all functions in the program.

- When a local variable has the same name as a global variable, the local variable *shadows* the global variable.

- A *value variable* always stores its own copy of a value.

- A *reference variable* stores a reference to a value. This allows multiple reference variables to *refer* to the same value.

- You can organize functions by storing them in separate files. To do that, you can store the function declarations in a *header file*, also known as an *interface file*, and you can store the function definitions in an *implementation file*.

- To prevent the compiler from including the same header twice, headers typically use the #ifndef, #define, and #endif preprocessor directives to define an *include guard*.

- A *namespace* provides a way to organize code to avoid naming conflicts. The functions defined within a namespace have *namespace scope*.

Exercise 7-1   Add functions to the Miles Per Gallon program

In this exercise, you'll add two functions to the Miles Per Gallon program that you worked on in exercise 5-2.

Open the program

1. Open the project or solution named mpg in this folder:
    `ex_starts\ch07_ex1_mpg`

2. Review the code and run the program to refresh your memory on how it works. Notice that, unlike the program in this chapter, this program lets the user perform more than one calculation, it stores the values the user enters in a text file, and it displays the total miles, total gallons, and average miles per gallon when the program starts and after each entry.

Add a function that calculates the miles per gallon

3. Define a function named calculate_mpg() before the main() function that calculates the miles per gallon. This function should accept two double values for the miles and gallons, round the result to two decimal places, and return the result as a double type.

4. Modify the code in the main() function so it uses the calculate_mpg() function. Note that the miles per gallon is calculated in three different places.

5. Move the definition for the calculate_mpg() function after the main() function. When you run the program, you'll get a compile-time error that the function is not found. To fix this problem, add a declaration for the calculate_mpg() function before the main() function.

Add a function that displays the totals

6. Declare a function named display_file_data() that will display the data in the text file. This function won't accept any parameters or return any data.

7. Define the display_file_data() function after the main() function. To do that, you can copy one of the occurrences of the code in the main() function that defines and opens the file and processes the data. Adjust the code as needed so it works within the function.

8. Modify the code in the main() function so it uses the display_file_data() function.

Exercise 7-2   Create a namespace with validation functions

In this exercise, you'll modify the Create Account program from exercise 6-2 so it uses two validation functions that are stored in a namespace.

Open the program

1. Open the project or solution named create_account in this folder:
   `ex_starts\ch07_ex2_create_account`

2. Review the code and run the program to refresh your memory on how it works.

Create a header file

3. Use your IDE to create a header file named validation.h.

4. Add the preprocessor directives to define an include guard. Use a name for the header file that consists of your first initial and last name, followed by "_VALIDATION_H".

5. Define a namespace named validation. Within this namespace, declare two functions named is_valid_password and is_valid_email. Each of these functions should accept a string and return a Boolean value that indicates if the string is valid. For this to work, you'll need to include the header file for the string class.

Create an implementation file

6. Use your IDE to create a file named validation.cpp that will implement the validation header file.

7. Add the code to implement the validation namespace and the two functions it contains. To do that, you can copy code from the main() function for the program and paste it into the function definitions. Then, you can adjust the code as necessary so it works within the functions. For this to work, you'll need to include the header files for the iostream and string classes.

Update the file that contains the main() function to use the header file

8. Add a using directive for the validation namespace to the file that contains the main() function.

9. Replace the code in the main() function that validates the password with a statement that calls the is_valid_password() function and assigns the return value to the valid_password variable.

10. Replace the code in the main() function that validates the email address with a statement that calls the is_valid_email() function and assigns the return value to the valid_email variable.

11. Test the program to see that it works the same as it did before. Now, though, the main() function should be easier to read and understand. In addition, the functions in the header file can be used by other programs.

8

How to test, debug, and deploy a program

As you develop a C++ program, you need to test it to make sure that it performs as expected. Then, if you encounter any problems, you need to debug the program to fix the problems. Finally, when you're done testing and debugging a program, you need to deploy it so your users can run it.

Basic skills for testing and debugging

When you *test* a program, you run it to make sure that it works correctly. As you test the program, you try every possible combination of input data and user actions to be certain that the program works in every case. In other words, the goal of testing is to make a program fail.

When you *debug* a program, you fix the errors (*bugs*) that you discover during testing. Each time you fix a bug, you test again to make sure that the change you made didn't affect any other aspect of the program. On a historical note, the term *bug* was popularized by early computing pioneer Grace Hopper when she found that a dead moth was causing her program to crash.

Typical test phases

When you test a program, you usually do so in phases. Figure 8-1 lists three common test phases.

In the first phase, you test the user interface. For a console program, that means you should make sure that the console displays the correct text and prompts the user for the correct data.

In the second phase, you test the program with valid data. To start, you can enter data that you would expect a user to enter. Then, you should enter valid data that tests all of the limits of the program.

In the third phase, you try to make the program fail. To do that, you can test every combination of invalid data that you can think of. That includes pressing the Enter key before entering any data at all.

The three types of errors

Three types of errors can occur as you test a program. These errors are described in figure 8-1.

Compile-time errors, also called *syntax errors*, prevent your program from compiling and running. This type of error is the easiest to find and fix. If you use an IDE like Visual Studio or Xcode, it automatically detects syntax errors as you type and gives you suggestions for how to fix them.

Unfortunately, some errors can't be detected until you run a program. These errors are known as *runtime errors*, and they can cause a program to crash.

Even if a program runs without crashing, it may contain *logic errors* that prevent the program from working correctly. This type of error is often the most difficult to find and correct. For example, the Future Value program in this figure has a logic error. Can you tell what it is?

The Future Value program with a logic error

```
The Future Value Calculator

INPUT
Monthly Investment:    100
Yearly Interest Rate: 3
Years:                 3

OUTPUT
Monthly Investment:    100.00
Yearly Interest Rate: 3.0
Years:                 3
Future Value:          3662.06

Continue? (y/n):
```

The goal of testing

- To find all errors (bugs) before the program is put into production.

The goal of debugging

- To fix all errors (bugs) before the program is put into production.

Three test phases

- Check the user interface to make sure that it works correctly.
- Test the program with valid input data to make sure the results are correct.
- Test the program with invalid data or unexpected user actions. Try everything you can think of to make the program fail.

The three types of errors that can occur

- *Compile-time errors* are caught by the IDE or compiler before you run the program. These errors are usually *syntax errors* that violate the rules for how statements must be written.
- *Runtime errors* don't violate the syntax rules, but they can cause the program to crash or to yield unexpected results.
- *Logic errors* are statements that don't cause syntax or runtime errors, but produce the wrong results.

Description

- To *test* a program, you run it to make sure that it works properly no matter what combinations of valid or invalid data you enter.
- When you *debug* a program, you fix all of the errors (*bugs*) that you find when you test the program.

Figure 8-1   An introduction to testing and debugging

Common C++ errors

Figure 8-2 presents some of the coding errors that are commonly made as you write a C++ program. If you study this figure, you'll have a better idea of what to watch out for. And if you did the exercises for the previous chapters, you've probably experienced some of these errors already.

The code at the top of this figure is the start of the code for the get_double() function of the Future Value program, but with four errors introduced. The first error is that a data type has not been declared for the variable named num. Unlike some other languages, C++ requires that you declare the data type for all variables.

The second error is a missing semicolon at the end of the statement that displays the prompt string on the console. As you know, C++ requires a semicolon at the end of every statement unless the statement contains a block of code that's enclosed in braces.

The third error is a missing closing parenthesis at the end of the condition for the if statement. Remember that every opening parenthesis, brace, or quotation mark must have a closing parenthesis, brace, or quotation mark.

The fourth error is that the statement that calls the clear() member function from the cin object uses improper capitalization. For this statement, "Clear" should be "clear" since C++ is case-sensitive.

This figure also describes the problem that C++ has with floating-point arithmetic. As you can see in the example near the bottom of this figure, floating-point arithmetic can produce strange results even with simple calculations. Here, you would think that 0.2 plus 0.7 would equal 0.9, but it doesn't. To prevent this type of problem with floating-point numbers, you can round the number to the specified number of decimal places or you can avoid using an equality comparison as described in chapter 6.

Code that contains syntax errors

```
double get_double(string prompt) {
    num;                                 // no data type declared
    while (true) {
        cout << prompt               // missing semicolon at end of statement
        cin >> num;
        if (cin.fail() {             // missing closing parenthesis
            cout << "Error! Invalid number. Try again.\n";
            cin.Clear();             // improper capitalization
            cin.ignore(1000, '\n');
            continue;
        }
        cin.ignore(1000, '\n');
        return num;
    }
}
```

Common syntax errors

- Misspelling keywords.
- Forgetting to declare a data type for a variable.
- Forgetting an opening or closing parenthesis, bracket, or brace.
- Forgetting an opening or closing quotation mark.
- Forgetting to code a semicolon at the end of a statement.

Problems with identifiers

- Misspelling or incorrectly capitalizing an identifier.
- Name collisions due to attempting to use a keyword, global constant, or global function as an identifier.

Problems with values

- Not checking that a value is the right data type before processing it. For example, you expect a number to be entered, but the user enters a non-numeric value instead.
- Using one equals sign (=) instead of two (==) when testing values for equality.

A problem with floating-point numbers

- Using floating-point numbers that can lead to arithmetic errors. For example:

```
double d = 0.2 + 0.7    // d = 0.8999999999999999
cout << d << endl;      // displays 0.9 because of cout's default rounding
if (d == .9)            // this is not true!
```

You can prevent errors like this by rounding or by not using the equality operator as described in chapter 6.

Figure 8-2   Common C++ errors

How to plan the test runs

When you test a program, you usually do so in at least two phases as shown in figure 8-3. In the first phase, you test the program with valid data. In the second phase, you test the program with invalid data.

As your programs become more complex, it helps to create a *test plan* for testing a program. This is simply a table or spreadsheet that shows what test data you're going to enter and what the results should be.

In the valid testing phase, you should start with test data that produces results that can be easily verified. This is illustrated by the Miles Per Gallon program in this figure. Here, the first test data entries are 325 miles driven and 10 gallons of gas used, so the result should clearly be 32.5 miles per gallon, and it is.

But don't stop there. You should also use test data that is more likely to produce an inaccurate result. For example, you could try 97.8 miles driven and 34.3 miles per gallon. Then, you can use a calculator or spreadsheet to determine that the result will be 2.851312, which the program should round to 2.9.

For the invalid testing phase, your test data should include all varieties of invalid entries. This is illustrated by the second and third examples in this figure.

The second example shows what happens when you enter invalid data in a program that doesn't validate the data. Here, the user has entered a string of "ten" at the first prompt of the Miles Per Gallon program. Since this program doesn't validate the data, the program attempts to work with the invalid data, which causes results that are inaccurate and don't make sense.

The third example shows what happens when you enter invalid data in a program that validates the data. Here, the example shows the start of a test run for the Future Value program that tests all aspects of the validation that's done by the program. When you create a test plan for invalid data, you try to make the program fail by testing every combination of invalid data and user action that you can think of. To start, the user enters a string of "ten" where a double value is expected. Then, the user enters a double value that's too small. Next, the user enters a double value that's too big. In each of these cases, the program displays an error message that describes why the data isn't valid and gives the user another chance to enter the data.

There's much more to testing than what's presented in this figure. However, in all programs, what's critical is (1) to test with as many of the possible combinations of data as you can, and (2) to make sure that the results are accurate by comparing them to results that you know are accurate.

The Miles Per Gallon program when it's tested with valid data

```
Miles Per Gallon Calculator

Enter miles driven:        325
Enter gallons of gas used: 10
Miles per gallon:          32.5
```

The Miles Per Gallon program when it's tested with invalid data

```
Miles Per Gallon Calculator

Enter miles driven:        ten
Enter gallons of gas used: Miles per gallon:        1
```

Starting to test the Future Value program with invalid data

```
The Future Value Calculator

INPUT
Monthly Investment:    ten
Error! Invalid number. Try again.
Monthly Investment:    0
Error! Number must be greater than 0. Try again.
Monthly Investment:    10000
Error! Number must be less than 10000. Try again.
Monthly Investment:    9999
Yearly Interest Rate:
```

The two critical test phases

1. Test the program with valid input data to make sure the results are correct.
2. Test the program with invalid data or unexpected user actions. Try everything you can think of to make the program fail.

How to make a test plan for the critical phases

1. List the valid entries that you're going to make and the correct results for each set of entries. Then, make sure that the results are correct when you test with these entries.
2. List the invalid entries that you're going to make. These should include entries that test the limits of the allowable values.

Two common testing problems

- Not testing a wide enough range of entries.
- Not knowing what the results of each set of entries should be and assuming that the answers are correct because they look correct.

Description

- It's easy to find compile-time errors because the program won't run until you fix them.
- Runtime errors and logic errors can slip through your tests if you don't check to make sure the results are correct, or if you don't test a wide enough range of entries.

Figure 8-3   How to plan the test runs

A simple way to trace code execution

Sometimes, the easiest way to find the cause of a runtime error or a logic error is to *trace* the execution of a program. One simple way to do that is to add statements to your code that display messages or variable values at key points in the code.

If, for example, you can't figure out why the future value that's calculated by the Future Value program is incorrect, you can add statements to the code as shown by the highlighted statements in figure 8-4. Here, the first highlighted statement displays a message that indicates that the calculate_future_value() function is starting. Then, the next three highlighted statements display the starting values of the monthly_investment, monthly_rate, and months variables. Finally, the last highlighted statement displays the value of the counter variable and the value of the future_value variable each time through the loop. That should help you determine where the calculation is going wrong. Then, when you find and fix the problem, you can remove the highlighted statements.

After you run the program, the data that's displayed by the highlighted statements clearly shows where the calculation is going wrong. Here, the loop is only executed 35 times for 3 years, but it should be executed 36 times. That means that the loop isn't coded correctly.

In this example, tracing helps you find a bug. However, you can also use tracing to make sure that the results are correct. For instance, you could easily assume that the future value result is correct without checking further, but tracing the execution of the statements in the loop shows that the result can't possibly be correct.

When you trace code execution by printing data to the console, you usually start by adding just a few statements to the code. Then, if that doesn't help you solve the problem, you can add more. This works well for simple programs, but it creates extra work for you because you have to add statements to your code and remove them later.

Later in this chapter, you'll learn how to use a tool known as a debugger to debug a program without having to add or remove statements. This is usually easier than adding and removing statements. However, you can use the technique shown in this figure if you prefer.

Code that traces execution by displaying messages on the console

```
double calculate_future_value(double monthly_investment,
    double yearly_interest_rate, int years) {
    cout << "calculate_future_value() starting...\n";

    // convert yearly values to monthly values
    double monthly_rate = yearly_interest_rate / 12 / 100;
    int months = years * 12;

    // calculate future value
    double future_value = 0;
    cout << "monthly_investment: " << monthly_investment << endl;
    cout << "monthly_rate: " << monthly_rate << endl;
    cout << "months: " << months << endl;
    for (int i = 1; i < months; ++i) {
        future_value = (future_value + monthly_investment) *
            (1 + monthly_rate);
        cout << "month " << i
            << " future_value: " << future_value << endl;
    }

    return future_value;
}
```

The data that's displayed on the console

```
The Future Value Calculator

INPUT
Monthly Investment:    100
Yearly Interest Rate: 3
Years:                 3

calculate_future_value() starting...
monthly_investment: 100
monthly_rate: 0.0025
months: 36
month 1 future_value: 100.25
month 2 future_value: 200.751
month 3 future_value: 301.503
month 4 future_value: 402.506
month 5 future_value: 503.763
...
month 35 future_value: 3662.06
OUTPUT
Monthly Investment:    100.00
Yearly Interest Rate: 3.0
Years:                 3
Future Value:          3662.06
```

Description

- A simple way to *trace* the execution of a program is to include statements at key points in the code that display debugging messages. These messages can indicate what code is being executed, and they may include the values of important variables.

Figure 8-4   A simple way to trace code execution

How to use Visual Studio to debug a program

Although you can find some programming errors by tracing program execution, it's usually easier to use a tool that's designed for just that purpose. Fortunately, most modern IDEs include a powerful tool called a *debugger* that can help you find and remove programming errors.

In the next few figures, you'll learn how to use Visual Studio's debugger. Of course, if you're using Xcode, you can skip these figures and go straight to the figures that show how to use Xcode's debugger. If you compare the debuggers for these two IDEs, you'll see that they work similarly. That's true for the debuggers for most IDEs.

How to set and remove breakpoints

The first step in debugging a program is to determine the cause of the bug. To do that, it's often helpful to view the values of the variables at different points in the program's execution.

The easiest way to view the variable values as a program is executing is to set a *breakpoint* as shown in figure 8-5. To set a breakpoint, you click in the bar to the left of the number for the line of code. Then, the breakpoint is marked by a red dot. Later, when you run the program with the debugger, execution will stop just prior to the statement at the breakpoint. Then, you will be able to view the variables that are in scope at that point in the program. You'll learn more about that in the next figure.

When debugging, it's important to set the breakpoint before the line in the program that's causing the bug. Often, you can figure out where to set a breakpoint by reading any error messages that are displayed when your program crashes. Sometimes, though, you will have to experiment before finding a good location to set a breakpoint.

After you set the breakpoint, you need to run the program with the debugger. To do that, you can press F5 or select the Start Debugging item from the Debug menu.

If you think you might use the breakpoint again, you can disable it by pointing to it with the mouse and clicking on Disable breakpoint icon. This causes the breakpoint icon to change to a hollow circle so you know it's not active. However, this makes it easy to find the breakpoint again. Then, if you want to enable the breakpoint, you can point to it and click on the Enable breakpoint icon.

Once you set a breakpoint, it remains set until you remove it. That's true even if you close the solution and exit from Visual Studio. To remove a breakpoint, you can click on its icon.

Visual Studio with a breakpoint

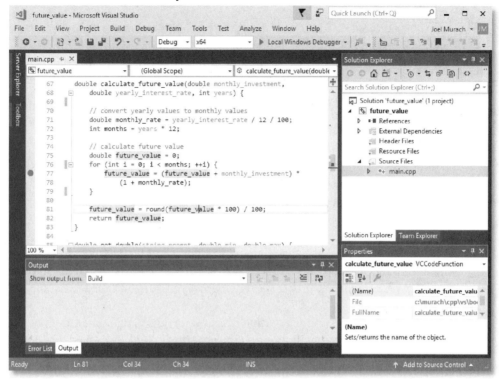

Description

- A *breakpoint* causes program execution to stop before the line that contains the breakpoint is executed.

- To set a breakpoint for a line of code, open the file in the code editor and click in the bar to the left of the line number. The breakpoint is identified by a red dot on the line where you clicked.

- To disable a breakpoint, point to the breakpoint icon with your mouse and click the Disable breakpoint icon that appears. To re-enable it, point to the breakpoint icon again and click on the Enable breakpoint icon that appears.

- To remove a breakpoint, click on the breakpoint icon.

- You can set and remove breakpoints either before you start debugging or while you're debugging. In most cases, you'll set at least one breakpoint before you start debugging.

- To start debugging for a project, press F5 or select the Debug→Start Debugging menu item.

Figure 8-5   How to set and remove breakpoints

How to step through code

When you run a program with the debugger and it encounters a breakpoint, execution stops just prior to the statement at the breakpoint. Once execution stops, a yellow arrow marks the next statement to be executed. In addition, Visual Studio opens the debugging windows shown in figure 8-6. In this figure, the Locals window shows the values of the variables that are in scope at the current point of execution.

Visual Studio also displays the Debug toolbar while you're debugging. You can click the Step Over and Step Into buttons on this toolbar repeatedly to step through a program one statement at a time. Then, you can use the Locals window to observe exactly how and when the variable values change as the program executes. That can help you determine the cause of a bug.

As you step through a program, you can click the Step Over button if you want to execute a function without stepping into it. Or, you can use the Step Out button to step out of any function that you don't want to step through. That includes any functions in C++ libraries that your program may step into. Since these functions probably won't make much sense to you, you can step out of them right away.

When you want to continue normal execution, you can click the Continue button. Then, the program will run until the next breakpoint is reached. Or, you can use the Stop Debugging button to end the program's execution.

These are powerful debugging features that can help you find the cause of serious programming problems. Stepping through a program is also a good way to understand how the code in an existing program works. If, for example, you step through the loop in the calculate_future_value() function, you'll get a better idea of how that loop works.

How to inspect variables

When you set breakpoints and step through code, the Locals window automatically displays the values of the variables that are in scope. In figure 8-6, the execution point is in the calculate_future_value() function of the Future Value program. Here, the Locals window shows the values of the three parameters that are defined by the function (monthly_investment, yearly_interest_rate, and years) and four local variables that are defined within the function (monthly_rate, months, future_value, and i).

For numeric variables and strings, the value of the variable is shown in the Locals window. However, when an object such as a vector is displayed in the Locals window, it doesn't display the values of its variables automatically. Instead, it displays a triangle symbol to the left of the object name. Then, you can view the values for the object by clicking on that triangle to expand it.

A debugging session with Visual Studio

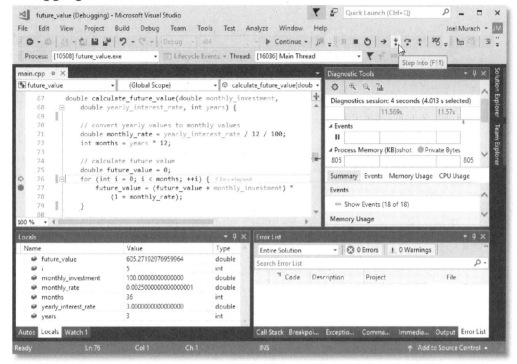

Some of the buttons on the Debug toolbar

Button	Keyboard shortcut	Description
Step Over	F10	Steps through the code one statement at a time, skipping over called functions.
Step Into	F11	Steps through the code one statement at a time, including statements in called functions.
Step Out	Shift+F11	Finishes executing the code in the current function and returns to the calling function.
Continue	F5	Continues execution until the next breakpoint.
Stop Debugging	Shift+F5	Stops debugging and exits the program.

Description

- When a breakpoint is reached, program execution is stopped before the line is executed.
- The arrow in the bar at the left side of the code editor window shows the line that will be executed next.
- The Locals window shows the values of the variables that are in scope for the current function. To display it, click on the Locals tab.
- The Autos window shows the values of the variables in the current line of code and the preceding line. To display it, click on the Autos tab.

Figure 8-6   How to step through code and inspect variables

How to inspect the stack trace

When you're debugging, it's sometimes helpful to view the *stack trace*, which is a list of functions in the reverse order in which they were called. By default, Visual Studio displays a stack trace in the Call Stack window that's displayed in the group of windows to the bottom right of the code editor.

In figure 8-7, for example, the Call Stack window shows that code execution is in the calculate_future_value() function. This window also shows that this function was called by line 35 of the main() function. At this point, you may want to display line 35 of the main() function to view the code that called the calculate_future_value() function. To do that, you can double-click the main() function in the stack trace.

In this figure, both functions are stored in the same file. However, it's common for a function in one file to call a function in another file. In chapter 7, for example, you learned how to code functions in header files. In that case, double-clicking on a function in the stack trace displays the source code for the other file in the code editor. If you experiment with this, you'll find that it can help you locate the origin of a bug.

A Visual Studio debugging session
with the Call Stack window displayed

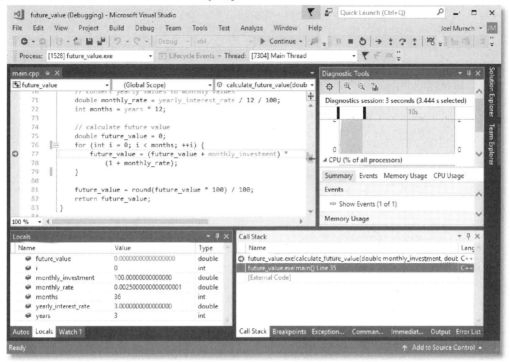

Description

- A *stack trace* is a list of the functions that have been called in the reverse order in which they were called.

- By default, Visual Studio displays a stack trace in the Call Stack window that's included in the group of windows on the bottom right side of the main window.

- To jump to a line of code in the code editor that's displayed in the stack trace, double-click on that line in the stack trace.

Figure 8-7   How to inspect the stack trace

How to use Xcode to debug a program

Although you can find some programming errors by tracing program execution, it's usually easier to use a tool that's designed for just that purpose. Fortunately, most modern IDEs include a powerful tool called a *debugger* that can help you find and remove programming errors.

In the next few figures, you'll learn how to use Xcode's debugger. Of course, if you're using Visual Studio, you can skip these figures. However, you might want to skim these figures to see how similarly the debuggers for these two IDEs work. That's true for the debuggers for most IDEs.

How to set and remove breakpoints

The first step in debugging a program is to determine the cause of the bug. To do that, it's often helpful to view the values of the variables at different points in the program's execution.

The easiest way to view the variable values as a program is executing is to set a *breakpoint* as shown in figure 8-8. To set a breakpoint, you click on the line number for the line of code. Then, the breakpoint is marked by a blue arrow that's placed over the breakpoint. Later, when you run the program, execution will stop just prior to the statement at the breakpoint. Then, you will be able to view the variables that are in scope at that point in the program. You'll learn more about that in the next figure.

When debugging, it's important to set the breakpoint before the line in the program that's causing the bug. Often, you can figure out where to set a breakpoint by reading any error messages that are displayed when your program crashes. Sometimes, though, you will have to experiment before finding a good location to set a breakpoint.

Once you set a breakpoint, it remains set until you deactivate it or remove it. That's true even if you close the project and exit from Xcode.

If you think you might use the breakpoint again, you can deactivate it by clicking on it. This greys out the breakpoint icon so you know it's not active. However, this makes it easy to find the breakpoint again. Then, if you want to activate the breakpoint, you can click on it.

If you want to remove a breakpoint, you can click on its icon while holding down the Control key. Then, you can remove the breakpoint by selecting the Delete Breakpoint item from the resulting menu.

Xcode with a breakpoint

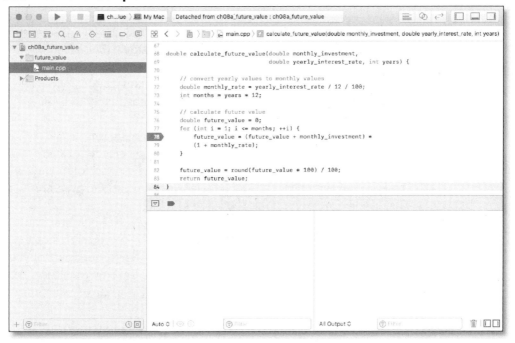

Description

- A *breakpoint* causes program execution to stop before the line that contains the breakpoint is executed.

- To set a breakpoint for a line of code, open the file in the code editor and click on the line number. The breakpoint is identified by a blue arrow that's placed over the line number.

- To deactivate a breakpoint, click on the breakpoint icon. To reactivate, click it again.

- To remove a breakpoint, hold down the Control button, click on the breakpoint icon, and select the Delete Breakpoint item from the resulting menu.

- You can set and remove breakpoints either before you start debugging or while you're debugging. In most cases, you'll set at least one breakpoint before you start debugging.

- To start debugging for a project, set a breakpoint and run the project as you normally would.

Figure 8-8   How to set and remove breakpoints

How to step through code

When you run a program and it encounters a breakpoint, execution stops just prior to the statement at the breakpoint. Once execution stops, the shaded line marks the next statement to be executed. In addition, Xcode opens the debugging windows shown in figure 8-9. In this figure, the Auto window at the bottom of the screen shows the values of the variables that you're most likely to be interested in at the current point of execution.

Xcode also displays the Debug toolbar while you're debugging. You can click the Step Over and Step Into buttons on this toolbar repeatedly to step through a program one statement at a time. Then, you can use the Auto window to observe exactly how and when the variable values change as the program executes. That can help you determine the cause of a bug.

As you step through a program, you can click the Step Over button if you want to execute a function without stepping into it. Or, you can use the Step Out button to step out of any function that you don't want to step through. When you want to continue normal execution, you can click the Continue button. Then, the program will run until the next breakpoint is reached. Or, you can use the Stop button in the Debug toolbar to end the program's execution.

These are powerful debugging features that can help you find the cause of serious programming problems. Stepping through a program is also a good way to understand how the code in an existing program works. If, for example, you step through the loop in the calculate_future_value() function, you'll get a better idea of how that loop works.

How to inspect variables

When you set breakpoints and step through code, the Auto window automatically displays the values of the variables that are most likely to be interesting to you. In figure 8-9, the execution point is in the calculate_future_falue() function of the Future Value program. Here, the Auto window shows the values of the three arguments that are passed to the function (monthly_investment, yearly_interest_rate, and years) and four local variables that are defined within the function (monthly_rate, months, future_value, and i). To make that easy to see, the arguments are marked with an A icon, and the local variables are marked with an L icon.

For numeric variables and strings, the value of the variable is shown in the Auto window. However, when an object such as a vector is displayed in the Auto window, it doesn't display the values of its variables automatically. Instead, it displays a triangle symbol to the left of the object name. Then, you can view the values for the object by clicking on that triangle to expand it.

A debugging session with Xcode

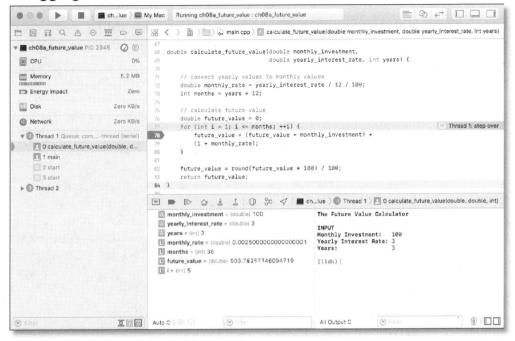

Some of the buttons on the Debug toolbar

Button	Keyboard shortcut	Description
Step Over	F6	Steps through the code one statement at a time, skipping over called functions.
Step Into	F7	Steps through the code one statement at a time, including statements in called functions.
Step Out	F8	Finishes executing the code in the current function and returns to the calling function.
Continue	Cmd+Ctrl+Y	Continues execution until the next breakpoint.

Description

- When a breakpoint is reached, program execution is stopped before the line is executed.
- The line that will be executed next is shaded in the code editor window.
- The Auto window shows the values of the variables that you're most likely to be interested in. To display it, select the Auto item from the list at the bottom of the Debug area.
- The Locals window shows the values of the local variables that are in scope for the current function. To display it, select the Locals item from the list at the bottom of the Debug area.
- To stop debugging and exit the program, click the Stop button that's in the Xcode toolbar at the top of the window, or select the Detach item from the Debug menu.

Figure 8-9   How to step through code and inspect variables

How to inspect the stack trace

When you're debugging, it's sometimes helpful to view the *stack trace*, which is a list of functions in the reverse order in which they were called. By default, Xcode displays a stack trace in the Debug navigator that's displayed on the left side of the main window.

In figure 8-10, for example, the stack trace shows that code execution is in the calculate_future_value() function. This window also shows that this function was called by the main() function. At this point, you may want to display the code in the main() function that called the calculate_future_value() function. To do that, you can click the main() function in the stack trace.

In this figure, both functions are stored in the same file. However, it's common for a function in one file to call a function in another file. In chapter 7, for example, you learned how to code functions in header files. In that case, clicking on a function in the stack trace displays the source code for the other file in the code editor. If you experiment with this, you'll find that it can help you locate the origin of a bug.

An Xcode debugging session with a stack trace displayed

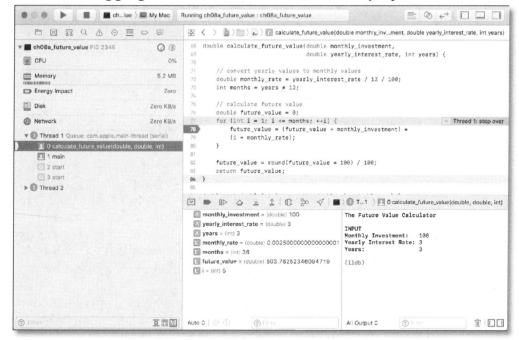

Description

- A *stack trace* is a list of the functions that have been called in the reverse order in which they were called.

- By default, when you begin a debugging session, Xcode displays the Debug navigator on the left side of the main window, and it displays a stack trace within this navigator.

- To jump to a line of code in the code editor that's displayed in the stack trace, click on that line in the stack trace.

- When you end a debugging session, you can display the Project navigator again by clicking on the Project navigator button that's above the Debug navigator.

Figure 8-10   How to inspect the stack trace

How to deploy and run a program

This chapter finishes by showing how to deploy a C++ program. Then, it shows how your users can run a C++ program that has been deployed.

How to deploy a program

When you are developing a C++ program with an IDE, the IDE creates an *executable file* that can run directly on the operating system for which it is compiled. As a result, deploying a program is as easy as finding the executable file and making it available to your users. If you have appropriate privileges, you can make a file available to your users by manually copying the file to their computers. If necessary, you can also include instructions for how to run the executable file, and tips for troubleshooting any problems they may encounter.

If you're using Visual Studio, it usually creates an executable file with an extension of .exe and stores it in a folder that's a subfolder of the project folder like the one shown in figure 8-11.

If you're using Xcode, it usually creates an executable file with no file extension and stores it in a folder like the one shown in this figure. Since this folder isn't a subfolder of the project folder, it can be hard to find. One easy way to find this folder is to use Xcode to expand the Products folder for the project. Then, you can Control click on the executable file and select the Show in Finder item from the resulting menu to view the file in Finder.

How to run a deployed program

In most cases, a user can run an executable file by using the Explorer (Windows) or Finder (Mac) to locate the file and double-click on it. Then, the operating system should start the program in the Command Prompt (Windows) or the Terminal (macOS). However, if Windows users run the executable by double-clicking on it, the console might close when your program exits. This might not allow those users to view the output of your program. To fix this, you can add the code shown in figure 8-11 to the end of your program. Then, the console will stay open until the user presses the Enter key.

Alternately, you may prefer to create programs that are designed to be run from the console. Then, you need to explain to your users that they must use the console to start the program. On Windows, for example, the user can start a Command Prompt window. Then, the user can use the cd command to change to the folder that contains the executable file as shown in this figure. Next, the user can enter the name of the executable file. Although the details are slightly different, you can use a similar technique to run a console program on other operating systems such as macOS or Linux.

You can also make the executable file for your program available from any folder by modifying the system's Path variable so it includes the folder for the executable. To find out how to do that, you can search the Internet.

Typical folder and filename of the executable file

For Visual Studio
```
C:\murach\cpp\vs\book_apps\ch08a_future_value\x64\Debug\future_value.exe
```

For Xcode
```
/Users/Username/Library/Developer/Xcode/DerivedData/ch08a_future_value/
Build/Products/Debug/ch08a_future_value
```

How to deploy an executable file

- Once you've created and found the executable file for a program, you can deploy it by making the executable file available to your users.

Two ways to run the executable file

- Use Explorer (Windows) or Finder (Mac) to locate the executable file. Then, double click on it.
- Start a Command Prompt (Windows) or Terminal (Mac), use the cd command to change to the folder that contains the executable file, and enter the name of the executable file.

Code that you can add to keep the console open
```
cin.ignore(1000, '\n');    // discard all extra data
cout << "Press [Enter] to exit...\n";
cin.ignore();
```

How to use the console to run an executable file on Windows
```
cd \murach\cpp\dist
future_value
```

How to use the console to run an executable file on macOS or Linux
```
cd \Documents/murach/cpp/dist
./future_value
```

Description

- Since C++ compiles the source code to an executable file, deploying a program is as easy as making the executable file available to your users.
- On Windows, if your users run the executable by double-clicking on it, the console might close when your program exits. Then, your users might not be able to view the output of your program. To fix this, you can add some code to the end of your program to keep it open until the user presses the Enter key.
- If your users open a console and use it to run the executable, the console stays open even after your program exits.
- With Xcode, you can find the location of your executable file by expanding the Products folder for the project, Control clicking on the executable file, and selecting the Show in Finder item from the resulting menu.
- If your program uses a file and no path is specified, the file must be located in the working directory, which is almost always the directory that contains the executable.

Figure 8-11   How to deploy and run a program

Perspective

Now that you've completed this chapter, you should have the skills you need to test a program to identify any bugs it may contain. Then, you should be able to use the debugging techniques presented in this chapter to determine the cause of those bugs.

However, you should know that the debuggers available from most IDEs provide some additional features that you can use to test and debug your programs. After reading this chapter, you should be able to learn more about those features on your own.

You should also know that the testing approaches described in this chapter are just the basics for getting you started. As you begin to develop more complex programs, you may want to learn more about other testing approaches such as Test Driven Development (TDD) and Behavior Driven Development (BDD). In addition, you may want to learn about other testing technologies such as unit testing, which is a way of creating tests for individual units of source code such as functions to make sure they work correctly.

Terms

test a program	test plan
debug a program	trace program execution
bug	debugger
compile-time error	breakpoint
syntax error	stack trace
runtime error	executable file
logic error	

Summary

- To *test* a program, you run it to make sure that it works properly no matter what combinations of valid or invalid data you enter.

- When you *debug* a program, you find and fix all of the errors (*bugs*) that you find when you test the program.

- *Compile-time errors* are caught by the compiler before you run the program. These errors are usually *syntax errors* that violate the rules for how statements must be written.

- *Runtime errors* don't violate the syntax rules, but they can cause the program to crash or to yield unexpected results.

- *Logic errors* are statements that don't cause syntax or runtime errors, but produce the wrong results.

- A *test plan* is a table or spreadsheet that shows the data entries that you can use for testing the program as well as the correct results for each set of entries. That way, you can verify that the program's results are correct.

- A simple way to *trace* the execution of a program is to include statements at key points in the code that display debugging messages.

- Most modern IDEs include a powerful tool known as a *debugger* that can help you find and fix errors.

- You can set a *breakpoint* on a line of code to stop code execution just before that line of code is executed. Then, you can step through the code and view the values of the variables as the code executes.

- A *stack trace* is a list of functions in the reverse order in which they were called.

- An *executable file* can be run directly by the operating system that it was compiled for. To deploy an executable file, you can distribute it to your users and show them how to run it.

Exercise 8-1   Test and debug a Test Scores program

In this exercise, you'll test and debug a variation of the Test Scores program of chapter 4.

1. Open the project or solution named test_scores in this folder:
    `ex_starts\ch08_ex1_test_scores`
    Then, review the code.

2. Create a test plan that thoroughly tests the program with valid data. This can be a handwritten table or a spreadsheet that includes the test data for three or four test runs as well as the expected results.

3. Use your test plan as a guide to testing the program. Then, note any inaccurate results that you discover during testing.

4. Debug any logic errors.

5. Test the program with the same data to be sure it works correctly.

Exercise 8-2   Test and debug the Future Value program

In this exercise, you'll use your IDE to find and fix syntax errors and logic errors in the Future Value program.

Correct syntax errors

1. Open the project or solution named future_value in this folder:
    `ex_starts\ch08_ex2_future_value`

2. Open the console.cpp file and notice that the get_double() function contains syntax errors.

3. Use your IDE to find and fix the errors.

Trace code execution

4. Display the main.cpp file, and scroll down to the definition of the calculate_future_value() function. Add a statement to the loop that displays the values of the month and the future value each time the loop is executed.

5. Run the program to see how the statement you just added works. Review the values that are displayed, and notice that the future value increases by too much each month.

6. Make the statement you added a comment so it no longer displays messages.

Step through the program

7. Set a breakpoint on the first statement in the calculate_future_value() function. Then, run the program with the debugger and enter values when prompted. The program should stop at the breakpoint.

8. View the values of the local variables and note that the monthly_investment, yearly_interest_rate, and years variables have been assigned values.

9. Click the Step Into button in the toolbar to execute the statement with the breakpoint, and notice the value that's been assigned to the monthly_rate variable. Is this value correct? If not, stop debugging and fix the error.

10. Run the program again with the debugger and enter the same values as before. When the program reaches the breakpoint, click the Step Into button to execute that statement. If you fixed the error, the value of the monthly_rate variable should now be correct.

11. Set another breakpoint on the statement within the for loop that calculates the future value. Then, step through the loop three or more times to see how the values of future_value and i variables change each time.

12. Remove both breakpoints from the calculate_future_value() function. Then, click the Step Out button to finish executing this function and return to the statement in the main() function that calls the calculate_future_value() function.

13. Click the Continue button to display the results of the calculation on the console.

14. Set a breakpoint on the first statement in the main() function.

15. At the console, enter "y" to continue. When the breakpoint is reached, use the Step Into, Step Out, and Step Over buttons to step through the code, entering values as prompted and experimenting as you go.

16. When you're done, use your IDE to end debugging.

Section 2

More skills as you need them

The chapters in this section are designed to add to the skills presented in section 1 of this book. Because these chapters are modular, you can read them in the sequence that you prefer. If, for example, you want to learn how to work with STL containers, you can skip to chapter 10. Or, if you want to learn how to work with exceptions, you can skip to chapter 13.

However, we recommend reading chapters 10 and 11 in sequence. In other words, chapter 10 is a prerequisite to chapter 11. Eventually, though, you'll want to read all of these chapters since they all describe skills that every C++ programmer should have.

9

How to work with structures and enumerations

This chapter begins by showing how to use a structure to group items of different data types into a single data type. Then, this chapter shows how to use an enumeration to group related constants. Both of these features make it easier to organize your code and work with related data.

Basic skills for working with structures

So far in this book, you've learned how to work with data types such as the string, double, int, and vector types. Sometimes, though, you need to organize your data by grouping related data types. For example, a product may consist of many data types, and you may want to group all of those data types into a single data type. To do that, you can create a structure.

How to get started with structures

Figure 9-1 shows how to define a *structure* that consists of multiple data types. To do that, you code the struct keyword, followed by the name of the structure and the data types it contains within braces. Notice in the syntax shown here that you must code a semicolon after the closing brace.

The example that follows defines a structure named Movie that contains two data types: a string for the title of the movie and an int value for the year that the movie was originally released. When working with structures, it's a common practice to start each word of a structure name with a capital letter, as in "Movie" and "CustomerInvoices".

After you define a structure, you can create an object from the structure by defining a variable of the structure type as shown in the second example. Here, the code defines a variable named movie of the Movie data type. Like other variable names, it's common to use lowercase letters for the names of variables that define structures.

Once you've created an object from a structure, you can access its *data members*, or just *members*, by using the dot operator. This works the same way it does for any other object such as the cout object. For instance, the third example shows how to assign values to the members of the Movie object, and it shows how to read values from the Movie object.

The fourth example shows that you can store one or more structure objects in a vector. Here, the first statement creates a vector of Movie objects named movies. Then, the second statement adds the Movie object named movie to the vector.

If you have a vector that contains one or more structure objects, you can use a range-based for loop to easily access the data in each object as shown by the fifth example. Here, the loop just displays the title and year for each movie in the vector.

Without a Movie structure, the code in the last two examples would be more difficult to develop and maintain. To start, you'd need a vector of strings for the title and a separate vector of integers for the year. Then, you'd need to make sure these vectors remained synchronized. To do that, you wouldn't be able to use a range-based for loop because you'd need an index to access the elements of each vector.

How to define a structure data type

The syntax for defining a structure

```
struct DataType {
    structure members ...
};
```

A Movie structure

```
struct Movie {
    string title;
    int year;
};
```

How to define a variable of a structure type

```
Movie movie;
```

How to access the members of a structure object

How to assign values directly

```
movie.title = "Wonder Woman";
movie.year = 2017;
```

How to assign values from the input stream

```
cout << "Please enter a movie title: ";
getline(cin, movie.title);

cout << "Please enter the year that movie was released: ";
cin >> movie.year;
```

How to read values

```
cout << movie.title << " was released in " << movie.year << ".\n";
```

How to create a vector of structure objects and add a structure object to it

```
vector<Movie> movies;
movies.push_back(movie);
```

How to loop through a vector of structure objects

```
for(Movie m: movies) {
    cout << m.title << " was released in " << m.year << ".\n";
}
```

Description

- You can use the struct keyword to define a *structure* that consists of one or more data types. When you define a structure, the definition ends with a semicolon.

- The data types that compose a structure type are called *data members*, or just *members*.

- When you define a variable of a structure type, an object of that type is created.

- You can use dot notation to access the data members of an object that's created from a structure.

- You can use a vector to store one or more objects created from a structure. Then, you can use a range-based for loop to easily access the data in each object.

Figure 9-1   How to get started with structures

How to initialize a structure

When you create an object from a structure, the members contain whatever values happen to be at the memory location where they are created. This can lead to unexpected results as shown by the first example in figure 9-2.

As a result, it's a best practice to *initialize* the members with starting data when you create an object. To do that, you can use an *initialization list* as shown by the second example. This example starts by showing the syntax of an initialization list. Then, it shows two Movie objects that are defined with initialization lists. When you use an initialization list, the assignment operator is optional, as illustrated by the second statement. Either way, the code assigns the first value in the list to the first member in the structure, it assigns the second value to the second member, and so on.

When you provide an initialization list, you don't have to include a value for every member. However, if you don't initialize a member, you can't initialize any subsequent members. This is illustrated by the third Movie object that's defined in this example. Here, the code assigns a title of "Casablanca" to the movie, but it doesn't assign any subsequent members. In this case, the only subsequent member is the year, but a Movie structure could potentially have many more subsequent members.

In C++11 and later, you can set default values in the structure definition. In the third example, for instance, the code defines a default title of an empty string and a default year of 0. These default values prevent unexpected results from occurring when you create a Movie object from this structure. As a result, this structure is easier to use than the Movie structure defined in the previous figure.

Code that displays the initial values of a Movie object's members

```
Movie movie;
cout << "MOVIE OBJECT INITIAL VALUES\n"
     << "Title: " << movie.title << endl
     << "Year: " << movie.year << endl;
```

The console

```
MOVIE OBJECT INITIAL VALUES
Title:
Year: 4201099
```

How to use an initialization list to initialize a structure

The syntax of an initialization list

```
DataType variable_name [=] { value1[, value2] ... };
```

Two Movie objects defined with initialization lists

```
Movie movie_1 = { "Casablanca", 1942 };   // optional assignment operator
Movie movie_2 { "Wonder Woman", 2017 };
```

A Movie object initialized with only a title

```
Movie movie_3 = { "Casablanca" };
```

How to set default member values as part of the structure definition

```
struct Movie {
    string title = "";
    int year = 0;
};
```

Description

- When you create an instance of a structure, the members contain whatever values happen to be at the memory location where they are created. This can lead to unexpected results.

- Due to possible unexpected results, it's generally considered a best practice to *initialize* the members with starting data when you create an object.

- You can use an *initialization list* to set the starting values of an object when you create it. When you use an initialization list, the assignment operator is optional.

- The first value in an initialization list is assigned to the first member in the structure, the second value is assigned to the second member, and so on.

- You don't have to include a value in the list for every member. However, if you don't initialize a member, you can't initialize any subsequent members.

- In C++11 and later, you can set default values in the structure definition.

Figure 9-2   How to initialize a structure

The Movie List 1.0 program

Now that you've seen some basic skills for working with a structure, you're ready to see a Movie List 1.0 program that uses these skills. Later in this chapter, you'll see a Movie List 2.0 program that expands on these skills.

Part 1 of figure 9-3 starts by showing the user interface for the Movie List 1.0 program. This program allows the user to enter one or more movies. Then, when the user is done entering movies, the program displays a list of all movies entered by the user.

Next, this figure shows the code for the Movie List 1.0 program. To start, this code defines a structure for a Movie object that contains a title and a year. This structure includes default values for the title and year, since the program doesn't initializes Movie objects when it creates them.

After defining the structure, the main() function displays the name of the program and prompts the user to enter a movie. Then, it defines a vector for storing Movie objects and enters a while loop that continues until the user decides to stop it by not entering a 'y' or 'Y'.

Within the loop, the first statement defines a Movie object named movie. Then, the code gets the title and year of the movie from the user and stores those values in the Movie object. Next, the code adds the Movie object to the vector of Movie objects.

The console

```
The Movie List program

Enter a movie...

Title: Casablanca
Year: 1942

Enter another movie? (y/n): y

Title: Wonder Woman
Year: 2017

Enter another movie? (y/n): n

TITLE                   YEAR
Casablanca              1942
Wonder Woman            2017
```

The code

```cpp
#include <iostream>
#include <iomanip>
#include <string>
#include <vector>

using namespace std;

// define a struct for a Movie object
struct Movie {
    string title = "";
    int year = 0;
};

int main() {
    cout << "The Movie List program\n\n"
         << "Enter a movie...\n\n";

    // get vector of Movie objects
    vector<Movie> movie_list;
    char another = 'y';
    while (tolower(another) == 'y') {
        Movie movie;

        cout << "Title: ";
        getline(cin, movie.title);

        cout << "Year: ";
        cin >> movie.year;

        movie_list.push_back(movie);

        cout << "\nEnter another movie? (y/n): ";
        cin >> another;
        cin.ignore();
        cout << endl;
    }
```

Figure 9-3   The Movie List 1.0 program (part 1 of 2)

When the user ends this loop by not entering 'y' or 'Y', the code in part 2 of figure 9-3 displays all Movie objects that have been stored in the vector. To do that, it uses the stream output manipulators to left align all data in two columns where the first column is 30 characters wide (10 * 3) and the second column is 10 characters wide.

As you review this code, note that the Movie List program doesn't validate any of the data entered by the user. That keeps the code listing short and focused on the code that works with the Movie structure.

The code (continued)

```
// display the Movie objects stored in the vector
const int w = 10;
cout << left
    << setw(w * 3) << "TITLE"
    << setw(w)      << "YEAR" << endl;
for (Movie movie : movie_list) {
    cout << setw(w * 3) << movie.title
        << setw(w)      << movie.year << endl << endl;
}
}
```

Figure 9-3   The Movie List 1.0 program (part 2 of 2)

More skills for working with structures

Now that you're familiar with the basic skills for working with structures, you're ready to learn more skills for working with structures. These skills include nesting structures, using structures with functions, comparing structures, and defining member functions.

How to nest structures

Figure 9-4 shows how to *nest* one structure within another structure. To do that, you code a structure variable as a data member. In this figure, the first example begins by defining a Date structure that uses int variables to store the year, month, and day of the date. Then, it defines an Invoice structure that uses an int variable for the invoice number, Date variables for the date and due date, and a double variable for the total. In other words, this code nests two Date structures within the Invoice structure.

The second example shows how to write code that works with these nested structures. Here, the first statement creates an Invoice object from the Invoice structure. Because this structure contains two members of the Date type, this also creates two Date objects. Then, this code assigns values to the Invoice object. To assign values to the nested objects, it uses dot notation to access the members of those objects. For example, it uses invoice.date.month to access the month member of the Date object that's stored in the Invoice object.

After assigning values to the Invoice object, this code also reads values from the Invoice object and displays them on the console. Again, to do that, this code uses the dot notation to access the members of the nested structures.

There is no limit to how deep you can nest structures. However, as with all nesting, it's best not to nest deeper than two or three levels. Otherwise, your code can become hard to understand and maintain.

An Invoice structure that nests two Date structures

```
struct Date {
    int year = 1900;
    int month = 1;
    int day = 1;
};

struct Invoice {
    int number = -1;
    Date date;
    Date due_date;
    double total = 0;
};
```

Code that uses these nested structures

```
// create the Invoice structure
Invoice invoice;

// assign values to the Invoice and Date structures
invoice.number = 1;
invoice.date.month = 1;
invoice.date.day = 2;
invoice.date.year = 2018;
invoice.due_date.month = 4;
invoice.due_date.day = 15;
invoice.due_date.year = 2018;
invoice.total = 1430.72;

// read values from the Invoice and Date structures
cout << "INVOICE\n"
     << "Number:   " << invoice.number << endl
     << "Date:     " << invoice.date.year << '-'
                     << invoice.date.month << '-'
                     << invoice.date.day << endl
     << "Due Date: " << invoice.due_date.year << '-'
                     << invoice.due_date.month << '-'
                     << invoice.due_date.day << endl
     << "Total:    " << invoice.total << endl << endl;
```

The console

```
INVOICE
Number:   1
Date:     2018-1-2
Due Date: 2018-4-15
Total:    1430.72
```

Description

- You can *nest* structures within other structures. To do that, you code a structure variable as a data member.

- You use dot notation to access the members of a nested structure.

- There is no limit to how deep you can nest structures.

Figure 9-4   How to nest structures

How to use structures with functions

Figure 9-5 shows how to use structures with functions. As you may remember from chapter 7, a function can't return multiple values. However, if a function returns a structure type, it can return multiple values as the data members of the structure. For instance, the first example in this figure creates a Movie object and stores two values in it (a string value and an int value) and returns that Movie object to the calling code.

By default, when you pass a structure type to a function, its data members are passed by value. That means a copy of each member is passed. Since that's not efficient, especially for a large structure with many members, it's common to pass structures by reference as shown in the second and third examples.

The second example, for instance, doesn't need to change any data members of the structure object. As a result, the parameter for the Movie object is defined as a constant reference parameter. That way, the statement within the display_movie() function can get the values of the data members, but it can't assign new values to them.

However, the third example does need to change a data member of the structure object. As a result, the parameter for the Movie object is defined as a reference parameter. That way, the second statement in the update_movie_year() function can assign a new value to the year member of the Movie object. Since this also modifies the Movie object in the calling code, there's no need to return the Movie object to the calling code.

The fourth example shows how to use the three functions defined by the first three examples. Here, the first statement gets a Movie object from user input. The second statement displays the Movie object to the user. The third statement allows the user to update the year for the movie. And the fourth statement displays the updated movie data.

Although the code in the third example is the most efficient way to update the data in a structure, some programmers consider it a better practice to pass structures by value as shown in the fifth example. To do that, the function in this example doesn't define the Movie parameter as a reference parameter. As a result, the Movie argument is passed by value. Then, the first two statements in this function update a copy of the Movie object and don't modify the Movie object in the calling code. As a result, this function must include a third statement that returns the Movie object to the calling code.

The sixth example shows how the calling code can use the function defined by the fifth example. Here, the statement passes a Movie object named movie to the function and assigns the updated Movie object to the same variable name. The advantage of this code is that it clearly shows that the Movie object in the calling code is being updated by this function. The disadvantage, as mentioned earlier, is that this code isn't as efficient. However, this is less of an issue as more compilers implement *return value optimization* (*RVO*), which eliminates the need to copy the object. Although the details of how this works are beyond the scope of this book, you can feel confident that in most situations, you can return a container without negatively impacting performance.

A function that returns a Movie object

```
Movie get_movie() {
    Movie movie;
    cout << "Enter title: ";
    getline(cin, movie.title);
    cout << "Enter year: ";
    cin >> movie.year;
    return movie;
}
```

A function that accepts a Movie object but doesn't update it

```
void display_movie(const Movie& movie) {
    cout << "MOVIE: " << movie.title << " (" << movie.year << ")\n\n";
}
```

A function that accepts a Movie object and updates it

```
void update_movie_year(Movie& movie) {
    cout << "Update Year: ";
    cin >> movie.year;
}
```

Code that uses these functions to work with movie data

```
Movie movie = get_movie();
display_movie(movie);
update_movie_year(movie);
display_movie(movie);
```

The output

```
Enter title: Wonder Woman
Enter year: 1917
MOVIE: Wonder Woman (1917)

Update Year: 2017
MOVIE: Wonder Woman (2017)
```

Another way to update a Movie object

```
Movie update_movie_year2(Movie movie) {
    cout << "Update Year: ";
    cin >> movie.year;
    return movie;
}
```

Code that uses this function to update a Movie object

```
movie = update_movie_year2(movie);
```

Description

- When you pass a structure object to a function, all the values in its data members are passed by value. That means a copy of each member is passed.

- If a function needs to access the same structure object as the calling code, the object must be passed by reference. This improves performance for large objects.

- A function can't return multiple values. However, if a function returns a structure type, it can return multiple values as the data members of the structure object.

Figure 9-5   How to use structures with functions

How to compare structures for equality

By default, a structure doesn't provide an equality operator (==). As a result, if you try to use the equality operator to compare two Movie objects, you'll get an error that indicates that the equality operator isn't available for comparing Movie objects. To illustrate, figure 9-6 starts by defining three Movie objects, the first two of which contain the same data. Then, the second example shows the error that's displayed by Visual Studio/MVSC when these two objects are tested for equality. You should get a similar message for other IDE/compiler combinations.

Instead of using the equality operator to compare structure objects, you can test whether two structure objects are equal by comparing the values of the data members. The third example in this figure illustrates how this works. Here, the code checks whether both the title and year members of two Movie objects are equal. If they are, the code displays a message that indicates that the objects are equal. Otherwise, the code displays a message that indicates that the objects are not equal.

The fourth example shows how you can store the result of an equality comparison in a Boolean variable. Here, the first statement defines a bool variable named duplicate. Then, the second statement checks whether the Movie objects named ww1 and ww2 contain the same data. Since they do, it sets the duplicate variable to a value of true. Next, the third statement checks whether the Movie objects named ww1 and cb contain the same data. Since they don't, it sets the duplicate variable to a value of false.

Three Movie objects for comparison

```
Movie ww1 {"Wonder Woman", 2017};
Movie ww2 {"Wonder Woman", 2017};
Movie cb {"Casablanca", 1942};
```

What happens if you try to compare structure variables for equality

The code

```
if (ww1 == ww2) {
    cout << "The movies are equal.\n";
}
```

A typical error message

```
no operator "==" matches these operands
```

How to compare the data members of the Movie objects for equality

An if statement that displays a message

```
if (ww1.title == ww2.title &&
    ww1.year  == ww2.year) {
    cout << "The movies are equal.\n";
} else {
    cout << "The movies are NOT equal.\n";
}
```

The console

```
The movies are equal.
```

Code that sets a Boolean variable

```
bool duplicate;
duplicate = (ww1.title == ww2.title &&
             ww1.year  == ww2.year);    // duplicate is true
duplicate = (ww1.title == cb.title &&
             ww1.year  == cb.year);     // duplicate is false
```

Description

- A structure doesn't define the equality operator (==) by default. As a result, if you try to use the equality operator to compare two structure variables, you'll get an error.

- To test whether two structure variables are equal, you can compare the values in the data members.

Figure 9-6   How to compare structures for equality

How to work with member functions

In addition to members that contain data, a structure can have *member functions* that operate on the data members. A member function works like a regular function, so it can accept parameters and return values.

In figure 9-7, the first example defines a Movie structure that includes a member function named equals(). This function accepts a Movie object named to_compare as an argument and returns a bool value. Within the body of this function, a single statement returns the bool value that results from checking whether the data members of the current Movie object are equal to the data members of the Movie object that's passed to the member function.

The second example shows that you can use the dot operator to call a member function. Here, the second statement uses the dot operator to call the equals() member function from the Movie object named ww1 defined in the previous figure. Then, it passes the Movie object named ww2, which was also defined in the previous figure, to this function. As a result, because these two Movie objects contain the same data, this function returns a bool value of true. The third statement, on the other hand, uses the equals() function to compare the Movie objects named ww2 and cb. As a result, this function returns a value of false.

As with regular functions, you can declare a function in the structure definition as shown by the third example. Then, you can define the function after the structure definition. To do that, you should prefix the function definition with the data type and the scope resolution operator (::). This tells the compiler that the function is a member of the structure.

How to work with member operators

You can also add operators that work with a structure. To do that, you can use the same skills for adding a function, but instead of coding the function name, you code the operator keyword and the operator. For instance, the fourth example shows how to define an equality operator (==) instead of the equals() member function shown in the first example.

The fifth example shows how to use the equality operator defined by the fourth example. As you review this example, you should realize that including an equality operator like this provides an easier way to compare structures for equality than the technique shown in the previous figure. As a result, if you find that you often need to compare structures for equality, you can add an equality operator like this one to your structure.

In this figure, the function for the operator is defined within the structure definition. However, if you want, you can declare the operator function within the structure definition, and you can code its definition after the structure definition. To do that, you can use the same skills for working with member functions that are illustrated in the third example.

A Movie data type with a member function

```
struct Movie {
    string title;
    int year;
    bool equals(const Movie& to_compare) {
        return (title == to_compare.title && year == to_compare.year);
    }
}
```

Code that calls the member function of a Movie object

```
bool duplicate;
duplicate = ww1.equals(ww2);      // duplicate is true
duplicate = ww1.equals(cb);       // duplicate is false
```

How to declare a member function prototype and define it later

```
struct Movie {
    string title;
    int year;
    bool equals(const Movie&);    // member function prototype
};
// member function definition
bool Movie::equals(const Movie& to_compare) {
    return (title == to_compare.title && year == to_compare.year);
}
```

How to add an operator to a data type

```
struct Movie {
    string title;
    int year;
    bool operator==(const Movie& to_compare) {
        return (title == to_compare.title && year == to_compare.year);
    }
};
```

Code that uses the equality operator with Movie objects

```
bool duplicate;
duplicate = (ww1 == ww2);        // duplicate is true
duplicate = (ww1 == cb);         // duplicate is false
```

Description

- In addition to members that contain data, a structure can have *member functions* that operate on its data members. A member function works like a regular function.

- To call a member function from a structure object, you use the dot operator.

- As with regular functions, you can declare a function in the structure definition and define it after the structure definition.

- To define a function outside of a structure definition, prefix the function definition with the data type and the scope resolution operator (::). That way, the compiler knows that this function is a member of the structure.

- You can also use member functions to add operators for your data type. To do that, you use the operator keyword and the operator you're adding when you define your function.

Figure 9-7   How to work with member functions and operators

The Movie List 2.0 program

Figure 9-8 presents a Movie List program that illustrates many of the skills that you've just learned. As the console shows, this program maintains a list of movies, and the user can view all the movies, add a movie to the list, or delete a movie from the list.

After the console, this figure shows the code for this program. By now, you should understand how most of this code works. To start, it defines a structure for a Movie object. This structure has three data members (title, year, and stars), and the declaration for a member function named equals().

Next is the definition for the equals() function. Here, it's important to note that this function only checks whether the title and year are the same, not whether the number of stars are the same. Then, this code defines a constant that stores the filename for the file that contains the data for the program.

The next function, shown in part 2 of figure 9-8, reads the movie data from the data file, stores this data in a vector of Movie objects, and returns that vector to the calling code. As you review this function, note that each line in the file stores the data for one movie with each data member separated by a tab character (\t). As a result, to get the movie title from the line, this code uses an overload of the getline() function that uses a third parameter to tell the function to stop reading the string when it encounters the next tab character (\t). That way, the code uses the getline() method to read the title for each line. Then, it uses the extraction operator (**>>**) to read the year and stars for each line.

Part 2 also includes two functions that accept the vector of Movie objects as a parameter. The first one writes the data in this vector to the movie file. The second one displays the data in this vector on the console, along with the number that's associated with each movie in the list.

Part 3 of figure 9-8 begins by showing the function that gets all of the data for a movie from the user. To do that, this function prompts the user to enter this data, and it stores the data in a Movie object. Then, it returns that Movie object to the calling code.

Next is a function that adds a Movie object to a vector of Movie objects. To make sure this works correctly, this code begins by checking if the Movie already exists in the vector. To do that, it uses the equals() member function of the Movie object. If the movie already exists in the vector, this code assumes that a different number of stars have been entered and it updates the number of stars for the movie. Then, it writes the vector of Movies to the movie file and displays a message that indicates that the movie was updated. However, if the movie doesn't already exist in the vector, this code adds the movie to the end of the vector, writes the vector to the movie file, and displays a message that indicates that the movie was added.

The last function in part 3 gets a number from the user that corresponds to a movie in the list of movies that's displayed on the console by the view command. This function starts by discarding any remaining characters in the input stream. Then, it uses a while loop to prompt the user for a number until the user enters a valid number. Here, the code checks whether the number is greater than 0 and less than or equal to the size of the vector. If so, the number is valid.

The console

```
The Movie List program

COMMANDS
v - View movie list
a - Add a movie
d - Delete a movie
x - Exit

Command: v
     TITLE                        YEAR    STARS
1    Casablanca                   1942    5
2    Wonder Woman                 2017    4

Command: a
Title: The Wizard of Oz
Year: 1939
Stars (1-5): 5
The Wizard of Oz was added.

Command: d
Number: 1
Casablanca was deleted.

Command: x
Bye!
```

The code

```cpp
#include <iostream>
#include <fstream>
#include <sstream>
#include <iomanip>
#include <string>
#include <vector>

using namespace std;

struct Movie {
    string title = "";
    unsigned int year = 0;
    unsigned int stars = 0;
    bool equals(Movie&);                    // member function declaration
};

// member function definition
bool Movie::equals(Movie& to_compare) {
    return (title == to_compare.title && year == to_compare.year);
}

const string movies_file = "movies.txt";
```

Figure 9-8   The Movie List 2.0 program (part 1 of 4)

The code (continued)

```cpp
vector<Movie> read_movies_from_file() {
    vector<Movie> movies;

    ifstream input_file(movies_file);
    if (input_file) {       // if file opened successfully...
        Movie movie;
        string line;
        while (getline(input_file, line)) {
            stringstream ss(line);

            getline(ss, movie.title, '\t');        // get title
            ss >> movie.year >> movie.stars;       // get year and stars
            movies.push_back(movie);               // add movie to vector
        }
        input_file.close();
    }
    return movies;
}

void write_movies_to_file(const vector<Movie>& movies) {
    ofstream output_file(movies_file);
    if (output_file) {       // if file opened successfully...
        for (Movie movie : movies) {
            output_file << movie.title << '\t'
                << movie.year << '\t'
                << movie.stars << '\n';
        }
        output_file.close();
    }
}

void view_movies(const vector<Movie>& movies) {
    int col_width = 8;
    cout << left
        << setw(col_width / 2) << " "
        << setw(col_width * 4) << "TITLE"
        << setw(col_width) << "YEAR"
        << setw(col_width) << "STARS" << endl;

    int number = 1;
    for (Movie movie : movies) {
        cout << setw(col_width / 2) << number
            << setw(col_width * 4) << movie.title
            << setw(col_width) << movie.year
            << setw(col_width) << movie.stars << endl;
        ++number;
    }
    cout << endl;
}
```

Figure 9-8   The Movie List 2.0 program (part 2 of 4)

The code (continued)

```cpp
Movie get_movie() {
    Movie movie;
    cout << "Title: ";
    cin.ignore(1000, '\n');
    getline(cin, movie.title);
    cout << "Year: ";
    cin >> movie.year;
    cout << "Stars (1-5): ";
    cin >> movie.stars;
    return movie;
}

void add_movie(vector<Movie>& movies) {
    Movie movie = get_movie();

    // check if movie already exists
    bool already_exists = false;
    for (Movie& m : movies) {
        if (m.equals(movie)) {
            already_exists = true;
            m.stars = movie.stars;
            break;
        }
    }

    if (already_exists) {
        write_movies_to_file(movies);
        cout << movie.title << " already exists and was updated.\n\n";
    }
    else {
        movies.push_back(movie);
        write_movies_to_file(movies);
        cout << movie.title << " was added.\n\n";
    }
}

int get_movie_number(const vector<Movie>& movies) {
    cin.ignore(1000, '\n');
    int number;
    while (true) {
        cout << "Number: ";
        cin >> number;
        if (number > 0 && number <= movies.size()) {
            return number;
        }
        else {
            cout << "Invalid movie number. Try again.\n";
        }
    }
}
```

Figure 9-8   The Movie List 2.0 program (part 3 of 4)

As a result, the function returns it to the calling code. This causes program execution to exit the loop and the function. Otherwise, the number is invalid. As a result, the code displays an appropriate error message. Then, program execution continues at the top of the loop, which prompts the user for another number.

Part 4 of figure 9-8 begins by defining a function that deletes a movie. This function begins by getting a number that corresponds with a movie in the list of movies that's displayed on the console. Then, this code gets the index for that movie by subtracting 1 from the number for the movie. Next, it uses the index to get the Movie object, delete it from the vector, write the movie data in the vector to a file, and display an appropriate message that includes the title of the movie that was deleted.

The next function in part 4 displays a menu of commands. This function consists of a single statement that displays the characters (v, a, d, and x). Then, the user can enter one of these characters to execute the commands (view, add, delete, and exit) for working with the program.

The last function is the main() function that runs when the program starts. This function begins by displaying the name of the program. Then, it displays the menu for the program, it reads the movie data from the text file for the program into a vector of movies, and it begins a while loop that continues until the user enters 'x' to exit. Within the loop, the code prompts the user to enter a command. Then, a switch statement executes the appropriate code depending on what command is entered. If the user enters 'v', 'a', or 'd', the function for viewing a movie, adding a moving, or deleting a movie is called. However, if the user enters 'x', the code displays a message of "Bye!", and program execution exits the loop, which causes the program to end. Or, if the user doesn't enter a valid command, the switch statement displays an appropriate error message, and program execution continues at the top of the loop, which prompts the user for another command.

As you review this code, note that the add_movie() and delete_movie() functions don't return the vector of movies after they change it. That's because these methods define the vector parameter as a reference variable. As a result, the code in the main() function refers to the same vector that's modified by the add_movie() and delete_movie() functions.

Also note that the write_movies_to_file(), view_movies(), and get_movie_number() functions accept the vector of movies as a reference parameter. That means these functions also work with the vector defined in the main() function. In addition, because these functions don't change the vector, the vector parameter is defined as a constant.

The code (continued)

```cpp
void delete_movie(vector<Movie>& movies) {
    int number = get_movie_number(movies);

    int index = number - 1;
    Movie movie = movies[index];
    movies.erase(movies.begin() + index);
    write_movies_to_file(movies);
    cout << movie.title << " was deleted.\n\n";
}

void display_menu() {
    cout << "COMMANDS\n"
        << "v - View movie list\n"
        << "a - Add a movie\n"
        << "d - Delete a movie\n"
        << "x - Exit\n\n";
}

int main() {
    cout << "The Movie List program\n\n";
    display_menu();
    vector<Movie> movies = read_movies_from_file();
    char command = 'v';
    while (command != 'x') {
        cout << "Command: ";
        cin >> command;
        switch (command) {
            case 'v':
                view_movies(movies);
                break;
            case 'a':
                add_movie(movies);
                break;
            case 'd':
                delete_movie(movies);
                break;
            case 'x':
                cout << "Bye!\n\n";
                break;
            default:
                cout << "Not a valid command. Please try again.\n\n";
                break;
        }
    }
}
```

Figure 9-8   The Movie List 2.0 program (part 4 of 4)

How to work with enumerations

In chapter 6, you learned how to use constants to store values that don't change as a program executes. In some cases, though, you may want to group related constants. For example, you might want to group constants that represent the seven days of the week. To do that, you can use an enumeration.

Basic skills for working with scoped enumerations

An *enumerated data type*, or *enumeration*, is a user-defined type that's composed of constant values. The constant values contained in an enumeration are called *enumerators*. By default, they are stored in memory as sequential integers starting at 0, which is usually what you want.

To define an enumeration, you use the syntax shown in figure 9-9. Here, the enum keyword is followed by the optional class keyword and the name of the enumeration. Then, the constants that make up the enumeration are coded within braces and separated by commas. Finally, a semicolon is coded after the closing brace. In this figure, for instance, the first example defines an enumeration named Operation that contains four enumerators (add, subtract, multiply, and divide).

With C++11 and later, it's generally considered a best practice to use the class keyword to define *scoped enumerations*, also known as *class enumerations*, as shown in this figure. However, it's also possible to define unscoped enumerations as shown in figure 9-11. This was a common practice prior to C++11. As a result, if you're working with legacy code, you may need to learn how unscoped enumerations work.

When you work with a scoped enumeration, you can access an enumerator by coding the name of the enumeration, the scope resolution operator (::), and the name of the enumerator. For instance, the second example shows how to access the add enumerator of the Operation enumeration.

Since a scoped enumeration defines a type, you can declare a variable of the enumeration as shown in the third example. Here, the code declares a variable named op of the Operation type.

The fourth example shows two ways to initialize a variable for an enumerator. This shows that you can use two statements or one statement, just as you can when initializing variables of other types.

The fifth example shows that a function can accept an enumeration as an argument. Here, the calculate() function accepts an Operation type as its first argument and double values for its second and third arguments. Within this function, the code uses a switch statement to determine the Operation enumerator that was passed to the function. Then, it executes the appropriate operation on the second and third arguments and returns the resulting value.

The sixth statement shows how to use the function defined in the fifth example. Here, the first statement defines two double values, and the second statement defines a variable of the Operation type that's initialized to the Operation::add enumerator. Then, the third statement calls the calculate() function and passes it the add enumerator and the two double values. This adds

How to define an enumeration

The basic syntax for creating an enumeration

```
enum [class] EnumerationName {
    constant_name_1[,
    constant_name_2] ...
};
```

An enumeration with four enumerators

```
enum class Operation { add, subtract, multiply, divide };
```

How to access an enumerator

```
Operation::add;
```

How to create a variable for an enumerator

```
Operation op;
```

How to create and initialize a variable for an enumerator

In two statements

```
Operation op;
op = Operation::add;
```

In one statement

```
Operation op = Operation::add;
```

A function that accepts an enumeration as an argument

```
double calculate(Operation op, double num1, double num2) {
    switch (op) {
        case Operation::add:
            return num1 + num2;
        case Operation::subtract:
            return num1 - num2;
        case Operation::multiply:
            return num1 * num2;
        case Operation::divide:
            return num1 / num2;
    }
}
```

Code that uses the function

```
double num1 = 50, num2 = 25;
Operation op = Operation::add;
cout << calculate(op, num1, num2) << endl;   // displays 75
op = Operation::subtract;
cout << calculate(op, num1, num2) << endl;   // displays 25
```

Description

- An *enumerated data type*, or *enumeration*, is a user-defined type that's composed of constant values. Enumerations can make your code more clear.

- The constant values contained in an enumeration are called *enumerators*. By default, they are stored in memory as sequential integers, starting at 0.

- To create a *scoped enumeration*, also known as a *class enumeration*, you code the class keyword. This keyword is available for enumerations with C++11 and later.

Figure 9-9   Basic skills for working with scoped enumerations

the values together. Next, the fourth statement assigns the subtract enumerator to the Operation variable. Finally, the fifth statement calls the calculate() function and passes it this enumerator and the two double values. This subtracts the second value from the first.

More skills for working with scoped enumerations

Figure 9-10 shows more skills for working with scoped enumerations. To start, the first example shows the enumeration that's used by the next three examples. Then, the second and third examples show how to convert an integer value to its corresponding enumerator and vice versa. To do that, you can use a static cast to explicitly perform the conversion. This is necessary because C++ won't do the conversion implicitly.

The fourth example shows how to use relational operators with an enumeration. This works because the enumerators correspond to integer values. Here, the code checks to make sure the enumerator stored in the variable named op is valid for the Operation enumeration. In most cases, you don't need to write code like this when you work with scoped enumerations. However, it may be necessary in some cases.

By default, enumerators correspond to int values that begin at 0 and continue sequentially. However, you can specify the values of the enumerators as long as you use an integer type, like int or char.

If you just want to start the enumerators at a value other than 0, you only need to specify the value for the first enumerator. For an enumeration of months like the one shown in the fifth example in this figure, you might want jan to correspond to 1, feb to correspond to 2, and so on. That way, the integer for the month matches the integer that's usually used for the month.

However, if you want to specify the values for all enumerators, you can do that too. You might want to do this to specify an integer value that corresponds better to each enumerator. For example, for an enumeration of payment terms, you might want net_due_20 to correspond to 20, net_due_30 to correspond to 30, and so on.

Since the char type is technically an integer type, you can create an enumeration of characters by assigning char values to the enumerators as shown in the sixth example. For example, for an enumeration of commands, you could assign 'v' to view, 'a' to add, 'd' to del, and 'x' to exit. (Note that you can't use "delete" as the name of an enumerator because it's a C++ keyword.) By default, these characters would be promoted to the int type, which uses 4 bytes. However, to save memory, you could change the underlying type to the char type, which uses 1 byte. To do that, just code a colon and the new underlying type immediately after the name of the enumeration as shown in this figure.

You can also convert a char value to one of the enumerators in the enumeration. To do that, you can use a static cast just as you do for an enumeration of int values.

An enumeration that uses indexes that start with zero

```
enum class Operation { add, subtract, multiply, divide };
```

Code that converts an integer to its corresponding enumerator

```
int choice = 0;
Operation op = static_cast<Operation>(choice);   // op is now Operation::add
```

Code that gets the corresponding integer of an enumerator

```
Operation op = Operation::divide;
choice = static_cast<int>(op);                    // choice is 3
```

Code that uses relational operators with an enumeration

```
if (op < Operation::add || op > Operation::divide) {
    cout << "Invalid operation!";
}
```

How to set the values of the enumerators

Specify the initial value

```
enum class Operation { add = 1, subtract, multipy, divide };
// add is 1, subtract is 2, multiply is 3, divide is 4

enum class Months { jan = 1, feb, mar, apr, may };
// jan is 1, feb is 2, mar is 3, apr is 4, and may is 5
```

Specify all the values

```
enum class Terms { net_due_20 = 20, net_due_30 = 30, net_due_60 = 60 };
enum class Flags { red = 1, orange = 2, yellow = 4, green = 8 };
```

How to work with char enumerators

Use the underlying int type to store char values (4 bytes per char)

```
enum class Command { view = 'v', add = 'a', del = 'd', exit = 'x' };
```

Change the underlying type to char (1 byte per char)

```
enum class Command : char { view = 'v', add = 'a', del = 'd', exit = 'x' };
```

Convert a character to its corresponding enumerator

```
char choice = 'a';
Command command = static_cast<Command>(choice);   // command is Command::add
```

Description

- To assign an integer value to an enumeration variable, or an enumeration value to an integer variable, you can use a static cast.

- Since enumerators correspond to integer values, you can use the relational operators with them.

- By default, the enumerator values are int values that begin at 0. However, you can specify the values of the enumerators as long as you use an integer type like int or char.

- You can also specify the integer type that the enumeration uses to store the underlying values.

Figure 9-10   More skills for working with scoped enumerations

How to work with unscoped enumerations

Prior to C++11, it was a common practice to create *unscoped enumerations*. Unscoped enumerations work much like scoped enumerations, but they can lead to several problems. As a result, it's considered a best practice to use scoped enumerations whenever possible.

Figure 9-11 begins by showing how unscoped enumerations work. Here, the first four examples show that you don't include the class keyword when you create an unscoped enumeration. In addition, to access an enumerator, you don't need to prefix it with the enumeration name and the scope resolution operator.

If you compare these examples with the examples in figure 9-9, you'll find that the code for unscoped enumerators is shorter and simpler. So, why wouldn't you want to use them all the time? Because they can cause problems like the three shown in this figure.

First, unscoped enumerations can lead to name collisions, which prevent your code from compiling. That's because a scoped enumeration provides its own scope for the enumerators, but an unscoped enumeration does not. As a result, with a scoped enumeration the Operation::add enumerator doesn't collide with the Command::add enumerator. However, with an unscoped enumeration, these two enumerators do collide.

Second, unscoped enumerations implicitly convert enumerators to int values, which isn't usually what you want. That's because you don't want to accidentally convert an enumerator to an integer type. As a result, it's generally considered a best practice to use a static cast to explicitly convert an enumeration type such as Operation to an integer type such as int. Scoped enumerations enforce this best practice by requiring an explicit cast, but unscoped enumerations do not.

Third, unscoped enumerations allow you to compare an enumerator to integer types using relational operators. Unfortunately, this can lead to code that's hard to read because the integer values that correspond to enumerators aren't as meaningful as enumerator names. Similarly, this often leads to code that's error-prone since it's easy to specify an integer value that doesn't correspond to any of the enumerators. Again, scoped enumerations enforce best practices by not allowing you to compare an enumerator to an integer value.

An unscoped enumeration

```
enum Operation { add, subtract, multiply, divide };
```

How to access an enumerator

```
add;
```

How to create and initialize a variable for an enumerator

```
Operation op = add;
```

A function that accepts an enumeration as an argument

```
double calculate(Operation op, double num1, double num2) {
    switch (op) {
        case add:
            return num1 + num2;
        case subtract:
            return num1 - num2;
        case multiply:
            return num1 * num2;
        case divide:
            return num1 / num2;
    }
}
```

Code that uses the function

```
double num1 = 50, num2 = 25;
Operation op = add;
cout << calculate(op, num1, num2) << endl;   // displays 75
op = subtract;
cout << calculate(op, num1, num2) << endl;   // displays 25
```

Problems with unscoped enumerations

They can lead to name collisions

```
enum Operation { add, subtract, multiply, divide };
enum Command { view, add, del, quit };   // error - name collision!
```

They implicitly convert enumerators to integers (not recommended)

```
Operation op = divide;
int choice = op;               // works, but an explicit cast would be better
```

They allow you to compare enumerators to integers (not recommended)

```
Operation op = divide;
if (op < 0 || op > 3) {        // works, but hard-to-read AND error-prone
    cout << "Invalid operation!\n";
}
```

Description

- Prior to C++11, it was a common practice to create *unscoped enumerations*. Unscoped enumerations work much like scoped enumerations, but they can lead to several problems. As a result, you should use scoped enumerations whenever possible.

Figure 9-11   How to work with unscoped enumerations

The Monthly Bonus Calculator program

Figure 9-12 shows a program that calculates the monthly bonus for an employee depending on the employee's department and performance. The code for this program uses an enumeration to enumerate each department in the company.

Part 1 begins by showing the console for this program. This console displays the name of the program and a menu of the four departments of the company where each department corresponds to an integer. Then, the program prompts the user to select a department by entering its corresponding number. Next, it prompts the user to answer a question that depends on the department that was selected. Finally, it displays a message that indicates whether the employee earned the bonus.

The code for the program begins by defining a scoped enumeration named Department for four departments (marketing, it, sales, and other). Here, it's important to note that this enumeration has been defined so the corresponding int values start at 1, not 0. As a result, the corresponding int values match the numbers on the menu that's displayed on the console.

After defining the enumeration, this code declares three functions. Of these functions, the get_department() function returns an enumeration of the Department type, and the check_criteria() function accepts an argument of the Department type.

The main() function begins by displaying the name of the program and the menu of departments. Then, it gets the department from the user and stores it in a variable named dept of the Department type. Next, this code passes the dept variable to the check_criteria() function to check if the user has earned a bonus for the month. If so, the code displays a message that indicates that the user has earned a bonus of $1000. Otherwise, the code displays a message that indicates that the user has not earned a bonus for the month.

The show_menu() function begins by displaying the DEPARTMENTS header on the console. Then, it displays one department for each enumerator in the Department enumeration. To do that, it gets the number for each department by casting each enumerator to its corresponding int value. Then, it displays the name of the corresponding department. For example, it displays "Marketing" to the right of the integer for the Department::marketing enumerator.

The console

```
The Monthly Bonus Calculator

DEPARTMENTS
1 - Marketing
2 - IT
3 - Sales
4 - Other

Enter department number: 2
How many trouble tickets did you close this month?: 11
Congrats! You earned the $1000 monthly bonus.
```

The code

```cpp
#include <iostream>

using namespace std;

enum class Department { marketing = 1, it, sales, other };

// function prototypes
void show_menu();
Department get_department();
bool check_criteria(Department);

int main() {
    cout << "The Monthly Bonus Calculator\n\n";
    show_menu();

    Department dept = get_department();
    bool bonus = check_criteria(dept);
    const double bonus_amt = 1000;
    if (bonus) {
        cout << "Congrats! You earned the $" << bonus_amt
            << " monthly bonus.\n\n";
    }
    else {
        cout << "Sorry! No bonus for you this month :(  Keep trying!\n\n";
    }

    return 0;
}

// function definitions
void show_menu() {
    cout << "DEPARTMENTS\n"
        << static_cast<int>(Department::marketing) << " - Marketing\n"
        << static_cast<int>(Department::it) << " - IT\n"
        << static_cast<int>(Department::sales) << " - Sales\n"
        << static_cast<int>(Department::other) << " - Other\n\n";
}
```

Figure 9-12   The Monthly Bonus Calculator program (part 1 of 2)

The get_department() function in part 2 of figure 9-12 starts by getting a number that corresponds to one of the Department enumerators. Then, this code explicitly casts that number to one of the Department enumerators. Next, the code checks whether the enumerator is less than Department::marketing or greater than Department::sales. This could be true if the user entered an invalid number such as 5 or 6. In that case, this code returns the Department::other enumerator. Otherwise, it returns the enumerator that corresponds to the number entered by the user.

The check_criteria() function accepts a Department enumerator and returns a Boolean value that indicates whether the user has earned a bonus. Within this function, a switch statement executes the appropriate code for the Department enumerator that's passed to this function. For each enumerator, the function asks the user a different question and returns a Boolean value that indicates whether the answer to the question is good enough to earn a bonus. For the marketing department, for instance, a bonus is earned if the number of viral campaigns is greater than or equal to 4. For IT, a bonus is earned if the number of closed trouble tickets is greater than or equal to 10. And so on.

The code (continued)

```cpp
Department get_department() {
    cout << "Enter department number: ";
    int choice = 0;
    cin >> choice;

    Department dept = static_cast<Department>(choice);
    if (dept < Department::marketing || dept > Department::sales) {
        return Department::other;
    }
    else {
        return dept;
    }
}

bool check_criteria(Department dept) {
    switch (dept) {
        case Department::marketing:
            int viral_campaigns;
            cout << "How many of your campaigns went viral "
                << "this month?: ";
            cin >> viral_campaigns;
            return viral_campaigns >= 4;
        case Department::it:
            int trouble_tickets;
            cout << "How many trouble tickets did you close "
                << "this month?: ";
            cin >> trouble_tickets;
            return trouble_tickets >= 10;
        case Department::sales:
            double sales;
            cout << "What were your total sales this month?: ";
            cin >> sales;
            return sales >= 1000;
        case Department::other:
            char supervisor_grade;
            cout << "What was your grade from your supervisor "
                << "this month?: ";
            cin >> supervisor_grade;
            return tolower(supervisor_grade) == 'a';
    }
}
```

Figure 9-12   The Monthly Bonus Calculator program (part 2 of 2)

Perspective

Now that you've finished this chapter, you should have all the skills that you need for defining any structures or enumerations that your programs require. These are critical skills that become increasingly valuable as the data requirements for your program become more complex. By applying these skills, you can make your programs easier to understand, test, debug, and maintain.

When you define a structure, you define a simple object. As a result, you can think of structures as your first step in using object-oriented programming. In section 3 of this book, you'll learn the rest of the skills that you'll need for working with object-oriented programming including how to define classes, how to work with inheritance, and more.

Terms

structure	enumeration
data member	enumerated data type
initialize	enumerator
initialization list	scoped enumeration
nested structure	class enumeration
return value optimization (RVO)	unscoped enumeration
member functions	

Summary

- A *structure* consists of one or more other data types.
- The data types that compose a structure are called the *data members*, or just *members*, of the structure.
- It's considered a best practice to *initialize* the members of a structure with starting data when you create an object from a structure.
- You can use an *initialization list* to set the starting values of an object when you create it. When you use an initialization list, the assignment operator is optional.
- You can *nest* structures within other structures. To do that, you code a structure variable as a data member.
- A structure can have *member functions* that work with the data members of the structure and operators that perform operations on its data members.
- An *enumerated data type*, or *enumeration*, is a user-defined type that consists of constant values.
- The constant values contained in an enumeration are called *enumerators*. By default, enumerators are stored in memory as sequential integers, starting at 0.
- With C++11 and later, it's generally considered a best practice to use the class keyword to create *scoped enumerations*, also known as *class enumerations*.
- Prior to C++11, it was a common practice to create *unscoped enumerations*.

Exercise 9-1   Use a structure with the Create Account program

In this exercise, you'll add a structure to a version of the Create Account program that accepts multiple accounts and saves the account data in a file. When you're done, a test run should look something like this:

```
Create Account List

Name                      Email
Grace Hopper              ghopper@yahoo.com
Margaret Hamilton         margarethamilton@mit.edu

First name: Dorothy
Last name: Vaughan
Password: 92010!SpaceMissions
Email: dvaughan@langley.com

dvaughan@langley.com was added for Dorothy Vaughan.

Enter another account? (y/n): y

First name: Grace
Last name: Hopper
Password: super#Secret456
Email: ghopper@yahoo.com
ghopper@yahoo.com already exists - account not added.

Enter another account? (y/n):
```

Open and run the program

1. Open the project or solution named create_account in this folder:
   ex_starts\ch09_ex1_create_account

2. Review the code in the main.cpp file, and then run the program to see how it works.

Add a structure and the functions that use it

3. Define a structure named Account that contains four string members for the first name, last name, password, and email that are initialized to empty strings.

4. Define a function named read_accounts_from_file() that creates an Account object for each account in the tab-delimited accounts.txt file, adds it to the end of a vector of Account objects, and then returns the vector.

5. Modify the display_accounts() function so it accepts the vector of Account objects as a parameter. Then, remove the code that gets the data from the accounts.txt file, and modify the remaining code so it uses a loop to display the data for each object in the vector.

6. Define a function named write_accounts_to_file() that accepts the vector of Account objects as a parameter. This function should write the data in each object to the accounts.txt file.

7. Define a function named get_account() that creates an Account object, gets the data for an account from the user and stores it in the Account object, and returns that object to the calling code. You can use the code in the main() function that gets the account data as a guide to coding this function.

Modify the main() function to use the structure

8. Modify the main() function so it uses the read_accounts_from_file() function to get the Account data and then stores that data in a vector of Account objects. Then, use the display_accounts() function to display the accounts in the vector.

9. Modify the while loop within the main() function so it uses the get_account() function to get each account the user enters, adds it to the vector, uses the write_accounts_to_file() function to update the accounts.txt file, and then displays a message indicating that the account has been added.

10. Remove any remaining code from the main() function that is no longer needed by the program.

Add a member function

11. Add a member function named equals() to the Account structure that allows you to compare the current Account object with another Account object. For two Account objects to be equal, their email members must be equal.

12. Add a loop within the while loop that uses the member function to check if the account a user enters is equal to an existing account.

13. If the account is equal to an existing account, display a message that the account already exists and wasn't added.

14. If the account isn't equal to an existing account, add the account to the end of the vector, update the accounts.txt file, and then display a message that the account was added.

Exercise 9-2   Use an enumeration with the Movie List program

In this exercise, you'll add an enumeration to the Movie List 2.0 program with four enumerators for the commands that a user can enter.

1. Open the project or solution named movie_list in this folder:
   `ex_starts\ch09_ex2_movie_list`

2. Define a scoped enumeration with four char enumerators that correspond to the four commands displayed in the menu.

3. Update the display_menu() function so it uses the enumeration. To do that, you can use a static cast to get the corresponding character for each enumerator.

4. Update the main() function so it uses the enumeration to test the command the user enters.

10

How to work with STL containers and iterators

In chapter 6, you learned how to work with a vector, which is a container object. In this chapter, you'll learn more about vectors, and you'll learn about some other container objects in the Standard Template Library (STL). In addition, you'll learn how to use iterators to access the elements in an STL container.

An introduction to STL containers and iterators

The *Standard Template Library (STL)* includes *containers* that store data and *iterators* that allow access to the data. It also includes algorithms that perform tasks on the data such as searching and sorting the data. You'll learn about algorithms in the next chapter.

A summary of STL containers

The STL containers share many characteristics. For example, they all store elements of the same data type. However, they can be divided into the two categories shown at the top of figure 10-1.

The *sequence containers* organize data sequentially by index. In other words, the elements are organized in the order that they're added, and an element is retrieved using an index that specifies its place in the sequence.

The *associative containers*, on the other hand, organize data by key. In other words, the order the elements are added has no bearing on how they're organized, and the elements are retrieved using their key values.

The second table in this figure presents five of the most common sequence containers. The vector and array objects store elements in *contiguous memory*, which is a consecutive block of memory with no gaps. The difference between them is that an array is a fixed size. This means its size must be known at compile time, and you can't add or remove elements after it's created. Like a vector, all of the other containers listed in this figure are *dynamic*. This means that you can add or remove elements at runtime.

The list and forward_list objects store elements linked by pointers in *non-contiguous memory*, which are unrelated memory locations. The list is *doubly linked* with both forward and backward pointers, while the forward list is *singly linked* with only forward pointers. Finally, the deque (pronounced "deck") object is a double-ended queue that stores its elements in a combination of contiguous and non-contiguous memory.

The third table presents two *container adapters*, which are objects that adapt an STL container to make it more specialized. The container adapters in this table adapt the deque container by default to create a queue or a stack. A queue provides *first-in, first-out (FIFO)* access to the elements it contains, and a stack provides *last-in, first-out (LIFO)* access to the elements it contains.

The last table presents five of the most common associative containers. All of these containers store their elements in non-contiguous memory. The pair container is a structure that stores a single *key/value pair*. This structure provides a way to work with the key/value pairs stored by the map and multimap containers. The set and multiset containers, by contrast, store keys only. The multiset and multimap containers allow multiple elements to have the same key, and the set and map containers require a unique key for each element.

In this chapter, you'll learn how to use most of these containers. In the meantime, you should know that this isn't a complete list of STL containers. To see a complete list, you can visit the URL shown in this figure.

Two types of STL containers

Type	Description
sequence	Elements are organized sequentially by index.
associative	Elements are organized by key.

Five of the sequence containers

Name	Description
`vector`	A collection of elements stored in contiguous memory.
`array`	A fixed-size collection of elements stored in contiguous memory.
`list`	A *doubly linked* collection of elements linked to other elements.
`forward_list`	A *singly linked* collection of elements linked to other elements.
`deque`	A double-ended queue that allows elements to be added to the front or the back.

Two container adapters

Name	Description
`queue`	A first-in first-out (FIFO) container.
`stack`	A last-in first-out (LIFO) container.

Five of the associative containers

Name	Description
`pair`	A structure that holds a key/value pair.
`map`	A collection of key/value pairs, sorted by key. The key values must be unique.
`set`	A collection of keys, sorted by key. The key values must be unique.
`multimap`	A collection of key/value pairs, sorted by key. The key values do not need to be unique.
`multiset`	A collection of keys, sorted by key. The key values do not need to be unique.

A URL for more documentation about containers

`http://en.cppreference.com/w/cpp/container`

Description

- The *sequence containers* store data sequentially by index, and the *associative containers* store data by key.
- The array and vector containers store data in *contiguous memory*, which is a consecutive block of memory with no gaps.
- The list, forward list, map, set, multimap, and multiset containers store data in *non-contiguous memory*, which are unrelated memory locations that may have gaps.
- The deque (pronounced "deck") container stores its elements in a combination of contiguous and non-contiguous memory.
- A *container adapter* adapts a container to make it more specialized.

Figure 10-1   A summary of STL containers

A summary of STL iterators

An *iterator* is an object that points to an element in a container. In addition, an iterator provides operations that allow it to change the element it points to and access the value of the element it points to. As a result, you can use iterators to access and traverse the elements in a container.

Every container in the STL provides an iterator object for working with its elements. Every STL container also provides the two member functions presented in the first table in figure 10-2.

The begin() function returns an iterator that points to the first element in a container. You might think, then, that the end() function would return an iterator that points to the last element in the container, but it doesn't. Instead, it returns an iterator that points one memory location past the last element, as illustrated by the graphical representation in this figure. Because of this, the iterator returned by end() is often called the *off-the-end* iterator.

The iterators returned by begin() and end() define a range, or *interval*. Specifically, they define a *half-open interval* that includes the element that the iterator returned by the begin() function points to through the element before the memory location that the iterator returned by the end() function points to. That makes sense because the end() function returns an iterator that points past the last element. In mathematics, this type of half-open interval can be represented by a range enclosed in a bracket and a parenthesis. For example, the interval [1:5] is 1, 2, 3, 4 because the last element in the range isn't included. As you'll see later in this chapter, some of the functions for working with containers use half-open intervals, so it's important for you to know how they work.

The second table in this figure presents the six types of iterators and indicates which objects or STL containers use them. These iterator types are hierarchical, which means that the higher iterator types inherit the operations defined by the lower ones. In this figure, the iterator types are listed from lowest (input/output) to highest (contiguous). As you can see, most of the STL containers use a bidirectional iterator or higher, so you can traverse them forwards or backwards. The exception is the forward list, which you can only traverse forwards.

The last table presents the operations provided by the iterators. The lowest iterators, input and output, only define operators that allow you to move forward one element, test iterators for equality, and access the value of the element the iterator points to. By contrast, the highest iterators, random-access and contiguous, inherit or define operators that allow you to move forward or backward one or more elements and randomly access individual elements by index. In the next figure, you'll learn more about how to perform these operations.

Note that the contiguous iterator, which was added in C++17, doesn't provide any more functionality than the random-access iterator does. Instead, it guarantees that the elements in the container are stored in contiguous memory. Because of that, it's typically implemented by the iterator provided by vectors and arrays.

Two member functions shared by all STL containers

Function	Description
begin()	Returns an iterator that points to the first element.
end()	Returns an iterator that points to one memory location past the last element.

An interval defined by the iterators returned by begin() and end()

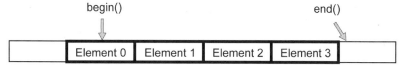

The six iterator types from lowest to highest

Type	Used by	Description
input	istream	Iterates forward only and reads each element only once.
output	ostream	Iterates forward only and writes each element only once.
forward	forward_list	Iterates forward only and reads or writes repeatedly.
bidirectional	list, map, set	Iterates forward or backward and reads or writes repeatedly.
random-access	vector, deque, array	Iterates forward or backward, reads or wrties repeatedly, and accesses individual elements in random order.
contiguous	vector, array	Available with C++17 and later. This iterator guarantees that elements are stored in contiguous memory.

Some of the operations provided by iterators

Operator	Provided by	Description
++	input, output	Moves forward one element.
==, !=	input, output	Tests iterators for equality.
*	input, output	Accesses the value the iterator is pointing to.
->	forward	Accesses members of the object the iterator is pointing to.
--	bidirectional	Moves backward one element.
[]	random-access	Allows access to individual elements by index.
+, +=, -, -=	random-access	Moves forward or backward the number of elements added or subtracted.

Description

- An *iterator object* allows you to access and traverse the elements in a container.
- The iterators returned by the begin() and end() functions define a range, or *interval*, that starts at the first element and ends one memory location past the last element. This is called a *half-open interval*, and can be represented by the mathematical notation [begin:end).
- The iterator returned by end() is sometimes called an *off-the-end* iterator.
- The six iterator types are hierarchical, where the input and output iterators are the lowest and the contiguous iterator is the highest.
- The iterators provide operations for working with elements. Each higher type *inherits* the operations provided by the lower ones and adds one or more operations of its own.

Figure 10-2   A summary of STL iterators

Basic skills for working with iterators

Each container provides a specific type of iterator. In figure 10-3, for instance, the first example defines a vector with a type of vector<double>. As a result, the iterator for that vector has a type of vector<double>::iterator as shown in the first statement of the second example. Because coding this type can be cumbersome, many programmers use the auto keyword when working with iterators as shown in the second statement.

The third example starts by using the auto keyword and the begin() function to get an iterator that points to the first element in the vector. Then, you can use the operations provided by the iterator to move the iterator so it points to other elements. However, the operations that are available depend on the type of iterator.

Because a vector provides a random-access iterator, you can use the + operator to advance the iterator the specified number of positions. In the third example, for instance, this operator is used to advance the iterator two positions so it points to the third element. If you're working with a lower iterator, though, you need to use the ++ operator to advance one position at a time. This is also shown by the third example.

The fourth example shows how to use a loop to advance an iterator that can only move one element at a time. Note that you can also accomplish this by using a helper function named advance() that's in the header file named iterator. However, to keep the focus on the basics, this chapter doesn't show how to use this header file.

When working with containers, you can easily get an iterator that points to the first element by using the begin() function. However, because the end() function returns an iterator that points to one memory location past the last element, it's slightly more difficult to get an iterator that points to the last element. The fifth example shows how to do that, depending on the type of iterator you're working with.

Since most containers provide an iterator that is bidirectional or higher, you can usually use the first technique. Here, the code gets the iterator returned by end() and then uses the -- operator to move the iterator back one element to the last element.

If you're using a forward list, however, you can't use this technique. That's because a forward list only has a forward iterator. In that case, you need to use begin() to get an iterator that points to the first element. Then, you can use the ++ operator in a for loop to advance to the last element.

The last example in this figure shows how to access the value in the element an iterator points to, which is referred to as *dereferencing* the iterator. Here, the first two statements get an iterator that points to the first element in a vector of strings. Then, the third statement uses the *indirection operator* (*) to get the element, which is the string "hello", and it calls the size() member function from that string. To do that, the iterator variable and indirection operator are enclosed in parentheses. Another way to accomplish this is to use the *member access operator* (->) as shown by the fourth statement. Both ways work equally well, but the member access operator results in code that's cleaner and easier to read.

The container that's used by the examples

```
vector<double> prices { 9.99, 18.99, 19.99, 23.99, 40.99 };
```

Two ways to define an iterator

```
vector<double>::iterator b1 = prices.begin();      // explictly define type
auto b2 = prices.begin();        // compiler infers vector<double>::iterator
```

How to get iterators that point to the first and third elements

```
auto iter = prices.begin();    // get iterator that points to first element
```

With a random-access iterator

```
iter = iter + 2;                 // use + operator to jump to third element
```

With an iterator that's lower than random-access

```
++iter;                          // use ++ operator to move to second element
++iter;                          // use ++ operator to move to third element
```

How to use the ++ operator in a loop to advance an iterator

```
int element_num = 4;
auto iter = prices.begin();
for (int i = 1; i < element_num; ++i) {
    ++iter;
}                                // points to fourth element when loop ends
```

How to get an iterator that points to the last element

With a bidirectional iterator or higher

```
auto last = prices.end();   // get iterator that points one past last element
--last;                          // use -- operator to move back one element
```

With a forward iterator or lower

```
auto iter = prices.begin();      // get iterator that points to first element
for (int i = 1; i < prices.size(); ++i) {
    ++iter;
}                                // points to last element when loop ends
```

How to access the value of the element that an iterator points to

```
vector<string> words { "hello", "world" };
auto b = words.begin();     // get iterator that points to first element

cout << *b << " has " << (*b).size() << " letters";   // indirection op
cout << *b << " has " << b->size() << " letters";     // member access op
// both statements display "hello has 5 letters"
```

Description

- An iterator for a container has a type that's related to the container's type. To simplify the code for declaring an iterator variable, many programmers use the auto keyword.

- An iterator *points* to an element in a container. To access the value an iterator points to, you can *dereference* the iterator with the *indirection operator* (*) or the *member access operator* (->). For more information about how this works, see chapter 17.

- You should avoid dereferencing the iterator that's returned by cnd(), since it can cause unexpected results from incorrect values to program crashes.

Figure 10-3   Basic skills for working with iterators

Member functions shared by the STL containers

One of the benefits of the STL is that the containers provide a similar *interface* for working with the elements they contain, even though they store the elements differently. This means that once you learn how to use one container, it's easy to learn how to use the others.

Except for the forward list and array containers, the containers in the STL share all of the member functions listed in figure 10-4. By now, you should be familiar with most of these functions. That's because you learned about many of them in chapter 6 when you learned about vectors.

To start, this figure shows the definitions of the two vectors named nums and neg_nums used by the examples. Then, the first example shows how to insert a single element into a vector. To do that, the insert() function accepts two arguments. The first argument is an iterator that indicates where the element should be inserted. Here, the code passes the iterator that's returned by the begin() function of the nums vector. This inserts the new element before the first element in that vector. The second argument is the value of the element to be inserted, in this case, 0.

The second example shows how to remove the single element that was just inserted into the nums vector. To do that, the erase() function accepts an iterator that points to the element to be removed. In this case, the iterator is retrieved using the begin() function so it points to the first element.

The third example shows how to insert a range of elements rather than a single element at the beginning of the nums vector. To do that, the insert() function accepts the iterator that's returned by the begin() function of the nums vector, as well as two iterators that define a half-open interval. Here, the iterators returned by the begin() and end() functions of the neg_nums vector are passed to the insert() function, so the interval is [begin: end). That causes all of the elements in the neg_nums vector to be inserted at the beginning of the nums vector.

The fourth example shows how to erase the range of elements that was just inserted. To start, the code gets an iterator that points to the element just past the ones that were inserted. To do that, it gets an iterator that points to the first element and then uses a loop that's compatible with all iterators to increment the iterator based on the size of the neg_nums vector. Then, the erase() function accepts two iterators that point to the first element of the nums vector and one past the element to be erased. This works because these iterators define a half-open interval that doesn't include the element at the end of the interval.

Note that since a vector uses a random-access iterator, you could replace the loop in this example with code that uses the += operator to advance the iterator. In other words, you could use code like this:

```
iter += neg_nums.size();
```

The fifth example shows how to swap the contents of two vectors. To do that, you pass one vector to the swap() function of the other vector.

The final example shows how to insert only some of the elements of a vector into another vector. Here, the code uses the ++ operator to advance the interval start one element and the -- operator to decrement the interval end one element.

Some more member functions shared by the STL containers

Function	Description
`size()`	Returns the number of elements in the container.
`empty()`	Returns a Boolean value indicating whether the container has any data.
`insert(i, val)`	Inserts the value before the iterator specified by i.
`insert(i, b, e)`	Inserts the interval [b:e) before the iterator specified by i.
`erase(i)`	Removes the element at the iterator specified by i.
`erase(b, e)`	Removes the interval [b:e).
`clear()`	Removes all the elements in the container.
`swap(container)`	Swaps the data with the data of the container passed to it.

Some examples of the member functions

```
vector<int> nums { 1, 2, 3, 4 };
vector<int> neg_nums { -2, -1 };

// insert a single int at the beginning of the vector
nums.insert(nums.begin(), 0);
// nums now contains 0, 1, 2, 3, 4

// erase a single int from the beginning of the vector
nums.erase(nums.begin());
// nums now contains 1, 2, 3, 4

// insert the elements of a vector at the beginning of another vector
nums.insert(nums.begin(), neg_nums.begin(), neg_nums.end());
// nums now contains -2, -1, 1, 2, 3, 4

// erase the interval just inserted at the beginning of the vector
auto iter = nums.begin();
for (int i = 0; i < neg_nums.size(); ++i) {
    ++iter;
}
nums.erase(nums.begin(), iter);
// nums now contains 1, 2, 3, 4

// swap the contents of two vectors
nums.swap(neg_nums);
// nums now contains -2, -1 and neg_nums now contains 1, 2, 3, 4

// insert some of the elements of a vector
nums.insert(nums.end(), ++neg_nums.begin(), --neg_nums.end());
// nums now contains -2, -1, 2, 3
```

Description

- The forward_list container and the array container don't support all of the functions that the rest of the STL containers do. For example, neither of these containers support the insert() or erase() functions, and forward_list doesn't support the size() function.

- The examples shown here use vectors, but they work with other containers too. That's because all the examples use operations provided by lower-level iterators.

Figure 10-4   Member functions shared by the STL containers

How to iterate the data in a container

In chapter 6, you learned how to use for loops and range-based for loops with vectors. Now, you'll review these skills and you'll learn how to use iterators to loop through the data in a container. In addition, you'll learn the pros and cons of each of these approaches.

Figure 10-5 starts by defining a vector of doubles and initializing it with five double values. All three of the examples that follow use this vector.

The first example uses a for loop. This loop defines a counter variable named i that's incremented by one each time through the loop until it's equal to the value returned by the size() function of the vector. Within the loop, the code uses the subscript ([]) operator and the counter variable to get the value of the current element. Note here that, as you learned in chapter 6, the indexes for a vector are zero-based.

This approach has several benefits. To start, it's familiar to most programmers. It also allows you to easily skip elements by changing the criteria in the for statement. For instance, you could get the value of every other element by incrementing the counter by two. In addition, you don't need to dereference an iterator to get the value of an element. Finally, the counter variable can be useful for some tasks such as displaying a number for each element.

On the other hand, this approach can only be used with the vector, deque, and array containers. That's because these are the only containers that provide the subscript operator. In addition, you could have out of bounds access if you don't code the loop correctly.

The second example uses a range-based for loop. As you learned in chapter 6, this kind of loop automatically iterates over every element in a container without specifically incrementing a counter. This approach also has the benefit of being available to all containers and not needing to use dereferencing. Because of that, you'll probably use range-based for loops with containers most of the time.

However, this approach has the drawback of being less flexible. For instance, if you want to iterate every other element, you'll need to write conditional code in the body of the loop. Or, if you want to display a number for each element, you'll need to define, initialize, and increment a counter variable.

Like the first example, the last example uses a for loop. However, this for loop doesn't define a counter variable. Instead, it defines an iterator that points to the first element in the sequence. It uses the ++ operator to advance the iterator one element at a time. And it uses the end() function to determine when to stop. This works because the iterator returned by end() points one past the last element. That way, when the loop iterator is advanced so it also points one past the last element, every element in the sequence has been iterated.

This approach has the benefit of being available to all containers. In addition, it's easy to skip elements by changing the loop criteria. The main drawback of this approach is that it works with iterators rather than values. So, you must use dereferencing to get the value of an element. If the code in the body of the loop needs to work with iterators rather than values, though, this can be a benefit.

Although it's not shown here, you should realize that you can also use a while loop to iterate the data in a container. However, the for loops shown here are more commonly used with containers.

The vector that's used by the examples

```
vector<double> prices { 9.99, 18.99, 19.99, 23.99, 40.99 };
```

How to use a for loop and subscripting to iterate the data in a container

```
for (int i = 0; i < prices.size(); ++i) {
    cout << prices[i] << ' ';
}
```

Pros

- You can easily skip elements by changing loop criteria.
- You don't need to dereference an iterator to get the value of an element.
- It uses a counter variable that can be useful for tasks such as displaying a number for each element.

Cons

- Out of bounds access is possible.
- Subscripting is not available to all containers.

How to use a range-based for loop to iterate the data in a container

```
for (auto p: prices) {
    cout << p << ' ';
}
```

Pros

- You don't need to dereference an iterator to get the value of an element.
- It's available to all containers.
- Out of bounds access is not possible.

Cons

- Extra code is required to skip elements.
- Extra code is required for a counter variable.

How to use iterators to iterate the data in a container

```
for (auto iter = prices.begin(); iter != prices.end(); ++iter) {
    cout << *iter << ' ';
}
```

Pros

- It's available to all containers.
- You can easily skip elements by changing loop criteria.
- It's useful if the code in the loop body needs to work with iterators rather than values.

Cons

- Out of bounds access is possible.
- You must dereference an iterator to get the value of an element.
- Extra code is required for a counter variable.

Description

- You can use a variety of techniques to iterate the elements in a container. Each of these techniques has its pros and cons.

Figure 10-5   How to iterate the data in a container

More skills for working with vectors

In chapter 6, you learned the basics of working with vectors. In the topics that follow, you'll learn more about vectors, including how a vector stores its data in memory and why the vector is the most recommended container in the Standard Template Library. First, though, you'll learn about some member functions that are shared by most of the sequence containers.

Member functions shared by the sequence containers

Figure 10-6 presents some member functions that are shared by most of the sequence containers. The exceptions, like before, are the forward list and array, which don't support all of the functions listed here.

The examples shown here start by defining a vector of chars named greeting and initializing it with ten characters (helloworld). Then, the next line of code uses the assignment operator to assign all the elements in the vector named greeting to a new vector named greeting2. This is an easy way to assign all the elements of one vector to another vector.

However, you may sometimes want to assign only some of the elements of a vector to another vector. In that case, you can use the assign() member function as shown here. The assign() function accepts two iterators that define a half-open interval that specifies the elements to assign. Here, the interval starts with the iterator returned by begin(), and ends with the iterator returned by advancing that iterator five positions. That moves the iterator to point to the sixth element, whose value is 'w'.

Remember, the end of a half-open interval is the off-the-end iterator. That means that the sixth element is one past the end of the interval to be assigned. Because of that, after the assign() function completes, the greeting2 vector contains the first five elements of the greeting vector (hello).

The next group of statements uses the member functions to change some of the existing elements. The first statement uses the pop_back() function to remove the last element. Then, the second statement uses the front() function to change the value of the first element, and the third statement uses the back() function to change the value of the last element. This shows that you can use front() and back() to change an element value as well as to retrieve it.

The next group of statements uses the push_back() function to add three characters to the vector. After these statements run, the greeting2 vector contains eight characters (welcome).

The final statement uses the resize() function to change the size of the original vector, greeting, to five. Since this value is smaller than the original size, the elements after the first five elements are destroyed. After this statement runs, the greeting vector contains five characters (hello).

Some member functions shared by the sequence containers

Function	Description
front()	Returns a reference to the first element.
back()	Returns a reference to the last element.
push_back(elem)	Adds a new element to the end, or back, of the sequence.
pop_back()	Removes the element at the end, or back, of the sequence.
resize(n)	Changes the current size to the size specified by n, destroying elements if needed.
assign(b, e)	Replaces the current content with interval [b:e) and adjusts the size accordingly.

Examples

```
vector<char> greeting {'h','e','l','l','o','w','o','r','l','d'};
vector<char> greeting2 = greeting;   // assign all elements to new vector
// both vectors now contain h e l l o w o r l d

// reassign greeting2 - this time only assign some elements
greeting2.assign(greeting.begin(), greeting.begin() + 5);
// greeting2 now contains h e l l o
// size has been adjusted - greeting2.size() now returns 5

// make changes to existing elements in greeting2
greeting2.pop_back();              // remove last element
greeting2.front() = 'w';           // change value of first element
greeting2.back() = 'c';            // change value of new last element
// greeting2 now contains w e l c

// add new elements to greeting2
greeting2.push_back('o');          // add element to back of sequence
greeting2.push_back('m');          // add element to back of sequence
greeting2.push_back('e');          // add element to back of sequence
// greeting2 now contains w e l c o m e

// resize greeting
greeting.resize(5);
// greeting now contains h e l l o
// greeting.size() returns 5
```

Description

- Some member functions are shared by all the containers in the STL, some are shared by the sequence containers, and some are shared by the associative containers.

- The forward_list container and the array container don't support all of the functions that the rest of the sequence containers do. For example, neither of these containers support the push_back() or pop_back() functions.

Figure 10-6 Member functions shared by the sequence containers

Member functions of a vector

The elements in a vector are stored in contiguous memory, as illustrated at the top of figure 10-7. This means that the elements are stored in physical memory next to each other. For instance, in the graphical representation here, element 0 is at memory address 100, element 1 is at memory address 101, and so on. You'll learn more about memory addresses in chapter 17. For now, just know that contiguous memory allows for fast access and fast iteration.

To maintain contiguous memory, a vector must sometimes move elements. For example, when you use insert() or erase() to add or remove elements at the front or in the middle of a sequence, the vector must move the remaining elements to make room or close up gaps.

Additionally, when you use push_back() to dynamically add elements at the end of a sequence, the vector sometimes runs out of room and must add capacity. To do that, it allocates a larger block of memory, moves all the elements to this new memory location, and deallocates the old block of memory.

Whenever a vector moves elements, any variable that holds an iterator can become invalid. That's because the memory location it points to may no longer contain the element it did before.

Even though the vector sometimes has to move elements like this, its contiguous memory still makes it the best performing container for most uses. In fact, Bjarne Stroustrup, the creator of the C++ language, recommends that you use a vector unless you have a good reason not to.

The tables in this figure present three of the member functions and one of the operators provided by the vector container. You learned about the at() function and the subscript operator ([]) in chapter 6. As you may recall, they both allow you to access the value of an element using an index that indicates its position in the sequence. However, the at() function throws an exception when you try to access an element that's out of bounds, and the subscript operator may not.

The capacity() function returns the number of elements the vector can store in memory. The size() function returns the number of elements the vector actually contains. And the reserve() function lets you set the capacity for the vector. In the next figure, you'll learn more about working with these member functions.

But first, this figure shows two ways to initialize a vector. To start, you can use an initialization list as you learned in chapter 6. The syntax and statements in the first example review this skill.

You can also use iterators to initialize a vector, as shown by the syntax and statement in the second example. To do that, you code the beginning and ending iterators for a half open interval between parentheses. Here, the statement uses iterators that point to elements in the vector named numbers2 to initialize a new vector named numbers3. Because the + operator is used to increment the iterator that's returned by the begin() function by 1, the first element of the numbers2 vector isn't included. Similarly, because the - operator is used to decrement the iterator that's returned by the end() function by 1, the last element of the numbers2 vector isn't included.

In this figure, the examples initialize vectors. However, these techniques also work with most of the other STL containers presented in this chapter.

A graphical representation of the contiguous memory of a vector

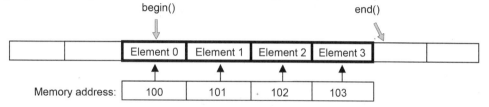

Some member functions of the vector container

Function	Description
`at(i)`	Returns the element at index i. Throws an out_of_range exception if i is out of bounds.
`capacity()`	Returns the number of elements the vector can currently store. This is different from size(), which returns the number of elements the vector actually contains.
`reserve(n)`	Increases the capacity of the vector to n elements. If n is less than the current capacity, this function doesn't do anything.

One of the operators defined by the vector container

Operator	Name	Description
`[i]`	subscript	Allows read/write access to the element at index i.

How to use a list of values to initialize a vector

The syntax

```
vector<type> name [=] { value1[, value2] ... };
```

Two statements that initialize a vector with a list of values

```
vector<int> numbers1 = { 1, 2, 3, 4, 5 };
vector<int> numbers2 { 1, 2, 3, 4, 5 };  // assignment operator is optional
```

How to use iterators to initialize a vector

The syntax

```
vector<type> name ( begin_iterator, end_iterator );
```

A statement that initializes a vector with values from another vector

```
vector<int> numbers3 ( numbers2.begin() + 1, numbers2.end() - 1 );
// skips first and last elements - numbers3 contains 2 3 4
```

Description

- The elements in a vector are stored in contiguous memory. This allows for random access and fast iteration.

- To maintain contiguous memory, a vector must sometimes move elements. When this happens, any iterators previously returned by begin() or end() become invalid.

- Although a vector must sometimes move elements, its contiguous memory makes it the best performing container for most uses.

- You can *initialize* a vector with an initialization list or with iterators. These techniques work with most of the other STL containers as well.

Figure 10-7   Member functions of a vector

How to set capacity to improve efficiency

The *capacity* of a vector is the amount of contiguous memory that's been allocated for its elements. In other words, the value returned by the capacity() function indicates how many elements it *can* store, not how many elements it contains. When you create an empty vector, both its size and its capacity are zero. Then, as you add elements, the capacity is increased as needed.

The first example in figure 10-8 shows how this works. Here, the first statement creates an empty vector. Then, a loop adds ten elements to the vector. Each time through the loop, the code displays messages about the capacity and size of the vector. These messages show that the vector automatically increases its capacity as the loop adds elements to it.

Each time the vector increases its capacity, it allocates new memory, moves its elements, and deallocates the old memory. To minimize the number of times the vector must reallocate memory and move elements, the vector begins to allocate enough capacity for extra elements as it gets larger. For example, after the code adds element 6, the capacity is increased from 6 to 9. This means that elements 7 and 8 can be added without moving any elements.

In this example, the vector automatically increases the capacity by 50%. However, this percentage may vary depending on the compiler that you're using. For example, many compilers double the capacity (increase it by 100%).

The code in this example allocates new memory, moves elements, and deallocates old memory seven times. When working with a small number of integers, this shouldn't lead to performance problems. When working with a vector that holds a large number of objects that are large or inefficient to copy, however, it might. In addition, when this code completes, the vector has allocated more memory than it needs. Again, since this is a small amount of memory, this shouldn't lead to performance problems. But, if a vector has allocated a huge amount of memory that it doesn't need, it might.

The second example shows how to use the reserve() function to allocate the memory that the vector is going to use. Here, the code allocates memory for ten elements. Then, when the loop runs, the vector doesn't need to increase its capacity. And when the loop ends, the vector has no extra capacity.

So, if you know the number of elements that you need to store, you can improve performance by using the reserve() function to allocate the correct amount of memory. However, if you don't know the number of elements in advance, the default behavior of the vector allocates memory in a way that leads to reasonably good performance.

Code that adds ten elements to an empty vector

```
vector<int> nums1;

for (int i = 0; i < 10; ++i) {
    nums1.push_back(i);
    cout << "Element " << i << '\t'
         << "Capacity " << nums1.capacity() << '\t'
         << "Size " << nums1.size() << endl;
}
```

The console: capacity increased seven times

```
Element 0        Capacity 1        Size 1
Element 1        Capacity 2        Size 2
Element 2        Capacity 3        Size 3
Element 3        Capacity 4        Size 4
Element 4        Capacity 6        Size 5
Element 5        Capacity 6        Size 6
Element 6        Capacity 9        Size 7
Element 7        Capacity 9        Size 8
Element 8        Capacity 9        Size 9
Element 9        Capacity 13       Size 10
```

How to create an empty vector with space for ten elements

```
vector<int> nums2;      // nums2 is empty
nums2.reserve(10);      // nums2 still empty but now has space for 10 elements

for (int i = 0; i < 10; ++i) {
    nums2.push_back(i);
    cout << "Element " << i << '\t'
         << "Capacity " << nums2.capacity() << '\t'
         << "Size " << nums2.size() << endl;
}
```

The console: capacity not increased

```
Element 0        Capacity 10       Size 1
Element 1        Capacity 10       Size 2
Element 2        Capacity 10       Size 3
Element 3        Capacity 10       Size 4
Element 4        Capacity 10       Size 5
Element 5        Capacity 10       Size 6
Element 6        Capacity 10       Size 7
Element 7        Capacity 10       Size 8
Element 8        Capacity 10       Size 9
Element 9        Capacity 10       Size 10
```

Description

- The *capacity* of a vector is the amount of contiguous memory that's been allocated for its elements.

- When you create an empty vector, both its size and its capacity are zero. Then, as you add elements, the capacity is increased as needed.

- You can specify the capacity of a vector by passing a value to the reserve() function. This doesn't create any elements. It just allocates memory for them.

Figure 10-8   How to set capacity to improve efficiency

The Movie Rankings 1.0 program

Figure 10-9 shows the Movie Ranking program, which displays a list of movies in ranked order with the best movie in the #1 position, the second best in the #2 position, and so on. Then, the program allows the user to change these rankings. To do that, the user selects a movie by entering its current rank. Then, the user enters a new ranking for the movie.

As usual, the code begins with include directives for the header files that the program needs, including the vector header, as well as a using directive for the std namespace. Then, the code declares three function prototypes, two of which accept a vector of strings.

Here, the display_rankings() function defines the vector as a constant reference parameter. That way, the function works directly with the vector passed to it, not with a copy, and it can't change any of the data in the vector. That makes sense because this function only needs to read the vector elements, not change them.

The change_ranking() function also defines the vector as a reference parameter so it can work directly with the vector passed to it. This time, though, the vector isn't defined as a constant. That makes sense because this function needs to change the sequence of the elements in the vector.

This is a common pattern when working with vectors, which can be large and inefficient to copy. In other words, it's common for a function to use a constant reference parameter for the vector when the function only needs to read the elements in the vector, and it's common for a function to use a variable reference parameter for the vector when the function needs to make changes to the vector.

The main() function starts by defining a vector of strings named movies. To keep this program simple, the code uses an initialization list to initialize this vector with five movie titles. However, in a more realistic program, this data would be read from a file or a database.

After initializing the vector, the code displays the program title and passes the vector of movie titles to the display_rankings() function that's shown in part 2 of this figure. This function displays the movie titles and their ranks as shown by the console in this figure.

Next, the code calls the get_choice() function that's shown in part 2 of this figure. This function asks users if they want to change a ranking, and it returns a char value that indicates the response.

The console

```
The Movie Rankings program

Movie Rankings
--------------
1 - Casablanca
2 - Wonder Woman
3 - The Godfather
4 - E.T.
5 - The Bridge on the River Kwai

Do you want to change any rankings? (y/n): y
Enter current ranking of a movie: 2
Enter new ranking of the movie: 4

Movie Rankings
--------------
1 - Casablanca
2 - The Godfather
3 - E.T.
4 - Wonder Woman
5 - The Bridge on the River Kwai

Do you want to change any rankings? (y/n): n
```

The code

```cpp
#include <iostream>
#include <iomanip>
#include <string>
#include <vector>

using namespace std;

void display_rankings(const vector<string>& movies);
char get_choice();
void change_ranking(vector<string>& movies,
                    int current_ranking, int new_ranking);

int main() {
    vector<string> movies { "Casablanca", "Wonder Woman", "The Godfather",
                            "E.T.", "The Bridge on the River Kwai" };

    cout << "The Movie Rankings program\n";
    display_rankings(movies);
    char choice = get_choice();
```

Figure 10-9   The Movie Rankings 1.0 program (part 1 of 2)

After checking whether the user wants to change a ranking, this code declares a while loop that runs if the user enters 'y' or 'Y' at the prompt. Within this loop, the code begins by getting the current ranking of the movie that the user wants to change. Then, it gets the new ranking for that movie. To keep the program simple, it doesn't validate the user entries for the rankings.

After getting the current and new rankings, this code passes these rankings along with the vector of movie titles to the change_ranking() function. This updates the vector so it stores the movies in the sequence of their rankings. Then, this code calls the display_rankings() function to display the updated rankings. Finally, the code uses the get_choice() function again to check whether the user wants to change any rankings. If the user enters 'y' or 'Y', the loop is executed again. Otherwise, the program ends.

The display_rankings() function starts by displaying "Movie Rankings" followed by a line of dashes that underlines this header. Then, it uses a for loop to iterate all the elements in the vector and display each movie's ranking and title. It calculates the ranking by adding 1 to the variable named i that indicates the movie's position in the vector, so the movie at index 0 has a ranking of 1, the movie at index 1 has a ranking of 2, and so on.

The get_choice() function starts by defining a char variable named choice. Then, it prints a message to the console that asks if the user wants to change a ranking. Next, it stores the user's response in the char variable. Finally, it discards any remaining characters from the input stream and returns the character entered by the user.

The change_ranking() function starts with an if statement that checks whether the current and new rankings entered by the user are in bounds. To do that, it uses relational and logical operators to make sure the values in the current_ranking and new_ranking variables are each greater than zero and less than or equal to the value returned by the size() function of the vector of movie titles.

If the two variables are in bounds, the code within the if statement decrements the rankings so they contain values that can be used as indexes for the vector. For example, if the current_ranking variable stores a value of 1, it's referring to the first movie title, which has an index of 0. Then, the code uses the subscript operator to get the movie title for the ranking the user wants to change, and it stores this string in a variable named movie.

After storing the title in the movie variable, the code calls the erase() function of the vector to remove the movie title from the vector. To do that, it calls the begin() function to get an iterator that points to the first element in the vector. Then, it uses the + operator and the current_ranking variable to advance that iterator to the element to be removed.

Finally, the code calls the insert() function of the vector to put the movie title back in the vector at the correct position for its new ranking. To do that, it again uses the begin() function to get an iterator for the first element and the + operator to advance the iterator to the correct position. But this time, it uses the new_ranking variable to advance to the correct position. In addition, it passes the value in the movie variable as the string value to insert.

The code (continued)

```
    while (tolower(choice) == 'y') {
        int current_ranking = 0;
        cout << "Enter current ranking of a movie: ";
        cin >> current_ranking;

        int new_ranking = 0;
        cout << "Enter new ranking of the movie: ";
        cin >> new_ranking;

        change_ranking(movies, current_ranking, new_ranking);
        display_rankings(movies);      // show updated rankings
        choice = get_choice();         // ask if user wants to continue
    }
}

void display_rankings(const vector<string>& movies) {
    cout << "\nMovie Rankings\n--------------\n";
    for (int i = 0; i < movies.size(); ++i) {
        cout << (i + 1) << " - " << movies[i] << endl;
    }
    cout << endl;
}

char get_choice() {
    char choice;
    cout << "Do you want to change any rankings? (y/n): ";
    cin >> choice;
    cin.ignore(10000, '\n');
    return choice;
}

void change_ranking(vector<string>& movies,
                    int current_ranking, int new_ranking) {

    // make sure rankings are in bounds
    if (current_ranking > 0 && new_ranking > 0 &&
        current_ranking <= movies.size() && new_ranking <= movies.size()) {

        // decrement rankings to create valid indexes
        --current_ranking;
        --new_ranking;

        // store element
        string movie = movies[current_ranking];

        // remove element at old location
        movies.erase(movies.begin() + current_ranking);

        // insert element at new location
        movies.insert(movies.begin() + new_ranking, movie);
    }
}
```

Figure 10-9   The Movie Rankings 1.0 program (part 2 of 2)

How to work with arrays

The Standard Template Library provides an array container that works much like the vector container. However, unlike a vector and the other containers described in this chapter, an array is not dynamic. Because of that, its size must be known at compile time. In addition, an array can't increase its capacity automatically to account for new elements, and it doesn't provide the push_back(), pop_back(), insert(), erase(), and clear() member functions that allow you to modify the elements of a vector.

Given these limitations, you may wonder why you would ever use an array instead of a vector. The answer is that, due to the way an array uses memory, it can perform significantly better than a vector. In addition, if you're working in a constrained environment that doesn't support dynamic containers, an array may be your only option. Constrained environments include embedded systems like the ones mentioned in chapter 1.

Basic skills for working with arrays

Figure 10-10 starts by showing the include statement for the STL array header file. Then, it shows the syntax for defining an array. To start, you code the name of the container class, array, followed by a pair of angle brackets and the name of the array.

Within the angle brackets, you specify the data type for the array, followed by a comma and a *size declarator* that declares the size of the array. This size must be known at compile time. As a result, you must use a literal value or a constant for the size declarator. If you try to use a variable, you'll get an error message and your code won't compile.

This figure also shows that you can use an initialization list to initialize an array object. This works much the same as it does with vectors. However, when working with an array, you must always explicitly specify the size of the array. In other words, you can't let the compiler infer the size of the array based on the number of elements in the initialization list. In addition, if you don't initialize an array, its elements won't be given default values. So you'll almost always want to initialize an array.

Once you've defined an array, you can use the subscript operator to get and set the elements that are stored in the array. This works the same as it does with vectors.

To loop through an array, you can use any of the loops presented in this book. For example, a range-based for loop is shown in this figure. This type of loop is commonly used to work with arrays. In the next figure, though, you'll see a while loop that works with an array.

Like a vector, an array allows out of bounds access. As a result, it's important for your code to check that it doesn't use indexes that are out of bounds. To do that, you can use the size() member function of an array to get the total number of elements in an array. Then, you can make sure to only use indexes from 0 to one less than the size of the array. Or, you can use a range-based for loop, since that type of loop prevents out of bounds access.

The header file for the array container

```
#include <array>
```

The syntax for defining an array

```
array<type, size> array_name;
```

Two examples that define an array

With a literal value for the size declarator

```
array<double, 5> prices;
```

With a constant value for the size declarator

```
const int size = 5;
array<double, size> prices;
```

The number of elements in an array must be known at compile time

```
int size;
cin >> size;
array<double, size> prices;              // Wrong! This will not work!
```

How to use an initialization list

```
array<int,7> grades1 { 98, 86, 100 };    // values are 98 86 100 0 0 0 0
array<int,7> grades2 { 0 };              // values are 0 0 0 0 0 0 0

const int size = 5;
array<double, size> prices { 0 };        // values are 0 0 0 0 0
```

How to access the elements in an array

```
prices[0] = 29.99;
prices[1] = 49.99;
prices[2] = 79.99;
cout << "Price: " << prices[2] << endl;  // displays "Price: 79.99"
```

How to loop through all of the values in an array

```
for (double price : prices) {
    cout << price << ' ';                // displays 29.99 49.99 79.99 0 0
}
```

Description

- An array contains a sequence of elements of the same data type. It stores the elements in contiguous memory, or consecutive blocks of memory with no gaps.

- The number of elements in an array is fixed and must be set at compile time. Therefore, you can only use a literal or constant value to specify the number of elements.

- You can use an initialization list to set the starting values for the elements of an array. If you don't, no starting values will be assigned.

- You can use the subscript operator ([]) to get and set elements in an array by specifying the element's index.

- You can use a range-based for loop, a traditional for loop, or a while loop to loop through the elements in an array.

- An array allows out of bounds access. To avoid this, you can use a range-based for loop or the size() member function of the array.

Figure 10-10   Basic skills for working with arrays

How to pass an array to a function

Figure 10-11 presents a Test Scores program that shows how to pass an array to a function. To do that, you typically code the size of the array as a global constant. That way, you can use the size constant to specify the size of the array in any function declarations or definitions and in the code that creates the array.

In this figure, for example, the code begins by declaring a global constant named len that stores a value of 10. Then, it uses that global constant as part of the code that defines the array parameter of the calculate_total() function. In addition, the main() function uses that global constant to create the array.

By default, an array is passed to a function by value. Since an array can contain a large amount of data, however, it often makes sense to define the parameter for an array as a reference parameter as it is in the calculate_total() function. Similarly, if you only need to read from the array, not modify it, it often makes sense to define the array parameter as a constant as it is in the calculate_total() function.

Within the calculate_total() function, the code begins by defining the total variable that's used to store the total of all scores. Then, this code uses a range-based for loop to add each score to the total. This works because the code in the main() function initializes all 10 elements in the array to 0. As a result, any elements that haven't been assigned a non-zero value don't increase the total.

The main() function shows several other techniques that are useful for working with arrays. To start, this function defines an array that can hold 10 scores and initializes each score to a value of 0. Then, this code displays the name of the program and a message that indicates that the user can enter 10 scores or -1 to exit. To do that, this code uses the global variable named len.

After displaying this message, the code defines and initializes a variable named score_count. This variable counts the number of valid scores that have been entered by the user. In addition, it is used as the index for the next score.

After defining the score_count variable, this code starts a loop that continues while the score count is less than the size of the array. To do that, this loop uses the size() member function of the array object to get the number of elements in the array. This prevents out of bounds access.

Within the loop, the code begins by getting a score from the user. Then, it checks if the score equals -1. If it does, this code exits the loop. If it doesn't, the code uses the subscript operator and the score_count variable to store the score in the array of scores. Then, it increments the score_count variable so it represents the correct number of scores. This also prepares the score_count variable to be used as the index for the next element in the array.

After the loop, the code calls the calculate_total() function to get the total of all scores. Then, it displays the score count and the score total and the program ends.

As you review this code, note that a vector would work better for this program than an array. To start, a vector would automatically increase its capacity to allow the user to enter more than 10 scores. In addition, a vector would automatically keep track of the number of scores that have been entered. So, unless you're working in a constrained environment or performance is critical, you probably won't want to use an array for this type of program.

The console

```
The Test Scores program

Enter 10 scores or -1 to exit.

Enter score: 98
Enter score: 92
Enter score: 95
Enter score: -1

Score count: 3
Score total: 285
```

The code

```cpp
#include <iostream>
#include <array>

using namespace std;

// define a constant to store the size of the array
const int len = 10;

// define the function that accepts an array argument
int calculate_total(const array<int, len>& scores) {
    int total = 0;
    for (int score : scores) {
        total += score;
    }
    return total;
}

int main() {
    array<int, len> scores { 0 };              // create and initialize the array

    cout << "The Test Scores program\n\n"
         << "Enter " << len << " scores or -1 to exit.\n\n";

    // get scores from user
    int score_count = 0;
    while (score_count < scores.size()) {
        int score;
        cout << "Enter score: ";
        cin >> score;
        if (score == -1) {
            break;
        }
        scores[score_count] = score;
        ++score_count;
    }
    cout << endl;

    int total = calculate_total(scores);    // call the function
    cout << "Score count: " << score_count << endl;
    cout << "Score total: " << total << endl;
}
```

Figure 10-11   How to pass an array to a function

How to work with lists

The Standard Template Library has two list containers: list and forward list. In the next few figures, you'll learn how these containers store data in memory, what their pros and cons are, when to use them, and how to use them.

An introduction to lists and forward lists

The elements in a list are stored in non-contiguous memory, as illustrated at the top of figure 10-12. This means that the elements are stored in physical memory locations that aren't related to each other. In the first diagram, for example, element 0 is at memory address 100, but element 1 is at memory address 108 and element 3 is at memory address 354.

Since the memory locations of the elements aren't related to each other physically, a list uses pointers to link each element to the other elements in the sequence. In the first diagram, the elements in the list object contain pointers that link to the next and previous elements in the sequence. This is called a *doubly linked list*. Because of these double links, the list object can traverse the sequence both forwards and backwards. That's why the list container can support the higher-level bidirectional iterator.

In the second diagram, the elements in the forward list object have pointers that link only to the next element in the sequence. This is called a *singly linked list*. Because these links only point forward, the forward list object can only traverse the sequence in a forward direction. That's why the forward list container must use the lower-level forward iterator.

Because lists don't need to maintain contiguous memory, they never need to move elements. That means that when you add or remove elements in a list, a variable that holds an iterator isn't invalidated unless it points to a removed element. This is the main advantage that lists have over vectors.

Lists can also be more efficient than vectors for inserting and removing elements in the middle of the sequence. However, this isn't always more efficient for two reasons. First, the overhead a list needs to allocate memory for elements and maintain pointers can be greater than the overhead a vector needs to occasionally allocate memory and move elements. Second, elements in contiguous memory are faster to access and iterate. Because of that, you should always make sure a list is the better choice before you choose it over a vector.

Because a forward list maintains fewer pointers, it is more efficient than a list. Keep in mind, though, that it also has less functionality since the elements can only be accessed in a forward direction.

The first code example shows how to include the header files for both the list and the forward list. Then, the second and third examples show how you can initialize a list with an initialization list or with iterators. One benefit of initializing with iterators is that you can fill a container with elements from another type of container. For instance, the third example shows how to initialize a list with the elements from a vector. Then, the last example shows how to use the assign() member function to replace the content of a list with elements from a vector.

A graphical representation of the non-contiguous memory of a list

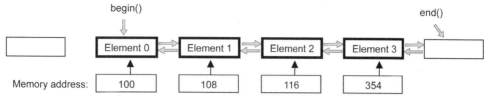

A graphical representation of the pointers of a forward list

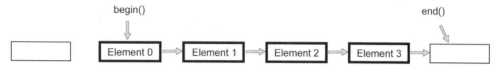

The header file for the list and forward list containers

```
#include <list>
#include <forward_list>
```

How to initialize a list and a forward list with a list of values

```
list<int> numbers1 { 1, 2, 3, 4, 5 };
forward_list<int> numbers2 { 6, 7, 8, 9 };
```

How to use the values of a vector to initialize a list

```
vector<int> nums { 1, 2, 3, 4, 5, 6 };
list<int> numbers3 (nums.begin(), nums.end());
// numbers3 contains 1 2 3 4 5 6
```

How to assign the values of a vector to a list

```
numbers3.assign(++nums.begin(), nums.end());   // skip first element
// numbers3 contains 2 3 4 5 6
```

Description

- The elements of both the list and the forward list are stored in non-contiguous memory, with *pointers* linking the elements.

- The elements of a list have pointers that link to the next element and the previous one. This is called a *doubly linked list* and it allows the iterator to be bidirectional.

- The elements of a forward list only have pointers that link to the next element. This is called a *singly linked list* and it only allows the iterator to move forward.

- A list never moves its elements. As a result, iterators that point to existing elements are never invalidated unless you remove the element from the list. This is the main advantage that lists have over vectors.

- A list can sometimes be more efficient than a vector for inserting or removing elements in the middle of the sequence. Before you choose a list over a vector, though, you should do performance testing to make sure the list is more efficient.

Figure 10-12   An introduction to lists and forward lists

Member functions of a list

Figure 10-13 presents some of the member functions of the list container. The push_front() and pop_front() functions work like the push_back() and pop_back() functions of the vector container. However, they work with the front of the sequence, not the back.

The reverse() function reverses the current order of the elements, and the sort() function arranges them in ascending order. On a related note, the vector doesn't provide a sort() function, but you can sort a vector using the sort() algorithm that's described in the next chapter.

The splice() function allows you to transfer some or all of the elements of another list before the element pointed to by an iterator. This is similar to the insert() function, with two important differences. First, you pass the list that contains the elements you want to transfer as an argument. Second, insert() makes copies of the elements being inserted, and splice() transfers them by rearranging pointers. Because of that, splicing removes the elements from the initial list.

The merge() function works similarly, transferring rather than copying elements. However, instead of using an iterator to determine position, it merges all the elements in both lists in ascending order. For this to work properly, you should call the sort() function for both lists before calling merge().

The remove() function removes elements by value rather than by iterator. And, it removes every element that contains that value.

The code examples show how these functions work. To start, the code defines and initializes three lists of int values named nums1, nums2, and nums3. Then, the code uses the splice() function to add all of the elements of nums3 to nums1. When this code runs, nums3 no longer has any elements because they've been transferred to nums1.

The second splice() function example adds some, but not all, of the elements of nums2 to nums1. To do that, the code passes a [b:e] interval that tells splice() which elements in the sequence to transfer. More specifically, it transfers the three middle elements but leaves the first and last elements in nums2.

The reverse() function example reverses the order of the elements in nums1, and the sort() function example arranges the elements in nums1 in ascending order. The next example calls the sort() function of the nums2 list. At this point, both lists are sorted. Then, this code passes nums2 to the merge() function of nums1. When this code runs, nums1 contains the elements that were in nums2 and nums2 is empty.

The last example passes a value of 5 to the remove() function of nums1. This removes both elements in the list that contain the value 5.

You can also use many of the skills presented in this figure with a forward list. However, you can't use them all. For example, you can't iterate backwards with the decrement operator (--). Instead, you can get an iterator for the first element and iterate forward to the correct element. Also, you can't use the splice() function to insert elements before the specified iterator. However, you can use the splice_after() function that's specific to forward lists to insert elements after the specified iterator.

Some member functions of the list container

Function	Description
push_front(elem)	Adds a new element to the front of the sequence.
pop_front()	Removes the element at the front of the sequence.
reverse()	Reverses the order of the elements.
sort()	Sorts elements in ascending order.
splice(i, list)	Transfers the elements in the list before the element pointed to by i.
splice(i, list, b, e)	Transfers the elements in the list in interval [b:e] before the element pointed to by i.
merge(list)	Merges two sorted lists. You should sort both lists before calling this function.
remove(value)	Removes the elements that are equal to value.

Examples

```
list<int> nums1 { 1, 2, 3, 4, 5 };
list<int> nums2 { 5, 6, 7, 8, 9 };
list<int> nums3 { 9, 10 };

nums1.splice(nums1.end(), nums3);
// nums1 now contains 1 2 3 4 5 9 10, and nums3 is empty

nums1.splice(nums1.begin(), nums2, ++nums2.begin(), --nums2.end() );
// nums1 now contains 6 7 8 1 2 3 4 5 9 10, and nums2 contains 5 9

nums1.reverse();
// nums1 now contains 10 9 5 4 3 2 1 8 7 6

nums1.sort();
// nums1 now contains 1 2 3 4 5 6 7 8 9 10

nums2.sort();
nums1.merge(nums2);
// nums1 now contains 1 2 3 4 5 5 6 7 8 9 9 10, and nums2 is empty

nums1.remove(5);
// nums1 now contains 1 2 3 4 6 7 8 9 9 10
```

Description

- The splice() and merge() functions don't make copies of their elements. Instead, they transfer elements by rearranging pointers. As a result, after these functions run, the elements passed to them are no longer in the initial list.

Figure 10-13   Member functions of a list

The Movie Rankings 2.0 program

Figure 10-14 shows a second version of the Movie Rankings program that was presented earlier in this chapter. To the user, this program works the same as the earlier version. However, the code for this program uses a list instead of a vector to store its data.

If you understand the code for the Movie Rankings 1.0 program, you shouldn't have much trouble understanding the code for the 2.0 version since it's mostly the same. One difference is that the fourth include directive specifies the header file for the list, not the header file for the vector. Another difference is that the display_rankings() and change_ranking() functions accept a list of strings instead of a vector of strings.

The console

```
The Movie Rankings program

Movie Rankings
--------------
1 - Casablanca
2 - Wonder Woman
3 - The Godfather
4 - E.T.
5 - The Bridge on the River Kwai

Do you want to change any rankings? (y/n): y
Enter current ranking of a movie: 2
Enter new ranking of the movie: 4

Movie Rankings
--------------
1 - Casablanca
2 - The Godfather
3 - E.T.
4 - Wonder Woman
5 - The Bridge on the River Kwai

Do you want to change any rankings? (y/n): n
```

The code

```cpp
#include <iostream>
#include <iomanip>
#include <string>
#include <list>

using namespace std;

void display_rankings(const list<string>& movies);
char get_choice();
void change_ranking(list<string>& movies,
                    int current_ranking, int new_ranking);
int main() {
    list<string> movies { "Casablanca", "Wonder Woman", "The Godfather",
                          "E.T.", "The Bridge on the River Kwai" };

    cout << "The Movie Rankings program\n";
    display_rankings(movies);
    char choice = get_choice();
    while (tolower(choice) == 'y') {
        int current_ranking = 0, new_ranking = 0;
        cout << "Enter current ranking of a movie: ";
        cin >> current_ranking;
        cout << "Enter new ranking of the movie: ";
        cin >> new_ranking;

        change_ranking(movies, current_ranking, new_ranking);
        display_rankings(movies);    // show new rankings
        choice = get_choice();       // ask if user wants to continue
    }
}
```

Figure 10-14   The Movie Rankings 2.0 program (part 1 of 2)

Part 2 of figure 10-14 shows the definitions of the three functions called by the main() function. The get_choice() function, which asks the user if they want to change the ranking for a movie, uses the same code as the Movie Rankings 1.0 program described earlier in this chapter. However, most of the code in the other two functions is different from the code in the 1.0 version.

After it displays an underlined heading for the rankings, the display_rankings() function uses a range-based for loop to iterate the list instead of a traditional for loop like the 1.0 version. That's because you can't use the subscript operator to access the elements in a list. In addition, this loop uses a counter variable named i. Then, within the body of the loop, this code uses the element value and the counter variable to display each movie's ranking and title.

Like the 1.0 version, the change_ranking() function starts by checking that the current and new rankings entered by the user are in bounds. The remaining code, though, is different from the code in the 1.0 version. To start, this code uses the auto keyword and the begin() member function of the list to get an iterator that points to the first element in the list. Then, it uses a for loop and the increment operator (++) to advance the iterator so it points to the element that contains the current ranking. It must use this operator rather than the addition operator (+) because the list uses a bidirectional iterator, and the addition operator isn't available to this type of iterator.

After this code advances the iterator to the correct element, the code defines a string variable named movie and uses the indirection operator (*) to get the movie title for the ranking the user wants to change. Then, it stores this title in the movie variable and calls the erase() function of the list to remove the movie title. Since the iterator variable already points to the correct element, this code passes that iterator to the erase() function.

At this point, the code needs to position the iterator variable so it points to the correct location for the new ranking. To do that, the code calls the begin() function again to move the iterator back to the first element. Then, it uses another for loop and the increment operator to advance the iterator to the position of the new ranking. Finally, the code calls the insert() function of the list to put the movie title back in the list at the correct position for its new ranking. To do that, this code passes the iterator and the movie variable to the insert() function.

As you can see, quite a few changes are necessary to get this program to work with a list instead of a vector. Most of these changes are necessary because a list uses a lower-level iterator than a vector. However, modifying the 2.0 version of this program so it works with a vector wouldn't require as many changes. That's because a higher-level iterator can work with any code that a lower iterator can.

This shows that it's possible to write code that can work with many types of containers. Of course, if you know that you're going to use a vector, as you probably would in this case, it can be much more convenient to just use the higher-level functionality that its random-access iterator provides.

The code (continued)

```cpp
void display_rankings(const list<string>& movies) {
    cout << "\nMovie Rankings\n--------------\n";
    int i = 1;
    for (string m: movies) {
        cout << i << " - " << m << endl;
        ++i;
    }
    cout << endl;
}

char get_choice() {
    char choice;
    cout << "Do you want to change any rankings? (y/n): ";
    cin >> choice;
    cin.ignore(10000, '\n');
    return choice;
}

void change_ranking(list<string>& movies,
                    int current_ranking, int new_ranking) {

    // make sure rankings are in bounds
    if (current_ranking > 0 && new_ranking > 0 &&
        current_ranking <= movies.size() &&
        new_ranking <= movies.size()) {

        // get iterator that points to first element
        auto iter = movies.begin();

        // increment iterator until it points to current ranking
        for (int i = 1; i < current_ranking; ++i) {
            ++iter;
        }

        // store value of element to be moved
        string movie = *iter;

        // remove element
        movies.erase(iter);

        // get first iterator again and then increment to new ranking
        iter = movies.begin();
        for (int i = 1; i < new_ranking; ++i) {
            ++iter;
        }

        // insert element at new location
        movies.insert(iter, movie);
    }
}
```

Figure 10-14   The Movie Rankings 2.0 program (part 2 of 2)

How to work with queues and stacks

The deque (pronounced "deck") container uses blocks of contiguous memory connected by pointers to store its data as illustrated in figure 10-15. This gives a deque some of the speed of a vector and allows for fast access at the front of the sequence as well as the back. Like a vector, however, a deque needs to move elements when an element is inserted or removed in the middle of the sequence. And, like a vector, this can cause iterators to be invalidated.

The Standard Template Library provides two container adapters, queue and stack, that adapt the deque to more specialized uses. This figure shows how to work with these container adapters.

How to work with queues

The queue container adapter provides *first-in, first-out (FIFO)* access. You can think of this as a line, or queue, at a movie theater. A new person lines up at the back of the line, and the first person in the line is the first person to get out of the line.

As a result, when used with a queue, the push() function adds an element to the back of the sequence, and the pop() function removes the element from the front. Additionally, as with other sequence containers, the front() function allows access to the first element in the sequence, and the back() function allows access to the last.

The queue example in this figure shows how these functions work. Note that, unlike the vector and list, you can't initialize a queue with an initialization list or iterators.

How to work with stacks

In contrast to the queue container adapter, the stack container adapter provides *last-in, first-out (LIFO)* access. You can think of this as a stack of books. A new book goes on the top of the stack, and the last book on the stack is also the first book out of the stack.

As a result, when used with a stack, the push() function adds an element to the top, or front, of the sequence, and the pop() function removes the element from the front. Unlike the other sequence containers, the stack doesn't have a front() or back() function. Instead, it has a top() function that allows access to the first element in the sequence.

The stack example in this figure shows how these functions work. Note that, like a queue, you can't initialize a stack with an initialization list or iterators.

The contiguous and non-contiguous memory of a deque

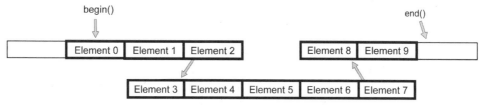

Some member functions of the queue container adapter

Function	Description
`push(value)`	Inserts an element at the back of the sequence.
`pop()`	Removes the first element in the sequence.
`front()`	Returns a reference to the value in the first element in the sequence.
`back()`	Returns a reference to the value in the last element in the sequence.

The header file for the queue container adapter

```
#include <queue>
```

An example of working with a queue

```
queue<int> q;
q.push(1);
q.push(2);
cout << "front = " << q.front() << " and back = " << q.back() << endl;
// displays "front = 1 and back = 2"

q.pop();
cout << "front = " << q.front() << " and back = " << q.back() << endl;
// displays "front = 2 and back = 2"
```

Some member functions of the stack container adapter

Function	Description
`push(value)`	Inserts an element at the front of the sequence.
`pop()`	Removes the first element in the sequence.
`top()`	Returns a reference to the value in the first element in the sequence.

The header file for the stack container adapter

```
#include <stack>
```

An example of working with a stack

```
stack<int> s;
s.push(1);
s.push(2);
cout << "top = " << s.top() << endl;
// displays "top = 2"

s.pop();
cout << "top = " << s.top() << endl;
// displays "top = 1"
```

Figure 10-15   How to work with queues and stacks

How to work with sets

A set is an associative container that stores and retrieves its elements based on the value of a *key*. A set, however, only stores keys. This key is often a string, but it can be any data type.

The Standard Template Library has two set containers: set and multiset. The multiset allows duplicate keys, but the set requires each key to be unique. Figure 10-16 presents some member functions that are shared by the associative containers and shows how to use them to work with sets.

Member functions of associative containers

Like a list, the elements in a set are stored in non-contiguous memory. However, when you add an element to a set, the set stores the element in sorted order. This is one of the main benefits of the set container.

Most C++ implementations of a set use a *balanced binary search tree* as shown by the diagram in this figure. Here, each parent node points to two nodes, one with a greater value and one with a lesser value. This allows the container to use a binary search to look for a specific key. Since a binary search can be more efficient than the linear search that a list has to use, sets can be more efficient for retrieving data.

Two member functions are shared by the associative containers. First, the find() function accepts a key and returns an iterator to the first element with the specified key. Or, if the key isn't in the container, find() returns the off-the-end iterator. Second, the count() function returns the number of elements in the container with the specified key.

Code examples that work with sets

The code examples in this figure show how to work with sets. To start, the first example shows how to include the header file for sets and multisets. Then, the second example shows how to define a set and use an initialization list to initialize it with some keys that are strings.

The third example shows how to use the insert() member function common to most containers to add keys to a set. Here, the second statement attempts to add a key of "AK". However, a set requires unique keys, and the key "AK" is already in the set. Therefore, this line of code doesn't add this key. However, if this code example used a multiset instead of a set, this statement would add the key and the container would have two keys with a value of "AK".

The fourth example shows how to use a range-based for loop to iterate the keys in the set. This displays the keys in alphabetical order, which shows that a set stores keys in sorted order, even when the keys aren't added in that order.

The fifth example shows how to find and remove a key. To do that, this code uses the find() function to get an iterator that points to the key. Then, it compares this iterator to the off-the-end iterator to determine if the key was found. If so, it uses the erase() function to remove the key.

A graphical representation of the non-contiguous memory of a set

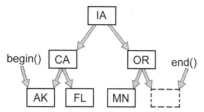

Some member functions shared by the associative containers

Function	Description
find(k)	Returns an iterator to the first element with a specified key. Or, if the specified key isn't found, it returns the off-the-end iterator.
count(k)	Returns the number of elements with a specified key.

The header file for the set and multiset containers

```
#include <set>
```

How to create a set with an initialization list

```
set<string> states { "CA", "OR", "AK" };
```

How to add keys to a set

```
states.insert("FL");    // added
states.insert("AK");    // not added because it already exists
states.insert("MN");    // added
states.insert("IA");    // added
```

How to iterate the elements in a set with a range-based for loop

```
for(string state: states) {
    cout << state << ' ';
}
// displays "AK CA FL IA MN OR ";
```

How to find and remove a value from a set

```
auto iter = states.find("FL");
if (iter == states.end()) {
    cout << "Not found\n";
} else {
    states.erase(iter);
}
// states now contains AK CA IA MN OR
```

Description

- The set and multiset store *keys* in ascending order in non-contiguous memory.
- When you add or remove a key, the pointers are rearranged to maintain the sort order but the data itself isn't moved. Because of that, iterators that point to existing elements aren't invalidated.

Figure 10-16   How to work with sets

How to work with maps

Like a set, a map is an associative container that stores and retrieves its elements based on the value of a key. Unlike a set, a map stores *key/value pairs*. In other words, it stores a key and a value that's associated with that key. Like a set, the key is often a string, but it can be any data type.

The Standard Template Library has two map containers: map and multimap. As you might expect, a map requires each key to be unique, and a multimap allows duplicate keys. The STL also provides a pair structure for working with maps.

Member functions and operators of a map

Like a set, the elements in a map are stored in sorted order in non-contiguous memory. Also like a set, most C++ implementations of a map use a balanced binary search tree as illustrated by the diagram in figure 10-17.

This figure begins by presenting three member functions of a map. First, the at() function works similarly to the at() function of a vector. However, this version accepts a key, not an index. Second, the insert() function accepts and inserts a key/value pair. Third, the insert_or_assign() function accepts a key and a value. If the key is not in the map, this function inserts an element with the key/value pair. Otherwise, it modifies the value associated with the key.

After the functions, this figure presents the subscript operator that's provided by a map. This operator provides read and write access to the values in the map, and it works similarly to the subscript operator provided by a vector. However, a map's subscript operator accepts a key, not an index. In addition, as you'll see in the next figure, you can use the subscript operator to insert a new element into a map.

The code examples in this figure show some basic skills for working with maps. To start, the first example shows how to include the header file that you use for both maps and multimaps.

The second example shows how to define a map and initialize it with a list of key/value pairs. When you define a map, you need to define the data type of both the key and the value. To do that, you code both types within the angle brackets that follow the class name and separate them with a comma. In this example, the key is a string and the value is an int. In addition, each key/value pair in an initialization list needs to be enclosed in its own pair of braces. Within these braces, the key and the value are separated by a comma.

The third example shows how to use a range-based for loop to iterate the key/value pairs in a map. To code the type for this loop, you can use the pair structure with the same data types as the map as shown here. However, you could also use the auto keyword for the type to simplify this code.

Within the for loop, you can use the two data members of the pair structure as shown here. The member named first stores the key, and the member named second stores the value. In this example, the code uses these data members to write the key and value to the console.

A graphical representation of the non-contiguous memory of a map

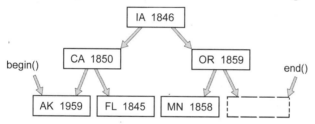

Some member functions of the map container

Function	Description
at(k)	Returns the value associated with the specified key. Throws an error if not found.
insert(p)	Inserts the specified key/value pair.
insert_or_assign(k, v)	Inserts an element with the specified key and value. If the key is already in the map, this function modifies the value.

One of the operators defined by the map container

Operator	Name	Description
[k]	subscript	Allows read/write access to the value with the specified key. In addition, it allows you to insert a key/value pair.

The header file for the map and multimap containers

```
#include <map>
```

How to create a map with an initialization list

```
map<string, int> states { {"CA", 1850}, {"OR", 1859}, {"AK", 1959} };
```

How to display the data in a map

```
for(pair<string, int> p: states) {
    cout << p.first << '(' << p.second << ") ";
}
// displays "AK(1959) CA(1850) OR(1859) ";
```

Description

- The map and multimap store *key/value pairs* in ascending order by key in non-contiguous memory.

- When you add or remove a key/value pair, the pointers are rearranged to maintain the sort order but the data itself isn't moved. Because of that, iterators that point to existing elements aren't invalidated.

- You use the pair structure to work with the keys and values of a map or multimap. The pair structure has a data member named first that contains the key and a data member named second that contains the value.

Figure 10-17   Member functions and operators of a map

How to insert key/value pairs and work with values by key

Figure 10-18 presents some code examples for working with maps. To start, the first example defines a map of string/int pairs and initializes it with three pairs. This map is used by the rest of the examples in this figure.

The second example shows how to use the subscript operator to insert key/value pairs and work with map values. Here, the first statement adds a new key/value pair to the map, and the second statement updates the value associated with that key. Then, the third statement uses the key to find and display the associated value.

The third example shows how to use the insert() function instead of the subscript operator to add a key/value pair to a map. To do that, you need to create a pair object and pass it to the insert() function. This example shows three ways to accomplish this. First, you can define and initialize a pair object in one statement and pass it to the insert() function in another. Note that you define and initialize a pair object using a technique that's similar to the one you use to define and initialize a map object. Because a pair consists of a single key and value, though, you code a single set of braces with that key and value.

When you use this first technique, you store the pair object in a variable. This is useful if you need to use the object again later. Otherwise, you can use one of the other two techniques shown here. First, you can define, initialize, and insert a pair object all in one statement. Second, you can create a pair object by passing a key and a value to the make_pair() function that's available from the utility header file, and then pass that pair object to the insert() function.

The fourth example shows how to use the insert_or_assign() function to insert key/value pairs and update map values. Here, the first statement adds a new key/value pair to the map. Then, because the second statement specifies the same key as the first statement, it updates the value for the element with that key.

The fifth example demonstrates an odd behavior you might run into if you try to use the subscript operator to retrieve a value from a map. For instance, this example attempts to retrieve the value associated with the key "WA" and store it in an int variable named year. However, there is no element with this key in the states map. Because of that, this unexpectedly adds an element with the key "WA" and a default value to the map. In this case, because the value has a data type of int, the element is given a value of 0. This value is also stored in the year variable.

Since this behavior isn't usually what you want, it's a better practice to use the find() member function to check whether a key is in a map before you retrieve its value as shown in the last example. Here, the code compares the iterator returned by the find() function to the off-the-end iterator to determine whether the key is in the map. If the key is not in the map, the code doesn't attempt to access its value. If the key is in the map, the code retrieves its value and stores it in the int variable named year.

The map of strings and ints used by the examples

```
map<string, int> states { {"CA", 1850}, {"OR", 1859}, {"AK", 1959} };
```

How to insert, read, and write values with the subscript operator

```
states["IA"] = 1946;                                    // adds key/value
states["IA"] = 1846;                                    // modifies value
cout << "Iowa entered union in " << states["IA"] << endl; // reads value
```

How to insert values with the insert() member function

Create a pair structure and then insert it

```
pair<string, int> florida {"FL", 1845};
states.insert(florida);
```

Create and insert a pair structure in one statement

```
states.insert(pair<string, int> {"FL", 1845});
```

Use the make_pair() function

```
states.insert(make_pair("FL", 1845));
```

How to insert and write values with the insert_or_assign() function

```
states.insert_or_assign("IL", 1828);        // adds key/value
states.insert_or_assign("IL", 1818);        // modifies value
```

How you can accidentally insert a key/value pair with the subscript operator

```
// states contains AK/1959 CA/1850 FL/1845 IA/1846 IL/1818 OR/1859

// attempt to retrieve the year Washington entered the union
int year = states["WA"];

// states now contains AK/1959 CA/1850 FL/1845 IA/1846 IL/1818 OR/1859 WA/0
// year is 0
```

How to use the find() member function to check whether a key is in the map

```
auto iter = states.find("WA");
if (iter == states.end()) {
    cout << "Not found\n";
} else {
    int year = states["WA"];
}
```

Description

- You can use the subscript operator, the insert() member function, or the insert_or_assign() member function to insert a new key/value pair in a map.

- When you use the insert() function, you can manually code a new pair structure, or you can use the make_pair() function.

- If you use the insert_or_assign() function and the key already exists, its value is changed.

- You can use the subscript operator to read or modify an existing value by key.

- When you use the subscript operator to access a value by key and the key isn't in the map, it's added with a value that's the default value of the data type. Because of that, it's safer to first use the find() member function to see if a key is in a map.

Figure 10-18   How to insert key/value pairs into a map and find a value by key

The Word Counter program

Figure 10-19 shows the Word Counter program. This program reads and processes text from a text file. It counts the total number of individual words, the total number of unique words, and the total number of times each word appears. The program displays the individual words in the order that it reads them, but it displays the unique words and the count per word in alphabetical order.

The code begins with include statements for the header files that the program needs, including the vector and map headers, and the using directive for the std namespace. Then, the code declares two function prototypes. Both of these functions return a container object. The load_words() function returns a vector of strings, and the get_word_count() function returns a map of string/int pairs.

You might wonder why these functions return containers instead of accepting existing containers by reference and updating them. After all, doesn't returning a container mean the function has to create a container and then return a copy of it? And isn't that a possible problem if the container is large or expensive to copy?

The reason you can safely return a container from a function is that, as you learned in chapter 9, most C++ compilers use *return value optimization (RVO)* to avoid the copy operation. The details of how RVO works are beyond the scope of this book. However, you can feel confident that in most situations, you can return a container without negatively impacting performance.

After the function prototypes, the main() function starts by displaying the program name. Then, it stores the name of the text file in a string variable named filename and passes that variable to the load_words() function. This loads all the words in the text file into a vector named words. Here, the code uses the auto keyword to allow the compiler to determine the data type instead of explicitly specifying a type of vector<string>. Next, the code uses a range-based for loop to display all the words in the vector.

After displaying all of the words in sequence, the code passes the vector of words to the get_word_count() function. This function loads each unique word as the key in a map named word_count, with the number of times each word appears in the file as the associated value. This code also uses the auto keyword instead of explicitly coding the map<string, int> type.

After getting the map named word_count, this code uses two range-based for loops to display the elements in the map. The first loop displays the unique words in the text file. To do that, this loop only displays the key for each pair. By contrast, the second loop displays the count for each unique word. To do that, this loop displays the key, which is the word, and the value, which is the word count. Both of these loops use the auto keyword to declare the data type for each pair instead of explicitly specifying a data type of pair<string, int>.

The console

```
The Word Counter program

60 WORDS: it was the best of times it was the worst of times it was
the age of wisdom it was the age of foolishness it was the epoch of
belief it was the epoch of incredulity it was the season of light
it was the season of darkness it was the spring of hope it was the
winter of despair

20 UNIQUE WORDS: age belief best darkness despair epoch foolishness
hope incredulity it light of season spring the times was winter
wisdom worst

COUNT PER WORD: age=2 belief=1 best=1 darkness=1 despair=1 epoch=2
foolishness=1 hope=1 incredulity=1 it=10 light=1 of=10 season=2
spring=1 the=10 times=2 was=10 winter=1 wisdom=1 worst=1
```

The code

```cpp
#include <iostream>
#include <fstream>
#include <string>
#include <vector>
#include <map>

using namespace std;

vector<string> load_words(string filename);
map<string, int> get_word_count(const vector<string>& words);

int main() {
    cout << "The Word Counter program\n\n";

    string filename = "dickens.txt";
    auto words = load_words(filename);

    cout << words.size() << " WORDS: ";
    for (string word : words) {
        cout << word << ' ';
    }
    cout << endl << endl;

    auto word_count = get_word_count(words);

    cout << word_count.size() << " UNIQUE WORDS: ";
    for (auto pair : word_count) {
        cout << pair.first << ' ';
    }
    cout << endl << endl;

    cout << "COUNT PER WORD: ";
    for (auto pair : word_count) {
        cout << pair.first << '='  << pair.second << ' ';
    }
    cout << endl << endl;
}
```

Figure 10-19   The Word Counter program (part 1 of 2)

Part 2 of figure 10-19 shows the definitions of the functions called by the main() function. First, the load_words() function starts by defining a vector of strings named words. Then, it defines an input file stream object and opens it by passing it the filename of the text file.

If the file opens successfully, the code uses a while loop to get each word in the text file. For each word, this code loops through each character in the word, discarding punctuation and converting any uppercase letters to lowercase. When that's done, this code uses the push_back() function to add the word to the vector.

After this code adds all of the words in the text file to the vector, it calls the close() function of the file stream to close the connection to the file. Then, it returns the vector of words to the calling code.

The get_word_count() function starts by defining a map of string/int pairs named word_count. Then, it uses a range-based for loop to process all the words in the vector.

Within this loop, the first statement passes the word from the vector as the key to the find() function of the map. Then, it compares the iterator returned by find() to the off-the-end iterator. If they're equal, that word isn't yet in the map. As a result, the code uses the subscript operator to add the key with a count value of 1. However, if the key is already in the map, the code uses the subscript operator to retrieve it and increment its associated count value by one. When the loop finishes, it returns the map of word/count pairs to the calling code.

The code (continued)

```cpp
vector<string> load_words(string filename) {
    vector<string> words;
    ifstream infile(filename);

    if (infile) {
        string word;
        while(infile >> word) {

            string new_word = "";
            for (char c : word) {
                if (c == '.' || c == ',') {
                    continue;                    // remove punctuation
                } else if (isupper(c)) {
                    new_word += tolower(c); // convert to lowercase
                } else {
                    new_word += c;
                }
            }
            words.push_back(new_word);         // add word
        }
        infile.close();
    }
    return words;
}

map<string, int> get_word_count(const vector<string>& words) {
    map<string, int> word_count {};

    for (string word : words) {
        auto search = word_count.find(word);
        if (search == word_count.end()) {
            word_count[word] = 1;    // not found - add word with count of 1
        } else {
            word_count[word] += 1;   // found - increment count for word
        }
    }
    return word_count;
}
```

Figure 10-19   The Word Counter program (part 2 of 2)

How to work with nested containers

Sometimes, you need to use an STL container to store instances of another STL container. In other words, you sometimes need to *nest* containers.

How to work with a vector of vectors

The first example in figure 10-20 shows how to define a vector of vectors. To do that, you code the inner vector as the data type for the outer vector. In this case, the outer vector holds other vectors of int values. In other words, the outer container has a data type of vector<int>.

Note that when you code nested vectors like this, some older compilers can interpret the closing angle brackets for the inner and outer vectors as the stream extraction operator (>>). To prevent this, you can code a space between the angle brackets as shown in this figure.

The second example shows how to use the push_back() function to add individual vectors to the vector of vectors. Here, values within the braces create a literal vector value and pass it to the push_back() function. In the first statement, the literal vector that's added contains three elements. In the second, the literal vector contains four elements.

The third example shows how to iterate a vector of vectors to access the elements contained within each vector. To do that, you can use nested loops. Here, an outer range-based for loop iterates through the nested vectors. Within that loop, a range-based for loop iterates through the elements in the nested vector.

The fourth example shows how to access a specific value within a vector of vectors. To do that, you code two subscripts. The first subscript is the index of the inner vector, and the second subscript is the index of the element within that vector. With two nested vectors, you can think of the first index as specifying the row of a table, and the second index as specifying the column.

How to work with a map of vectors

Figure 10-20 also shows how to work with a map of vectors. The first example defines a map that stores string/vector pairs where the vectors store int values. Again, the code shown here includes a space between the closing angle brackets to avoid problems with older compilers.

The second example shows how to use the subscript operator to add a string key and a vector value to the map of vectors. Here, the student's name is the key.

The third example shows how to iterate the map of vectors to access the elements contained within each vector. Like before, this code uses nested loops. Since the map automatically sorts the keys, this code displays the student names in alphabetical order.

The fourth example shows how to access a specific value within a map of vectors. Just as with a vector of vectors, you provide two subscripts. This time, though, the first subscript is the key associated with the vector, not an index.

How to work with a vector of vectors

How to define a vector of vectors

```
vector<vector<int> > student_grades;
```

How to add vectors to a vector of vectors

```
student_grades.push_back( {78, 56, 90} );
student_grades.push_back( {89, 85, 87, 83} );
```

How to iterate the elements in a vector of vectors

```
cout << "Total number of students: " << student_grades.size() << endl;
for (auto grades: student_grades) {
    cout << "This student has " << grades.size() << " grades:   ";
    for (auto grade: grades) {
        cout << grade << ' ';
    }
    cout << endl;
}
```

```
Total number of students: 2
This student has 3 grades:   78 56 90
This student has 4 grades:   89 85 87 83
```

How to access a specific value in a vector of vectors

```
int grade = student_grades[1][0];          // grade is 89
```

How to work with a map of vectors

How to define a map of vectors

```
map<string, vector<int> > student_grades;
```

How to add vectors to a map of vectors

```
student_grades["joe"] = {78, 56, 90};
student_grades["amy"] = {89, 85, 87, 83};
```

How to iterate the elements in a map of vectors

```
cout << "Total number of students: " << student_grades.size() << endl;
for (auto grades: student_grades) {
    cout << grades.first << " has " << grades.second.size() << " grades: ";
    for (auto grade: grades.second) {
        cout << grade << ' ';
    }
    cout << endl;
}
```

```
Total number of students: 2
amy has 4 grades:   89 85 87 83
joe has 3 grades:   78 56 90
```

How to access a specific value in a map of vectors

```
int grade = student_grades["amy"][0];   // grade is 89
```

Description

- When you *nest* containers, it's a best practice to code a space between the closing angle brackets so older compilers don't interpret them as the stream extraction operator (>>).

Figure 10-20   How to work with nested containers

Perspective

Now that you've completed this chapter, you should have the skills you need to work with the containers and iterators of the Standard Template Library. In the next chapter, you'll learn how to use the STL algorithms to perform common tasks with the data in a container, such as searching and sorting the elements in a container.

Terms

Standard Template Library (STL)	initialize a vector
container	capacity
iterator	size declarator
sequence container	pointer
associative container	doubly linked list
contiguous memory	singly linked list
non-contiguous memory	first-in, first-out (FIFO) access
container adapter	last-in, first-out (LIFO) access
interval	key
half-open interval	balanced binary search tree
off-the-end iterator	key/value pair
dereference an iterator	return value optimization (RVO)
indirection operator	nested containers
member access operator	

Summary

- The *Standard Template Library (STL)* includes *containers* that store data and *iterators* that allow access to the data.

- The *sequence containers* store data in sequence by index, and the *associative containers* store data by *key*.

- The array and vector containers store data in *contiguous memory*, which is a consecutive block of memory with no gaps.

- The list, forward list, and associative containers store data in *non-contiguous memory*, which are unrelated memory locations that may have gaps.

- An *iterator* allows you to access and traverse the elements in a sequence.

- The iterators returned by a container's begin() and end() functions define a range that starts at the first element and ends one past the last element. This is called a *half-open interval*, and can be represented by the mathematical notation [begin:end).

- The iterator returned by a container's end() function is sometimes called an *off-the-end* iterator.

- There are six types of iterators, and they are hierarchical. Each higher iterator *inherits* the operations provided by the lower ones.

- An iterator *points to* an element in a container. To access the value an iterator points to, you can *dereference* the iterator with the *indirection operator* (*) or the *member access operator* (->).

- The *capacity* of a vector is the amount of contiguous memory that's been allocated for its elements.

- An array stores its elements in contiguous memory, but its size must be known at compile time and can't be increased dynamically at runtime.

- A deque (pronounced "deck") is a double-ended queue that stores its elements in a combination of contiguous and non-contiguous memory and allows elements to be added to the front or the back.

- A *container adapter* adapts a container to make it more specialized.

- A queue adapts the deque and provides *first-in, first-out (FIFO)* access.

- A stack adapts the deque and provides *last-in, first-out (LIFO)* access.

- Both the list and the forward list store their elements in non-contiguous memory, with *pointers* linking the elements.

- A list where each element has pointers that link to the next element and the previous one is known as a *doubly linked list*.

- A list where each element only has pointers that link to the next element is known as a *singly linked list*.

- The set and multiset containers store *keys* in ascending order in non-contiguous memory.

- The map and multimap containers store *key/value pairs* in ascending order by key in non-contiguous memory.

- Most C++ compilers use *return value optimization (RVO)* to avoid the copy operation when they return containers.

Exercise 10-1 Use a list with the Movie List program

In this exercise, you'll modify the Movie List 2.0 program from chapter 9 so it uses a list instead of a vector. You'll also add a function for modifying a movie. When you're done, a test run should look something like this:

```
The Movie List program

COMMANDS
v - View movie list
a - Add a movie
d - Delete a movie
m - Modify a movie
x - Exit

Command: v
        TITLE                        YEAR     STARS
1    Casablanca                      1942     5
2    Wonder Woman                    2017     4
3    Wizard of Oz                    1939     5

Command: m
Number: 2
Enter new number of stars (1-5) for Wonder Woman: 3
Wonder Woman was updated.

Command: v
        TITLE                        YEAR     STARS
1    Casablanca                      1942     5
2    Wonder Woman                    2017     3
3    Wizard of Oz                    1939     5

Command: x
Bye!
```

Open and review the program

1. Open the project or solution named movie_list in this folder:
   `ex_starts\ch10_ex1_movie_list`

2. Review the code. Then, run the program to refresh your memory on how it works.

Modify the program to use a list instead of a vector

3. Modify the main() function so it stores the list that's returned by the read_movies_from_file() function in a list of Movie objects instead of a vector of Movie objects. Then, modify the read_movies_from_file() function so it returns a list.

4. Modify the other functions called by the main() function so they accept a list of Movie objects. You'll also need to modify the delete_movie() function so it uses an iterator instead of an index to get and erase the movie.

Add the code for modifying a movie

5. Add another command to the menu that lets the user modify a movie.

6. Add a function named modify_movie() that accepts a list of Movie objects. This function should get the number of the movie to be modified and the Movie object for that movie. Be sure to store the Movie object in a reference variable so it points to the Movie object in the list. Then, get the new number of stars for the movie, update the Movie object, and update the movies file.

7. Add a case label to the switch statement in the main() function that lets the user modify a movie.

8. Modify the add_movie() function so that if a movie already exists, it displays an appropriate message but doesn't modify the movie.

Exercise 10-2   Create a program that uses a map

In this exercise, you'll write the code for a program called Country Codes that uses a map. This program displays a list of country codes, lets the user enter a code, and then displays the country name for that code. When you're done, a test run should look something like this:

```
The Country Codes Program

Country codes: CA MX US

Enter a country code: mx
You selected Mexico!

Continue (y/n)?: y

Enter a country code: PR
Country code not found.

Continue (y/n)?: n
```

1. Open the project or solution named country_codes in this folder:
    `ex_starts\ch10_ex2_country_codes`

2. Review the main.cpp file to see that it contains the code for a function named get_choice() as well as the starting code for two functions named display_codes() and display_country(). In addition, the main() function defines a map whose key/value pairs contain country codes and names.

3. Add code to the display_codes() function so it displays the country codes as shown above.

4. Add code to the display_country() function so it gets an iterator for the element whose key is equal to the code. If the code isn't found, display an appropriate message. Otherwise, display the country name as shown above. Because the map parameter is defined as a constant, you'll need to use the at() member function to do that, not the subscript operator.

5. Add code to the main() function that calls the display_codes() function to display the country codes when the program starts. In addition, add code that calls the display_country() function to display country names as long as the user indicates they want to continue.

Exercise 10-3   Use a multiset and a set with the Word Counter program

In this exercise, you'll modify the Word Counter program so it stores all of the words in the text file in a multiset and all of the unique words in a set. When you're done, a test run should look something like this:

```
The Word Counter program

FILE TEXT: It was the best of times, it was the worst of times,
it was the age of wisdom, it was the age of foolishness, it was
the epoch of belief, it was the epoch of incredulity, it was the
season of Light, it was the season of Darkness, it was the spring
of hope, it was the winter of despair...

WORD COUNT: 60

20 UNIQUE WORDS: age belief best darkness despair epoch foolish-
ness hope incredulity it light of season spring the times was
winter wisdom worst

COUNT PER WORD: age=2 belief=1 best=1 darkness=1 despair=1 epoch=2
foolishness=1 hope=1 incredulity=1 it=10 light=1 of=10 season=2
spring=1 the=10 times=2 was=10 winter=1 wisdom=1 worst=1
```

1. Open the project or solution named word_counter in this folder:
   ex_starts\ch10_ex3_word_counter

2. Change the name of the load_words() function to display_and_load_words(), and modify it so it creates and returns a multiset instead of a vector.

3. Add code to the display_and_load_words() function that displays each word without modification as it's retrieved from the file.

4. Modify the code in the main() function so it displays the count of words that have been loaded into the multiset.

5. Add a function named get_unique_words() that accepts the multiset and returns a set that contains just the unique words.

6. Modify the main() function so it uses the get_unique_words() function to get a set of unique words.

7. Modify the main() function so it displays the number of words in the set that's returned by the get_unique_words() function, followed by each of the words in that set.

8. Modify the main() function so it displays the words in the set that's returned by the get_unique_words() function, followed by a count of the number of times each word in the set occurs in the multiset.

9. Comment out or delete any code that is no longer used by the program.

11

How to work with STL algorithms

In chapter 10, you learned how to use the containers of the Standard Template Library to store and work with elements. You also learned how to use the iterators of the STL to access and traverse the elements in those containers.

In this chapter, you'll learn how to use algorithms provided by the STL to perform tasks on the elements in a container. In addition, you'll see how the STL provides a framework that makes it easy to work with a wide variety of containers and algorithms. Because this chapter assumes that you already know how to work with containers and iterators, you'll want to be sure to read chapter 10 before reading this chapter.

An introduction to STL algorithms

The *Standard Template Library (STL)* contains three types of objects: *containers* that store data, *iterators* that allow access to the data, and *algorithms* that perform tasks on the data. In the previous chapter, you learned about the STL containers and iterators. Now, this chapter introduces STL algorithms.

The relationship between containers, iterators, and algorithms

The STL algorithms perform common tasks on the elements in a container, such as finding an element with a specified value or copying all the elements to another container. However, the algorithms don't work directly with containers. Instead, they use iterators to perform their tasks as shown in figure 11-1.

Because algorithms work with iterators, they don't need to know anything about how the elements in a container are stored to work with the container. For instance, an algorithm doesn't care if a container uses contiguous or non-contiguous memory. This is known as *abstraction*.

To use an STL algorithm with a container, the container must provide iterators that define a half-open, or [b:e), interval. As you learned in the last chapter, this is a range in which the beginning iterator points to the first element and the ending iterator points one memory location past the last element. The STL containers have begin() and end() member functions that provide a half-open interval, as does the string object, which is not an STL container. Although the C++ built-in array doesn't have begin() and end() functions, it can still provide a half-open interval. You'll learn more about that in chapter 12.

The code examples in this figure illustrate how the same STL algorithm can work with several different types of containers. These examples use the count() algorithm, which returns the number of times a specified value occurs in an interval.

The first example defines five containers that hold char data and initializes each container with the characters 'h', 'e', 'l', 'l', and 'o'. The first statement defines a vector, the second defines an STL array, the third defines a list, and the fourth defines a multiset. These are all STL containers, and they all store and retrieve their elements differently. The fifth statement defines a string object, which isn't an STL container but provides iterators that define a [b:e) interval.

The second example counts the number of times the character 'l' appears in each container. Again, the implementation details of the containers are different, but that doesn't matter. In each case, the algorithm accepts the iterators and does its work.

Because containers and algorithms don't need to know anything about each other, it's possible to create your own custom containers and algorithms. You just need to make sure that a custom container provides iterators that define a half-open interval and that a custom algorithm works with iterators that define a half-open interval. In chapter 19, you'll learn how to define custom containers and algorithms.

The STL algorithms work with iterators rather than directly with containers

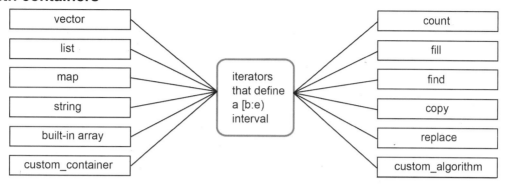

Examples that use the same algorithm with five different container types

The containers

```
vector<char> vec   { 'h', 'e', 'l', 'l', 'o' };
array<char, 5> arr { 'h', 'e', 'l', 'l', 'o' };
list<char> lst     { 'h', 'e', 'l', 'l', 'o' };
multiset<char> mst { 'h', 'e', 'l', 'l', 'o' };
string str = "hello";
```

The algorithm that counts how many times a value appears in a container

```
int c;
c = count(vec.begin(), vec.end(), 'l');     // c is 2
c = count(arr.begin(), arr.end(), 'l');     // c is 2
c = count(lst.begin(), lst.end(), 'l');     // c is 2
c = count(mst.begin(), mst.end(), 'l');     // c is 2
c = count(str.begin(), str.end(), 'l');     // c is 2
```

Description

- The STL *algorithms* don't perform operations directly on a specific container. Instead, they perform operations on a half-open, or [b:e), interval that's defined by iterators. This provides *abstraction* between the algorithms and the containers.

- The STL algorithms are commonly used with STL containers. However, they can also be used with non-STL containers like strings, built-in arrays, and custom objects.

- As long as an object provides iterators that define a half-open interval, and those iterators define the operations required by the algorithm, the algorithm can perform its task.

Figure 11-1   The relationship between containers, iterators, and algorithms

How to call an algorithm

The STL contains dozens of algorithms. In this chapter you'll learn to work with a few of the algorithms in the algorithm header file. However, there are more algorithms in that header file as well as in other header files. For more information, you can visit the URL shown at the top of figure 11-2.

An STL algorithm is a function. Because of that, you call it by coding its name, followed by a set of parentheses with any arguments it requires. Also like other functions, some of the STL algorithms return a value, and some don't.

The code examples in this figure show how to call some of the STL algorithms. To start, the first example includes the algorithm header file. Then, the second example defines and initializes a vector of int values that's used by the rest of examples in this figure.

The third example calls the sort() algorithm. This algorithm accepts two iterators that define an interval and rearranges the elements in that interval in ascending order. For this algorithm to work correctly, you must pass it a high-level, random-access iterator. However, most algorithms work correctly with lower-level iterators. As you progress through this chapter, you'll learn more about the type of iterator that's required by each algorithm.

The fourth and fifth examples call the count() algorithm. This algorithm accepts iterators that define an interval as well as another argument that indicates the value to count. Note that, unlike sort(), count() returns a value. These examples show that you can define the [b:e) interval to include all the elements in a container or just some of them. This shows the flexibility of using iterators and algorithms.

The sixth example calls the find() algorithm. This algorithm returns an iterator that points to the search value, or it returns the off-the-end iterator if the search value isn't found. As a result, you can determine whether the search value is found by comparing the iterator that's returned to the off-the-end iterator as shown in this example.

How to pass a function as an argument

Some of the STL algorithms accept functions as arguments. For instance, the optional third argument of the sort() algorithm is a function that lets you customize how the sort operation is performed. This is a useful technique that lets you customize the way an algorithm works.

The last code example in figure 11-2 shows how this works. This example starts with a function named sort_descending() that accepts two int values and returns a Boolean value. In the body of the function, the code returns true if the first int value is greater than the second int value. Otherwise, it returns false.

After the sort_descending() function, a single statement calls the sort() algorithm and passes the sort_descending() function as the third argument. Note that no parentheses are included after the function name. If they were, the statement would call the function rather than pass it. Then, the algorithm calls this function to sort the elements in descending order rather than the default ascending order.

A URL that lists all of the STL algorithms

```
http://en.cppreference.com/w/cpp/algorithm
```

The header file for many of the STL algorithms

```
#include <algorithm>
```

A vector of integers that's used in the following examples

```
vector<int> nums { 5, 7, 34, 6, 1, 890, 17 };
```

An algorithm that accepts two iterators and doesn't return a value

```
sort(nums.begin(), nums.end());
// nums now contains 1 5 6 7 17 34 890
```

An algorithm that accepts two iterators plus a third argument and returns a value

```
int c = count(nums.begin(), nums.end(), 6);          // c is 1
```

An algorithm that accepts a smaller range than the sequence in a container

```
int c = count(nums.begin() + 3, nums.end(), 6);      // c is 0
```

An algorithm that returns an iterator

```
auto iter = find(nums.begin(), nums.end(), 6);
if (iter == nums.end()) {
    cout << "Value not found.\n";
}
else {
    cout << "Value found.\n";
}
```

An algorithm that accepts a function as an argument

```
// create a function to perform the comparison
bool sort_descending(int a, int b) {
    return a > b;
}
// pass the function as the third argument to the sort algorithm
sort(nums.begin(), nums.end(), sort_descending);
// nums now contains 890 34 17 7 6 5 1
```

Description

- When you call an algorithm, you pass it the iterators that define a half open interval as well as any other arguments the algorithm requires.

- The type of iterator an algorithm requires determines which containers can use it.

- Many algorithms accept a function as an argument. This allows you to customize how the algorithm performs its operation.

- To pass a function as an argument, you just code the function name. If you include parentheses and arguments, you are calling the function, not passing it.

Note

- Unless otherwise noted, this chapter presents algorithms in the algorithm header file.

Figure 11-2   How to call an algorithm and pass a function as an argument

Basic skills for working with algorithms

The next four topics present examples that show some basic skills for working with some of the STL algorithms. Unless otherwise noted, these algorithms are available from the algorithm header file.

How to use the non-modifying algorithms

Figure 11-3 shows how to use four of the STL algorithms. These are called *non-modifying algorithms* because they don't change the interval that's passed to them.

All of the algorithms presented in this figure accept lower-level iterators. In fact, all but search() accept the lowest iterator, input. This means that all of the sequence containers you learned about in the last chapter work with these algorithms. As you progress through this chapter, you'll find that most of the algorithms also work with low-level iterators such as forward and input.

In addition, both the find() and search() algorithms return an iterator if they find what they're looking for. If they don't find what they're looking for, they return an off-the-end iterator. This is a common way for the STL algorithms to indicate that they haven't found what they're looking for.

The code examples show how to use these non-modifying algorithms. The first example uses the count() algorithm to determine how many times the value 6 is found in a vector of double values.

The second example begins by defining a function named display() that accepts a string value and displays it on the console. Then, this code defines and initializes a set container named states with several string values that represent state codes. Next, the code calls the for_each() algorithm and passes it three arguments. The first two define a half-open interval and the third is the display() function. When this code runs, it passes the value of every element in the interval to the display() function. As a result, this example displays each element in the interval on the console.

The third example starts by initializing a list of int values. Then, it uses the find() algorithm to retrieve an iterator that points to the first element whose value is 3. This code passes three arguments to the find() algorithm. The first two arguments are the iterators that define the interval to be searched, and the third argument is the value to find. Since find() returns the off-the-end iterator if the value isn't found, this example finishes by using the off-the-end iterator to check whether the search was successful.

The last example initializes a vector of int values and a set of int values. Then, it uses the search() algorithm to check whether the interval contained in the set can be found in the vector. Again, the first two arguments are the iterators that define the interval to be searched. Then, the next two arguments are the iterators that define the interval to search for. Like find(), search() returns the off-the-end iterator if the interval it's looking for isn't found. As a result, you can use an if statement to check whether the search was successful.

Non-modifying operations

Algorithm	Iterator	Description
`count(b, e, val)`	Input	Returns the number of times that val occurs in interval [b:e].
`for_each(b, e, func)`	Input	Passes each element in interval [b:e] to func.
`find(b, e, val)`	Input	Returns an iterator that points to the first occurrence of val in interval [b:e]. Returns the off-the-end iterator if val isn't found.
`search(b, e, b2, e2)`	Forward	Searches for the first occurrence of the interval [b2:e2] in interval [b:e] and returns an iterator that points to the first element. Returns the off-the-end iterator if the interval isn't found.

How to count the number of occurrences of an element

```
vector<double> nums { 6.0, 4.5, 34.1, 6.7, 6 };
int c = count(nums.begin(), nums.end(), 6);              // c is 2
```

How to display each element in an interval

```
void display(string value) {
    cout << value << ' ';
}

set<string> states { "OR", "WA", "CA", "AK", "HI" };
for_each(states.begin(), states.end(), display);
// displays "AK CA HI OR WA "
```

How to find a specific element in an interval

```
list<int> target { 1, 2, 3, 4, 5 };
auto iter = find(target.begin(), target.end(), 3);
if (iter == target.end()) {
    cout << "Not Found!\n";
}
```

How to search for a range of elements in an interval

```
vector<int> target { 1, 2, 3, 4, 5 };
set<int> to_find { 3, 4, 5, 6 };
auto iter = search(target.begin(), target.end(),
                   to_find.begin(), to_find.end());
if (iter == target.end()) {
    cout << "Not Found!\n";
}
```

Description

- The *non-modifying algorithms* don't change the values or the order of the elements in an the interval.

- The find() and search() algorithms perform a *linear search*, which means that they start at the first element and continue in order until they either find what they're looking for or reach the end of the interval.

Figure 11-3   How to use the non-modifying algorithms

How to use the modifying algorithms

The table in figure 11-4 presents four more of the STL algorithms. These are called *modifying algorithms* because they *do* change the interval that's passed to them by adding, replacing, or removing elements.

The code examples show how to use the modifying algorithms. The first example uses the replace() algorithm to replace all instances of a dash character in a string with a space character. The first two arguments define the interval that the algorithm will work with. Then, the third argument identifies the value to find, and the fourth argument specifies the replacement value. Note that this example works with a sequence of elements in a string, which is not an STL container. Again, this shows the flexibility of the STL algorithms.

The second example begins by initializing a vector of int values. Then, it uses the fill() algorithm to set the value of all its elements to zero. Again, the first two arguments define the interval the algorithm works with. Then, the third argument specifies the value to assign to the elements in the interval.

The third example shows how to use the copy() algorithm. It starts by initializing a list of int values. Then, it uses the size() function of that list to define a vector of the same size. This is necessary because the vector must be able to accommodate all of the elements being copied from the list. And, in this case, all of the elements will be copied.

After initializing the two containers, this example calls the copy() algorithm and passes it three arguments. The first two arguments are the iterators that define the interval to be copied, and the third argument is an iterator that points to the first element to be copied to. Note that you don't need to pass the ending iterator for this interval because the algorithm can determine it based on the interval that's being copied.

The fourth example initializes a vector of int values. Then, it uses the remove() algorithm to remove all instances of a value from the vector. Here, the first two arguments define the interval to be searched, and the third argument defines the value to be removed.

When working with the remove() algorithm, it's important to understand that this algorithm doesn't delete the elements from the container. That's because this algorithm doesn't know anything about the internal workings of the container. As a result, it can't delete elements from it. Instead, it moves the elements to the end of the interval and returns an iterator that points to the first of these elements. To delete these elements, the code can pass this iterator as the first argument of the container's erase() function, and it can pass the same ending iterator used by the remove() algorithm as the second argument.

You can also code the remove and erase operations in one statement as shown by the fifth example. To do that, you can nest the call to the remove() algorithm within the call to the container's erase() function.

Modifying operations

Algorithm	Iterator	Description
replace(b, e, val, val2)	Forward	Replaces the elements in [b:e) that are equal to val with val2.
fill(b, e, val)	Forward	Assigns val to every element in [b:e).
copy(b, e, b2)	Input	Copies the values in [b:e) to the interval beginning with b2.
remove(b, e, val)	Forward	Removes the elements in [b:e) that are equal to val.

How to replace a value in an interval with another value

```
string cc_number = "4012-881022-88810";
replace(cc_number.begin(), cc_number.end(), '-', ' ');
cout << cc_number << endl; // displays "4012 881022 88810"
```

How to assign a value to every element in an interval

```
vector<int> scores { 89, 34, 78, 100, 45, 68, 92};
fill(scores.begin(), scores.end(), 0);
// scores now contains 0 0 0 0 0 0 0
```

How to copy the elements of an interval

```
list<int> nums { 1, 4, 5, 2, 3, 1 };
vector<int> numbers(nums.size());  // same size as nums
copy(nums.begin(), nums.end(), numbers.begin());
// numbers now contains 1 4 5 2 3 1
```

How to remove and erase elements from an interval

```
vector<int> times { 1800, 1845, 0, 2000, 0, 1745, 1600, 0, 1530 };
auto iter = remove(times.begin(), times.end(), 0);
times.erase(iter, times.end());
// times now contains 1800 1845 2000 1745 1600 1530
```

How to remove and erase in one statement

```
vector<int> times { 1800, 1845, 0, 2000, 0, 1745, 1600, 0, 1530 };
times.erase(remove(times.begin(), times.end(), 0), times.end());
// times now contains 1800 1845 2000 1745 1600 1530
```

Description

- The *modifying algorithms* change the elements in an interval by adding, replacing, or removing values.

- The copy() algorithm requires that the container being copied to has at least as many elements as the interval being copied.

- The remove() algorithm moves the removed elements to the end of the interval and returns an iterator that points to the first removed element. You can then pass this iterator to a container's erase() member function to remove the elements from the container.

Figure 11-4   How to use the modifying algorithms

How to use the min and max algorithms

The first table in figure 11-5 presents two STL algorithms that return an iterator that points to the smallest or largest value in an interval. The first four code examples show how to use these algorithms.

To start, the first example initializes a vector of int values that's used in the rest of this figure. Then, the second example finds and displays the minimum value, and the third example finds and displays the maximum value. To do that, both of these examples get the value that the iterator points to by using the indirection operator (*) to dereference the iterator.

The fourth example shows how to use the iterator returned by max_element() to determine the index of the maximum value. Here, the iterator returned by the begin() function of the vector is subtracted from the iterator returned by the max_element() algorithm. This technique only works with a random-access or higher iterator, since the random-access iterator is the lowest iterator that supports the subtraction operator.

How to use the numeric algorithms

So far, this chapter has presented algorithms that are available from the algorithm header file. Now, the second table in figure 11-5 presents three algorithms that are available from the numeric header file. As the name suggests, the algorithms in this header file perform tasks on numbers.

The code examples below this table show how to use these algorithms. To start, the first example shows how to include the numeric header file. Then, the second example uses the iota() algorithm to fill a vector of int values with values that increase sequentially. The first two arguments define the interval to be filled, and the third argument specifies the value to assign to the first element in the interval. Then, this algorithm increments the value by 1 before assigning it to each remaining element.

The third example shows how to use the first version of the accumulate() algorithm. The first two arguments define the interval whose values are to be totaled, and the third argument specifies the initial value of the total. In this case, the code specifies an initial value of 0, which is a common initial value.

The fourth example shows how to use the second version of the accumulate() algorithm. This algorithm accepts a fourth argument that lets you customize how the algorithm totals the values. Here, the code begins by defining a function named total_even() that accepts an accumulator variable and the value of the current element in the interval. Within this function, the code only adds the element value to the accumulator variable if the value is an even number. Then, the statement after the function passes the function to the accumulate() algorithm. As a result, this statement only totals the even numbers.

Minimum/maximum operations

Algorithm	Iterator	Description
`min_element(b, e)`	Forward	Returns an iterator that points to the smallest value in [b:e).
`max_element(b, e)`	Forward	Returns an iterator that points to the largest value in [b:e).

A vector of int values used in the following examples

```
vector<int> nums { 89, 34, 78, 100, 45, 68 };
```

How to find the minimum value in an interval

```
auto min_iter = min_element(nums.begin(), nums.end());
cout << "Min is " << *min_iter << endl;    // displays "Min is 34"
```

How to find the maximum value in an interval

```
auto max_iter = max_element(nums.begin(), nums.end());
cout << "Max is " << *max_iter << endl;    // displays "Max is 100"
```

How to find the index of the maximum value in an interval

```
int index = max_iter - nums.begin();        // index is 3
```

Numeric operations

Algorithm	Iterator	Description
`iota(b, e, val)`	Forward	Fills the interval [b:e) with values that start with val and are incremented by 1.
`accumulate(b, e, val)`	Input	Returns the total of the values in [b:e), with val as the initial value of the total.
`accumulate(b, e, val, func)`	Input	Returns the total of the values in [b:e), with val as the initial value of the total. Passes each element to func to determine how to add it to the total.

The header file for the numeric algorithms

```
#include <numeric>
```

How to fill an interval with sequentially increasing values

```
iota(nums.begin(), nums.end(), 5);    // nums now contains 5 6 7 8 9 10
```

How to total all the values in an interval

```
auto total = accumulate(nums.begin(), nums.end(), 0);
                                        // total is 45
```

How to total all the even-numbered values in an interval

```
// a function that only adds even numbers to an accumulator value
int total_even(int accumulator, int current_val) {
    if (current_val % 2 == 0)
        accumulator += current_val;
    return accumulator;
}
total = accumulate(nums.begin(), nums.end(), 0, total_even);
                                        // total is 24
```

Figure 11-5   How to use the min and max algorithms and the numeric algorithms

How to use the sort and binary search algorithms

Figure 11-6 presents two versions of a sort() algorithm as well as an algorithm that performs a binary search. The binary_search() algorithm, like the other algorithms you've seen so far, accepts a lower-level iterator. Because of that, it works with any STL container. However, the sort algorithms require a random-access iterator, which is a high-level iterator. So, the sort() algorithms don't work with STL containers that provide bidirectional or forward iterators. Fortunately, they work with vectors and strings.

The code examples show how to use these algorithms. The first example initializes a vector of strings that's used by the sort examples. Then, the second example uses the first version of the sort() algorithm to sort the elements in the vector in ascending order.

The third and fourth examples show how to use the second version of the sort() algorithm. This version accepts a function argument that allows you to specify the sort order of the elements.

The third example sorts the elements in descending order. To start, it defines a function that accepts two string variables. Then, within the body of the function, it returns a true value if the first string is greater than the second string. Otherwise, it returns a false value.

The fourth example, on the other hand, uses the length of the string to determine the sort order. Like the third example, this example begins by defining a function that accepts two string variables. Then, within the body of the function, it returns a true value if the size of the first string is greater than the size of the second string. Otherwise, it returns a false value.

The fifth example shows how to use the binary_search() algorithm. This algorithm can work more efficiently than the find() and search() algorithms described earlier in this chapter. That's because the find() and search() algorithms perform a linear search. A *linear search* starts at the first element and iterates through the elements until it finds the value or interval it's looking for. This can be inefficient when you're doing multiple searches of a large interval.

In contrast to the way a linear search works, a *binary search* starts by looking at the midpoint of a sorted interval. Then, the algorithm discards half the interval, depending on whether the search value is greater or less than the midpoint value. But, for it to work properly, the interval must be sorted first.

The code in the fifth example begins by defining a list of double values. Then, it sorts them. To do that, it calls the sort() member function of the list. That's necessary because a list doesn't support the sort() algorithm, since it uses a bidirectional iterator. Next, the code calls the binary_search() algorithm. This algorithm returns a Boolean value that indicates whether the search value was found. This works differently than the find() and search() algorithms, which return iterators that point to the first element that contains the search value.

Sort and binary search operations

Algorithm	Iterator	Description
sort(b, e)	Random-access	Sorts the elements in [b:e) in ascending order.
sort(b, e, func)	Random-access	Sorts the elements in [b:e) according to the sort criteria in the specified function.
binary_search(b, e, val)	Forward	Returns true if val is found in interval [b:e). This only works if the elements in [b:e) are sorted.

A vector of strings to be used in the sort examples

```
vector<string> names { "grace", "bjarne", "steve", "ada", "katherine" };
```

How to sort an interval in ascending order

```
sort(names.begin(), names.end());
// order is now ada bjarne grace katherine steve
```

How to sort an interval in descending order

```
int sort_descending(string a, string b) {
    return a > b;
}

sort(names.begin(), names.end(), sort_descending);
// order is now steve katherine grace bjarne ada
```

How to sort an interval by length of string

```
int sort_by_length(string a, string b) {
    return b.size() > a.size();
}

sort(names.begin(), names.end(), sort_by_length);
// order is now ada steve grace bjarne katherine
```

How to use a binary search to see if an element is in an interval

```
list<double> prices { 9.99, 5.78, 34.25, 4.99, 125, 77.99, 15.20 };
prices.sort();            // sort elements before calling binary_search()
bool is_found = binary_search(prices.begin(), prices.end(), 15.20); // true
```

Description

- The sort() algorithm requires a random-access iterator, so it can't be used with a list, set, or map. However, the list container has a sort() member function, and the map and set containers are sorted by key by default.

- Like the sort() algorithm, the sort() member function of the list container accepts an optional function that lets you determine the sort criteria.

- The binary_ search() algorithm returns a Boolean value, not an iterator to an element.

- The binary_search() algorithm performs a *binary search* by repeatedly selecting the midpoint of a sorted interval and discarding the half that doesn't contain the search value.

Figure 11-6   How to use the sort and binary search algorithms

The Number Cruncher program

Figure 11-7 shows the Number Cruncher program. This program generates a sequence of random integers. Then, it performs a series of operations on them. The console for this program shows that the program sorts the numbers, calculates a total and average, gets the maximum and minimum values, and counts how many times the number 10 appears in the sequence.

The code begins with include statements for the header files that the program needs, including the algorithm and numeric header files, and the using directive for the std namespace. After that, the code defines a function named display_int() that accepts an int value and displays it on the console.

The main() function starts by displaying the name of the program. Then, it defines a vector of int values named numbers, and it uses the reserve() function of the vector to allocate space in memory for 11 elements.

Next, the code uses a for loop to add random numbers to the vector. To do that, it iterates the elements in the vector as long as the capacity() function of the vector is less than the counter variable. Within the loop, it gets a random number from 0 to 29 and then uses the push_back() function of the vector to add the random number to the vector. When this loop completes, the vector named numbers contains eleven random integers. Then, the code uses the for_each() algorithm and the display_int() function to display those numbers.

After displaying the unsorted random numbers, the code uses the sort() algorithm to sort the numbers in the vector in ascending order. This works because the vector provides the high-level, random-access iterator that the sort() algorithm requires. Then, the code uses the for_each() algorithm and the display_int() function to display the sorted numbers.

Next, the code uses the accumulate() algorithm to total all the numbers in the vector, it stores the result in a variable named sum, and it displays the sum. Then, it calculates the average of these numbers by dividing the sum by the size of the vector, and it displays the average.

The console

```
The Number Cruncher program

11 RANDOM NUMBERS: 12 25 10 3 0 8 8 1 10 16 15
11 SORTED NUMBERS: 0 1 3 8 8 10 10 12 15 16 25
Sum = 108 Average = 9 Max = 25 Min = 0

The number 10 occurs 2 time(s).
```

The code

```cpp
#include <iostream>
#include <cstdlib>
#include <ctime>
#include <vector>
#include <algorithm>
#include <numeric>

using namespace std;

void display_int(int num) {
    cout << num << ' ';
}

int main() {
    cout << "The Number Cruncher program\n\n";

    // create an empty vector with space for 11 elements
    vector<int> numbers;
    numbers.reserve(11);

    // fill the vector with random numbers
    srand(time(nullptr));
    for (int i = 0; i < numbers.capacity(); ++i) {
        int number = rand() % 30;
        numbers.push_back(number);
    }

    cout << numbers.size() << " RANDOM NUMBERS: ";
    for_each(numbers.begin(), numbers.end(), display_int);
    cout << endl;

    sort(numbers.begin(), numbers.end());
    cout << numbers.size() << " SORTED NUMBERS: ";
    for_each(numbers.begin(), numbers.end(), display_int);
    cout << endl;

    int sum = accumulate(numbers.begin(), numbers.end(), 0);
    cout << "Sum = " << sum << ' ';

    int avg = sum / numbers.size();
    cout << "Average = " << avg << ' ';
```

Figure 11-7   The Number Cruncher program (part 1 of 2)

Part 2 of figure 11-7 begins by using the max_element() and min_element() algorithms to retrieve iterators that point to the largest and smallest elements in the vector. This code uses the auto keyword to define the variables named max_iter and min_iter that store the iterators returned by these algorithms so the code is more concise. It also displays the minimum and maximum values on the console. To do that, it uses the indirection operator (*) to get the values that min_iter and max_iter point to.

After getting the maximum and minimum values, the code checks how many times the number 10 occurs in the vector of random numbers. To do that, it starts by defining an int variable named num and initializing it with the number 10. Then, it uses the binary_search() algorithm to check whether this number exists in the vector.

For the binary_search() algorithm to work correctly, the interval that's passed to it must be sorted. In this case, the numbers in the vector were sorted before the various calculations were performed. As a result, the numbers are still in sorted order, and the algorithm works correctly.

If the binary search finds the number, the code uses the count() algorithm to get a count of the number of times the number occurs in the vector, and it displays this number on the console. Otherwise, this code displays a message indicating that the number 10 isn't in the vector.

As you review this code, you should realize that this chapter has only presented some of the many variations of these STL algorithms. For instance, the count_if() algorithm is similar to the count() algorithm, but it accepts a function that determines which values to count. And the for_each_n() algorithm is similar to the for_each() algorithm, but it accepts a numeric value rather than an ending iterator to determine the elements that are included in the interval. Variations with the suffix _if or _n are common. To learn more about these variations, you can visit the URL shown in figure 11-2.

The code (continued)

```
auto max_iter = max_element(numbers.begin(), numbers.end());
cout << "Max = " << *max_iter << ' ';

auto min_iter = min_element(numbers.begin(), numbers.end());
cout << "Min = " << *min_iter << ' ';
cout << endl;

int num = 10;
bool num_exists = binary_search(
    numbers.begin(), numbers.end(), num);
if (num_exists) {
    int c = count(numbers.begin(), numbers.end(), num);
    cout << "The number " << num << " occurs " << c
        << " time(s).\n";
}
else {
    cout << "These numbers do NOT include " << num << ".\n";
}
}
```

Figure 11-7   The Number Cruncher program (part 2 of 2)

More skills for working with algorithms

So far, this chapter has presented the skills you need to work with the STL algorithms in most situations. However, in some situations, you may need some of the additional skills that are presented in the next two topics.

How to use algorithms with intervals of key/value pairs

As you learned in the last chapter, an STL map or multimap contains key/value pairs that are stored in pair objects. Each pair object has a data member named first that holds the key and a data member named second that holds the value.

However, the STL algorithms don't know how the pair object works. To use the STL algorithms with the data in a map or multimap, then, you often need to pass a function to the algorithm that specifies the task that you want to perform on each pair object.

The code examples in figure 11-8 show how this works. The first example initializes a map of string/double pairs named products. In this map, the key is a product's name and the value is a product's price.

The second example shows how to use the for_each() algorithm to display the key and value for each pair object. To start, this code defines a display() function that accepts a pair object. Within this function, the code uses the first data member to display the key and the second data member to display the value. After the function, the code calls the for_each() algorithm and passes it a half-open interval for the map and the display() function. This displays the key and value for each pair object in the map.

The third example shows how to use the accumulate() algorithm to sum the prices in the products map. This code starts by defining a sum_products() function that accepts an accumulator variable named total and a pair object for the current element in the map. Within this function, the code uses the second data member to add the price of the current product to the total. After the function, this code calls the accumulate() algorithm and passes it a half-open interval for the map, the initial value of the accumulator variable, and the sum_products() function. This returns the total price of all products in the map.

The last example shows how to use the count_if() algorithm to count the number of products in the map whose price meets a certain criteria. This algorithm works like the count() algorithm, but it accepts a function that lets you specify which elements to count. To start, this code defines a function named under_500() that accepts a pair object and returns a Boolean value. Within the function, the code returns true if the pair's value is under 500. Otherwise, it returns false. After this function, the code calls the count_if() algorithm and passes it a half-open interval for the map as well as the under_500() function. This returns a count of all products in the map with a price that's less than 500.

A map of strings and doubles to be used in the following examples

```
map<string, double> products { {"guitar", 199.99},
                               {"piano", 799.99},
                               {"drums", 249.99},
                               {"violin", 489.99} };
```

How to display the pairs in a map

```
void display(pair<string, double> p) {
    cout << p.first << " $" << p.second << "   ";
}
```

```
for_each(products.begin(), products.end(), display);
// "drums $249.99   guitar $199.99   piano $799.99   violin $489.99 "
```

How to total the values in a map

```
double sum_products(double total, pair<string, double> p) {
    return total + p.second;
}
```

```
double sum = accumulate(
    products.begin(), products.end(), 0.0, sum_products);
                                             // sum is 1739.96
```

How to count the pairs in a map that meet a criteria

```
bool under_500(pair<string, double> p) {
    return p.second < 500;
}
```

```
int num_low = count_if(
    products.begin(), products.end(), under_500); // num_low is 3
```

Description

- When you use the STL algorithms with maps and multimaps, you often need to use the versions that accept a function argument. This provides a way for you to tell the algorithm how to work with the data members of the pair structure.

Figure 11-8   How to use algorithms with intervals of key/value pairs

How to use algorithms with nested containers

At the end of the previous chapter, you learned how to nest a container within another container. Specifically, you learned how to work with a vector of vectors and a map of vectors.

When you work with nested vectors, you often want to use STL algorithms to perform tasks on the data they contain. However, you can encounter some of the same problems you do when you work with key/value pairs. Namely, the algorithms don't know how to work with the containers you're passing to them. As you learned in the last figure, the solution to this problem is to pass a function to the algorithm that defines the task that you want to perform on the nested containers.

The examples in figure 11-9 show how this works. The first example initializes a map whose key is a string and whose value is a vector of doubles. In this map, the key is a student's name and the value is a collection of grades for that student.

The second example shows how to use the accumulate() algorithm to sum the values in all vectors in the map. You might do this, for instance, so you can calculate the average grade for all the students.

The code starts by defining a sum_grades() function that accepts an accumulator variable named total and a pair object that's the current element in the map. Note that the key in the pair object is a string and the value is a vector of doubles. Within the function, the first statement uses the second data member to get the vector of double values. Then, the second statement uses the accumulate() algorithm to total all the grades in the vector. Finally, the third statement adds the total for the student to the accumulator variable and returns the result.

After the sum_grades() function, the next statement calls the accumulate() algorithm and passes it the begin() and end() iterators for the map, a starting accumulator value of 0.0, and the sum_grades() function. As you review this code, you can think of the accumulate() algorithm as being nested too. In other words, the accumulate() algorithm for the map calls a function that calls the accumulate() algorithm for each vector in the map.

The third example shows how to use the accumulate() algorithm to count the number of elements in all the vectors in the map. Again, you might do this so you can calculate the average grade for all the students.

The code starts by defining a count_grades() function that accepts an accumulator variable named count and a pair object that's the current element in the map. Within the function, the code adds the size of the vector to the accumulator variable and returns the result.

After the count_grades() function, the next statement calls the accumulate() algorithm and passes it the begin() and end() iterators for the map, a starting accumulator value of 0, and the count_grades() function. This time, there's no "nested" algorithm. That's because the count_grades() function uses the size() function of the vector to get a count of the grades.

A map of strings and vectors to be used in the following examples

```
map<string, vector<double> > grades;    // space for pre-C++11 compilers
grades["Joe"] = { 89, 67, 78 };
grades["Stacey"] = { 93, 88, 94, 91 };
grades["Pat"] = { 79, 86, 83 };
```

How to total the values in all the vectors in the map

```
double sum_grades(double total, pair<string, vector<double> > p) {
    vector<double> g = p.second;
    double sum_per_student = accumulate(g.begin(), g.end(), 0.0);
    return total + sum_per_student;
}

double sum = accumulate(
    grades.begin(), grades.end(), 0.0, sum_grades);        // sum is 848
```

How to count the number of elements in all the vectors in the map

```
int count_grades(int count, pair<string, vector<double> > p) {
    return count + p.second.size();
}

int count = accumulate(
    grades.begin(), grades.end(), 0, count_grades);        //  count is 10
```

Description

- When you use the STL algorithms with nested containers, you often need to use the versions that accept a function argument. This provides a way for you to tell the algorithm how to work with the nested container.

Figure 11-9   How to use algorithms with nested containers

More skills for passing functions to algorithms

So far, you've learned the basic skills for passing a function as an argument to an algorithm. Now, you'll learn some additional skills for passing a function as an argument that can make your code more concise and flexible.

How to work with function templates

So far in this chapter, you've seen three different versions of a function that displays a value on the console. One displayed an int value like the one shown at the top of figure 11-10, one displayed a string value, and one displayed the key and value in a key/value pair. Instead of coding a separate function for each data type or for each combination of data types in a key/value pair, wouldn't it be nice to code one function that could accept any data type and another function that could accept any combination of data types in a key/value pair? Fortunately, C++ lets you do just that by using *function templates*.

To create a function template, you start by coding the template keyword. Then, within angle brackets, you code either the typename or the class keyword to declare one or more *generic data types* separated by commas. Because these keywords work identically in most cases, the one you use is mostly a matter of preference.

The two examples below the syntax summary show how to create two function templates for a function named display(). The first function template identifies a generic type named T, which represents the data type of its single parameter. Theoretically, this display() function can accept any data type. Realistically, any data type passed to this function must implement the stream insertion operator (<<). Otherwise, the code in the body of the function will fail.

The second version of the display() function identifies two types, K and V. This function accepts a pair object whose key is of type K and whose value is of type V. As in the first example, any data types passed to this function must implement the stream insertion operator.

The rest of the examples show how to use these function templates. The first of these examples defines and initializes a list of int values, a vector of double values, and a map of string/int pairs. The second of these examples iterates each of these containers with a range-based for loop and passes each element to the display() function. And the last example accomplishes the same task as the previous example by calling the for_each() algorithm and passing the display() function as the third argument. Note that when you pass a function template as an argument to an algorithm, you need to include the data type in angle brackets.

When coding a generic type, it's common to use a single uppercase letter like T as the name for the type. But, you can use any name you like. In many cases, giving a generic type a more descriptive name can make your code clearer.

A function that displays an int value

```
void display(int value) {
    cout << value << ' ';
}
```

The syntax for creating a function template

```
template<typename|class name [, typename|class name2] ...>
```

A function template that can display multiple data types

```
template<typename T>
void display(T value) {
    cout << value << ' ';
}
```

A function template that can display key/value pairs of multiple types

```
template<typename K, typename V>
void display(pair<K, V> p) {
    cout << p.first << '=' << p.second << ' ';
}
```

Three container objects used by the following examples

```
list<int> nums { 5, 7, 34, 6, 1, 890, 17 };
vector<double> prices { 9.89, 45.6, 34.98, 23.12 };
map<string, int> states { {"CA", 1850}, {"OR", 1859}, {"AK", 1959} };
```

Code that calls the function templates directly

```
for (int i: nums) {
    display(i);
}
// displays "5 7 34 6 1 890 17 "

for (double d: prices) {
    display(d);
}
// displays "9.89 45.6 34.98 23.12 "

for (pair<string, int> p: states) {
    display(p);
}
// displays "AK=1959 CA=1850 OR=1859 "
```

Code that passes a function template as an argument to an algorithm

```
for_each(nums.begin(), nums.end(), display<int>);
for_each(prices.begin(), prices.end(), display<double>);
for_each(states.begin(), states.end(), display<string, int>);
```

Description

- You can use the template keyword with the typename or class keywords to create *function templates* with *generic data types*. This allows the functions to accept a variety of data types.

- When you call a function template directly, you call it as you would a regular function.

- When you pass a function template as an argument to an algorithm, you need to specify the data type(s) in angle brackets (<>).

Figure 11-10   How to work with function templates

How to work with function objects

The under_500() function at the top of figure 11-11 was presented earlier in this chapter. This function checks whether the value in a key/value pair is less than 500. But, what if the cut-off value you need to check varies? In that case, you could write a separate function for each cut-off value, but the code for each function would be almost identical.

A better solution would be to use a *function object*, also called a *functor*. A function object is a structure or class that overloads the function call operator (()). This operator defines the function that's called when the function object is passed to a function. This allows an object of the structure or class to be called like a function. But, because it's an object, it can have data members to store data, or *state*, that it needs to complete its task.

The second code example in this figure presents a function object named Under. Since this book hasn't presented classes yet, this figure uses a structure to define this object. It has a data member named limit that contains a double value, and it has a *constructor* function that sets the value of the limit member. In chapter 14, you'll learn more about constructors. For now, just know that a constructor has the same name as the structure or class that it's in, and you can call it to create an object from that structure or class. So, when you call the Under constructor and pass it an argument, it creates an Under object and stores the argument in the limit member of that object.

The Under structure also overloads the function call operator (()) with a function that's similar to the under_500() function. However, this function uses the limit data member in its comparison, not a hard-coded value. As a result, this function is more flexible than the code for the under_500() function. In addition, this function includes the const keyword at the end of the function declaration. This prevents the member function from modifying the data in the Under object, which is typically what you want.

The third and fourth examples show how to use a function object with an algorithm. The third example defines and initializes a map of string/double pairs. Then, the fourth example shows how to pass an Under function object to the count_if() algorithm. Here, the first statement passes a function object with a limit of 500.0, and the second statement passes a function object with a limit of 200.0.

As you review this code, you might be confused by the way it passes the Under function object to the algorithm. After all, throughout this chapter, the examples don't include parentheses when they pass a function because that would call the function, not pass it. However, when you use a function object, the parentheses don't call the function that's stored in the object. Instead, they call the constructor function that creates the object. Then, the algorithm calls the function that's defined by the () operator.

In this figure, the limit data member of the Under function object can be accessed from outside that object. This is adequate for most purposes, but it's generally considered a better practice to code these data members so they can only be accessed from within the object. To do that, you can use a class instead of a structure as described in chapter 14.

A function that checks if a pair value is less than 500

```cpp
bool under_500(pair<string, double> p) {
    return p.second < 500;
}
```

A function object that checks if a pair value is less than a varying amount

```cpp
struct Under {
    double limit;

    // constructor function that accepts a value
    Under(double max) {
        limit = max;
    }

    // overload () operator
    bool operator () (pair<string, double> p) const {
        return p.second < limit;
    }
};
```

A map of strings and doubles to be used in the following examples

```cpp
map<string, double> products { {"guitar", 199.99},
                               {"piano", 799.99},
                               {"drums", 249.99},
                               {"violin", 489.99} };
```

Code that uses the function object with the count_if() algorithm

```cpp
auto num_low = count_if(
    products.begin(), products.end(), Under(500.0));    // num_low is 3

num_low = count_if(
    products.begin(), products.end(), Under(200.0));    // num_low is 1
```

Description

- A *function object*, or *functor*, is an object that you can pass as a function argument. This works because the object overloads the function call operator (()) to define the function that's called when the object is passed to a function.

- Function objects let you avoid writing multiple functions for varying search criteria.

- A function object usually has a *constructor* that lets you set the value of one or more data members. You'll learn more about constructors in chapter 14.

Figure 11-11   How to work with function objects

How to work with lambda expressions

If a function that you need to pass to an algorithm is simple or it's only used once, it may not make sense to code it as a separate function. In that case, you can use a feature of C++11 called *lambda expressions* to code the function inline as part of the algorithm. Figure 11-12 shows you how lambda expressions work.

This figure starts by presenting the syntax of a lambda expression. Then, the two tables that follow expand on this syntax.

A lambda expression starts with a *capture specifier*, which is a pair of square brackets. It serves two purposes. First, it tells the compiler that what follows is a lambda expression. Second, it tells the compiler which external variables, if any, to capture for the lambda expression's use.

After the capture specifier, a lambda expression has a parameter list that works like the parameter list for any function. Then, a lambda can include the -> operator and the return type. However, this part of a lambda is only needed if the compiler can't infer the return type from the body of the expression. Because of that, lambdas often don't include it. Finally, a lambda includes one or more statements within curly braces that work like the body of any function.

The second table in this figure shows how you can use the capture specifier to capture external variables for use within the body of the lambda. If you leave the square brackets empty, nothing is captured. But if you code one of the captures presented here, you can capture external variables either by reference or by making a copy. And you can indicate whether all variables or just specified variables should be captured.

The first code example shows how to code a lambda expression as the third argument of the for_each() algorithm. Here, the lambda expression defines a parameter named val of the int type that's used in the body of the lambda.

If a lambda expression will be used more than once, you can store it in a variable as illustrated by the second code example. Here, the first statement stores the same lambda expression as in the first example in a variable named display. Note that the auto keyword defines the type for this variable. Then, the second statement passes this variable to the for_each() algorithm.

The third example shows how to capture an external variable. Here, an int named limit is initialized to 500. Then, a variable named under is initialized with a lambda expression that captures the limit variable that's used in the body of the lambda by reference. Because this lambda expression returns a value, the -> operator is included to indicate the data type of that value. This operator is optional, though, because the compiler can infer the return type from the body of the lambda expression.

After storing the lambda expression in the under variable, the code in this example calls the count_if() algorithm with the under variable. Then, it changes the value of limit and calls count_if() again.

Note that capturing an external variable like this is similar to using a function object to store data in a member of the object, as you saw in the last

The syntax of a lambda expression

```
[ captures ] ( parameter_list ) [-> return_type] { statements }
```

The parts of a lambda expression

Syntax	Name	Description
[]	Capture specifier	Notifies the compiler of a lambda expression and tells the compiler whether to capture external variables.
()	Parameter list	Zero or more arguments that are passed to the body.
->	Return	Indicates the return type. This is required only if the compiler can't infer the type.
{}	Body	The statements to be executed.

How to tell the compiler whether and how to capture variables

Capture	Description
[]	Capture nothing.
[&]	Capture any external variable by reference.
[=]	Capture any external variable by making a copy.
[=, &var]	Capture any external variable by making a copy, but capture the named variable by reference.
[var]	Capture the named variable by making a copy, but nothing else.

How to code a lambda expression inline

```
vector<int> nums { 89, 93, 79, 92, 86 };
for_each( nums.begin(), nums.end(), [](int val) { cout << val << ' '; } );
```

How to store a lambda expression in a variable for reuse

```
auto display = [](int val) { cout << val << ' '; };
for_each(nums.begin(), nums.end(), display);
```

How to capture an external variable in a lambda expression

```
map<string, double> products { { "guitar", 199.99 }, { "piano", 799.99 },
                               { "drums", 249.99 }, { "violin", 489.99 } };

int limit = 500;                 // external variable
auto under = [&] (pair<string, double> p) -> double {
    return p.second < limit; };
auto num_low = count_if(products.begin(), products.end(), under);
                         // num_low is 3

limit = 200;                     // change the value of the external variable
num_low = count_if(products.begin(), products.end(), under);
                         // num_low is 1
```

How to allow varying data types (C++2014 and later)

```
auto under = [&] (auto p) { return p.second < limit; };
```

Description

- *Lambda expressions* allow you to code functions inline or store them in variables. A lambda expression can capture external variables to use in its body.

- You can use the auto keyword to allow a lambda to accept multiple data types.

Figure 11-12   How to work with lambda expressions

figure. Although using a function object may be somewhat more straightforward, using a lambda expression has the benefit of not requiring you to define a separate function object.

The last example in figure 11-12 shows how you can use the auto keyword to allow a lambda to accept multiple data types. This ability was added in C++14 and is the functional equivalent of coding a templated lambda expression. In this case, the body of the lambda expression calls the data member named second. As a result, it only works for containers such as maps that have a data member named second. But, it works for maps that store different types of data.

The Uptime Percentage program

Figure 11-13 shows the Uptime Percentage program. This program reads uptime data about servers in several geographical regions from a text file. Then, it computes the average uptime for each region as well as across all regions. To do that, it uses a map with a nested vector, a function template, the for_each() algorithm, and the accumulate() algorithm.

The code begins with include statements for the header files that the program needs, as well as the using directive for the std namespace. Then, it declares three function prototypes. The display() function is a function template that accepts a single value of type T. The load_uptimes() function accepts a filename and returns a map of string/vector pairs. And the process_uptimes() function accepts a map of string/vector pairs by constant reference.

After the function prototypes, the main() function starts by defining a string constant that specifies the filename for the text file that contains the uptime data. Then, it displays a message indicating that the program is processing the regional uptimes in the specified text file. Next, it calls the load_uptimes() function, passes it the filename, and stores the value returned by the function in a variable named uptimes. To keep this code concise, the auto keyword is used to define the type for the uptimes variable. As you can see by the prototype for the load_uptimes() function, though, it returns a type of

```
map<string, vector<double> >
```

After loading the map of uptimes, this code checks if the map is empty. If it is, the code displays a message that indicates that the program wasn't able to get any data. Otherwise, it calls the process_uptimes() function and passes it the map of string/vector pairs.

After the main() function, the code defines the templated display() function. This function works similarly to the templated display() function presented earlier in this chapter. However, this version appends a percent sign and two spaces to the end of the value it receives.

The console

```
Processing regional uptimes in uptimes.txt...

Central:
    Avg uptime - 98.73%
    Daily: 100.0%   99.9%   100.0%   98.2%   99.4%   96.9%   96.7%
    Sorted: 96.7%   96.9%   98.2%   99.4%   99.9%   100.0%   100.0%
Eastern:
    Avg uptime - 98.66%
    Daily: 96.6%   98.5%   100.0%   100.0%   98.2%
    Sorted: 96.6%   98.2%   98.5%   100.0%   100.0%
Mountain:
    Avg uptime - 98.75%
    Daily: 96.7%   100.0%   97.8%   99.7%   98.3%   100.0%
    Sorted: 96.7%   97.8%   98.3%   99.7%   100.0%   100.0%
Western:
    Avg uptime - 97.59%
    Daily: 99.8%   99.3%   100.0%   89.0%   99.4%   98.9%   96.7%
    Sorted: 89.0%   96.7%   98.9%   99.3%   99.4%   99.8%   100.0%

Avg uptime across all regions - 98.40%
```

The code

```cpp
#include <iostream>
#include <iomanip>
#include <fstream>
#include <sstream>
#include <string>
#include <vector>
#include <map>
#include <algorithm>
#include <numeric>

using namespace std;

template<typename T> void display(T value);
map<string, vector<double> > load_uptimes(string filename);
void process_uptimes(const map<string, vector<double> >& uptimes);

int main() {
    const string filename = "uptimes.txt";
    cout << "Processing regional uptimes in " << filename << "...\n\n";
    auto uptimes = load_uptimes(filename);

    if (uptimes.empty()) {
        cout << "No data or unable to open file.\n\n";
    }
    else {
        process_uptimes(uptimes);
    }
}

template<typename T>
void display(T value) {
    cout << value << "%  ";
}
```

Figure 11-13   The Uptime Percentage program (part 1 of 2)

Part 2 of figure 11-13 shows the remaining two function definitions. The load_uptimes() function returns a map of string/vector pairs. Remember, it's efficient to return an STL container from a function because most compilers move the data to the calling code rather than copying it.

Within the function, the code starts by declaring the map that stores the uptime data. Then, the function creates an input file stream object named datafile and opens it by passing it the filename parameter. Next, this code checks whether the file was opened successfully.

If the file was opened successfully, the code uses a while loop to get each line from the file. Then, it uses that line to create a string stream object named row. Next, the code stores the first value in the row in a string variable named region, and it uses a while loop to add the rest of the values in the row to a vector of double values named times. After this code extracts all the values in the string stream, it uses the subscript operator to add the region and vector of uptimes to the map, with the region as the key and the vector of uptimes as the value.

Once this code processes all the lines in the text file, it closes the input file stream object and returns the map to the calling code. However, if the file stream doesn't open successfully, this code returns an empty map.

The process_uptimes() function accepts a map of string/vector pairs by constant reference. Within this function, the code starts by using a range-based for loop to iterate through the pairs in the map. Within the loop, the first statement uses the first data member of the current pair object to get the region, and the second statement uses the second data member to get the vector of double values. Then, the third statement uses the accumulate() algorithm to total all the values in the vector and store the result in a variable named sum.

After getting the total for the region, this code displays the name of the region. Then, it calculates and displays the average uptime for that region. Next, it uses the for_each() algorithm and the templated display() function to display the daily uptimes for the region. Finally, it sorts the uptimes with the sort() algorithm and uses the for_each() algorithm and the templated display() function again to display the sorted uptimes for the region.

When the loop completes, the code calculates the average uptime across all regions. To do that, it needs to calculate the sum of all the uptimes in all the vectors in the map, and it needs to get a count of all the uptimes in all the vectors in the map. This code uses the accumulate() algorithm with a lambda expression for both of these tasks.

Both lambda expressions pass an accumulator variable and a pair object to the body of the expression. Then, the first lambda expression uses the accumulate() algorithm again to get the total of all the uptimes in the vector, adds this total to the accumulator variable, and returns that variable. The second lambda expression adds the size of the vector of uptimes to the accumulator variable and returns that variable. Once the code calculates the total and count of all uptimes, it calculates and displays the average of all uptimes.

The code (continued)

```cpp
map<string, vector<double> > load_uptimes(string filename) {
    map<string, vector<double> > uptimes;
    ifstream datafile(filename);

    if (datafile) {
        string line;
        while (getline(datafile, line)) {    // for each line in file...
            istringstream row(line);          // create string stream

            string region;                    // get region
            row >> region;

            vector<double> times;             // get uptimes
            double uptime;
            while (row >> uptime) {
                times.push_back(uptime);
            }
            uptimes[region] = times;          // add to map
        }
        datafile.close();
    }
    return uptimes;
}

void process_uptimes(const map<string, vector<double> >& uptimes) {
    for (auto p : uptimes) {
        string region = p.first;
        vector<double> times = p.second;      // get vector of uptimes
        double sum = accumulate(times.begin(), times.end(), 0.0);

        cout << region;
        cout << "\n\tAvg uptime - " << fixed << setprecision(2);
        cout << (sum / times.size()) << '%';

        cout << "\n\tDaily: " << setprecision(1);
        for_each(times.begin(), times.end(), display<double>);

        sort(times.begin(), times.end());
        cout << "\n\tSorted: ";
        for_each(times.begin(), times.end(), display<double>);
        cout << endl;
    }

    cout << "\nAvg uptime across all regions - ";
    double uptime_total = accumulate(uptimes.begin(), uptimes.end(), 0.0,
        [] (double total, auto p) {
            return total + accumulate(
                p.second.begin(), p.second.end(), 0.0);
        }
    );
    int uptime_count = accumulate(uptimes.begin(), uptimes.end(), 0,
        [] (int count, auto p) { return count + p.second.size(); }
    );
    cout << setprecision(2) << (uptime_total / uptime_count) << "%\n\n";
}
```

Figure 11-13   The Uptime Percentage program (part 2 of 2)

Perspective

Now that you've completed this chapter, you should understand how to use the STL algorithms to work with STL containers and string objects. That includes how to pass functions to algorithms. In the next chapter, you'll learn how to use STL algorithms with built-in arrays. In addition, you'll learn how to write your own algorithms for searching and sorting built-in arrays. Finally, in chapter 19, you'll learn how to write your own algorithms for working with STL containers.

Terms

Standard Template Library (STL)	binary search
container	function template
iterator	generic data type
algorithm	function object
abstraction	functor
non-modifying algorithm	constructor
modifying algorithm	lambda expression
linear search	capture specifier

Summary

- The *Standard Template Library (STL)* contains three types of objects: *containers* that store data, *iterators* that allow access to the data, and *algorithms* that perform tasks with the data.

- To provide *abstraction* between the algorithms and the containers, the algorithms perform operations on a half-open interval rather than directly on a specific container.

- The find() and search() algorithms perform a *linear search* that starts at the first element and continues sequentially until it finds the search value or reaches the end of the interval.

- The binary_search() algorithm performs a *binary search* that selects the midpoint of a sorted interval and discards the half that doesn't contain the search value. This continues until the search value is found or the end of the interval is reached.

- You can use the template keyword to create *function templates* with *generic data types*. This allows a function argument to accept a variety of data types.

- A *function object*, or *functor*, is an object that you can pass as a function argument.

- A function object usually has a *constructor* that lets you set the value of one or more data members of the object.

- A *lambda expression* allows you to code functions inline or store them in variables.

- A lambda expression can use a *capture specifier* to capture external variables to use in its body.

Exercise 11-1   Use algorithms with the Test Scores program

In this exercise, you'll modify the Test Scores program from chapter 6 so it uses some of the algorithms presented in this chapter. When you're done, a test run should look something like this:

```
The Test Scores program

Enter test scores from 0 to 100.
To end the program, enter -1.

Enter score: 96
Enter score: 88
Enter score: 100
Enter score: 95
Enter score: 89
Enter score: 100
Enter score: -1

100 100 96 95 89 88
Highest score: 100
Lowest score: 88
This student has 2 perfect score(s)!

Score count:   6
Score total:   568
Average score: 94.7
```

1. Open the project or solution named test_scores in this folder:
    `ex_starts\ch11_ex1_test_scores`

2. Modify the program so it sorts the scores in descending sequence. To do that, use the sort() algorithm with a function that specifies the sort order.

3. Add code that displays the sorted scores as shown above. To do that, use the for_each() algorithm with a function that displays a score.

4. Add code that gets and displays the highest and lowest scores.

5. Add code that gets the number of scores that are equal to 100. Then, display that number.

6. Modify the code that gets the total of the scores so it uses the accumulate() algorithm instead of a range-based for loop.

Exercise 11-2   Use algorithms with the Word Counter program

In this exercise, you'll modify the Word Counter program from chapter 10 so it uses algorithms with the pairs of values in the map that contains the words and the count of each word. When you're done, a test run should look something like this:

```
The Word Counter program

60 WORDS: it was the best of times it was the worst of times it was
the age of wisdom it was the age of foolishness it was the epoch of
belief it was the epoch of incredulity it was the season of light
it was the season of darkness it was the spring of hope it was the
winter of despair

20 UNIQUE WORDS: age belief best darkness despair epoch foolishness
hope incredulity it light of season spring the times was winter
wisdom worst

COUNT PER WORD: age=2 belief=1 best=1 darkness=1 despair=1 epoch=2
foolishness=1 hope=1 incredulity=1 it=10 light=1 of=10 season=2
spring=1 the=10 times=2 was=10 winter=1 wisdom=1 worst=1

8 DUPLICATE WORDS
```

Open the program and review the code

1. Open the project or solution named word_counter in this folder:
   `ex_starts\ch11_ex2_word_counter`

2. Review the code and run the program to refresh your memory on how it works.

Add the functions to be used by the algorithms

3. Code a prototype for a function named display() that accepts a pair of string/int values and does not return a value. Then, code the definition of this function. It should display the string and int values in the pair as shown above for the count per word.

4. Code a prototype for a function named over_1() that accepts a pair of string/int values and returns a Boolean value. Then, code the definition of this function. It should return true if the int value in the pair is greater than 1 and false otherwise.

Use the functions in algorithms

5. Modify the code in the main() function that displays the count per word so it uses the for_each() algorithm with the display() function.

6. Add code to the main() function that uses the count_if() algorithm with the over_1() function to get a count of the number of words that occur more than once. Then, display that count as shown above.

Exercise 11-3   Use a function object and a lambda expression with the Test Scores program

In this exercise, you'll modify the Test Scores program from exercise 11-1 so it uses a function object to get the count of scores that are greater than or equal to two different values. Then, you'll replace the function object with a lambda expression. When you're done, a test run should look something like this:

```
The Test Scores program

Enter test scores from 0 to 100.
To end the program, enter -1.

Enter score: 95
Enter score: 88
Enter score: 92
Enter score: 80
Enter score: 76
Enter score: -1

95 92 88 80 76
Highest score: 95
Lowest score: 76
Scores 90 or above: 2
Scores 80 or above: 4

Score count:   5
Score total:   431
Average score: 86.2
```

Use a structure to count the scores with a minimum value

1. Open the project or solution named test_scores in this folder:

    `ex_starts\ch11_ex3_test_scores`

2. Define a structure named MinScore with a member named minimum that stores an integer value. The constructor for this structure should accept an int and assign it to the minimum member.

3. Overload the function call operator for the structure so it accepts an int value and returns a Boolean value that indicates if the int is greater than or equal to the value of minimum. Be sure to include code that prevents the value of minimum from being modified.

4. Comment out the code in the main() function that gets and displays a count of the number of scores that are equal to 100.

5. Add code that uses the count_if() algorithm with the MinScore structure to get the number of scores that are 90 and above. Then, display that count as shown above. To make that easier to do for varying values, you can store the minimum value in a variable.

6. Repeat step 5, but get the number of scores that are 80 and above.

Use a lambda expression to count the scores with a minimum value

7. Comment out the structure you just added.

8. Make a copy of the code that uses the function object. Then, comment out the original code.

9. Modify the code that uses a function object so it uses a lambda expression instead. To start, define a lambda expression that accepts an int and returns a Boolean value that indicates if the int is greater than or equal to the minimum value.

10. Modify the two statements that call the count_if() algorithm so they use the lambda expression instead of the MinScore structure.

12

How to work with built-in arrays and C strings

In the last two chapters, you learned how to use the containers of the Standard Template Library. You can use these containers for the vast majority of coding tasks. However, in some cases, the STL containers require too much overhead. In an embedded environment, for example, you may not be able to use STL objects. Also, you may sometimes need to maintain legacy C++ code that was developed before the STL. In these cases, you may need to work with built-in arrays.

Similarly, if you're working in an embedded environment or with legacy code, you might not be able to use string objects as described in chapter 6. Instead, you can use an array of characters. This is known as a C string, or C-style string, because that's how the C programming language works with strings.

Basic skills for built-in arrays

This chapter begins by presenting the basic skills for working with built-in arrays. These skills include creating an array, initializing it, accessing its elements, passing it to a function, copying it, and comparing it to another array.

How to create an array and access its elements

A *built-in array* contains a sequence of elements of the same data type. If this sounds similar to the definition of a vector, that's because a vector uses a built-in array under the hood to store its elements. In chapter 19, you'll learn more about how this works by coding your own custom vector.

Figure 12-1 starts by showing the syntax for creating a built-in array. Then, the first example shows how to create an array that stores seven elements of the int type in a variable named week. To do that, this example declares the data type and the array name followed by the number of elements within brackets. The number within the brackets is sometimes called the *size declarator*.

The graphical representation of this array shows the space allocated in memory for the array. Like a vector, an array stores its element in *contiguous memory*, meaning that the elements are stored in consecutive memory locations with no gaps.

When you create an array, the number of elements is fixed. This means that once you create an array, you can't change the number of elements it contains.

Additionally, the number of elements in an array must be known at compile time. Otherwise, the compiler doesn't know how much memory to allocate. This means that you must use either a numeric literal or a constant to define an array as shown by the second example. If you try to set the size of the array at runtime as shown by the third example, you'll get an error.

Each element in an array is assigned an *index* where the first index is 0, the second index is 1, and so on. This figure shows how you can use the *subscript operator* (`[]`) to access each element in an array by its index. This should be familiar to you from the chapters on working with vectors.

Also like a vector, you can have *out of bounds access* if your code specifies a subscript that's outside the range of valid subscripts. As you may remember, this leads to unexpected results that vary depending on the compiler. Because of that, you should always write code that prevents out of bounds access.

The syntax for creating a built-in array

```
type array_name[number_of_elements];
```

Code that creates a built-in array of type int with 7 elements

The code

```
int week[7];
```

A graphical representation of the space allocated in memory

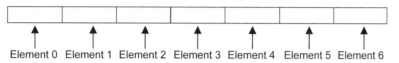

Two examples that create a built-in array

With a literal value for the size declarator

```
double prices[5];
```

With a constant value for the size declarator

```
const int size = 5;
double prices[size];
```

The number of elements in an array must be known at compile time

```
int size;
cin >> size;
double prices[size]; // Wrong! This will not work!
```

How to access the elements in an array

```
double prices[3];
prices[0] = 29.99;
prices[1] = 49.99;
prices[2] = 79.99;
cout << "The third element contains the value " << prices[2];
// displays "The third element contains the value 79.99"
```

Description

- A *built-in array* contains a sequence of elements of the same data type. It stores the elements in *contiguous memory*, or consecutive blocks of memory with no gaps.

- The number of elements in an array is fixed and must be set at compile time. Therefore, you can only use a literal or constant value to specify the number of elements.

- Each element in an array has an *index*, where the first element has an index of 0, the second an index of 1, and so on. To access an individual element, you use the *subscript operator* (`[]`) to specify the element's index.

Figure 12-1   How to create an array and access its elements

How to initialize an array

Figure 12-2 shows how to initialize the values in an array when you define it. To do that, you can use an *initialization list* as shown by the syntax in this figure.

The first code example shows how this works. Here, the first statement defines a constant that can be used to declare the size of the array.

The second statement creates an array with three elements and initializes those elements with the values 1, 2, and 3. It does this by coding an array variable followed by the assignment operator (=) and a list of values within braces.

The third statement works like the second, except that it doesn't include the assignment operator. This shows that the assignment operator is optional.

The fourth statement works like the third, except that it doesn't include a size declarator. When you omit the size declarator, the compiler infers the size of the array from the number of values in the initialization list. However, you still need to include the square brackets to tell the compiler that the variable is an array.

The second example shows that you can include fewer values in the initialization list than there are elements in the array. This example creates an int array with seven elements, but it only includes values for the first three. When you only include some of the values like this, the values of the remaining elements are initialized with the default value for the data type. In this case, the default value for the int data type is 0, so the rest of the elements are filled with a value of 0.

The third code example works like the second, but it shows how to initialize all the elements in an array to a default value. Here, the value in the list is assigned to the first element, and the rest of the elements are assigned the default value for the int data type. In general, it's considered a good practice to initialize arrays in this way. Otherwise, the array will initially hold random values that happen to be at the memory locations where the array is allocated. This can make a program hard to debug and lead to unexpected results.

How to loop through an array

Figure 12-2 also shows how to loop through the elements in an array. To start, the first example defines a size constant that contains a value of 5. Then, the second example uses a for loop to display all elements in an array, and the third example uses a while loop to add elements to an array. These loops are similar to the ones that you've already seen for working with STL containers such as vectors.

However, a built-in array doesn't have a size() member function that gets the number of elements in the array. As a result, the loops in both of these examples use the size constant to determine when to end the loop. In some cases, it's possible to use range-based for loops with arrays. However, they don't work correctly when you pass an array to a function. Because of that, it's more common to use traditional for loops with arrays.

In the while loop example, the code uses the increment operator (++) as a postfix to the counter variable named i. As a result, the increment operation takes place after all other operations. So, the first time through the loop, the array index is 0. The second time through the loop, the index is 1. And so on.

How to initialize an array

The syntax for initializing an array with a list of values

```
element_type array_name[[array_size]] [=] {val1[, val2] ...}
```

Three ways to initialize an array with a list of values

```
const int size = 3;
int numbers1[size] = { 1, 2, 3 }; // element values are 1 2 3
int numbers2[size] { 1, 2, 3 };   // assignment operator is optional
int numbers3[] { 1, 2, 3 };       // size declarator is optional - compiler
                                  // infers array size of three elements
```

How to initialize an array with three values and the rest default values

```
int grades[7] { 98, 86, 100 };    // element values are 98 86 100 0 0 0 0
```

How to set all the elements in an array to a default value

```
int grades[7] { 0 };              // element values are 0 0 0 0 0 0 0
```

How to loop through all the elements in an array

Define a constant for the size

```
const int size = 5;
```

A for loop that displays all elements in an array

```
double prices[size] { 9.99, 49.99, 79.99 }; // initialize with three values
for (int i = 0; i < size; ++i) {
    cout << prices[i] << ' ';                // displays 9.99 49.99 79.99 0 0
}
```

A while loop that gets element values from the user

```
int scores[size];
int i = 0;
int score;
while (cin >> score && i < size) {
    // postfix so subscript operation occurs before increment operation
    scores[i++] = score;
}
```

Description

- You can use an *initialization list* to set the starting values of an array. When you do, both the assignment operator and the *size declarator* are optional. If you don't supply the size declarator, the compiler sizes the array based on the number of values in the list.

- The first value in an initialization list is assigned to the first element in the array, the second value is assigned to the second element, and so on.

- If the initialization list doesn't specify a value for every element, the rest of the elements are initialized to the default value for the data type.

- You can use a for loop or a while loop to iterate the elements in an array. Like a vector, an array allows *out of bounds access*. To avoid that, you can use a constant to define the size of an array and use that constant value to prevent out of bounds access.

- You can also use a range-based for loop with an array. However, this type of loop doesn't work correctly with arrays that are passed to functions. As a result, it's more common to use traditional for loops with arrays.

Figure 12-2   How to initialize and loop through an array

How to pass an array to a function

To code a function that accepts an array as an argument, you code the subscript operator (`[]`) after the parameter name. This is shown by the first example in figure 12-3. However, this is only the first step toward working effectively with arrays in functions because arrays behave differently than other data types when they're passed to functions.

In chapter 7, you learned that an argument is passed to a function by value unless the function uses the & symbol to indicate that the parameter is a reference parameter. However, an array isn't passed to a function by value. Instead, it's converted to a *pointer* to the first element in the array. In chapter 17, you'll learn more about pointers. For now, just know that a pointer contains a *memory address* for a value, not the value itself. In other words, a pointer indicates the location in memory where a value is stored.

When you pass an array to a function, then, the function doesn't receive the array itself. Instead, it receives a pointer to the memory address of the first element of the array along with the data type of the array. This is called *array decay* because the array *decays* to a pointer and significant information about the array, such as the number of elements it contains, is lost.

Fortunately, the function can still use the subscript operator to access the elements of the array. That's possible because the compiler knows the size of the data type, and it knows that the elements are stored in contiguous memory. As a result, it can advance from the memory address of the first element as many bytes as necessary to access subsequent elements.

For instance, on most systems, an int uses four bytes of memory. So, for an array of ints, it can advance four bytes from the memory address of the first element to access the second element, it can advance eight bytes to access the third element, and so on. Unfortunately, the compiler doesn't know the array's size, so it doesn't know when it's moved past the last element in the array.

To prevent the out of bounds access that occurs if you move past the end of an array, you can pass the number of elements in the array to the function. In this figure, for instance, the display_array() function has a size parameter that specifies the number of elements in the array. This function begins by using the sizeof() operator to display the amount of memory that's used by the array parameter. Then, it uses a loop to display the value of each element in the array. This loop uses the size parameter to determine when to end.

After the display_array() function, the main() function begins by defining an int array with five elements. Then, it displays the amount of memory that's used by the array. Next, it passes the array and its size to the display_array() function.

The console shows that the array uses 20 bytes of memory (four bytes per element multiplied by the five elements). However, after being passed to the function, the size of the array is eight bytes. On most systems, that's the size of the pointer that contains the memory address of the first element. Nevertheless, because of the size parameter, the function can still display all of the elements in the array.

How to code a function with an array as a parameter

```
void do_something(int arr[]) {
    // body of function
}
```

What happens to an array when it's passed to a function

A function that accepts an array and iterates its elements

```
void display_array(int nums[], int size) {
    cout << "The array AFTER passing to function:    "
        << (sizeof(nums)) << " bytes.\n";

    cout << "The elements: ";
    for (int i = 0; i < size; ++i) {
        cout << nums[i] << ' ';
    }
    cout << endl;
}
```

Code that creates an array and passes it to the function

```
int main() {
    const int size = 5;
    int nums[size] = { 1, 2, 3, 4, 5 };
    cout << "The array BEFORE passing to function: "
        << (sizeof(nums)) << " bytes.\n";

    display_array(nums, size);
}
```

The console

```
The array BEFORE passing to function: 20 bytes.
The array AFTER passing to function:  8 bytes.
The elements: 1 2 3 4 5
```

What happens to an array when it's used in an expression

```
int nums[] = { 1, 2, 3, 4, 5 };
cout << nums << endl;  // displays memory address of first element
```

Description

- To create a function that accepts an array, you code the subscript operator ([]) after the parameter name. This subscript operator should not include a size declarator.

- An array isn't passed to a function by value. Instead, C++ converts it to a *pointer* to the first element in the array. A pointer contains the *memory address* of a value, not the value itself.

- This conversion to a pointer is known as *array decay*, because information about the array, including its size, is lost.

- You can still access the elements of the array with the subscript operator ([]). However, to avoid out of bounds access, you need to know the number of elements. That's why it's common to pass the number of elements as a separate argument.

- Array decay can also occur when an array variable is used in an expression.

Figure 12-3   How to pass an array to a function

Array decay can also occur when you use an array in an expression. For instance, the last example defines an array and uses it in a stream insertion expression. Here, the array decays to a pointer. As a result, this statement displays the memory address of the first element in the array.

How to compare and copy arrays

Because arrays decay to pointers in many expressions, you can't use assignment operators or relational operators with arrays. For instance, if you try to use the equality operator (==) to check whether two arrays are equal, the arrays decay to pointers. So, this checks whether the memory addresses for the first elements of each array are the same. Unless both array variables point to the same location in memory, comparing the variables for equality always returns false even if the arrays contain identical elements.

Similarly, if you try to use the greater than operator (>) to check whether one array is greater than another, you are actually comparing whether the memory address of the first element in the first array is greater than the memory address of the first element in the second array. Since this may or may not be true, depending on where the memory for the arrays was allocated, it yields unpredictable results.

Finally, if you try to use the assignment operator (=) to copy one array to another, you are actually attempting to assign a new memory address to an array. Since this isn't allowed, it causes a compile-time error.

So, when working with arrays, you need to work directly with the elements of the arrays to perform these types of operations as shown by the examples in figure 12-4. The first example shows how to compare two arrays for equality. This example starts by defining a constant with a value of 5 that can be used to declare the size of an array. Then, the code uses this constant to define two char arrays named grades1 and grades2, and it initializes these arrays with three characters.

Next, this example defines a Boolean flag variable named equal that's initialized to true. Then, a for loop compares each value in the two arrays. If the two values aren't the same, the two arrays aren't the same. As a result, the code sets the flag to false and exits the loop. Otherwise, the loop continues. When the loop ends, the value of the flag indicates whether the arrays are equal.

The second example shows how to copy the values of one array to another. Like the first example, this example starts by coding a constant value of 5 as a size declarator. Then, it uses that constant to define two int arrays named scores1 and scores2, and it initializes the first array with five int values. However, it doesn't initialize the second array.

After defining the two arrays, this code uses a for loop to assign the value of each element in the scores1 array to an element in the scores2 array. When the loop ends, the values in scores2 are the same as the values in scores1. To illustrate, the second for loop displays the values in the scores2 array on the console.

How to check whether two arrays are equal

```
const int size = 5;
char grades1[size]{ 'A', 'B', 'B' };
char grades2[size]{ 'A', 'C', 'B' };

bool equal = true;
for (int i = 0; i < size; ++i) {
    if (grades1[i] != grades2[1]) {
        equal = false;
        break;    // no need to continue, exit loop
    }
}

if (equal) {
    cout << "The arrays are equal.\n";
}
else {
    cout << "The arrays are NOT equal.\n";
}
```

The console

```
The arrays are NOT equal.
```

How to copy the values of one array to another

```
const int size = 5;
int scores1[size]{ 89, 92, 78, 68, 87 };
int scores2[size];

for (int i = 0; i < size; ++i) {
    scores2[i] = scores1[i];
}

// display the values of the scores2 array
for (int i = 0; i < size; ++i) {
    cout << scores2[i] << ' ';
}
cout << endl;
```

The console

```
89 92 78 68 87
```

Description

- Arrays don't provide relational operators or assignment operators.
- To compare two arrays, you can use a loop to compare the values in each element of the two arrays.
- To copy an array, you can use a loop to copy the values in the elements of one array to the elements of another array.

Figure 12-4   How to compare and copy arrays

The Test Scores program

Figure 12-5 shows the Test Scores program. This program lets the user enter up to 50 test scores. To indicate that all test scores have been entered, the user enters -1. Then, the program computes and displays the number of scores entered, the sum of all the scores, and the average score.

This code begins with include statements for the header files that the program needs. Since the array is a built-in type, this code doesn't need to specify an include statement for it. This shows that working with arrays requires less overhead than working with vectors or other STL containers.

After the using directive for the std namespace, this code declares a function prototype named calculate_total() that includes two parameters. The first parameter specifies an array of int values named scores, and the second specifies an int variable named score_count.

After the function prototype, the main() function starts by declaring a constant named capacity that stores a value of 50. Then, it uses the capacity constant as the size declarator to create an array of int values named scores. As a result, this program can store a maximum of 50 scores.

Since this program uses an array, not a vector, it's necessary to specify a maximum number of scores. That's because the size of the array must be specified at compile time, but you don't know how many scores the user will enter until runtime. The trick with this technique is to make sure the array is large enough for the purposes of the program without being so large that it uses an excessive amount of memory.

The statement that defines the array includes an initialization list with a single value, which is the default value for the int data type. As a result, this statement fills all the elements of the array with that default value.

After initializing the scores array, this code displays some messages to the user that explain how the program works. Then, it defines and initializes a variable named score_count to keep track of how many scores the user has entered, and it defines a variable named score that holds the current score.

The console

```
The Test Scores program

Enter test scores (50 max).
Make sure each score is between 0 and 100.
To end the program, enter -1.

Enter score: 89
Enter score: 78
Enter score: 92
Enter score: 88
Enter score: -1

Score count:    4
Score total:    347
Average score: 86.8
```

The code

```cpp
#include <iostream>
#include <cmath>

using namespace std;

double calculate_total(int scores[], int score_count);

int main() {
    const int capacity = 50;
    int scores[capacity] { 0 };  // set each element in array to 0

    cout << "The Test Scores program\n\n";

    cout << "Enter test scores (" << capacity << " max).\n"
         << "Make sure each score is between 0 and 100.\n"
         << "To end the program, enter -1.\n\n";

    // initialize variables
    int score_count = 0, score = 0;
```

Figure 12-5   The Test Scores program (part 1 of 2)

Part 2 of figure 12-5 starts by defining a while loop that runs as long as two conditions are true. The first is that the user hasn't entered -1 to end the program. The second is that the number of scores entered is less than the capacity of the array. This prevents the user from entering more scores than the array can hold.

Within the loop, the code extracts the score entered by the user from the standard input stream and checks it. If the extraction failed, the code notifies the user, clears the input stream, and jumps to the top of the loop. If the score is within the appropriate range, the code adds it to the array, increments the score count, and jumps to the top of the loop. If the score is outside the appropriate range, the code notifies the user and jumps to the top of the loop.

Once the while loop completes, either because the user entered -1 or the maximum number of scores has been entered, the code checks the score count. If it's zero, the user didn't enter any valid scores. In this case, the code displays an appropriate message and the program ends.

Otherwise, the score count is greater than zero, so the user entered one or more valid scores. In this case, the code passes the scores array and the score_count variable to the calculate_total() function and stores the return value in a double variable named total. Then, the code uses this value to calculate the average score. Finally, the code displays the score count, the score total, and the average score on the console.

After the main() function, this code defines the calculate_total() function. This function starts by defining a double variable named total and initializing it to zero. Then, it uses the score_count parameter in a for loop that iterates the array of scores. Within this loop, the code adds each score to the total. When the loop completes, the function returns the total to the calling code.

As you review this code, note that the code in the main() function that calls the calculate_total() function stores the int value that's returned in a double variable. This allows the statement that follows that calculates the average score to use decimal division, not integer division.

The code (continued)

```
        // prevent out of bounds access by making sure
        // score count is less than array capacity
        while (score != -1 && score_count < capacity) {
            cout << "Enter score: ";
            cin >> score;

            if (cin.fail()) {
                cin.clear();                // clear bad input flag
                cin.ignore(1000, '\n');     // discard input up to end of line
                cout << "Invalid number. Try again.\n";
            }
            else if (score > 100) {
                cout << "Score must be from 0 to 100. Try again.\n";
            }
            else if (score < -1) {
                cout << "Score can't be a negative number. Try again.\n";
            }
            else if (score > -1) {
                scores[score_count] = score;   // store score in array
                ++score_count;                 // increment score count
            }
        }
        cout << endl;

        if (score_count == 0) {
            cout << "No scores entered.\n\n";
        }
        else {
            // calculate total and average scores
            double total = calculate_total(scores, score_count);
            double average = total / score_count;
            average = round(average * 10) / 10;

            // display the score count, score total, and average score
            cout << "Score count:   " << score_count << endl
                 << "Score total:   " << total << endl
                 << "Average score: " << average << endl << endl;
        }

        return 0;
}

double calculate_total(int scores[], int score_count) {
        double total = 0.0;
        for (int i = 0; i < score_count; ++i) {
            total += scores[i];
        }
        return total;
}
```

Figure 12-5   The Test Scores program (part 2 of 2)

How to work with C strings

A *string* is a sequence of characters. So far, this book has only shown how to use string objects that are part of the C++ standard library to work with strings. Since a string object provides many member functions that make it easy to work with strings, this is typically how you want to work with strings.

Sometimes, though, a string object can use too much overhead. For example, you may not be able to use string objects in an embedded environment. And, sometimes, you may need to maintain legacy C++ code that was developed before the string object was available. In these cases, you'll need to use C strings to work with an array of characters. This is how the C language handles strings.

An introduction to C strings

A *C string*, also known as a *C-style string*, is a built-in array of characters that ends with a *null terminator*, also known as a *null character*. This null terminator is the ASCII code 0. When working with null terminators, it's important to understand that the ASCII code 0 is *not* the same as the character literal '0', which is ASCII code 48. Instead, to specify a null terminator, you can use the character literal '\0'.

The first example in figure 12-6 shows two ways to create a C string. First, you can code a char array with an initialization list whose last value is the null terminator. Second, you can code a char array and initialize it with a string literal. Then, C++ automatically adds the null terminator to the end of the array. Either way, the compiler infers the size of the array from the initialization list or the string literal. In other words, you don't need to include a size declarator.

The second example shows that it's possible to code a partially filled C string. This example includes a size declarator of 15 and a string literal with five characters. The graphical representation below this example shows that this code produces a C string with 15 characters and that all elements after the first five characters contain the null terminator.

An *empty string* is a C string whose elements are all initialized with the null terminator. This is similar to initializing the elements of an int array with the default value for the int type, which is 0. The third example shows three ways to code an empty C string. To do that, you can code an empty string literal, an initialization list that contains ASCII code 0 (no single quotes), or an initialization list that contains the character literal for ASCII code 0 (single quotes).

When you're working with string literals, you don't need to code the null terminator value in your code. However, the fourth example shows how to make sure it's there. To start, this code uses the sizeof() operator to show that a C string of 5 characters uses 6 bytes: 1 byte for each character plus 1 byte for the null terminator. Then, this code uses a loop to display the ASCII code for each character, including the null terminator, on the console.

The fifth example shows two char arrays that aren't C strings. Remember, if a char array doesn't end with a null terminator, it's not a C string. Here, the first array isn't initialized so it doesn't contain any values, and the initialization list for the second array doesn't include a null terminator.

How to create a C string
With an initialization list
```
char greeting[] = {'h','e','l','l','o', '\0'}; // explicit null terminator
```
With a string literal
```
char greeting[] = "hello";                      // implicit null terminator
```
A graphical representation of the C string

h	e	l	l	o	\0

How to initialize a partially filled C string
```
char greeting[15] = "hello";   // include a size declarator
```
A graphical representation of the partially filled C string

h	e	l	l	o	\0	\0	\0	\0	\0	\0	\0	\0	\0	\0

Three ways to initialize an empty C string
```
char greeting[15] = "";        // string literal
char greeting[15] = {0};       // ASCII code 0 - no single quotes
char greeting[15] = {'\0'};    // character literal for ASCII code 0
```
A graphical representation of the empty C string

\0	\0	\0	\0	\0	\0	\0	\0	\0	\0	\0	\0	\0	\0	\0

Code that shows the extra element for the null terminator
```
char greeting[] = "hello";                        // 5 characters
int num_bytes = sizeof(greeting);                 // num_bytes is 6
for (int i = 0; i < num_bytes; ++i) {
    cout << static_cast<int>(greeting[i]) << ' '; // display ASCII code
}
cout << endl;
```
The console
```
104 101 108 108 111 0
```

Two char arrays that are not C strings
```
char arr[5];                              // no null terminator, not a C string
char arr[] = {'h','e','l','l','o'};       // no null terminator, not a C string
```

Description
- A *string* is a sequence of characters. In previous chapters, you learned how to use the string object that's available from the C++ standard library to work with strings.

- A *C string*, or *C-style string*, is a char array that ends with a *null terminator*, also called a *null character*.

- The null terminator is a char that contains the ASCII code 0. You can code it with the number zero (no single quotes) or with a character literal.

- A C string contains one element for each character in the string, plus an additional element for the null terminator.

- In C++, string literals are actually C strings, not string objects.

Figure 12-6   An introduction to C strings

How to use C strings with input streams

As you just learned, a string literal is a C string. As a result, you already know how to use a C string with an output stream. For instance, this code

```
cout << "Welcome to the Test Scores program";
```

sends a C string to the console output stream.

Using a C string with an input stream, on the other hand, requires a technique like the one shown in the first example in figure 12-7. This example uses a C string with an input stream to get a two-character abbreviation for a state from the user. To start, this code defines a char array with three elements and initializes it to an empty string. That way, the array is a C string that initially contains three null terminators, which means there's room for two characters and a null terminator.

In this example, the stream extraction operator (>>) retrieves two characters from the standard input stream and stores them as the first two characters of the C string. Then, the code sends the C string to the standard output stream.

This example works because the code requested two characters, and the user entered two characters. But what if the user entered "ORE" or "Oregon"? Or, what if you needed to get a string that varies in length? For example, what if you needed to get the full name of a state? In these cases, you can make the C string a maximum size and partially fill it with the string the user enters.

However, two potential problems remain. First, what happens if the user enters a state name with a space like "South Carolina"? Second, what happens if the user enters more characters than the maximum size of the C string?

To address these problems, you can use the getline() member function of the input stream. Note that this isn't the getline() function you learned about in chapter 2. That getline() function is a stand-alone function provided by the iostream header that accepts an input stream object and a string object as arguments. By contrast, the getline() member function described here is a member of the input stream and accepts a C string rather than a string object.

When you call the getline() member function of an input stream, the first argument is the C string that will store the characters entered by the user, and the second argument is the number of characters to extract, including the null terminator. Optionally, you can pass a third argument that indicates the delimiter that ends the line. The default value for this argument is the newline character.

The second code example shows how this works. It uses the getline() member function to get a state name from a user. The code begins by creating an empty C string with 15 characters and prompts the user to enter a state name. Then, this code passes the C string and the string size to the getline() function of the cin object. After using getline() to get characters from the user, the code checks the fail() function of the input stream. That's because the failbit is set to true if the user enters too many characters. In this case, the code calls the clear() and ignore() functions to reset the stream.

On the console, you can see that the user enters a state with spaces in its name that has more than the maximum number of characters. However, the getline() function only extracts the first 14 characters entered by the user (13 letters plus the space) and the null terminator (ASCII code 0).

Code that gets a fixed-length C string with no spaces

```
const int size = 3;     // 2 characters plus null terminator
char state[size] = "";
cout << " Enter 2-letter state code: ";
cin >> state;
cout << "State code is " << state << endl << endl;
```

The console

```
Enter 2-letter state code: OR
State code is OR
```

The syntax of the getline() member function of an input stream object

```
stream.getline(cstring, character_limit, [delimiter='\n']);
```

Code that gets a variable-length C string with possible spaces

```
const int size = 15;    // 14 characters plus null terminator
char state[size] = "";
cout << "Enter state name: ";
cin.getline(state, size);
if (cin.fail()) {       // if user entered too many characters...
    cin.clear();
    cin.ignore(1000, '\n');
}
cout << "State name is " << state << endl << endl;

// display ASCII code for each character in C string
for (int i = 0; i < size; ++i) {
    cout << static_cast<int>(state[i]) << ' ';
}
```

The console

```
Enter state name: South Carolina Rulzzz!
State name is South Carolina

83 111 117 116 104 32 67 97 114 111 108 105 110 97 0
```

Description

- The stream insertion operator (<<) can write a C string to an output stream.

- The stream extraction operator (>>) can read characters from an input stream and automatically add a null terminator to create a valid C string.

- If you know the number of characters a string will have, you should size the C string for that number of characters, plus one for the null terminator. Otherwise, you can size the C string for the maximum number of allowable characters, plus one for the null terminator.

- If a user enters more characters than a C string can hold, the program can crash. To prevent this, you can use the getline() member function of the input stream.

- When using the getline() member function of an input stream, the failbit is set if the user enters more characters than specified in the second argument. However, you can use the clear() and ignore() functions of the input stream to reset the stream.

Figure 12-7   How to use C strings with input streams

Some utility functions for working with C strings

The C++ standard library provides several utility functions for working with C strings. Figure 12-8 begins by showing how to include the cstring header file that contains these functions. Then, it presents four of these functions and examples of how to use them.

The strlen() function accepts a C string as an argument and returns the number of characters in the string. This return value represents the total number of characters, not the total number of elements. For instance, the first code example defines a C string with 20 elements and initializes it with a string literal of 12 characters (including the space). As a result, the strlen() function returns a value of 12 because that's the number of characters in the string, not including null terminators.

The strncat() function accepts two C string arguments and a size argument. Then, it concatenates the two strings, up to the limit in the size argument. In other words, it appends the characters in the second string to the end of the first string, as long as the first string has no more than the specified number of characters. For instance, the second code example appends the 6 characters in s2 to the end of the 6 characters in s1 for a total of 12 characters. The size limit passed to the function is the size of the first C string minus 1, or 19 characters. This makes sure the first C string can end with the null terminator. That way, if s2 contained 30 characters, only the first 13 would be appended to s1.

The strncpy() function accepts two C string arguments and a size argument. Then, it copies the characters in the second string to the first string, up to the limit in the size argument. This overwrites any characters already in the first C string. For instance, the third code example copies the characters in s2 to s1 and overwrites the characters that were already in s1. As before, the size limit passed to the function is the size of the first C string minus 1. That way, you can be sure that the first C string ends with the null terminator.

Note that, unlike the getline() member function described in the previous figure, the strncat() and strncpy() functions don't automatically adjust for the null terminator. Instead, the size argument must provide for that adjustment.

If you're using Visual Studio and the MSVC compiler and you attempt to use the strncat() or strncpy() function, your code might not compile and you might get a warning. That's because Microsoft has deprecated these functions. For example, for strncpy(), you might get a warning that says, "This function or variable may be unsafe. Consider using strncpy_s instead." However, strncpy_s() is not part of the C++ standard, so it makes your code less portable. As a result, we recommend solving this issue by editing the project properties so the SDL checks property is set to No. This turns off additional Security Development Lifecycle (SDL) checks so these warnings are ignored and the code is compiled.

The strcmp() function accepts two C string arguments and compares the alphabetical order of the characters in the two strings. Then, it returns 0 if they are equal, 1 if the first string comes after the second, or -1 if the first string comes before the second. For instance, the fourth code example uses the strcmp() function in an if statement to determine whether two strings contain the same value.

The include statement for the cstring header file

```
#include <cstring>
```

Some of the functions for working with C strings

Function	Description
`strlen(s)`	Provides the number of characters in the string. Note this is often less than the total number of elements in the char array.
`strncat(s1, s2, size)`	Concatenates the characters in the second string to the end of the first string, up to the limit passed as the size argument.
`strncpy(s1, s2, size)`	Copies the characters in the second string to the first string, up to the limit passed as the size argument.
`strcmp(s1, s2)`	Compares the alphabetical order of two strings. Returns 0 if they are equal, 1 if s1 comes after s2, and -1 if s1 comes before s2.

Code that determines the length of a string

```
const int size = 20;
char cstring[size] = "Grace Hopper";
cout << size << " elements, string length of " << strlen(cstring);
// Displays "20 elements, string length of 12"
```

Code that concatenates two strings

```
const int size = 20;
char s1[size] = "Grace ";
char s2[size] = "Hopper";
strncat(s1, s2, size - 1);    // s1 now contains Grace Hopper
```

Code that assigns one string to another

```
const int size = 20;
char s1[size] = "Ada ";
char s2[size] = "Grace ";
strncpy(s1, s2, size - 1);    // s1 now contains "Grace "
```

Code that compares two strings for equality

```
char string1[] = "Grace";
char string2[] = "Hopper";
if (strcmp(string1, string2) == 0) {
    cout << string1 << " and " << string2 << " match!\n";
} else {
    cout << string1 << " and " << string2 << " aren't the same.\n";
}
```

Description

- Like other arrays, you can't use assignment or relational operators with C strings. However, the cstring header provides several functions for these types of operations.

- The strncat() and strncpy() functions don't automatically adjust to account for the null terminator. Instead, you need to write code that manually adjusts for the null terminator.

- To use the strncat() and strncpy() functions with Visual Studio/MSVC, you may need to disable Security Development Lifecycle (SDL) checks. To do that, display the Property Pages dialog (Project→Properties), expand the C/C++ group, select the General item, and set the SDL checks property to No.

Figure 12-8   Some utility functions for working with C strings

Beyond the functions presented in this figure, the cstring header also provides functions named strcat() and strcpy(). These functions work similarly to strncat() and strncpy() functions, but they don't accept a numeric value to limit the number of characters in the resulting C string. This is why these functions don't have an 'n' in their names. Using these functions is dangerous because you can end up overwriting the null terminator with a character, thus transforming a C string into an ordinary char array. Because this can lead to problems, it's generally considered a better practice to use the strncat() and strncpy() functions.

How to loop through a C string

The null terminator identifies the end of a C string. As a result, you can use the null terminator to determine when to end the loop when you're looping through all the characters in a C string.

Figure 12-9 shows two ways to use the null terminator to loop through the characters in a C string. In the first example, the strlen() function gets the number of characters in the string. Then, a for loop uses that number to determine when to stop the loop. This code doesn't explicitly use the null terminator, but the strlen() function uses the null terminator to determine the string's length.

In the second example, both loops check each character in the C string. When the character equals the null terminator, represented here by the character literal of '\0', the code knows it has reached the end of the string and the loop ends.

When you code a function that accepts an array, you typically need to include a size parameter so the function can determine the end of the array and prevent out of bounds access. However, when you code a function that accepts a C string, you don't need to include a size parameter. That's because a C string uses the null terminator to define the end of the string. As a result, the function can use the null terminator to determine the end of the string and prevent out of bounds access as shown by the third example.

In the third example, a function named capitalize() accepts a char array argument, but no size argument. Then, the function uses the strlen() function to determine the string's size, and it uses this size value to loop through the characters in the string and capitalize each character. In the main() function, the code calls the capitalize() function to capitalize a C string that stores the characters for a name.

For the third example to work correctly, the array of characters that's passed to the function must be a C string. If it's possible that the array isn't a C string, the function should also accept a size argument.

Code that uses the value returned by strlen() to traverse a C string

```
char name[] = "Grace Hopper";
int len = strlen(name);
for (int i = 0; i < len; ++i) {
    name[i] = toupper(name[i]);
}
cout << name << endl;              // Displays GRACE HOPPER
```

Code that checks for the null terminator to traverse a C string

Using a while loop

```
char name[] = "Grace Hopper";
int i = 0;
while (name[i] != '\0') {
    name[i] = toupper(name[i]);
    ++i;
}
cout << name << endl;              // Displays GRACE HOPPER
```

Using a for loop

```
char name[] = "Grace Hopper";
for (int i = 0; name[i] != '\0'; ++i) {
    name[i] = toupper(name[i]);
}
cout << name << endl;              // Displays GRACE HOPPER
```

How to work with a function that accepts a C string

A function that capitalizes a C string

```
void capitalize(char cstr[]) {  // no array size parameter needed
    int len = strlen(cstr);
    for (int i = 0; i < len; ++i) {
        cstr[i] = toupper(cstr[i]);
    }
}
```

Code that calls the function

```
int main() {
    char name[] = "Grace Hopper";
    capitalize(name);
    cout << name << endl;         // Displays GRACE HOPPER
}
```

Description

- You can use the strlen() function to determine the number of characters in a C string.

- You can use the null terminator to determine when you've reached the end of a C string.

- When coding a function that accepts a C string as an argument, you don't need to include a parameter for the string length because you can get that information from the C string.

Figure 12-9   How to loop through a C string

The Create Account program

Figure 12-10 presents a version of the Create Account program from chapter 6 that works with C strings instead of string objects. This program accepts a full name and a password from the user that can both be a maximum of 50 characters. Data validation is performed on both entries to make sure they meet specific criteria.

The code begins with include statements for the header files that the program needs, including the cstring header file, as well as the using directive for the std namespace. After that, the code declares several function prototypes, most of which accept one or more C strings as arguments. Only the find_space() function returns a value, and only the get_name() and get_password() functions require a size argument.

After the function declarations, the main() function starts by displaying the name of the program. Then, it defines a constant integer named size and initializes it with a value of 51. Next, it uses this constant to define three C strings named full_name, first_name, and password. Since each of these C strings can store 51 characters, each has room for 50 characters plus the null terminator.

After defining the three C strings, the code gets the name entered by the user by calling the get_name() function and passing it the first_name and full_name variables and the size constant. Then, it gets the password entered by the user by calling the get_password() function and passing it the password and size variables. Parts 2 and 3 of this figure show that these functions perform data validation when getting the name and password from the user.

After getting the name and password from the user, the code capitalizes the initial letter of the first name entered by the user. To do that, this code calls the capitalize_initial_letter() function and passes it the first_name variable. Since you can be sure that the first_name variable is a C string, this function doesn't need to include a parameter for the size of the string. Finally, the code displays a message that uses the first_name variable to welcome the user and thank the user for creating an account.

As you review this code, note that some of the functions that are declared aren't used in the main() function. In particular, the main() function doesn't call the trim_leading_whitespace(), find_space(), or reset_stream() functions. That's because these functions are helper functions that are used by the get_name() and get_password() functions shown in parts 2 and 3 of this figure.

The console

```
Create Account

Enter full name (50 chars max): grace
You must enter your full name. Try again.

Enter full name (50 chars max): grace  hopper

Enter password (50 chars max): debugger
Password must meet the following criteria:
 - at least 8 characters long
 - at least one number
 - at least one special character
Try again.

Enter password (50 chars max): d3bugg3r!

Hi Grace,
Thanks for creating an account!
```

The code

```cpp
#include <iostream>
#include <cstring>  // for C string utility functions

using namespace std;

// function declarations
void get_name(char first_name[], char full_name[], int size);
void get_password(char password[], int size);
void trim_leading_whitespace(char cstring[]);
int find_space(char cstring[]);
void capitalize_initial_letter(char cstring[]);
void reset_stream();

int main()
{
    cout << "Create Account\n\n";

    const int size = 51;  // space for 50 characters plus null terminator
    char full_name[size] = "", first_name[size] = "", password[size] = "";

    get_name(first_name, full_name, size);
    get_password(password, size);
    capitalize_initial_letter(first_name);

    // display welcome message
    cout << "\nHi " << first_name << ",\n"
        << "Thanks for creating an account!\n\n";

    return 0;
}
```

Figure 12-10   The Create Account program (part 1 of 3)

Part 2 of figure 12-10 presents the first three function definitions. The get_name() function starts with a while loop that runs until the break keyword stops it. This technique allows the function to continue to ask users to try again if they enter invalid data.

Within the loop, the code asks the user to enter a full name and displays the maximum number of characters allowed. To get this maximum number of characters, the code subtracts 1 from the size variable. This reserves space for the null terminator.

After prompting the user, the code calls the getline() function of the cin object and passes it the full_name parameter and the size variable. Then, this code handles the situation that occurs if the user enters too many characters by calling the reset_stream() function that's defined in part 3 of this figure.

Next, the code trims any leading whitespace, such as spaces and tabs, from the beginning of the name. To do that, it passes the full_name variable to the trim_leading_whitespace() function.

After trimming any leading whitespace, the code gets the first name from the full name entered by the user. To do that, it passes the full_name variable to the find_space() function to get the index of the first space in the string. If the index is -1, there's no space. As a result, the code asks the user to enter a full name, and the loop repeats.

However, if the C string contains a space, the code uses the strncpy() function to copy the characters of the first name from the full_name variable to the first_name variable. To do that, this code passes the index of the space after the first name to the strncpy() function so the copy operation stops at that index. Then, the break keyword ends the loop.

The trim_leading_whitespace() function begins by using the isspace() function to check whether the C string it receives has leading whitespace. If not, the function ends. However, if the C string does have leading whitespace, this function defines an int index named i and initializes it to 0. Then, a while loop runs as long as the character in the C string at the index is a whitespace character. Within the body of the loop, the index is incremented. This advances the index to the first non-whitespace character.

After getting the index of the first non-whitespace character, the code declares a second index named j and initializes it to 0. Then, a second while loop uses the first index to iterate through the rest of the elements of the C string. Within the body of this loop, the first statement copies the character at the first index to the second index. This shifts the character to the left by the number of whitespace characters that the function skipped. Next, the code increments both the i and j variables.

When this second loop ends, the code adds the null terminator to the end of the cstring variable. At this point, there may be non-null characters after the null terminator, but they don't prevent the C string from working correctly with the other functions for this program.

The find_space() function starts by setting a Boolean flag to false. Then, it uses the strlen() function to loop through each character in the string. When it finds a space, it sets the flag to true and exits the loop. Finally, the code checks the flag to determine whether a space was found. If so, it returns the index of the space. Otherwise, it return a value of -1 to indicate that no space was found.

The code (continued)

```
// function definitions
void get_name(char first_name[], char full_name[], int size) {
    while (true) {
        cout << "Enter full name (" << size - 1 << " chars max): ";
        cin.getline(full_name, size);
        reset_stream();

        trim_leading_whitespace(full_name);

        // get first name
        int index = find_space(full_name);
        if (index == -1) {
            cout << "You must enter your full name. Try again.\n\n";
        } else {
            strncpy(first_name, full_name, index);
            break;
        }
    }
}

void trim_leading_whitespace(char cstring[]) {
    if (isspace(cstring[0])) {
        // increment index until first non-space character found
        int i = 0;
        while (isspace(cstring[i])) {
            ++i;
        }

        // start manual copy at index of first non-space character
        int j = 0;
        while (cstring[i] != '\0') {
            cstring[j] = cstring[i];   // shift chars to the left
            ++i;                       // increment both counters
            ++j;
        }

        // add null terminator to string
        cstring[j] = '\0';
    }
}

int find_space(char cstring[]) {
    bool space_found = false;
    int i, len = strlen(cstring);
    for (i = 0; i < len; ++i) {
        if (isspace(cstring[i])) {
            space_found = true;
            break;             // exit loop
        }
    }
    if (space_found)
        return i;
    else
        return -1;
}
```

Figure 12-10   The Create Account program (part 2 of 3)

Part 3 of figure 12-10 presents the last three function definitions. The get_password() function starts with a while loop that runs until the break keyword stops it. Within the loop, the code asks the user to enter a password and displays the maximum number of characters allowed.

After prompting the user to enter a password, this code calls the getline() function of the cin object and passes it the password parameter and the size variable. Then, the code handles the situation that occurs if the user enters too many characters by calling the reset_stream() function.

Next, the code validates the password entered by the user. To start, it uses the strlen() function to get the number of characters in the password. Then, it uses that value in a conditional expression that sets the a Boolean flag named has_length to true or false. If the password is less than 8 characters, the flag is set to false. Otherwise, it's set to true.

The code also checks that the password contains at least one number. To do that, it defines a Boolean flag named has_number and initializes it to false. Then, it uses a for loop to pass each character in the C string to the isdigit() function. If that function returns true, the code sets the has_number flag to true and exits the loop. However, if isdigit() never returns true, the flag remains set at its initial value of false when the loop ends.

Finally, the code checks that the password contains at least one special character. To do that, it defines a Boolean flag named has_special_char and initializes it to false. Then, it uses a for loop to pass each character in the C string to the ispunct() function. If that function returns true, the code sets the has_special_char flag to true and exits the loop. However, if ispunct() never returns true, the flag remains set at its initial value of false when the loop ends.

After all three Boolean flags have been set, the code tests these flags to check whether the user has entered a password that is at least 8 characters long and contains a number as well as a special character. If so, the code exits the outer while loop, which exits the function. Otherwise, the code notifies the user of the password criteria and the while loop repeats, which prompts the user to enter another password.

The capitalize_initial_letter() function starts by using the toupper() function to capitalize the first character in the C string that's passed to it. Then, it uses a for loop to make sure the remaining characters are lower case. To do that, it uses the strlen() function to get the number of characters in the C string, and it uses this value to determine the number of times the for loop iterates. This for loop starts at the index of 1, which is the second character in the C string. As a result, the loop iterates through all characters in the C string, starting at the second character. Within the for loop, the code uses the tolower() function on each character.

The reset_stream() function starts by using the fail() member function of the standard input stream to check the state of the stream. If the failbit is set, the function resets it by calling the stream's clear() function. Then, it uses the stream's ignore() function to discard any remaining characters in the console input stream.

The code (continued)

```cpp
void get_password(char password[], int size) {
    while (true) {
        cout << "Enter password (" << size - 1 << " chars max): ";
        cin.getline(password, size);
        reset_stream();

        // make sure password has at least 8 characters
        int len = strlen(password);
        bool has_length = (len < 8) ? false : true;

        // make sure password includes a number
        bool has_number = false;
        for(int i = 0; i < len; ++i) {
            if (isdigit(password[i])) {
                has_number = true;
                break;                          // exit inner loop
            }
        }

        // make sure password includes a special character
        bool has_special_char = false;
        for (int i = 0; i < len; ++i) {
            if (ispunct(password[i])) {
                has_special_char = true;
                break;                          // exit inner loop
            }
        }

        // if all tests pass, exit outer loop
        if (has_length && has_number && has_special_char) {
            break;    // exit outer loop
        } else {
            cout << "Password must meet the following criteria:\n"
                 << " - at least 8 characters long\n"
                 << " - at least one number\n"
                 << " - at least one special character\n"
                 << "Try again.\n\n";
        }
    }
}

void capitalize_initial_letter(char cstring[]) {
    cstring[0] = toupper(cstring[0]);        // upper case for first letter
    int len = strlen(cstring);
    for (int i = 1; i < len; ++i) {
        cstring[i] = tolower(cstring[i]);  // lower case for the rest
    }
}

void reset_stream() {
    if (cin.fail()) {
        cin.clear();
        cin.ignore(10000, '\n');
    }
}
```

Figure 12-10   The Create Account program (part 3 of 3)

Advanced skills for built-in arrays

Now that you know the basic skills for working with arrays of elements and C strings, you're ready to learn some more skills for working with arrays. These skills include searching and sorting arrays. This is sometimes necessary in constrained environments where you can't use STL algorithms. In addition, it's good conceptual background for understanding the strategies that the STL uses for searching and sorting.

How to search an array

An *algorithm* is a specification of how to solve a problem. For example, an algorithm can perform a calculation, process data, or automate reasoning tasks. In chapter 11, you learned how the STL provides algorithms for working with the data in a container, such as searching and sorting that data.

Now, figure 12-11 presents two functions that implement algorithms for searching a sequence of elements for a specific value. To start, the algorithm for a *linear search* specifies that the search starts at the beginning of a sequence and advances one element at a time.

In this figure, the linear_search() function starts by looping through each element in the array and checking if the search value is equal to the current value. If it is, the code returns the current index, which exits the loop and the function. However, if the search value isn't in the array, the loop completes, and the function returns a value of -1 to indicate that the value was not found.

On the other hand, the algorithm for a *binary search* specifies that the search starts in the middle of a sequence and discards half of the elements each time through. A binary search can be more efficient than a linear search. However, for it to work, the elements must be sorted before performing the search.

In this figure, the binary_search() function starts by defining and initializing three int variables named first, middle, and last. Then, it uses a loop that continues while the first variable is less than or equal to the last variable.

Within the loop, the code sets the middle variable to the index of the element halfway between the first and last indexes. Then, it compares this value to the search value. If the values are equal, the middle variable stores the index of the search value. As a result, this code returns the middle variable to the calling code, which exits the loop and the function.

If, however, the middle value is greater than the search value, the search value is in the lower half of the sequence. In that case, the code sets the last variable to one less than the middle value. This discards the elements in the upper half of the sequence for the next iteration of the loop.

Conversely, if the middle value is less than the search value, the search value is in the upper half of the sequence. In that case, the code sets the first variable to one more than the middle value. This discards the elements in the lower half of the sequence for the next iteration of the loop.

If the loop never finds the value, it ends after it has processed all of the indexes. Then, the statement after the loop returns a value of -1 to indicate that it did not find the value.

A function that uses a linear search to find an element in an array of ints

```
int linear_search(const int arr[], int size, int value_to_find) {
    for (int i = 0; i < size; ++i) {
        if (arr[i] == value_to_find) {
            return i;  // value found - return index
        }
    }
    return -1;           // value not found - return -1
}
```

Code that calls this function

```
const int size = 6;
int numbers[size] = { 1, 2, 3, 5, 7, 11 };
int search_for = 3;
int index = linear_search(numbers, size, search_for);  // index is 2
```

A function that uses a binary search to find an element in an array of ints

```
int binary_search(const int arr[], int size, int value_to_find) {
    int first = 0;
    int middle = 0;
    int last = size - 1;
    while (first <= last) {
        middle = (first + last) / 2;
        if (arr[middle] == value_to_find) {
            return middle;         // value found - return index
        }
        else if (arr[middle] > value_to_find) {
            last = middle - 1;   // value is in lower half
        }
        else {
            first = middle + 1;  // value is in upper half
        }
    }
    return -1;                      // value not found - return -1
}
```

Code that calls this function

```
const int size = 6;
int numbers[size] = { 1, 2, 3, 5, 7, 11 };
int search_for = 3;
int index = binary_search(numbers, size, search_for);  // index is 2
```

Description

- A *linear search* algorithm searches the elements in a sequence in ascending order until it finds the search value.

- A *binary search* algorithm divides the elements in a sequence in half, determines which half the search element is in, and discards the other half. It repeats this process until it finds the search element. For this to work, the elements in the sequence must be sorted.

- A binary search can be more efficient than a linear search, but there's a cost if the list must be sorted first. If the list is not sorted, and you're only searching once, use a linear search. If the data is already sorted, or if you're going to perform multiple searches after sorting, use a binary search.

Figure 12-11   How to search an array

How to sort an array

Figure 12-12 presents two common algorithms for sorting the elements in a sequence. The first example implements an algorithm that performs a *bubble sort*. This algorithm states that the code should loop repeatedly through a sequence and swap adjacent elements until they are in order.

In this figure, the bubble_sort() function starts by defining a Boolean flag named is_swap and an int variable named temp. Then, it starts a do-while loop. Within this loop, the first statement sets the is_swap flag to false. Next, the code starts an inner for loop. Within this loop, the code compares the value of the current element to the value of the next one. This inner loop stops at the second to last element. That's so it doesn't attempt to compare the last element to the next element, which doesn't exist.

If the current element is greater than the next element, this code swaps the values and sets the is_swap flag to true. Then, the while clause checks the flag. If it's false, no swaps occurred, which means that the sequence is in order and the do-while loop can end. Otherwise, the do-while loop continues.

Below the bubble_sort() function, this figure shows the swaps that occur during each iteration of the outer loop when the function sorts the sequence 2 7 5 1. The first pass swaps the values 7 and 5 and the values 1 and 7. The second pass swaps the values 1 and 5. And the third pass swaps the values 1 and 2. The last iteration doesn't swap any values, so the loop ends.

The second example implements an algorithm that performs a *selection sort*, which loops once through a sequence and uses an inner loop to move each element directly to its final position. A selection sort can be more efficient than a bubble sort because the inner loop iterates fewer elements each time, and because it often needs fewer swaps.

In this figure, the selection_sort() function starts by defining int variables named min_index and min_value. Then, the code starts an outer for loop. Like the bubble sort, this for loop stops at the second to last element. This time, though, that's because all elements are in their correct order by the time the loop finishes with the second to last element.

The outer for loop starts by storing the index and value of the current element as the minimum. Then, it starts an inner for loop that iterates the rest of the elements. Within this loop, if an element is less than the current minimum, it replaces the minimum. So, when this inner loop finishes, min_index and min_value contain the index and value of the lowest remaining element.

After the inner for loop ends, the code swaps the current and minimum elements. As a result, the code assigns the smallest value to the first element, the second smallest value to the second element, and so on. Also, the outer loop only iterates the elements once, and the inner loop iterates fewer and fewer elements each time.

Below the selection_sort() function, this figure shows the sort order after each iteration of the outer loop when the function sorts the sequence 2 7 5 1. The first pass moves the value 1 to the first position by swapping it with the value 2. The second pass moves the value 2 to second position by swapping it with 7. The third pass doesn't need to perform a swap, but the code doesn't know that, so it still ends up swapping the value 5 with itself.

A function that uses the bubble sort algorithm to sort an array of ints

```
void bubble_sort(int arr[], int size) {
    bool is_swap;
    int temp;
    do {
        is_swap = false;                    // reset swap flag each iteration
        for (int i = 0; i < (size - 1); ++i) {  // stop at 2nd to last
            if (arr[i] > arr[i + 1]) {   // if current greater than next
                temp = arr[i];           // swap current and next values
                arr[i] = arr[i + 1];
                arr[i + 1] = temp;
                is_swap = true;          // set flag to show swap occurred
            }
        }
    } while (is_swap); // if a swap occurred, continue loop
}
```

The swaps that occur at each iteration of a bubble sort

```
Initial sequence:          (2 7 5 1)
First iteration:  2 swaps (2 5 7 1) then (2 5 1 7)
Second iteration: 1 swap  (2 1 5 7)
Third iteration:  1 swap  (1 2 5 7)
Fourth iteration: no swaps - end loop
```

A function that uses the selection sort algorithm to sort an array of ints

```
void selection_sort(int arr[], int size) {
    int min_index, min_value;
    for (int i = 0; i < (size - 1); ++i) {        // stop at 2nd to last
        min_index = i;          // get index of current element
        min_value = arr[i];     // get value of current element

        // loop remaining elements and find the lowest value
        for (int j = (i + 1); j < size; ++j) {
            if (arr[j] < min_value) {
                min_index = j;
                min_value = arr[j];
            }
        }
        // swap values so lowest value is in current position
        arr[min_index] = arr[i];
        arr[i] = min_value;
    }
}
```

The sort order after each iteration of a selection sort

```
Initial sequence: (2 7 5 1)
First iteration:   (1 7 5 2)   move 1 to first position by swapping with 2
Second iteration:  (1 2 5 7)   move 2 to second position by swapping with 7
Third iteration:   (1 2 5 7)   swap 5 with itself
```

Description

- A *bubble sort* algorithm loops through a sequence, comparing adjacent elements and swapping values as needed. It loops until it doesn't need to swap any more elements.

- A *selection sort* algorithm loops through a sequence once, moving each element to its final position. A selection sort can be more efficient for large sequences.

Figure 12-12   How to sort an array

How to use STL algorithms with built-in arrays

If your environment supports STL algorithms, you can use them with built-in arrays. That way, you don't need to write your own functions to implement algorithms for tasks such as searching and sorting the elements in an array.

As you should know by now, a built-in array doesn't provide the begin() and end() functions that return the iterators needed by most STL algorithms. So, how can you use STL algorithms with a built-in array? To start, you can use array decay to get a pointer to the first element. Then, you can use *pointer arithmetic* to get a pointer to another element in the array. Figure 12-13 shows how this works.

The first example defines and initializes a built-in array of double values. To do that, it also defines a constant integer named size that defines the number of elements in this array. This constant and the built-in array of doubles are used by the rest of the examples in this figure.

The second example shows how to use array decay to get a pointer to the first element. To do that, the first statement assigns the built-in array to a variable named ptr. This causes the built-in array to decay to a pointer that points to the first element in the array. Then, the second statement uses the indirection operator (*) to get the value that the pointer points to.

The third example shows how to use pointer arithmetic to get the pointer to point to different elements of the array. To do that, you can increment or decrement the pointer. Or, you can add or subtract integers from the pointer. When you do that, you can use the size constant to make sure that you don't return a pointer that causes out of bounds access.

The fourth example shows how to get an off-the-end iterator that points to one memory address past the last element. To do that, the statement adds the size constant to the array variable. This works because referring to the array variable causes it to decay to a pointer to the first element.

The fifth example shows two ways to pass pointers that define a [begin:end) interval to an STL algorithm. First, you can store the pointers in variables such as the begin and end variables in this figure. Then, you can pass those variables to the STL algorithm. Second, you can skip the variable names and pass the pointers directly to the algorithm. To do that, you can pass the built-in array variable to get the pointer to the first element, and you can pass an expression that uses pointer arithmetic to get the pointer to the off-the-end element.

The last group of examples shows some additional ways of using STL algorithms with built-in arrays. Here, the first example shows how to use the find() algorithm to get the iterator for an element with a specified value. The second example shows how to use the accumulate() algorithm to get the total of the elements in an array. The third example shows how to use the min_element() algorithm to get an iterator for the element with the minimum value. And the fourth example shows how to use the sort() algorithm to sort the elements in an array and the for_each() algorithm to display the values in an array. This should give you a good idea of the types of operations you can perform on arrays.

A built-in array of double values

```
const int size = 5;
double prices[size] {9.99, 87.99, 5.99, 32.99, 15.99};
```

How to use array decay to get a pointer to the first element

```
auto ptr = prices;           // array decays to pointer to first element
cout << '$' << *ptr << endl; // dereference to get value - displays $9.99
```

How to use pointer arithmetic to change the element that's pointed to

```
++ptr;                     // ptr now points to second element (87.99)
--ptr;                     // ptr points to first element again (9.99)
ptr = ptr + 3;             // ptr now points to fourth element (32.99)
ptr = ptr - 2;             // ptr now points to second element (87.99)
ptr = prices;              // ptr points to first element again (9.99)
ptr = ptr + (size - 1);    // ptr now points to last element (15.99)
```

How to use pointer arithmetic to get a pointer to one past the last element

```
auto end = prices + size;
```

Two ways to pass the pointers to an STL algorithm

Store pointers in variables and pass them to the algorithm

```
auto begin = prices;
auto end = prices + size;
int c = count(begin, end, 9.99);                    // c is 1
```

Pass pointers directly to algorithm

```
int c = count(prices, prices + size, 9.99);         // c is 1
```

More examples that use STL algorithms with built-in arrays

Find the iterator for the specified element

```
auto iter = find(prices, prices + size, 19.99);
if (iter == prices + size) {
    cout << "Not Found!\n";                          // displays "Not Found!"
}
```

Total just the first three elements

```
double sum = accumulate(prices, prices + 3, 0.0);    // sum is 103.97
```

Find the iterator for the minimum element

```
auto min_iter = min_element(prices, prices + size);
cout << "Min is " << *min_iter << endl;              // displays "Min is 5.99"
```

Sort and display all elements

```
sort(prices, prices + size);
for_each(prices, prices + size,
    [](double d) { cout << '$' << d << ' '; });
// displays "$5.99 $9.99 $15.99 $32.99 $87.99"
```

Description

- To use an STL algorithm, you need iterators that define a [begin:end) interval.

- With a built-in array, you can use array decay to get a pointer to use as the begin iterator. Then, you can use *pointer arithmetic* to get a pointer to use as the end iterator.

Figure 12-13   How to use STL algorithms with built-in arrays

How to work with a two-dimensional array

So far, this chapter has shown how to work with *one-dimensional (1D) arrays*. Now, the next two topics show how to work with *two-dimensional (2D) arrays*. You can think of a 2D array as a *table* made up of *rows* and *columns* where each element in the array is at the intersection of a row and a column.

The first code example in figure 12-14 shows how to create a two-dimensional array. To do that, you code two subscript operators after the array name. Then, you specify the number of rows in the first subscript operator and the number of columns in the second. As a result, this example defines a 2D array with 3 rows and 4 columns like the graphical representation in this figure.

To refer to the elements in a two-dimensional array, you use the two subscript operators to specify two index values. The first value refers to the row index, and the second value refers to the column index. For instance, the second code example assigns values to two elements within the 2D array.

You can also define and initialize a 2D array in a single statement as shown by the third code example. To do that, you use an initialization list that's similar to the initialization list for a 1D array. However, for a 2D array, each row of elements is coded within braces. As a result, this example creates a scores array with three rows where each row contains four elements.

When coding this initialization list, the inner brackets are optional. For instance, you could code the initialization list in this example like this:

```
double scores[rows][cols] =
    {88,87,91,86,93,96,89,95,82,77,79,83};
```

Then, the number of elements in each row is determined by the value in the subscript operator for the row. However, the technique shown in the figure makes your code easier to read.

To process the elements in a two-dimensional array, it's common to use nested loops as shown in the fourth code example. Here, the outer loop uses an index named row to process each row of the array, and the inner loop uses an index named col to process each column within the current row.

In addition to two-dimensional arrays, you can code *multi-dimensional arrays* with 3 dimensions, 4 dimensions, and so on. To do that, you simply code one subscript operator for each dimension. There's no technical limit to the number of dimensions an array can have. As a practical matter, though, an array becomes harder to work with the more dimensions it has.

The last example in this figure shows how to work with an array of C strings. Remember, a C string is an array of chars that has a null terminator. Because of that, an array of C strings is a 2D array. In this example, the first two statements define constants named size and len. The names of these constants should help you think of the 2D array as an array of C strings rather than as a table of data.

After the constants, the third statement initializes the array of C strings. This statement also demonstrates that the inner brackets are optional in an initialization list for a 2D array. Then, a for loop displays the C strings on the console. Notice that this code doesn't use a nested loop. That's because the statement within the loop displays the entire string. However, if you wanted to process the individual characters of the strings, you could use a nested loop to do that.

How to create a two-dimensional array

```
const int rows = 3, cols = 4;
int table[rows][cols];
```

Graphical representation of a two-dimensional array

	col 0	col 1	col 2	col 3
row 0				
row 1				
row 2				

How to access the elements in a two-dimensional array

```
table[0][0] = 89;    // assigns int 89 to first column in first row
table[1][3] = 100;   // assigns int 100 to fourth column in second row
```

How to initialize a two-dimensional array

```
double scores[rows][cols] = {{88,87,91,86}, {93,96,89,95}, {82,77,79,83}};
```

How to process a two-dimensional array with a nested for loop

```
for (int row = 0; row < rows; ++row) {         // process each row
    double total = 0;
    cout << "Student " << (row + 1) << ": ";
    for (int col = 0; col < cols; ++col) {     // process each column
        cout << scores[row][col] << ' ';
        total += scores[row][col];
    }
    cout << "\tAvg score: " << (total / cols) << endl;
}
```

The console

```
Student 1: 88 87 91 86    Avg score: 88
Student 2: 93 96 89 95    Avg score: 93.25
Student 3: 82 77 79 83    Avg score: 80.25
```

A two-dimensional array of C strings

```
const int size = 3;   // array holds three C strings
const int len = 10;   // each C string max 9 chars (plus null terminator)

char medals[size][len] = { "Gold", "Silver", "Bronze" };

for (int i = 0; i < size; ++i) {
    cout << medals[i] << ' ';
}
```

Description

- A *one-dimensional (1D) array* holds one set of data, such as all the test scores for a single student.

- A *two-dimensional (2D) array* holds multiple sets of data, such as all the test scores for multiple students. 2D arrays can be thought of as a *table* of *rows* and *columns*.

- You use two subscripts to access elements in a 2D array and nested loops to iterate them.

- When you use initialization lists, it's best to separate the sets with inner brackets.

- A 2D array of C strings is like a 1D array unless you need to access individual characters.

Figure 12-14   How to work with a two-dimensional array

How to pass a two-dimensional array to a function

Earlier in this chapter, you learned how to pass an array to a function. Now, figure 12-15 shows how to pass a two-dimensional array to a function. This code example begins by defining and initializing global constants named rows and cols to store the number of rows and columns for the 2D array. Then, it declares a prototype for the display_scores() function.

The display_scores() function accepts a 2D array as an argument, and it uses the global constant named cols as the size declarator for the second subscript operator. This size declarator is required and must be specified at compile time. Otherwise, the function won't be able to determine the amount of memory to allocate for each row of the 2D array.

The main() function begins by defining and initializing a 2D array with 3 rows and 4 columns. To do that, this function uses the global rows and cols constants as the size declarators for the number of rows and columns. Here, each row represents a group of scores for a student. Then, this code passes the 2D array to the display_scores() function.

The display_scores() function uses the global constant named cols as the size declarator for the second subscript operator. This shows that both the function declaration and the definition require a size declarator for the second subscript operator. Within this function, the code uses nested loops to display the scores on the console. Since each row of scores is associated with a specific student, the outer loop displays the student number. To do that, it uses the global rows constant for the number of rows. Then, the inner loop displays the scores for the student and accumulates a total of all scores for the student. After the inner loop finishes, the outer loop calculates and displays the average score for the student.

Code that passes a two-dimensional array to a function

```
// global constants
const int rows = 3;
const int cols = 4;

// function declaration
void display_scores(double scores[][cols]);

int main() {
    double scores[rows][cols] = { {88,87,91,86},
                                  {93,96,89,95},
                                  {82,77,79,83} };
    display_scores(scores);
}

// function definition
void display_scores(double scores[][cols]) {
    for (int row = 0; row < rows; ++row) {
        double total = 0;
        cout << "Student " << (row + 1) << ": ";
        for (int col = 0; col < cols; ++col) {
            cout << scores[row][col] << ' ';
            total += scores[row][col];
        }
        cout << "\tAvg score: " << (total / cols) << endl;
    }
}
```

The console

```
Student 1: 88 87 91 86  Avg score: 88
Student 2: 93 96 89 95  Avg score: 93.25
Student 3: 82 77 79 83  Avg score: 80.25
```

Description

- When you code a function parameter that accepts a two-dimensional array, you need to include a size declarator for the second subscript.

- When you code a multi-dimensional array, you need to include a size declarator for every subscript except the first one.

- Any required size declarator must be known at compile time. Because of that, it must be a literal value or a constant. If it's a constant, it should be a global constant so the code that defines the array and the function that accepts the array can both use it.

Figure 12-15   How to pass a two-dimensional array to a function

The Top Five program

Figure 12-16 shows the Top Five program. This program lets a user enter their top five items in a category. It begins by prompting the user to specify a category, in this case, cities. Then, the program accepts five items from the user. Finally, it sorts the items and displays them in alphabetical order.

The code begins with include statements for the header files that the program needs as well as the using directive for the std namespace. Note that this program includes the cstring header that has utility functions for working with C strings.

Next, this code defines a global constant named item_length for the maximum number of characters for the C strings the user will enter. This constant is initialized to a value of 51, which allows for 50 characters plus the null terminator.

After the global constant, this code declares two function prototypes. The alpha_sort() function accepts a two-dimensional array. This 2D array uses the item_length constant as the size declarator for its second subscript. However, since this program doesn't code a constant for the first subscript, the alpha_sort() function also accepts the size of the 2D array (the number of rows) as its second argument.

The reset_stream() function doesn't accept any arguments. It's used to clear the input stream if the user enters more than 50 characters for an item.

The main() function begins by creating a two-dimensional array named list. To do that, it uses a local constant named size and the global constant named item_length.

After creating the 2D array, this code creates a C string named item_type and initializes it with an empty string. Then, it prompts the user to enter a category, and uses the getline() function of the console input stream to get the category and store it in the item_type C string. Next, the reset_stream() function makes sure the input stream is in a good state, even if the user enters too many characters.

After getting the category from the user, this code loops through the 2D array and gets five C strings from the user. Again, this code makes sure to reset the stream if the user enters too many characters. This loop shows that even though an array of C strings is a 2D array, it often behaves like a 1D array.

The console

```
What kind of items are going to be in your list? cities

Please enter your top 5 cities:
#1: Portland
#2: New York
#3: Cologne
#4: Victoria, B.C.
#5: Amsterdam

Your top 5 cities, sorted alphabetically:
---------------------------------------
Amsterdam
Cologne
New York
Portland
Victoria, B.C.
```

The code

```cpp
#include <iostream>
#include <cstring>

using namespace std;

// global constant
const int item_length = 51;

// function declarations
void alpha_sort(char items[][item_length], int size);
void reset_stream();

int main() {
    // create 2D array to hold C strings from user
    const int size = 5;
    char list[size][item_length];

    char item_type[item_length] = "";
    cout << "What kind of items are going to be in your list? ";
    cin.getline(item_type, item_length);
    reset_stream();
    cout << endl;

    // get list from user
    cout << "Please enter your top " << size << " " << item_type << ":\n";
    for (int i = 0; i < size; ++i) {
        cout << "#" << (i + 1) << ": ";
        cin.getline(list[i], item_length);
        reset_stream();
    }
    cout << endl;
```

Figure 12-16   The Top Five program (part 1 of 2)

Part 2 of figure 12-16 begins by passing the 2D array and the local size constant to the alpha_sort() function. Then, it uses a loop to display the sorted C strings on the console.

After the main() function, this code defines the alpha_sort() function. Like the function's declaration, the definition uses the global constant item_length as the size declarator for the second subscript operator.

The body of the alpha_sort() function uses the bubble sort algorithm to sort the C strings in the two-dimensional array named items. This is similar to the bubble sort function presented in figure 12-12. However, since this function works with C strings rather than integers, the temp variable that temporarily stores elements is a C string. In addition, the code uses utility functions from the cstring header to compare and swap the C string elements. Remember, though, that these utility functions don't automatically adjust for the null terminator like the getline() function does. Because of that, this code manually adjusts for the null terminator by subtracting 1 from the item_length global constant.

As you review this code, take a moment to look at how it swaps the elements. To start, it uses the strcmp() function to compare the current element to the next element. Remember, strcmp() returns 1 if the first argument is greater than the second argument. So, this code checks if the current element is greater than the next. If it is, the code executes the body of the if statement.

In the body of the if statement, three code statements use the strncpy() function to swap the current element and the next element. The first statement copies the characters from the current element to the temp variable. The second statement copies the characters from the next element to the current element. And the third statement copies the characters from the temp variable to the next element.

The definition for the reset_stream() function starts by using the fail() function of the standard input stream to check the state of the stream. If the failbit is set, the function clears it and discards any remaining characters in the stream.

The code (continued)

```cpp
        // sort and display the items in the list
        alpha_sort(list, size);
        cout << "Your top " << size << " " << item_type
             << ", sorted " << "alphabetically:\n"
             << "----------------------------------------\n";
        for (int i = 0; i < size; ++i) {
            cout << list[i] << endl;
        }
    }

    // an alphabetical bubble sort
    void alpha_sort(char items[][item_length], int size) {
        bool is_swap;
        char temp[item_length] = "";   // temporary C string
        do {
            is_swap = false;                              // reset flag to false

            for (int i = 0; i < (size - 1); ++i) {  // stop at 2nd to last
                if (strcmp(items[i], items[i + 1]) > 0) {
                    // swap current and next values
                    strncpy(temp, items[i], item_length - 1);
                    strncpy(items[i], items[i + 1], item_length - 1);
                    strncpy(items[i + 1], temp, item_length - 1);

                    // set flag to indicate a swap occurred
                    is_swap = true;
                }
            }
        } while (is_swap); // if a swap occurred, continue loop
    }

    void reset_stream() {
        if (cin.fail()) {
            cin.clear();
            cin.ignore(10000, '\n');
        }
    }
```

Note

- To get this program to compile with Visual Studio, you may need to set the SDL checks property for the project to No as described in figure 12-8.

Figure 12-16   The Top Five program (part 2 of 2)

Perspective

Now that you've completed this chapter, you should have a good idea of how to work with the built-in array, including how to work with C strings. In most cases, you shouldn't need to use built-in arrays or C strings. Still, it's good to understand how they work in case you need to work in a resource constrained environment, or you need to maintain legacy code.

Terms

built-in array	null character
contiguous memory	empty string
index	algorithm
subscript operator	linear search
initialization list	binary search
size declarator	bubble sort
out of bounds access	selection sort
pointer	pointer arithmetic
memory address	one-dimensional (1D) array
array decay	two-dimensional (2D) array
string	table
C string	rows
C-style string	columns
null terminator	multidimensional array

Summary

- A *built-in array* contains a sequence of elements of the same data type. It stores the elements in *contiguous memory*, or consecutive blocks of memory with no gaps.

- Each element in an array has an *index*, where the first element has an index of 0, the second an index of 1, and so on.

- To access an individual element, you use the *subscript operator* ([]) to specify the element's index.

- You can use an *initialization list* to set the starting values of an array.

- When you create an array, you can use a *size declarator* to specify the size of an array.

- Like a vector, an array allows *out of bounds access*. To avoid this, you can use a constant to define the size of an array and use that constant to prevent out of bounds access.

- When you pass an array to a function, C++ converts it to a *pointer* that points to the *memory address* of the first element in the array, not to the value itself. This is known as *array decay*, because information about the array is lost.

- A *string* is a sequence of characters.

- A *C string*, also known as a *C-style string*, is an array of characters that ends with a *null terminator*, also known as a *null character*.

- An *empty string* is a C string whose elements are all initialized with the null terminator.

- An *algorithm* is a specification of how to solve a problem. For example, an algorithm can perform a calculation, process data, or automate reasoning tasks.

- A *linear search* algorithm iterates through the elements in a sequence until it finds the search element.

- A *binary search* algorithm divides the elements in a sequence in half, determines which half the search element is in, and discards the other half. It repeats this process until it finds the search element.

- A *bubble sort* algorithm loops through a sequence repeatedly and swaps adjacent elements until they are in order.

- A *selection sort* algorithm loops through a sequence once and uses an inner loop to move each element directly to its final position.

- After you use array decay to get a pointer to the first element in an array, you can use *pointer arithmetic* to get pointers to other elements in the array.

- A *one-dimensional*, or *1D*, *array* holds one set of data, such as all the test scores for a single student.

- A *two-dimensional*, or *2D*, *array* holds multiples sets of data, such as all the test scores for multiple students. 2D arrays can be thought of as defining a *table* that contains *rows* and *columns*.

- A *multidimensional array* has three or more dimensions. Although there's no limit to the number of dimensions an array can have, arrays with too many dimensions are impractical.

Exercise 12-1 Use an array with a Product Sales program

In this exercise, you'll write the code for a Product Sales program that uses an array to store sales data. When you're done, a test run should look something like this:

```
The Product Sales program

Enter product sales from 0 to 10,000.
To end the program, enter -1.

Enter sales amount: 2756.28
Enter sales amount: 4285.32
Enter sales amount: 3527.58
Enter sales amount: 3897.40
Enter sales amount: -1

Sales count:   4
Sales total:   14466.6
Average sales: 3616.65
```

1. Open the project or solution named product_sales in this folder:
    `ex_starts\ch12_ex1_product_sales`

2. Review the code for this program and then run it to see that it works much like the Test Scores program.

3. Define a constant that can be used as the size declarator for an array that can store up to twelve elements.

4. Replace the vector named sales with an array, and initialize the elements of the array with the default value for a double type.

5. Define a variable named sales_count that can be used to count the number of sales entries, and initialize this variable to 0.

6. Modify the while loop so it won't accept more sales entries than can be stored by the array.

7. Modify the code that's executed for a valid sales entry so the sales amount is stored in the next element in the array and the sales_count variable is increased by one.

8. Modify the code that checks if sales were entered so it works for the modified code.

9. Modify the code that calculates the average sales and displays the number of sales entries so it uses the sales_count variable.

Exercise 12-2   Use C strings with the Word Jumble program

In this exercise, you'll modify the Word Jumble program from chapter 6 so it uses C strings and an array of C strings instead of string objects and a vector.

1. Open the project or solution named word_jumble in this folder:
    `ex_starts\ch12_ex2_word_jumble`

2. Define two constants that can be used as the size declarators for a two-dimensional array. Assign values to these constants so they will accommodate the data that's currently stored in the words vector.

3. Replace the words vector with a two-dimensional array of C strings.

4. Modify the code that gets a random word from the array so the word is stored in a C string. To do that, you can use a loop to assign each character of the randomly selected word from the two-dimensional array to the C string.

5. Modify the code that jumbles the word so the jumbled word is stored in a C string. To do that, you can use the strncpy() function to copy the randomly selected word to the jumbled word.

6. Modify the code that gets the user guesses so the guess is stored in a C string and the strcmp() function is used to compare the guess to the other strings.

Exercise 12-3   Use a two-dimensional array with the Test Scores program

In this exercise, you'll modify the Test Scores program presented in this chapter so it uses a two-dimensional array to store a fixed number of scores for multiple students. When you're done, a test run should look something like this:

```
The Test Scores program

Enter test scores (3 per student, 20 max students.)
Make sure each score is between 0 and 100.
To end the program, enter -1.

Student 1
Enter score: 92
Enter score: 89
Enter score: 95

Student 2
Enter score: 85
Enter score: 88
Enter score: 76

Student 3
Enter score: -1

Student 1: 92 89 95      Avg score: 92
Student 2: 85 88 76      Avg score: 83
```

1. Open the project or solution named test_scores in this folder:
   ex_starts\ch12_ex3_test_scores

2. Modify the code in the main() function so it defines a two-dimensional array that can store scores for up to ten students with three scores per student.

3. Modify the instructions for the program so they indicate the maximum number of students and scores per student.

4. Modify the while loop so it continues until the user enters -1 or until the user enters the maximum number of students. To do that, use a counter variable to count the number of students that have been entered.

5. Within this while loop, add a nested while loop that continues until the user has entered all scores for the student or -1. This nested loop should contain the code that gets the scores for each student, and it should store each score in the appropriate element of the array.

6. Add any additional code for the while loops to work correctly. That includes initializing and incrementing counter variables.

7. Modify the code that checks if any scores have been entered so it checks the counter variable for the number of students.

8. Modify the code that's executed if scores have been entered so it loops through the array for each student that has scores and displays those scores and the average score on the console as shown above.

13

How to work with exceptions

All programs can encounter errors when they run. For example, a user may enter data that's not valid, or a file that your program needs may get moved or deleted. These types of errors may cause a poorly-coded program to crash and cause the user to lose data. In contrast, when an error occurs in a well-coded program, the program notifies the user and attempts to recover from the error. If it can't recover, it saves as much data as possible, cleans up resources, and exits the program as smoothly as possible.

In the old days of programming, handling errors was difficult because programming languages didn't provide a standard way to check for errors, and they didn't provide a standard way to communicate errors to other parts of the program that might need to know about them. To address this problem, most modern programming languages, including C++, provide exceptions. Exceptions allow you to write code that can handle errors more easily and reliably.

How to get started with exceptions

This chapter starts by showing you the basic skills for working with exceptions. But first, to illustrate the need for exceptions, it shows you a function that doesn't use exceptions.

A function that doesn't use exceptions

In the early days of C++, it was a common practice for a function to return an *error code* such as -1 or NULL to signal that an error had occurred. Then, the calling code could check the return value and proceed accordingly. For instance, the first example in figure 13-1 defines a calculate_mpg() function that returns a value of -1.0 to indicate that the calling code passed an invalid argument to the function. That way, the code that calculates the miles per gallon isn't executed. This avoids dividing by zero, which is an illegal mathematical operation that can yield unexpected results.

The second example calls the calculate_mpg() function and passes it an invalid value of 0 for the gallons argument. However, it doesn't check the value that's returned by the function to determine whether an error occurred. Instead, it displays a value of -1 on the console. Although this value indicates that an error occurred, it's possible for some programmers to mistake this value for the result of the calculation.

The third example also calls the calculate_mpg() function and passes it an invalid value of 0 for the gallons argument. In this case, the code checks the value that's returned by the function to determine whether an error occurred. If it did, the code displays an appropriate error message on the console.

Unfortunately, this technique makes it easy for other programmers to use a function incorrectly. That's because the program doesn't crash when an error occurs. Instead, the calling function just gets bad data. As a result, this makes it more likely that the program may just process the bad data instead of handling the error appropriately. However, if the program crashed when the error occurred, the programmer would discover the error during testing and handle it appropriately.

A function that returns -1.0 to signal that an error has occurred

```
double calculate_mpg(double miles, double gallons) {
    if (miles <= 0.0) {
        return -1.0;
    }
    if (gallons <= 0.0) {
        return -1.0;
    }
    double mpg = miles / gallons;
    mpg = round(mpg * 10) / 10;     // round to 1 decimal place
    return mpg;
}
```

Calling code that displays an invalid result

```
double mpg = calculate_mpg(100, 0);
cout << "Miles per gallon: " << mpg << "\n\n";
```

The console

```
Miles per gallon: -1
```

Calling code that uses the return value to check for an error

```
double mpg = calculate_mpg(100, 0);
if (mpg == -1.0) {
    cout << "Error! Unable to calculate miles per gallon\n\n";
} else {
    cout << "Miles per gallon: " << mpg << "\n\n";
}
```

The console

```
Error! Unable to calculate miles per gallon
```

Description

- Before exceptions were available to C++, it was common for a function to signal that an *error* had occurred by returning a value such as -1 or NULL that represented an *error code*. Then, the calling code could check the return value and proceed accordingly. Unfortunately, this practice made it easy for other programmers to use a function incorrectly.

Figure 13-1   A function that doesn't use exceptions

How to throw an exception

In C++, an *exception* is an object that represents an error that has occurred and contains information about the error. In most cases, you create an exception from the exception class or one of its subclasses. All exception classes are derived from the exception class as shown by the diagram in figure 13-2.

The exception class is the most general type of exception because it's the *parent class* of the logic_error and runtime_error classes, which define more specific exceptions. Conversely, the logic_error and runtime_error classes are *child classes* of the exception class, although they are also parent classes of even more specific child classes.

When you're coding a function, you may sometimes need to throw an exception. To do that, you code a throw statement that throws an object of an exception class. To create this object, you code the name of the exception class, followed by a set of parentheses. Within the parentheses, you usually code an error message that's stored within the object. However, this error message is optional.

To illustrate, the calculate_mpg() function shown in this figure throws an exception if the calling code passes it an invalid argument. To start, this function defines two parameters, miles and gallons. Within this function, the code begins by checking whether the miles parameter is less than or equal to 0. If it is, this code creates an exception object from the invalid_argument class. Then, it throws this object to the calling code. After checking the miles parameter, this function uses a similar technique to check the gallons parameter. In general, it's a good coding practice for any function to throw an invalid_argument exception if any of its parameters have unacceptable values.

The hierarchy of predefined exception classes

```
exception
    logic_error
        invalid_argument
        out_of_range
    runtime_error
        range_error
        overflow_error
        underflow_error
```

The syntax for creating an exception object

```
class_name([error_message])
```

The syntax of the throw statement

```
throw exception_object;
```

A function that throws a predefined exception

```
double calculate_mpg(double miles, double gallons) {
    if (miles <= 0.0) {
        throw invalid_argument("Error! Miles must be > 0.");
    }
    if (gallons <= 0.0) {
        throw invalid_argument("Error! Gallons must be > 0.");
    }
    double mpg = miles / gallons;
    mpg = round(mpg * 10) / 10;    // round to 1 decimal place
    return mpg;
}
```

Calling code that passes an invalid argument

```
double mpg = calculate_mpg(100, 0);    // causes the program to crash!
cout << "Miles per gallon: " << mpg << "\n\n";
```

Description

- An *exception* is an object that represents an error that has occurred and contains information about that error. In most cases, you create an exception from one of the classes in the exception hierarchy.

- You use the throw statement to *throw* an exception. You can throw any object, but it usually makes sense to throw objects created from one of the predefined exception classes.

- The predefined exception classes all have a constructor that allows you to specify an error message for the object that you're creating.

- In the hierarchy of the predefined exceptions, the exception class is the *parent class* of the other exception classes. These classes in turn can be referred to as *child classes* of the exception class, but they can also be the parent class of other more specific exception classes.

Figure 13-2   How to throw an exception

How to catch an exception

To *catch* exceptions like the ones thrown by the function in the previous figure, you use a try statement as shown in figure 13-3. As the syntax summary shows, you start by coding a try clause that contains one or more statements that may throw an exception. Then, you code a catch clause that contains one or more statements that should be executed if any statements in the try clause throw an exception.

The first example in this figure shows how to use a try statement to catch the exception that might be thrown by the calculate_mpg() function. Here, the calculate_mpg() function is coded within a try clause, and a catch clause is coded for the exception named invalid_argument. Then, if the miles and gallons variables contain valid values, the calculate_mpg() function returns the result of the calculation, and the next statement displays the result on the console. After that, the program skips over the catch clause and executes the statement after the catch clause that displays "Bye!" on the console.

However, if the miles or gallons variable contains an invalid value, the calculate_mpg() function throws an invalid_argument exception. As a result, program execution skips the second statement in the try clause and executes the statement in the catch clause. In this case, the catch clause just displays the error message that's stored in the exception object. After that, execution continues with the statement after the catch clause that displays "Bye!" on the console.

In this example, the catch clause specifies the invalid_argument exception so it is only executed if that type of exception occurs. By contrast, the second example specifies the exception class. As a result, this catch clause is executed if any exception in the exception hierarchy occurs. Then, the catch clause displays the error message stored in that object.

In general, it's a good practice to code the name of the most specific exception in the catch clause. That way, your code can handle the exception in the way that's best for that particular type of exception. You'll learn more about this in a moment.

In this figure, both catch clauses get the error message that's stored in the exception object by calling the object's what() member function. Both of these catch clauses also provide a name of e for the exception object. That's a common coding convention, but you can specify any name you like for the exception object. In addition, both of these catch clauses define the exception object as a constant reference type. That's generally considered a best practice, although it's also possible to pass the exception object as a value type.

Although the examples in this figure show how to catch exceptions that are thrown by user-defined functions, you should realize that some of the C++ functions also throw exceptions. For example, the at() function of the vector container that you learned about in chapter 6 throws an out_of_range exception if an element doesn't exist at the index that's passed to the function. In some cases, you'll want to catch exceptions thrown by C++ functions by using try statements as shown here. In other cases, though, you'll want to write code that prevents these exceptions from being thrown as shown later in this chapter.

The syntax for a try/catch statement that catches an exception

```
try {
    statements that might throw an exception
}
catch (exception_type object_name) {
    statements that handle the exception
}
```

The what() function that's available from all exception objects

Function	Description
what()	Displays the error message that's stored in the exception object.

How to handle an invalid_argument exception

```
double mpg;
try {
    mpg = calculate_mpg(miles, gallons);
    cout << "Miles per gallon: " << mpg << "\n";
}
catch (const invalid_argument& e) {
    cout << e.what() << "\n";
}
cout << "Bye!\n\n";
```

The console for 100 miles and 4 gallons

```
Miles per gallon: 25.0
Bye!
```

The console for 100 miles and 0 gallons

```
Error! Gallons must be > 0.
Bye!
```

A catch clause that handles all predefined exceptions

```
double mpg;
try {
    mpg = calculate_mpg(miles, gallons);
    cout << "Miles per gallon: " << mpg << "\n";
}
catch (const exception& e) {
    cout << e.what() << "\n";
}
cout << "Bye!\n\n";
```

Description

- In a try statement, you code a try clause that contains any statements that might throw an exception. Then, you code a catch clause that *catches* and handles any exceptions that have been thrown. This is known as *exception handling*.

- If you code the exception class as the exception type in the catch clause, the catch clause catches all types of exceptions that can occur.

- When an exception occurs, C++ skips any remaining statements in the try clause and executes the statements in the catch clause.

Figure 13-3   How to catch an exception

A program that catches exceptions

Figure 13-4 presents another version of the Miles Per Gallon program presented in previous chapters. This version has a calculate_mpg() function that throws an exception if the user enters an invalid value for miles or gallons. Then, the code in the main() function handles these exceptions.

The console shows how the program handles invalid user input. If the user enters an invalid amount for miles or gallons, such as 0 or -100, the program displays an appropriate error message and exits the program. However, if the user enters valid amounts for miles and gallons, the program displays the miles per gallon.

Because the code for this program is mostly the same as the Miles Per Gallon program presented in chapter 7, this figure highlights the code that has been added to handle exceptions. To start, the calculate_mpg() function throws an invalid_argument exception that contains an appropriate message if the calling code passes an invalid value to either of its arguments. Then, the statement that calls the calculate_mpg() function in the main() function is coded within a try clause, and the catch clause catches and handles any invalid_argument exceptions that have been thrown.

For this program, the code handles the exception by displaying its error message on the console and allowing the program to exit normally. Alternately, you might want to handle this exception by giving the user another chance to enter valid data as shown in the next figure.

The console

```
The Miles Per Gallon program

Enter miles:      100
Enter gallons:    0
Error! Gallons must be > 0.

Bye!
```

The code

```cpp
#include <iostream>
#include <cmath>

using namespace std;

void display_title() {
    cout << "Miles Per Gallon Calculator\n\n";
}

double calculate_mpg(double miles, double gallons) {
    if (miles <= 0.0) {
        throw invalid_argument("Error! Miles must be > 0.");
    }
    if (gallons <= 0.0) {
        throw invalid_argument("Error! Gallons must be > 0.");
    }
    double mpg = miles / gallons;
    mpg = round(mpg * 10) / 10;     // round to 1 decimal place
    return mpg;
}

int main() {
    display_title();

    double miles;
    cout << "Enter miles driven:       ";
    cin >> miles;

    double gallons;
    cout << "Enter gallons of gas used: ";
    cin >> gallons;

    double mpg;
    try {
        mpg = calculate_mpg(miles, gallons);
        cout << "Miles per gallon:        " << mpg << "\n\n";
    }
    catch (const invalid_argument& e) {
        cout << e.what() << "\n\n";
    }
    cout << "Bye!\n\n";
    return 0;
}
```

Figure 13-4   A program that catches exceptions

A program that prevents exceptions from being thrown

Figure 13-5 presents another version of the Miles Per Gallon program shown in the previous figure. This version prevents the calculate_mpg() function from throwing any exceptions. To do that, the main() function uses the get_double() function of the console namespace presented in chapter 7 to always get double values that are greater than 0.0. This improves the efficiency of the code, and it provides better functionality by continuing to prompt the user for a valid number until the user enters one.

At this point, you may be wondering why the calculate_mpg() function needs to contain code that throws these exceptions. After all, doesn't the main() function prevent these exceptions from being thrown? The reason is that the code in the calculate_mpg() function that throws these exceptions makes sure that the program always passes valid data to this function. So, if the program is later modified so it's possible for invalid data to be passed to this function, the program will crash because the exceptions aren't caught. Then, when the program is tested and it crashes, it will be obvious that the code needs to be fixed.

In other words, when you're testing and debugging a program, it's good for a function to throw an exception if it encounters a situation it can't handle. At first, this may cause the program to crash when you test it. But, that's good because it makes it obvious what's causing the problem. At that point, you can modify the calling code to fix the problem. Ideally, you can modify the calling code so the exception is never thrown. However, there are times when it will be necessary for you to use a try statement to catch the exception and handle it.

The console

```
Miles Per Gallon Calculator

Enter miles driven:          0
Error! Number must be greater than 0. Try again.
Enter miles driven:          10
Enter gallons of gas used: -5
Error! Number must be greater than 0. Try again.
Enter gallons of gas used: 2
Miles per gallon:            5

Bye!
```

The code

```cpp
#include <iostream>
#include <cmath>
#include "console.h"       // the console namespace from chapter 7

using namespace std;

void display_title() {
    cout << "Miles Per Gallon Calculator\n\n";
}

double calculate_mpg(double miles, double gallons) {
    if (miles <= 0.0) {
        throw invalid_argument("Error! Miles must be > 0.");
    }
    if (gallons <= 0.0) {
        throw invalid_argument("Error! Gallons must be > 0.");
    }
    double mpg = miles / gallons;
    mpg = round(mpg * 10) / 10;     // round to 1 decimal place
    return mpg;
}

int main() {
    display_title();

    // use console namespace to get valid values
    double miles =
        console::get_double("Enter miles driven:          ", 0.0);
    double gallons =
        console::get_double("Enter gallons of gas used: ", 0.0);

    // calculate and display mpg
    double mpg = calculate_mpg(miles, gallons);
    cout << "Miles per gallon:            " << mpg << "\n\n";

    // exit program
    cout << "Bye!\n\n";
    return 0;
}
```

Figure 13-5   A program that prevents exceptions from being thrown

More skills for working with exceptions

So far, this chapter has presented the skills for working with exceptions that you'll use most of the time. Now, the topics that follow present some more exception handling skills that you may need now and then. Then, this chapter finishes by presenting some conceptual information that should help you visualize how exception handling works with C++.

How to catch multiple exceptions

When the code in a try clause can throw multiple types of exceptions, you may want to code a try statement with a catch clause for each type of exception. That way, you can handle each type of exception in an appropriate way.

Figure 13-6 shows how to code a try statement with multiple catch clauses. When you do that, the catch clauses must be coded in sequence from the most specific exception to the most general exception. For instance, the example shown here assumes that the try clause contains code that could throw an invalid_argument exception or a runtime_error exception. As a result, the first two catch clauses are coded for these types of exceptions. Then, the third catch clause is coded for any other exceptions in the exception hierarchy that aren't caught by the first two clauses.

Note that the sequence of exceptions applies only when the exceptions are in the same branch of the exception hierarchy. If you look back to figure 13-2, for example, you'll see that the invalid_argument exception and the runtime_error exception are from different branches of the exception hierarchy. Because of that, you could code the catch clause for the runtime_error exception in this example before the catch clause for the invalid_argument exception.

In this example, the code just displays a different message for each type of exception. However, the code in a catch clause could do more than that. In some cases, for example, you might want to save as much data as possible and shut down the program as smoothly as possible.

Keep in mind that some exceptions are caused by programming errors like attempting to use an invalid index to access an item in a vector. Although this type of coding error can cause exceptions, you don't usually want to handle these exceptions with try statements. Instead, you should fix your code to prevent these exceptions from occurring in the first place.

The syntax for a try statement with multiple catch clauses

```
try {
    statements that might throw an exception
}
catch (most_specific_exception object_name) {
    statements that handle the most specific exception type
}
[catch (less_specific_exception object_name) {
    statements that handle a less specific exception type
}]...
```

Code that throws different types of predefined exception objects

```
throw invalid_argument("Miles must be > 0.");
throw runtime_error();
throw exception();
```

Code that handles multiple predefined exceptions

```
try {
    // statements that might throw predefined exceptions
}
catch (const invalid_argument& e) {
    cout << "Invalid argument!\n\n";
}
catch (const runtime_error& e) {
    cout << "An unexpected runtime error occurred!\n\n";
}
catch (const exception& e) {
    cout << "An unexpected exception occurred.\n\n";
}
```

The console when an invalid_argument exception occurs

```
Invalid argument!
```

The console when a runtime_error occurs

```
An unexpected runtime error occurred!
```

The console when any other type of predefined exception occurs

```
An unexpected exception occurred!
```

Description

- When a try statement includes multiple catch clauses, the clauses for exceptions within the same branch of the exception hierarchy must be coded in sequence starting with the most specific exception and ending with the least specific exception.

Figure 13-6   How to catch multiple exceptions

How to rethrow an exception

In some situations, you may need or want to code a catch clause that catches an exception, performs some processing for that exception, and *rethrows* the exception. To rethrow an exception, you can just code a throw statement in a catch clause without specifying the exception object's name, as shown by the syntax presented at the top of figure 13-7.

To illustrate, the first example shows a load_temps() function that throws an exception if its code isn't able to open the file with the specified filename. For this example, you can assume that the filename is specified as a global constant. If the code that calls this function is coded correctly, the function should be able to open the file. However, it's always possible that the file was moved or deleted. In that case, the code throws a runtime_error exception that can be handled by the calling code.

The second example shows a load_temps_with_check() function that calls the load_temps() function. If this doesn't cause a runtime_error exception, this code displays a message that indicates that the temperatures have been loaded. However, if this causes a runtime_error exception, the catch clause processes the exception.

In this case, the code begins by displaying the error message from the runtime_error exception that indicates that the code wasn't able to open the file. It also displays a message that the code wasn't able to load the temperatures. Then, it asks if the user would like to create a new file. If so, the code allows the user to add new temperatures. Then, a file with a name that's specified by the program could be created, and the temperatures the user enters could be stored in that file.

If the user doesn't want to create a new file, the code displays a message that contains information that's intended to help the user locate the file. Then, this code rethrows the exception.

Although this code illustrates how to rethrow an exception, you might wonder why you would code two separate functions like this instead of just a single function. After all, if you did that, you wouldn't need to rethrow the exception. The reason for coding two functions is that it allows you to separate the code that loads the data from the code that works with the console. That means that you could use the load_temps() function in a console program as shown here or in a GUI program, which makes this function more flexible. In fact, this function might even be coded in a separate header file that only contains functions for working with the data of the program.

The syntax for rethrowing an exception

```
catch (exception_type object_name) {
    // code that performs some processing on the exception
    throw;   // rethrow the exception
}
```

A function that throws an exception

```
void load_temps(vector<double>& low_temps,
    vector<double>& high_temps) {
    double low, high;
    ifstream input_file(filename);
    if (input_file) {
        while (input_file >> low >> high) {
            low_temps.push_back(low);
            high_temps.push_back(high);
        }
        input_file.close();
    }
    else {
        throw runtime_error("Error! Unable to open file: " + filename);
    }
}
```

A function that rethrows an exception

```
void load_temps_with_check(vector<double>& low_temps,
    vector<double>& high_temps) {
    try {
        load_temps(low_temps, high_temps);
        cout << "Temperatures have been loaded.\n\n";
    }
    catch (const runtime_error& e) {
        cout << e.what() << endl;
        cout << "Unable to load temperatures from file.\n";

        char choice;
        cout << "Would you like to create a new file? (y/n): ";
        cin >> choice;
        cout << endl;

        if (choice == 'y') {
            cout << "OK. You can add temperatures now.\n";
        }
        else {
            cout << "Please make sure the file exists and try again.\n"
                 << "You may need to specify a full path to file.\n";
            throw;
        }
    }
}
```

Description

- In some situations, you may need or want to code a catch clause that catches an exception, performs some processing for that exception, and *rethrows* the exception.

Figure 13-7   How to rethrow an exception

The Temperature Manager program

Figure 13-8 presents another version of the Temperature Manager program presented in chapter 7. This version handles the exceptions that may occur if the program isn't able to read the file that stores the data.

Because the code for this program is mostly the same as the Temperature Manager program from chapter 7, this figure highlights the code in the main() function that has changed. Here, a try statement has been added, and the load_temps_with_check() function from the previous figure is called within the try clause of this statement to load the temperatures. Remember that this function calls the load_temps() function from the previous figure, and that function might throw a runtime_error exception. Because of that, the try statement includes a catch clause that catches this exception.

If the load_temps() function is able to open the file and load the temperatures, it doesn't throw an exception. Then, the load_temps_with_check() function displays a message that indicates that the temperatures have been loaded, as shown by the first console in this figure.

However, if the load_temps() function isn't able to open the file and load the temperatures, it throws a runtime_error exception. Then, the load_temps_with_check() function catches this exception and displays two error messages. These error messages are followed by a prompt that asks whether the user wants to create a new file. This is shown by the second console.

If the user wants to create a new file, this code displays a message that indicates that the user can add new temperatures. Then, the code continues by displaying a command prompt that allows the user to enter a command from the menu.

But if the user doesn't want to create a new file, this code displays a message that attempts to help the user find the file. Then, it rethrows the exception to the main() function, and that exception is handled by the catch clause. Since the program can't work correctly if it can't write to a file to store its data, the catch clause displays a message that says "Bye!" and uses a return statement to exit the program normally.

At this point, the user could attempt to find the missing temps.txt file and move it to the correct directory. During development, this is typically the directory that contains the source code for the program. On some systems, though, it may be the directory that stores the executable file for the program. That's the case, for example, if you're using Xcode.

The console for no exceptions

```
The Temperature Manager program

COMMANDS
v - View temperatures
a - Add temperatures
r - Remove temperatures
x - Exit

Temperatures have been loaded.

Command:
```

The console if load_temps() throws an exception

```
The Temperature Manager program

COMMANDS
v - View temperatures
a - Add temperatures
r - Remove temperatures
x - Exit

Error! Unable to open file: temps.txt
Unable to load temperatures from file.
Would you like to create a new file? (y/n): n

Please make sure the file exists and try again.
You may need to specify a full path to this file.
Bye!
```

The code for the main() function

```cpp
int main()
{
    cout << "The Temperature Manager program\n\n";

    display_menu();

    // get temps from file
    vector<double> low_temps, high_temps;
    try {
        load_temps_with_check(low_temps, high_temps); // from fig 13-7
    }
    catch (runtime_error e) {
        cout << "Bye!\n\n";
        return 0;
    }

    // the rest of the code for the main() function
    ...
    ...
}
```

Figure 13-8   The Temperature Manager program

How to work with custom exceptions

Although the C++ standard library provides some predefined exceptions, you may encounter a situation where none of those exceptions describe your exception accurately. In that case, you can code a structure that defines a custom exception, create an object from it, and throw it as described in figure 13-9.

The first example shows that C++ allows any object to be an exception object. Here, the code throws a string object that's created from the string class of the standard library. Although this is allowable, it's not considered a good practice since the name of the class doesn't accurately describe the type of exception.

The second example shows how to use a structure to create a custom exception. This structure has a name of NegativeGallons that clearly identifies the type of the exception. In addition, it has a data member that stores an error message and another data member that stores the number of gallons that caused the exception.

The third example shows code that creates and throws a NegativeGallons exception. Here, the code checks if the number of gallons is less than zero. If it is, the code creates a NegativeGallons object named error. Then, it sets the error message and the number of gallons in the exception object. Finally, it throws the exception object to the calling code.

This figure also shows the syntax for a catch clause that catches all exceptions, even if they aren't part of the predefined exception hierarchy. To do that, you can code a catch clause that has three dots within its parentheses.

When you code this type of catch clause, it catches all exceptions, including system errors that can cause the environment to become unstable. As a result, it's generally considered a good practice to rethrow the exception after you process it, as shown by the fourth example. Here, the code displays a message to the console indicating that an unexpected error occurred. Then, it rethrows the exception to the calling code.

The fourth example also shows how to catch the string and NegativeGallons objects that were thrown by the first and third examples. Here, the catch clause for the string object just displays the string on the console. That's all that's needed since the exception object is a string.

However, the catch clause for the NegativeGallons object begins by displaying the message that's stored in the exception object. Then, it displays the number of gallons that caused the exception to be thrown. In some cases, this extra information can be helpful in determining the cause of the exception.

Code that throws a string object

```
throw string("Error! Gallons must be > 0.");
```

Code that defines a custom exception object

```
struct NegativeGallons {
    string message;
    double gallons;
};
```

Code that creates a custom exception object and throws it

```
if (gallons < 0) {
    NegativeGallons error;                              // create object
    error.message = "Error! Gallons must be > 0.";  // set message
    error.gallons = gallons;                            // set gallons
    throw error;                                        // throw object
}
```

The syntax for a catch clause that catches all exceptions

```
catch (...) {
    statements that handle all exceptions (predefined and custom)
}
```

Code that handles multiple custom exceptions

```
try {
    // statements that might throw custom exceptions
}
catch (const string& message) {
    cout << message << "\n\n";
}
catch (const NegativeGallons& e) {
    cout << e.message << "\n"
         << "You entered: " << e.gallons << "\n\n";
}
catch (...) {
    cout << "An unexpected exception occurred!\n\n";
    throw;
}
```

The console when the string object is thrown

```
Error! Gallons must be > 0.
```

The console when the NegativeGallons object contains -1 gallons

```
Error! Gallons must be > 0.
You entered: -1
```

The console when any other type of exception is thrown

```
An unexpected exception occurred!
```

Description

- To catch all exceptions, even if they aren't part of the predefined exception hierarchy, you can code a catch clause with three dots within the parentheses.

Figure 13-9   How to work with custom exceptions

504 Section 2 More skills as you need them

How exception handling works

Figure 13-10 shows how the exception handling mechanism works in C++. To start, when a function encounters a problem that it can't handle, it throws an exception. Once a function throws an exception, the runtime system begins looking for a function that can handle the exception. To do that, it searches through the *call stack*, which is the list of functions that have been called in the reverse order that they were called. In this figure, for example, when the code in functionC() executes, the call stack is functionC(), functionB(), functionA(), and main().

This figure shows that the main() function calls functionA(), which calls functionB(), which calls functionC(). Here, functionC() may throw an exception. If it does, the exception is thrown up the call stack to functionB(), which passes it to functionA(), which passes it to the main() function, which catches it. If you throw an exception and it isn't caught by any other functions in the call stack, including the main() function, the program crashes. Then, information about the exception is typically displayed on the console.

The call stack after four functions have been called

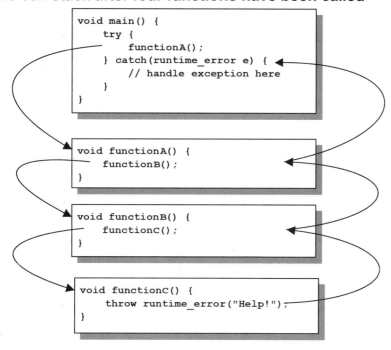

Description

- The *call stack* lists the functions that have been called in reverse order.
- When a function encounters a condition it can't handle, it should throw an exception. This allows other programmers to handle the exception in a way that's appropriate for their programs.
- When a function calls another function that may throw an exception, the function can catch the exception and handle it, or it can allow the exception to continue further up the stack trace.
- When an exception is thrown, the runtime system looks through the call stack until it finds a function that catches and handles the exception.
- If an exception is thrown and isn't caught and handled somewhere in the program, the runtime system aborts execution of the program. This causes the program to crash.

Figure 13-10   How exception handling works

Perspective

In this chapter, you have learned some of the best practices for handling exceptions in C++. As a result, you should now be able to write code that handles exceptions so your programs don't crash. And that's what you need to do in a professional program.

At this point, you're ready to read section 3 to learn how to develop object-oriented programs. When you're done with that section, you'll have a better understanding of how an exception class defines an exception object and how the hierarchy of exception classes works. In addition, you'll learn how to define a custom exception class by inheriting one of the classes in the exception hierarchy. In most cases, that's preferable to using a structure to define an exception as shown in this chapter.

Terms

error	throw an exception
error code	catch an exception
exception	exception handling
parent class	rethrow an exception
child class	call stack

Summary

- In the early days of C++, it was a common practice for a function to signal that an *error* had occurred by returning an *error code* such as -1 or NULL.

- An *exception* is an object that represents an error that has occurred and contains information about that error. In most cases, you create an exception from one of the classes in the exception hierarchy.

- In the hierarchy of predefined exceptions, the exception class is the *parent class* of the other exception classes. These classes can be referred to as *child classes* of the exception class, but they can also be the parent class of other child classes.

- You can use the throw statement to *throw* an exception object.

- In a try statement, you code a try clause that contains any statements that might throw an exception. Then, you code a catch clause that *catches* and handles any exceptions that have been thrown. This is known as *exception handling*.

- Sometimes, you need to code a catch clause that catches an exception, performs some processing for that exception, and *rethrows* the exception.

- The *call stack* lists the functions that have been called in reverse order. When an exception is thrown, the runtime system looks through the call stack until it finds a function that catches and handles the exception.

Exercise 13-1 Add exception handling to the Convert Temperatures program

In this exercise, you'll add exception handling to the Convert Temperatures program from chapter 7. When you're done, a test run should look something like this if the user enters an invalid temperature:

```
Convert Temperatures

MENU
1. Fahrenheit to Celsius
2. Celsius to Fahrenheit

Enter a menu option: 1
Enter degrees Fahrenheit: 0
Error! Temperature must be from 32 to 212.

Convert another temperature? (y/n):
```

1. Open the project or solution named temperature_converter in this folder:
    ex_starts\ch13_ex1_temperature_converter

2. Modify the to_celsius() function so an invalid argument is thrown if the temperature is less than 32 (the freezing point of water) or greater than 212 (the boiling point of water).

3. Modify the to_fahrenheit() function so an invalid argument is thrown if the temperature is less than 0 or greater than 100.

4. Modify the convert_temp() function so it catches the exceptions thrown by the to_celsius() and to_fahrenheit() functions. The code that handles the exceptions should simply display the message that's stored in the exception object.

Exercise 13-2   Add a custom exception to the Word Counter program

In this exercise, you'll add a custom exception to another version of the Word Counter program from chapter 10 that accepts a filename from the user. When you're done, a test run should look something like this when the file the user enters isn't found:

```
The Word Counter program

Enter a file name: dicken.txt
File not found.
You entered: dicken.txt.
Exiting program...
```

1. Open the project or solution named word_counter in this folder:
    ex_starts\ch13_ex2_word_counter

2. Define a structure named FileNotFound with data members that can store an error message and a filename.

3. Modify the load_words() function so the vector of words is returned only if the file is found.

4. Add code to the load_words() function that's executed if the file isn't found. This code should create a FileNotFound object, assign values to its members, and then throw the object.

5. Add a try statement to the main() function so the try clause contains the statement that calls the load_words() function. For this to work, you will need to define the words vector before the try statement so it can be used by the code after the try statement.

6. Code a catch clause that catches and handles a FileNotFound exception. This code should end by exiting the program.

7. Code another catch clause that catches and handles any other exceptions that might occur. This code should end by throwing the exception.

Section 3

Object-oriented programming

So far in this book, you have learned how to create objects from the classes that are available from the C++ standard library, like the string and vector classes. In addition, you have learned how to organize your programs into a series of functions that process the data of your program. This is known as *procedural programming*.

In the next three chapters, you'll learn how to define your own classes and use objects created from those classes. This allows you to group the data for your programs and the procedures for operating on that data into an object. This is known as *object-oriented programming*, and it can speed the development of large programs and make your code more reusable.

To start, chapter 14 presents the basic skills for defining and using classes. That includes using the fundamental concept of encapsulation. Then, chapter 15 shows you how to work with two more fundamental concepts of object-oriented programming: inheritance and polymorphism. Finally, chapter 16 presents some additional object-oriented programming skills, including how to work with static members and functions and how to overload operators.

Because chapter 14 presents the basic skills for using object-oriented programming, it's a prerequisite to chapters 15 and 16. However, chapters 15 and 16 aren't prerequisites for the chapters in section 4. If you want to, then, you can go on to the chapters in section 4 after reading chapter 14. But, at some point, you'll want to be sure to read chapters 15 and 16 because they present critical object-oriented programming skills.

14

How to define classes

In this chapter, you'll learn the basic skills for defining your own classes. In addition, you'll learn how to create objects from those classes and use them in your programs. As you'll see, this works the same as creating and using objects from the classes provided by C++.

An introduction to object-oriented programming

When you use *object-oriented programming (OOP)*, you group related variables and functions into *data structures* called *objects*. In chapter 9, for example, you learned how to define structures that use *data members* to store the data of an object. In addition, you learned how to code *member functions* that work with the data members of an object.

A Movie structure that doesn't provide encapsulation

To review how structures work, figure 14-1 starts by presenting a structure that defines a Movie object that has two data members: the title of the movie and the year that the movie was made. In addition, it includes a member function named equals() that compares the current Movie object with another Movie object and returns a Boolean value that indicates whether the two objects store the same data.

The example that follows creates a Movie object from the structure and then uses that object. The first statement creates the Movie object. Then, the second and third statements access the data members of the Movie object directly to set the title and year in the object. And the fourth statement accesses the data members directly to get the title and year from the Movie object and display them on the console.

This is a good way to get started with object-oriented programming, and it's an approach that's adequate for many programs. Unfortunately, this approach can allow other programmers to use the objects that you define in ways that may cause them to not work properly. In addition, it can make it more difficult for other programmers to figure out how to use your objects, which makes your objects less user-friendly and reusable. If you encounter these types of problems, you can use *encapsulation* to control access to your data members. This allows you to hide the data members of an object from other code that uses the object, which is known as *data hiding*.

To provide encapsulation, you typically use a class as shown in the next figure. A *class* can be thought of as a blueprint from which objects are created. Like a structure, a class provides data members and member functions. However, the members and functions of a class can't be accessed directly by default. This allows you to control access to these members.

When working with object-oriented code, you're likely to encounter a wide range of terminology. For example, programmers often say that an object is an instance of a class or structure. That means that you can create multiple objects from a single class or structure. The process of creating an object from a class or structure is sometimes called *instantiation*. Once you create an object, the object has an *identity* (a unique address), a *state* (the data that it stores), and *behavior* (the functions that it provides). As a program runs, an object's state may change.

A Movie structure

```
struct Movie {
    string title = "";              // data member
    int year = 0;                   // data member
    bool equals(const Movie&);      // member function declaration
};

// member function definition
bool Movie::equals(const Movie& to_compare) {
    return (title == to_compare.title && year == to_compare.year);
}
```

Code that creates an object from the Movie structure and uses it

```
Movie movie;                                // create Movie object
movie.title = "Roundhay Garden Scene";      // set title
movie.year = 1776                           // set year - invalid - too old

cout << "MOVIE DATA\n"
     << "Title: " << movie.title << endl    // get title
     << "Year:  " << movie.year << endl;    // get year
```

The console

```
MOVIE DATA
Title: Roundhay Garden Scene
Year:   1776
```

Description

- *Object-oriented programming* (*OOP*) groups related variables and functions into *data structures* called *objects*.

- A *structure* can be thought of as a blueprint from which objects are created.

- The *data members* of a structure store the data of an object.

- The *member functions* of a structure define the tasks that an object can perform. Often, these functions provide a way to work with the data members of an object.

- Once you create an object from a structure, the object has an *identity* (a unique address), a *state* (the data that it stores), and *behavior* (the functions that it provides). As a program runs, an object's state may change.

- An object is an *instance* of a structure. In other words, you can create multiple objects from a single structure. The process of creating an object from a structure is sometimes called *instantiation*.

- *Encapsulation* allows you to hide the members of an object from other code that uses the object. This is also known as *data hiding*.

- Like a structure, a *class* defines the data members and member functions of an object. However, by default, the members of a class can't be accessed from outside the class. As a result, classes are typically used to provide encapsulation.

- Structures work fine for most purposes, but allowing direct access to members can sometimes lead to problems. To prevent these problems, you can use classes to provide encapsulation as shown in the next figure.

Figure 14-1   A Movie structure that doesn't provide encapsulation

A Movie class that provides encapsulation

Figure 14-2 shows a Movie class that stores the same data as the Movie structure presented in the previous figure. However, this Movie class prevents direct access to its data members. This is known as encapsulation, and it's generally considered a good practice.

To start, the Movie class defines the title and year data members in a private section. This prevents code outside the class from directly accessing these data members. Instead, the Movie class provides four public member functions that allow other code to get and set the values of these two data members.

These four member functions, along with the equals member function, provide the *interface* that programmers can use to work with a Movie object. This allows programmers to use a Movie object correctly without understanding its internal code. For example, the set_year() function checks the year parameter to make sure that it's greater than or equal to 1888, because that's the year that the first movie was made. If the year is less than 1888, this code throws an exception. This forces the programmer to handle this exception. One way to do that is to modify the calling code so it doesn't pass invalid values to the Movie object.

The example that follows shows code that creates an object from the Movie class and then uses that object. Here, the first statement creates a Movie object. Then, the second and third statements uses the object's set_title() and set_year() functions to set the title and the year. And the fourth statement uses the object's get_title() and get_year() functions to get the title and the year. Note that this code can't directly access the title or year data members since they're private. Similarly, if this code passed an invalid year such as 1776 to the set_year() function, that function would throw an exception.

If the interface of an object remains the same, a programmer can change the source code that implements the object without needing to change or recompile any of the code that uses the object. For example, let's say you want to modify the set_title() function so it only allows titles that have less than 120 characters. To do that, you could modify the code for the body of the set_title() function, and you wouldn't need to change any of the code for working with the object. On the other hand, if the Movie class provided direct access to the title member, you wouldn't be able to add validation code like this.

Now that you've seen both a structure and a class, you should realize that the only difference between the two is that the members of a structure are public by default, and the members of a class are private by default. As a result, structures are typically used when you don't need to provide encapsulation, and classes are typically used when you do need to provide encapsulation. However, you can declare private and public sections like the ones shown in this figure in either a structure or a class. In fact, the code in this figure would work exactly the same if it used a structure instead of a class.

A Movie class

```cpp
class Movie {
private:                            // data members are private
    string title = "";
    int year = 0;
public:                            // member functions are public
    void set_title(string);
    string get_title();
    void set_year(int);
    int get_year();
    bool equals(const Movie&);
};

// member function definitions
void Movie::set_title(string title_param) {
    title = title_param;
}
string Movie::get_title() {
    return title;
}

void Movie::set_year(int year_param) {
    if (year_param < 1888) {
        throw invalid_argument("Year must be 1888 or later.");
    }
    year = year_param;
}
int Movie::get_year() {
    return year;
}

bool Movie::equals(const Movie& to_compare) {
    return (title == to_compare.title && year == to_compare.year);
}
```

Code that creates an object from the Movie class and uses it

```cpp
Movie movie;
movie.set_title("Roundhay Garden Scene"); // set title
// movie.year = 1776;                      // illegal - no direct access
// movie.set_year(1776);                   // invalid - throws exception
movie.set_year(1888);                      // set year

cout << "MOVIE DATA\n"
    << "Title: " << movie.get_title() << endl    // get title
    << "Year:  " << movie.get_year() << endl;    // get year
```

Description

- An *interface* allows a programmer to use an object without understanding its internal code.
- If the interface for an object remains the same, a programmer can change the source code that implements the object without needing to change or recompile any of the code that uses the object.

Figure 14-2   A Movie class that provides encapsulation

How to define private data members

Figure 14-3 shows how to define the private data members of a class. As you know, the data members of a class are private by default, which means that they can be used only within the class that defines them. In the two examples in this figure, for instance, the title and year data members can only be accessed by code within the Movie class.

Notice that the first example doesn't use the private keyword to define a private section at the beginning of the class. That's because a class starts with a private section by default. As a result, defining a private section here is optional. However, many programmers consider it a good practice to explicitly define a private section at the beginning of a class to improve the readability of the code.

After defining the private data members, the first example uses the public keyword to define a public section that contains the declarations for the five data members of the class. That means that the member functions can be called by code outside of the Movie class. As a result, these member functions provide an indirect way to access the data members, which is often what you want.

The second example shows that it's possible to code a class that starts with a public section and ends with a private section. Some programmers prefer this approach because the interface that's exposed by the class is listed first, followed by the data members that are hidden by the class.

It's also possible to alternate between private and public sections. However, this makes it more difficult for other programmers to determine which members are private and which are public. In general, then, this isn't considered a good practice.

The syntax for defining private and public members

```
class ClassName {
[private:]
    // private members go here

public:
    // public members go here

[private:
    // you can also code private members here]
};
```

A class that places all private members before public members

```
class Movie {
    string title;              // private members
    int year;
public:                        // public members
    void set_title(string);
    string get_title();
    void set_year(int);
    int get_year();
    bool equals(const Movie&);
};
```

A class that places all public members before private members

```
class Movie {
public:                        // public members
    void set_title(string);
    string get_title();
    void set_year(int);
    int get_year();
    bool equals(const Movie&);
private:                       // private members
    string title;
    int year;
};
```

Description

- To prevent the calling code from directly accessing a data member, define it in a private section of the class. Then, if you want, you can code public member functions that provide indirect access to the data member.

- To allow the calling code to directly access a data member, define it in a public section of the class.

- By default, the members of a class are private until the public keyword is coded. As a result, you don't need to code the private keyword at the beginning of a class. However, it's generally considered a good practice to include this keyword to clearly identify all private members.

Figure 14-3   How to define private data members

How to define getter and setter functions

Figure 14-4 shows how to code the definitions for the member functions that get and set the data members of a class. This is similar to the way you code any function. However, you must code the name of the class followed by the scope resolution operator (::) just before the name of the function. In this figure, for example, the Movie class and the scope resolution operator are coded for all four functions.

Since a function name should describe the action that the function performs, it's a common coding practice to start each function name with a verb. For example, functions that set the value of a data member usually begin with set and are known as *setters*. And, because they change the data that's stored in an object, they're also known as *mutators*. Conversely, functions that return the value of a data member usually begin with get and are known as *getters*. Because they let you access the values of data members, they're also known as *accessors*.

When you code getter and setter functions, you can access private data members just by coding their names. In the first example, for instance, the set_title() function sets the data member named title to the value that's stored in the parameter named title_param.

The exception is if a setter function has a parameter with the same name as a data member. Then, you can identify the data member by prefixing it with the *this* keyword and using the member access operator (->), as shown in the second example. This works because the *this* keyword provides a pointer to the current object, and the member access operator allows you to access data members from the pointer. In general, this approach isn't considered a good practice because forgetting to prefix the data member name with the *this* keyword and member access operator can lead to an error that isn't detected by the compiler.

The third example is for the set_year() function. It works like the first example, but it includes code that makes sure the calling code passes a valid argument. To start, the code for this function checks if the year parameter is less than 1888, which is the year the first movie was made. If it is, the code throws an exception that indicates that the year must be 1888 or later. When coding setters, it's typical to include validation code like this. This technique makes sure that any code that uses your object passes it valid data or handles the exception that's thrown.

When you code a getter function, it's considered a good practice to include the const keyword after the function's parentheses as shown by the fourth and fifth examples. This defines the function as a constant function, which means that the function can't modify any data members of the class. In general, that's considered a best practice since getter functions should only get data, not modify data. For this to work, you must code the const keyword in both the declaration and the definition.

The sixth example shows some code that creates a Movie object and then calls these functions. By now, you shouldn't have any trouble understanding how this code works.

A setter function

```
void Movie::set_title(string title_param) {
    title = title_param;
}
```

Another way to code this setter function

```
void Movie::set_title(string title) {
    this->title = title;
}
```

A setter function that validates data

```
void Movie::set_year(int year_param) {
    if (year_param < 1888) {
        throw invalid_argument("Year must be 1888 or later.");
    }
    year = year_param;
}
```

A getter function that returns a string

```
string Movie::get_title() const {
    return title;
}
```

A getter function that returns an int value

```
int Movie::get_year() const {
    return year;
}
```

Code that calls these functions

```
Movie movie;
movie.set_title("Roundhay Garden Scene");
movie.set_year(1888);
string title = movie.get_title();
int year = movie.get_year();
```

Description

- When you name a function, you should start each name with a verb. It's a common coding practice to use the verb *set* for functions that set the values of data members and to use the verb *get* for functions that return the values of data members.

- Functions that access the value stored in a data member are commonly referred to as *getters* or *accessors*.

- Functions that change the value stored in a data member are commonly referred to as *setters* or *mutators*.

- When you code a getter function, it's considered a good practice to include the const keyword after the function's parentheses. You must do this in both the declaration and the definition.

- When you code functions, you can access private data members just by coding their names. However, if a setter function has a parameter with the same name as a data member, you can identify the data member by prefixing it with the *this* keyword and the member access operator (->).

Figure 14-4   How to define getter and setter functions

The Movie List 1.0 program

Figure 14-5 shows a Move List program that uses a Movie class to store its data. This program prompts the user to enter the title and year of one or more movies. Then, it displays a list of all movies entered by the user.

The code for this program begins by including all of the header files needed by the program, as well as a using directive for the standard namespace. Then, it defines a Movie class that uses encapsulation to provide indirect access to its data members. To start, this class defines two private data members, title and year. Then, it declares four public member functions that provide the getters and setters for the two data members.

After declaring the members functions within the class, this code defines the four functions that implement these declarations. By now, you shouldn't have any trouble understanding how these functions work. However, you should note that these functions use a suffix of _param to identify the names of the parameters. This prevents the parameter names from colliding with the names of the data members. The code in this chapter uses this convention because it clearly identifies the parameter. However, this convention yields a long parameter name that many programmers might prefer to shorten. For example, some might prefer using a suffix of _p or even a suffix of a single underscore.

The console

```
The Movie List program

Enter a movie...

Title: Roundhay Garden Scene
Year: 1888

Enter another movie? (y/n): y

Title: Arrival of a Train
Year: 1895

Enter another movie? (y/n): n

TITLE                          YEAR
Roundhay Garden Scene          1888
Arrival of a Train             1895
```

The code

```cpp
#include <iostream>
#include <iomanip>
#include <string>
#include <vector>

using namespace std;

class Movie {
private:
    string title;
    int year;
public:
    void set_title(string);
    string get_title() const;
    void set_year(int);
    int get_year() const;
};

void Movie::set_title(string title_param) {
    title = title_param;
}

string Movie::get_title() const {
    return title;
}

void Movie::set_year(int year_param) {
    if (year_param < 1888) {
        throw invalid_argument("Year must be 1888 or later.");
    }
    year = year_param;
}
```

Figure 14-5   The Movie List 1.0 program (part 1 of 2)

After the function definitions for the class, this code presents the main() function. This function begins by displaying the title of the program and prompting the user to enter a movie. Then, it defines a vector to store Movie objects. Next, it enters a while loop that continues while the user enters 'y' or 'Y'.

Within this loop, the first statement creates a Movie object. Then, it gets the title of the movie and uses the set_title() function to store this title in the Movie object. Next, it gets the year of the movie and uses the set_year() function to store the year in the Movie object. Since this function will throw an exception if the user enters an invalid year, this code catches the exception and handles it. To keep things simple, this program handles the exception by displaying an error message and exiting the program normally. However, a more robust program would display an error message and give the user another chance to enter a year.

After setting the title and year in the Movie object, this code adds the movie to the end of the vector. Then, it asks whether the user would like to enter another movie. If so, the loop executes again. If not, the loop ends.

After the while loop, the code displays the movies in two columns where the first column is three times as wide as the second column (30 characters and 10 characters). Here, the second statement displays column headers for TITLE and YEAR. Then, a for loop displays the title and year for each Movie object stored in the vector. After this for loop, the program ends.

The code (continued)

```cpp
int Movie::get_year() const {
    return year;
}

int main() {
    cout << "The Movie List program\n\n"
         << "Enter a movie...\n\n";

    // get movies from user
    vector<Movie> movies;
    char another = 'y';
    while (tolower(another) == 'y') {
        Movie movie;

        string title;
        cout << "Title: ";
        getline(cin, title);
        movie.set_title(title);

        int year;
        cout << "Year: ";
        cin >> year;
        try {
            movie.set_year(year);
        }
        catch (const invalid_argument& e) {
            cout << e.what() << "\n";
            cout << "Exiting program...\n\n";
            return 0;
        }

        movies.push_back(movie);

        cout << "\nEnter another movie? (y/n): ";
        cin >> another;
        cin.ignore();
        cout << endl;
    }

    // display the movies
    const int w = 10;
    cout << left
         << setw(w * 3) << "TITLE"
         << setw(w) << "YEAR" << endl;
    for (Movie movie : movies) {
        cout << setw(w * 3) << movie.get_title()
             << setw(w) << movie.get_year() << endl;
    }
    cout << endl;
}
```

Figure 14-5   The Movie List 1.0 program (part 2 of 2)

More skills for coding member functions

At this point, you should understand how to code a class that provides encapsulation by using private data members and public member functions. Now, you'll learn some more skills for defining classes.

How to work with private member functions

If you need to code a member function but you don't want to make it available outside of the class, you can declare it in a private section. Then, the member function is private and can be used by other member functions. As a result, it's known as a private *helper function*.

In figure 14-6, for instance, the first example declares three member functions that could be added to the Movie class presented in the previous figure. Here, the to_upper() member function is declared in a private section. As a result, it's a helper function that can be used by the get_title_upper() and iequals() member functions that are declared in the public section.

The second example presents the code that implements the private to_upper() function. To start, it declares a string variable named str_upper to store the upper-case string. Then, this code loops through each character in the string parameter, converts the character to uppercase, and adds it to the str_upper variable. Finally, this function returns the uppercase string.

The third example presents the code that implements the get_title_upper() function. This function uses the to_upper() helper function to convert the title data member to uppercase. Then, it returns the uppercase title. Since this function is public, it provides an easy way for anyone using a Movie object to get the movie's title in uppercase.

The fourth example presents the code that implements the iequals() function. This function performs a case-insensitive comparison of the current Movie object and another Movie object. In the function name, *i* is for *insensitive*. This function works much like the equals() function presented earlier in this chapter. However, before comparing the movie titles, it uses the to_upper() helper function to convert the titles to uppercase. As a result, this function returns true if comparing two Movie objects that have the same year and the same title, regardless of the case of the titles.

As you review this code, note that the iequals() function can access the private title and year data members because it's coded in the same class as those data members. Similarly, this function can access the private to_upper() function because it's coded in the same class as that member function.

The fifth example shows some code that calls the public functions. To start, it creates two Movie objects, sets the titles to "Test" and "test", and sets both years to 2018. Then, it uses the iequals() function to compare these two Movie objects. Since this performs a case-insensitive comparison, this function returns a true value, and the if statement displays a message that indicates that these objects are equal. After that, the code uses the get_title() and get_title_upper() functions to print the title that's stored in the first Movie object as well as that title after it has been converted to uppercase.

The declarations for three more functions for the Movie class

```
private:
    string to_upper(string);        // helper function
public:
    string get_title_upper() const;
    bool iequals(const Movie&);
```

A private function that converts a string to uppercase

```
string Movie::to_upper(string str) {
    string str_upper;
    for (char c : str) {
        str_upper.push_back(toupper(c));
    }
    return str_upper;
}
```

A public function that returns the title in uppercase

```
string Movie::get_title_upper() const {
    return to_upper(title);
}
```

A public function that performs a case-insensitive equality comparison

```
bool Movie::iequals(const Movie& to_compare) {
    return (to_upper(title) == to_upper(to_compare.title) &&
            year == to_compare.year);
}
```

Code that calls the public functions

```
Movie m1;
Movie m2;
m1.set_title("Test");
m1.set_year(2018);
m2.set_title("test");
m2.set_year(2018);
if (m1.iequals(m2)) {
    cout << "The test movies are equal (case-insensitive).\n";
}

// m1.to_upper()     // illegal - can't call private member function
cout << "The title is " << m1.get_title() << endl;
cout << "The uppercase title is " << m1.get_title_upper() << endl;
```

The console

```
The test movies are equal (case-insensitive).
The title is Test
The uppercase title is TEST
```

Description

- If you need to code a member function but you don't want to make it available outside of the class, you can declare it as private. Since a private function can be used by other member functions, it's known as a private *helper function*.

Figure 14-6   How to work with private member functions

How to convert between numbers and strings

When you define a class, it sometimes helps to provide setter functions for the same data member that accept different types of data. To do that, you can code overloaded functions. As you learned in chapter 7, overloaded functions have the same name but different signatures. The signatures of two functions can be different because they have a different number of parameters or because they have the same number of parameters but different data types for those parameters.

When working with overloaded setter functions, any function that accepts a parameter with a data type that's different from the type of the data member must convert the parameter to the correct type before storing it in the data member. To convert from one data type to another, you can use functions like the ones shown in figure 14-7 for converting between numbers and strings.

Here, the to_string() function converts a number to a string, the stoi() function converts a string to an integer, and the stod() function converts a string to a double. To help you remember what the stoi() and stod() functions do, just remember that the names stand for *string to i*nteger and *string to d*ouble. Note that if either of these functions isn't able to convert a string to the specified numeric data type, it throws an exception. For example, if you attempt to use the stoi() function to convert a string of "ten" to a number, it will throw an exception.

To illustrate how to use these functions with overloaded setters, this figure shows the declarations and definitions for two versions of the set_year() function for the Movie class. By now, you should already understand how the first set_year() function works. This function accepts a year parameter of the int type. Then, it checks the year parameter to make sure it's in a valid range. If so, it sets the year data member, which is also of the int type, to the value stored in the year parameter.

The second set_year() function accepts a year parameter of the string type. As a result, before this parameter can be stored as an integer, this function must use the stoi() function to convert the string to an int value. Then, the code can pass the int value to the first set_year() function for validation. If the year is in a valid range, this sets the year data member to the int value.

Although you could also use the to_string() function to convert a number to a string before storing it in a data member, you're more likely to convert strings to numbers. However, it is common to use this function to convert a number to a string so it can be concatenated with other strings. This is illustrated by the to_str() function shown in this figure.

Here, the to_str() function uses the to_string() function to convert the year data member from the int type to the string type. This allows the to_str() function to return a string that includes the movie title followed by its year in parentheses.

Three functions for converting between numbers and strings

Function	Description
`to_string(num)`	Converts the specified number to a string and returns the string.
`stoi(str)`	Converts the specified string to an int value and returns that value. If this function can't perform the conversion, it throws an exception.
`stod(str)`	Converts the specified string to a double value and returns that value. If this function can't perform the conversion, it throws an exception.

The declarations for more functions for the Movie class

```
public:
    void set_year(int year_param);
    void set_year(string year_param);
    string to_str() const;
```

A set_year() function that accepts an int value

```
void Movie::set_year(int year_param) {
    if (year_param < 1888) {
        throw invalid_argument("Year must be 1888 or later.");
    }
    year = year_param;
}
```

An overload of the set_year() function that accepts a string

```
void Movie::set_year(string year_param) {
    int yr = stoi(year_param);               // string to int
    set_year(yr);
}
```

A function that returns a string representation of an object

```
string Movie::to_str() const {
    return title + " (" + to_string(year) + ')';  // int to string
}
```

Code that calls the three public functions

```
Movie movie;
movie.set_title("Arrival of a Train");
movie.set_year("1895");
cout << movie.to_str() << endl;
```

The console

```
Arrival of a Train (1895)
```

Description

- When you define a class, you should consider coding overloaded setter functions that accept different data types.

- If a setter function accepts a parameter with a data type that's different from the type of the data member, you can use the functions shown above to convert the parameter to the appropriate type.

- The to_string() function is typically used to convert a number to a string so it can be concatenated with other strings.

Figure 14-7   How to convert between numbers and strings

How to define constructors

A *constructor* is a special type of member function that's automatically called when you create (construct) an object. Figure 14-8 shows how to define constructors.

To start, a constructor must use the same name and capitalization as the name of the class. For instance, the first example shows that the name of the constructor for the Movie class must be Movie in both its declaration and its definition. In addition, this example shows that a constructor does not include a return type.

The constructor in the first example has zero parameters. As a result, it's known as the *default constructor*. However, the constructor in the second example has two parameters with default values. Because it provides default values, no arguments need to be passed to it when it's used to create an object. As a result, it can accept arguments and also act as the default constructor. If it's used as the default constructor, it initializes the title data member to an empty string, and it initializes the year data member to a value of 1888.

If you don't code any constructors, C++ creates a default constructor for your class. However, there's no guarantee that the compiler will initialize the data members of the class to default values. In that case, the data members would point to whatever old values happen to be in memory. Because of that, it's generally considered a best practice to include a default constructor that initializes all data members to default values.

If you code one or more constructors but don't code a default constructor, C++ doesn't create a default constructor for your class. Instead, it forces you to use one of the non-default constructors. As a result, you can't use the abbreviated syntax to call a constructor, which is the syntax you've seen so far. Instead, you must use a syntax that allows you to pass arguments to the constructor.

The third example shows three ways that you can call a default constructor. Here, the first statement creates a Movie object by explicitly calling its default constructor. Then, it assigns this Movie object to a Movie variable named m1. By contrast, the second and third statements don't explicitly call the default constructor. Instead, the second statement uses a partially abbreviated syntax that includes parentheses after the variable name, and the third statement uses an abbreviated syntax that doesn't include the parentheses.

If you want to pass arguments to a constructor, you can't use the abbreviated syntax. Instead, you have to use the full syntax or the partially abbreviated syntax as shown in the fourth example. Here, the first and second statements pass one argument to the Movie constructor. Then, the third and fourth statements pass two arguments to the Movie constructor.

In some cases, you may want to create an object without assigning it to a variable. To do that, you can call the constructor of a class by coding the name of the class followed by a set of parentheses. Within those parentheses, you can code any arguments that you want to send to the constructor. In the fifth example, for instance, a single statement creates a Movie object by passing its constructor a title and a year and then adds that object to the end of a vector of Movie objects.

A default constructor (zero parameters)

The declaration

```
Movie();
```

The definition

```
Movie::Movie() {
    title = "";
    year = 1888;
}
```

Another way to code a default constructor (zero required parameters)

The declaration

```
Movie(string title = "", int year = 1888);
```

The definition

```
Movie::Movie(string title, int year) {
    set_title(title);
    set_year(year);
}
```

Three ways to call the default constructor (no arguments)

```
Movie m1 = Movie();     // full syntax
Movie m2();             // partially abbreviated syntax
Movie m3;               // abbreviated syntax
```

Examples that pass arguments to a constructor

```
Movie m4 = Movie("Wizard of Oz");           // passes 1 argument
Movie m5("Wizard of Oz");                   // passes 1 argument
Movie m6 = Movie("Wizard of Oz", 1939);     // passes 2 arguments
Movie m7("Wizard of Oz", 1939);             // passes 2 arguments
```

An example that creates an object and stores it in a vector

```
movies.push_back(Movie("Wizard of Oz", 1939));
```

Description

- A *constructor* is a special type of member function that's automatically called when you create (construct) an object.
- A constructor must use the same name and capitalization as the name of the class.
- A constructor does not include a return type.
- A *default constructor* has zero required parameters.
- If you provide default values for each parameter of a constructor, the constructor can accept arguments and can also act as the default constructor.
- If you don't code any constructors, C++ creates a default constructor for your class. However, this default constructor might not initialize data members. As a result, the data members might point to whatever old values happen to be in memory.
- If you code one or more constructors but don't code a default constructor, C++ doesn't create a default constructor for your class.

Figure 14-8   How to define constructors

How to define destructors

A *destructor* is a special type of member function that's automatically called when an object is destroyed. C++ automatically destroys most objects when they go out of scope. Figure 14-9 shows how to define destructors.

You code a destructor using a technique that's similar to the technique for coding a constructor. However, the name of a destructor must be preceded by a tilde character (~) and a destructor can't accept any arguments. In addition, a class can only contain one destructor.

A common use for a destructor is to free system resources that an object is using. For example, if an object's constructor dynamically allocates memory as described in chapter 17, the object's destructor should free this memory.

The first example in this figure shows how to code the declaration and definition for a destructor for the Movie class. Since this class doesn't allocate any memory or use any other system resources, the destructor for this class just contains a comment that indicates that you could add code to free system resources here. Although it's a relatively common practice to code destructors that don't contain any code, and many IDEs generate code like this when you create a class, the programs in this book only use destructors when they're needed to release system resources.

The second example begins by showing the declaration for a MovieList class that works with a file, which requires a system resource. Then, this example shows the code for the constructor. This code uses the open() function of the fstream class to open the file named movies.txt. Next, this example shows the code for the destructor. This code begins by using the is_open() function of the fstream class to check if the file is open. If it is, this code uses the close() function of the fstream class to close the connection to the file, which frees the system resource.

A destructor

The declaration

```
~Movie();
```

The definition

```
Movie::~Movie() {
    // code that frees system resources goes here
}
```

An example of a class with a destructor

The declaration

```
class MovieList {
private:
    string filename = "movies.txt";
    fstream file;
    vector<Movie> movies;
public:
    MovieList();
    ~MovieList();
    void add_movie(Movie);
    void delete_movie(Movie);
};
```

The definition for the constructor

```
MovieList::MovieList() {
    file.open(filename, ios::in);     // open a system resource
}
```

The definition for the destructor

```
MovieList::~MovieList() {
    if (file.is_open())
        file.close();                 // close a system resource
}
```

Description

- A *destructor* is a special type of member function that's automatically called when an object is destroyed. C++ automatically destroys most objects when they go out of scope.

- A destructor must use the same name and capitalization as the name of the class and be preceded by a tilde character (~).

- A destructor can't include a return type.

- A destructor can't accept any arguments.

- A class can only contain one destructor.

- A common use for a destructor is to free system resources that an object is using.

Figure 14-9   How to define destructors

How to store a class in header and source files

When you code classes, it's common to store them in separate header and source files. This makes it easier to reuse a class, which is one of the primary benefits of using classes.

The header and source files for a Movie class

Figure 14-10 presents the header and source files for a Movie class. To start, it presents the code for the header file. This code is stored in the Movie.h file.

Like the header files presented in chapter 7, this header file uses an *include guard* to prevent the compiler from including the same header file twice. To do that, it uses the #ifndef, #define, and #endif preprocessor directives to check whether a constant named MURACH_MOVIE_H has been defined. For this to work correctly, this constant must have a unique name.

After including the string header file, the Movie.h header file declares a class named Movie. To start, this class has a private section that defines three data members (title, year, and stars) and a helper function named to_upper(). Then, this class has a public section that declares a constructor and seven functions.

The constructor provides default values for all three data members. As a result, none of these data members are required when an object is created, so this constructor can be the default constructor. In addition, it allows you to pass arguments to specify the data members. This is a flexible and concise way to code a constructor.

Of the seven member function declarations, the first six are getters and setters for the three data members. Then, the iequals() function provides a way to perform a case-insensitive comparison of two Movie objects.

Note that this header file follows the best practice of not providing any using directives or declarations. That way, other classes that include this header file won't have any objects or functions imported into its namespace. For example, instead of coding a using declaration for the string class, this code uses the scope resolution operator (::) to fully qualify the string class every time it's used in the header file.

The Movie.cpp file contains the definitions for the functions declared in the header file. In other words, this file implements these functions. As a result, the Movie.cpp file is sometimes called the *implementation file*. On the other hand, the header file provides the interface for using the class. As a result, it's sometimes called the *interface file*.

The source file begins by including all necessary header files, including the Movie.h header file. Then, it includes two using declarations that make it easy to use the std::string and std::invalid_argument classes. Next, it defines the private to_upper() function that works like the to_upper() function described earlier in this chapter.

After the private function, this code declares the constructor for the class. This constructor sets the data members by passing its parameters to the

The Movie.h file

```cpp
#ifndef MURACH_MOVIE_H
#define MURACH_MOVIE_H

#include <string>

class Movie {
private:
    std::string title;
    int year;
    int stars;

    std::string to_upper(std::string);
public:
    Movie(std::string title = "", int year = 1888, int stars = 1);

    Movie set_title(std::string);
    std::string get_title() const;

    Movie set_year(int);
    int get_year() const;

    Movie set_stars(int);
    int get_stars() const;

    bool iequals(const Movie&);
};

#endif // MURACH_MOVIE_H
```

The Movie.cpp file

```cpp
#include "Movie.h"
#include <string>

using std::string;
using std::invalid_argument;

// private function
string Movie::to_upper(string str) {
    string str_upper;
    for (char c : str) {
        str_upper.push_back(toupper(c));
    }
    return str_upper;
}

// public functions
Movie::Movie(string title, int year, int stars) {
    set_title(title);
    set_year(year);
    set_stars(stars);
}
```

Figure 14-10   The header and source files for a Movie class (part 1 of 2)

appropriate setter functions. For example, it passes the year parameter to the set_year() function. That way, the setter function can validate the value that's passed to it.

The definitions for the next six functions work as you would expect. Here, all of the setter functions validate their parameters. This helps to make sure that a Movie object stores valid data. For example, this code makes sure the title string is 120 characters or less. Similarly, it makes sure that the number of stars for a movie ranges from one to five.

The iequals() function provides a way to perform a case-insensitive comparison of two Movie objects. To do that, it uses the private to_upper() function to convert both movie titles to uppercase before comparing them. However, this function doesn't include the number of stars in the comparison. As a result, the two movies are considered equal if the titles are equal (not including case) and the years are equal.

The Movie.cpp file (continued)

```cpp
void Movie::set_title(string title_param) {
    if (title_param.size() > 120) {
        throw invalid_argument(
            "Title must not have more than 120 chars.");
    }
    title = title_param;
}

string Movie::get_title() const {
    return title;
}

void Movie::set_year(int year_param) {
    if (year_param < 1888) {
        throw invalid_argument("Year must be 1888 or later.");
    }
    year = year_param;
}

int Movie::get_year() const {
    return year;
}

void Movie::set_stars(int stars_param) {
    if (stars_param < 1 || stars_param > 5) {
        throw invalid_argument("Stars must be from 1 to 5.");
    }
    stars = stars_param;
}

int Movie::get_stars() const {
    return stars;
}

bool Movie::iequals(const Movie& to_compare) {
    return (to_upper(title) == to_upper(to_compare.title) &&
        year == to_compare.year);
}
```

Description

- It's a common practice to store the interface for a class in a header file and the source code that implements the interface in another file. This works much like storing functions in header and source files as described in chapter 7.

Figure 14-10   The header and source files for a Movie class (part 2 of 2)

When and how to use inline functions

In the previous figure, all of the member function declarations for the Movie class were coded in the header, and all of the function definitions were coded in the source file. But, as figure 14-11 shows, you can also code the definition of a member function in the header file. In that case, the function is known as an *inline function*.

When you code an inline function, you are giving the compiler a hint that you would like it to optimize the executable file by replacing each function call with the code in the function itself. This process is known as *inline expansion*. Although inline expansion can reduce the overhead needed to call a function, it can also cause the code for the function to be duplicated in multiple places in the executable file, which increases the size of the executable file.

One advantage of inline functions is that they can make your code more concise since they allow you to declare and define the function in the same place. Another advantage is that they can result in improved performance since they avoid the overhead that's needed to call a function.

However, there are several disadvantages to using inline functions. To start, because an inline function's code is duplicated in the executable file, the size of the executable file is increased. This larger file size can sometimes degrade performance. In addition, it's necessary to recompile the header file if you change any of the implementation code of the inline function.

When you code an inline function, there is no guarantee that the compiler will use your hint. In other words, the compiler may decide that the best way to optimize the executable file is to not use inline expansion for the function. Conversely, modern compilers may use inline expansion automatically, even for functions that aren't coded as inline functions. In other words, they may decide that they can optimize the executable file by using inline expansion on a regular function.

So, when should you use inline functions? Unfortunately, there's no simple answer because it depends on your system. In general, though, it makes sense to use inline functions for functions that are short and are unlikely to change. That's the case for the header file for the Movie class shown here, which uses inline get_title() and get_year() functions. The main benefit of this approach is that it results in code that's concise and easy to read. It also results in code that should work well with older compilers or modern ones.

On the other hand, the set_title() and set_year() functions are longer and more likely to change since they contain code that validates the data that's passed to them. That's why this header file just declares these functions and leaves it to the source file to implement them.

A Movie.h file that uses inline function definitions

```
#ifndef MURACH_MOVIE_H
#define MURACH_MOVIE_H

#include <string>

class Movie {
private:
    std::string title;
    int year;
    int stars;
    std::string to_upper(std::string);
public:
    Movie(std::string title = "", int year = 1888, int stars = 1);

    void set_title(std::string);
    std::string get_title() const { return title; }    // inline function

    void set_year(int);
    int Movie::get_year() const { return year; } // inline function

    // other function declarations go here
};

#endif // MURACH_MOVIE_H
```

Pros of inline functions

- More concise code due to function being declared and defined in the same place.
- Possible improved performance due to avoiding function call overhead.

Cons of inline functions

- Larger executable file size because the inline function is duplicated each time it's called.
- Possible degraded performance due to larger executable file size.
- Header file must be recompiled if you change any of the implementation code of the inline function.

Description

- If you code the definition of a member function in the header file, the function is known as an *inline function*.
- When you code an inline function, you are giving the compiler a hint that you would like it to optimize the executable file by using a process known as *inline expansion*. Inline expansion replaces each function call with the code in the function itself.
- When you code an inline function, there is no guarantee that the compiler will use your hint.
- Modern compilers often use inline expansion automatically, even for functions that aren't coded as inline functions.

Figure 14-11   When and how to use inline functions

The Movie List 2.0 program

Figure 14-12 presents another version of the Movie List program. This program is similar to the Movie List 2.0 program presented in chapter 9. However, it uses a Movie class to store the data for the movie, not a Movie structure. Because of that, this figure highlights the code that works with the Movie object that's created from the Movie class.

To start, this code imports the Movie.h header file presented earlier in this chapter. As a result, this code can use the Movie class defined by that header.

The console

```
The Movie List program

COMMANDS
v - View movie list
a - Add a movie
d - Delete a movie
x - Exit

Command: v
      TITLE                        YEAR    STARS
1     Casablanca                   1942    5
2     Wonder Woman                 2017    4

Command: a
Title: The Wizard of Oz
Year: 1939
Stars (1-5): 5
The Wizard of Oz was added.

Command: d
Number: 1
Casablanca was deleted.

Command: x
Bye!
```

The code

```cpp
#include <iostream>
#include <fstream>
#include <sstream>
#include <iomanip>
#include <string>
#include <vector>
#include "Movie.h"

using namespace std;

const string movies_file = "movies.txt";

vector<Movie> read_movies_from_file() {
    vector<Movie> movies;

    ifstream input_file(movies_file);
    if (input_file) {      // if file opened successfully...
        string line;
        while (getline(input_file, line)) {
            stringstream ss(line);
```

Figure 14-12   The Movie List 2.0 program (part 1 of 4)

In part 2 of figure 14-12, the code uses a single statement to add the Movie objects to the vector of Movie objects. To do that, this code calls the constructor of the Movie class and passes it the title, year, and stars that have been read from the file. Then, it passes the movie to the push_back() function of the vector.

In the write_movies_to_file() function, the code uses the getter functions to get the data from the Movie object. This is necessary because the data members of the Movie class are private. As a result, you can't access them directly. Instead, you must use these getter functions to get values from the data members. Similarly, the view_movies() function uses the getter functions to get the values from the data members.

In part 3, the get_movie() function creates a Movie object and stores it in a variable named movie. To do that, it passes the title, year, and stars entered by the user to the constructor of the Movie class. Then, the next statement returns the Movie object. Alternately, this code could return the Movie object without creating a variable for it by coding the return statement like this:

```
return Movie(title, year, stars);
```

In the add_movie() function, the code uses the iequals() function to compare the current Movie object with every movie in the vector of Movie objects. If the current Movie already exists in the vector, this code uses the set_stars() and get_stars() functions to set the number of stars for the existing movie to the number of stars for the new movie. In other words, it doesn't add a new movie to the list since the title and year are the same. Instead, it updates the number of stars, which might be different.

The rest of the code in this listing works mostly as described in chapter 9. As a result, you shouldn't have much trouble understanding how it works. The only difference of any significance is that the add_movie() and delete_movie() functions use the get_title() function to get the title of the movie instead of directly accessing the data member.

As you review this code, you may wonder why it doesn't use a try statement to catch the exceptions that might be thrown by the constructor of the Movie class. In the read_movies_from_file() function, this isn't necessary if the data in the file is valid. However, in the get_movie() function, it would be a good practice to catch these exceptions and handle them. It would be an even better practice to prevent these exceptions from being thrown in the first place by validating user input so no invalid data is passed to the Movie object. To do that, you could use functions from the console namespace described in chapter 7.

The code (continued)

```cpp
            string title;
            int year;
            int stars;
            getline(ss, title, '\t');          // get title
            ss >> year >> stars;               // get year and stars

            // add movie to vector
            movies.push_back(Movie(title, year, stars));
        }
        input_file.close();
    }
    return movies;
}

void write_movies_to_file(const vector<Movie>& movies) {
    ofstream output_file(movies_file);
    if (output_file) {       // if file opened successfully...
        for (Movie movie : movies) {
            output_file << movie.get_title() << '\t'
                << movie.get_year() << '\t'
                << movie.get_stars() << '\n';
        }
        output_file.close();
    }
}

void view_movies(const vector<Movie>& movies) {
    int col_width = 8;
    cout << left
        << setw(col_width / 2) << " "
        << setw(col_width * 4) << "TITLE"
        << setw(col_width) << "YEAR"
        << setw(col_width) << "STARS" << endl;

    int number = 1;
    for (Movie movie : movies) {
        cout << setw(col_width / 2) << number
            << setw(col_width * 4) << movie.get_title()
            << setw(col_width) << movie.get_year()
            << setw(col_width) << movie.get_stars() << endl;
        ++number;
    }
    cout << endl;
}

Movie get_movie() {
    string title;
    cout << "Title: ";
    cin.ignore(1000, '\n');
    getline(cin, title);

    int year;
    cout << "Year: ";
    cin >> year;
```

Figure 14-12   The Movie List 2.0 program (part 2 of 4)

The code (continued)

```cpp
    int stars;
    cout << "Stars (1-5): ";
    cin >> stars;

    Movie movie(title, year, stars);
    return movie;
}

void add_movie(vector<Movie>& movies) {
    Movie movie = get_movie();

    // check if movie already exists
    bool already_exists = false;
    for (Movie& m : movies) {
        if (m.iequals(movie)) {
            already_exists = true;
            m.set_stars(movie.get_stars());
            break;
        }
    }

    if (already_exists) {
        write_movies_to_file(movies);
        cout << movie.get_title() << " was updated.\n\n";
    }
    else {
        movies.push_back(movie);
        write_movies_to_file(movies);
        cout << movie.get_title() << " was added.\n\n";
    }
}

int get_movie_number(const vector<Movie>& movies) {
    int number;
    while (true) {
        cout << "Number: ";
        cin >> number;
        if (number > 0 && number <= movies.size()) {
            return number;
        }
        else {
            cout << "Invalid movie number. Try again.\n";
        }
    }
}
```

Figure 14-12   The Movie List 2.0 program (part 3 of 4)

The code (continued)

```cpp
void delete_movie(vector<Movie>& movies) {
    int number = get_movie_number(movies);

    int index = number - 1;
    Movie movie = movies[index];
    movies.erase(movies.begin() + index);
    write_movies_to_file(movies);
    cout << movie.get_title() << " was deleted.\n\n";
}

void display_menu() {
    cout << "COMMANDS\n"
        << "v - View movie list\n"
        << "a - Add a movie\n"
        << "d - Delete a movie\n"
        << "x - Exit\n\n";
}

int main() {
    cout << "The Movie List program\n\n";
    display_menu();
    vector<Movie> movies = read_movies_from_file();
    char command = 'v';
    while (command != 'x') {
        cout << "Command: ";
        cin >> command;
        switch (command) {
            case 'v':
                view_movies(movies);
                break;
            case 'a':
                add_movie(movies);
                break;
            case 'd':
                delete_movie(movies);
                break;
            case 'x':
                cout << "Bye!\n\n";
                break;
            default:
                cout << "Not a valid command. Please try again.\n\n";
                break;
        }
    }
}
```

Figure 14-12   The Movie List 2.0 program (part 4 of 4)

How to work with UML diagrams

An introduction to UML diagrams

When working with classes, it's common to use a diagram known as a *class diagram* to plan and document the data members and functions of a class. To do that, it's common to use *Unified Modeling Language* (*UML*), a modeling language that's the industry standard for working with all object-oriented programming languages including C++.

Figure 14-13 presents two UML diagrams. The first diagram is for the Movie class that was presented in figure 14-10. The second diagram is for the Product class that's presented later in this chapter.

The diagram for the Movie class contains three data members and nine member functions. Here, the minus sign (-) identifies private members that are available only within the current class. Conversely, the plus sign (+) identifies public members that are available to other classes. For example, all three data members are private, but only the to_upper() member function is private. The rest of the member functions, including the constructor, are public.

The diagram for the Product class contains three data members and seven member functions. Here, the first data member is public. As a result, this class doesn't need to include getter and setter functions for this data member. However, the second and third data members are private. As a result, this class includes public getter and setter functions for them. In addition, it includes a constructor and two other functions named get_discount_amount() and get_discount_percent().

These get_discount_amount() and get_discount_percent() functions get data that can't be set in the object. As a result, these functions are known as *read-only functions*. These functions calculate the values that they return from other data members.

As you review these diagrams, note that the name of each function is followed by a set of parentheses. Within the parentheses, these diagrams specify the names of the parameters of the function. However, they don't specify the data types for these parameters. Similarly, these diagrams don't specify the return types for the functions.

In most cases, you can guess the data types from the names. For example, a parameter named title is most likely a string, a parameter named year is most likely an int, and a function named get_price() most likely returns a double value. However, if you want to explicitly specify data types in your diagrams, you can do that by using the notation described in the next figure.

A UML diagram for the Movie class from figure 14-10

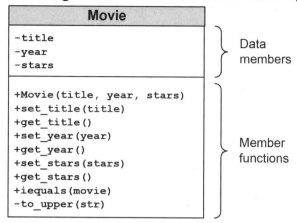

A UML diagram for the Product class from figure 14-15

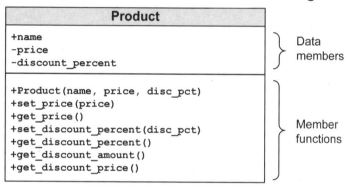

Description

- *UML* (*Unified Modeling Language*) is the industry standard used to describe the classes and objects of an object-oriented program.
- A UML *class diagram* describes the data members and member functions of one or more classes.
- The minus sign (-) marks the private members that can't be accessed by other classes, and the plus sign (+) marks the public members that can be accessed by other classes.
- For each member function, the name is followed by a set of parentheses. Within the parentheses, the class diagram specifies the parameters of the function.
- When a member function provides a way to get data that can't be set in the object, it's known as a *read-only function*.

Figure 14-13   An introduction to UML diagrams

UML diagrams with data types

Figure 14-14 presents the same Movie and Product diagrams from the last figure. In this figure, however, these diagrams also specify the data types used by the data members and the member functions. To do that, these diagrams specify a colon and the data type after the name of the data member or function parameter. Or, to specify the return type of a function, these diagrams include the colon and the data type after the parentheses of the function.

If you compare these diagrams to the diagrams in the previous figure, you'll find that the data types clutter the diagram and make it a little harder to read. As a result, if you don't need to specify the data types, you might want to leave them out. Or, as a middle ground, you might want to only specify them for the data members. Of course, this depends on what you're using the class diagrams for and how detailed you need your documentation or specification to be.

A UML diagram for the Movie class from figure 14-10

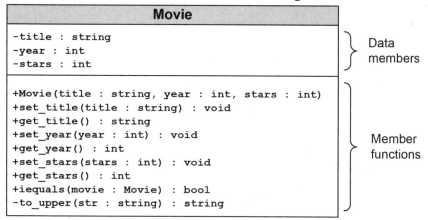

A UML diagram for the Product class from figure 14-15

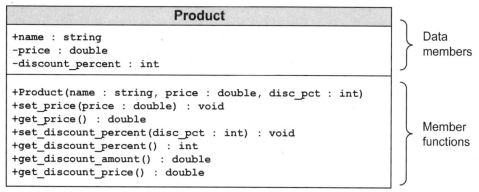

Description

- After the names of the data members and function parameters, these class diagrams specify a colon and the data type.

- After the parentheses of a function, these class diagrams specify a colon and the return type for the function.

Figure 14-14   UML diagrams with data types

A Product class that implements a UML diagram

To round out your understanding of UML, figure 14-15 shows a Product class that implements the diagram presented in the previous two figures. Note that this class doesn't encapsulate the name data member. Instead, it only encapsulates the product's price and discount percent.

Part 1 of this figure shows the header file for the Product class. To start, the private section declares the two data members that are encapsulated. Then, the public section declares the public data member, the constructor, the four getter and setter functions, and the two read-only functions. As you review this code, note that both of the getter functions are coded as inline functions.

The Product.h file

```
#ifndef MURACH_PRODUCT_H
#define MURACH_PRODUCT_H

#include <string>

class Product {
    double price;
    int discount_percent;

public:
    std::string name;
    Product(std::string name = "", double price = 0.0,
            int discount_pct = 0);

    void set_price(double);
    double get_price() const {
        return price;
    }

    void set_discount_percent(int);
    int get_discount_percent() const {
        return discount_percent;
    }

    double get_discount_amount();
    double get_discount_price();
};

#endif // MURACH_PRODUCT_H
```

Figure 14-15   A Product class that implements ta UML diagram (part 1 of 2)

Part 2 of figure 14-15 shows the code that implements the header file for the Product class. To start, this code defines the constructor for this class. This code assigns the first parameter to the name data member by directly accessing this data member. Then, it assigns the second parameter to the price data member by passing it to the set_price() function. Similarly, it assigns the third parameter to the discount_percent data member by passing it to the set_discount_percent() function. That way, the class can validate the data being assigned to these data functions.

As you review this code, note that it doesn't need to implement the getter functions for the price and discount_percent data members. That's because these functions were defined as inline functions in the header file. As a result, the header file contains the implementation for these functions.

Also, note that the get_discount_amount() and get_discount_price() functions don't get or set any data members. Instead, they use the data members to calculate a result. Then, they return the result of that calculation. For example, the get_discount_amount() function calculates the discount amount by multiplying the price by the discount percent. Similarly, the get_discount_price() function calculates the discount price by subtracting the discount amount from the price. This is a good example of how a class can include functions that operate on its data members.

The Product.cpp file

```cpp
#include <string>
#include <cmath>
#include "Product.h"

using std::string;
using std::invalid_argument;

Product::Product(string p_name, double price, int discount_percent) {
    name = p_name;
    set_price(price);
    set_discount_percent(discount_percent);
}

void Product::set_price(double p_price) {
    if (p_price >= 0.0)
        price = round(p_price * 100) / 100;
    else
        throw invalid_argument("Price can't be negative.");
}

void Product::set_discount_percent(int p_discount_percent) {
    if (p_discount_percent >= 0 && p_discount_percent <= 100)
        discount_percent = p_discount_percent;
    else
        throw invalid_argument("Invalid range for discount percent.");
}

double Product::get_discount_amount() {
    double discount_amount = price * discount_percent / 100;
    return round(discount_amount * 100) / 100;
}

double Product::get_discount_price() {
    double discount_price = price - get_discount_amount();
    return round(discount_price * 100) / 100;
}
```

Figure 14-15   A Product class that implements ta UML diagram (part 2 of 2)

The Product Viewer program

Figure 14-16 shows a simple but complete program named Product Viewer that uses objects created from the Product class. This program begins by displaying a numbered list of three products. Then, the user can view the data for a product by entering its number.

To start, the code in part 1 includes the header file for the Product class presented in the previous figure. Then, it defines a function named show_products() that displays a numbered list of products. This function accepts a vector that contains one or more Product objects. To display these Product objects, a range-based for loop iterates through the vector. Within the loop, the code increments the counter variable named number. In addition, it displays this number followed by the name that's stored in the current Product object. To get this name, the code directly accesses the name data member.

The show_product() function displays the data for a product. To do that, it accepts a constant reference parameter that's a Product object. Then, it uses the name data member to display the name. Next, it uses the two getter functions to display the price and discount percent. Finally, it uses its two read-only functions to display the discount amount and discount price.

The console

```
The Product Viewer program

PRODUCTS
1. Stanley 13 Ounce Wood Hammer
2. National Hardware 3/4" Wire Nails
3. Economy Duct Tape, 60 yds, Silver

Enter product number: 1

PRODUCT DATA
Name:              Stanley 13 Ounce Wood Hammer
Price:             12.99
Discount percent: 62
Discount amount:  8.05
Discount price:   4.94

View another product? (y/n):
```

The code

```cpp
#include <iostream>
#include <string>
#include <vector>
#include "Product.h"

using namespace std;

void show_products(const vector<Product>& products) {
    cout << "PRODUCTS\n";
    int number = 0;
    for (Product product : products) {
        cout << ++number << ". " << product.name << endl;
    }
    cout << endl;
}

void show_product(const Product& p) {
    cout << "PRODUCT DATA\n"
        << "Name:              " << p.name << endl
        << "Price:             " << p.get_price() << endl
        << "Discount percent: " << p.get_discount_percent() << endl
        << "Discount amount:   " << p.get_discount_amount() << endl
        << "Discount price:    " << p.get_discount_price() << "\n\n";
}
```

Figure 14-16   The Product Viewer program (part 1 of 2)

In part 2 of figure 14-16, the main() function begins by displaying the title of the program. Then, it creates a vector of Product objects. Note that this code doesn't assign the Product objects it creates to variables. Instead, it calls the constructor of the Product class to create each object, and it stores each object in the vector without going through the intermediate step of creating a variable to store the object.

After creating the vector of Product objects, this code passes that vector to the show_products() function defined in part 1 of this figure. This displays the numbered list of products. Then, this code uses a while loop to display the information for one or more products. To do that, the code in the loop prompts the user to enter a number that corresponds to a product. Next, it checks if the number entered by the user corresponds to a Product object from the vector of Product objects. If it does, the code passes that Product object to the show_product() function. This displays the data for the product object.

The code (continued)

```cpp
int main() {
    cout << "The Product Viewer program\n\n";

    vector<Product> products;
    products.push_back(
        Product("Stanley 13 Ounce Wood Hammer", 12.99, 62));
    products.push_back(
        Product("National Hardware 3/4\" Wire Nails", 5.06, 0));
    products.push_back(
        Product("Economy Duct Tape, 60 yds, Silver", 7.24, 0));

    show_products(products);

    char choice = 'y';
    while (choice == 'y') {
        int number;
        cout << "Enter product number: ";
        cin >> number;
        cout << endl;

        if (number > 0 && number <= products.size()) {
            Product product = products[number - 1];
            show_product(product);
        }
        else {
            cout << "There is no product with that number.\n\n";
        }

        cout << "View another product? (y/n): ";
        cin >> choice;
        cout << endl;
    }
    cout << "Bye!\n\n";
}
```

Figure 14-16   The Product Viewer program (part 2 of 2)

How to work with object composition

So far in this chapter, you have learned how to define a class that has data members with types from the C++ standard library, like string and double. However, you can also define a class that stores one or more user-defined objects. To do that, you can use *object composition* to combine simple objects into more complex data structures.

To illustrate how object composition works, the topics that follow start by presenting a class named Die that can store information about a single die. Then, they present a class named Dice that can store multiple Die objects. Finally, they present a simple Dice Roller program that uses both the Die and Dice objects.

A Die class

Figure 14-17 begins by showing a UML diagram for a Die class that defines a single six-sided die. This class has a single private data member named value that has a public getter function. In addition, the class provides a default constructor for the class, as well as a public function named roll() that sets the value data member to a random value from 1 to 6.

The header file for the Die class defines the private data member and declares all of the public functions in the UML diagram. Then, the source code file implements these functions. To start, it imports the header files that it needs to get a random number, as well as the header file for the Die class.

The constructor for the Die class uses the srand() function to seed the rand() function that's used in the roll() member function. Then, the constructor initializes the value of the die to 1. As a result, when you first create a Die object, its value is set to 1.

The roll() function begins by using the rand() function with the modulus operator (%) to get a value from 0 to 5. Then, the next statement increments this value so it's from 1 to 6.

As you would expect, the get_value() function returns the value. This provides a way for the calling code to get the value after the roll() function has been called.

A UML diagram for a Die class

Die
-value : int
+Die() +roll() : void +get_value() : int

The Die.h file

```
#ifndef MURACH_DIE_H
#define MURACH_DIE_H

class Die {
private:
    int value;

public:
    Die();
    void roll();
    int get_value() const;
};

#endif // MURACH_DIE_H
```

The Die.cpp file

```
#include <cstdlib>
#include <ctime>
#include "Die.h"

Die::Die() {
    srand(time(nullptr));    // seed the rand() function
    value = 1;
}

void Die::roll() {
    value = rand() % 6;      // value is >= 0 and <= 5
    ++value;                 // value is >= 1 and <= 6
}

int Die::get_value() const {
    return value;
}
```

Figure 14-17   A Die class

A Dice class

Figure 14-18 begins by presenting a UML diagram that shows how object composition works. More specifically, this diagram shows that a Dice object is composed of one or more Die objects. To show this relationship, this diagram connects the two classes with a line, and it places a diamond connector next to the Dice class to show that it's the object that's composed of other objects. It may not seem like much, but being able to define an object that's composed of other user-defined objects is a powerful feature that allows you to create complex data structures that you can customize for each program that you develop.

The header file for the Dice class starts by including the header files it needs. This includes the header file for the Die class, which shows that the Dice class uses Die objects. Then, the Dice header file defines a single private data member named dice that's initialized to an empty vector of Die objects. Finally, it declares the public functions in the UML diagram, including a default constructor.

The source code file for the Dice class implements these functions. To start, it defines a default constructor. This constructor doesn't perform any initialization because the dice data member doesn't need to be initialized. However, if you later wanted to initialize the vector by setting its capacity, you could add that code here.

The add_die() function adds a Die object to the vector. To do that, this function calls the push_back() function of the Dice object to add the Die object to the end of the vector.

The roll_all() function rolls all of the Die objects that have been added to the vector. To do that, this code loops through the Die objects in the Dice object and calls the roll() function for each one.

The get_dice() function is a getter function for the dice data member. It returns the vector of Die objects that's stored in that data member. This provides a way for the calling code to get the value from each Die object in the Dice object.

A UML diagram for two classes that use composition

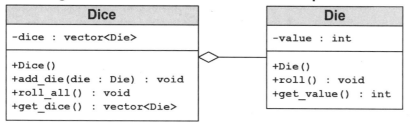

The Dice.h file

```
#ifndef MURACH_DICE_H
#define MURACH_DICE_H

#include <vector>
#include "Die.h"

class Dice {
private:
    std::vector<Die> dice;
public:
    Dice();
    void add_die(Die die);
    void roll_all();
    std::vector<Die> get_dice() const;
};

#endif // MURACH_DICE_H
```

The Dice.cpp file

```
#include "Dice.h"

Dice::Dice() {}

void Dice::add_die(Die die) {
    dice.push_back(die);
}

void Dice::roll_all() {
    for (Die& die : dice) {
        die.roll();
    }
}

std::vector<Die> Dice::get_dice() const {
    return dice;
}
```

Description

- *Object composition* is a way to combine simple objects into more complex ones. For example, one Dice object can store multiple Die objects.
- In a UML diagram, you can use the diamond connector to identify the object that is composed of other objects.

Figure 14-18   A Dice class

The Dice Roller program

Figure 14-19 shows a program named Dice Roller that uses the Die and Dice classes. To start, the code for this program includes the header files for the Die and Dice classes.

After the using directive, the main() function starts by displaying the title of the program. Then, it prompts the user to enter the number of dice to roll. Next, it creates a Dice object and uses a loop to create the correct number of Die objects and add them to the Dice object. To do that, this code uses the abbreviated syntax to call the default constructors for these objects.

After creating the Dice object, the code enters a loop that continues while the user enters 'y'. This loop begins by calling the roll_all() function of the Dice object to roll all of the dice. Then, it loops through each of the Die objects and prints the value of each Die object to the console. To do that, this code calls the get_dice() function to get the vector of Die objects from the Dice object.

After displaying the roll, this code asks if user wants to roll again. If the user enters 'y' for yes, the condition at the top of the loop evaluates to true, so the loop is executed again. Otherwise, the condition at the top of the loop evaluates to false, so the loop ends. Then, a goodbye message is printed and the program ends.

At this point, you may realize that you could accomplish the same results with less code by not using the Die and Dice objects. So, why bother creating these objects?

One advantage of using these objects is that it shields the programmer who uses these classes from the technical details of how the classes work. In this case, the Die class shields the programmer who uses that class from how the random value is generated. In other words, the programmer doesn't need to know how to use the srand() and rand() functions to get a random value from 1 to 6. That might not be a big selling point for a simple class like the Die class, but it is for classes where the underlying technical details are more complex.

Another advantage is that these objects promote code reusability. In other words, the Dice Roller program isn't the only program that can use Die and Dice objects. Other programs that need to roll six-sided dice can also use these classes, especially if you continue to improve their functionality and ease of use.

The console

```
The Dice Roller program

Enter the number of dice to roll: 5
YOUR ROLL: 1 5 1 2 6

Roll again? (y/n): y
YOUR ROLL: 1 1 4 3 4

Roll again? (y/n): y
YOUR ROLL: 5 4 6 2 2

Roll again? (y/n): n
Bye!
```

The code

```cpp
#include <iostream>
#include "Die.h"
#include "Dice.h"

using namespace std;

int main() {
    cout << "The Dice Roller program\n\n";

     // get number of dice from user
    int count;
    cout << "Enter the number of dice to roll: ";
    cin >> count;

    // create Dice object and add Die objects to it
    Dice dice;
    for (int i = 0; i < count; ++i) {
        Die die;
        dice.add_die(die);
    }

    char choice = 'y';
    while (choice == 'y') {
        // roll the dice
        dice.roll_all();
        cout << "YOUR ROLL: ";
        for (Die die : dice.get_dice()) {
            cout << die.get_value() << " ";
        }
        cout << endl;

        cout << "Roll again? (y/n): ";
        cin >> choice;
    }
    cout << "Bye!\n\n";
}
```

Figure 14-19   The Dice Roller program

The Pig Dice game

This chapter finishes by presenting a Pig Dice game that uses an object to store all variables related to the state of the game. This makes it easy to pass the game state from one function to another.

In addition, this Pig Dice game uses the Die class described earlier in this chapter. This shows that the Die class can be used in multiple programs.

The console

Figure 14-20 begins by showing the console for the Pig Dice game. The console begins by displaying the rules for the game. Then, it prompts the user to roll the die or hold the die. If the user holds, the total of all the points rolled for that turn are added to the overall total and the turn ends. If the user rolls and the roll is a 1, though, the turn ends and the points rolled for that turn are lost. The game continues for as many turns as it takes for the player to get to at least 20 points.

The code

The code begins by including the header file for the Die class shown earlier in this chapter. Then, the code defines a structure for the GameState object. This structure defines six public data members to store the state of the game, and it initializes these data members to values that are appropriate for a new game. For example, the turn data member is set to 1, the score data member is set to 0, and the game_over data member is set to false. In addition, the die data member is initialized by using the abbreviated syntax to call the default constructor of the Die class.

At this point, you may wonder why this program doesn't use a class instead of a structure. The answer is that the GameState object applies to this program and isn't designed to be reused by other programs. It just provides a way to combine some related data members that are needed by the program. Also, it doesn't need to provide encapsulation for these data members. As a result, it's a good candidate to be a structure instead of a class.

After defining the GameState structure, this code declares five functions that are used to organize the code. Of these functions, the last four accept the GameState object as a reference parameter. As a result, the code within these functions can get any of the data members of the GameState object to check the state of the game, and it can set any of these data members to change the state of the game.

The console

```
Let's Play PIG!

* See how many turns it takes you to get to 20.
* Turn ends when you hold or roll a 1.
* If you roll a 1, you lose all points for the turn.
* If you hold, you save all points for the turn.

TURN 1
Roll or hold? (r/h): r
Die: 5
Roll or hold? (r/h): r
Die: 4
Roll or hold? (r/h): r
Die: 5
Roll or hold? (r/h): h
Score for turn: 14
Total score: 14

TURN 2
Roll or hold? (r/h): r
Die: 6
Roll or hold? (r/h): h
Score for turn: 6
Total score: 20

You finished in 2 turns!

Game over!
```

The code

```cpp
#include <iostream>
#include "Die.h"

using namespace std;

// a struct for game variables
struct GameState {
    int turn = 1;
    int score = 0;
    int score_this_turn = 0;
    bool turn_over = false;
    bool game_over = false;
    Die die;
};

// declare functions
void display_rules();
void play_game(GameState&);
void take_turn(GameState&);
void roll_die(GameState&);
void hold_turn(GameState&);
```

Figure 14-20   The Pig Dice game (part 1 of 3)

In part 2 of figure 14-20, the main() function begins by calling the display_rules() function to display the welcome message and rules for the game. Then, it creates a GameState object and passes it to the play_game() function.

The play_game() function contains the code that's called when the game is started. This code starts the main loop for the game. This loop continues until the game_over data member of the GameState object is set to true. Within this loop, a single statement calls the take_turn() function and passes it the GameState object.

The take_turn() function begins by printing the turn number. To do that, it gets the turn from the GameState object. Then, it resets the turn_over data member. This isn't necessary on the first turn, but it is necessary for subsequent turns. Next, it begins a while loop that continues until the turn_over data member is set to true.

Within the loop, the code starts by prompting the user to choose whether to roll or hold. If the user chooses to roll, this code calls the roll_die() function and passes the GameState object to it. If the user chooses to hold, this code calls the hold_turn() function and passes the GameState object to it.

The code (continued)

```cpp
int main() {
    display_rules();
    GameState game;
    play_game(game);
}

// define functions
void display_rules() {
    cout << "Let's Play PIG!\n"
         << "\n"
         << "* See how many turns it takes you to get to 20.\n"
         << "* Turn ends when you hold or roll a 1.\n"
         << "* If you roll a 1, you lose all points for the turn.\n"
         << "* If you hold, you save all points for the turn.\n\n";
}

void play_game(GameState& game) {
    while (!game.game_over) {
        take_turn(game);
    }
    cout << "Game over!\n";
}

void take_turn(GameState& game) {
    cout << "TURN " << game.turn << endl;
    game.turn_over = false;
    while (!game.turn_over) {
        char choice;
        cout << "Roll or hold? (r/h): ";
        cin >> choice;

        if (choice == 'r')
            roll_die(game);
        else if (choice == 'h')
            hold_turn(game);
        else
            cout << "Invalid choice. Try again.\n";
    }
}
```

Figure 14-20   The Pig Dice game (part 2 of 3)

In part 3 of figure 14-20, the roll_die() function begins by getting the Die object from the GameState object and calling its roll() function. This updates the value that's stored in the Die object. Next, this code displays the value that's stored in the Die object on the console.

After that, the roll_die() function checks if the value in the die is 1. If it is, the code changes several data members of the GameState object. Specifically, it sets the score_this_turn member to 0, it increments the turn member by 1, and it sets the turn_over member to true. In other words, it discards all points for this turn and ends the turn. Then, it displays a message on the console that indicates that the turn is over and that there was no score for this turn. However, if the die is not 1, this code increments the score_this_turn data member by the value of the die.

The hold_turn() function begins by changing two data members of the GameState object. Specifically, it increments the score data member by the score_this_turn data member, and it sets the turn_over data member to true. In other words, this code saves the score for the turn and ends the turn. Then, the code displays the score for the turn and the total score on the console. Next, the code resets the score_this_turn data member to 0 so it's ready for the next turn.

After that, the hold_turn() function checks if the score is greater than or equal to 20. If it is, this code sets the game_over variable to true and displays a message that indicates how many turns it took to finish the game. Otherwise, this code increments the turn data member by 1.

The code (continued)

```cpp
void roll_die(GameState& game) {
    game.die.roll();

    cout << "Die: " << game.die.getValue() << endl;
    if (game.die.getValue() == 1) {
        game.score_this_turn = 0;
        game.turn += 1;
        game.turn_over = true;
        cout << "Turn over. No score.\n\n";
    }
    else {
        game.score_this_turn += game.die.getValue();
    }
}

void hold_turn(GameState& game) {
    game.score += game.score_this_turn;
    game.turn_over = true;
    cout << "Score for turn: " << game.score_this_turn << endl;
    cout << "Total score: " << game.score << "\n\n";
    game.score_this_turn = 0;

    if (game.score >= 20) {
        game.game_over = true;
        cout << "You finished in " << game.turn << " turns!\n\n";
    }
    else {
        game.turn += 1;
    }
}
```

Figure 14-20   The Pig Dice game (part 3 of 3)

Perspective

This chapter has presented the most useful skills for working with classes and objects. In addition, it has presented the most important principle of object-oriented programming: encapsulation. In the next chapter, you'll learn about two more important principles of OOP: inheritance and polymorphism.

When you're first getting started with OOP, it can be hard to see its advantages over procedural programming. For now, you can focus on just two. First, dividing the code into classes often makes it easier to reuse code. For example, the Die and Dice classes presented in this chapter could be reused by many programs. Second, using classes helps you separate the different layers of a program. That can simplify the development of the program and make the program easier to maintain and enhance later on.

Terms

object-oriented programming (OOP)	getter
data structure	accessor
object	setter
structure	mutator
data member	helper function
member function	constructor
identity	default constructor
state	destructor
behavior	inline function
instance	inline expansion
instantiation	UML (Unified Modeling Language)
encapsulation	class diagram
data hiding	read-only function
class	object composition
interface	

Summary

- *Object-oriented programming* (*OOP*) groups related variables and functions into *data structures* called *objects*.

- A *structure* or *class* can be thought of as a blueprint from which objects are created.

- The *data members* of a structure or class store the data of an object.

- The *member functions* of a structure or class define the tasks that an object can perform. Often, these functions provide a way to work with the data members of an object.

- Once you create an object from a structure or class, the object has an *identity* (a unique address), a *state* (the data that it stores), and *behavior* (the functions that it provides). As a program runs, an object's state may change.

- An object is an *instance* of a structure or class. In other words, you can create multiple objects from a single structure or class. The process of creating an object from a structure or class is sometimes called *instantiation*.

- *Encapsulation* allows you to hide the members of an object from other code that uses the object. This is also known as *data hiding*.

- An *interface* allows a programmer to use an object without understanding its internal code.

- Functions that access the value stored in a data member are commonly referred to as *getters* or *accessors*.

- Functions that change the value stored in a data member are commonly referred to as *setters* or *mutators*.

- If you need to code a member function but you don't want to make it available outside of the class, you can declare it as private. Since this private function can be used by other member functions, it's known as a private *helper function*.

- When you define a class, it sometimes helps to code overloaded setter functions for a data member that accept different types of data. Then, you can use functions such as stoi(), stod(), and to_string() to convert the value that's passed to a setter function to the appropriate type.

- A *constructor* is a special type of member function that's automatically called when you create (construct) an object.

- A *default constructor* has zero required parameters.

- A *destructor* is a special type of member function that's automatically called when an object is destroyed. C++ automatically destroys most objects when the object goes out of scope.

- If you code the definition of a member function in the header file, the function is known as an *inline function*.

- Inline functions are compiled and executed differently than regular functions. The compiler uses a process known as *inline expansion* to replace each function call with the code in the function itself. This can reduce the overhead needed to call a function.

- *UML* (*Unified Modeling Language*) is the industry standard used to describe the classes and objects of an object-oriented program.

- A UML *class diagram* describes the data members and member functions of one or more classes.

- When a member function provides a way to get data that can't be set in the object, it's known as a *read-only function*.

- *Object composition* is a way to combine simple objects into more complex ones.

Exercise 14-1   Enhance the Dice Roller program

In this exercise, you'll enhance the Dice Roller program by making some improvements to its classes. When you're done, rolling two dice should look something like this:

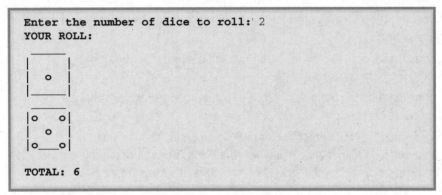

Open and test the program

1. Open the project or solution named dice_roller in this folder:
   `ex_starts\ch14_ex1_dice_roller`

2. Review the code and run the program to make sure it works correctly. Note that it starts by displaying an image for each of the six possible die values.

Improve the Die class

3. In the Die class, add a member function named get_image() that gets a string for an image that represents the die's current value. For example, the console above displays images that represent a roll of 1 and 5.

4. Modify the code that displays the roll so it uses the new get_image() function to display an image for each die instead of displaying the value.

5. In the Die class, add a set_value() function that allows you to set the value data member by passing an int value to it. This function should throw an exception if this int value isn't from 1 to 6.

6. In the main() function for the program, modify the code that displays the six die images so it uses a loop to create a Die object for each valid number and to display its image. This reduces code duplication since the code that defines the image is only stored in one place now, in the Die class.

Improve the Dice class

7. In the Dice class, add a function named get_total() that gets the total value of all Die objects currently stored in the Dice object.

8. Add code that displays the total each time the user rolls the dice.

Exercise 14-2   Create an object-oriented Convert Temperatures program

In this exercise, you'll modify the Convert Temperatures program presented in chapter 7 so it uses object-oriented programming instead of procedural programming.

Open and test the program

1. Open the project or solution named temperature_converter in this folder:

    `ex_starts\ch14_ex2_temperature_converter`

2. Review the code for the program and note how it uses functions to convert the temperatures.

3. Run the code to make sure it works correctly.

Define a Temp object that can store a temperature

4. Use your IDE to create a header file and an implementation file for a class named Temp.

5. In the header file, define two private data members to store the degrees Fahrenheit and Celsius.

6. Declare and define a default constructor that sets the private data members to the temperature where water freezes, which is 0 degrees Celcius or 32 degrees Fahrenheit.

7. Declare and define getter functions for the private data members. Each of these functions should round the number that it returns to 1 decimal place. To do that, you can copy code from the main.cpp file.

8. Declare and define setter functions for the private data members. When you set one unit of temperature, it should also calculate and set the other unit of temperature. For example, when you set degrees Fahrenheit, it should also calculate and set degrees Celsius. If you want, you can copy the code that performs these calculations from the main.cpp file.

Modify the program so it uses the Temp object

9. In the main.cpp file, delete the to_fahrenheit() and to_celsius() functions.

10. In the main.cpp file, add a statement that includes the header file for the Temp class.

11. In the convert_temp() function, create a Temp object and use it to set and get the temperature.

12. In the main.cpp file, remove any code that's unnecessary, including any unnecessary include directives.

Exercise 14-3   Create an object-oriented Circle Calculator program

This exercise guides you through the process of converting the Circle calculator program from chapter 2 from a procedural program to an object-oriented program.

Open and test the program

1. Open the project or solution named circle_calculator in this folder:
    `ex_starts\ch14_ex3_circle_calculator`

2. Review the code for the program and run it to make sure it works correctly.

Create and use a Circle object

3. Use your IDE to create a header file and an implementation file for a class named Circle.

4. In the Circle class, add a private data member for the radius. Then, define a private data member for pi that stores a constant value of 3.14159.

5. Code a default constructor that sets the radius to a value of zero.

6. Code public getter and setter functions that allow you to get and set the radius. You can code both of these functions as inline functions.

7. In the header file, declare getter functions that calculate the diameter, circumference, and area of the circle and return a double value for each result. Then, define these functions in the implementation file. If you want, you can get the code for these calculations from the main.cpp file.

8. In the main.cpp file, modify the code for the main() function so it creates a Circle object and sets its radius to the value entered by the user.

9. In the main() function, modify the code that calculates the diameter, circumference, and area so it uses the functions of the Circle object to perform these calculations. However, the code in this function should still round the circumference and area to 1 decimal place.

10. In the main.cpp file, remove any code that's unnecessary, including any unnecessary include directives.

11. Run the program and test it with valid data. It should calculate and display the diameter, circumference, and area for a circle just as it did before.

Overload the constructor

12. Open the Circle class. Then, modify the constructor so it accepts an optional parameter for the radius and supplies a default value of zero for that parameter. This constructor should set the radius data member to the value supplied by the parameter.

13. In the main() function, modify the code so it uses the constructor to set the radius data member.

14. Run the program and test it to make sure it still works correctly.

15

How to work with inheritance

In the previous chapter, you learned how to work with encapsulation, one of the fundamental concepts of object-oriented programming. In this chapter, you'll learn how to work with two more fundamental concepts of object-oriented programming: inheritance and polymorphism.

Inheritance is typically used by the developers of large programs to develop a consistent set of classes. When used correctly, inheritance can simplify the design of a program and reduce code duplication. However, when used incorrectly, inheritance can violate encapsulation and create unwanted dependencies between classes.

In this chapter, you'll begin by learning *how* inheritance works. Then, at the end of this chapter, you'll learn *when* it makes sense to use inheritance.

How to get started with inheritance

Inheritance allows you to create a new class that's based on an existing class. Along with encapsulation, it is a fundamental concept of object-oriented programming.

How inheritance works

With inheritance, a *subclass* inherits the public data members and member functions of a *superclass* as shown by the diagram in figure 15-1. Then, when you create an object from the subclass, that object can use these data members and member functions. The subclass can also add new data members and member functions to the superclass, and it can change the way the data members and member functions of the superclass work by *overriding* them and providing new code for them.

The UML diagram in this figure shows how this works. Here, the superclass is the Product class. This class has three data members. Of these data members, the first one has *protected* access. This means that it's available to the current class and its subclasses, but not to any code that's outside of these classes. To indicate that a member is protected, a UML diagram typically uses the hash symbol (#). The other two data members are private. As a result, they are only available within the Product class.

In addition, the Product class has seven public member functions. The first six member functions work the same as the Product class presented in the previous chapter. However, the get_description() function is a new function that's described in the next figure.

This diagram contains two subclasses: Book and Movie. These classes inherit the protected data member and the seven member functions from the Product superclass. Then, each subclass adds a new data member. The Book class adds the author data member, and the Movie class adds the year data member. Next, each subclass adds getter and setter functions that provide indirect access to its new private data member. In addition, they both change the way the get_description() member function of the Product class works by overriding it.

In this book, we use *superclass* to refer to a class that another class inherits and *subclass* to refer to a class that inherits another class. However, a superclass can also be called a *base* or *parent class*, and a subclass can also be called a *derived* or *child class*.

A UML diagram for three classes that use inheritance

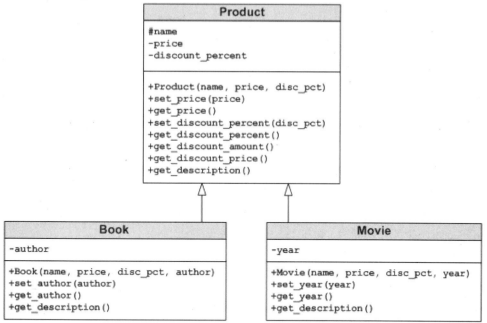

Description

- *Inheritance* lets you create a new class based on an existing class. Then, the new class *inherits* the public data members and member functions of the existing class.

- A class that another class inherits is called a *base class*, *parent class*, or *superclass*.

- A class that inherits another class is called a *derived class*, *child class*, or *subclass*.

- A superclass can include protected members that are only available to the current class and its subclasses.

- A subclass can add new data members and functions to the superclass. It can also *override* a function from the superclass by providing its own version of the function.

UML diagramming note

- To indicate that a member is protected, a UML diagram typically uses the hash symbol (#).

- To indicate that a class inherits another class, a UML diagram typically uses an arrow with an open (not shaded) arrowhead.

Figure 15-1   How inheritance works

How to define a superclass

Figure 15-2 shows how to create a class that can be used as a superclass for one or more subclasses. To do that, you define the data members and member functions of the class just as you would for any other class.

This figure starts by summarizing several *access modifiers* you can use to specify whether members of a superclass are accessible to code outside the class. By now, you should be familiar with the private and public access modifiers. To review, you use the private keyword for any members that you only want to be available within the current class. In contrast, you use the public keyword for any members that you want to be available to all calling code.

Beyond that, you may occasionally want to use the protected keyword to code protected members. A protected member can be accessed within the current class and its subclasses, but not by any code outside of these classes. This lets subclasses access certain parts of the superclass without exposing those parts to other classes. For example, the Product class in this figure uses protected access for the name data member. As a result, any subclass of the Product class can access this data member directly, but no other calling code can.

The Product class shown in this figure includes a get_description() member function. The declaration for this function begins with the virtual keyword. This identifies this function as a function that subclasses can *override*.

The definition for the get_description() function returns the name data member. This is a concise and easy-to-read representation of this object that also works for subclasses. As a result, any subclass of this class can use this get_description() member function. Or, it can override the get_description() member function to provide its own code for that member function.

If you don't include the virtual keyword for the get_description() function, any subclass that provides this function *redefines* the get_description() function in the superclass instead of overriding it. Unfortunately, this prevents polymorphism from working correctly. So, if you want polymorphism to work correctly as described in figure 15-5, you need to use the virtual keyword to identify the functions that are designed to be overridden, not redefined.

You should also code the virtual keyword for a destructor of a superclass. Otherwise, the destructor won't work correctly for subclasses. This isn't an issue for a class like the Product class that's shown in this figure, but you should be aware of it in case you ever need to use a class like the HeapArray class described in section 4 as a superclass.

Access modifiers

Keyword	Description
private	Available to the current class.
protected	Available to the current class and its subclasses.
public	Available to the current class, its subclasses, and all other classes.

The Product.h file for the Product superclass

```
#ifndef MURACH_PRODUCT_H
#define MURACH_PRODUCT_H

#include <string>

class Product {
protected:
    std::string name;       // protected data member
private:
    double price;
    int discount_percent;
public:
    Product(std::string name = "", double price = 0.0,
            int discount_pct = 0);

    void set_price(double);
    double get_price() const { return price; }

    void set_discount_percent(int);
    int get_discount_percent() const { return discount_percent; }

    double get_discount_amount() const;
    double get_discount_price() const;

    // virtual function - necessary for polymorphism
    virtual std::string get_description() const;
};

#endif // MURACH_PRODUCT_H
```

The get_description() function in the Product.cpp file

```
string Product::get_description() const {
    return name;
}
```

When coding a superclass...

- You can declare protected members that are only available to the current class and its subclasses.

- You can use the virtual keyword to identify functions that are designed to be overridden by subclasses.

- You should declare the destructor, if one exists, as virtual. Otherwise, the destructor won't work correctly for subclasses.

Figure 15-2   How to define a superclass

How to define a subclass

Figure 15-3 starts by showing some syntax that's helpful for working with subclasses. Then, it presents two examples that use this syntax.

The first example shows the complete code for the Book class. To indicate that this class is a subclass, the name of the class is followed by a colon, the public keyword, and the name of the class that you want to inherit. Here, the Book class inherits the Product class. In other words, the Book class is a subclass of the Product superclass.

After you declare the subclass, you can add functionality to the superclass by adding data members and member functions. For example, the Book subclass adds a new data member named author, getter and setter functions for that data member, and a new constructor. In addition, it overrides the get_description() member function defined by the Product class.

The constructor for the Book subclass accepts four arguments. The first three are the same as the Product class, but the fourth provides the value for the author data member. This constructor calls the Product class constructor and passes it the first three arguments. This initializes the three data members that are defined by the Product class. Then, the statement in the body of the constructor initializes the author data member of the Book class to the value of the author parameter.

To override a virtual function of the superclass, you begin by coding a member function with the same name and signature as the function in the super-class. In this case, the get_description() function of the Book class overrides the virtual get_description() function of the Product class. The code within this function returns a string that's created by concatenating the name data member of the Product object with "by" and the author data member of the Book object.

In the first example, the get_description() function accesses the name data member directly. This is possible because the Product class declares that data member as protected. However, that doesn't mean this is always the best way to access this data member. For example, it often makes sense to begin by calling the member function in the superclass as shown by the second example. That way, if you change the member function in the superclass later, the member function in the subclass will reflect that change.

When you define subclasses, you typically code the public keyword before the name of the superclass as shown in this figure. That way, an object created from the subclass has the same access to the members of the superclass as an object created from the superclass. However, if that's not what you want, you can use the protected and private keywords instead to restrict access to the members of the superclass.

For example, if you coded the protected keyword before the name of the Product class, public and protected members of the Product class would become protected in the Book class. As a result, subclasses of the Book class would still be able to directly access these members, although these subclasses would be using protected access, not public access. However, if you coded the private keyword, the public members would become protected, and the protected members would become private. As a result, subclasses of the Book class would not be able to directly access the protected data member.

The syntax for working with subclasses

To define a subclass

```
class SubclassName : public|protected|private SuperclassName {}
```

To define a subclass constructor that calls a superclass constructor

```
SubclassName([parameterList]) : SuperclassName(argumentList) {}
```

To call a superclass member function

```
SuperclassName::function_name(argumentList);
```

The Book.h file for the Book subclass

```cpp
#ifndef MURACH_BOOK_H
#define MURACH_BOOK_H

#include <string>
#include "Product.h"

class Book : public Product {
private:
    std::string author;
public:
    Book(std::string name = "", double price = 0.0,
         int disc_pct = 0, std::string author_param = "") :
         Product(name, price, disc_pct) {
        author = author_param;
    }

    void set_author(std::string author_param) {
        author = author_param;
    }
    std::string get_author() const { return author; }

    std::string get_description() const {
        return name + " by " + author;
    }
};
#endif // MURACH_BOOK_H
```

Another way to code the get_description() function

```cpp
string get_description() const {
    return Product::get_description() + " by " + author;
}
```

When coding a subclass...

- You can add new members that aren't in the superclass.

- You can override virtual member functions in the superclass by coding member functions that have the same name and signature.

- You can directly access public and protected members of the superclass.

- You can call member functions of the superclass by coding the name of the superclass, the scope resolution operator (::), and the name of the function.

Figure 15-3   How to define a subclass

How to define another subclass

Figure 15-4 shows how to define another subclass named Movie. This class works much like the Book subclass described in the previous figure, except that this subclass defines a product that is a movie, not a book.

To start, the Movie class declares that it inherits the Product class. Then, the Movie class adds a private data member named year, getter and setter functions for that data member, and a constructor that calls the constructor of the Product class. In addition, the Movie class overrides the get_description() member function defined by the Product class so it returns the name of the movie followed by the year in parentheses.

Now that you've seen the Book and Movie subclasses, you should note that all of the implementation for these classes is included in the header files. Because of that, no implementation files are needed. In many cases, however, you'll want to declare the functions of a subclass in the header file and define them in the implementation file. For example, if you wanted to validate the year before storing it in the year data member of a Movie object as shown in the last chapter, you would typically define the set_year() function in the implementation file.

The Movie.h file for the Movie subclass

```
#ifndef MURACH_MOVIE_H
#define MURACH_MOVIE_H

#include <string>
#include "Product.h"

class Movie : public Product {
private:
    int year;
public:
    Movie(std::string name = "", double price = 0.0, int disc_pct = 0,
            int year_param = 1888) : Product(name, price, disc_pct) {
        year = year_param;
    }

    void set_year(int year_param) {
        year = year_param;
    }
    int get_year() const { return year; }

    std::string get_description() const {
        return name + " (" + std::to_string(year) + ')';
    }
};

#endif // MURACH_MOVIE_H
```

Note

- Because the Movie subclass and the Book subclass in the previous figure are fully implemented in their header files, no implementation files are required.

Figure 15-4   How to define another subclass

How polymorphism works

Polymorphism lets you treat objects of different types as if they were the same type by referring to a superclass that's common to the objects. For example, figure 15-5 defines a show_product() function that treats Book and Movie objects as if they were Product objects. Like encapsulation and inheritance, polymorphism is a fundamental feature of object-oriented programming.

One benefit of polymorphism is that you can write generic code that's designed to work with a superclass. Then, you can use that code with objects that are created from any subclass of the superclass. For instance, the first example in this figure shows the get_description() member functions for the Product, Book, and Movie classes. The Book version of the get_description() member function adds the author to the end of the product's description. Similarly, the Movie version adds the year to the end of the product's description.

The second example shows a function named show_product() that accepts a Product object by constant reference. Since Book and Movie objects are a type of Product object, this function also accepts Book and Movie objects. Within this function, the code shows the product by displaying the string that's returned by the get_description() member function as well as the value that's returns by the get_discount_price() member function.

The main() function presented in the third example shows how this works. To start, the first three statements create a Product object, a Book object, and a Movie object. Then, the next three statements pass these three objects to the show_product() function.

When you run this code, C++ uses polymorphism to call the correct get_description() member function from each object. The console in this figure shows that this works correctly. Here, the description for the Book object includes the author's name, and the description for the Movie object includes the year that the movie was made.

The key to polymorphism is that C++ decides which member function to call at runtime. This is known as *dynamic binding* or *late binding*, and it's made possible by the virtual keyword that's coded in the superclass. If you don't declare the get_description() function as a virtual function in the superclass, C++ decides which member function to call at compile time. This is known as *static binding* or *early binding*. In this example, static binding would cause C++ to call the get_description() function of the Product class for the Book and Movie objects. As a result, this code would not display the author's name for a Book object or the year for a Movie object.

In summary, *overriding* a virtual member function allows polymorphism to work because it uses dynamic binding. On the other hand, *redefining* a member function that isn't a virtual function doesn't allow polymorphism to work because it uses static binding.

Three definitions of the get_description() function

In the Product superclass

```
string Product::get_description() const {
    return name;
}
```

In the Book subclass

```
string get_description() const {
    return name + " by " + author;
}
```

In the Movie subclass

```
string get_description() const {
    return name + " (" + std::to_string(year) + ')';
}
```

A function that calls the virtual function

```
void show_product(const Product& p) {
    cout << "Description:    " << p.get_description() << '\n';
    cout << "Discount Price: " << p.get_discount_price() << "\n\n";
}
```

Code that passes three different object types to the function

```
int main() {
    Product product("Stanley 13 Ounce Wood Hammer", 12.99, 62);
    Book book("The Big Short", 15.95, 34, "Michael Lewis");
    Movie movie("The Wizard of Oz", 14.99, 50, 1939);

    show_product(product);
    show_product(book);
    show_product(movie);
}
```

The console

```
Description:    Stanley 13 Ounce Wood Hammer
Discount Price: 4.94

Description:    The Big Short by Michael Lewis
Discount Price: 10.53

Description:    The Wizard of Oz (1939)
Discount Price: 7.49
```

Description

- *Polymorphism* is a feature of inheritance that lets you treat objects of subclasses as if they were objects of the superclass.

- If you access a function of a superclass object and the function is overridden in the subclasses of that class, polymorphism determines which function is executed based on the object's type.

Figure 15-5   How polymorphism works

The Product Viewer program

To show how the Product, Book, and Movie classes can work together, figure 15-6 presents another version of the Product Viewer program that was presented in the previous chapter. To start, the code for this program imports the header files it needs, including the header files for the Product, Book, and Movie classes defined in the previous figures.

After importing the header files, this code defines three constants, one for each of the available products. Of these three products, one object is of the Product type, one is of the Book type, and one is of the Movie type. Then, this code defines the three functions of the program.

The show_products() function calls the get_description() member function to display the data for the three products on the console. Since this function calls the get_description() function directly from the object, C++ uses static binding to determine which get_description() function to call. As a result, it doesn't use polymorphism.

The console

```
PRODUCTS
1. Stanley 13 Ounce Wood Hammer
2. The Big Short by Michael Lewis
3. The Wizard of Oz (1939)

Enter product number: 2

PRODUCT DATA
Name:              The Big Short by Michael Lewis
Price:             15.95
Discount percent: 34
Discount amount:  5.42
Discount price:   10.53

View another product? (y/n): y

Enter product number: 3

PRODUCT DATA
Name:              The Wizard of Oz (1939)
Price:             14.99
Discount percent: 50
Discount amount:  7.5
Discount price:   7.49

View another product? (y/n): n

Bye!
```

The code

```cpp
#include <iostream>
#include <string>
#include "Product.h"
#include "Book.h"
#include "Movie.h"

using namespace std;

const Product p1("Stanley 13 Ounce Wood Hammer", 12.99, 62);
const Book p2("The Big Short", 15.95, 34, "Michael Lewis");
const Movie p3("The Wizard of Oz", 14.99, 50, 1939);

void show_products() {
    cout << "PRODUCTS\n"
         << "1. " << p1.get_description() << endl
         << "2. " << p2.get_description() << endl
         << "3. " << p3.get_description() << endl << endl;
}
```

Figure 15-6   The Product Viewer program (part 1 of 2)

The show_product() function, on the other hand, calls the get_description() function from an object that has been passed to a function that accepts a Product object. As a result, C++ uses dynamic binding and polymorphism to determine which get_description() function to call. This function works like the show_product() function shown in the previous figure. However, it displays more information about each product, such as the discount percent, discount amount, and discount price.

The main() function begins by displaying the title of the program. Then, it calls the show_products() function to display the numbered list of products. Next, this function prompts the user to enter a number that corresponds to a product. After the user enters a number, this code uses a switch statement to pass the corresponding Product object to the show_product() function. This displays the data for the product object, which varies based on the object type.

The code (continued)

```cpp
void show_product(const Product& p) {
    cout << "PRODUCT DATA\n"
        << "Name:              " << p.get_description() << endl
        << "Price:             " << p.get_price() << endl
        << "Discount percent: " << p.get_discount_percent() << endl
        << "Discount amount:  " << p.get_discount_amount() << endl
        << "Discount price:    " << p.get_discount_price() << "\n\n";
}

int main() {
    cout << "The Product Viewer program\n\n";

    show_products();

    char choice = 'y';
    while (choice == 'y') {
        int number;
        cout << "Enter product number: ";
        cin >> number;
        cout << endl;

        switch (number) {
            case 1:
                show_product(p1);
                break;
            case 2:
                show_product(p2);
                break;
            case 3:
                show_product(p3);
                break;
            default:
                cout << "Invalid product number.\n\n";
                break;
        }

        cout << "View another product? (y/n): ";
        cin >> choice;
        cout << endl;
    }
    cout << "Bye!\n\n";

    return 0;
}
```

Figure 15-6   The Product Viewer program (part 2 of 2)

More skills for working with inheritance

Now that you've learned the basic skills for working with inheritance and polymorphism, you're ready to learn some more skills for working with inheritance. You might not need to use these skills often, but they are sometimes helpful.

How to define an abstract class

An *abstract class* is a class that can't be instantiated. In other words, you can't create an object directly from an abstract class. Instead, you can code a class that inherits an abstract class, and you can create an object from that class.

Figure 15-7 shows how to work with abstract classes. To make a class abstract, you declare one of its functions as a *pure virtual function* by coding an equal sign (=) and a zero at the end of the function declaration and by not including a function definition. In this figure, for instance, the first example declares the get_description() function of the Product class as a pure virtual function, and it doesn't provide code that defines this function. As a result, this Product class is an abstract class.

When you code a class that inherits an abstract class, you must override any pure virtual functions in the abstract class as shown by the second example. Here, classes named Book and Movie that inherit the Product class override the pure virtual member function named get_description().

When you work with an abstract class, you can't create an instance of the abstract type. In this figure, for example, you can't create a Product object. Instead, you must use a Book or Movie object.

So, why would you use abstract classes? One common use is to implement most, but not all, of the functionality of a class as a convenience to the programmer. That way, the programmer only needs to supply code for the pure virtual functions. In this figure, for example, the Book and Movie subclasses only need to supply code for the pure virtual get_description() function of the Product class, but they can use the other functions of the Product class such as get_price(), set_price(), and so on.

A pure virtual function in the Product.h file

```
class Product {
protected:
    std::string name;        // protected data member

private:
    double price;
    int discount_percent;

public:
    // other public functions and constructors

    // pure virtual function
    virtual std::string get_description() const = 0;
};
```

Two subclasses that override the pure virtual function

In the Book subclass

```
std::string get_description() const {
    return name + " by " + author;
}
```

In the Movie subclass

```
std::string get_description() const {
    return name + " (" + std::to_string(year) + ')';
}
```

Code that attempts to create Product, Book, and Movie objects

```
// Compile-time error! Cannot instantiate abstract Product class
Product p1("Stanley 13 Ounce Wood Hammer", 12.99, 62);

// Success! Can instantiate Book and Movie classes
Book p2("The Big Short", 15.95, 34, "Michael Lewis");
Movie p3("The Wizard of Oz", 14.99, 50, 1939);
```

Description

- An *abstract class* is a class that can be inherited by other classes but that you can't use to create an object.

- To create an abstract class, declare one of its virtual functions as a *pure virtual function* by coding "= 0" at the end of the function declaration.

Figure 15-7   How to define an abstract class

How to control overriding

Figure 15-8 shows how to use the override and final keywords to help control overriding. Both of these keywords were introduced with C++11. As a result, they don't work with older compilers. Although these keywords are optional, they can help prevent errors that are hard to detect if you don't use them.

You can use the override keyword to explicitly identify a function as a function that overrides a virtual function. To do that, you code the override keyword at the end of the function declaration as shown by the first example. This clearly shows that the get_description() functions of the Book and Movie classes override the virtual get_description() function of the Product class. Although this keyword isn't required, it makes your code easier to understand for other programmers, and it allows the compiler to make sure that the get_description() function of the Product class is a virtual function.

You can use the final keyword to prevent subclasses from overriding an inherited virtual function. To do that, you can code the final keyword at the end of the function declaration as shown by the second example. Here, the get_description() functions of the Book and Movie classes can't be overridden by any classes that inherit these classes.

When necessary, you can use both the override and final keywords at the end of the same function declaration as shown by the third example. This clearly indicates that the get_description() function of the Book subclass overrides the virtual get_description() function of the Product class. In addition, it prevents subclasses of the Book class from overriding this function

Two functions that explicitly override another function

In the Book subclass

```cpp
string get_description() const override {
    return name + " by " + author;
}
```

In the Movie subclass

```cpp
string get_description() const override {
    return name + " (" + std::to_string(year) + ')';
    }
```

A function that can't be overridden

In the Book subclass

```cpp
string get_description() const final {
    return name + " by " + author;
}
```

In the Movie subclass

```cpp
string get_description() const final {
    return name + " (" + std::to_string(year) + ')';
}
```

A function that explicitly overrides and can't be overridden

In the Book subclass

```cpp
string get_description() const override final {
    return name + " by " + author;
}
```

Description

- To explicitly identify a function as a function that overrides a virtual function with the same name, you can code the override keyword at the end of the function declaration. This is optional, but it can help prevent errors that are hard to detect and fix.

- To prevent subclasses from overriding an inherited virtual function, you can code the final keyword at the end of the function declaration.

- When necessary, you can use the override and final keywords in the same function declaration.

- The override and final keywords were introduced with C++11.

Figure 15-8   How to control overriding

How to work with multiple inheritance

Multiple inheritance allows a class to inherit multiple classes. C++ is one of the few programming languages to support multiple inheritance.

Multiple inheritance can lead to good program design, but it can lead to problems such as the dreaded "diamond problem", sometimes called the "deadly diamond of death". If you want to learn more about this problem, a quick web search should lead to a description of it as well as ways to solve it. But first, you should learn the basic skills for working with multiple inheritance.

How multiple inheritance works

Figure 15-9 presents a UML diagram that shows how multiple inheritance works. Here, the DayIO class inherits the DayReader and DayWriter classes. As a result, you can call the load_temps() and save_temps() functions from an object created from the DayIO class.

This figure also shows the code for the Day structure that's used by the DayReader and DayWriter classes. You can create a Day object from this structure, and you can store the low and high temperatures for the day within this object. Then, you can use the DayReader and DayWriter classes to load or save a vector of Day objects.

The DayReader superclass

Figure 15-10 shows the code in the header and implementation files for the DayReader superclass. To start, the header file includes the header for the Day structure. Then, it declares a private data member to store the filename for the file that contains the data. Next, it declares a constructor that provides a way to set the filename. In addition, it declares a load_temps() function that provides a way to load a vector of Day objects with the data that's stored in the specified file.

By now, you should be able to understand most of the code in the definition for the load_temps() function. Note, however, that this code throws an exception named DayIOError if it can't open the specified file. This works as described in chapter 13, but it uses a custom DayIOError class that's described later in this chapter. To make this work, the implementation file includes the header file for the DayIOError class.

The DayWriter superclass

Figure 15-11 shows the code in the header and implementation files for the DayWriter superclass. This works much like the code for the DayReader superclass. However, the files for the DayWriter class declare and define a save_temps() function that provides a way to save the data that's stored in a vector of Day objects to the specified file.

A UML diagram for a class that uses multiple inheritance

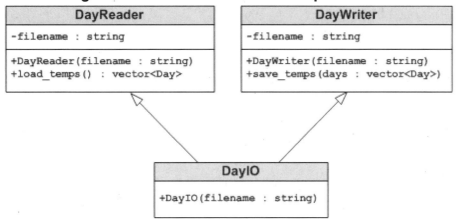

The Day structure

```
#ifndef MURACH_DAY_H
#define MURACH_DAY_H

struct Day {
    double low_temp;
    double high_temp;
};

#endif // MURACH_DAY_H
```

Description

- *Multiple inheritance* allows a class to inherit multiple classes.
- The Day structure defines a Day object that stores the low and high temperatures for the day.
- The DayReader and DayWriter classes work with a vector of Day objects.
- The DayIO class inherits the DayReader and DayWriter classes. As a result, the load_temps() and save_temps() functions are available from a DayIO object.

Figure 15-9   How multiple inheritance works

The DayReader superclass

The DayReader.h file

```cpp
#ifndef MURACH_DAYREADER_H
#define MURACH_DAYREADER_H

#include <string>
#include <vector>
#include "Day.h"        // include Day structure

class DayReader {
private:
    std::string filename;
public:
    DayReader(std::string filename = "");
    std::vector<Day> load_temps();
};

#endif // MURACH_DAYREADER_H
```

The DayReader.cpp file

```cpp
#include <fstream>
#include <vector>
#include "DayReader.h"
#include "DayIOError.h"

using namespace std;

DayReader::DayReader(std::string filename_param) {
    filename = filename_param;
}

vector<Day> DayReader::load_temps() {
    vector<Day> days;
    Day day;
    ifstream input_file(filename);
    if (input_file) {
        while (input_file >> day.low_temp >> day.high_temp) {
            days.push_back(day);
        }
        input_file.close();
        return days;
    }
    else {
        throw DayIOError("Unable to open file: " + filename);
    }
}
```

Figure 15-10   The DayReader superclass

The DayWriter superclass

The DayWriter.h file

```cpp
#ifndef MURACH_DAYWRITER_H
#define MURACH_DAYWRITER_H

#include <string>
#include <vector>
#include "Day.h"    // include Day structure

class DayWriter {
private:
    std::string filename;
public:
    DayWriter(std::string filename = "");
    void save_temps(const std::vector<Day>& temps);
};

#endif // MURACH_DAYWRITER_H
```

The DayWriter.cpp file

```cpp
#include <fstream>
#include <vector>
#include "DayWriter.h"

using namespace std;

DayWriter::DayWriter(std::string filename_param) {
    filename = filename_param;
}

void DayWriter::save_temps(const vector<Day>& days) {
    ofstream output_file(filename);
    for (Day day : days) {
        output_file << day.low_temp << '\t' << day.high_temp << '\n';
    }
    output_file.close();
}
```

Figure 15-11   The DayWriter superclass

The DayIO subclass

Figure 15-12 starts by showing the code for the header and implementation files for the DayIO subclass. The header file includes the header files it needs, including the header files for the DayReader and DayWriter classes. Then, it declares that the DayIO class inherits both the DayReader and DayWriter classes. To do that, this code separates the names of the two superclasses with a comma. Next, it declares a constructor for the DayIO class that accepts a filename as an argument.

At this point, the implementation file doesn't need to do anything except implement the constructor. To do that, it just calls the constructors of the DayReader and DayWriter classes and passes them the filename parameter of the current constructor. Here, it separates the calls to the two superclass constructors with a comma.

Code that uses the DayIO subclass

Figure 15-12 finishes by showing some code that uses the DayIO subclass. Here, the first statement creates a DayIO object by passing a filename to the constructor of the DayIO class. Then, it assigns this DayIO object to a variable named dayIO.

The second statement calls the load_temps() function that's available from the DayIO object to read data from the file and store it in a vector of Day objects. Then, it assigns the vector of Day objects to the variable named days. At this point, a program such as the Temperature Manager program from chapter 13 could display or modify the data stored in this vector.

The third statement calls the save_temps() function that's available from the DayIO object to write data from the vector of Day objects to the file. If a program such as the Temperature Manager program from chapter 13 had modified the vector of Day objects, this would provide a way for that program to save these changes.

The DayIO subclass

The DayIO.h file

```
#ifndef MURACH_DAYIO_H
#define MURACH_DAYIO_H

#include <string>
#include "DayReader.h"
#include "DayWriter.h"

class DayIO : public DayReader, public DayWriter
{
public:
    DayIO(std::string filename = "");
};

#endif // MURACH_DAYIO_H
```

The DayIO.cpp file

```
#include <string>
#include "DayIO.h"

DayIO::DayIO(std::string filename) : DayReader(filename),
                                     DayWriter(filename)
{}
```

Code that uses the DayIO subclass

Code that creates a DayIO object

```
DayIO dayIO("temps.txt");
```

Code that uses the DayIO object to get a vector of Day objects

```
vector<Day> days = dayIO.load_temps();
```

Code that uses the DayIO object to save a vector of Day objects

```
dayIO.save_temps(days);
```

Figure 15-12   The DayIO subclass

When to use inheritance

To develop simple programs like the ones in this book, you typically don't need to use inheritance. If you continue with programming, though, you'll eventually need to use inheritance. In addition, if you ever design a larger or more complex program, you'll need to learn when it makes sense to use inheritance and when you should use object composition instead.

How to use inheritance with custom exceptions

In chapter 13, you learned how to create a custom exception by defining a structure with data members for the error information you want to store. Another way to create a custom exception, though, is to create a class that inherits one of the classes in the exception hierarchy. This is shown in figure 15-13, and this is a good example of when it makes sense to use inheritance in your programs.

To start, this figure shows the hierarchy for some common exceptions. By now, you should have a pretty good idea of how this inheritance hierarchy works. For example, it should be clear to you that the invalid_argument class is a subclass of the logic_error class, which is a subclass of the exception class.

The first code example defines a class named DayIOError that inherits the runtime_error class. The body of this class defines a constructor that can be used to set an error message. To set that error message, this constructor calls the constructor of the runtime_error class and passes it the message parameter. As a result, the DayIOError class works like the runtime_error class.

It's important to note, though, that the DayIOError class has a different name and a different position in the inheritance hierarchy than the runtime_error class. This is important because the name of the error provides information about the error. In addition, the position in the inheritance hierarchy provides the flexibility to handle a DayIOError differently than other types of exceptions.

The second code example shows how to throw a custom exception. Here, the load_temps() function attempts to read temperature data from a file and return a vector of Day objects. However, if it can't open the file, this function throws a DayIOError object with an appropriate message.

The third code example shows how to catch a custom exception. Here, the try clause calls the load_temps() function that might throw the custom DayIOError exception. Then, the catch clause catches this exception and handles it. To do that, it starts by calling the what() function from the DayIOError object to display the error message in that object. This function is available to the DayIOError object because the DayIOError class inherits the runtime_error class, which provides the what() function. Next, the catch clause displays a message that indicates that the program is ending, and it uses the return statement to end the program normally.

As you review this code, note that the custom DayIOError class makes the calling code easier to read and understand. That's because it clearly identifies the type of exception that's being handled by the catch clause. In particular, it shows that this catch clause is handling the DayIOError that might be thrown by the load_temps() function that's available from the DayIO object.

The hierarchy for some common exceptions

```
exception
    logic_error
        invalid_argument
        out_of_range
    runtime_error
        range_error
        overflow_error
        underflow_error
```

A DayIOError.h file that defines a class for a custom exception

```cpp
#ifndef MURACH_DAYIOERROR_H
#define MURACH_DAYIOERROR_H

#include <iostream>
#include <string>

class DayIOError : public std::runtime_error {
public:
    DayIOError(std::string message = "") : runtime_error(message) {};
};

#endif // MURACH_DAYIOERROR_H
```

Code that throws the custom exception

```cpp
vector<Day> DayReader::load_temps() {
    vector<Day> days;
    Day day;
    ifstream input_file(filename);
    if (input_file) {
        // code that reads data from the file goes here
        return days;
    }
    else {
        throw DayIOError("Unable to open file: " + filename);
    }
}
```

Code that catches a custom exception

```cpp
vector<Day> days;
try {
    days = dayIO.load_temps();
}
catch (const DayIOError& e) {
    cout << e.what() << "\n"
         << "Exiting program. Bye!\n\n";
    return 0;
}
```

Description

- To define a custom exception, you can code a class that inherits one of the built-in exception classes. Then, you can use the custom exception as you would any other exception.

Figure 15-13   How to use inheritance with custom exceptions

Guidelines for using inheritance

Figure 15-14 begins by listing three guidelines for when it makes sense to use inheritance in your programs. First, it makes sense to use inheritance when the subclass *is a* type of the superclass. For example, this chapter has presented a Book object that *is a* type of a Product object.

Second, it makes sense to use inheritance when both classes are part of the same logical domain. For example, the Product, Book, and Movie objects shown in this chapter are all in the same domain. In other words, they're all part of a domain that's attempting to define the different types of products for a system.

Third, it makes sense to use inheritance when the subclass primarily adds features to the superclass. In other words, it makes sense when a subclass adds new data members or member functions to the superclass that are only needed in the subclass. In addition, a subclass may override some member functions to change the behavior of the subclass. However, if the subclass needs to override many member functions, or if you find yourself wishing that you could remove some member functions from the superclass, you are probably better off using object composition instead of inheritance.

To illustrate, this figure shows a version of the Dice class that was presented in the previous chapter that inherits the vector class. When coding a container class like the Dice class, this type of approach is tempting because it's so easy. You just inherit the vector class, add a constructor, and add a roll_all() member function. Then, you can use all the features of the vector class to work with a vector of Die objects. However, this approach breaks the guidelines for when it makes sense to use inheritance and it leads to several problems.

First, the Dice object presented in this figure is *not* a type of vector object. A vector stores an ordered sequence of any data type. A Dice object stores one or more Die objects and provides member functions for working with them. It's more accurate to say that the Dice object *has a* vector object that it uses to work with multiple Die objects. As a result, the Dice object should use object composition as shown in the previous chapter, not inheritance.

Second, the Dice class is *not* part of the same logical domain as the vector class. The Dice and Die objects are part of a logical domain that's used to model dice objects that programmers can use in games. The vector class is a class that provides a standard container that can be used by any program.

Third, the interface for the Dice object is too complex. Ideally, this object should only provide the member functions necessary to use it. This helps to make the Dice object easy for other programmers to use. Instead, this object includes all of the operators and member functions for working with the vector class. Unfortunately, this extra functionality makes it more difficult for other programmers to figure out how to use the Dice object.

Fourth, it violates encapsulation. That's because it allows other programmers to directly access the vector that stores the Die objects. But this is an implementation detail that should be hidden from other programmers. Instead, you should be able to change the vector to another container such as a list without changing the interface of the Dice object. That way, other programmers can continue to use the Dice object without needing to modify their code.

It makes sense to use inheritance when...

- One object *is a* type of another object.

- Both classes are part of the same logical domain.

- The subclass primarily adds features to the superclass.

A Dice class that inherits the vector class (not recommended)

The Dice.h file

```
#include <vector>
#include "Die.h"

class Dice : public std::vector<Die>
{
public:
    Dice() : vector<Die>() {};
    void roll_all();
};
```

The Dice.cpp file

```
#include "Dice.h"

void Dice::roll_all() {
    for (int i = 0; i < size(); ++i) {  // calls vector size() function
        Die& die = at(i);               // calls vector at() function
        die.roll();
    }
}
```

Code that uses this Dice class

```
Dice dice = Dice();
dice.push_back(Die());                      // function from vector class
dice.push_back(Die());                      // function from vector class
dice.roll_all();
Die die = dice[0];                          // operator from vector class
dice.insert(dice.begin(), Die());           // function from vector class
dice.pop_back();                            // function from vector class
cout << "Die value: " << die.get_value() << endl;
cout << "Dice count: " << dice.size() << endl;
```

A few problems with this approach

- The Dice object is not a type of vector object.

- Both classes are not part of the same logical domain.

- The interface is too complex.

- It violates encapsulation.

Description

- If an object *is a* type of another object, it typically makes sense to use inheritance to create the relationship between the two classes.

- If an object *has a* type of another object, it typically makes sense to use object composition to create the relationship between the two classes.

Figure 15-14   Guidelines for using inheritance

Perspective

Conceptually, this is one of the most difficult chapters in this book. Although the basic idea of inheritance is easy enough to understand, figuring out how to use it to benefit your programs can be difficult. So if you find yourself a bit confused right now, don't be disheartened.

Fortunately, when you're getting started, you typically don't need to code classes that inherit other classes. But, as you learn more about programming, you'll see more examples of how to use inheritance and your understanding of it should grow. The good news is that you don't have to understand every nuance of how inheritance works to use it. For example, when you learned about the C++ exception hierarchy in chapter 13, you didn't need to understand that the invalid_argument class inherits the logic_error class, which inherits the exception class. But now that you realize that these classes use inheritance, you should understand how they work a little better.

If you continue with programming, you'll learn how to inherit other classes to create more complex programs. For example, you'll use inheritance to create graphical user interfaces (GUIs), web programs, and mobile apps. In addition, as you learn more about object-oriented design, it will become clearer when it makes sense to use inheritance.

Terms

inheritance
superclass
subclass
base class
derived class
parent class
child class
access modifier
protected access
virtual function
override a function
redefine a function
polymorphism
dynamic binding
static binding
late binding
early binding
abstract class
pure virtual function
multiple inheritance

Summary

- *Inheritance* lets you create a new class based on an existing class. Then, the new class *inherits* the public data members and member functions of the existing class.
- A class that another class inherits is called a *base class, parent class*, or *superclass*.
- A class that inherits another class is called a *derived class*, *child class*, or *subclass*.
- A class can use *access modifiers* to specify whether members of a superclass are accessible to subclasses. A *protected* member of a class is available to the current class and its subclasses, but not to any code that's outside of these classes.
- A subclass can add new data members and functions that aren't in the superclass.
- A subclass can *override* a virtual function from the superclass by providing its own version of that function.
- A subclass can *redefine* a non-virtual function from the superclass by providing its own version of that function.
- *Polymorphism* is a feature of inheritance that lets you treat objects of subclasses as if they were objects of the superclass.
- Overriding a virtual function allows polymorphism to work because it allows C++ to determine which function to call at runtime. This is known as *dynamic binding* or *late binding*.
- Redefining a function that isn't virtual prevents polymorphism from working because it forces C++ to determine which function to call at compile time. This is known as *static binding* or *early binding*.
- An *abstract class* is a class that objects can't be created from but that can be inherited by other classes.
- To create an abstract class, you declare one of its virtual functions as a *pure virtual function* by coding "= 0" at the end of the function declaration.
- *Multiple inheritance* allows a class to inherit multiple classes.
- If an object *is a* type of another object, it makes sense to use inheritance to create the relationship between the two classes.
- If an object *has a* type of another object, it makes sense to use object composition to create the relationship between the two classes.
- Encapsulation, inheritance, and polymorphism are three of the fundamental concepts of object-oriented programming (OOP).

Exercise 15-1   Enhance the Product Viewer program

In this exercise, you'll enhance the Product Viewer program shown in this chapter so the Movie and Book classes include another data member that stores the media format. Then, you'll add a Media class to store the format. Finally, you'll add an Album class that provides for another type of product that stores information about a music album. When you enter the product number for an album, it should print the data to the console like this:

```
Enter product number: 4

PRODUCT DATA
Name:              Rubber Soul (The Beatles) - CD
Price:             9.99
Discount percent: 10
Discount amount:   1
Discount price:    8.99
```

Open and test the program

1. Open the project or solution named product_viewer in this folder:
    `ex_starts\ch15_ex1_product_viewer`

2. Review the code and run the program to make sure it works correctly.

Improve the Movie and Book classes

3. In the Movie class, add a private data member named format that stores the format of the product. For example, the format could be Blu-ray, DVD, Stream HD, or Stream SD.

4. Modify the constructor so it includes a parameter that allows you to set the format data member.

5. Modify the get_description() function so it appends the format to the end of the product description, after the year of the movie.

6. In the main() function for the program, modify the code that creates the Movie object so it stores "Stream HD" as the format data member. Then, run the program to make sure it works correctly.

7. Repeat steps 3-6 for the Book class. You can use Hardcover as the format for the book. Or, if you prefer, you can specify a different type of book format such as Paperback or Ebook.

Add a Media class

8. Add a header file for a class named Media that inherits the Product class. This Media class should add a protected data member named format.

9. Add a constructor to this class that passes all necessary arguments to the Product class and also includes a format parameter and uses that parameter to set the value of the data member. This should work much like the constructor of the Movie class.

10. Modify the Movie and Book classes so they include and inherit the Media class, not the Product class. This should create a class hierarchy that looks like this:

```
Product
    Media
            Movie
            Book
```

11. Delete the format data member from the Movie and Book classes.

12. Modify the constructors of the Movie and Book classes so the format argument is passed to the constructor of the Media class. In other words, these classes should set the format data member by calling the constructor of the Media class. Note how this reduces code duplication.

13. Run the program to make sure it still works correctly.

Add an Album class

14. Add a class named Album that inherits the Media class. The Album class should work much like the Book class, but it should include a data member for storing the artist, not a data member for storing the author.

15. In the main.cpp file, modify the code that creates the objects so it creates an Album object in addition to a Product, Book, and Movie object. This object should store the data for a music album that you like.

16. Modify the show_products() function so the program displays the description for the Album object when it starts.

17. Modify the main() function so it passes the Album object to the show_product() function if the user enters the correct number for the album. This should display the Album object as shown at the beginning of this exercise.

Exercise 15-2   Work with abstract classes and control overriding

In this exercise, you'll convert the Product class into an abstract class and use the override and final keywords to control overriding.

Open and test the program

1. Open the project or solution named product_viewer in this folder:
   `ex_starts\ch15_ex2_product_viewer`

2. Review the code and run the program to make sure it works correctly.

Use an abstract class

3. Open the header file for the Product class. Then, modify the declaration for the get_description() function so it is a pure virtual function. This makes the Product class an abstract class.

4. Attempt to run the program. This should display an error message that indicates that you can't create an object from the abstract Product class.

5. Open the main.cpp file. Then, modify the code that attempts to create the Product object so it creates a Book object instead. For data, you can use the name and author of one of your favorite books.

6. Run the program to make sure it works correctly.

Use the override and final keywords

7. In the Movie and Book classes, add the override and final keywords to the get_description() function. This shows that this function overrides the pure virtual function of the Product class and that this function can't be overridden by other subclasses.

8. Create the header file for a new class named UsedBook that inherits the Book class.

9. Code a constructor that accepts the same four arguments as the constructor for the Book class and passes those arguments to the constructor of the Book class. The body of this constructor doesn't need to contain any code.

10. Code a get_description() function that attempts to override the get_description() function of the Book class. This function should append "(Used)" to the end of the description.

11. In the main.cpp file, modify the code that creates the first object so it creates a UsedBook object instead of a Book object.

12. Attempt to run the program. This should display an error message that indicates that the get_description() function can't be overridden because it is final.

13. In the Book class, remove the final keyword from the get_description() function.

14. Run the program. This time, it should work correctly.

16

More skills for object-oriented programming

The last two chapters presented the fundamental skills and concepts for working with object-oriented programming (OOP). Now, this chapter presents a few more skills for working with object-oriented programming. In particular, it shows how to work with static members, how to work with friend members, and how to overload operators so they work correctly with objects that you define.

How to work with static members

In the last two chapters, you learned how to code data members and member functions that belong to the object that's created from the class. Because these members belong to an instance of the class, they're sometimes referred to as instance variables and object functions. Now, the topics that follow show how to code *static data members* and *static member functions*. These members belong to the class itself, not the object created from the class. As a result, they're sometimes called *class data members* or *class member functions*.

How to code static data members and functions

To code static members, you code the static keyword before the data member or member function. This is illustrated by the Product class presented in figure 16-1. This class is similar to the Product class presented in chapter 14, but it includes a static data member and a static member function.

The header file for this class declares a static data member named object_count that's used to count the number of Product objects that are created from the Product class. This data member is declared as private so calling code can't access it directly. Then, the header file declares and defines a static member function named get_object_count() that returns the static object_count data member. This member function is declared as public so calling code can access it.

The implementation file begins by initializing the static object_count data member to a value of 0. Since this data member is a static member that belongs to the Product class, not a Product object, this code must qualify the data member with the name of its class and the scope resolution operator. Then, the implementation file defines a constructor that increments the static data member. As a result, after the first object is created from the Product class, the object_count member of the Product class contains a value of 1. When the second object is created, the object_count member contains a value of 2. And so on.

When you code a static function such as the get_object_count() function, you can only use static data members and any local variables that are defined in the function. You can't use regular data members in a static function because they belong to an object, not to the class. In other words, you can't code the get_object_count() function like this:

```
static int get_object_count() {    // static function
    return discount_percent;   // non-static data member - ERROR!
}
```

Code like this would result in a compile-time error that says something like, "illegal reference to non-static member."

When you code a class that mixes non-static members with static members, it's a good practice to organize these members in a way that allows you to easily determine which members are non-static and which members are static. For example, you might want to code static members after the non-static members as shown in this figure. Or, you may prefer to code static members before non-static

The Product class with a static data member and a static function

The Product.h file

```
#ifndef MURACH_PRODUCT_H
#define MURACH_PRODUCT_H

#include <string>

class Product {
private:
    double price;
    int discount_percent;
    static int object_count;  // static data member

public:
    Product(std::string name = "", double price = 0.0,
            int discount_percent = 0);

    std::string name;

    void set_price(double);
    double get_price() const { return price; }
    void set_discount_percent(int);
    int get_discount_percent() const { return discount_percent; }
    double get_discount_amount() const;
    double get_discount_price() const;

    static int get_object_count() {   // static function
        return object_count;
    }
};

#endif // MURACH_PRODUCT_H
```

Code in the Product.cpp file that works with the static data member

```
int Product::object_count = 0;  // initialize static data member

Product::Product(string name_param, double price, int discount_pct) {
    name = name_param;
    set_price(price);
    set_discount_percent(discount_pct);
    ++object_count;     // increment static data member
}
```

Description

- You can use the static keyword to code *static data members* and *static functions* that belong to the class, not to an object created from the class.

- Static data members and static member functions are sometimes called *class data members* and *class member functions*.

- When you code a static function, you can only use static data members and local variables that are defined in the function. You can't use regular data members in a static function because they belong to an object created from the class, not to the class itself.

Figure 16-1   How to code static data members and functions

members. For small classes, grouping members like this isn't critical. However, as your classes get larger, grouping the members of a class in a logical way makes your code easier to read and maintain.

How to access static data members and functions

Figure 16-2 begins by showing two ways to access a static data member. To access a static member directly from a class, you can code the name of the class, the scope resolution operator (`::`), and the name of the data member as shown by the first syntax and example. Or, you can access a static data member from an object by coding the name of the object, the dot operator (`.`), and the name of the data member as shown by the second example.

Both of these techniques also work for calling a static member function. However, for a static member function, you also need to code the parentheses after the function name and the argument list within these parentheses. This is shown by the third and fourth syntaxes and examples.

How to access a static data member from a class

Syntax
```
ClassName::data_member_name
```

Example
```
int product_count = Product::object_count  // if object_count is public
```

How to access a static data member from an object

Syntax
```
object_name.data_member_name
```

Example
```
Product p;
int product_count = p.object_count;        // if object_count is public
```

How to call a static member function from a class

Syntax
```
ClassName::function_name([argument_list])
```

Example
```
int product_count = Product::get_object_count();
```

How to call a static member function from an object

Syntax
```
object_name.function_name([argument_list])
```

Example
```
Product p;
int product_count = p.get_object_count();
```

Description

- You can use the scope resolution operator (::) to access a static data member or function directly from the class without creating an object.

- You can use the dot operator (.) to access a static data member or function from an object created from a class.

Figure 16-2   How to access static data members and functions

The Console class

If a function doesn't use the data members of a class, you may want to make the function static. That way, it can be called directly from the class or from an object created from the class as shown by the previous figure. For example, figure 16-3 presents a Console class that provides three static functions that get user input from the console.

The code for these static functions works similarly to the code provided by the console namespace described in chapter 7. In this figure, however, these functions are available from the Console class, not the console namespace. This shows that a class prevents name collisions in the same way that a namespace does.

The header for the Console class begins by defining a default constructor for the class. Since this class doesn't need to initialize any data members, this constructor doesn't do anything. As a result, you could rely on the compiler to automatically generate this constructor. However, it's considered a good practice to provide a default constructor because it makes it easy for other programmers to see what, if anything, this constructor does. In this case, the constructor clearly shows that it doesn't do anything.

After defining the default constructor, the header file declares three public member functions that are static. These member functions work as described in chapter 7. The first one displays a prompt to the user and gets a double value within the specified range. The second one works similarly, except it gets an int value, not a double value. And the third one displays a prompt to the user, gets the first character that the user enters, discards any remaining characters, and optionally displays a blank line after the prompt.

The implementation file begins by defining three helper functions that are used by the three static functions of this class. Since these three helper functions aren't declared in the header file, they aren't available to other classes. Then, this class defines the three static functions. Next, it defines the three helper functions. The code for all of these functions is the same as the code in the console namespace described in chapter 7. As a result, this figure doesn't show the code again.

A Console class that provides static functions

The console.h file

```cpp
#ifndef MURACH_CONSOLE_H
#define MURACH_CONSOLE_H

#include <string>
#include <limits>

class Console {
public:
    Console() {};    // define default constructor

    // declare static functions
    static double get_double(std::string prompt,
        double min = std::numeric_limits<double>::min(),
        double max = std::numeric_limits<double>::max());
    static int get_int(std::string prompt,
        int min = std::numeric_limits<int>::min(),
        int max = std::numeric_limits<int>::max());
    static char get_char(std::string prompt,
        bool add_blank_line = true);
};

#endif // MURACH_CONSOLE_H
```

The console.cpp file

```cpp
#include <iostream>
#include <string>
#include <limits>
#include "console.h"

// declare helper functions
void discard_remaining_chars();
void handle_invalid_number();
bool check_range(double num, double min, double max);

// define public functions
double Console::get_double(std::string prompt, double min, double max) {
    // same as code from console namespace in chapter 7
}

int Console::get_int(std::string prompt, int min, int max) {
    // same as code from console namespace in chapter 7
}

char Console::get_char(std::string prompt, bool add_blank_line) {
    // same as code from console namespace in chapter 7
}

// define private functions
// same as code from console namespace in chapter 7
```

Figure 16-3   The Console class

Code that uses the Console class

Figure 16-4 presents two code examples that use the Console class. The first example uses the scope resolution operator to call three static functions directly from the Console class. The advantage of this approach is that you don't have to create an object from the Console class. Also, it clearly indicates that you're calling a static function from the Console class.

The second example begins by creating a Console object from the Console class and storing it in a variable named c. Then, this example uses the dot operator to call three static functions from this Console object. The advantage of this approach is that it yields code that's more concise. That doesn't make much of a difference when calling just a few functions. However, it might make a difference if you needed to call dozens of functions from this class.

The console presented in this figure reviews how the functions of the Console class work. If the user enters an invalid number such as "x", the console displays an appropriate message and prompts the user again. Similarly, if the user enters a number outside the specified range, the console displays an appropriate message and prompts the user again.

If the user enters a double value when an integer is expected, the get_int() function converts the double value to an int value by truncating the decimal digits. Similarly, if the user enters a string where a single character is expected, the get_char() function gets the first character in the string and discards the rest of the characters.

Code that calls static functions directly from the Console class

```
double mi = Console::get_double("Monthly Investment:   ", 0, 10000);
int years = Console::get_int("Years:                 ", 0, 100);
char choice = Console::get_char("Continue? (y/n): ")
```

Code that calls static functions from a Console object

```
Console c;
double mi = c.get_double("Monthly Investment:   ", 0, 10000);
int years = c.get_int("Years:                 ", 0, 100);
char choice = c.get_char("Continue? (y/n): ");
```

The console for both examples

```
Monthly Investment:   x
Error! Invalid number. Try again.
Monthly Investment:   100
Years:                1000
Error! Number must be less than 100. Try again.
Years:                3
Continue? (y/n): no
```

Description

- If a function doesn't use the data members of a class, you may want to make the function static. That way, it can be called directly from the class or from an object created from the class.

Figure 16-4   Code that uses the Console class

How to work with a friend function

When designing classes, you may sometimes want to allow a function outside of a class to access private members of a class. To do that, you can use a friend function as described in the next two topics. Note that using friend functions breaks encapsulation. In some cases, though, this may be the best way to accomplish a task.

The FuelTank class

Figure 16-5 presents a FuelTank class that's designed to keep track of the amount of fuel that's stored in a tank. Internally, this class stores the amount of fuel in gallons, but it provides functions that allow the user to get the amount of fuel in gallons or liters.

At this point, the FuelTank class only uses skills that were presented in chapter 14. However, the next figure adds a friend function to this class so another class can access its private data member.

To start, the header file for the FuelTank class declares a private data member named gallons. Then, it declares a constructor that can set this data member, public getter and setter functions for this data member, and a get_liters() function that gets the amount of fuel in liters.

The implementation file provides the definition of the get_liters() function. This function converts the gallons data member to liters. Then, it returns the result to the calling code.

The code example shows how this works. Here, the first statement creates a FuelTank object and uses its constructor to set the gallons to 100. Then, the second statement displays the amount of fuel in the tank on the console as measured in both gallons and liters.

A FuelTank class

The FuelTank.h file

```
#ifndef MURACH_FUEL_TANK_H
#define MURACH_FUEL_TANK_H

#include <iostream>

class FuelTank {
private:
    double gallons;
public:
    FuelTank(double gallons_param = 0) { gallons = gallons_param; }
    void set_gallons(double gallons_param) { gallons = gallons_param; }
    double get_gallons() const { return gallons; }
    double get_liters() const;
};
#endif // MURACH_FUEL_TANK_H
```

The FuelTank.cpp file

```
#include <iostream>
#include "FuelTank.h"

using namespace std;

double FuelTank::get_liters() const {
    double liters = gallons * 3.7854;
    return liters;
}
```

Code that uses the FuelTank class

```
FuelTank tank1(100);

cout << "TANK 1" << endl
     << "  Gallons: " << tank1.get_gallons() << endl
     << "  Liters:  " << tank1.get_liters() << endl << endl;
```

The console

```
TANK 1
  Gallons: 100
  Liters:  378.54
```

Description

- The FuelTank class can be used to store the amount of fuel in the tank. Internally, this class stores the amount of fuel in gallons, but it allows the user to get the amount of fuel in gallons or liters.

Figure 16-5   The FuelTank class

A friend function that works with two classes

Figure 16-6 begins by showing the header file for a FuelCan class that has a *friend function* named pour() that's designed to work with the FuelTank and FuelCan classes. To do that, the declaration for the pour() function begins with the friend keyword. Then, it defines one reference parameter for a FuelTank object and another for a FuelCan object.

To make it possible for the FuelCan class to compile, it must include a *forward declaration* for the FuelTank class. This forward declaration tells the compiler that the FuelTank class will be defined and compiled later. This is similar to the way that a header file declares functions that can be defined later in the implementation file.

This figure also shows a FuelTank class that includes a friend function named pour(). The declaration for this function is the same as the declaration in the FuelCan class. In addition, the header file for the FuelTank class needs to include the FuelCan header file. That way, the FuelCan class is available to the FuelTank class.

The implementation for the pour() function accesses the private data members of FuelTank and FuelCan objects. Within its body, the first statement adds all of the fuel in the can to the fuel that's already in the tank. Then, since all the fuel has been poured from the can into the tank, the second statement sets the amount of fuel in the can to zero. To accomplish this task, this code accesses the private gallons data member of the FuelCan object and the private gallons data member of the FuelTank object.

A friend function works much like a static function, but it has a scope that's larger than the class. In this figure, for example, the pour() function is declared within the FuelCan and FuelTank classes, but it is defined outside of either of these classes. In other words, it has the scope of a regular function that's declared outside of a class. As a result, a friend function can't access the data members of a class directly. However, it can access the data members from any of its parameter objects that declare this function as a friend.

With this simple example, it would probably be better not to use friend functions at all. In that case, you could just use the public setter and getter functions within the pour() function like this:

```
void pour(FuelTank& tank, FuelCan& can) {
    tank.set_gallons(tank.get_gallons() + can.get_gallons();
    can.set_gallons(0);
}
```

That way, you wouldn't need to declare the pour() function in the FuelCan and FuelTank classes, and those classes would remain encapsulated.

However, for more complicated classes and functions, it may sometimes be convenient to be able to access private data members. In addition, there may be times when a function may need to access private members to work correctly. At the end of this chapter, for example, you'll see a friend function for an operator that shows when using a friend function is necessary.

The header file for a FuelCan class that declares a friend function

```
#ifndef MURACH_FUEL_CAN_H
#define MURACH_FUEL_CAN_H

class FuelTank;    // forward declaration of a class

class FuelCan {
private:
    double gallons = 0;
public:
    FuelCan(double gallons_param = 0) { gallons = gallons_param; }
    double get_gallons() { return gallons; }
    friend void pour(FuelTank& tank, FuelCan& can);
};
#endif // MURACH_FUEL_CAN_H
```

The header file for a FuelTank class that declares a friend function

```
#ifndef MURACH_FUEL_TANK_H
#define MURACH_FUEL_TANK_H

#include "FuelCan.h"

class FuelTank {
private:
    double gallons;
public:
    FuelTank(double gallons_param = 0) { gallons = gallons_param; }
    void set_gallons(double gallons_param) { gallons = gallons_param; }
    double get_gallons() const { return gallons; }
    double get_liters() const;
    friend void pour(FuelTank& tank, FuelCan& can);
};
#endif // MURACH_FUEL_TANK_H
```

The implementation for the friend function

```
#include "FuelCan.h"
#include "FuelTank.h"

void pour(FuelTank& tank, FuelCan& can) {
    tank.gallons += can.gallons;    // access private data members
    can.gallons = 0;                // access private data memeber
}
```

Code that uses the friend function

```
FuelCan can(2);        // can has 2 gallons
FuelTank tank(500);    // tank has 500 gallons
pour(tank, can);       // tank has 502 gallons, can has 0 gallons
```

Description

- You can use the friend keyword to declare *friend functions* that exist outside of a class. These functions can access the private members of a class.

- A *forward declaration* declares a class or function so it can be defined and compiled later.

Figure 16-6   A friend function that works with two classes

How to overload operators

In chapter 9, you learned how to overload the equality operator (==) for a structure. Now, this chapter shows that the same principles apply to overloading the operators of a class. In the topics that follow, you'll learn how to overload some of the most common operators. However, you can use the techniques described here to overload any of the operators provided by C++. By overloading these operators, you can allow your classes to work more like the built-in types.

How to overload arithmetic binary operators

Figure 16-7 shows how to overload arithmetic binary operators such as the addition (+) and subtraction (-) operators. To overload these operators, you can code a special function known as an *operator function* that defines the behavior of an operator for an object. To start, this figure shows how to overload the addition operator so it works with FuelTank objects.

The header file for the FuelTank class declares an addition operator that accepts a FuelTank object as a constant reference and returns a FuelTank object. Here, instead of coding a name for the function, you code the operator keyword followed by the operator that you're declaring. When doing this, it's common to code the operator immediately after the operator keyword as shown by the first example. However, if you prefer, you can code a space between the operator keyword and the operator as shown in the second example.

The implementation file for the FuelTank class provides the definition of the addition operator. Within this function, the first statement creates a new FuelTank object named t. Then, the second statement adds the gallons in the FuelTank parameter object to the gallons in the current object, and it sets the result in the newly created FuelTank object named t. Finally, the third statement returns this FuelTank object. Note that the parameter in this example is named right because it's used as the right operand for the operation.

After the definition for the addition operator, this figure presents some code that uses this operator. Here, the first statement creates a FuelTank object that stores 100 gallons, the second creates a FuelTank object that stores 200 gallons, and the third adds the two FuelTank objects together to get a third FuelTank object that stores 300 gallons. This shows that the addition operator needs to create a third FuelTank object because it wouldn't make sense for this operation to change the values stored in the first two FuelTank objects.

This figure also shows that you can call the addition operator with a syntax that's similar to calling a function. Here, the code calls the operator+() function. This shows that using an operator is really just a shorthand way of calling a function. In other words, an operator is really just a special kind of function that can provide a more concise and intuitive way to work with objects.

After showing how to use the addition operator, this figure shows how to use the subtraction operator. If you compare the code for this operator to the addition operator, you'll see that all the same techniques and concepts apply to the subtraction operator. In addition, the same techniques and concepts apply to other arithmetic binary operators, such as the multiplication and division operators.

The addition operator for the FuelTank class

The declaration in the FuelTank.h file

```
FuelTank operator+ (const FuelTank& right);
```

The same declaration but with a space after the operator keyword

```
FuelTank operator + (const FuelTank& right);
```

The definition in the FuelTank.cpp file

```
FuelTank FuelTank::operator+ (const FuelTank& right) {
    FuelTank t;
    t.set_gallons(gallons + right.gallons);
    return t;
}
```

Code that uses the addition operator

```
FuelTank tank1(100);
FuelTank tank2(200);
FuelTank tank3 = tank2 + tank1;            // tank3 has 300 gallons
```

Another way to code the third statement

```
FuelTank tank3 = tank2.operator+(tank1);   // tank3 has 300 gallons
```

The subtraction operator for the FuelTank class

The declaration in the FuelTank.h file

```
FuelTank operator- (const FuelTank& right);
```

The definition in the FuelTank.cpp file

```
FuelTank FuelTank::operator- (const FuelTank& right) {
    FuelTank t;
    t.set_gallons(gallons - right.gallons);
    return t;
}
```

Code that uses the subtraction operator

```
FuelTank tank1(100);
FuelTank tank2(200);
FuelTank tank3 = tank2 - tank1;            // tank3 has 100 gallons
```

Another way to code the third statement

```
FuelTank tank3 = tank2.operator-(tank1);   // tank3 has 100 gallons
```

Description

- An *operator function* is a function that defines the behavior of an operator for an object.

- The arithmetic binary operators should create and return a new object because they shouldn't modify the state of the objects used in the operation.

Figure 16-7   How to overload the arithmetic binary operators

How to overload arithmetic unary operators

Figure 16-8 shows how to overload the increment operator (++), which is an arithmetic unary operator. However, the skills for overloading this operator can be applied to other arithmetic unary operators such as the decrement operator (--).

To start, this figure shows how to overload the prefix increment operator so it works with the FuelTank class. Here, the header file for the FuelTank class declares an increment operator that doesn't accept any arguments and returns a FuelTank object by reference. Then, the implementation file defines this operator. Within its body, the first statement increments the number of gallons stored in the current object. Then, the second statement returns a reference to the FuelTank object. To do that, this code uses the indirection operator (*) with the *this* keyword to get a reference to the object.

The code that uses the prefix increment operator begins by creating a FuelTank object that stores 100 gallons of fuel. Then, the code uses the prefix increment operator to increase the amount of fuel in the tank to 101 gallons and to display the result on the console. This shows that the prefix increment operator increments the FuelTank object before C++ executes the rest of the expression that displays the gallons on the console.

To declare the postfix increment operator, the header file for the FuelTank class declares an increment operator that accepts an int value and returns a FuelTank object. This int parameter is a *dummy parameter* that isn't used by the function for the operator. Instead, it identifies the overload as the postfix overload, not the prefix overload.

The implementation file defines the postfix increment operator. Within the body of this operator, the first statement makes a copy of the current FuelTank object. Then, the second statement increments the number of gallons stored in the current object. Finally, the third statement returns the copy of the FuelTank object that contains the values that haven't been incremented.

If you want the postfix operator to behave correctly, it's necessary to create a copy of the current object for the postfix operator as shown here. This allows the postfix operator to return the copy of the object without incremented values. Then, after the increment operation is performed, the code can access the object with its incremented values.

Conversely, you don't need to make a copy of the object for the prefix operator to behave correctly. That's why the prefix operator returns a reference to the current object and the postfix operator doesn't. That's also why the prefix operator is more efficient than the postfix operator and why it's generally considered a good practice to use the prefix operator whenever possible.

The second definition for the postfix operator shows another way to code this operator. The body of this function uses the prefix operator defined earlier in this figure to increment the current object. This approach makes sure that the same code for incrementing is used for both the prefix and postfix operators. In this example, the prefix operator only increments a single data member, the gallons member. As a result, it's easy to duplicate the code in both the prefix and postfix operators. However, if the prefix operator incremented multiple data members, it would make sense to use the second technique.

The prefix increment operator for the FuelTank class

The declaration in the FuelTank.h file

```
FuelTank& operator++ ();
```

The definition in the FuelTank.cpp file

```
FuelTank& FuelTank::operator++ () {
    ++gallons;                  // increment data member
    return *this;               // return current object
}
```

Code that uses the prefix increment operator

```
FuelTank tank1(100);
cout << ++tank1.get_gallons() << endl; // displays 101
```

The postfix increment operator for the FuelTank class

The declaration in the FuelTank.h file

```
FuelTank operator++ (int unused_param);
```

The definition in the FuelTank.cpp file

```
FuelTank FuelTank::operator++ (int unused_param) {
    FuelTank temp = *this;     // make copy of current object
    ++gallons;                 // increment the current object
    return temp;               // return the pre-increment copy
}
```

Another definition that works better for incrementing multiple data members

```
FuelTank FuelTank::operator++ (int unused_param) {
    FuelTank temp = *this;     // make copy of current object
    ++*this;                   // increment the current object
    return temp;               // return the pre-increment copy
}
```

Code that uses the postfix increment operator

```
FuelTank tank1(100);
cout << tank1++.get_gallons() << endl; // displays 100
cout << tank1.get_gallons() << endl;   // displays 101
```

Description

- You can use the *this* keyword to get a pointer to the location of an object in memory. You can use the indirection operator (*) to access the object.

- The postfix overload uses a *dummy parameter* to identify the overload as the postfix overload rather than the prefix overload.

- A postfix operator should return a copy of the object *before* the increment operation.

- A prefix operator should return a reference to the object *after* the increment operation.

- Because the prefix operator doesn't need to make a copy of an object, it is more efficient than the postfix operator.

- The techniques shown in this figure also work with the decrement operator (--).

Figure 16-8   How to overload the arithmetic unary operators

How to overload relational operators

Figure 16-9 shows how to overload relational operators such as the greater than (>), less than (<), and equality (==) operators. These operators return a Boolean value that indicates the result of the comparison. Since these operators should not modify their parameters, you can define them as constant reference parameters.

To start, this figure shows how to overload the less than operator so it works with the FuelTank class. The header file for the FuelTank class declares a less than operator that accepts a FuelTank object by constant reference and returns a Boolean value.

The implementation file defines the less than operator. The body of this operator uses an if statement to check whether the gallons data member in the current object is less than the gallons data member in the FuelTank parameter. If it is, this operator returns true. Otherwise, it returns false. As a result, one FuelTank object is less than another FuelTank object if it has fewer gallons than the other FuelTank object.

Since the condition in this if statement evaluates to a Boolean value, you can code this definition more concisely by returning the result of the comparison. The second definition for the less than operator uses this technique.

The same principles for overloading the less than operator also apply to the other relational operators. As a result, if you understand how to code a less than operator like the one shown in this figure, you shouldn't have any trouble coding the greater than or equality operators shown in this figure. In addition, you should be able to code other equality operators not shown here, such as the greater than or equal to (>=) and less than or equal to (<=) operators.

The code that uses the relational operators uses an if statement to check whether one FuelTank object is less than, greater than, or equal to another FuelTank object. Then, this code displays an appropriate message depending on the result.

The less than operator for the FuelTank class

The declaration in the FuelTank.h file

```
bool operator< (const FuelTank& right);
```

The definition in the FuelTank.cpp file

```
bool FuelTank::operator< (const FuelTank& right) {
    if (gallons < right.gallons)
        return true;
    else
        return false;
}
```

A more concise definition for this operator

```
bool FuelTank::operator< (const FuelTank& right) {
    return (gallons < right.gallons);
}
```

The greater than operator for the FuelTank class

The declaration in the FuelTank.h file

```
bool operator> (const FuelTank& right);
```

The definition in the FuelTank.cpp file

```
bool FuelTank::operator> (const FuelTank& right) {
    return (gallons > right.gallons);
}
```

The equality operator for the FuelTank class

The declaration in the FuelTank.h file

```
bool operator== (const FuelTank& right);
```

The definition in the FuelTank.cpp file

```
bool FuelTank::operator== (const FuelTank& right) {
    return (gallons == right.gallons);
}
```

Code that uses the relational operators

```
if (tank1 < tank2) {
    cout << "Tank 1 has less fuel than tank 2.\n\n";
}
else if (tank1 > tank2) {
    cout << "Tank 1 has more fuel than tank 2.\n\n";
}
else if (tank1 == tank2) {
    cout << "Tank 1 has the same amount of fuel as tank 2.\n\n";
}
```

Description

- The relational operators return a Boolean value that indicates the result of the comparison. Since these operators should not modify their parameters, you can define them as constant reference parameters.

Figure 16-9   How to overload the relational operators

How to overload the insertion and extraction operators

Figure 16-10 shows how to overload the insertion (<<) and extraction operators (>>) so they work correctly with the FuelTank class presented earlier in this chapter.

The functions for the insertion and extraction operators are actually defined by the ostream and istream classes that are available from the C++ standard library. As a result, the header for the FuelTank class must declare these functions as friend functions of the ostream and istream classes. Otherwise, you'll get an error when you try to overload the insertion and extraction operators. For example, this figure declares that the insertion operator is a friend of the insertion operator of the ostream class, and it declares the extraction operator is a friend of the extraction operator of the istream class, which is what you typically want.

The insertion operator declares two parameters, an ostream object and a FuelTank object. This allows the insertion operator to work with a FuelTank object. Here, the ostream object is passed by reference since you need to modify it by inserting data into it, and the FuelTank object is passed by constant reference since you shouldn't modify this object. In addition, this operator returns an ostream object by reference. This makes it possible to chain multiple calls to this operator together within a single statement as shown in this figure.

The body for the insertion operator begins with a single statement that inserts a message that includes the number of gallons and liters stored in the FuelTank object into the insertion stream. To do that, this code uses the insertion operator to insert data into the ostream parameter named out. Then, this code returns the ostream object to the calling code.

The extraction operator works much like the insertion operator. However, the extraction operator needs to be able to modify the FuelTank parameter. As a result, this parameter is passed by reference, not by constant reference.

The body for the extraction operator begins by prompting the user to enter the number of gallons. Then, the second statement stores the number of gallons entered by the user in the gallons data member of the FuelTank object. To do that, this code uses the extraction operator to extract data from the istream parameter named in. Finally, the third statement returns the istream object to the calling code.

The code that uses the insertion and extraction operators begins by creating two FuelTank objects. Then, the second statement chains together two calls to the extraction operator to set the gallons in both of these FuelTank objects. Finally, the third statement chains together four calls to the insertion operator to display headings and data for both FuelTank objects on the console. As you review this code, note that you wouldn't be able to use chaining within these operators if they didn't return the appropriate stream object.

The insertion operator for the FuelTank class

The declaration in the FuelTank.h file

```
friend std::ostream& operator<< (std::ostream&, const FuelTank&);
```

The definition in the FuelTank.cpp file

```
ostream& operator<< (ostream& out, const FuelTank& tank) {
    out << "    Gallons: " << tank.gallons << endl
        << "    Liters:  " << tank.get_liters() << endl
        << endl;
    return out;
}
```

The extraction operator for the FuelTank class

The declaration in the FuelTank.h file

```
friend std::istream& operator>> (std::istream&, FuelTank&);
```

The definition in the FuelTank.cpp file

```
istream& operator>> (istream& in, FuelTank &tank) {
    cout << "Enter gallons: ";
    in >> tank.gallons;
    return in;
}
```

Code that uses the insertion and extraction operators

```
FuelTank tank4, tank5;
cin >> tank4 >> tank5;          // chains 2 extraction operators together
cout << "TANK 4\n" << tank4
     << "TANK 5\n" << tank5;    // chains 4 insertion operators together
```

The console

```
Enter gallons: 400
Enter gallons: 500
TANK 4
    Gallons: 400
    Liters:  1514.16

TANK 5
    Gallons: 500
    Liters:  1892.7
```

Description

- An operator that accepts and returns an object by reference allows you to *chain* calls to the operator together within a single statement.

Figure 16-10   How to overload the insertion and extraction operators

Perspective

Now that you've finished this chapter, you have a solid foundation in object-oriented programming. At this point, you have most of the object-oriented skills you need for understanding how various C++ libraries such as the Standard Template Library (STL) work. In fact, the next three chapters show how to use the skills you learned in chapter 14 to define classes that implement custom containers that work much like the vector and list containers that are available from the STL. As you read the remaining chapters of this book, you'll reinforce your existing knowledge of object-oriented programming, and you'll learn a few more object-oriented skills.

Terms

static data member
static member function
class data member
class member function
forward declaration
friend function
operator function
dummy parameter
chaining

Summary

- Within a class, you can use the static keyword to code *static data members* and *static member functions* that belong to the class, not the object that's created from the class.

- Static data members and static functions are sometimes called *class data members* and *class member functions*.

- A f*orward declaration* declares a class or function so it can be defined and compiled later.

- Within a class, you can use the friend keyword to declare *friend functions* that are defined outside of the class. These friend functions can accept objects created from the class that they can use to access the private members of the class.

- An *operator function* is a function that defines the behavior of an operator for an object.

- To overload the postfix operator, you code a *dummy parameter* that isn't used by the function except to create a different signature that identifies the overload as the postfix overload, not the prefix overload.

- An operator that accepts and returns an object by reference allows you to *chain* calls to the operator together within a single statement.

Exercise 16-1   Enhance the Future Value program

This exercise guides you through the process of modifying the Future Value program from chapter 7 so it uses a Console class that provides static functions instead of a console namespace.

Open and test the program

1. Open the project or solution named future_value in this folder:
    `ex_starts\ch16_ex1_future_value`

2. Review the code and run the program to make sure it works correctly. Note that this program uses the console namespace to declare and define the get_double(), get_int(), and get_char() functions.

Add the Console class

3. Open the header file for the console namespace. Then, modify the code so it stores the function declarations in a class named Console instead of the console namespace. When you do that, declare all three functions as static and with public access. Also, make sure to include a semicolon at the end of the class declaration.

4. Open the implementation file for the console namespace. Then, modify the code so it provides the function definitions for the Console class. To do that, you can delete the code that defines the console namespace and qualify the get_double(), get_int(), and get_char() functions with the Console class.

5. In the main.cpp file, modify the main() function so it calls static functions directly from the Console class. Then, run the program to make sure it still works correctly.

6. In the main.cpp file, modify the main() function so it creates an object from the Console class named c and calls static functions from this object. Then, run the program to make sure it still works correctly.

Add the Finance class

7. Create a header file and an implementation file for a class named Finance.

8. Move the declaration for the calculate_future_value() function from the main.cpp file to the header file for the Finance class. When you do, make sure to declare this function as static and with public access.

9. Move the definition for the calculate_future_value() function from the main.cpp file to the implementation file for the Finance class. Then, qualify the name of the function with the name of the class.

10. Modify the main.cpp file so it uses the static calculate_future_value() function that's stored in the Finance class. Then, run the program to make sure that it still works properly.

Exercise 16-2   Add operators to a Circle object

In this exercise, you'll add some of the operators described in this chapter to
a Circle object. Then, you'll code a program that tests these operators. When
you're done, running the program should display this:

```
CIRCLE 1:
radius=20|diameter=40|circumference=125.664|area=1256.64

CIRCLE 2:
radius=10|diameter=20|circumference=62.8318|area=314.159

CIRCLE 3 (CIRCLE1 + CIRCLE2):
radius=30|diameter=60|circumference=188.495|area=2827.43

CIRCLE 4 (CIRCLE1 - CIRCLE2):
radius=10|diameter=20|circumference=62.8318|area=314.159

CIRCLE 4 after ++:
radius=11|diameter=22|circumference=69.115|area=380.132
```

Open and test the program

1.   Open the project or solution named circle_tester in this folder:

   ex_starts\ch16_ex2_circle_tester

2.   Review the code and note how the Circle class defines functions for getting
   the diameter, circumference, and area based on the value of the radius. Also,
   note that the code in the main.cpp file includes a display() function that you
   can use to display a Circle object on the console.

3.   Run the program to make sure it works correctly. At this point, it should only
   display the first two Circle objects shown above.

Add the addition and subtraction operators

4.   In the header file for the Circle class, add a declaration for the addition
   operator. Then, in the implementation file, add a definition for this operator
   that adds the radius of one Circle object to another circle object.

5.   In the main.cpp file, add code that uses the addition operator to add the first
   two Circle objects together to get a third Circle object. Then, use the display()
   function to display that object on the console as shown above.

6.   Repeat step 4 for the subtraction operator. Then, in the main.cpp file, add code
   that uses the subtraction operator to subtract the second Circle object from the
   first Circle object to get a third Circle object, and use the display() function to
   display that object on the console as shown above.

Add the prefix increment operator

7.   In the header file for the Circle class, add a declaration for the prefix increment operator. Then, in the implementation file, add a definition for this
   operator that increases the radius by 1.

8. In the main.cpp file, add code that uses the prefix increment operator to increment the fourth Circle object. Then, use the display() function to display that object on the console as shown above. At this point, the console should look like the console shown above.

Add the insertion operator

9. In the header file for the Circle class, add a declaration for the insertion operator.

10. In the implementation file, add a definition for this operator. To do that, you can copy the code that displays the Circle object from the display() function in the main.cpp file. For this to work, you need to include the iostream header, so this definition can work with the std::ostream class.

11. In the main.cpp file, modify the code so it uses the insertion operator instead of the display() function to display the Circle objects on the console. To make sure this code is no longer using the display() function, comment out the display() function when you're done.

Section 4

Skills for legacy and generic programming

So far, this book has presented the skills that you need to write modern C++ programs, and it has presented many sample programs that use these skills. Most of these programs use reference variables to work with memory safely and efficiently. In addition, these programs use the containers that are available from the STL (Standard Template Library). If you're using a modern version of C++, that's typically the approach that you want to take.

However, if you need to work with legacy C++ or C code, or if you need to work in an embedded environment, you may need to use pointers to work with memory at a low level as described in chapter 17. In addition, if you want to allow your classes and functions to support multiple data types, you may need to work with templates as described in chapter 18. Once you have those skills, you can define custom containers that work like the containers of the STL as described in chapter 19.

Because chapters 17 and 18 present skills that are used in chapter 19, they are prerequisites to chapter 19. Similarly, chapter 17 presents some skills that are used in chapter 18. As a result, we recommend reading these three chapters in sequence.

17

How to work with memory and pointers

In chapter 12, you were introduced to some skills for working with pointers that you need to work with built-in arrays. Now, you'll review those skills and learn much more about working with pointers.

But first, you should know that it's often a good practice to avoid using pointers when you're working with modern versions of C++. That's because using pointers can be difficult and error prone. Fortunately, C++ has evolved over the years so that it's usually possible to avoid pointers by using reference variables and STL vectors instead of pointers and built-in arrays.

However, you can't always avoid pointers. For example, if you work with legacy C++ or C code, you are likely to encounter them. Also, if you are working in an environment with constrained resources, such as an embedded environment, you might need to use pointers.

An introduction to memory and pointers

In C++, a pointer is an object that works at the level of the physical memory. As a result, before you can understand how pointers work, you need to understand how physical memory works.

How physical memory works

Physical memory is a sequence of bytes as shown by the graphical representation at the top of figure 17-1. Each byte in the sequence is assigned a number, usually ranging from zero to one less than the size of the memory. This number is called a *memory address*.

In C++, you typically allocate memory by defining variables that have a data type as shown by the first example. Here, the first statement defines a char variable named letter, and the second defines an int variable named num. These statements direct the system to set aside enough bytes to store a char value and an int value. On most systems, that means that 1 byte is allocated for the letter variable and 4 bytes are allocated for the num variable.

At this level, the only difference between a char type and an int type is the number of bytes of physical memory that's allocated for them. This is illustrated by the graphical representation below the two statements.

The second example provides a single statement that defines an array variable that holds five elements of the int type. This statement directs the system to set aside enough bytes to hold the elements of the array. On most systems, that's 5 elements of 4 bytes each for a total of 20 bytes. At this level, the only difference between this variable and the variables from the first example is the number of bytes that are allocated. Again, this is illustrated by the graphical representation below the statement.

Remember, each byte in physical memory is assigned a unique memory address. That means that when you define a variable and memory for it is allocated by the system, each byte that's allocated has a unique address. With C++, you can use the *address of operator* (**&**) to retrieve this memory address. Specifically, the address of operator returns the memory address of the first byte of the memory location of the *object*, which in this context is anything that's stored in memory.

The third example shows how this works. Here, the first statement displays the memory address of the first byte of the 4 bytes the system allocated for the int variable named num. Then, the second statement displays the memory address of the first byte of the 20 bytes the system allocated for the int array variable named nums.

The notation used to display the memory addresses varies by system, but most systems use some variation of *hexadecimal* (or *hex*). In this figure, for example, Visual Studio/MSVC and Xcode/Clang use different variations of hexadecimal notation to display the memory address. Since the notation used by Xcode/Clang is shorter, this is the notation we'll use in the next figure. Of course, your system will likely produce different hexadecimal values than these.

A graphical representation of the sequence of bytes in physical memory

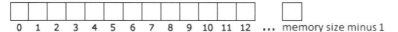

How to allocate memory by defining two variables

```
char letter;    // sets aside 1 byte of memory (usually) for variable letter
int num;        // sets aside 4 bytes of memory (usually) for variable num
```

A graphical representation of these variables

How to allocate memory by defining an array variable

```
int nums[5];    // sets aside enough memory for variable nums
                // (usually 20 bytes: 4 bytes times 5 elements)
```

A graphical representation of this array

How to use the address of operator to get the memory address of an object

```
cout << &num << endl;    // displays memory address of first of 4 bytes
cout << &nums << endl;   // displays memory address of first of 20 bytes
```

The hexadecimal notation displayed by Visual Studio/MSVC

`00000093670FFD34`

The hexadecimal notation displayed by Xcode/Clang

`0x28ff2c`

Description

- The physical memory of a computer is a sequence of bytes.

- Each byte is a physical location and is represented by a number, also called a *memory address*. On most systems, the numbers range from zero to one less than the memory size.

- The notation for memory addresses varies by system, but it's common for systems to use *hexadecimal*, or *hex*, notation. Hex notation is a base 16 numbering system that uses sixteen distinct symbols, typically 0-9 for zero to nine and A-F for ten to fifteen.

- You can use the *address of operator* (**&**) to get the memory address of an *object*, which can be thought of as anything that's stored in memory. This returns the address of the first byte of the location of the object in memory.

Figure 17-1   How physical memory works

How to define and use pointers

As you just learned, each object in C++ is allocated a specific location in physical memory. Further, you learned that you can use the address of operator to retrieve the memory address of the first byte of that location. Once you've retrieved a memory address, you can store it in a special variable called a *pointer variable*, also known as a *pointer*. In other words, a pointer is an object that stores the memory address of another object.

The first example in figure 17-2 shows how to define a pointer variable. Here, the first statement defines an int variable named num whose value is 200. Then, the second statement defines a pointer variable named ptr whose value is the memory address of the num variable. More precisely, the value of the ptr variable is the memory address of the first byte of the location where the num value is stored. As a result, the ptr variable *points to* the num variable.

It's important to understand that a pointer variable is itself an object. As a result, it has its own memory address as shown by the graphical representation below the code example. In addition, the second code example displays this memory address on the console.

In addition to having a memory address, a pointer variable has a data type. In this figure, for example, the pointer named ptr has a data type of *pointer to int* since it points to an int data type. This is a *compound type* that's created from an underlying type, and it allows you to use the pointer to indirectly access and work with the underlying value.

To access the underlying value of a pointer, you can use the *indirection operator* (*) as shown by the third code example. Here, the first statement uses the indirection operator to display the underlying value on the console. This is the value that's stored in the num variable. Then, the second statement uses the indirection operator to change the underlying value. To show that this works, the third statement displays the num variable on the console.

As you review the third example, note that the first example uses the asterisk (*) to define the pointer named ptr. Then, the third example uses the asterisk as the indirection operator. In other words, the operation of the asterisk changes depending where it's coded. Similarly, the asterisk becomes the multiplication operator if it's coded between two numbers.

To access a member function of an object, you can use the *member access operator* (->). For instance, the fourth example defines a string and a pointer named sptr that points to that string. Then, the fifth example uses the member access operator to call the size() member function of the string object. It's also possible to use the indirection operator here like this:

```
cout << (*sptr).size() << endl;   // displays 5
```

However, the member access operator is cleaner and less error prone. As a result, you should use it whenever possible.

Code that defines an int variable and a pointer to that int object

```
int num = 200;       // defines and initializes int variable named num
int* ptr = &num;     // defines and initializes pointer to int named ptr
```

A graphical representation of the relationship between these two variables

How to display the value stored by the pointer

```
cout << ptr << endl;        // displays 0x28ff2c
```

How to use the indirection operator to work with a pointer

To retrieve the underlying value

```
cout << *ptr << endl;       // displays 200
```

To change the underlying value

```
*ptr = 1000;                // assigns new value to underlying object
cout << num << endl;        // displays 1000
```

Code that defines a string variable and a pointer to the string object

```
string s = "hello"; // defines and initializes string variable
string* sptr = &s;  // defines and initializes pointer to string vari-
able
```

How to use the member access operator to call a function

```
cout << sptr->size() << endl;    // displays 5
```

Description

- A *pointer variable*, or *pointer*, is an object that stores the memory address of another object. In other words, the pointer *points to* the other object.

- The value of a pointer is a memory address, but a pointer is also an object in its own right with its own memory address.

- You can use the address of operator (&) to get an address that you can use to initialize a pointer variable.

- A pointer variable stores a memory address and has a data type that depends on the data type it points to. For example, a pointer to an int data type is of the *pointer to int* type. This is referred to as a *compound type*.

- You can use the *indirection operator* (*) to *dereference* a pointer. This allows you to access the value of the object that a pointer points to.

- You can use the *member access operator* (->) to access public data members and functions of the object that a pointer points to.

Figure 17-2   How to define and use pointers

More skills for defining and using pointers

Figure 17-3 begins by showing the three syntaxes for defining a pointer. The first syntax is the one you saw in the last figure, and you'll learn more about it and the other syntaxes in just a minute. But first, you should notice that regardless of which syntax you use, you can initialize a pointer variable when you define it. This is considered a best practice, since uninitialized pointers are a common cause of errors.

The first code example defines three variables that are used by the other examples. Here, the first two statements define variables of the int type, and the third statement defines a variable of the double type.

The second code example shows the three places that you can code the asterisk when defining a pointer. First, you can code it immediately after the data type. This style makes it clear that the type is a compound type, and it makes it easier to distinguish between code that defines a pointer and code that dereferences a pointer. As a result, the code examples in this book use this placement of the asterisk in most cases.

Second, you can code the asterisk immediately before the variable name. This style makes it easier to remember to include the asterisk when defining multiple pointers as shown in the third example of this figure. However, this placement of the asterisk looks similar to code that dereferences a pointer.

Third, you can code the asterisk with spaces between it, the data type, and the variable name. This style is the least common, partly because it looks like the placement of the asterisk for a multiplication expression.

The third example shows how to define multiple pointers on one line of code. To do that, you need to make sure that each variable has an asterisk before it. Otherwise, you'll accidentally define some regular variables instead of pointers. For instance, without the asterisk before it, the p2 variable would be an int variable, not a pointer. Because of that, some programmers consider it a best practice to code one pointer per line.

The fourth example shows how to define a null pointer. With C++11 and later, it's generally considered a best practice to define a null pointer by using the nullptr keyword to assign a value to the pointer. Prior to C++11, it was common to assign NULL or 0 to create a null pointer. Once you define a null pointer, you shouldn't attempt to dereference it. To avoid that, you can check whether a pointer is null as shown in figure 17-5.

The fifth example shows how to use the address of operator to change the object that a pointer points to. Here, the first statement changes the address of the pointer named iptr so it points to the grade variable instead of the num variable. This works because both of these variables are of the int type.

The last example shows that you can't change a pointer so it points to a different data type. This might seem odd, since memory addresses are just numbers. Remember, though, that a pointer only contains the memory address of the first byte of an object's location. It uses the data type of the pointer to determine how many more bytes have been allocated for that object. For instance, a pointer to an int variable knows it contains the memory address for the first of 4 bytes. If you changed that memory address to the first of 8 bytes of a double, the

The three syntaxes for defining a pointer

```
type* name [= &object];
type *name [= &object];
type * name [= &object];
```

Three variables used in this figure

```
int num = 200;
int grade = 88;
double pi = 3.14;
```

Three places to code the asterisk when defining a pointer

```
int* iptr = &num;      // immediately after the data type
int *iptr2 = &num;     // immediately before the variable name
int * iptr3 = &num;    // with spaces before and after
```

How to define multiple pointers on one line

```
int *p1 = &num, *p2 = &grade;  // each declaration must have a * symbol
```

Three ways to define a null pointer

```
int* ip1 = nullptr;    // C++11 and later
int* ip2 = NULL;       // prior to C++11
int* ip3 = 0;          // prior to C++11
```

How to change the object a pointer points to

```
iptr = &grade;         // iptr now points to the grade object
cout << *iptr << endl; // displays 88
```

An error that can occur when changing the object a pointer points to

```
iptr = &pi;            // ERROR: cannot convert from double* to int*
```

Description

- When defining a pointer, you can code the asterisk immediately after the data type, immediately before the variable name, or with spaces before and after the asterisk.

- It's recommended that you initialize a pointer when you define it, since uninitialized pointers are a common cause of errors.

- When defining multiple pointers on one line, make sure each variable has an asterisk.

- With C++11 and later, it's a best practice to define a null pointer by assigning it the nullptr keyword. Prior to C++11, you can define a null pointer by assigning it a value of NULL or 0.

- Once you define a null pointer, you shouldn't try to dereference it.

Figure 17-3   More skills for defining and using pointers

pointer would still think it pointed to an object that was 4 bytes. Because this could lead to problems, the compiler displays an error if you try to do this.

How pointer variables compare to reference variables

In chapter 7, you learned how to work with reference variables. As you may have noticed in this chapter, pointer variables are similar to reference variables in some ways. Both types of variables allow you to indirectly access another object. However, figure 17-4 describes several important differences between the two.

First, a pointer is an object with its own memory address. A reference, by contrast, is another name, or *alias*, for the object it refers to. In other words, a reference variable doesn't have its own memory address.

Second, you typically need to use operators to assign a memory address to a pointer and to access the object a pointer points to. In particular, you typically need to use the address of operator to assign a memory address to a pointer variable, and you typically need to use the indirection operator to access the underlying value. By contrast, you can use the same syntax as a regular variable to assign a value to a reference variable and to access the value that it refers to.

Third, a pointer variable can be null and the memory address it stores can change. In other words, a pointer can point to nothing and the object that it points to can change. A reference variable, by contrast, must always refer to an object, and once it refers to an object it can't be changed to refer to a different object.

The examples below the table show the values and memory addresses of a regular variable, a reference variable, and a pointer variable. These examples show some of the differences presented in the table. In particular, the first example shows that you must use the address of operator to assign a value to a pointer variable. Then, the second example shows that you must use the indirection operator to access the value stored by a pointer variable. Finally, the third example shows that when you use the address of operator with a pointer variable, you get the memory address of that variable rather than the memory address of the object that it points to.

In general, working with reference variables is easier and less error prone than working with pointer variables. As a result, you should use reference variables whenever they provide the functionality that you need. However, if you need to store a null value or change the object a variable points to, you'll need to use pointers.

How pointer variables compare to reference variables

Pointer	Reference
Is an object with its own memory address	Is an alias without its own memory address
Must dereference to access underlying value	Can access underlying value automatically
Must use address of operator to assign value	No extra operators necessary to assign value
Can store a null value	Can't store a null value (must refer to an object)
Can change the object it points to	Can't change the object it refers to

Define and initialize a regular, reference, and pointer variable

```
double pi = 3.14;      // regular variable
double& dref = pi;     // reference variable
double* dptr = &pi;    // pointer variable - requires address of operator
```

Display the underlying value of each variable

```
cout << pi << endl;      // displays 3.14
cout << dref << endl;    // displays 3.14
cout << *dptr << endl;   // displays 3.14 - requires indirection operator
```

Display the memory address of each variable

```
cout << &pi << endl;     // displays memory address of pi
cout << &dref << endl;   // displays memory address of pi
cout << &dptr << endl;   // displays memory address of dptr
```

Description

- In general, pointer variables are more difficult to work with than reference variables. As a result, it's generally considered a best practice to use reference variables unless you need the functionality of a pointer variable.

Figure 17-4   How pointer variables compare to reference variables

How to use pointers with functions

At this point, you should understand the basics of how memory and pointers work. Now, you're ready to learn how to use pointers with functions and when it makes sense to do that.

How and when to pass pointers to functions

You can use pointers to pass objects to functions by reference instead of by value. The first example in figure 17-5 shows how this works. Here, the square() function defines a parameter named val that's a pointer to a double object.

Within this square() function, the code uses the pointer to work with the underlying double object. To start, this code uses an if statement to make sure the val parameter isn't a null pointer. That's because attempting to dereference a null pointer causes problems. Then, the code uses the indirection operator to get the value that the val parameter points to, square that value, and update the value that the val parameter points to.

Below the square() function is some code that calls it. Here, the first statement defines a double variable named d and initializes it to a value of 4.0. Then, the second statement calls the square() function and passes it a pointer to the double value. To do that, this statement uses the address of operator to get the address of the double value. Finally, the third statement displays the new value of d, which is 16.0.

The code in this first square() function is complicated. To start, it must include an if statement to make sure it doesn't try to dereference a null pointer. Even worse, asterisks appear in the second line three times, twice as the indirection operator and once as part of a compound assignment operator. Finally, the code calling the function has to use the address of operator.

By contrast, the code in the second square() function is simpler. That's because it uses a reference variable instead of a pointer variable. In this version of the function, you don't have to check for null because a reference variable can't be null. You don't have to dereference the variable to get its value. And you don't have to use the address of operator to pass the reference variable.

When you compare these two functions, it's obvious why it typically makes sense to use reference parameters rather than pointer parameters. In most cases, you should only use pointer parameters when you need to be able to pass a null value or change the object that the pointer points to. However, some programmers prefer to use pointer parameters for clarity. That's because you have to code the address of operator in the calling code when you pass the argument, and that makes it clear that the argument is being passed by reference and might be changed. Of course, you can weigh whether you think this benefit offsets the drawbacks of using pointer parameters.

As you learned in chapter 12, a built-in array decays to a pointer when it's passed to a function. As a result, it's common to code function parameters for built-in arrays as pointers as shown by the third example. And since a built-in array automatically decays to a pointer, you don't need to use the address of operator when passing it to the function.

The square() function with a pointer parameter

```
void square(double* val) {
    if (val != nullptr) {    // make sure pointer isn't null
        *val *= *val;        // dereference value and perform calculation
    }
}
```

Code that calls the function

```
double d = 4.0;
square(&d);                  // use address of operator to pass argument
cout << d << endl;           // displays 16
```

The square() function with a reference parameter

```
void square(double& val) {
    val *= val;              // perform calculation
}
```

Code that calls the function

```
double d = 4.0;
square(d);                   // pass argument normally
cout << d << endl;           // displays 16
```

The display_array() function with a pointer parameter for a built-in array

```
void display_array(int* arr, int size) {
    if (arr) {                   // same as (arr != nullptr)
        for (int i = 0; i < size; ++i) {
            cout << arr[i] << ' ';  // can subscript without dereference
        }
        cout << endl;
    }
}
```

Code that calls the function

```
const int size = 10;
int arr[size] = {0};
display_array(arr, size);        // pass argument normally
                                 // displays 0 0 0 0 0 0 0 0 0 0
```

When to use a pointer parameter rather than a reference parameter

- You need to be able to pass a null value to the function.
- The function needs to be able to change the object the parameter points to.
- You want to make it clear in the calling code that the argument is not being passed by value and that the function might change it.
- The parameter is a built-in array.

Description

- To pass an argument to a function by reference, you can use a reference parameter or a pointer parameter.
- In general, reference parameters are easier to work with. As a result, you should use reference parameters unless you've got a good reason to use a pointer parameter.

Figure 17-5   How and when to pass pointers to functions

How to use the *this* pointer in a member function

Every object has a pointer whose value is its own memory address. The *this* keyword is used to refer to this pointer. As a result, each member function of an object has access to a pointer that points to the current object.

To illustrate this concept, figure 17-6 presents a Calculator class that uses this pointer. To start, this class defines a private data member named result. Then, it defines three public member functions named multiply(), square_result(), and get_result(). The get_result() function returns an int value, but the other two functions return a reference to a Calculator object.

The multiply() member function defines two int parameters named a and b. Then, the body of this function multiplies these parameters and stores the result in the private data member named result.

To do that, this code uses the *this* keyword to access the pointer to the current object, and it uses the member access operator (`->`) to access the data member of the current object named result. For this class, this isn't necessary. Instead, this function could use a simpler statement like this:

```
result = a * b;
```

However, some programmers prefer to use the *this* keyword and the member access operator to clearly show that the object they're working with is a member of the current object.

After performing its calculation, the multiply() function uses the *this* keyword to return a reference to the current object. In other words, it returns a reference to the specific Calculator object that it's a member of. To do that, it dereferences the pointer named *this* and returns a reference to that object. This is known as returning a *self-reference*, and it's often used to make it possible to *chain* member functions as shown later in this figure.

In the Calculator class, the square_result() member function squares the value of the private data member named result. Then, it also returns a reference to the current object. The get_result() function, by contrast, just returns the int value of result.

The second code example shows how to use the Calculator class without function chaining. Here, the first statement creates a Calculator object. Then, the next three statements call the multiply(), square_result(), and get_result() functions. This works, but it takes three lines of code and requires you to code the name of the Calculator object three times.

The third example shows how to use the Calculator class with function chaining. Here, the first statement creates a Calculator object. Then, the second statement calls the multiply(), square_result(), and get_result() functions of the Calculator object. This works because multiply() returns a Calculator object that the square_result() function can be called from, and square_result() returns a Calculator object that get_result() can be called from. Note that this only takes one line of code and only requires you to code the name of the Calculator object once. Code that chains function calls like this is sometimes called *fluent* because it often reads fluently, like a sentence.

A Calculator class whose member functions use the this pointer and return self-references

```
class Calculator {
private:
    int result;
public:
    Calculator& multiply(int a, int b) {
        this->result = a * b;            // this-> is optional
        return *this;                    // return a self-reference
    }

    Calculator& square_result() {
        this->result *= this->result;    // this-> is optional
        return *this;                    // return a self-reference
    }

    int get_result() {
        return this->result;             // this-> is optional
    }
};
```

Code that uses the Calculator class

```
Calculator calc;
calc.multiply(2, 5);
calc.square_result();
int result = calc.get_result();
cout << result << endl;                  // displays 100
```

Code that uses the Calculator class with function chaining

```
Calculator calc;
int result = calc.multiply(2,5).square_result().get_result();
cout << result << endl;                  // displays 100
```

Description

- Every object has a pointer named *this* whose value is its own memory address.
- When you define member functions in a class or structure, you can use the pointer named this to access the members of the current object.
- When coding member functions, you can use the member access operator (->) of the pointer named this to access other members of the object. However, unless you need to do this to prevent a naming conflict, this technique is optional.
- When coding member functions, you can return a reference to the current object. This is known as a *self-reference*, and it's useful for creating member functions that can be *chained* together.
- To return a self-reference, use the indirection operator (*) to return the underlying value of the pointer named this.

Figure 17-6   How to use the this pointer in a member function

The Step Counter 1.0 program

Figure 17-7 shows the Step Counter 1.0 program. This program begins by prompting the user to enter the number of steps walked for each day of the week. After the user enters this data, the program calculates the total number of steps for the week and the average number of steps per day.

The code begins by including the iostream header file. However, it doesn't include a using directive for the std namespace. Instead, it fully qualifies the calls to iostream objects.

Next, the code declares two functions. The first function, get_weekly_steps(), defines a pointer to an int parameter, a pointer to a char parameter, and an int parameter, and it doesn't return any data. The second function, get_total(), defines a pointer to an int parameter and an int parameter, and it returns a double value.

The main() function starts by defining an int constant named num_days for the number of days in a week. Then, it defines two built-in arrays. The first is an array of characters named days that's initialized with a string literal that contains one character for each day of the week. Remember from chapter 12 that this makes this array a C string. The second array is an array of int values named steps with one element for each day of the week. The single value in the initialization list means that each element in the array is initialized to zero.

After defining the built-in arrays, the code displays a welcome message. Then, it calls the get_weekly_steps() function to get the steps for each day from the user. To do that, it passes this function the steps array, the days C string, and the num_days constant.

Next, this code calls the get_total() function and stores the return value in a double variable named total. To do that, it passes this function the steps array and the num_days constant. Then, the code calculates the average number of steps per day. Finally, it displays the total steps for the week and the daily average on the console.

The definition for the get_weekly_steps() function starts by checking if the steps pointer or the days pointer is null. If so, the function ends without executing any other statements. Otherwise, the function executes a loop for each day of the week. Within the loop, the first statement displays the current character in the days array to prompt the user to enter the steps for that day. Then, the second statement gets the number of steps the user enters and stores them in the current element of the steps array.

The definition for the get_total() function starts by defining an accumulator variable named total and initializing it to zero. Then, it makes sure the steps pointer is not null. However, it uses a shortcut to do that. You could also code the Boolean expression in the if statement like this:

```
if (steps != nullptr)
```

Either way, if the steps pointer is not null, the function loops through the elements in the array and adds them to the accumulator variable. After the loop finishes, the function returns this variable. Note that if the steps pointer is null, the loop doesn't run and the function returns the initial accumulator value of zero, which is probably what you want.

The console

```
Welcome to the Weekly Step Counter program!

Please enter your steps for the week:
M: 10000
T: 8900
W: 8800
T: 7000
F: 5700
S: 10000
S: 12000


Total steps for the week:   62400
Average daily steps:        8914.29
```

The code

```cpp
#include<iostream>

void get_weekly_steps(int* steps, char* days, int num_days);
double get_total(int* steps, int num_days);

int main() {
    const int num_days = 7;
    char days[] = "MTWTFSS";      // built-in array for the days argument
    int steps[num_days] = { 0 }; // built-in array for the steps argument

    std::cout << "Welcome to the Weekly Step Counter program!\n\n"
              << "Please enter your steps for the week:\n";

    get_weekly_steps(steps, days, num_days);
    double total = get_total(steps, num_days);
    double avg = total / num_days;

    std::cout << "Total steps for the week:  " << total << '\n'
              << "Average daily steps:       " << avg << "\n\n";
}

void get_weekly_steps(int* steps, char* days, int num_days) {
    if (steps == nullptr || days == nullptr) return;
    for (int i = 0; i < num_days; ++i) {
        std::cout << days[i] << ": ";
        std::cin >> steps[i];
    }
    std::cout << '\n';
}

double get_total(int* steps, int num_days) {
    double total = 0;
    if (steps) {                              // same as (steps != nullptr)
        for (int i = 0; i < num_days; ++i) {
            total += steps[i];
        }
    }
    return total;
}
```

Figure 17-7   The Step Counter 1.0 program

The Step Counter 2.0 program

Figure 17-8 shows the Step Counter 2.0 program. Like the 1.0 version, the 2.0 version prompts the user to enter the number of steps walked for each day of the week. Then, it calculates and displays the total number of steps for the week and the average number of steps per day.

The code for the Step Counter 2.0 program starts by including the iostream and vector header files. Like the 1.0 verison, this code doesn't specify a using directive for the std namespace. Instead, it fully qualifies the calls to iostream and vector objects.

Next, this code declares a class named Counter. This class defines a private data member named steps, which is a vector of int values. Then, this class defines a public data member named days, which is a vector of chars, initialized with one character for each day of the week. Finally, it declares two public member functions. The first, get_weekly_steps(), returns a reference to a Counter object. The second, get_total(), returns a double value.

The main() function starts by displaying a welcome message. Then, it defines a Counter object named steps. Next, it defines a double variable named total and assigns it the value that's returned by chaining calls to the get_weekly_steps() and get_total() functions of the Counter object. This gets the steps from the user, stores those steps in the object, and gets the total steps from the object.

After getting the total number of steps, this code calculates the average number of steps. To do that, it calls the size() member function from the days data member. This works because the days data member is public and is a vector. Finally, this code displays the total number of steps and the average daily steps.

The definition for the get_weekly_steps() member function starts by defining an int variable named daily_steps. Then, it loops through the elements in the days data member. The condition for the loop uses the *this* pointer and the member access operator to access the days data member. However, this is optional and would typically be omitted.

Within the loop, the first statement prompts the user to enter the number of steps for the day. To do that, this statement gets the character for the current day from the days vector, and it displays that character. Then, the second statement gets the number of steps the user enters, stores them in the daily_steps variable, and passes that variable to the push_back() function of the steps vector.

When the loop completes, the steps vector contains one element for each day of the week. At this point, the code dereferences the *this* pointer to return a self-reference. This makes it possible to chain a call to another member function to the get_weekly_steps() function.

The definition for the get_total() member function starts by coding an accumulator variable named total and initializing it to zero. Then, the function loops through the elements in the steps vector and adds each element to the accumulator variable. Finally, the function returns this variable.

This version of the Step Counter program shows that even when you're working with high-level objects like vectors, you may still need to use the *this* pointer. In this case, using the *this* pointer to return a self-reference makes it possible to chain function calls to the Counter object.

The console

```
Welcome to the Weekly Step Counter program!

Please enter your steps for the week:
M: 10000
T: 8900
W: 8800
T: 7000
F: 5700
S: 10000
S: 12000


Total steps for the week:  62400
Average daily steps:       8914.29
```

The code

```cpp
#include<iostream>
#include<vector>

class Counter {
private:
    std::vector<int> steps;
public:
    std::vector<char> days = { 'M','T','W','T','F','S','S' };
    Counter& get_weekly_steps();
    double get_total();
};

int main() {
    std::cout << "Welcome to the Weekly Step Counter program!\n\n"
              << "Please enter your steps for the week:\n";
    Counter steps;
    double total = steps.get_weekly_steps().get_total();    // chaining
    double avg = total / steps.days.size();
    std::cout << "Total steps for the week:  " << total << '\n'
              << "Average daily steps:       " << avg << "\n\n";
}

Counter& Counter::get_weekly_steps() {
    int daily_steps;
    for (char day : this->days) {
        std::cout << day << ": ";
        std::cin >> daily_steps;
        this->steps.push_back(daily_steps);  // this-> is optional
    }
    std::cout << '\n';
    return *this;                            // return a self-reference
}

double Counter::get_total() {
    double total = 0;
    for (int s : this->steps) {              // this-> is optional
        total += s;
    }
    return total;
}
```

Figure 17-8   The Step Counter 2.0 program

How to use pointers to work with dynamic memory

One of the most common uses of pointers is to allocate *dynamic memory*, which is memory that's allocated at runtime. Now, you'll learn about the different types of memory. Then, you'll learn how to use pointers to work with dynamic memory.

An overview of the types of storage

When a program starts, the system sets aside memory for that program. Four of the types of memory, also known as *storage*, are described at the top of figure 17-9.

The first three types of storage are allocated for specific purposes. *Code storage*, as its name implies, is memory that's allocated for the program code itself. *Static storage* is memory that's allocated for global variables, like the ones you learned about in chapter 7. And *automatic storage* is memory that's allocated for functions and local variables.

With automatic storage, the system automatically allocates memory when you create an object and automatically deallocates it when the object goes out of scope. To manage the local variables and functions, automatic storage uses a last-in-first-out (LIFO) stack. That's why automatic storage is also known as *stack storage*, *stack memory*, the *call stack*, or the *stack*.

One of the benefits of automatic storage is that you can use it just by declaring a variable. Another benefit is that it can be accessed quickly.

One of the drawbacks of automatic storage is that it can be inflexible. For instance, you must know the size of a built-in array at compile time. Another drawback is that the amount of available stack storage is limited. If you try to use more than what's available, you'll get a *stack overflow* error. For example, this error can occur if you define a built-in array that's larger than the memory the stack has available.

Free store storage, or the *free store*, is the remaining memory that's set aside for a program but that's not yet allocated. This type of storage is also called *heap memory* or the *heap*.

One of the benefits of the free store is that there's much more of it than there is stack memory. Another benefit is that it's flexible. In fact, the free store is what gives the vector and string objects their flexibility and the ability to hold large amounts of data.

One of the drawbacks of the free store is that it can't be accessed as quickly as automatic storage. Another drawback is that the programmer must add code to manually allocate and deallocate memory. If the programmer fails to properly deallocate free store memory, it can lead to memory leaks or heap corruption. You'll learn more about that later in this chapter.

Types of storage set aside for a program when it starts

Name	Description
Code storage	Memory allocated for the program code itself.
Static storage	Memory allocated for global variables.
Automatic storage	Memory allocated for local variables and functions. This memory uses a last-in-first-out (LIFO) *stack* to manage local variables and functions. As a result, it's also called *stack storage*, *stack memory*, the *call stack*, or the *stack*.
Free store	The remaining, unallocated memory. This memory is also called *heap memory* or the *heap*.

Automatic storage (stack)

Benefits

- Access is fast.
- Allocation and deallocation of memory is handled by the system automatically.

Drawbacks

- Less flexible. For instance, the size of an array must be known at compile time.
- The memory allocated for the stack is limited, so you can run out of automatic storage. Running out of stack memory is known as *stack overflow*.

Free store (heap)

Benefits

- More flexible.
- Much more available memory.

Drawbacks

- Access is slower.
- Allocation and deallocation of memory must be handled manually by the program code. Failure to properly deallocate free store memory can lead to *memory leaks* or *heap corruption*.

Description

- When a program starts, the system sets aside memory for the program code, global and local variables, and functions. It also sets aside memory that can be allocated as the program runs.
- *Dynamic memory* is memory that's allocated at runtime. The free store is a type of dynamic memory.
- Unlike stack memory, free store memory is *not* automatically deallocated when the code goes out of scope. Instead, the program must manually deallocate it.

Figure 17-9   An overview of the types of storage

How to allocate and deallocate free store memory

To work with free store memory, you use the new and delete keywords. The new keyword allocates memory on the free store and returns a pointer to the location where the memory is allocated. The delete keyword deallocates that memory and returns it to the free store so it can be used again.

The example in figure 17-10 shows how this works. Here, the first two statements show how to allocate a single object. To start, the first statement uses the new keyword to allocate memory for a double object and return a pointer to it. This assigns that pointer to the variable named pi. The second statement works similarly, but it includes an initial value for the double object that's created.

The next two statements show how to allocate memory to an array of objects. Here, the first statement uses the new keyword to create an array of 10 doubles and return a pointer to it that's assigned to the variable named arr. The second statement works similarly, but it includes a list of initial values for the array.

As you learned in chapter 12, a built-in array on the stack decays to a pointer. This pointer points to the first element in the array and doesn't know how many elements the array contains. A pointer to an array on the heap works similarly, except that it can be allocated at runtime. As a result, you don't have to code the size of the array as a constant.

Once you use the new keyword to allocate objects on the free store, you need to use the delete keyword to deallocate them. This is important because, unlike automatic storage, an object that's allocated on the free store is *not* automatically deallocated when it goes out of scope. Instead, you must write code to deallocate the memory yourself.

The second example shows how to use the delete keyword to deallocate memory. Here, the first statement uses the delete keyword to deallocate the memory for the object that the pointer named pi points to. Then, the second statement uses the delete keyword followed by square brackets ([]) to deallocate the memory for the array that the pointer named arr points to.

Although this seems easy enough, in practice, using the new and delete keywords can cause problems. For example, if you forget to call delete, the memory is never returned to the free store and can't be used again. This is known as a *memory leak* and it's shown by the third example. If the program runs for a short time, it may not matter because all memory is returned when a program ends. But for long-running programs, memory leaks can build up and degrade performance over time.

Unfortunately, you can't fix a memory leak just by coding the delete keyword throughout your code. That's because attempting to deallocate memory that's already been deallocated can corrupt that memory. This is known as *heap corruption*, and it's shown by the fourth example.

If you work with legacy C or C++ code, you may find that it uses the malloc and free keywords to allocate and deallocate memory. This is an older technique that's not considered a best practice for new development, but you might need to use it to maintain old code. If you do that, however, you should make sure not to use the malloc/free keywords and the new/delete keywords in the same program as that can lead to serious problems.

How to use the new keyword to allocate free store memory

Allocate a single object of type double

```
double* pi = new double;              // returns pointer to double
double* price = new double(5.99);     // include initial value
```

Allocate a dynamic array of doubles

```
double* arr = new double[10];      // returns pointer to first element
double* prices = new double[3]{5.99,6.99,7.99};
                                   // include initial values
```

How to use the delete keyword to deallocate free store memory

Deallocate a single object

```
delete pi;
```

Deallocate an array

```
delete[] arr;
```

A function that could lead to a memory leak

```
int* create_array(unsigned int size) {
    return new int[size]{0};  // returns pointer to array on free store
}
```

This code neglects to call delete[ ] on the pointer returned by the function

```
void main() {
    int* arr = create_array(20);
    /* code that works with the array goes here */
}
```

A function that could lead to heap corruption

```
void display_array(int* arr, unsigned int size) {
    for (int i = 0; i < size; ++i) {
        cout << arr[i] << ' ';
    }
    delete[] arr;             // deletes array when done
}
```

This code calls delete on a pointer to stack memory

```
int arr[5]{0};            // allocate memory on stack
display_array(arr, 5);    // function calls delete on stack memory
```

This code calls delete twice on a pointer to heap memory

```
int* arr = new int[5]{0}; // allocate memory on heap
display_array(arr, 5);    // function calls delete on heap memory
delete[] arr;             // statement calls delete on heap memory again
```

Description

- You can use the new keyword to allocate free store memory. This keyword returns a pointer to the newly allocated memory.

- You can use the delete keyword to deallocate a single object, and you can use the delete keyword followed by square brackets ([]) to deallocate an array.

Figure 17-10   How to allocate and deallocate free store memory

How to avoid memory leaks and corruption

When you allocate and deallocate memory, it's possible to write code that leaks or corrupts memory. The topics that follow present two techniques that can help you avoid these problems.

How to use RAII (Resource Acquisition Is Instantiation)

When you define an object on the stack, the system automatically calls its constructor to create it. Then, when that stack object goes out of scope, the system automatically calls its destructor to destroy it.

RAII (*Resource Acquisition Is Instantiation*) is a programming pattern that takes advantage of this process to safely allocate and deallocate free store memory used by an object. Basically, RAII states that you should allocate free store memory in the constructor of an object and deallocate that memory in the destructor of that object. That way, the free store memory is automatically managed by the processes of stack storage, and the programmer can just use the object without needing to manually manage the free store memory that it uses.

Figure 17-11 defines a class named MyContainer that shows how this works. To start, this class defines two private data members, a pointer to an int variable named elements and an int variable named size. This class also defines public constructor and destructor functions.

Within the constructor, the new keyword allocates an array on the free store. This returns a pointer to the dynamic array that's assigned to the data member named elements. Then, this constructor displays a message on the console that indicates that the memory has been allocated.

Within the destructor, the delete[] keyword deallocates the free store memory that was allocated in the constructor. Then, this destructor displays a message on the console that indicates that the memory has been deallocated.

This illustrates how an object created from the MyContainer class handles its free store memory cleanly. When you create a MyContainer object, it allocates memory for an int array with ten elements. In other words, a *resource* is *acquired* when the object is *instantiated*. Then, when that object goes out of scope, the system calls the destructor, which deallocates the memory.

In the second example, for instance, free store memory is allocated when the main() function defines a MyContainer object. Then, when the main() function ends and this object goes out of scope, the memory is automatically deallocated.

Because RAII doesn't mention freeing the resource, some programmers have proposed more descriptive names like Constructor Acquires Destructor Releases (CADRe) or Scope-Based Resource Management (SBRM). However, RAII is the most common name for this pattern.

When using RAII, you should know that some C++ compilers don't automatically call destructors when an exception occurs. This can keep your automatic deallocation from occurring. To correct for this, you can put all code in the main() function within a try/catch block that handles all exceptions.

A MyContainer class that uses RAII

```
class MyContainer {
private:
    int* elements;
    int size = 10;
public:
    // constructor
    MyContainer() {
        elements = new int[size];                           // allocate memory
        cout << "memory allocated for MyContainer object\n";
    }

    // destructor
    ~MyContainer() {
        delete[] elements;                                  // deallocate memory
        cout << "memory deallocated for MyContainer object\n";
    }
};
```

Code that uses the MyContainer class

```
int main() {
    cout << "main() function starting...\n";
    MyContainer mine;
    cout << "main() function ending...\n";
}
```

The console

```
main() function starting...
memory allocated for MyContainer object
main() function ending...
memory deallocated for MyContainer object
```

Description

- When you create an object on the stack, the object's constructor runs when the object is created and its destructor runs when it goes out of scope.

- *RAII* (*Resource Acquisition Is Instantiation*) is a programming pattern that takes advantage of the way the stack creates and destroys objects to allocate and deallocate free store memory automatically.

- For RAII to work, the object must be created on the stack. If the object is created on the heap, its destructor won't be called when it goes out of scope.

- RAII can also be used to work with other system resources such as file handles.

- Some C++ compilers don't call destructors (sometimes called *unwinding the stack*) when an unhandled exception is thrown. To account for this, you can code a try/catch statement around all code in the main() function of your program that handles all exceptions.

Figure 17-11   How to use RAII (Resource Acquisition Is Instantiation)

How to implement the Rule of Three with RAII

When you define a class in C++, if you don't explicitly define a destructor, a copy constructor, and a copy assignment operator, the compiler automatically generates default versions for you. Often, these default functions work fine. Sometimes, though, they don't. For example, if your class has a data member that's a pointer, the default copy constructor and copy assignment operator copy the pointer rather than the object that the pointer points to. This is called a *shallow copy*, and in most instances that's not what you want for this constructor and operator. When the default functions don't work, you need to write your own.

The *Rule of Three* states that if you need to define your own destructor, copy constructor, or copy assignment operator, you should define all of them as indicated by the table at the top of figure 17-12. In the previous figure, you learned that RAII requires you to define your own constructor and destructor to allocate and deallocate free store memory. Therefore, according to the Rule of Three, you should also define your own copy constructor and copy assignment operator when you use RAII.

The MyContainer class in this figure is an enhanced version of the MyContainer class from the previous figure that implements the Rule of Three. To start, the constructor and destructor shown here are the same as the constructor and destructor from the previous figure, except that they don't print messages to the console.

The copy constructor accepts a MyContainer object by constant reference. Then, the constructor uses this parameter to initialize itself. First, it uses the new keyword to allocate an array on the free store and stores the pointer to this array in the elements data member. Then, it makes a *deep copy* of the MyContainer object that's passed to it. To do that, it loops through the elements in the MyContainer parameter and copies those elements to the data member array.

This deep copy is critical. The default copy constructor generated by the compiler would just make a copy of the element pointer. In that case, both objects would have pointers that point to the same location on the heap. This would lead each object to call delete[] on the same heap memory when they went out of scope, which could cause memory corruption.

The copy assignment operator also accepts a MyContainer object by constant reference. Then, this function uses this parameter to update itself. First, it uses the new keyword to allocate an array on the free store and stores the pointer to this array in a temporary variable named temp. Then, it makes a deep copy of the MyContainer object that's passed to it and stores it in the temp variable. Next, it deallocates the memory that the elements pointer points to and updates that pointer so it points to the new array. Finally, it returns a reference to itself, which is what the default copy constructor that's generated by the compiler does.

This copy assignment operator could assign the pointer to the newly allocated memory directly to the elements data member and then perform the copy operation. However, it uses a temporary variable instead to provide exception safety. That way, if an exception occurs during the copy operation, the state of the container doesn't change. This avoids a situation where some, but not all, of the elements are changed and is generally considered a best practice.

The member functions required by the Rule of Three

Function	Description
destructor	Deallocates the memory allocated for the container's data.
copy constructor	Copies the data in the container passed to the constructor. Copied container is unchanged.
copy assignment operator	Copies the data in the container on the right side of the assignment operator (=). Copied container is unchanged.

The MyContainer class updated to implement the Rule of Three

```cpp
class MyContainer {
private:
    int* elements = nullptr;
    int size = 10;
public:
    // constructor
    MyContainer() {
        elements = new int[size];
    }

    // destructor
    ~MyContainer() {
        delete[] elements;
    }

    // copy constructor
    MyContainer(const MyContainer& tocopy) {
        elements = new int[size];
        for (int i = 0; i < size; ++i) {          // deep copy
            elements[i] = tocopy.elements[i];
        }
    }

    // copy assignment operator
    MyContainer& operator= (const MyContainer& tocopy) {
        auto temp = new int[size];                // allocate new array
        for (int i = 0; i < size; ++i) {          // deep copy
            temp[i] = tocopy.elements[i];
        }
        delete[] elements;                        // delete old
        elements = temp;                          // assign new
        return *this;                             // return self-reference
    }
};
```

Description

- When you define a class, the compiler creates default copy constructor and copy assignment operator functions. In classes that use pointers, these functions copy the pointers, not the underlying objects. This is known as making a *shallow copy*.

- When you use RAII, you must define a constructor and destructor. With the *Rule of Three*, if you define (1) a destructor, you should also define (2) a copy constructor and (3) a copy assignment operator. With RAII, the copy constructor and assignment operator must copy the underlying objects, not the pointers. This is known as making a *deep copy*.

Figure 17-12   How to implement the Rule of Three with RAII

How to implement the Rule of Five with RAII

C++11 added a feature known as *move semantics* to the C++ language. This feature allows you to transfer data from one object to another rather than making copies of the data. As you might expect, moving data is more efficient than copying data, especially with large objects that are expensive to copy.

To implement move semantics in your own classes, you need to define a move constructor and a move assignment operator. These functions are described at the top of figure 17-13.

The addition of move semantics expands The Rule of Three to The Rule of Five. The *Rule of Five* states that if you need to define your own destructor, copy constructor, copy assignment operator, move constructor, or move assignment operator, you should define all of them.

As you've learned, RAII requires you to define your own destructor to deallocate free store memory. Therefore, according to the Rule of Five, if you want to include move semantics, you should also define your own copy constructor, copy assignment operator, move constructor, and move assignment operator when you use RAII.

The code example in this figure presents the MyContainer class from the last figure updated to implement the Rule of Five. The constructor, destructor, copy constructor, and copy assignment operator in this class are the same as in the previous figure. As a result, this figure doesn't show them again.

The move constructor accepts an *rvalue reference* to a MyContainer object. An rvalue reference identifies an object that can be moved. To declare a rvalue reference, you can use the *rvalue reference declarator* (**&&**).

Within the move constructor, the first statement copies the elements pointer of the parameter object to the elements pointer of the current object. At this point, both objects have pointers that point to the same memory address, which is the address where the array is stored. Then, the second statement sets the elements pointer of the parameter object to null so it no longer points to the array. This completes the move operation.

This move operation is more efficient than the copy operation shown in the previous figure. In that operation, the copy constructor allocated new memory and then copied each element in an array. Here, the move constructor doesn't need to allocate any new memory. Instead, it just reassigns the pointers that point to an existing array.

The move assignment operator also accepts an rvalue reference to a MyContainer object. Then, it uses this parameter object to update itself. To do that, it begins by using the delete[] keyword to deallocate the memory pointed to by the elements pointer of the current object. Next, it copies the elements pointer from the parameter object to the current object and sets the parameter object's pointer to null. Finally, it returns a reference to itself.

This move assignment operation is more efficient than the copy assignment operation in the previous figure. That's because this operation doesn't need to allocate new memory. Instead, it only needs to reassign the pointers to existing memory.

The additional member functions required by the Rule of Five

Function	Description
move constructor	Moves the data from the container passed to the constructor. Moved container is emptied.
move assignment operator	Moves the data from the container on the right side of the assignment operator (=). Moved container is emptied.

The MyContainer class updated to implement the Rule of Five

```
class MyContainer {
private:
    int* elements = nullptr;
    int size = 10;
public:
    // constructor is the same as in the previous figure
    // destructor is the same as in the previous figure
    // copy constructor is the same as in the previous figure
    // copy assignment operator is the same as in the previous figure

    // move constructor
    MyContainer(MyContainer&& tomove) {
        elements = tomove.elements;        // assign pointer to data
        tomove.elements = nullptr;         // remove pointer to data
    }

    // move assignment operator
    MyContainer& operator= (MyContainer&& tomove) {
        delete[] elements;                 // deallocate existing memory
        elements = tomove.elements;        // assign pointer to data
        tomove.elements = nullptr;         // remove pointer to data
        return *this;                      // return self-reference
    }
};
```

Description

- C++11 and later provide *move semantics* that enable you to move existing data. This is more efficient than copying existing data.

- The *rvalue reference declarator* (&&) indicates that the data of an object can be moved.

- To implement move semantics in your classes, you need to code a move constructor and a move assignment operator.

- When you use RAII, you must define a constructor and destructor. With the *Rule of Five*, if you define (1) a destructor, you should also define (2) a copy constructor, (3) a move constructor, (4) a copy assignment operator, and (5) a move assignment operator.

Figure 17-13   How to implement the Rule of Five with RAII

How to work with smart pointers

If you just want to do something simple like allocate an array in free store memory, it may not make sense to create all the member functions you need when using RAII, the Rule of Three, and the Rule of Five. Fortunately, with C++11 and later, you can use *smart pointers* instead. Unlike the *raw pointers* that you've worked with so far in this book, a smart pointer uses RAII under the hood to deallocate the free store memory automatically.

The top of figure 17-14 shows how to include the memory header file that contains the smart pointers. Then, it describes three of the smart pointers introduced in C++11. To start, unique_ptr objects can only point to one memory location. When this type of pointer goes out of scope, the system deallocates the memory. Because this type of pointer must be unique, it can't be copied, but it can be moved.

By contrast, shared_ptr objects can point to the same memory location. To do that, shared_ptr maintains a reference count. Then, when the reference count goes to zero, the system deallocates the memory. Because this type of pointer allows multiple pointers to point to the same location, it can be copied or moved.

You can create a weak_ptr object as a copy of a shared_ptr object. However, this type of pointer doesn't add to the reference count. Typically, weak_ptr objects are used with shared_ptr objects to avoid circular references that keep the reference count from ever reaching zero.

A unique_ptr has less overhead than a shared_ptr and is appropriate for most purposes. As a result, the examples in this figure show how to work with unique_ptr objects. However, the skills for working with shared_ptr and weak_ptr objects are similar.

The first example shows how to create a smart pointer that points to a single object or to an array of objects. When you define a smart pointer, you code the data type that the pointer refers to within angle brackets. To identify an array, you code square brackets after the data type. Then, you code the name of the pointer followed by a set of parentheses. Within these parentheses, you code the new keyword and the data type to allocate the free store memory. After that, you can work with the smart pointer just as you would a raw pointer, except that you can't use pointer arithmetic.

The second example shows how to use the make_unique() function, added in C++14, to create a unique_ptr to a single object or an array of objects. First, you code the auto keyword, the pointer name, and the assignment operator. Then, you call the make_unique() function with the data type within angle brackets. For an array, you code square brackets after the data type within the angle brackets. Then, you pass the number of elements as an argument to the function. The advantage of this function is that you can use the auto keyword, and you don't have to use the new keyword.

The last two examples work with a create_array() function that returns a unique_ptr to an array. This function works like the create_array() function presented in figure 17-10. However, that version returned a raw pointer to memory that needed to be deallocated manually. With this version, the smart pointer deallocates the memory automatically when the smart pointer to the array goes out of scope.

How to include the memory header file

```
#include <memory>
```

Three smart pointers in the memory header (C++11 and later)

Smart Pointer	Description
`unique_ptr`	Only one unique_ptr object can point to allocated memory. When unique_ptr is destroyed or goes out of scope, memory is deallocated.
`shared_ptr`	Multiple shared_ptr objects can point to allocated memory. Maintains a reference count and deallocates memory when count is zero.
`weak_ptr`	Created as a copy of a shared_ptr, but does not add to the reference count.

How to use unique_ptr to work with free store memory

Code that creates a smart pointer to an int

```
unique_ptr<int> ptr(new int);      // create smart pointer to int
*ptr = 4;                          // dereference and assign value
*ptr *= *ptr;                      // dereference and square value
cout << *ptr << endl;              // displays 16
```

Code that creates a smart pointer to a built-in array

```
unique_ptr<int[]> arr(new int[10]); // create smart pointer to array
for(int i = 0; i < 10; ++i) {       // set values of array elements
    arr[i] = i;
}
```

How to use the make_unique() function (C++14 and later)

```
auto ptr = make_unique<int>();      // create smart pointer to int
auto arr = make_unique<int[]>(10);  // create smart pointer to array
```

A create_array() function that returns a smart pointer to a built-in array

```
unique_ptr<int[]> create_array(unsigned int size) {
    auto arr = make_unique<int[]>(size);
    return arr;
}
```

Code that uses the create_array() function

```
int main() {
    unsigned int size = 0;
    cout << "Please enter the size of the array: ";
    cin >> size;

    auto arr = create_array(size);
    for (int i = 0; i < size; ++i) {
        cout << arr[i] << ' ';
    }
}  // the smart pointer automatically deallocates memory for the array
```

Description

- With C++ 11 and later, you can use *smart pointers* to manage memory automatically.

- The weak_ptr type is often used with the shared_ptr type to avoid circular references.

- There is also an auto_ptr type, but it was deprecated in C++11.

Figure 17-14   How to work with smart pointers

The Sensor Analysis program

Figure 17-15 shows the Sensor Analysis program. This program simulates a sensor that takes one reading per second. To start, this program asks the user how many days of readings to analyze. Then, it retrieves the correct number of readings, simulates some data for each reading, performs calculations on the readings, and displays the results to the user.

To do its work, this program uses a custom HeapArray object. As the name implies, this object creates an array on the free store, or heap. This is necessary for two reasons. First, the program asks the user how many days of sensor readings to analyze. As a result, the size of the array that stores the sensor readings isn't known at compile time, so the array needs to use dynamic memory that can be allocated at runtime. Second, if the user selects a large number of days, the array may need more room than is available on the stack. As a result, the memory for the array needs to be allocated on the heap.

Of course, the easiest way to overcome these issues would be to use a vector. For the purposes of this chapter, though, assume that you can't use a vector for technical reasons.

The code for this figure begins by presenting the header file for the HeapArray class. This class has two private data members. The first is an int named array_size that stores the number of elements in the array. The second is a pointer to an int named arr that stores the pointer to the dynamic array that will be allocated on the heap.

After the private data members, this code declares three constructors and a destructor. The first constructor accepts an int, the second accepts a constant HeapArray object by reference, and the third accepts a HeapArray rvalue reference. Then, this code declares two assignment operator functions. The first accepts a constant HeapArray object by reference, and the second accepts a HeapArray rvalue reference. Both functions return a HeapArray object by reference.

As you review these six public functions, you can see that the HeapArray class declares a destructor, a copy constructor, a move constructor, a copy assignment operator, and a move assignment operator. In other words, it implements the Rule of Five.

After the assignment operators, this code declares a subscript operator that accepts an int by value and returns an int by reference. This function allows the HeapArray class to provide the subscripting that you would expect from an array.

Finally, the header file declares three member functions. To start, the size() function returns an int value. Then, the begin() and end() functions return pointers to int values. These functions allow the HeapArray class to work like an STL container. In addition, the begin() and end() functions allow a HeapArray object to be used with STL algorithms.

After the header file, this figure presents the source file for the HeapArray class. This code starts by including the HeapArray header file. Then it defines the first constructor. This constructor accepts an int named size and stores that value in the private array_size data member. Then, it uses the array_size value to allocate an array of int values on the free store and it stores the pointer to this

The console

```
The Sensor Analysis program
Enter the number of days you'd like to analyze: 5

Number of sensor readings over 5 days: 432000
Average reading: 67.0863
Lowest reading: 17
Highest reading: 111
```

The HeapArray.h file

```cpp
#ifndef MURACH_HEAPARRAY_H
#define MURACH_HEAPARRAY_H

class HeapArray {
    private:
        int array_size;
        int* arr = nullptr;

    public:
        // constructors
        HeapArray(const int);
        HeapArray(const HeapArray& tocopy);      // copy constructor
        HeapArray(HeapArray&& tomove);           // move constructor

        // destructor
        ~HeapArray();

        // assignment operators
        HeapArray& operator= (const HeapArray& tocopy);  // copy assignment
        HeapArray& operator= (HeapArray&& tomove);       // move assignment

        // subscript operator
        int& operator[] (int i);

        // Member functions
        int size() const;
        int* begin();
        int* end();
};

#endif /* MURACH_HEAPARRAY_H */
```

The HeapArray.cpp file

```cpp
#include "HeapArray.h"

// ----- CONSTRUCTORS ----- //
HeapArray::HeapArray(const int size) {
    array_size = size;                // set array size property
    arr = new int[array_size]{0};     // allocate memory on heap
}
```

Figure 17-15   The Sensor Analysis program (part 1 of 3)

array in the private data member named arr. In addition, this code initializes all the elements of the array to a value of zero.

Part 2 of figure 17-15 presents the rest of the source file for the HeapArray class. It starts with the definition for the copy constructor function. This constructor accepts a constant HeapArray object by reference. Then, it uses the array_size value of the HeapArray parameter to set its own array_size value. Next, it uses that array_size value to allocate an array of integers on the free store and stores the pointer to the array in the arr data member.

Unlike the previous constructor, the copy constructor doesn't use an initialization list to initialize the array. Instead, it initializes the array by looping through the elements in the HeapArray parameter and copying each value to its own array. This works because you can use the subscript operator with a pointer to an array to access that array's elements.

The definition for the move constructor function accepts a HeapArray rvalue reference. As with the copy constructor, it starts by using the array_size value of the parameter object to set its own array_size value. Then, it assigns the parameter arr member to its own arr member. Next, to make sure that only one pointer points to that array, it assigns a null pointer to the parameter arr data member and sets the parameter's array_size value to zero. This shows that the HeapArray parameter object has no elements after the move operation is completed.

The definition for the destructor function deallocates the free store memory that the arr data member points to. This works even when the arr member has been set to null by a move constructor. That's because you can call delete on a null pointer without causing any problems.

The definition for the copy assignment operator works similarly to the copy constructor. It accepts a constant HeapArray object by reference. Then, it uses this HeapArray parameter to set its own array_size data member, to allocate an array on the free store, and to copy the elements of the parameter array to the new array. The difference is that the copy assignment operator uses a temporary pointer variable named new_arr to provide for exception safety.

After the elements are copied, the function deallocates the free store memory pointed to by the arr data member. Then, it assigns the pointer to the newly allocated memory to the arr member. Finally, it returns a self-reference.

The definition for the move assignment operator accepts a HeapArray rvalue reference. This function starts by making sure it doesn't try to perform a move operation on itself. To do that, this code checks to make sure the HeapArray parameter is not equal to the pointer to the current object. Then, it uses the array_size value of the parameter object to set its own array_size value, it deallocates the memory pointed to by its own arr data member, and it assigns the array pointer from the parameter object to its own arr member. Next, it empties the HeapArray parameter by setting its arr member to null and its array_size member to zero. Finally, it returns a self-reference.

The last four definitions in the source file should be easy for you to understand. The subscript operator accepts an index value and returns the array element at that index. The size() function returns the value of the private array_size data member. The begin() function returns the private arr data member, which is a pointer to the first element. And the end() function returns a pointer that points one past the last element. To do that, this function uses pointer arithmetic, which is presented in chapter 12 and reviewed later in this chapter.

The HeapArray.cpp file (continued)

```cpp
HeapArray::HeapArray(const HeapArray& tocopy) {                    /* COPY */
    array_size = tocopy.array_size;           // copy size
    arr = new int[array_size];                // allocate memory on heap

    for (int i = 0; i < array_size; i++) {    // copy array values
        arr[i] = tocopy.arr[i];
    }
}

HeapArray::HeapArray(HeapArray&& tomove) {                         /* MOVE */
    array_size = tomove.array_size;           // copy size
    arr = tomove.arr;                         // reset array pointer

    tomove.arr = nullptr;                     // empty parameter array
    tomove.array_size = 0;
}

// ----- DESTRUCTOR ----- //
HeapArray::~HeapArray() {
    delete[] arr;                             // deallocate memory
}

// ----- ASSIGNMENT OPERATORS ----- //
HeapArray& HeapArray::operator= (const HeapArray& tocopy) {      /* COPY */
    array_size = tocopy.array_size;           // copy size
    int* new_arr = new int[array_size];       // allocate memory on heap

    for (int i = 0; i < array_size; ++i) {    // copy array values
        new_arr[i] = tocopy.arr[i];
    }

    delete[] arr;                             // deallocate old memory
    arr = new_arr;                            // assign pointer to new memory
    return *this;                             // return a self-reference
}

HeapArray& HeapArray::operator= (HeapArray&& tomove) {           /* MOVE */
    if (this != &tomove) {                    // don't move if passed self
        array_size = tomove.array_size;       // copy size
        delete[] arr;                         // deallocate old memory
        arr = tomove.arr;                     // reset array pointer

        tomove.arr = nullptr;                 // empty HeapArray param
        tomove.array_size = 0;
    }
    return *this;                             // return a self-reference
}

// ----- SUBSCRIPT OPERATOR ----- //
int& HeapArray::operator[] (int i) { return arr[i]; }

// ----- MEMBER FUNCTIONS ----- //
int HeapArray::size() const { return array_size; }
int* HeapArray::begin() { return arr; }
int* HeapArray::end() { return arr + array_size; }
```

Figure 17-15   The Sensor Analysis program (part 2 of 3)

Part 3 of figure 17-15 presents the code for the main.cpp file for the Sensor Analysis program. To start, this code includes the header files it needs. That includes the cstdlib and ctime headers it needs to generate random numbers to simulate the sensor data, as well as the HeapArray header file that it needs to work with HeapArray objects.

After a using directive for the std namespace, this code declares a function named load_sensor_data(). This function accepts a HeapArray object by reference and doesn't return any data. From this, you can infer that this function updates any HeapArray objects that are passed to it.

The main() function starts by displaying a welcome message on the console. Then, it gets the number of days to analyze from the user. Next, it defines a constant that stores the number of seconds in a 24-hour day (86400), and it calculates the total number of seconds for the number of days entered by the user.

The code then creates a HeapArray object named data and passes the total number of seconds to its constructor. This creates a dynamic array on the free store with one element for each second. Then, the code passes the HeapArray object to the load_sensor_data() function. This loads the sensor reading for each second into the HeapArray object.

Next, the code uses STL algorithms to analyze the sensor readings. First, it calls the accumulate() algorithm to get the total of all the readings. Second, it calls the min_element() algorithm to get the lowest reading. Third, it calls the max_element() algorithm to get the highest reading. Each of these algorithms uses the pointers returned by the begin() and end() functions of the HeapArray object to do its work.

The main() function ends by displaying the results of the sensor analysis. It uses the size() function of the HeapArray object to display the number of sensor readings and also to calculate the average of the readings. In addition, it dereferences the iterators returned by the min_element() and max_element() algorithms to display the lowest and highest readings.

The definition of the load_sensor_data() function starts by seeding the random number. Then, it defines an int variable named adjust. This variable is initialized to a random number between 10 and 70 and is used just to make the simulated readings more interesting. Without it, the low reading is almost always 1, the high is almost always 100, and the average is always approximately 50.

Finally, this function ends by looping through each element in the HeapArray parameter that's received by reference. Within the loop, it generates a random number between 1 and 100 that's stored in an int variable named num. Then, it uses the conditional operator to adjust that random number and assign it to the current array element. It adjusts the number by checking if it's less than the value in the adjust variable. If it is, the function adds the adjust value to the random number.

As you review this function, note that the loop uses the size() function and subscript operator of the HeapArray object. Specifically, it uses the size() function to determine when to end, and it uses the subscript operator to update each element. Also, note that you could easily update this loop to read numbers from a file or other data source without having to change any of the code in the main() function.

The main.cpp file

```cpp
#include <iostream>
#include <cstdlib>
#include <ctime>
#include <algorithm>
#include <numeric>
#include "HeapArray.h"

using namespace std;

void load_sensor_data(HeapArray& data);

int main() {
    cout << "The Sensor Analysis program\n\n";

    int num_days = 0;
    cout << "Enter the number of days you'd like to analyze: ";
    cin >> num_days;
    cout << endl;

    const int seconds_per_day = 86400;
    int total_seconds = num_days * seconds_per_day;

    HeapArray data(total_seconds);
    load_sensor_data(data);

    double total = accumulate(data.begin(), data.end(), 0);
    auto min = min_element(data.begin(), data.end());
    auto max = max_element(data.begin(), data.end());

    cout << "Number of sensor readings over " << num_days
        << " days: " << data.size() << endl;
    cout << "Average reading: " << (total / data.size()) << endl;
    cout << "Lowest reading: " << *min << endl;
    cout << "Highest reading: " << *max << endl << endl;
}

// load simulated sensor data
void load_sensor_data(HeapArray& data) {
    srand(time(nullptr));                   // seed random number
    int adjust = rand() % 70 + 10;          // number between 10 - 70

    int num = 0;
    for (int i = 0; i < data.size(); ++i) {
        num = rand() % 100 + 1;                 // number between 1 - 100
        data[i] = (num < adjust) ? num + adjust : num;   // adjust number
    }
}
```

Figure 17-15   The Sensor Analysis program (part 3 of 3)

More skills for working with pointers

So far, this chapter has presented the skills for working with pointers that you'll need most of the time. Now, it will present some more skills for working with pointers that you may need occasionally.

How to compare pointers

You can use the comparison operators to compare pointers of the same data type. This compares the memory addresses of the objects the pointers point to, *not* the values of those objects. The first example in figure 17-16 shows how this works.

This example starts by defining two pointers named p1 and p2 that point to the same memory address and a third pointer named s that points to a different address. Then, the first statement that follows uses the equality operator (==) to check whether p1 and p2 are equal. Since these pointers both point to the same memory address, this comparison returns a value of 1 (true).

The second and third statements check whether p1 and s are equal. Although these pointers provide access to the same underlying value, they point to different memory addresses. As a result, the second comparison returns a value of 0 (false). However, the third statement dereferences p1 and s to check whether the underlying values are equal. As a result, this comparison returns a value of 1.

How to use pointer arithmetic

The +, -, ++, --, +=, or -= operators move a pointer forward or backward along the sequence of bytes in memory to point to a different memory address. This is called *pointer arithmetic*. Technically, you can do this with any pointer. However, it typically only makes senses with pointers that point to arrays.

With pointer arithmetic, the compiler uses the data type of the pointer to determine how many bytes to move. For example, if you add 1 to a pointer to an int type, the compiler advances the pointer by 4 bytes.

The second example in figure 17-16 starts by defining an int array with five elements. Then, it uses array decay to get a pointer to the first element. After that, it uses arithmetic operators to move the pointer to point to different elements in the array. Finally, this code attempts to move the pointer outside the bounds of the array. This is possible, but it will cause problems. As a result, when working with pointer arithmetic, make sure to stay within the bounds of the array.

How to work with void pointers

You can use the void keyword to create a *void pointer* that can point to any data type. However, because the data type isn't known, you can't dereference it or use pointer arithmetic unless you first cast the void pointer to a pointer with a data type. The last two examples in figure 17-16 show how this works.

How to compare pointers

```
double price = 89.99, score = 89.99;
double *p1 = &price, *p2 = &price, *s = &score;

cout << (p1 == p2);    // displays 1 - pointers point to the same object
cout << (p1 == s);     // displays 0 - values match but objects are different
cout << (*p1 == *s);   // displays 1 - values match
```

How to use pointer arithmetic in an array

```
int arr[] { 2, 4, 6, 8, 10 };
int* i = arr;          // i points to first element
cout << *i << endl;    // displays 2

++i;                   // advances 1 element to point to second element
cout << *i << endl;    // displays 4

i = i + 2;             // advances 2 elements to point to fourth element
cout << *i << endl;    // displays 8

i = i - 3;             // moves back 3 elements to point to first element
cout << *i << endl;    // displays 2

--i;                   // DANGER! you've moved outside the array bounds!
cout << *i << endl;    // displays ????
```

How to define a void pointer and point to different types

```
double pi = 3.14;
int i = 0;

void* ptr = &pi;       // define void pointer that points to a double
ptr = &i;              // change void pointer to point to an int
cout << *ptr << endl;  // ERROR - can't dereference - data type unknown
```

How to cast a void pointer to a pointer to a type

```
int* iptr = static_cast<int*>(ptr);
cout << *iptr << endl; // SUCCESS - displays 0
```

Description

- You can use the equality operator (==) to compare pointers of the same data type. This checks whether the pointers point to the same memory address, not whether the objects store the same value.

- *Pointer arithmetic* allows you to use arithmetic operators to move a pointer forward or backward along a sequence of bytes to point to a different memory address. You usually do this only with pointers that point to arrays.

- A *void pointer*, also known as a *generic pointer*, can point to an object of any data type. In most cases, you should avoid using void pointers because they often lead to errors. However, you may encounter them when working with legacy C++ or C code.

- You can compare void pointers, pass them to a function, and return them from a function.

- You can't dereference void pointers or use pointer arithmetic with them. However, if you want to perform these operations on a void pointer, you can cast it to a pointer to a specific data type.

Figure 17-16   More skills for working with pointers

How to use pointers with inheritance

In chapter 15, you learned how to work with inheritance and polymorphism. In that chapter, you learned how to define the Product superclass as well as Book and Movie subclasses shown by the inheritance hierarchy at the top of figure 17-17.

To refresh your memory about how these classes work, the Product superclass defines a virtual get_description() member function. Then, the Book subclass inherits the Product class and overrides the get_description() function so it includes the author's name as part of the description. The Movie subclass also inherits the Product class and overrides the get_description() function so it includes the year as part of the description.

Now, this figure shows how you can use pointers when working with inheritance. For instance, the first code example shows that a pointer that points to a superclass object can also point to a subclass object. Here, the first statement creates a Product object on the free store. The second statement creates a Book object on the free store. And the third statement creates a Movie object on the free store. Each of these statements stores the pointer returned by the new keyword in a pointer to the Product type. This shows that a pointer to a superclass can store the memory address of a superclass or a subclass object.

When working with a pointer to a superclass, you can only call members of the superclass, not members of the subclass. In the second example, for instance, the code in the show_product() function can't call the get_author() member function from the pointer to the Product object because that function is only available from the Book object. However, this function can call a virtual member of the superclass such as the get_description() function. Then, if you pass a pointer to a subclass object to this function, C++ uses polymorphism to call the overridden function from the correct subclass. This is illustrated by the statements that calls the show_product() function. Here, for example, the second statement causes C++ to call the get_description() function of the Book class. That's because this statement passes a pointer to a Book object to the function.

The third example shows that you can store superclass pointers in a vector. That's useful because it lets you create a vector that can store pointers to any objects created from the superclass or any of its subclasses. In this example, the vector named products can store pointers to any objects created from the Product, Book, or Movie classes.

Once you create a vector of superclass pointers, you can pass it to a function like the one shown in the fourth example. When you do, that function can use polymorphism to call the correct get_description() function from any of the objects that are passed to that function. This causes the description for Book objects to include the author and the description for Movie objects to include the year as shown by the console in this figure.

To save space and focus on inheritance, the examples in this figure use the new keyword to store objects in the free store, but they don't subsequently use the delete keyword to deallocate memory. In a production program, of course, you would also deallocate the memory. Better yet, you'd use RAII and the Rule of Five as described earlier in this chapter.

The Product hierarchy

```
Product   - defines   virtual get_description() function
   Book   - overrides virtual get_description() function to add author
  Movie   - overrides virtual get_description() function to add year
```

How to use a superclass pointer to store addresses of subclass objects

```
Product* p1 = new Product("Stanley 13 Ounce Wood Hammer", 12.99, 62));
Product* p2 = new Book("The Big Short", 15.95, 34, "Michael Lewis"));
Product* p3 = new Movie("The Wizard of Oz", 14.99, 50, 1939));
```

How to code a function that accepts a superclass pointer

```
void show_product(const Product* p) {
    cout << "Name:              " << p->get_description() << endl
         << "Price:             " << p->get_price() << endl
         << "Discount percent: " << p->get_discount_percent() << "\n\n";
}
```

Code that calls this function

```
show_product(p1);   // calls get_description() function of the Product class
show_product(p2);   // calls get_description() function of the Book class
show_product(p3);   // calls get_description() function of the Movie class
```

How to create a vector of superclass pointers

```
vector<Product*> products = vector<Product*>();
products.push_back(new Product("Stanley 13 Ounce Wood Hammer", 12.99, 62));
products.push_back(new Book("The Big Short", 15.95, 34, "Michael Lewis"));
products.push_back(new Movie("The Wizard of Oz", 14.99, 50, 1939));
```

How to code a function that accepts a vector of superclass pointers

```
void show_products(const vector<Product*>& products) {
    int number = 0;
    for (int i = 0; i < products.size(); ++i) {
        Product* p = products[i];
        cout << ++number << ". " << p->get_description() << endl;
    }
    cout << endl;
}
```

Code that calls this function

```
show_products(products);
```

The console

```
1. Stanley 13 Ounce Wood Hammer
2. The Big Short by Michael Lewis
3. The Wizard of Oz (1939)
```

Description

- When working with inheritance, a pointer to a superclass can store the memory address of a subclass object.

- When working with a pointer to a superclass, you can only call members of the superclass, not members of the subclass. However, if you call a virtual member of the superclass, C++ uses polymorphism to call the overridden function of the subclass.

Figure 17-17   How to use pointers with inheritance

How complex compound types work

A pointer is an object with a memory address. This means that you can have a pointer to a pointer or a reference to a pointer. You can have pointers that are constant or pointers that point to constants. And you can combine these variations to create even more *complex compound types*. However, because a reference variable doesn't have its own memory address, you can't have a pointer to a reference.

Typically, you don't need to use compound types that are this complex. However, you might come across code that uses complex compound types. When that happens, it's important to be able to decipher that code. That's why figure 17-18 presents some skills that should help you understand how to read these complex compound types.

The first example shows how to create a pointer to a pointer. First, the code defines an int object named i. Then, it uses a single asterisk to create a *pointer to int* named p that points to i. Next, it uses two asterisks to create a *pointer to pointer to int* named pp that points to the pointer p.

The second example shows how to dereference the pointers in the first example. First, it uses one indirection operator to display the value of p, which is the memory address of i. Then, it uses two indirection operators to display the value of i, which is 2000.

There is no technical limit to the number of pointers to pointers you can have. For example, you can use three asterisks to code a pointer to a pointer to a pointer. However, this would be extremely rare.

The third example shows how to create a reference to a pointer by coding both an asterisk and an ampersand after the data type. This ref variable is another name, or alias, for the pointer p. As a result, they both point to the same value.

The fourth example shows how to work with constants and pointers. Here, the location of the const keyword determines whether the pointer is constant, the object pointed to is constant, or they both are.

If you code the const keyword after the data type and asterisk, the variable is a *constant pointer*. This means that you can change the value of the object that's pointed to, but you can't change the pointer so it points to a different object.

Conversely, if you code the const keyword before the data type and asterisk, the variable is a *pointer to a constant*. This means that you can't change the value of the object that's pointed to, but you can change the pointer so it points to a different object.

Finally, if you code the const keyword in both places, it's a *constant pointer to a constant*. This means that you can't change the pointer so it points to a different object, and you can't change the value of the object that the pointer points to.

Complex compound types can be easier to understand if you read them from right to left as shown by the fifth example. For instance, you can read the third statement as "r1 is a reference to a pointer to a constant int". Similarly, you can read the fourth statement as "p5 is a constant pointer to an int".

How to define a pointer to a pointer

```
int i = 2000;          // an int (value = 2000)
int* p = &i;           // a pointer to int (value = address of i)
int** pp = &p;         // a pointer to pointer to int (value = address of p)
```

How to dereference a pointer to a pointer

```
cout << *pp << endl;   // one indirection operator - displays address of p
cout << **pp << endl;  // two indirection operators - displays 2000
```

How to code a reference to a pointer

```
int*& ref = p;         // a reference to p
cout << p << endl;     // displays the address of i
cout << ref << endl;   // also displays the address of i
```

How to use the const keyword with pointers

Description	Change pointer?	Change underlying object?
constant pointer	no	yes
pointer to constant	yes	no
constant pointer to constant	no	no

Examples that use the const keyword with pointers

```
double price = 5.99;          // a double
const double pi = 3.14;       // a constant double

double* const p1 = &price;    // a constant pointer to a double
const double* p2 = &pi;       // a pointer to a constant double
const double* const p3 = &pi; // a constant pointer to a constant double
```

Examples that use compound types

```
const int ci = 2000;          // a constant int
const int* p4 = &ci;          // a pointer to a constant int
const int*& r1 = p4;          // a reference to a pointer to a constant int
int* const p5 = &i;           // a constant pointer to an int
const int* const p6 = &ci;    // a constant pointer to a constant int
const int* const & r2 = p6;   // a reference to a constant pointer to
                              // a constant int
```

Description

- You can combine pointers, references, and constants to create *complex compound types*.

- It can be easier to understand a complex compound type if you read it from right to left.

Figure 17-18   How to understand complex compound types

Perspective

Now that you've completed this chapter, you should have a good understanding of how pointers work. However, there's more to learn about pointers than what's presented in this chapter. For example, this chapter didn't present a common pattern called PIMPL (Pointer IMPLementation) that's often used with interfaces and libraries. However, this chapter should provide a solid foundation for you to research these more advanced concepts on your own. It should also prepare you for chapter 19, which shows you how to create your own custom containers, iterators, and algorithms.

Terms

memory address	free store
hexadecimal (hex) notation	heap memory (heap)
address of operator	memory leaks
pointer variable (pointer)	heap corruption
indirection operator	RAII (Resource Acquisition Is
dereference a pointer	Instantiation)
compound type	unwinding the stack
member access operator	shallow copy
alias	deep copy
self-reference	Rule of Three
function chaining	move semantics
dynamic memory	rvalue reference
storage	rvalue reference declarator
code storage	Rule of Five
static storage	smart pointers
automatic storage	raw pointer
stack storage	pointer arithmetic
stack memory	void pointer
call stack (stack)	generic pointer
stack overflow	complex compound type

Summary

- Each byte of memory is a physical location that's represented by a number, also called a *memory address*.

- The notation for memory addresses varies by system, but it's common for systems to use *hexadecimal*, or *hex*, notation.

- You can use the *address of operator* (&) to get the memory address of an object. This returns the address of the first byte of the location of the object in memory.

- A *pointer variable*, or *pointer*, is an object that contains the memory address of another object. In other words, a pointer *points to* another object.

- You can use the *indirection operator* (*) to *dereference* a pointer. This allows you to access the value of the object that a pointer points to.

- You can use the *member access operator* (->) to access public data members and functions of the object that a pointer points to.

- A reference is another name, or *alias*, for the object it refers to.

- Every object has a pointer named *this* whose value is its own memory address.

- When coding member functions of a class, you can return a reference to the current object. This is known as a *self-reference*, and it's useful for creating member functions that can be *chained* together.

- When a program starts, the system sets aside memory, also known as *storage*, for that program.

- *Code storage* is memory that's allocated for the program code itself.

- *Static storage* is memory that's allocated for global variables.

- *Automatic storage* is memory that's allocated for local variables and functions. This memory uses a last-in-first-out (LIFO) *stack* to manage local variables and functions. As a result, it's also called *stack storage*, *stack memory*, the *call stack*, or the *stack*.

- *Stack overflow* occurs when a program runs out of stack memory.

- *Dynamic memory* is memory that's allocated and deallocated manually at runtime. *Free store storage*, also known as the *free store*, is a type of dynamic memory. This memory is also called *heap memory* or the *heap*.

- Failure to properly deallocate free store memory can lead to *memory leaks* or *heap corruption*.

- *RAII* (*Resource Acquisition Is Instantiation*) is a programming pattern that takes advantage of the way the stack creates and destroys objects to allocate and deallocate free store memory automatically.

- Some C++ compilers don't call destructors (sometimes called *unwinding the stack*) when an unhandled exception is thrown. To account for this, you can code a try/catch statement around all code in the main() function of your program that handles all exceptions.

- A *shallow copy* copies a pointer to an object. A *deep copy* copies the object that a pointer points to.

- The *Rule of Three* states that if you need to code (1) a destructor, (2) a copy constructor, or (3) a copy assignment operator, you should code all three.

- C++11 and later provide *move semantics* that enable you to move existing data. This is more efficient than copying existing data.

- An *rvalue reference* identifies an object that can be moved and is declared with the *rvalue reference declarator* (&&).

- The *Rule of Five* states that if you need to code (1) a destructor, (2) a copy constructor, (3) a move constructor, (4) a copy assignment operator, or (5) a move assignment operator, you should code all five.

- With C++ 11 and later, you can use *smart pointers* to manage memory safely.

- *Pointer arithmetic* allows you to use arithmetic operators to move a pointer forward or backward along a sequence of bytes to point to a different memory address. You usually do this only with pointers that point to arrays.

- A *void pointer*, also known as a *generic pointer*, can point at an object of any data type.

- You can combine pointers, references, and constants to create *complex compound types*.

Exercise 17-1   Use pointers with built-in arrays

In this exercise, you'll code a program that gets a starting weight for each month of the year from the user, stores the weights and month names in built-in arrays, and uses pointers to work with the arrays. When you're done, a test run should look something like this:

```
Welcome to the Weight Tracker program!

Please enter your weight at the beginning of each month:
Jan: 172.4
Feb: 170.8
Mar: 167.4
Apr: 168.8
May: 166.5
Jun: 165.7
Jul: 163.6
Aug: 165.9
Sep: 163.3
Oct: 162.5
Nov: 159.7
Dec: 158.2

Maximum weight: 172.4
Minimum weight: 158.2
Average weight: 165.4
```

Open and review the project

1. Open the project or solution named weight_tracker in this folder:
   ex_starts\ch17_ex1_weight_tracker

2. Review the main.cpp file to see that it contains the required header files and a using statement for the std namespace. In addition, the main() function defines a constant for the number of months and a built-in array of strings for the month name abbreviations. It also contains the code that displays the messages on the console when the program starts.

Define the weights array and the functions that work with it

3. Define another built-in array named weights that can store a value for each month, and initialize the values to 0.0.

4. Declare a function named get_monthly_weights() that accepts a pointer to the weights array, a pointer to the months array, and the number of months and doesn't return a value.

5. Declare another function named get_total() that accepts a pointer to the weights array and the number of months and returns a double type.

6. Code the definition for the get_monthly_weights() function. This function should prompt the user for a weight for each month by displaying the month abbreviation in the months array, and then store the values that are entered in the weights array. Be sure to check that neither the months or weights array contains a null pointer before using it.

7. Code the definition for the get_total() function. This function should calculate the total of all the values in the weights array. Be sure to check that the weights array doesn't contain a null pointer before using it.

Modify the main() function to use the weights array

8. Add code to the main() function that calls the get_monthly_weights() function.

9. Add code to the main() function that calls the get_total() function.

10. Add code to the main() function that calculates and displays the average weight.

11. Use the max_element() and min_element() algorithms to get pointers to the elements in the weights array that contain the maximum and minimum weights. Then, display the values of those elements.

12. Modify the main() function so it uses the accumulate() algorithm to get the total of the weights instead of calling the get_total() function.

Exercise 17-2   Implement the Rule of Three

In this exercise, you'll modify another version of the Step Counter program that uses a HeapArray class so that class implements the Rule of Three.

Open, review, and test the program

1. Open the project or solution named step_counter in this folder:
    `ex_starts\ch17_ex2_step_counter`

2. Review the main.cpp file to see that it stores the steps for each day of the week in a HeapArray object instead of a built-in array. Also notice that the HeapArray object is passed to the get_weekly_steps() function by value. Because of that, a copy of this object will be passed to the function, and the modified HeapArray object is returned by the function.

3. Review the HeapArray.cpp file to see that its constructor and destructor use RAII to allocate and deallocate memory for an array on the heap. Notice also that it includes a subscript operator and size(), begin(), and end() member functions that are used by the Step Counter program.

4. Run the program and enter the number of steps for each day of the week. When you do, an error will occur because the default copy operation for the HeapArray object copies the pointer to the array, not the array itself.

Implement the Rule of Three

5. Open the HeapArray.h file and add the declaration for a copy constructor that accepts a constant reference to a HeapArray object.

6. Also in the HeapArray.h file, add the declaration for a copy assignment operator that accepts a constant reference to a HeapArray object and returns a reference to a HeapArray object.

7. Open the HeapArray.cpp file and add the definition for the copy constructor. This constructor should create a HeapArray object with a pointer to an array that's a copy of the array in the HeapArray object that's passed to it.

8. Also in the HeapArray.cpp file, add the definition for the copy assignment operator. This should work like the copy constructor, but it should store the new array in a temporary variable to provide for exception safety and it should return a self-reference. When you code this function, be sure to deallocate the old memory for the array before you assign a pointer to the new memory.

9. Run the program again. This time, it should work correctly.

18

How to work with templates

In chapters 10 and 11, you learned how to use the containers and algorithms of the Standard Template Library (STL). These containers and algorithms use a feature know as templates to allow them to be flexible enough to work with different data types. That's why it's called the Standard *Template* Library. In this chapter, you'll learn how to use templates to code your own containers and algorithms that can work with multiple data types.

Some of the examples in this chapter use built-in arrays as described in chapter 12 and pointers as described in chapter 17. As a result, you should read those chapters before reading this chapter. Otherwise, you may find it difficult to understand parts of this chapter.

How to work with function templates

A *function template* provides a way to allow a function to work correctly with different data types. For example, the STL algorithms use function templates to allow a function to work with the different container types. This is more flexible and efficient than overloading a function.

An overloaded function

In chapter 12, you learned how to code a linear_search() function like the first one shown in figure 18-1. This function implements the linear search algorithm to find a specified int in an array of int values. Unfortunately, this function only works with the int type. However, you could *overload* this function to get it to work correctly with different data types. For example, this figure shows how to overload this function so it also works with the char type.

When you overload a function, the compiler must compile all of the function overloads. That's true even if one or more overloads aren't used by the program. For example, if you included both overloads of the linear_search() function shown in this figure in a header file but a program only worked with an array of int values, the program would still compile the overload for working with an array of char values. Obviously, this isn't as efficient as it could be. Instead of using function overloads, then, you can use function templates to provide for multiple data types.

A function that's overloaded for two data types

The int type

```
int linear_search(const int arr[], int counter, int value_to_find) {
    for (int i = 0; i < counter; ++i) {
        if (arr[i] == value_to_find) {
            return i;   // value found - return index
        }
    }
    return -1;          // value not found - return -1
}
```

The char type

```
int linear_search(const char arr[], int counter, char value_to_find) {
    for (int i = 0; i < counter; ++i) {
        if (arr[i] == value_to_find) {
            return i;   // value found - return index
        }
    }
    return -1;          // value not found - return -1
}
```

Code that calls these functions

```
const int size = 6;
int numbers[size] = { 1, 2, 3, 5, 7, 11 };
int index = linear_search(numbers, size, 11);   // index is 5

char letters[size] = { 'a', 'e', 'i', 'o', 'u', 'y' };
index = linear_search(letters, size, 'o');      // index is 3
```

Description

- You can *overload* a function to get it to work correctly with different data types.

- When you overload a function, you must code one function overload for each data type.

- When you overload a function, the compiler must compile all of those functions, even if they aren't used by the program.

Figure 18-1   An overloaded function

A function template

Figure 18-2 begins by showing the linear_search() function presented in the previous figure after it has been converted to a function template. A *function template* allows a function to work correctly with any data type that supports the operators and functions that are used by the template. In this case, the linear_search() function uses the equality operator (==), so this function will work with any data type that supports this operator. As a result, this function works correctly with most data types, including the built-in data types and classes.

If you review the code for the function template, you'll notice that the function is prefixed by a line of code that defines the function as a template with a type parameter named T. Then, the function uses this type parameter to specify the type for the elements of the array and the value to find. Other than that, the code for the linear search is the same as the code shown in the overloaded functions in the previous figure. However, the code doesn't have to be duplicated for each data type.

After the function template, this figure shows code that calls the linear_search() function template three times, each time using a different data type. With each call, the compiler generates a function with the appropriate data types and compiles that function. Specifically, the first call generates the first overloaded function presented in the previous figure that works with the int type. The second call generates the second overloaded function presented in the previous figure that works with the char type. And the third call generates another function that works with the double type.

Since the function in the previous figure didn't provide an overload for working with the double type, that function isn't capable of working with the double type. As a result, this clearly shows that using a function template is more flexible than overloading a function.

In addition, because the compiler only generates the functions that are used by the program, function templates can result in smaller executable files. As a result, using a function template is typically more efficient than overloading a function. The compiler also generates these functions at compile time, not at runtime, so there's no performance penalty for using templates.

As you gain experience with C++, you'll find that function templates are often used to allow algorithms like the linear search algorithm to work with multiple data types instead of just a single data type. In general, templates provide a way to convert a function that uses a specific type such as the int type to a function that uses a generic type. As a result, working with templates is also referred to as *generic programming* or *generics*.

A function template

```
template<typename T>
int linear_search(const T arr[], int counter, T value_to_find) {
    for (int i = 0; i < counter; ++i) {
        if (arr[i] == value_to_find) {
            return i;   // value found - return index
        }
    }
    return -1;          // value not found - return -1
}
```

Code that calls this function template

```
const int size = 6;
int numbers[size] = { 1, 2, 3, 5, 7, 11 };
int index = linear_search(numbers, size, 11);   // index is 5

char letters[size] = { 'a', 'e', 'i', 'o', 'u', 'y' };
index = linear_search(letters, size, 'o');      // index is 3

double prices[size] = { 9.99, 19.99, 24.99 };
index = linear_search(prices, size, 19.99);     // index is 1
```

The function that's generated by the first call to the template

```
int linear_search(const int arr[], int counter, int value_to_find) {
    for (int i = 0; i < counter; ++i) {
        if (arr[i] == value_to_find) {
            return i;   // value found - return index
        }
    }
    return -1;          // value not found - return -1
}
```

Description

- You can code a single *function template* to get a function to work correctly with all data types that support the operators and functions used by the function template.

- When the compiler encounters a call to a function template, it generates a function with the appropriate data types and compiles that function.

- Function templates are often used to allow algorithms to work with multiple data types instead of just a single data type.

- Function templates are typically more flexible than function overloading.

- Function templates often reduce code duplication when compared to function overloading.

- Since the compiler generates functions from a template at compile time, not at runtime, there's no performance penalty for using templates.

- Since the compiler only generates functions that are called by the program, function templates often result in smaller executable files than function overloading.

- Templates provide a way to convert a function that uses a specific type to a function that uses a generic type. As a result, working with templates is also referred to as *generic programming* or *generics*.

Figure 18-2   A function template

How to code a function template with one type parameter

Figure 18-3 starts by showing a simple display() function that accepts an int value and displays it on the console followed by a space. Then, it shows how to convert that function to a function template that can accept any data type that supports the stream insertion operator (<<).

When creating function templates, it's often helpful to start by coding a function that works with a specific type. Then, you can convert that function to a function template. To do that, the first step is to code a *template prefix* before the function. This prefix consists of the template keyword followed by a pair of angle brackets (<>). Within the angle brackets, you specify a *type parameter* that the function template can use anywhere in its declaration or definition.

To specify a type parameter, you begin by coding the typename or class keyword. The older class keyword provides backwards compatibility with the C language and has a long history of use in C++. However, the newer typename keyword more accurately indicates that the type parameter can be a built-in type such as the int type or a class that defines another data type such as the string class of the C++ standard library or the Product class described in chapter 14. Since the typename keyword describes the code more accurately, this book uses this keyword. However, it's common to see the class keyword in online examples and legacy code.

After the typename or class keyword, you code the name of the type parameter. It's a common convention to use a single capital letter for this name, such as T for *type*. However, you can also use a longer name such as Type or Object. You could even use a lowercase name such as type or object, although it's a common convention to use an initial cap for type parameter names.

The first two examples in this figure after the syntax for a template prefix show two different definitions for the display() function template. The first one uses the typename keyword and the second one uses the class keyword. You can also separate the declaration and definition of a function template just as you can a standard function. The third example, for instance, shows a declaration for the display() function template that uses the typename keyword.

In most cases, the compiler can deduce the type of data that's passed to a function template when it's called. As a result, you can typically call a function template without specifying the data type, as shown by the first group of statements that call the display() function template. Here, the first statement passes an int value, the second statement passes a string object, and the third statement passes a double value.

Although it's not usually necessary to explicitly specify the data type when you call a function template, you may need to do that in some rare situations when your code won't compile. You may also want to do that to make it clear to other programmers what type of value you're passing to the function template. To explicitly specify the data type, you can code it in angle brackets between the function name and the parentheses for the function as shown by the second group of statements that call the display() function template.

A function that accepts an int value

```
void display(int value) {
    cout << value << ' ';
}
```

The syntax for a template prefix with a single type parameter

```
template<class|typename name>
```

A function template that uses a single type parameter

```
template<typename T>
void display(T value) {
    cout << value << ' ';
}
```

Another way to code the same function template

```
template<class T>
void display(T value) {
    cout << value << ' ';
}
```

A declaration for the first function template

```
template<typename T>
void display(T value);
```

How to use type deduction when you call a function template

```
display(1);
display("Hammer");
display(19.99);
```

The console

```
1 Hammer 19.99
```

How to explicitly specify the type when you call a function template

```
display<int>(1);
display<string>("Hammer");
display<double>(19.99);
```

Description

- To create a function template, you code a *template prefix* before the function. This prefix consists of the template keyword followed by a pair of angle brackets (`<>`).

- Within the angle brackets, you specify a *type parameter* that the function template can use anywhere in its declaration or definition.

- The typename and class keywords that you can use to specify a type parameter are synonymous.

- It's a common convention to use a single capital letter such as T for *type* for the name of a type parameter.

- The compiler can typically deduce the correct data type when you call a function template. However, you can also explicitly specify the data type in angle brackets.

Figure 18-3   How to code a function template with one type parameter

How to code a function template with multiple type parameters

Now that you understand the syntax for coding a function template that uses a single type parameter, you're ready to learn how to code a function template that uses multiple type parameters. To do that, you can use commas to separate the parameters as shown by figure 18-4.

This figure starts by showing a display() function that accepts arguments of two data types, a string argument for a key and an int argument for a value. This function displays the key and value on the console, separated by an equals sign and followed by a new line character. However, it only works for a string key and an int value.

Next, this figure shows how to convert this display() function to a function template that can accept any data type for the key or the value. To do that, you begin by coding a template prefix before the function. This template prefix specifies two data types, one for the key and one for the value. Then, you substitute the type parameters for the string and int types used by the function.

After you define the function template, you can use almost any data type as the key or value. In this figure, for example, the first call to the display() function template passes a string and an int value, the second call passes an int value and a string, and the third call passes a string and a double value.

You can also explicitly specify the data types when you call a function template with multiple type parameters, as shown by the last example in this figure. Just as you can when you call a function template with a single type parameter, though, you typically don't need to do that.

Although this figure only shows how to code a template that uses two type parameters, you can extend this syntax to code as many type parameters as you need. However, it's rare to need more than two type parameters.

A function that accepts a string and an int value

```
void display(string key, int value) {
    cout << key << '=' << value << '\n';
}
```

Code that calls the function

```
display("mary", 217);
```

The console

```
mary=217
```

The syntax for a template prefix with multiple type parameters

```
template<class|typename name1[, class|typename name2] ...>
```

The same function after it has been converted to a function template

```
template<typename K, typename V>
void display(K key, V value) {
    cout << key << '=' << value << '\n';
}
```

How to use type deduction when you call a function template

```
display("mary", 217);
display(1, "Hammer");
display("price", 19.99);
```

The console

```
mary=217
1=Hammer
price=19.99
```

How to explicitly specify type when you call a function template

```
display<string, int>("mary", 217);
```

Description

- You can code a template prefix that defines multiple type parameters. To do that, use commas to separate the parameters.

Figure 18-4   How to code a function template with multiple type parameters

How to work with class templates

A *class template* provides a way to get a class to work correctly with different data types. For example, the STL container classes such as the vector class use class templates to allow them to work with the different data types. Most of the skills for working with function templates also apply to class templates. As a result, once you understand how function templates work, you're well on your way to understanding class templates.

How to code a simple class template

Figure 18-5 shows how to code a simple class template. To do that, you code a template prefix before the class definition that specifies one or more type parameters. Then, you can use the type parameters in your class definition.

The first example shows how to define a class named Dyad that uses a single type parameter named T. Here, the class has two private data members that are of the same type, which is the type specified by the type parameter. The class contains a constructor that allows you to set the values of the two data members. The class also has two member functions that get the first and second data members. As you review this code, note that it works because this class uses the type parameter named T to specify the data type for the data members, the type for each parameter of the constructor, and the return type for the two getter functions.

The second example uses the Dyad class defined by the first example. Here, the first statement creates a Dyad object named name that can store two strings. To do that, this code includes angle brackets (<>) after the name of the class, and it includes the string data type within those brackets. In addition, this statement uses the constructor of the class to set the first string to "Bjarne" and the second string to "Stroustrup". Then, the second statement uses the two member functions to print those strings to the console.

The third and fourth statements perform a similar task. However, they work with a Dyad object named xy that stores two int values of 10 and 20. This shows that the Dyad class can work with different data types.

The third example works much like the first example. However, it defines a class named MixedDyad that uses a template prefix that specifies two data types named T1 and T2. This class uses T1 as the type for the first data member, and it uses T2 as the type for the second data member.

As a result, the MixedDyad class can store two different data types as shown by the fourth example. Here, the first two statements work with a MixedDyad object named row that stores a string in the first data member and a double value in the second data member. Similarly, the last two statements work with a MixedDyad object named product that stores an int value as the first data member and a string as the second data member.

A class template that defines one type parameter

```
template<typename T>
class Dyad {
private:
    T one, two;
public:
    Dyad(T val1, T val2) {
        one = val1;
        two = val2;
    }
    T get_first() { return one; }
    T get_second() { return two; }
};
```

Code that calls the class template

```
Dyad<string> name("Bjarne", "Stroustrup");
cout << name.get_first() << ' ' << name.get_second() << endl;
Dyad<int> xy(10, 20);
cout << xy.get_first() << ' ' << xy.get_second() << endl;
```

The console

```
Bjarne Stroustrup
10 20
```

A class template that defines two type parameters

```
template<typename T1, typename T2>
class MixedDyad {
private:
    T1 one;
    T2 two;
public:
    MixedDyad(T1 val1, T2 val2) {
        one = val1;
        two = val2;
    }
    T1 get_first() { return one; }
    T2 get_second() { return two; }
};
```

Code that calls the class template

```
MixedDyad<string, double> row("Price", 19.99);
cout << row.get_first() << ": $" << row.get_second() << endl;
MixedDyad<int, string> product(1, "Hammer");
cout << product.get_first() << ' ' << product.get_second() << endl;
```

The console

```
Price: $19.99
1 Hammer
```

Description

- You can use a *class template* to get a class to work with different type parameters.

- To code a class template, code the template prefix before the class definition. Then, you can use the type parameter in your class definition.

Figure 18-5   How to code a simple class template

How to code a more complex class template

In the previous chapter, you learned how to code a HeapArray class that allows you to store an array of int values on the heap. That class provides many features that one would expect from a container class of the STL. However, the HeapArray class from the previous chapter can only store int values.

Now, figure 18-6 shows the HeapArray class after it has been converted to a class template. This allows the HeapArray class to work with most data types, which makes this class more flexible and useful.

Classes like the HeapArray class are often designed to be used by multiple programs. As a result, they're typically coded in their own header files. In addition, some compilers require a class template to be declared and defined within a single compilation unit. Because of that, it's generally considered a best practice to put both the declarations and definitions for a class template in the header file so a separate implementation file isn't required. In this figure, for example, all of the code for the HeapArray class is stored in a header file.

Part 1 of this figure begins with the include guard for the header file. Then, the template prefix defines a type parameter named T that can be used throughout the HeapArray class. This class begins by using this type parameter to define a pointer to an array whose type will be specified later.

After the private data members, the HeapArray class declares functions for three constructors, a destructor, and two assignment operators. These declarations work the same as described in the previous chapter.

Next, the HeapArray class provides inline definitions for the subscript operator ([]) and the size(), begin(), and end() functions. Here, the subscript operator returns a reference to the array element that's stored at the specified index. The begin() function returns a pointer to the first element in the array. And the end() function returns a pointer to one past the end of the array. Note that the subscript operator and the begin() and end() functions all use the type parameter to specify the type for the element that's returned.

When coding short functions like these, it often improves efficiency to use inline functions. In addition, inline functions are easier to code since you don't have to define the function in another place. As a result, it often makes sense to use inline functions for short functions.

After the inline definitions, this header file continues by providing the definitions for the functions (constructors, destructor, and operators) that have been declared but not yet defined. To do that, the code provides a template prefix before each function definition. This makes the type parameter available to the function definition. Then, each function name is qualified with HeapArray<T> to indicate that it's a member of that class.

For example, the first constructor uses T to specify the type of the array and T() to call the default constructor for that type. This creates a default object from that type. Similarly, the copy constructor uses T to specify the type of the array that it creates. However, the move constructor doesn't need to specify the type anywhere. As a result, the code for this constructor is the same as the code from the previous chapter.

The header file for the HeapArray class template

```cpp
#ifndef MURACH_HEAP_ARRAY_H
#define MURACH_HEAP_ARRAY_H

template<typename T>
class HeapArray {
private:
    int array_size;
    T* arr;

public:
    // declarations
    HeapArray(const int);                       // constructor
    HeapArray(const HeapArray& tocopy);         // copy constructor
    HeapArray(HeapArray&& tomove);              // move constructor
    ~HeapArray();                               // destructor
    HeapArray& operator=(const HeapArray& tocopy);   // copy assignment
    HeapArray& operator=(HeapArray&& tomove);        // move assignment

    // inline definitions
    T& operator[](int i) { return arr[i]; } // subscript operator
    int size() const { return array_size; } // member functions
    T* begin() { return arr; }
    T* end() { return arr + array_size; }

};

// ----- CONSTRUCTORS ----- //
template<typename T>
HeapArray<T>::HeapArray(const int size) {
    array_size = size;                          // set array size property
    arr = new T[array_size];                    // allocate memory on heap
    for (int i = 0; i < array_size; i++) {      // initialize array values
        arr[i] = T();
    }
}

template<typename T>
HeapArray<T>::HeapArray(const HeapArray& tocopy) {           // COPY
    array_size = tocopy.array_size;             // copy size
    arr = new T[array_size];                    // allocate memory on heap
    for (int i = 0; i < array_size; i++) {      // copy array values
        arr[i] = tocopy.arr[i];
    }
}

template<typename T>
HeapArray<T>::HeapArray(HeapArray&& tomove) {                // MOVE
    array_size = tomove.array_size;             // copy size
    arr = tomove.arr;                           // reset array pointer
    tomove.array_size = 0;                      // empty passed in container
    tomove.arr = nullptr;
}
```

Figure 18-6   How to code a more complex class template (part 1 of 2)

Except for the template prefix and the HeapArray<T> qualification, the code for the destructor and the move assignment operator is also the same as the code from the previous chapter. However, the copy assignment operator uses the type parameter named T to specify the type of the new array that it creates.

The header file for the HeapArray class template (continued)

```cpp
// ----- DESTRUCTOR ----- //
template<typename T>
HeapArray<T>::~HeapArray() {
    delete[] arr;  // deallocate memory - safe to run delete on nullptr
}

// ----- ASSIGNMENT OPERATORS ----- //
template<typename T>
HeapArray<T>& HeapArray<T>::operator= (const HeapArray& tocopy) {
                                                            // COPY
    array_size = tocopy.array_size;        // copy size
    T* new_arr = new T[array_size];        // allocate memory on heap
    for (int i = 0; i < array_size; ++i) { // copy array values
        new_arr[i] = tocopy.arr[i];
    }
    delete[] arr;                          // deallocate old memory
    arr = new_arr;                         // assign new memory
    return *this;                          // return a self-reference
}

template<typename T>
HeapArray<T>& HeapArray<T>::operator= (HeapArray&& tomove) { // MOVE
    if (this != &tomove) {                 // don't move if passed self
        array_size = tomove.array_size;    // copy size
        delete[] arr;                      // deallocate old memory
        arr = tomove.arr;                  // reset array pointer
        tomove.array_size = 0;             // empty passed in container
        tomove.arr = nullptr;
    }
    return *this;                          // return a self-reference
}

#endif // MURACH_HEAP_ARRAY_H
```

Description

- Some compilers require a class template to be declared and defined within a single compilation unit. As a result, it's generally considered a best practice to put all code for the class template in a header file.
- You can use function templates to define the member functions.
- You can often improve efficiency by coding member functions inline.

Figure 18-6   How to code a more complex class template (part 2 of 2)

How to use a complex class template

Figure 18-7 shows code that uses the HeapArray class template. To start, this code includes the header file named HeapArray.h that stores the code for the HeapArray class template.

Within the main() function, the first statement uses the first constructor of the HeapArray class to create a HeapArray object that can store 11 int values. To do that, this code includes angle brackets (<>) after the name of the class and specifies the int type for the class template. Then, this code uses a loop to store int values of 10 through 110 in that array, and it displays the first two int values on the console.

The second group of statements uses the first constructor of the HeapArray class to create a HeapArray object that can store 3 strings. Then, it uses three statements to store three strings in the array, and two more statements to display the first two strings on the console.

When you create a HeapArray object for a specific data type, the compiler uses a process known as *specialization* to generate a specific class from the template. For example, HeapArray<int> and HeapArray<string> are specializations of the HeapArray class template. Similarly, vector<char> and vector<Movie> are specializations of the vector class.

Code that uses the HeapArray class template

```
#include <iostream>
#include <string>
#include "HeapArray.h"

using namespace std;

int main() {
    HeapArray<int> nums(11);
    for (int i = 0; i < nums.size(); ++i) {
        nums[i] = (i + 1) * 10;
    }
    cout << "First number: " << nums[0] << endl;
    cout << "Second number: " << nums[1] << endl;

    HeapArray<string> words(3);
    words[0] = "hello";
    words[1] = "good";
    words[2] = "buddy";
    cout << "First word: " << words[0] << endl;
    cout << "Second word: " << words[1] << endl;
}
```

The console

```
First number: 10
Second number: 20
First word: hello
Second word: good
```

Description

- When you create an object from a class template, you must code angle brackets
  (<>) after the name of the class. Within those brackets, you must code the data
  types required by the class template.

- The process of generating classes from a class template is called *specialization*.
  For example, HeapArray<int> and HeapArray<string> are specializations of
  HeapArray. Similarly, vector<char> and vector<Movie> are specializations of
  vector.

Figure 18-7   How to use a complex class template

How to code a function template that works with a class template

If you want to pass an object that's created from a class template to a function, you need to code a function template that defines a class template as a parameter as shown in figure 18-8. Before the main() function, this code declares a function template named display() that accepts a reference to a HeapArray<T> object.

After the main() function, this code defines the display() function. Within this definition, the code uses the type parameter named T to work with elements that are stored in the HeapArray object. Specifically, this code uses the type parameter named T within a range-based for loop to display each element on the console, followed by a space. Then, after the loop, the function starts a new line on the console.

Within the main() function, the code creates a HeapArray object for an array of 11 int values, and it uses the display() function to display those int values on the console. Then, it creates a HeapArray object for an array of 3 strings, and it uses the display() function to display those string objects on the console.

Although it isn't shown in this figure, you can also use a function template to return an object created from a class template. For example, this function declaration:

```
HeapArray<T> bubble_sort(HeapArray<T> arr);
```

is for a function template that accepts, sorts, and returns a HeapArray<T> object.

A function template that works with a class template

```cpp
#include <iostream>
#include <string>
#include "HeapArray.h"

using namespace std;

// declaration
template<typename T>
void display(HeapArray<T>&);

int main() {
    HeapArray<int> nums(11);
    for (int i = 0; i < nums.size(); ++i) {
        nums[i] = (i + 1) * 10;
    }
    display(nums);      // call function template

    HeapArray<string> words(3);
    words[0] = "hello";
    words[1] = "good";
    words[2] = "buddy";
    display(words);    // call function template
}

// definition
template<typename T>
void display(HeapArray<T>& arr) {
    for (T elem : arr) {
        cout << elem << ' ';
    }
    cout << endl;
}
```

The console

```
10 20 30 40 50 60 70 80 90 100 110
hello good buddy
```

Description

- You can use a function template to work with a class template. To do that, the function template can accept arguments of a class template object or return an object created from a class template.

Figure 18-8   How to code a function template that works with a class template

The Sensor Analysis program

In the previous chapter, you learned how to code a Sensor Analysis program that used a HeapArray class that could only store int values. Now, figure 18-9 shows this Sensor Analysis program after it has been converted to use the HeapArray class template presented earlier in this chapter.

To start, this code includes the header file named HeapArray.h that stores the code for the HeapArray class template. Then, before the main() function, this program declares a function named load_sensor_data() that accepts a reference to a HeapArray<int> object. After the main() function, this code defines the load_sensor_data() function. This shows that this function is designed to work with an array of int values. In other words, this is not a function template. Instead, it is a regular function that accepts a specialization of the HeapArray class template.

Within the main() function, the code creates a HeapArray object for an array of int values. This array is big enough to store one sensor reading for each second required by the program. Then, this array is passed to the load_sensor_data() function.

At this point, you may be wondering why you would bother using a template for the HeapArray class if this program only works with int values. The reason is that using a class template makes it more likely that you'll reuse the HeapArray class in other programs. For example, you could use it in a program that works with an array of strings or double values. In short, it makes your code more flexible and reusable.

The console

```
The Sensor Analysis program

Enter the number of days you'd like to analyze: 2

Number of sensor readings over 2 days: 172800
Average reading: 65.27
Lowest reading: 39
Highest reading: 100
```

The code

```cpp
#include <iostream>
#include <cstdlib>
#include <ctime>
#include <algorithm>
#include <numeric>
#include "HeapArray.h"

using namespace std;

void load_sensor_data(HeapArray<int>& data);

int main() {
    cout << "The Sensor Analysis program\n\n";
    int num_days = 0, total_seconds = 0;

    cout << "Enter the number of days you'd like to analyze: ";
    cin >> num_days;
    cout << endl;

    const int seconds_per_day = 86400;
    total_seconds = num_days * seconds_per_day;
    HeapArray<int> data(total_seconds);
    load_sensor_data(data);

    double total = accumulate(data.begin(), data.end(), 0);
    auto min = min_element(data.begin(), data.end());
    auto max = max_element(data.begin(), data.end());

    cout << "Number of sensor readings over " << num_days
        << " days: " << data.size() << endl;
    cout << "Average reading: " << (total / data.size()) << endl;
    cout << "Lowest reading: " << *min << endl;
    cout << "Highest reading: " << *max << endl << endl;
}

void load_sensor_data(HeapArray<int>& data) { // simulate sensor data
    srand(time(nullptr));                      // seed random number
    int num, adjust;
    adjust = rand() % 70 + 10;                 // get number from 10 - 70
    for (int i = 0; i < data.size(); ++i) {
        num = rand() % 100 + 1;                // get number from 1 - 100
        data[i] = (num < adjust) ? num + adjust : num;  // adjust number
    }
}
```

Figure 18-9   The Sensor Analysis program

Perspective

Now that you've completed this chapter, you should understand how to work with templates. In particular, you should understand how to define a class template for a container or a function template for an algorithm. In the next chapter, you'll learn how to use templates to define other custom classes and algorithms. In particular, you'll learn how to define your own class templates for a custom vector and a custom list, and you'll learn how to define your own algorithms that work with those containers or the STL containers.

Terms

overload a function
function template
generic programming
generics
template prefix
type parameter
class template
specialization

Summary

- You can *overload* a function to get it to work correctly with different data types.

- You can code a *function template* to get a function to work correctly with all data types that support the operators and functions used by the template. This is more flexible than overloading a function.

- Templates provide a way to convert a function that uses a specific type such as the int type to a function that uses a generic type. As a result, working with templates is also referred to as *generic programming* or *generics*.

- To create a function template, you code a *template prefix* before the function. This prefix consists of the template keyword followed by a pair of angle brackets (<>).

- Within the angle brackets of a template prefix, you can specify a *type parameter* that the function template can use in its declaration or definition.

- You can use a *class template* to get a class to work correctly with different type parameters.

- The process of generating classes from a class template is called *specialization*.

Exercise 18-1   Create a function template

In this exercise, you'll convert a function that sorts an array of int values to a function template that can sort an array of any type that supports the greater than operator (>). When you're done, running the program should display this:

```
Temperatures: 75 64 92 88 57
Sorted temperatures: 57 64 75 88 92

Prices: 18.99 9.99 12.99 24.99 15.99
Sorted prices: 9.99 12.99 15.99 18.99 24.99
```

1. Open the project or solution named sort_array in this folder:
    `ex_starts\ch18_ex1_sort_array`

2. Open the main.cpp file and review its code. Note that this program includes the bubble_sort() function from chapter 12 that sorts an array of int values. Also note that this function uses the greater than operator (>).

3. Run the program to see that it displays the temperatures, the sorted temperatures, and the prices as shown above.

4. Convert the bubble_sort() function to a function template. In addition to adding a type parameter, be sure to change the name of the variable that refers to an individual element to something more generic.

5. Modify the code in the main() function so it uses the bubble_sort() function to sort the array of prices. Then, print the sorted array as shown above. This shows that the bubble_sort() function can now be used with the double data type, since is supports the greater than operator.

Exercise 18-2   Add a function to the HeapArray class template

In this exercise, you'll modify the HeapArray class template from this chapter so it includes a function for performing a linear search. Then, you'll use this function from the Sensor Analysis program. When you're done, a test run should look something like this:

```
The Sensor Analysis program

Enter the number of days you'd like to analyze: 5

Number of sensor readings over 5 days: 432000
Average reading: 92.0921
Lowest reading: 65 first found at 176 seconds
Highest reading: 129 first found at 118 seconds
```

1. Open the project or solution named sensor_analysis in this folder:
    `ex_starts\ch18_ex2_sensor_analysis`

2. Open the HeapArray.h file and review its code.

3. Add the declaration for a function named linear_search() that accepts the value to be found for any type that supports the equality operator.

4. Add the definition for the linear_search() function. Because this function will use the type parameter, be sure to include the template prefix. Also be sure to qualify the name of the function with the name of the class.

5. Add code to the linear search function that loops through the array in the elements data member using the array_size data member, returns the index of the value if it's found, and returns -1 if it isn't found.

6. Open the main.cpp file and add code to the main() function that uses the linear_search() function to get the index of the first element with the minimum sensor reading and the index of the first element with the maximum sensor reading.

7. Modify the code that displays the minimum and maximum values so it also displays the second where these values first occur.

Exercise 18-3   Use a class template with a function template

In this exercise, you'll modify two function templates so they use the HeapArray class template from this chapter. When you're done, running the program should display this:

```
Numbers array: 10 20 30 40 50 60
The number 40 was found at index 3

Prices array: 0.99 1.99 2.99 3.99 4.99 5.99
The price 1.99 was found at index 1
```

1. Open the project or solution named linear_search in this folder
    `ex_starts\ch18_ex3_linear_search`

2. Review the code in the main.cpp file and run the program to be sure it works correctly.

3. In the main.cpp file, modify the two function template declarations and definitions so they work with a HeapArray object by reference instead of a constant built-in array.

4. Modify the code in the main() function so the numbers and prices variables are defined as HeapArray objects instead of built-in arrays. Note that you can't initialize the HeapArray objects like you can the arrays.

5. Run the program again to see that it works like it did before.

How to code custom containers, iterators, and algorithms

In chapters 10 and 11, you learned how to use some containers, iterators, and algorithms that are available from the Standard Template Library. Now, you'll learn to code your own custom containers, iterators, and algorithms. In addition, you'll learn how to code these custom objects so they're compatible with STL objects. This allows you to use your custom objects with STL objects. For example, you can use STL algorithms with your custom container, or you can use your custom algorithm with STL containers.

The custom containers, iterators, and algorithms presented in this chapter use pointers and templates, which were covered in chapters 17 and 18, respectively. As a result, you should read those chapters before reading this chapter. Otherwise, you may find it difficult to understand this chapter.

How to code a custom container

Chapters 17 and 18 showed how to code a custom container named HeapArray that provides some standard STL features such as the size(), begin(), and end() functions. This made it possible to use STL algorithms like accumulate() with a HeapArray object.

The topics that follow show how to code a custom container that provides many of the same features as a vector from the STL. This should reinforce many of the skills presented in the previous two chapters. In addition, it should give you some valuable insights into how the STL vector works.

How to work with member types

The STL containers define several common types. For instance, the return type of the size() member function that's common to many STL containers is *not* the int type or the unsigned int type. Instead, the size() function returns a type named size_type that's specific to the container itself. In other words, each STL container provides its own member types. For example, the size() function of a vector of int values has a return type of

```
vector<int>::size_type
```

Similarly, the size() function of a list of double values has a return type of

```
list<double>::size_type
```

These common types are known as *member types*, and they make it possible to write generic code that can work with any container. For example, suppose you have a function template that can accept any STL container. In addition, suppose that your function needs to know the type of the elements in the container. Fortunately, an STL container provides a type called value_type that provides this information.

Some of the most common member types provided by the STL containers are presented in the table at the top of figure 19-1. These include types that define the type of elements in the container, the type for the container's size, the reference and pointer types for the elements, and the type of the iterator provided by the container. When you create a custom container, you should provide some or all of these member types. This makes your container compatible with the STL.

To create a member type for your container, you create an *alias* for each type. The first two examples show how this works. The first example uses the typedef keyword to define an alias of size_type for the unsigned int type. This is an older technique that was commonly used prior to C++11. The second example uses the using keyword to do the same thing. This is a newer technique that's available with C++11 and later.

The C++ standard library provides a type named size_t that's returned by the sizeof operator presented in chapter 6. Most containers use std::size_t as the data type for their size_type member. For instance, the third example presents a class named MyContainer that defines a size_type alias for the size_t type. Then, this class defines a size() member function that returns a value of this type.

Some of the member types provided by the STL containers

Type	Description
value_type	The data type of an element.
size_type	The type for the size of the container. This type is typically defined with std::size_t, which is an unsigned integer type.
difference_type	The type for the difference between iterators. This type is typically defined with std::ptrdiff_t, which is a signed integer type.
reference	The reference type of an element.
const_reference	The constant reference type of an element.
pointer	The pointer type of an element.
const_pointer	The constant pointer type of an element.
iterator	The type of the iterator provided by the container.
const_iterator	The type of the constant iterator provided by the container.

The size types for two STL containers

Container type	Return type of size() function
vector<int>	vector<int>::size_type
list<double>	list<double>::size_type

How to create an alias with the typedef keyword (prior to C++11)

```
typedef unsigned int size_type;
```

How to create an alias with the using keyword (C++11 and later)

```
using size_type = unsigned int;
```

Code that creates a MyContainer class with a size_type type

```
class MyContainer {
public:
    // member type
    using size_type = std::size_t;

    // function that uses member type as return type
    size_type size() { return 0; }
};
```

Code that uses the MyContainer::size_type member type

```
MyContainer products;
MyContainer::size_type size = products.size();   // size is 0
```

Description

- The STL containers define several common types, sometimes known as *member types*. Each type of container provides its own member types. These types make it possible to write generic code that can work with any container type.

- With C++11 and later, you can create an *alias* for a member type with the using keyword. Prior to C++11, it was common to use the typedef keyword to create an alias for a member type.

Figure 19-1   How to work with member types

The MyVector class declaration

The next few figures present a class named MyVector that defines a container. As the name implies, this container works much like the STL vector container. Although the MyVector container doesn't provide all of the functionality of the STL vector, it provides enough of that functionality to give you an idea of how the STL vector works.

Figure 19-2 presents the declaration for the MyVector class. To start, this code declares the class as a template. As a result, it can store any type of object.

The MyVector class defines three private data members. The elem data member is a pointer to type T. This is the pointer to the free store memory that's dynamically allocated to store the elements in the container.

The array_size and space data members are both of the size_t type. These data members store the number of elements currently stored in the container and the amount of memory allocated to store elements.

After the private data members, this class defines six of the member types described in the previous figure. To save space and keep things simple, this code doesn't define all of the member types.

The reference member type is defined as a reference to T, and the iterator member type is defined as a pointer to T. As a result, the iterator returned by the MyVector class is a raw pointer to an element. This works for the purposes of this class. However, it's sometimes necessary to create custom iterator classes as shown later in this chapter.

This class declares five constructors and a destructor. The first constructor is defined inline. It's the default constructor, and it just sets the elem member to a null pointer and the array_size and space members to zero. The second and third constructors declare the copy and move constructors required by the Rule of Five. The last two constructors allow the user to set an initial size or to use an initialization list. Finally, the destructor makes sure memory allocated in the constructors is deallocated as required by RAII.

This class declares two overloads for the assignment operator to provide the copy and move assignment required by the Rule of Five. Then, it provides inline definitions for two overloads for the subscript operator for passing a MyVector object by reference. These definitions return a reference to the element at the specified index. To do that, their return types use the reference and const_reference member types defined earlier in the class.

Finally, the class declares several member functions also provided by the STL vector. Many of these functions use the member types defined earlier in this class to specify their return types. Some of these member functions are simple enough that they have been defined inline. For instance, the size() function returns the array_size member. The capacity() function returns the space member. The begin() function returns the elem member. And the end() function uses pointer arithmetic to return a pointer to one past the last element.

Like the subscript operator, the at() function can return a reference or a constant reference. Similarly, the cbegin() and cend() functions work like the begin() and end() functions, except that they return a constant iterator, not a regular iterator.

The MyVector class declaration

```cpp
template <typename T>
class MyVector {
private:
    T* elem = nullptr;        // pointer to memory for elements
    std::size_t array_size;   // actual number of elements (size)
    std::size_t space;        // space allocated for elements (capacity)
public:
    // Member types
    using size_type = std::size_t;
    using value_type = T;
    using reference = T&;
    using const_reference = const T&;
    using iterator = T*;
    using const_iterator = const T*;

    // Constructors
    MyVector() {                              // default - inline
        elem = nullptr;
        array_size = 0;
        space = 0;
    }
    MyVector(const MyVector& tobecopied);    // copy constructor
    MyVector(MyVector&& tobemoved);          // move constructor
    MyVector(int initial_size);              // set initial size
    MyVector(std::initializer_list<T> list); // initialization list

    // Destructor
    ~MyVector();

    // Assignment operator
    MyVector& operator=(const MyVector& tobecopied); // copy assignment
    MyVector& operator=(MyVector&& tobemoved);       // move assignment

    // Subscript operator
    reference operator[](int i) { return elem[i]; }        // inline
    const_reference operator[](int i) const { return elem[i]; }// inline

    // Member functions
    size_type size() const { return array_size; }          // inline
    size_type capacity() const { return space; }           // inline

    reference at(int index);
    const_reference at(int index) const;

    void reserve(int new_size);
    void push_back(T val);
    void resize(int new_size);

    iterator begin() { return elem; }                      // inline
    const_iterator cbegin() const { return elem; }         // inline
    iterator end() { return elem + array_size; }           // inline
    const_iterator cend() const { return elem + array_size; }  // inline
};
```

Figure 19-2   The MyVector class declaration

The constructor and destructor definitions

Figure 19-3 presents the definitions for the constructor and destructor functions of the MyVector class. Because the default constructor was defined inline in the class declaration, that constructor isn't presented here.

The first definition is for the copy constructor. It accepts a MyVector object by constant reference and uses its array_size data member to set this container's array_size and space data members. This code does *not* use the space data member of the MyVector parameter because the parameter might have more space allocated than is being used, but this constructor is only going to allocate enough space for the current number of elements. Next, this constructor allocates free store memory for the elements and stores the pointer that's returned by the new keyword in the elem data member. Finally, it copies the elements from the parameter object to the newly allocated memory.

The second definition is for the move constructor. It accepts an rvalue reference to a MyVector object and uses it to set this container's array_size and space data members. Unlike the copy constructor, the move constructor *does* use the space data member of the object it receives. That's because this constructor uses the memory already allocated by this object, which might be more than the space that's needed for actual elements. Next, the constructor assigns the pointer in the MyVector parameter to this container's elem pointer. Finally, it empties the MyVector object by setting its array_size and space data members to zero and its elem data member to a null pointer.

The third definition is for the constructor that accepts a value for the initial size. It uses this value to set the container's array_size and space data members by chaining these variables with assignment operators. Next, the constructor allocates free store memory for the elements and stores the pointer to that memory in the elem data member. Finally, it sets each element in the newly allocated memory to the default value of the container's data type. To do that, this code assigns the data type followed by a set of parentheses to each element.

The fourth definition is for the constructor that uses an initialization list. It accepts a constant reference of the std::initializer_list type. This type was introduced in C++11 and is the type that C++ automatically converts a brace-enclosed initialization list to. As a result, you can use it as a parameter type, although you must include the data type of the list in angle brackets. Here, the constructor uses the size() function of the std::initializer_list parameter to set this container's array_size and space data members. Next, the constructor allocates free store memory for the elements and stores the pointer to that memory in the elem data member. Finally, it copies the elements from the initialization list to the newly allocated memory. It does this by indexing the iterator returned by the begin() function of std::initializer_list.

The last definition is for the destructor. The code for the destructor calls delete[] on the elem data member to deallocate the memory allocated in the constructor. Fortunately, this code works correctly, even if the elem member is a null pointer. As a result, there's no need to do any checking on the elem member before executing this code.

The constructor and destructor definitions

```cpp
// copy constructor
template <typename T>
MyVector<T>::MyVector(const MyVector& tobecopied) {
    array_size = tobecopied.array_size;    // copy size
    space = tobecopied.array_size;         // set capacity
    elem = new T[array_size];              // allocate memory for array

    // copy the elements of tobecopied's array (could also use std::copy)
    for (int i = 0; i < array_size; ++i) {
        elem[i] = tobecopied.elem[i];
    }
}

// move constructor
template <typename T>
MyVector<T>::MyVector(MyVector&& tobemoved) {
    array_size = tobemoved.array_size; // copy size
    space = tobemoved.space;           // copy capacity
    elem = tobemoved.elem;             // point to existing elements

    // empty the passed in vector
    tobemoved.array_size = 0;
    tobemoved.space = 0;
    tobemoved.elem = nullptr;
}

// constructor that accepts an integer value for initial size
template <typename T>
MyVector<T>::MyVector(int initial_size) {
    array_size = space = initial_size; // set initial size and capacity
    elem = new T[array_size];          // allocate memory for array

    // initialize the array with default value of type
    for (int i = 0; i < initial_size; ++i) {
        elem[i] = T();
    }
}

// constructor that accepts an initialization list
template <typename T>
MyVector<T>::MyVector(std::initializer_list<T> list) {
    array_size = space = list.size();  // set initial size and capacity
    elem = new T[array_size];          // allocate memory for array

    // copy the elements in the list (could also use std::copy)
    for (int i = 0; i < array_size; ++i) {
        elem[i] = list.begin()[i];
    }
}

// destructor
template <typename T>
MyVector<T>::~MyVector() {
    delete[] elem;  // OK even if elem is nullptr
}
```

Figure 19-3   The constructor and destructor definitions

The assignment operator definitions

Figure 19-4 presents the definitions for the copy assignment operator and the move assignment operator of the MyVector class.

The definition for the copy assignment operator accepts a MyVector object by constant reference and uses its array_size data member to set the current container's array_size and space data members. Then, it allocates free store (heap) memory for the elements and stores the pointer to that memory in a temporary variable named new_elem. This is a common pattern for copy assignment that provides some exception safety in the event of an error.

After allocating memory for the new array, this code copies the elements from the MyVector parameter to the newly allocated memory. When that's done, it deallocates the memory that the elem member currently points to and sets the elem member so it points to the newly allocated memory. Finally, this code returns a self-reference.

The definition for the move assignment operator accepts an rvalue reference to a MyVector object. To start, it checks that the parameter is not a reference to the current object. If it isn't, it uses the MyVector parameter to set this container's array_size and space data members. Then, it deallocates the memory that elem currently points to and sets elem so it points to the elem data member of the MyVector parameter. Next, it empties the MyVector parameter by setting its array_size and space data members to zero and its elem data member to a null pointer. Finally, it returns a self-reference.

The assignment operator definitions

```cpp
// copy assignment
template <typename T>
MyVector<T>& MyVector<T>::operator=(const MyVector& tobecopied) {
    array_size = tobecopied.array_size; // copy size
    space = tobecopied.array_size;      // set capacity

    // allocate new space
    T* new_elem = new T[array_size];

    // copy elements (could also use std::copy)
    for (int i = 0; i < array_size; ++i) {
        new_elem[i] = tobecopied.elem[i];
    }

    // deallocate old space
    delete[] elem;

    // assign new space
    elem = new_elem;

    // return a self-reference
    return *this;
}

// move assignment
template <typename T>
MyVector<T>& MyVector<T>::operator=(MyVector&& tobemoved) {
    if (this != &tobemoved) {
        array_size = tobemoved.array_size;   // copy size
        space = tobemoved.space;             // copy capacity

        // deallocate old space and then point to existing elements
        delete[] elem;
        elem = tobemoved.elem;

        // empty the passed in vector
        tobemoved.array_size = 0;
        tobemoved.space = 0;
        tobemoved.elem = nullptr;
    }

    // return a self-reference
    return *this;
}
```

Figure 19-4   The assignment operator definitions

The member function definitions

Figure 19-5 presents the definitions for the at(), reserve(), push_back(), and resize() member functions of the MyVector class. Remember that the size(), capacity(), begin(), and end() member functions were already defined inline in the class declaration.

The first two definitions are for the at() function and its constant overload. Both of these functions begin with the typename keyword. That's because these functions return member types defined by the container, but the compiler might not recognize MyVector<T>::reference as a type. As a result, you include the typename keyword to let the compiler know that what comes next is a type.

Both versions of the at() member function start by checking that the index it receives is within bounds. If it isn't, the function throws an out_of_range exception. Otherwise, it returns a reference to the element at that index. This works much like the inline definitions for the subscript operator, but it provides bounds checking where the subscript operator does not.

The third definition is for the reserve() member function. It accepts a value for the new size and then checks if the new size is less than the current size. If it is, the function returns without doing anything. This prevents the amount of memory allocated from ever being decreased. Otherwise, the function allocates free store memory for the new size and stores the pointer to that memory in a temporary variable named new_elem. Then, it copies the old elements to the newly allocated memory. When that's done, it deallocates the memory that elem currently points to and sets elem so it points to the newly allocated memory. Finally, it sets the space data member to the new size.

The fourth definition is for the push_back() member function. This function accepts an item of type T. It starts by checking the allocated space and uses the reserve() function to reserve more if necessary. If the space value is zero, this function passes a new size of 1 to reserve(). If the space is equal to the number of elements already in the vector, this function increases capacity by doubling the value of space and passing it to reserve(). Once the function has established that there is adequate capacity for the new item, it adds it to the end of the array that elem points to and increments the array_size data member.

The last definition is for the resize() function. This function accepts an int value that specifies the new size of the vector. First, it calls the reserve() function and passes it the new_size argument. Remember that if the new size is smaller than the current size, the reserve() function doesn't change the size. However, if the new size is larger than the current size, this code increases the capacity and adds the new elements. To do that, this code uses a loop that begins with an index that is equal to the value in the array_size data member. This makes sure that the loop starts at the end of the existing elements and at the beginning of the new capacity that was added by the reserve() function. Finally, the resize() function sets the new value for array_size so it includes any new elements that have just been added.

So, what's the difference between the reserve() and resize() functions? In short, the reserve() function can increase the capacity but doesn't add any new elements. By contrast, the resize() function can increase the capacity and add new elements to fill the newly added capacity.

The member function definitions

```
// at()
template <typename T>
typename MyVector<T>::reference MyVector<T>::at(int i) {
    if (i < 0 || i >= array_size)
        throw std::out_of_range("MyVector<T>::at() - index out of range");
    else
        return elem[i];
}

template <typename T>
typename MyVector<T>::const_reference MyVector<T>::at(int i) const {
    if (i < 0 || i >= array_size)
        throw std::out_of_range("MyVector<T>::at() - index out of range");
    else
        return elem[i];
}

// reserve()
template <typename T>
void MyVector<T>::reserve(int new_size) {
    if (new_size <= space) return;         // never decrease allocation
    T* new_elem = new T[new_size];         // allocate new space
    for (int i = 0; i < array_size; ++i) { // copy old elements
        new_elem[i] = elem[i];
    }
    delete[] elem;                         // deallocate old space
    elem = new_elem;                       // assign new space
    space = new_size;                      // set new capacity
}

// push_back()
template <typename T>
void MyVector<T>::push_back(T item) {
    if (space == 0)                  // if array empty,
        reserve(1);                  // start with capacity of 1
    else if (array_size == space)    // if array full,
        reserve(2 * space);          // add more capacity (doubling is common)

    elem[array_size] = item;         // add item at end
    ++array_size;                    // increment variable that tracks size
}

// resize()
template <typename T>
void MyVector<T>::resize(int new_size) {
    reserve(new_size);     // set new capacity (won't make smaller)
    for (int i = array_size; i < new_size; ++i) {  // init new elements
        elem[i] = T();
    }

    // reset size variable to indicate new size (
    if (new_size > array_size)
        array_size = new_size;
}
```

Figure 19-5   The member function definitions

The Task Manager 1.0 program

Figure 19-6 shows the Task Manager program. This program asks the user to enter one or more tasks. After the user has entered 'x' to exit the program, the program sorts the tasks in alphabetical order and displays them.

As usual, the code begins with include directives for the header files that the program needs and a using directive for the std namespace. This time, though, the code includes the "MyVector.h" header file that contains the code for the MyVector class presented in previous figures.

The main() function starts by displaying the name of the program along with instructions on how to use the program. Then, it defines a MyVector container named tasks to hold strings, and it defines a string variable named task.

Next, this code begins a while loop that continues until it encounters the break statement. Within the loop, the first statement displays a message on the console that asks the user to enter a task. Then, the second statement uses the getline() function to retrieve the task entered by the user. Next, the code checks whether the value of the task string is 'x'. If so, the break statement ends the loop. Otherwise, the code uses the push_back() function of the MyVector object to add the task entered by the user and the loop continues.

When the loop ends, the code uses the STL sort() algorithm to put the tasks in alphabetical order. This is possible for two reasons. First, the MyVector object is STL compliant, so it can be used with STL algorithms. Second, the iterator returned by begin() is a pointer to a built-in array, which uses a random-access iterator. As a result, it can be used with the sort() function, which requires a random-access iterator.

Finally, the code ends by looping through the elements in the MyVector container and displaying them. To do that, it uses a for loop and some of the features provided by the MyVector class, such as the size() member function and the subscript operator.

The console

```
The Task Manager program
Enter tasks and enter 'x' when done.

Enter task:  Go to store
Enter task:  Feed cats
Enter task:  Check email
Enter task:  x

My Task List
-----------
1) Check email
2) Feed cats
3) Go to store
```

The code

```cpp
#include <iostream>
#include <string>
#include <algorithm>
#include "MyVector.h"

using namespace std;

int main() {
    cout << "The Task Manager program\n";
    cout << "Enter tasks and enter 'x' when done.\n\n";

    MyVector<string> tasks;
    string task = "";
    while (true) {
        cout << "Enter task:  ";
        getline(cin, task);
        if (task == "x") {
            break;
        }
        else {
            tasks.push_back(task);
        }
    }
    cout << endl;

    sort(tasks.begin(), tasks.end());

    cout << "My Task List\n"
         << "-----------\n";
    for (int i = 0; i < tasks.size(); ++i) {
        cout << (i + 1) << ") " << tasks[i] << endl;
    }
}
```

Description

- This Task Manager program uses the custom MyVector object to store tasks entered by the user. Because MyVector is STL compliant, this program can use it with the STL sort() algorithm.

Figure 19-6   The Task Manager 1.0 program

How to code a custom iterator

So far, this chapter has presented a MyVector class that uses a built-in array to store data internally and then uses pointers to that array as iterators. However, data may also be stored internally in ways that don't provide such a ready-made iterator object. For example, because a list container stores data in non-contiguous memory, the container can't use a pointer as an iterator. In that case, you need to create a custom iterator. Before you learn how to do that, you need to learn how to work with iterator traits.

How to work with iterator traits

When you implement a custom iterator, you want it to be STL compliant. In other words, you want the algorithms of the STL to be able to use it. To provide for that, you need to implement the five *iterator traits* presented in the first table of figure 19-7.

Most of the iterator traits presented here are similar to the member types presented in figure 19-1. The exception is the iterator_category trait, which specifies the functionality that the iterator provides. This trait uses the iterator category tags presented in the second table in this figure. These tags indicate whether the iterator is an input, forward, bidirectional, or random-access iterator. As you learned in chapter 11, the type of the iterator determines the STL algorithms that you can use with the iterator.

The first code example shows a custom iterator class named MyIterator that implements iterator traits. As with the member types, you can use either the typedef keyword or the using keyword to code your iterator traits. However, this example presents the using keyword because it's a newer approach that was introduced in C++11. In this example, each using statement creates an alias for the data type of each iterator trait.

The second code example shows another way to implement iterator traits. With this approach, the MyIterator class inherits the std::iterator class. Then, the custom iterator class passes the iterator traits as part of the class template. When you implement iterator traits this way, the last three traits are optional.

If you compare these two approaches, the second one appears more convenient at first glance, since it doesn't require you to type out full alias statements and it allows you to skip the last three iterator traits. However, this leads to code that's difficult to understand. To compensate for this, programmers would often type comments to explain the code. This, of course, negated the benefits of less typing. As a result, the std::iterator class was deprecated in C++17. You may still see it in online examples, but it's a better practice to use the "longhand" method of the first example in your own code. This leads to code that's self-documenting and easy to understand.

The five iterator traits needed for an iterator class to be STL compliant

Trait	Description
`iterator_category`	A tag that indicates the functionality the iterator provides.
`value_type`	The data type of an element.
`difference_type`	The type for the difference between iterators.
`reference`	The reference type of an element.
`pointer`	The pointer type of an element.

The iterator category tags

Tag	Indicates iterator provides...
`std::random_access_iterator_tag`	random access iterator functionality
`std::bidirectional_iterator_tag`	bidirectional iterator functionality
`std::forward_iterator_tag`	forward iterator functionality
`std::input_iterator_tag`	input iterator functionality

An iterator class that implements iterator traits (C++11 and later)

```
class MyIterator {
    public:
        using iterator_category = std::bidirectional_iterator_tag;
        using value_type = int;
        using difference_type = std::ptrdiff_t;
        using reference = int&;
        using pointer = int*;

        // rest of class
};
```

How to inherit from std::iterator (deprecated in C++17)

```
class MyIterator : std::iterator<std::bidirectional_iterator_tag,
                                 int,                // value_type
                                 std::ptrdiff_t,     // difference_type
                                 int&,               // reference
                                 int*>               // pointer
{
        // rest of class
};
```

Description

- When you create your own container, you can use pointers as iterators as shown earlier in this chapter, or you can define a custom iterator class as shown in this figure.

- If you want your custom iterator class to be able to be used by STL algorithms, you need to implement five *iterator traits*.

- You can create a customer iterator by inheriting the std::iterator class. To do that, you pass the five iterator traits as part of the class template, with the last three being optional. This approach is convenient but leads to code that's difficult to read and maintain. As a result, it was deprecated in C++17.

Figure 19-7   How to work with iterator traits

The Link structure

A list container stores elements in non-contiguous memory. As a result, a pointer to an element in a list doesn't automatically know where the next and previous elements are since they aren't stored adjacent to the current element in memory.

To provide a way for an element in non-contiguous memory to connect, or link, to the previous and next elements in a list, you can define a Link structure like the one presented in figure 19-8. This structure is a template that defines an element in a list that can store any type of data. The data member named value stores the value of the element. Then, the data members named prev and next store pointers to the previous and next Link objects in the list.

The Link structure

```
template <typename T>
struct Link {
    T value;                // the value in the link
    Link* prev;             // pointer to the previous link
    Link* next;             // pointer to the next link

    Link(T val) {           // constructor
        value = val;
        prev = nullptr;
        next = nullptr;
    }
};
```

Description

- The Link structure represents an element in a list container that can link to the previous and next elements.

Figure 19-8   The Link structure

The MyIterator class

The MyIterator class presented in figure 19-9 defines a bidirectional iterator that can work with a list. Like the Link structure, the MyIterator class is a template. This class template defines a single private data member named current that's a pointer to the Link object for the current element.

The public section of the MyIterator class starts by defining the five iterator traits. Here, the iterator_category trait is set to std::bidirectional_iterator_tag. This means that MyIterator is a bidirectional iterator. The rest of the traits indicate that the value type is T, the reference type is a reference to T, and the pointer type is a pointer to T. The difference_type trait uses the standard std::ptrdiff_t, which is similar to the std::size_t type you learned about in figure 19-1. This is a common way to define the difference type trait.

After the iterator traits, the class defines a constructor that accepts a pointer to a Link object. It uses this value to set the value of its current data member. Then, the rest of the class defines the operators that it needs to perform its iterator tasks. Many of these operators return a self-reference.

The assignment operator accepts a MyIterator object by constant reference and uses it to set the current data member of the current MyIterator object. The indirection operator uses the member access operator to return the value of the current element. The equal and not equal operators each accept a MyIterator object by constant reference and return the result of comparing that object's current data member for equality or inequality.

The increment operator works differently for its prefix and postfix versions. The prefix operator moves to the next element and returns a self-reference. The postfix operator stores a self-reference in a temporary variable, moves to the next element, and returns the temporary variable. In addition, the postfix operator accepts a dummy int argument that's only used to tell the compiler that this operator is the postfix operator, not the prefix operator.

The prefix and postfix versions of the decrement operator work much like the prefix and postfix versions of the increment operator. However, the decrement operator moves to the previous element, not the next element.

The MyIterator class

```cpp
#include "Link.h"

template<typename T>
class MyIterator {
private:
    Link<T>* current = nullptr;
public:
    // iterator traits
    using iterator_category = std::bidirectional_iterator_tag;
    using value_type = T;
    using difference_type = std::ptrdiff_t;
    using reference = T&;
    using pointer = T*;

    // constructor
    MyIterator(Link<T>* curr) {
        current = curr;
    }

    // operators
    MyIterator& operator=(const MyIterator& tobecopied) { // assignment
        current = tobecopied.current;
        return *this;
    }

    T& operator*() const { return current->value; }        // indirection

    bool operator==(const MyIterator& other) const {       // equal
        return current == other.current;
    }

    bool operator!=(const MyIterator& other) const {       // not equal
        return current != other.current;
    }

    MyIterator& operator++() {                             // increment - prefix
        current = current->next;
        return *this;
    }

    MyIterator operator++(int unused) {                   // increment - postfix
        auto temp = *this;
        current = current->next;
        return temp;
    }

    MyIterator& operator--() {                             // decrement - prefix
        current = current->prev;
        return *this;
    }

    MyIterator operator--(int unused) {                   // decrement - postfix
        auto temp = *this;
        current = current->prev;
        return temp;
    }
};
```

Figure 19-9   The MyIterator class

The MyList class declaration

Figure 19-10 presents the class declaration for a custom container named MyList that stores data in non-contiguous memory. Like the MyVector class, the MyList class is a template so it can store any type of object.

As the name implies, this container is a version of the list that's available from the STL. This version, though, is much simpler and doesn't recreate all of the functionality of the STL list. However, it should give you an idea of how a list works.

Most of the code in this figure consists of declarations. Then, the definitions are presented later in this chapter. However, this figure does contain a few inline definitions.

The MyList class defines three private data members and a private helper function. The head and tail data members are pointers to Link objects that are dynamically allocated in free store memory. The head data member points to the first Link object in the list. The tail data member points to the last Link object in the list. The list_size data member stores the number of elements in the container. And the initialize() helper function sets the head and tail pointers to null and the list size to zero.

After the private members, the MyList class defines the public member types. Here, the iterator member type is defined as a MyIterator of type T. This allows the iterator to work with the same data type as the container.

The constructor for this class is defined inline. This is the default constructor, and it calls the initialize() helper function to set the pointers to null and the list size to zero.

Unlike the MyVector class presented earlier in the chapter, the MyList class doesn't implement the Rule of Five. This saves space and keeps the focus on working with custom iterators. However, in the real world, you *would* implement the Rule of Five, or at least the Rule of Three. Otherwise, your container will throw errors when it's passed by value.

The member functions for the MyList class define member functions that are also provided by the STL list. First, this class defines the size() function inline, which returns the list_size value. Then, it declares the push_back(), pop_back(), at(), and remove() functions but doesn't define them. Finally, it defines the begin() and end() functions inline.

The begin() and end() functions both have a return type of iterator. This is a member type that's defined as MyIterator<T>.

The begin() function calls the constructor of the MyIterator class and passes it the head pointer. Then, it returns the result of that function call. As a result, begin() returns a MyIterator<T> object whose current data member points to the first element in the list.

The end() function calls the constructor of the MyIterator class and passes it the nullptr keyword. Then, it returns the result of that function call. As a result, end() returns a MyIterator<T> object whose current data member is null. This is the functional equivalent of pointing one past the last element in a sequence.

Unlike the MyVector class presented earlier in this chapter, the MyList class doesn't include the cbegin() and cend() functions. Again, this saves space and keeps the focus on working with custom iterators.

The MyList class declaration

```cpp
#include "MyIterator.h"

template <typename T>
class MyList {
private:
    Link<T>* head;          // A pointer to the first link in the list
    Link<T>* tail;          // A pointer to the last link in the list
    std::size_t list_size;  // The number of nodes in the list

    // helper function
    void initialize() {
        head = nullptr;
        tail = nullptr;
        list_size = 0;
    }

public:
    // Member types
    using size_type = std::size_t;
    using value_type = T;
    using reference = T& ;
    using iterator = MyIterator<T>;

    // Constructor
    MyList() { initialize(); }                      // inline

    // Destructor
    ~MyList();

    // Member functions
    size_type size() const { return list_size; }   // inline
    void push_back(T);
    void pop_back();
    reference at(int index);
    void remove(T);

    iterator begin() { return iterator(head); }     // inline
    iterator end() { return iterator(nullptr); }    // inline
};
```

Description

- The MyList class stores pointers to Link objects that represent the first and last elements in the list.

- The iterator defined by MyList is of type MyIterator<T>. As a result, the begin() and end() functions return MyIterator<T> objects.

- To save space and keep the focus on working with iterators, the MyList class shown here doesn't implement the Rule of Five. As a result, you can't pass a MyList object by value. To fix this, you should implement the Rule of Five, or at least the Rule of Three.

Figure 19-10   The MyList class declaration

The destructor definition

Figure 19-11 begins by presenting the definition for the destructor of the MyList class. The default constructor was defined inline in the class declaration, so that constructor isn't presented in this figure.

Unlike the destructor for MyVector, this destructor can't deallocate all the memory at once by calling delete[]. That's because MyList doesn't store its elements in contiguous memory. Instead, this destructor must traverse all the elements in the list and call delete on each one.

The destructor starts by defining two pointers to Link objects of type T. The pointer named iter is used to traverse the elements in the list, and the pointer named next points to the element that's next in the list.

To start, the head pointer is assigned to the iter variable. As a result, the iter variable points to the first element. Then, a loop starts that continues while the iter variable is not null. Within the loop, the first statement stores the pointer to the next element in the next variable, the second statement deletes the memory that iter points to, and the third statement stores the pointer to the next element in the iter variable.

This continues until the iter variable points to the last element in the list. At that point, the next element stores a value of nullptr. Then, when the code assigns the nullptr value to the iter variable, the loop ends.

The member function definitions

After the destructor, figure 19-11 continues by presenting the definitions for the push_back(), pop_back(), at(), and remove() member functions of the MyList class. Remember that the size(), begin(), and end() member functions were defined inline in the class declaration, so they aren't presented in this figure.

The push_back() member function accepts an item of type T. It starts by using the new keyword to allocate free store memory for a new Link of type T. To create the Link object, this code passes the item argument to the constructor of the Link class. This sets the value of the Link object and stores this new object in a temporary variable named new_link. Next, the function checks whether there are any elements in the list. If not, it updates both the head and tail pointers so they both point to the new Link object. Otherwise, it adds the new Link object to the end of the list by rearranging the pointers of the Link objects for the tail and the newly added link. Finally, it increments the size of the list.

The pop_back() function doesn't accept any arguments or return any data. It begins by checking if the tail points to a Link object. If so, the list is not empty. In that case, the code checks if the head and tail pointers refer to the same Link object. If so, the list only contains one element. In that case, the code deallocates memory for that element and calls the initialize() helper function. This sets the head and tail pointers to null and sets the size of the list to zero.

However, if multiple elements exist, the code gets a pointer to the Link object for the tail and stores it in a temporary variable named todelete. Then, it removes the last Link object in the list by rearranging the pointers of the Link objects. Next, it deallocates memory for the last Link object in the list. Finally, it decrements the size of the list.

The destructor definition

```
template <typename T>
MyList<T>::~MyList() { // deallocate the memory for each element in the
list

    Link<T>* iter;      // to traverse the list
    Link<T>* next;      // to point to the next link in the list

    iter = head;
    while (iter) {       // while iter != nullptr
        next = iter->next;
        delete iter;
        iter = next;
    }
}
```

The member function definitions

```
// push_back()
template <typename T>
void MyList<T>::push_back(T item) {
    Link<T>* new_link = new Link<T>(item);  // allocate memory

    if (!head) {                             // if empty
        head = new_link;
        tail = new_link;
    }
    else {                                   // if elements exist
        auto curr_tail = tail;               // store current tail link

        curr_tail->next = new_link;          // connect current tail
        new_link->prev = curr_tail;          // and new link

        tail = new_link;                     // set new link as new tail
    }
    ++list_size;
}
```

```
// pop_back()
template <typename T>
void MyList<T>::pop_back() {
    if (tail) {                              // if elements exist
        if (head == tail) {                  // if one element
            delete head;
            initialize();
        }
        else {                               // if multiple elements
            Link<T>* todelete = tail;
            tail = tail->prev;
            tail->next = nullptr;
            delete todelete;
            --list_size;
        }
    }
}
```

Figure 19-11   The destructor and member function definitions (part 1 of 2)

The at() function accepts an int argument that specifies the index of the element, and it returns the reference member type of the MyList<T> object. To inform the compiler that the return type is a type, the function definition begins with the typename keyword. Otherwise, the compiler might not recognize the reference member type as a type.

In the body of this function, the code begins by checking whether the index parameter is out of bounds. If so, the function throws an out_of_range exception. Otherwise, the function returns a reference to the element at that index.

Since the elements of MyList aren't stored in an array, the code can't use the subscript operator to get the element at the specified index. Instead, the code defines a pointer to a Link object named iter. Then, it uses a for loop to iterate through the elements in the list to the one specified by the index. Each time the loop executes, the code modifies the iter variable so it points to the next Link object in the list. When the iter variable points to the element at the specified index, the loop ends. Then, the function returns the value of the element that's pointed to by the iter variable.

The remove() member function accepts an element of type T that might be in the list. Then, the function removes all elements in the list that match the element specified by the parameter. To do that, the body of the function begins by defining a pointer to a Link object named iter and initializing it to the first element in the list. Then, it uses a while loop to iterate through all elements in the list.

Within the loop, the code begins by checking whether the value of the iter pointer is equal to the value of the val parameter. If it isn't, the code simply moves to the next link. If it is, however, the code removes the Link object that's pointed to by the iter pointer.

To do that, the code begins by checking whether there's only one Link object in the list. In that case, the code deallocates the memory for that Link object. Then, it calls the initialize() helper function to empty the list. Next, it uses the break statement to end the loop since there are no more objects in the list.

However, if there are multiple links, the code does some more checking to determine whether the element is stored in the first link of the list, the last link of the list, or somewhere in the middle of the list. If it's stored in the first link, this code changes the head data member so it points to the next link of the list. Then, it sets the prev pointer of the head link to nullptr, since this link is now the first link in the list.

The code that's executed if the element is stored in the last link of the list is similar. It changes the tail data member so it points to the previous link of the list. Then, it sets the next pointer of the tail link to nullptr.

If the element is stored in a link between the first and last links, this code must change the previous and next links so they point to each other rather than to the current link. To do that, the first two statements get iterators that point to the links before and after the current link. Then, the third statement changes the next pointer of the before link so it points to the after link, and the fourth statement changes the prev pointer of the after link so it points to the before link.

After the pointers are rearranged, the code stores a pointer to the next link in a temporary Link object named next. Then, it deallocates the memory for the Link object pointed to by the iter variable, it assigns next to iter, and it decrements the size of the list.

The member function definitions (continued)

```
// at()
template <typename T>
typename MyList<T>::reference MyList<T>::at(int index) {
    if (index < 0 || index >= list_size) {
        throw std::out_of_range("MyLinkedList<T>::at() - out of range");
    }
    else {
        Link<T>* iter = head;                  // start at first link
        for (int i = 0; i < index; ++i) {      // iterate to desired link
            iter = iter->next;
        }
        return iter->value;                    // return value of link
    }
}


// remove()
template <typename T>
void MyList<T>::remove(T val) {
    Link<T>* iter = head;                      // pointer to traverse list

    while (iter) {
        if (iter->value == val) {
            if (head == tail) {                // if only one link
                delete head;
                initialize();
                break;
            }
            else {                             // if multiple links
                // rearrange connecting pointers
                if (iter == head) {            // if first of multiple links
                    head = iter->next;
                    head->prev = nullptr;
                }
                else if (iter == tail) {       // if last of multiple links
                    tail = iter->prev;
                    tail->next = nullptr;
                }
                else {                         // if between other links
                    // get the links before and after the current link
                    auto before_iter = iter->prev;
                    auto after_iter = iter->next;

                    // connect before and after links to each other
                    before_iter->next = after_iter;
                    after_iter->prev = before_iter;
                }
                // remove current link
                Link<T>* next = iter->next;    // store next element in link
                delete iter;                   // deallocate memory
                iter = next;                   // move to next link
                --list_size;                   // decrement size
            }
        }
        else  // current element doesn't match
            iter = iter->next;                 // move to next link
    }
}
```

Figure 19-11   The destructor and member function definitions (part 2 of 2)

The Task Manager 2.0 program

Figure 19-12 shows the Task Manager 2.0 program. Like the previous version, it asks the user to enter one or more tasks. This time, though, it doesn't order the elements alphabetically before it displays them. That's because the STL sort() algorithm requires a random-access iterator, but the MyIterator object used by the MyList class is only a bidirectional iterator. As a result, the STL sort() algorithm doesn't work for a MyList object.

As usual, the code begins with include directives for the header files that the program needs and a using directive for the std namespace. This time, though, one of the header files is the "MyList.h" file that contains the declarations and definitions presented in the previous figures.

The main() function starts by displaying the name of the program and instructions on how to use the program. Then, it defines a MyList object named tasks that holds strings, along with a string variable named task that's initialized to an empty string.

Next, the code executes a while loop that runs until it encounters the break statement. Within the while loop, the first statement displays a message on the console that asks the user to enter a task. Then, the getline() function gets the task entered by the user.

After getting the task from the user, this code checks the value of the task string. If it's 'x', the code uses a break statement to end the loop. Otherwise, the code passes the task entered by the user to the push_back() function of the MyList object and the loop continues.

When the while loop ends, the code displays the tasks in the list. To do that, the code uses a range-based for loop to iterate through the elements in the MyList object. This works because the begin() and end() functions of the MyList class both provide a bidirectional iterator that the range-based for loop can use to iterate through the elements of the MyList object. These bidirectional iterators are MyIterator objects.

If you need to gain more control over these iterators, you can code them explicitly in a for loop like this:

```
for (auto iter = tasks.begin(); iter != tasks.end(); ++iter) {
    cout << ++num << ") " << *iter << endl;
}
```

Here, the code explicitly uses the increment and indirection operators provided by the MyIterator class.

So, why can't this for loop just use an index and subscripting like the previous Task Manager program did? Because the MyIterator object provided by MyList is a bidirectional iterator, not a random-access iterator. Like most bidirectional iterators, the MyIterator object doesn't support subscripting.

The console

```
The Task Manager program
Enter tasks and enter 'x' when done.

Enter task:  Go to store
Enter task:  Feed cats
Enter task:  Check email
Enter task:  x

My Task List
------------
1) Go to store
2) Feed cats
3) Check email
```

The code

```cpp
#include <iostream>
#include <string>
#include "MyList.h"

using namespace std;

int main() {
    cout << "The Task Manager program\n";
    cout << "Enter tasks and enter 'x' when done.\n\n";

    MyList<string> tasks;
    string task = "";
    while (true) {
        cout << "Enter task:  ";
        getline(cin, task);
        if (task == "x") {
            break;
        }
        else {
            tasks.push_back(task);
        }
    }
    cout << endl;

    cout << "My Task List\n";
    cout << "------------\n";
    int num = 0;
    for (string task : tasks) {
        cout << ++num << ") " << task << endl;
    }
}
```

Description

- This Task Manager program uses the MyList object to store tasks, and it uses operations provided by the MyIterator class to display the elements.

Figure 19-12   The Task Manager 2.0 program

How to code a custom algorithm

In addition to creating custom containers with iterators that you can use with the STL algorithms, you can create custom algorithms that you can use with the STL containers or your own custom containers. Now, you'll learn how.

The find_midpoint() algorithm

STL algorithms don't work directly with the STL containers. Instead, the STL containers provide iterators that define a half-open interval. Then, the STL algorithms work with these iterators to perform their tasks. If you read chapter 11, this should sound familiar to you.

This architecture makes it easy for you to write your own STL-compliant algorithms. For example, figure 19-13 presents a custom algorithm named find_midpoint() that returns a pointer to the midpoint of a sequence of elements. This algorithm is a function template, which means that it can work with a sequence of elements of any data type.

The template prefix uses a name of BidirIter for the type parameter instead of the traditional name of T. This name clearly indicates the type of iterator that your algorithm requires. In this case, this name makes it clear that the find_midpoint() algorithm requires an iterator that is bidirectional or higher.

The find_midpoint() algorithm accepts two iterators that define the begin and end of a half-open interval, and it returns an iterator that points to the element that's at the midpoint of the container. To start, this algorithm checks whether the two iterator parameters are equal. If so, the sequence is empty, and the algorithm returns the off-the-end iterator. Remember from chapter 11 that this is a common way for an algorithm to indicate that a value wasn't found.

If the sequence isn't empty, the code defines an int counter variable and initializes it to zero. Then, it starts a while loop that continues until begin and end iterators point to the same element. Within the loop, the code checks whether the counter variable is an even or odd number. If the counter is even, the code moves the end iterator back one element. If the counter is odd, the code moves the begin iterator forward one element. Either way, the code increments the counter.

This continues until the begin and end iterators both point to the same element in the sequence. At this point, the loop ends, and the algorithm returns a pointer to that element. If the sequence contains an odd number of elements, the pointer that's returned will point to the middle element. If the sequence contains an even number of elements, though, it doesn't have a middle element. In that case, the find_midpoint() algorithm returns a pointer to the element that's closer to the end of the sequence. For example, if the sequence has six elements, this algorithm will return the fourth element. That makes sense if you remember that the end iterator points one past the last element in the sequence.

This figure also presents some code that uses the find_midpoint() algorithm. To start, this code defines an STL vector of int values and initializes it with seven values. Then, it finds and displays the element at the midpoint, which is an int value of 6. Next, it uses the STL sort() algorithm to arrange the vector's elements in ascending order. Finally, this code finds and displays the element at the midpoint. This time, the element at the midpoint is an int value of 8.

The find_midpoint() algorithm

```
template<typename BidirIter>
BidirIter find_midpoint(BidirIter begin, BidirIter end) {
    // if range is empty, return the off-the-end iterator
    if (begin == end) {
        return end;
    }

    // alternate decrementing end iterator
    // and incrementing begin iterator
    // until both point to the same element
    int counter = 0;
    while (begin != end) {
        if (counter % 2 == 0) {  // counter is even
            --end;
        }
        else {                        // counter is odd
            ++begin;
        }
        ++counter;
    }
    return begin;
}
```

Code that uses this algorithm with an STL vector

```
vector<int> numbers { 5, 8, 2, 6, 11, 9, 34 };
auto iter = find_midpoint(numbers.begin(), numbers.end());
cout << *iter << endl;                        // displays 6

sort(numbers.begin(), numbers.end());  // sequence is now 2 5 6 8 9 11 34
iter = find_midpoint(numbers.begin(), numbers.end());
cout << *iter << endl;                        // displays 8
```

Description

- In the template for an algorithm, you can use the type name to indicate the kind of iterator your algorithm expects. This makes it easier for other programmers to understand how to use the algorithm.

Figure 19-13   The find_midpoint() algorithm

The Number Cruncher program

Figure 19-14 shows another version of the Number Cruncher program that was originally presented in chapter 11. This program generates a sequence of random integers. Then, it performs a series of operations on them. The console for this program shows that the program sorts the numbers, calculates a total and average, gets the maximum and minimum values, and gets the midpoint and median values.

In chapter 11, the Number Cruncher program used STL algorithms to work with an STL vector. The version of the Number Cruncher program presented in this figure works similarly, but it uses a custom MyVector object to store the random numbers, and it uses the custom find_midpoint() algorithm defined in the previous figure as well as STL algorithms. However, if you wanted, you could modify this program so it used an STL vector instead of the custom vector. That would work because the find_midpoint() algorithm works correctly with STL containers or custom containers.

As usual, the code for the program begins with the include directives for the header files that the program needs and a using directive for the std namespace. This time, though, one of the header files is the "MyVector.h" file and another is the "find_midpoint.h" file.

The main() function starts by displaying the name of the program. Then, it defines a MyVector object of int values named numbers, and it uses the reserve() function of the MyVector object to allocate space in memory for 11 elements.

Next, the code uses a for loop to add random numbers to the custom vector. To do that, it iterates the elements in the vector as long as the capacity() function of the vector is less than the counter variable. Within the loop, it gets a random number from 0 to 29 and then uses the push_back() function of the vector to add the random number to the vector. When this loop ends, the vector named numbers contains eleven random integers. Then, the code uses the for_each() algorithm and the display_int() function to display those numbers.

After displaying the unsorted random numbers, the code uses the sort() algorithm to sort the numbers in the custom vector in ascending order. This works because the MyVector class provides the high-level, random-access iterator that the sort() algorithm requires. Then, the code uses the for_each() algorithm and the display_int() function to display the sorted numbers.

Next, the code uses the accumulate() algorithm to total all the numbers in the custom vector, it stores the result in a variable named sum, and it displays the sum. Then, it calculates the average of these numbers by dividing the sum by the size of the vector, and it displays the average.

The console

```
The Number Cruncher program

11 RANDOM NUMBERS: 1 1 10 26 5 29 2 17 28 26 21
11 SORTED NUMBERS: 1 1 2 5 10 17 21 26 26 28 29
Sum = 166 Average = 15
Min = 1 Max = 29
Midpoint = 17 Median = 17
```

The code

```cpp
#include <iostream>
#include <cstdlib>
#include <ctime>
#include "MyVector.h"
#include <algorithm>
#include <numeric>
#include "find_midpoint.h"

using namespace std;

void display_int(int num) {
    cout << num << ' ';
}

int main() {
    cout << "The Number Cruncher program\n\n";

    // create an empty vector for a specified number of elements
    MyVector<int> numbers;
    numbers.reserve(11);    // 11 elements

    // fill the vector with random numbers
    srand(time(nullptr));
    for (int i = 0; i < numbers.capacity(); ++i) {
        int number = rand() % 30;
        numbers.push_back(number);
    }

    // use STL algorithms
    cout << numbers.size() << " RANDOM NUMBERS: ";
    for_each(numbers.begin(), numbers.end(), display_int);
    cout << endl;

    sort(numbers.begin(), numbers.end());
    cout << numbers.size() << " SORTED NUMBERS: ";
    for_each(numbers.begin(), numbers.end(), display_int);
    cout << endl;

    int sum = accumulate(numbers.begin(), numbers.end(), 0);
    cout << "Sum = " << sum << ' ';

    int avg = sum / numbers.size();
    cout << "Average = " << avg << '\n';
```

Figure 19-14   The Number Cruncher program (part 1 of 2)

Part 2 of figure 19-14 begins by using the min_element() and max_element() algorithms to retrieve iterators that point to the largest and smallest elements in the custom vector. This code uses the auto keyword to define the variables named max_iter and min_iter that store the iterators returned by these algorithms so the code is more concise. It also displays the minimum and maximum values on the console. To do that, it uses the indirection operator (*) to get the values that min_iter and max_iter point to.

After getting the maximum and minimum values, the code uses the custom find_midpoint() algorithm to retrieve the iterator that points to the element at the midpoint of the vector. This is consistent with the way that the min_element() and max_element() algorithms of the STL work. Then, it displays the value of the midpoint on the console.

Next, the code calculates the median value of the elements in the sequence. To start, it defines a double variable named median. Then, it checks whether the numbers container has an odd or even number of elements. If the container has an odd number of elements, the iterator returned by find_midpoint() is at the exact middle of the sequence. As a result, the code simply dereferences the iterator and assigns the value to the median variable.

However, if the container has an even number of elements, the iterator returned by find_midpoint() isn't at the middle of the sequence and the code needs to calculate the median. To do that, it gets the value of the midpoint and the value of the previous element, adds those values together, and divides them by two. That makes sense if you remember that the find_midpoint() algorithm returns an iterator that points one element closer to the end of the container than to the beginning of the container if the container has an even number of elements. So, by getting the value of the previous element, you now have the values of the two elements in the middle of the container.

To get the two values, the code assigns the value of the iterator returned by the find_midpoint() algorithm to a double variable named mid_val. Then, it assigns the value of the previous iterator to a double variable named prev_val. To do this, the code decrements the iterator returned by the algorithm, uses the indirection operator to get the value of that iterator, and uses parentheses to make sure these operations are performed in the correct order.

After storing the two values in their respective variables, this code adds them together, divides the result by two, and assigns the result to the median variable. Like the previous statement, this statement uses parentheses to make sure that these operations take place in the correct order. Finally, this code displays the median on the console.

The code (continued)

```
auto min_iter = min_element(numbers.begin(), numbers.end());
cout << "Min = " << *min_iter << ' ';

auto max_iter = max_element(numbers.begin(), numbers.end());
cout << "Max = " << *max_iter << '\n';

// use custom algorithm
auto mid_iter = find_midpoint(numbers.begin(), numbers.end());
cout << "Midpoint = " << *mid_iter << ' ';

// calculate median
double median;
if (numbers.size() % 2 != 0) {  // odd - median is same as midpoint
    median = *mid_iter;
}
else {    // even - median is sum of midpoint and prev divided by 2
    double mid_val = *mid_iter;
    double prev_val = *(--mid_iter);
    median = (mid_val + prev_val) / 2;
}
cout << "Median = " << median << "\n\n";
}
```

Description

- The Number Cruncher program sorts the numbers in a sequence so that they're in ascending order. Then, it uses the find_midpoint() custom algorithm to find the number at the midpoint of the sequence.

- When the number of elements is odd, the midpoint is the same as the median. When the number of elements is even, the program calculates the median by adding the midpoint to the value of the previous element and dividing by two.

Figure 19-14   The Number Cruncher program (part 2 of 2)

Perspective

In this chapter, you learned how to create custom containers, iterators, and algorithms that are compatible with the Standard Template Library. These custom classes also provide a good example of how object-oriented programming is used in the real world.

Of course, there's still plenty more to learn about C++. For example, you may want to learn how to use C++ with the Qt library to create a GUI (Graphical User Interface) for a desktop application. You may want to learn how to use C++ to develop video games that perform extensive graphics processing. Or, you may want to learn how to use C++ to work with embedded systems, big data, or artificial intelligence. Whatever you decide to learn next, you now have a skillset that you can build on.

Terms

member types
alias
iterator traits

Summary

- The STL containers define several commonly used types, sometimes known as *member types*. These types make it possible to write generic code that can work with any container type.

- With C++11 and later, you can create an *alias* for a member type with the using keyword. Prior to C++11, it was common to use the typedef keyword to create an alias for a member type.

- If you want to use your custom iterator class with STL algorithms, you need to implement five *iterator traits*.

Exercise 19-1   Test the MyVector class

This exercise guides you through the process of testing some of the constructors, operators, and functions of the MyVector class. When you're done with this exercise, the console for the program should look something like this:

```
TESTING
Init:          Go to store|Feed cats|Check email|
capacity():    3
push_back():   Go to store|Feed cats|Check email|Brush teeth|
capacity():    6
size():        4
at(0):         Go to store
at(size-1):    Brush teeth
resize(20)
capacity():    20
size():        20
```

Open and test the program

1. Open the project or solution named vector_tester in this folder:

    ex_starts\ch19_ex1_vector_tester

2. Open the MyVector.h file and review its code. Note that it provides all the constructors, operators, and functions described in this chapter.

3. Open the main.cpp file and review its code. Note that it uses the initialization list constructor to initialize the vector so it stores three strings. Then, it displays some messages on the console. Note also that it uses a function named display() that tests the copy constructor by accepting a MyVector<T> object by value.

4. Run the program. At this point, it should display just some of the information shown above since not all of the functionality has been implemented. For example, because the push_back() function isn't called to add another string to the vector, the second call to the capacity() function should still be 3.

Complete the code that tests the vector

5. In the main.cpp file, add code that uses the push_back() function to add a fourth string to the vector. Then, run the program to test this code. This should cause the second call to the capacity() function to be 6 since it should double the capacity from 3.

6. In the main.cpp file, add code that uses the at() function to get the first and last strings in the vector. This shows that you can use the at() function or the subscript operator to get items from a MyVector object.

7. In the main.cpp file, add a statement that uses the resize() function of the vector to change its size and capacity to 20. This shows that you can use the resize() function to allocate more memory for a specified number of elements.

8. If you have time or you're instructed to do so, experiment by adding code that tests other constructors, operators, and functions of the MyVector object.

Exercise 19-2   Test the MyList class

This exercise guides you through the process of testing some of the functions of the MyList class. When you're done with this exercise, the console for the program should look something like this:

```
TESTING
Go to store|Feed cats|Check email|Feed cats|Brush teeth|
size():      5
pop_back(): Go to store|Feed cats|Check email|Feed cats|
at(0):       Go to store
at(size-1): Feed cats
remove():    Go to store|Check email|
size():      2
```

Open and test the program

1. Open the project or solution named list_tester in this folder:
    `ex_starts\ch19_ex2_list_tester`

2. Open the MyList.h file and review its code. Note that it provides all the constructors and functions described in this chapter.

3. Open the main.cpp file and review the code. Note that it uses the push_back() function to add five strings to the list, including two strings of "Feed cats". Then, it displays some messages on the console.

4. Run the program. At this point, it should start by displaying five strings, but the rest of the console shouldn't match the console shown above because not all of the functionality has been implemented.

Complete the code that tests the list

5. In the main.cpp file, add code that uses the pop_back() function to remove the last string from the list. Next, run the program to test this code.

6. In the main.cpp file, add code that uses the at() function to get the first and last strings in the list. This shows that you can use the at() function to get the item at the specified index of a MyList object.

7. In the main.cpp file, add a statement that uses the remove() function of the list to remove both strings of "Feed cats". This shows that you can use the remove() function to remove one or more items from a MyList object.

8. If you have time or you're instructed to do so, experiment by adding code that tests other constructors and functions of the MyList object.

Exercise 19-3   Create a new custom algorithm

In this exercise, you'll modify the Number Cruncher program presented in this chapter so it uses a custom algorithm to calculate the median.

Open and test the program

1. Open the project or solution named number_cruncher in this folder:

    `ex_starts\ch16_ex3_number_cruncher`

2. Review the code in the main.cpp file, and note that it uses the custom find_midpoint() algorithm to get the midpoint. However, it manually calculates the median.

3. Run the code to make sure it works correctly for 11 numbers. Note that the midpoint and the median are always the same.

Modify the code so it generates 12 numbers and test it

4. In the main.cpp file, modify the code so it generates 12 numbers, not 11.

5. Run the code to make sure it works correctly for 12 numbers. It should calculate the median by adding the middle two numbers together and dividing by 2. Note that this number is usually different from the midpoint, which is the second of the two middle numbers.

Add the custom calc_median() algorithm

6. Add a header file named calc_median.h to the project.

7. In the calc_median.h file, add include guards and a calc_median() function. The calc_median() function should work much like the custom find_midpoint() algorithm. However, it should calculate the median and return it as a double value.

8. To code the calc_median() function, you can start by copying code from the body of the find_midpoint() algorithm to find the midpoint. Then, you can copy the code from the main.cpp file that calculates the median. Next, you can modify the code so the calc_median() function works correctly.

9. In the main.cpp file, modify the code so it includes the calc_median.h header file and uses the calc_median() algorithm to calculate the median.

10. Run the code to make sure it still works correctly.

Appendix A

How to set up Windows for this book

This appendix shows how to install the software that we recommend for developing C++ applications on a Windows system. Then, it shows how to install the source code for this book.

As you read this appendix, please remember that most websites are continually updated. As a result, some of the procedures may have changed since this book was published. Nevertheless, these procedures should still be good guides to installing the software. And if there are significant changes to these setup instructions, we will post updates on our website (www.murach.com).

How to install the Visual Studio IDE

Figure A-1 shows how to install the Community edition of the Visual Studio IDE (Integrated Development Environment). By default, installing this IDE also installs and configures the Microsoft Visual C++ (MSVC) compiler. This is the compiler that Visual Studio uses by default to compile C++ programs.

When you install the Visual Studio IDE, you need to be sure to select the "Desktop development with C++" option as shown in this figure. In addition, because the programs in this book target Windows 10, you should make a note of the Windows 10 SDK version that's being installed. This version is included by default in the Optional list at the right side of the installation dialog box. You'll learn why you may need to know the version that's installed in chapter 1 of this book.

The main page for installing Visual Studio Community

The download page for Visual Studio Community

https://www.visualstudio.com/vs/community/

How to install the Visual Studio IDE

1. Find the download page for Visual Studio Community by going to the URL above or by searching the Internet for "Visual Studio Community download".

2. Click the appropriate Download button to download the setup program for Visual Studio to your hard disk. This setup file should be an exe file.

3. Run the setup program and respond to the resulting dialog boxes. When the dialog box above is displayed, be sure to select the "Desktop development with C++" option.

Description

- Visual Studio Community is a free IDE that you can use to create C++ programs. It runs on Windows and macOS but is typically used for Windows.

- When you install Visual Studio, the Microsoft Visual C++ (MSVC) compiler is also installed. This is the compiler that Visual Studio uses by default to compile C++ programs.

- The procedure above installs the current version of Visual Studio, which was Visual Studio 2017 at the time of this printing. However, this book will work equally well with later versions of Visual Studio.

- For more information about installing and using Visual Studio, you can refer to the Visual Studio website. Chapter 1 also presents an introduction to using Visual Studio for Windows development.

Figure A-1   How to install the Visual Studio IDE

How to install the source code for this book

Figure A-2 shows how to download and install the source code for this book. This includes the source code for the applications that are presented in this book. In addition, it includes the source code for the starting points and solutions for the exercises that are presented at the end of each chapter.

When you finish this procedure, the book applications, exercise starts, and exercise solutions should be in the folders shown in this figure. Then, you can review the applications that are presented in this book, and you'll be ready to do the exercises in this book.

The Murach website

`www.murach.com`

The folder that contains the Visual Studio projects

`C:\murach\cpp\vs`

The subfolders

Folder	Description
book_apps	The applications that are presented throughout this book.
ex_starts	The starting points for the exercises at the end of each chapter.
ex_solutions	The solutions to the exercises.

How to download and install the files for this book

1. Go to www.murach.com, and go to the page for *Murach's C++ Programming*.
2. If necessary, scroll down to the FREE Downloads tab. Then, click on it.
3. Click the DOWNLOAD NOW button for the exe file, and respond to the resulting pages and dialog boxes. This should download an installer file named cpls_allfiles.exe.
4. Use Windows Explorer or File Explorer to find the exe file.
5. Double-click this file and respond to the dialog boxes that follow. This should install the files for the Visual Studio projects for this book in folders that start with C:\murach\cpp\vs.

How to use a zip file instead of a self-extracting zip file

- Although we recommend using the self-extracting zip file (cpls_allfiles.exe) to install the downloadable files as described above, some systems won't allow self-extracting zip files to be downloaded. In that case, you can download a regular zip file (cpls_allfiles.zip) from our website. Then, you can extract the files stored in this zip file into the C:\murach folder. If the C:\murach folder doesn't already exist, you will need to create it.

Figure A-2   How to install the source code for this book

Appendix B

How to set up macOS for this book

This appendix shows how to install the Xcode IDE that we recommend for developing C++ applications for the macOS operating system. Then, this appendix shows how to install the source code for this book. In addition, it describes how this source code includes some extra code that isn't shown in the book that makes it easier to use Xcode to work with files that store data.

As you read this appendix, please remember that most websites are continually updated. As a result, some of the procedures in this appendix may have changed since this book was published. Nevertheless, these procedures should still be good guides to installing the software. And if there are significant changes to these setup instructions, we will post updates on our website (www.murach.com).

How to install the Xcode IDE

Figure B-1 shows how to install the Xcode IDE (Integrated Development Environment). By default, installing this IDE also installs and configures the Clang compiler. This is the compiler that Xcode uses by default to compile C++ programs.

The download page for Xcode

`https://developer.apple.com/download/`

How to install the Xcode IDE

1. Find the download page for Xcode by going to the URL above or by searching the Internet for "Xcode download".

2. Sign in with your Apple Developer ID and password. If you don't have an Apple Developer ID, you can create one for free.

3. Click the Download button for Xcode to go to the Mac App Store.

4. Click the Get button.

5. Click the Install Now button.

6. Click the Open button to finish the installation and start Xcode.

Description

- Xcode Community is a free IDE that you can use to create C++ programs. It runs on macOS and is typically used to develop applications for Apple platforms.

- When you install Xcode, the Clang compiler is also installed. This is the compiler that Xcode uses by default to compile C++ programs.

- For more information about installing and using Xcode, you can refer to the Xcode website.

Figure B-1   How to install the Xcode IDE

How to install the source code for this book

Figure B-2 shows how to download and install the source code for this book. This includes the source code for the applications that are presented in this book. In addition, it includes the source code for the starting points and solutions for the exercises that are presented at the end of each chapter.

When you finish this procedure, the book applications, exercise starts, and exercise solutions should be in the directories shown in this figure. Then, you can review the applications that are presented in this book, and you'll be ready to do the exercises in this book.

As you work with the Xcode projects, you may find that some of them display warnings about the code. However, these warnings typically don't cause any problems with the programs presented in this book. As a result, you can usually ignore them. Or, if you prefer, you can attempt to resolve each warning by editing your code. As you progress through this book and learn more about C++, it should become easier to understand and fix these warnings.

The Murach website

www.murach.com

The directory that contains the Xcode projects

/Documents/murach/cpp/xcode

The subdirectories

Directory	Description
book_apps	The applications that are presented throughout this book.
ex_starts	The starting points for the exercises at the end of each chapter.
ex_solutions	The solutions to the exercises.

How to download and install the files for this book

1. Go to www.murach.com, and go to the page for *Murach's C++ Programming*.

2. If necessary, scroll down to the FREE Downloads tab. Then, click on it.

3. Click the Download Now button for the zip file for the book applications and exercises. Then, respond to the resulting pages and dialog boxes. This should download a zip file named cpls_allfiles.zip to your hard drive.

4. Move this zip file from your Downloads directory into your Documents directory. Then, double-click on the zip file to extract the book_apps, ex_starts, and ex_solutions directories that contain the Xcode projects for this book into the murach/cpp/xcode directory.

A note about right-clicking

- This book sometimes instructs you to right-click, because that's common in Windows. On macOS, right-clicking is not enabled by default. However, you can enable right-clicking by editing the system preferences for your mouse.

A note about warnings

- As you use Xcode to work with the source code for this book, it may display some warnings. However, these warnings don't typically cause any problems with the programs presented in this book. As a result, you can usually ignore them.

Figure B-2   How to install the source code for this book

How the source code makes it easier for Xcode projects to store data in files

Most IDEs set the working directory to the same directory as the directory that stores the source code for the project. This makes it possible for a program that stores its data in a file to access that file just by specifying its filename, not a full path to the file.

However, Xcode sets the working directory for a project to a directory that's different from the directory that stores the source code for a project. To illustrate, figure B-3 shows the source code directory and the working directory for an Xcode project named ch05a_temperature_manager. As a result, since this Xcode project stores its data in a file, it must specify a full path to that file, not just a filename. To make it easy to do that, the download for this book adds code like the code shown in this figure to every Xcode project that uses a file.

The code that's added to these projects attempts to automatically set a full path to the file for the project. In most cases, this should work correctly. If so, the Xcode project can automatically access the file without any problems. As a result, you don't need to take any action, although you should be aware that these projects are automatically working with the files in the murach/cpp/files directory described in this figure.

If the code that's added to these projects doesn't work correctly, you can manually edit the "/Users/username" string so it points to the appropriate user. To do that, you just need to change "username" so it's correct for your system. Typically, this should be set to your name or your computer's name.

If you don't want to use code to set a full path to the file, you can open the project in Xcode and set a custom working directory as described in the last bullet in this figure. Then, you can delete any code that attempts to set a full path to the file and just specify the filename. When you do, Xcode looks for the file in the custom working directory that you specified. For projects that already specify a full path, like the ones for this book, you probably don't need to specify a custom working directory. But, you might want to set one when creating new projects.

The source code directory for an Xcode project

```
/Users/username/Documents/murach/cpp/xcode/book_apps
/ch05b_temperature_manager/temperature_manager
```

The working directory for the project

```
/Users/username/Library/Developer/Xcode/DerivedData
/ch05b_temperature_manager-GENERATED_KEY/Build/Products/Debug
/temperature_manager
```

The directory that contains the files for most programs in this book

```
/Users/username/Documents/murach/cpp/files
```

The subdirectories

Directory	Description
temp_manager	The temps.txt file for all Temperature Manager programs.
temp_analyzer	The temps.txt file for all Temperature Analyzer programs.

Code that has been added to the Xcode source code

```cpp
string filename = "temps.txt";

// set a full path to the correct file
const char* home = getenv("HOME");
string user_home = "";
if (home) {
    user_home = home;
}
else {
    // if home isn't found, edit 'username' so it's correct for your system
    user_home = "/Users/username";
}
string file_path = "/Documents/murach/cpp/files/temp_manager/";
filename = user_home + file_path + filename;
```

Description

- By default, Xcode sets the working directory for a project to a subdirectory that's different from the directory for the project's source code. As a result, if an Xcode project uses a file to store its data, it must specify a full path to that file, not just the filename of the file.

- In the download for this book, every Xcode project that works with data in a file includes code that attempts to automatically set a full path to that file. If this code can't set a full path automatically, you can manually edit the path so it's correct for your system.

- The code that attempts to automatically set a full path to the data file varies from project to project, but the general idea is always the same.

- If you don't want to use the code that automatically sets the full path to the file, you can change the working directory for a project by opening the project and selecting the Product→Scheme→Edit Scheme item. Then, you can select the Run category, check the Use Custom Working Directory box, and specify the working directory.

Figure B-3   How the source code makes it easier for Xcode projects to store data in files

Index

D